D0020114

P8 - BYR - 274

Madagascar
& Comoros

David Andrew
Becca Blond & Aaron Anderson
Tom Parkinson

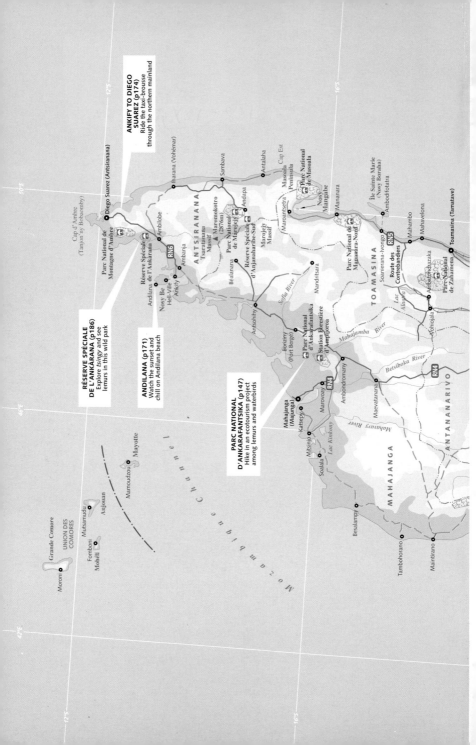

RÉSERVE SPÉCIALE DE L'ANKARANA (p186)
Explore *tsingy* and see lemurs in this wild park

ANDILANA (p171)
Watch the sunset and chill on Andilana beach

PARC NATIONAL D'ANKARAFANTSIKA (p147)
Hike in an ecotourism project among lemurs and waterbirds

ANKIFY TO DIEGO SUAREZ (p174)
Ride the taxi-brousse through the northern mainland

Cap d'Ambre (Tanjon' ny Bobaonby)

Diego Suarez (Antsiranana)

Parc National de Montagne d'Ambre

Réserve Spéciale de l'Ankarana

Andilana de l'Ankarana

Nosy Be
Hell-Ville
Arikity

Iharana (Vohémar)

Ambanja

Ambilobe

RN6

A N T S I R A N A N A

Tsaratanana Massif
Marromokotro (2876m)

Parc National de Marojejy

Réserve Spéciale d'Anjanaharibe-Sud

Andapa

Sambava

Antalaha

Cap Est

Bealanana

Sofia River

Antsohihy

Mandritsara

Parc National de Masoala

Maroantsetra

Masoala Peninsula

Nosy Mangabe

Mananara

Parc National de Mananara-Nord

Île Sainte Marie (Nosy Boraha)

Ambodifotatra

T O A M A S I N A

Soanierana-Ivongo

Route des Contrebandiers

RN5

Ambodiriana

Mahambo

Mahavelona

Toamasina (Tamatave)

Lac Alaotra

Ambatondrazaka

Parc National de Zahamena

Vohidiala

Boriziny (Port Bergé)

Parc National d'Ankarafantsika

Station Forestière d'Ampijoroa

Mahajamba River

Betsiboka River

RN4

A N T A N A N A R I V O

Ambondromamy

Maevatanana

Mahajanga (Majunga)

Katsepy

RN4

Marovoay

Mahavavy River

Mitsinjo

Lac Kinkony

Soalala

M A H A J A N G A

Besalampy

Tambohorano

Maintirano

Grande Comore

Moroni

UNION DES COMORES

Mutsamudu

Fomboni
Mohéli

Anjouan

Mamoudzou

Mayotte

M o z a m b i q u e   C h a n n e l

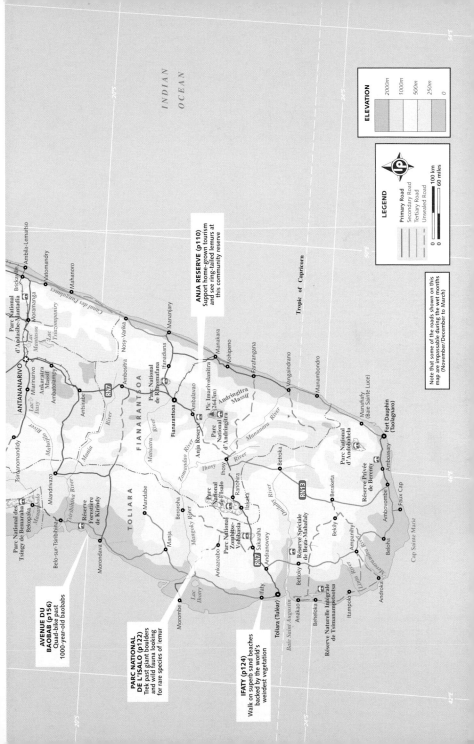

INDIAN OCEAN

ANTANANARIVO

ANJA RESERVE (p110)
Support home-grown tourism and see ring-tailed lemurs at this community reserve

Tropic of Capricorn

AVENUE DU BAOBAB (p156)
Quad-bike past 1000-year-old baobabs

PARC NATIONAL DE L'ISALO (p122)
Trek past giant boulders and wild fauna looking for rare species of lemur

IFATY (p124)
Walk on superb sand beaches backed by the world's weirdest vegetation

Note that some of the roads shown on this map are impassable during the wet months (November/December to March)

ELEVATION
2000m
1000m
500m
250m
0

LEGEND
Primary Road
Secondary Road
Tertiary Road
Unsealed Road

0 — 100 km
0 — 60 miles

Parc National des Tsingy de Bemaraha
Réserve Forestière de Kirindy
Parc National Zombitse-Vohibasia
Réserve Spéciale de Bezà-Mahafaly
Réserve Naturelle Intégrale de Tsimanampetsotsa
Parc National de l'Isalo
Parc National d'Andringitra
Parc National d'Andohahela
Réserve Privée de Berenty
Parc National d'Andasibe-Mantadia

Andringitra Massif
Pic Imarivolanitra (2643m)

Ankaratra Massif

TOLIARA
FIANARANTSOA

Fianarantsoa
Toliara (Tuléar)
Fort Dauphin (Taolagnaro)

Baie Sainte Augustin
Cap Sainte Marie

On the Road

TOM PARKINSON

Tom was originally the sole author for this 6th edition of *Madagascar & Comoros*. Tragically for everyone who knew him, Tom passed away unexpectedly in January 2007, aged 28. While conducting research for the book, Tom managed to find time to complete the full Maroantsetra–Cap Est trek (p224); this is the end-of-trip team photo. Tom is pictured 5th from the left.

A TRIBUTE TO TOM FROM BECCA

Aaron and I had the opportunity to travel to the SOS Children's Village (p99) outside Antsirabe to which Tom Parkinson's parents had chosen to donate money in his name. We asked to visit the school to take some photos for his parents, but the director was so honoured to have 'delegates from Lonely Planet', as he called us, that he organised an entire ceremony in our honour that included planting a tree in Tom's name. It was a heart-wrenching experience, laying that small tree into the earth, then listening to the director speak about the Parkinsons' generosity and how the money they had donated allowed the school to construct more buildings, including a centre to teach older children the technical skills, such as welding, construction and carving, they will need to get a job in Madagascar's sluggish economy. My speech, given in broken French, was not nearly as eloquent.

AARON ANDERSON

It was an absolutely gorgeous Monday on Andilana beach (p171). The sun was hot and I had been researching hard for the last week straight, so was treating myself to a day of snorkelling in the clear blue water in front of me, and lazing on Chez Loulou's beach chairs drinking Three Horses beer while reading Upton Sinclair's *The Jungle*. The dog in the picture befriended Becca and me, and would sprint across the beach and up a steep flight of stairs every time he saw us.

BECCA BLOND

I love animals, so I was really stoked when I got a chance to see my first lemur. This picture was taken in Anja Reserve (p110). It's a small community-run reserve that protects a big colony of ring-tailed lemurs. The park is small so you have a pretty good chance of getting close enough to a lemur for a photo like this one. Although the hiking isn't technical it involves lots of rock scrambling and tight spaces – not easy with a broken ankle, but I was determined to see one of these creatures. The park was started by a guide named Adrien, who was a friend of Tom's and took him trekking when Tom was researching this guide. He started to cry when I told him of Tom's passing.

For author bios, see p303.

Madagascar Highlights

Madagascar is Noah's ark adrift in the Indian Ocean, an island peopled by seafarers and colonised by the French. 'Unique' is almost too simple a word for its creatures, its cultures and its landscapes. We asked travellers about the unmissable experiences in Madagascar. They've swum and boated in the turquoise waters to the north, passed weeks bumping to the end of the red roads in the south, feasted on French cuisine and trekked the mountains in search of ring-tailed lemurs. Here are the top picks from Lonely Planet authors, staff and travellers.

TOM PARKINSON

1 CHILLING OUT ON ANDILANA BEACH

Becca and I couldn't get enough of Andilana beach (p171). A few nights at the Au Belvedere hotel, perched high on a cliff overlooking the perfect turquoise crescent of sea, watching the sunset from the bed in our super-breezy room, made our troubles melt away. We snorkelled around the headland, read on the beach and dined on Chez Loulou's delicious fresh seafood.

Aaron Anderson, Author

EATING WELL

Consoling myself over another miserly *petit déjeuner* by re-living past glories: musing over the etymology of the French *ecrévisse* and 'crayfish' while tucking into a plate of the boiled crustaceans at Ranomafana; the long list of chocolate desserts at Esterel in Toliara; melted goat's cheese with herbs on toast and a cold beer at Arboretum d'Antsokay; tender, juicy zebu shashliks along the highway at Ranohira; Tana, where you are simply spoilt for choice…

David Andrew, Author

3

GREG ELMS

2

RAY TIPPER

IFATY

Ifaty's white-sand beach (p124) with coral just offshore, fresh seafood for lunch and dinner, and spiny desert with the world's strangest vegetation a short walk away…

David Andrew, Author

4

MARGIE POLITZER

AMBALAVAO

Gabled roofs poking through the treetops in Ambalavao (p109) give the illusion of a European alpine village, only to be dispelled by the noise of hundreds of zebu at the country's biggest livestock market; elegant Malagasy people in their felt hats and finery; and the roar of *ramba-rambas* (carts) being pushed through the streets.

David Andrew, Author

RIVER TRIP

My daughter offered me three days canoeing and camping down the Tsiribihina River (p149) as a highlight to my 70th birthday holiday – and so it was! We hired our own *piroguier* in Miandrivazo (p150), bought colourful raffia sun hats (made from rice leaves) in the market and set off for an adventure. The tranquillity of the broad river was pure joy. We had sightings of the riverside birds, a sleeping crocodile with a baby, workers in the rice fields, wading fishermen in the shallows, and a family of Verreaux's sifakas flying between enormous fluted fig trees with young on board.

Sylvia Mercer, Traveller

ANDERS BLOMQVIST

A DAY IN THE RÉSERVE SPÉCIALE DE L'ANKÀRANA

This reserve (p186) makes a wonderful day trip from Diego Suarez and features some truly bizarre scenery. We couldn't get enough photos of the strange spires of ruby-red *tsingy* (limestone pinnacle formations) and we got more than excited when we spotted one of the nearly a dozen species of lemur living in this still-wild reserve.

Becca Blond, Author

TOM PARKINSON

OLIVIER CIRENDINI

VANILLA PODS

Madagascan vanilla is sold the world over. The pod comes from the vanilla orchid plant, originally from Mexico, which is converted via a long, complicated process. The northeast of Madagascar is where sweet vanilla can be smelled as it is tied in bundles.

Eizzi, Traveller

ANDERS BLOMQVIST

8 FIANAR TO MANAKARA BY TRAIN

I like to be among local life rather than see it as a tourist and I love train journeys, so the 12-hour trip (p108) from Fianarantsoa to the seaside with Malagasy workers and families, through tea and coffee plantations, banana forests and 48 dark tunnels, and past hills and waterfalls, was just the ticket. Hordes of villagers at all 17 stations sell their produce: cooked meat, live crayfish, fruit and my favourite, rice-flour fairy buns baked in tins on the top of roadside burners. One long picnic outing!

Eveline Rose, Traveller

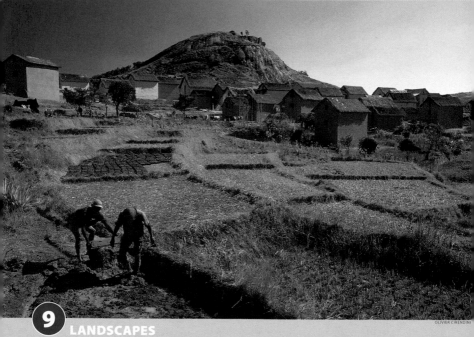

OLIVIER CIRENDINI

9 LANDSCAPES

Red soil and incredibly green rice fields in the highlands, deserted beaches and rainforests in the east, dry hills in all shades of brown around Lac Alaotra…

Munkel, Traveller

Contents

Regional Map Contents

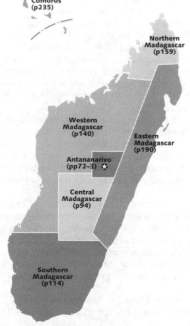

Comoros
(p235)

Northern
Madagascar
(p159)

Western
Madagascar
(p140)

Eastern
Madagascar
(p190)

Antananarivo
(pp72–3) ✿

Central
Madagascar
(p94)

Southern
Madagascar
(p114)

Destination Madagascar & Comoros

They don't make places like Madagascar any more – and they never did, for *la Grande Île* is like nowhere else on earth. Cast adrift from Africa about 165 million years ago, its cargo of strange animals and plants has been evolving in isolation ever since. Most famous are the acrobatic lemurs and bizarre chameleons, but the island's extraordinary plants include forests of spiny 'octopus' trees and bottle-shaped baobabs.

The country's biodiversity may have ancient affinities with Africa but its people definitely don't: they are descended from Indo-Malayan seafarers who arrived here along Indian Ocean trade routes a mere 2000 years ago. Their staple crop is rice grown on terraced hillsides that would be reminiscent of Indonesia – if it weren't for the villages of European-looking multistorey brick houses with shuttered windows and carved balconies. The language also has affinities with Southeast Asia, but Malagasy culture is steeped in its own brand of taboo and magic: you can still see highland families dance with their dead relatives in the 'turning of the bones' ceremony.

All this forms the backdrop to a country striving to shake off a French colonial legacy under the leadership of a sharp-suited yogurt baron named Marc Ravalomanana. Since independence, Madagascar has struggled under one incompetent and corrupt government after another; it is still one of the poorest countries in the world. President Ravalomanana's tenure began in 2002 with a controversial election win that left his opponents smarting. But so far the new boy has been as good as his word: he has repaired the main highways and introduced a new currency; his expansion of Madagascar's national park system has been met with worldwide approval; and Unesco granted the country a third World Heritage site in 2006. Growing confidence in the economy has seen $20 billion wiped from Madagascar's foreign debt by the World Bank.

All this in four short years – a pace of reform almost unheard of in nearby Africa. Ravalomanana has clearly got his sights set on attracting foreign investment and has promised to use his entrepreneurial flair to fight poverty and hunger. Of course change comes slowly for the average citizen, but despite protestations from his political opponents public optimism was high enough to return Ravalomanana to a second term in office late in 2006.

Meanwhile the president's former rival, Didier Ratsiraka, is licking his wounds under French protection after a Malagasy court sentenced him to 10 years' jail *in absentia* for corruption. This decision had chins wagging in the capital, Antananarivo, but of more pressing concern to some has been the recovery of Madagascar's vanilla crop after devastating cyclones in 2003. Madagascar grows half the world's supply of the fragrant beans, but rival producers such as Uganda are shaping up as serious competition.

With a recent history that sounds like a Graham Greene satire, it's business as usual in the Comoros as squabbling politicians use inter-

FAST FACTS

Madagascar

Population: 19,448,815

GDP per capita: €652

Average annual income per capita: €565

Average life expectancy: 62 years

Annual rate of inflation: 12%

Degrees a chameleon can swivel its eyes: 180

Length of an aye-aye's tail: 45cm

Comoros

Population: 711,417

Average annual income per capita: €464

Average life expectancy: 62.7 years

Annual rate of inflation: 5%

Fruit-bat population: 1200

island rivalry to secure their own powers. A peace accord between the three islands of the Union des Comores allowed for better definition of the role of the central government: each island retains its own president but presidency of the union is now shared on a rotating basis. In May 2006 a businessman and Islamic moderate educated in the Middle East, Ahmed Abdallah Sambi, was elected as the second island president, taking over from President Assoumani Azali.

In Mayotte political discussion continues to revolve around the island being recognised as a French *département d'outre mer* (overseas territory) in the coming few years, a move sought by local leaders for its economic benefits.

Getting Started

If you were brought up on tales of exotic wayfarers such as Gerald Durrell and Dervla Murphy, you probably have a mental image of Madagascar as a hot, sticky land where nothing works properly and nobody moves after midday, and where diabolical roads cause long delays for nearly everything. Well you're in for a surprise, as this is one of the most pleasant and charming countries you'll ever visit. The colonial legacy has left just enough Gallic order to keep transportation, banking and other necessities moving, without ruining this naturally fascinating land and its endemic culture. Sure, things go wrong, as they do everywhere in the developing world: bridges fall into rivers, cyclones destroy villages and buses break down. But just as some roads are slow and bumpy, many are new and smooth; taxis-brousses (bush taxis) break down with monotonous regularity but Air Madagascar flies shiny new planes; and you may get sick of rice in the *hauts plateaux* (highlands) but you can feast on seafood on the coast. There's none of the random menace that mars so many African destinations and – *merci, bon Dieu* – the food is excellent.

The main problem is deciding how to make the best use of your time – each of Madagascar's fascinating corners offers something different, but the island is so large that travel (or, if you don't use a travel agent, organising transport) will take up a fair chunk of your time. Decide whether your priority is bumming around on beaches, hiking pristine rainforests in search of lemurs, climbing bizarre rock formations or canoeing down a river for several days – to suggest but a few. Key points to remember are that you should definitely book ahead during European holiday periods, and that you will need to speak at least some French, even if it's only enough to cope with basic comforts.

The following information is intended to point you in the right direction while planning your trip – please refer to the Directory (p263) for more detailed information. Perhaps the most useful advice we can offer is to get into the mindset of the locals, who believe that what can't be changed isn't worth worrying about. The Malagasy phrase '*mora mora*' (slowly, slowly) pretty much sums up the attitude of the Malagasy to impatient or demanding travellers.

The Comoros have an indolent, carefree atmosphere, but chances are that if you're visiting these tropical islands you'll already have time on your hands and a sense of adventure anyway. The islands' small size and good roads make them pretty easy to travel around, but you'd still be well advised to prepare yourself for some frustrating moments: travelling between the islands, for example, can sometimes mean delays and it would be wise to have some time up your sleeve in case you have to stay longer than planned.

WHEN TO GO

Because Madagascar is so large, it experiences several climates simultaneously. For example, you could be pegged out on a beach in the southwest and a few days later be rugged up against the cold in the *hauts plateaux*. In general, the best time to travel in most areas is April and October/November. The only time you should avoid is January to March, when heavy rain can make many roads muddy and impassable, and when there's a high risk of cyclones in the east and northeast. The coolest time to travel is during the winter months (May to October), when the Central Highlands (including Antananarivo) can get cold, wet and windy, although it can still be hot and sunny in the west and southwest.

The west and southwest get searingly hot during the summer, but winter in these regions is pleasantly cool, with blue skies and little rain. Fort Dauphin

See Climate Charts (p267) for more information.

DON'T LEAVE HOME WITHOUT...

Antimalarials Most of Madagascar, and all of the Comoros, is a high-risk malaria area (p289).

Insect repellent Better still, don't let the blighters bite you in the first place (p292).

Waterproofs and warm clothing Much of Madagascar is colder and wetter than you think.

A decent tent with a groundsheet Tents can be hired in Madagascar, but they're not always good quality.

Water purifiers Better to treat your own water (p292) than lug litres along with you on hikes.

Modest clothing Your skimpy little number won't be appreciated in the Islamic Comoros.

Torch (flashlight) You'll need it for night walks, cave explorations and unlit camping grounds, and during power cuts.

Earplugs Taxi-brousse drivers love their radios, and cheap hotels are usually noisy, too.

Tampons Not easy to find in many places, and often expensive.

---

can experience rain as late in the year as July. In the east and northeast be prepared for rain and overcast skies at any time; on the Masoala Peninsula and around Maroantsetra the wettest months are from July to September.

Hotels, popular tourist attractions and all forms of transport, including planes and buses, fill up during European holiday periods, ie July to August, Christmas and Easter. Prices also go up at these times. The period between June and October is vanilla season on the east coast, so flights between towns such as Maroantsetra, Mananara and Antalaha often fill up far in advance.

The Comoros are hot and sticky year-round. If you're visiting between October and April, be prepared for torrential monsoon rains. The coolest part of the year is between April and September. In July and August plane tickets to the Comoros are expensive and hard to come by, thanks to expat Comorians returning from Europe for their annual holiday. During the holy Muslim month of Ramadan (dates vary from year to year), shops open for only a couple of hours a day, and many restaurants, bars and discos are closed.

COSTS & MONEY

Madagascar is a pretty cheap travel destination and by global standards represents good value for money, although transport is getting more expensive due to the rising cost of fuel. A couple staying in midrange hotels (solo travellers will mostly have to pay for double rooms in hotels), eating at fairly decent restaurants and travelling mostly by public transport, with the odd domestic flight, could reckon on about €40 per person per day. However, to get off the beaten track you may want to hire a 4WD for a few days, which will set you back another €90 or so per day (plus fuel). Most hotels offer significant discounts for children under 12. Budget travellers camping or sleeping in very cheap hotels, eating street meals and going everywhere by public transport can get by on about €20 per day. For both food and lodging, prices in Antananarivo and Nosy Be are a bit higher than elsewhere in the country.

Price-conscious travellers could be in for a nasty shock in the Comoros, particularly in Mayotte: fixed exchange rates and imported goods make these islands some of the most expensive destinations in the Indian Ocean. Hotel rooms, however basic, rarely fall below €25, while private taxi charters cost around €40. Meals at Comorian restaurants cost at least €7 for a main course and in Mayotte the cost is usually even higher, with pizzas costing €12 not being unheard of!

TRAVEL LITERATURE

Most books are published in different editions by different publishers in different countries. As a result, a book might be a hard-cover rarity in one country, but readily available in paperback in another. Some of the following

HOW MUCH?

Madagascar

Cup of coffee €0.80

Seafood feast €12

Shared-taxi ride €0.90

50km bus trip €2.10

A zebu €180

Comoros

One dive €28.50

Seafood feast €12.25

Shared-taxi ride €0.80

Half-day canoe hire €14.65

A goat €20.35

See also the Lonely Planet Index on the inside front cover.

titles may be hard to come by – your bookshop or library can advise you on availability – but we guarantee they will be almost impossible to find in Madagascar or the Comoros, so stock up on reading material before you go.

Maverick in Madagascar, by Mark Eveleigh, is a quirky tale of the author's travels on foot down Madagascar's northwest coast and the infamous western 'Zone Rouge'.

Zoo Quest to Madagascar, by David Attenborough, is a marvellously dated account of the intrepid TV presenter's trip to Madagascar in the 1960s.

The Aye-Aye and I, by Gerald Durrell, is another golden oldie – the irrepressible Durrell took his team of long-suffering naturalists and filmmakers to Madagascar to capture the island's rarest lemur.

The Coelacanth: A Fish Out of Time, by Samantha Weinberg, is a fascinating account of a quest to find the prehistoric coelacanth and has lots of good background material on the Comoros.

The Eighth Continent: Life, Death, and Discovery in the Lost World of Madagascar, by Peter Tyson, is a blend of scientific journalism, conservation politics and travelogue. The author accompanied four scientists on their journeys through Madagascar.

Lemurs of Madagascar is a pocket-sized field guide, published by Conservation International, with superb illustrations that will help you identify every lemur species.

Muddling Through Madagascar, by Dervla Murphy, is the eccentric travel writer's account of an accident-prone trip to Madagascar with her 14-year-old daughter.

INTERNET RESOURCES

Internet sites on Madagascar and the Comoros are fairly numerous, but most are in French and few are entirely up to date. The following have some or all of their content in English as well as French.

8th Continent (www.ucpzone.com.madagascar/en/) This site should convince you to visit Madagascar and support its ecotourism projects, and contribute to a greater understanding of the land and its environment.

Angap (www.parcs-madagascar.com) The official website of Madagascar's national parks association has maps and information on each park and reserve in the country.

BBC Country Profiles (http://news.bbc.co.uk/1/hi/world/africa/country_profiles) Comprehensive background information and the latest news headlines on both Madagascar and the Comoros.

Comoros Home Page (www.ksu.edu/sasw/comoros/comoros.html) Comprehensive, if slightly random, information and a long list of links, plus some photos.

Lonely Planet (www.lonelyplanet.com) General information on Madagascar and the Comoros, with links to traveller reports and useful websites.

Visit Madagascar (www.visitmadagascar.org) A very professionally produced website with lots of information on Madagascar and its people, landscapes and wildlife.

World Factbook (www.cia.gov/library/publications/the-world-factbook/geos/ma.html) Reams of rather dry statistical information on every aspect of the country. Pretty comprehensive, but this site is run by the CIA…

LANGUAGE

'If you don't speak French, you are strongly advised to learn some or travel with someone who does'

French is the official language in both Madagascar and the Comoros. In Madagascar it is widely spoken all over the island, although in some remote areas only Malagasy is spoken and written on menus, signs etc. If you don't speak French, you are strongly advised to learn some or travel with someone who does – especially if you're planning to travel independently off the beaten track. English is not spoken by anyone much at all, except in some hotels in major tourist centres, and that usually includes any travellers you might meet along the way. It's also extremely helpful to

TOP PICKS

Antananarivo
MADAGASCAR
Mozambique
Channel

LEMUR-WATCHING SPOTS

You won't see these fabulous primates anywhere else, so make the most of it! Beady eyes, luxuriant fur and treetop acrobatics are all on offer at the following places.

- Parc National d'Andasibe-Mantadia (p192)
- Parc National de Ranomafana (p103)
- Réserve Spéciale de l'Ankàrana (p186)
- Réserve Privée de Berenty (p136)
- Station Forestiére d'Ampijoroa (p147)

TROPICAL BEACH PARADISES

After days slogging through the jungle slipping on mud or wedged into a taxi-brousse, here are the perfect spots to kick back and indulge your inner sloth.

- Anakao, near Toliara (p127)
- Nosy Iranja, off Nosy Be (p174)
- Île aux Nattes, off Île Sainte Marie (p215)
- Lokaro Peninsula, near Fort Dauphin (p134)
- Itsandra beach, near Moroni, Grande Comore (p242)

HIKES & TREKS

Madagascar is a walker's destination. Conditions and levels of difficulty vary, but most visitors will be strapping on their walking boots at some point. These are some of the most breathtaking walks on the island.

- Grotte des Portugais, Parc National de l'Isalo (p123)
- Grands Tsingy, Parc National des Tsingy de Bemaraha (p151)
- Peninsula circumambulation, Masoala Peninsula (p223)
- Ascent of Pic Imarivolanitra, Parc National d'Andringitra (p110)
- Parc National de Mananara-Nord, northeast coast (p217)

use a travel agency or tour operator where some English is spoken – you'll find it invaluable if a flight is cancelled or something else goes wrong. Similarly, if you hire a car ask for an English-speaking driver; even if they have only basic English they will be a great asset to your trip.

You should be able to get by on high-school French and if you haven't spoken it for a while it'll soon come back to you as you'll get plenty of practice. Carrying Lonely Planet's *French Phrasebook* is a good start: the gentle, charming Malagasy can be rather reserved and a phrase or two in a language they understand will go a long way towards breaking the ice. Try to master a few basics, such as numbers, how to obtain food and accommodation, and – pretty important, this – how to get online at an internet café (once you log on to Google you're away, but French-language keyboards are the Devil's work and you'll need to negotiate log-ins and time limits).

Itineraries

CLASSIC ROUTES

THE NORTH
Two weeks / Diego Suarez to Nosy Be

The remote north of Madagascar offers rainforest hikes, spectacular rock formations and white beaches just waiting to be lazed upon.

Spend a few days hiking or rock climbing around colonial **Diego Suarez** (p175), then head out to sleepy **Joffreville** (p183) for a trek in the magical forest of **Parc National de Montagne d'Ambre** (p184).

Return to Diego before setting out for three days in **Réserve Spéciale de l'Ankàrana** (p186), a wilderness of caves, pinnacles and canyons.

At the end of your trip, you could continue to **Ambilobe** (p188); from there it's easy enough to find onward transport to **Ambanja** (p174) and on to **Ankify** (p174). From here you can catch a ferry across to **Nosy Be** (p160), Madagascar's premier beach destination.

On the 'big island', head north from **Hell-Ville** (p165) to **Andilana** (p171) to find the best beaches. Factor in a few days to enjoy the coral reefs and white sand of outlying islands such as **Nosy Iranja** (p174; the place to splurge on a luxury hotel), **Nosy Komba** (p172) or **Nosy Sakatia** (p173).

The north route is around 250km, plus a bit more for Parc National de Montagne d'Ambre and Réserve Spéciale de l'Ankàrana. Flying between Diego and Nosy Be will save time.

ROUTE DU SUD   One month / Antananarivo to Toliara
The lovely smooth tarmac of the Route Nationale 7 (RN7), commonly known as the Route du Sud, will whisk you from Antananarivo down to Toliara, stopping en route for some fantastic trekking opportunities.

Begin in **Antananarivo** (p70), with a few days to adjust to Malagasy life and take in the sights. From **Antsirabe** (p95), with its wide colonial streets and hordes of colourful rickshaws, it's a short journey to **Ambositra** (p100), the shopping capital of Madagascar, where you can take your time to choose a few souvenirs from myriad carved handicrafts. Excellent side-trips include hiking or cycling to Zafimaniry villages around **Antoetra** (p102), but allow at least three days if you want to get off the beaten track.

Further south you'll pass through spectacular mountain scenery until you reach **Fianarantsoa** (p105), but there's no real reason to linger here – backtrack to **Parc National de Ranomafana** (p103) for a pristine rainforest experience. Time your visit to the beautiful highland town of **Ambalavao** (p109) to coincide with the noises and smells of Madagascar's largest zebu market, then spend a few days hiking among the granite peaks of **Parc National d'Andringitra** (p110). **Ranohira** (p119) is an ideal base for three or four days' trekking in nearby **Parc National de l'Isalo** (p122), with its jagged sandstone massifs, cool canyons and endless plains.

After some pretty hard travelling and trekking, peg yourself out on the perfect beaches of **Anakao** (p127) or **Ifaty** (p124), near **Toliara** (p115); from there you can fly back to Antananarivo or travel on to Fort Dauphin (p130) or Morondava (p153).

The Route du Sud is 941km of tarmac, plied by numerous taxis-brousses (bush taxis) as far as Toliara. You can speed it up by leaving out some of the treks en route.

EAST COAST
                                              One month / Antananarivo to Île Sainte Marie

Tripping down the dizzy escarpment to the east coast, you can take in some of the country's best wildlife watching, from wailing lemurs to leaping whales, plus pirate graveyards, superb beaches and diving. Unless you take your own car all the way, you'll need to be flexible enough to travel by taxi-brousse (bush taxi), canal boat and even dugout canoe!

Begin in **Antananarivo** (p70), spending a few days strolling along the cobbled streets. Then head east along the surfaced Route Nationale 2 (RN2) to the charming village of **Andasibe** (p195), jumping-off point for the luxuriant, misty rainforests of **Parc National d'Andasibe-Mantadia** (p192). Spend at least a couple of days waking to the cries of the legendary indri (Madagascar's largest lemur species), hiking and bird-watching before winding down the RN2 again to the coast. At **Brickaville** (p197) rent a car or hitch to the tiny villages of **Ambila-Lemaitso** (p230) or **Manombato** (p230). From here, take to the waterways and lakes of the French-built **Canal des Pangalanes** (p228), stopping off at **Palmarium Reserve** (p229), or the tranquil fishing villages on the way north.

Stroll among the crumbling colonial grandeur of **Toamasina** (p197), have close encounters with semi-tame lemurs at **Parc Zoologique Ivoloina** (p203) and seek out white beaches at **Mahavelona** (p204), **Mahambo** (p205) and **Fenoarivo-Atsinanana** (p205). Or head straight to **Soanierana-Ivongo** (p206), from where you can catch a boat across to **Île Sainte Marie** (p206). Should you need some serious R&R you could splash out on a fabulous luxury hotel, soak up the island's torrid pirate history, watch breaching whales or go diving. The brave-hearted can seek further adventures by continuing further north on the Vanilla Coast (p216).

> The east coast route is around 500km of road, track, canal and sea! A shorter version leaves out the resorts north of Toamasina and heads straight for Île Sainte Marie.

ROADS LESS TRAVELLED

THE VANILLA COAST   **One month / Île Sainte Marie to Diego Suarez**

The crazy world of the Vanilla Coast is tailor-made for travellers with plenty of time and a well-developed sense of adventure. Those who do attempt this journey will not regret it.

Begin with a few days relaxing in **Île Sainte Marie** (p206) to fortify yourself for the mission ahead. From here, fly or catch a cargo boat to **Mananara** (p218) for a trip to remote **Parc National de Mananara-Nord** (p216), or spend a night on **Aye-Aye Island** (p218). Fly, trek or catch another cargo boat northwards to **Maroantsetra** (p220), the base for visiting the lost world of **Nosy Mangabe** (p219) and its dramatic surrounding coastline. From here, it's on to the stunning **Masoala Peninsula** (p223), where you can have the privilege of hiking or mountain-biking around the little-visited rainforests flanked by marine parks. The less energetic can spend a few days sea-kayaking or snorkelling at Cap Masoala or Tampolo. Return to Maroantsetra and fly across to **Antalaha** (p225), or trek all the way to **Cap Est** (p225).

Once in Antalaha, a good road leads to the dramatic beaches at **Sambava** (p226), with a side trip to charming **Andapa** (p227) and **Parc National de Marojejy** (p227) or **Réserve Spéciale d'Anjanaharibe-Sud** (p227). These are hard hiking areas, so factor in some recovery time, or opt for easier walks in the region of Andapa. From Sambava, you can fly or continue by taxi-brousse to **Diego Suarez** (p175).

This route is around 900km, much of it without proper roads. Between June and October rough seas make cargo boats dangerous, so you'll have to walk or fly some sections.

THE WILD WEST   Two weeks / Antsirabe to Morondava

Travel in Madagascar's harsh western region, home of the fiercely proud Sakalava people, can be daunting at first, but a number of organised tours (p97) are available if you want to make things easier on yourself.

Begin in **Antsirabe** (p95), a genteel and civilised town in the Central Highlands and the best place to find a group if you're looking to do an organised tour. The hot little town of **Miandrivazo** (p150) nearby is the push-off point for canoe trips down the **Tsiribihina River** (p149). It takes around three days to drift down to the village of Antsiraraka, then three hours by 4WD to **Belo-sur-Tsiribihina** (p151).

From Belo, continue south to **Morondava** (p153), or take the rough road north to **Parc National des Tsingy de Bemaraha** (p151). Once there you can explore the Grands and Petits Tsingy, before the long day's drive back to Morondava, stopping to get those sunset photos at the impressive **Avenue du Baobab** (p156). Morondava itself is a laid-back seaside town that makes a good base for a visit to the **Réserve Forestière de Kirindy** (p156), home to the elusive *fosa* and the giant jumping rat, or a pirogue ride down the coast to the fishing village of **Belo-sur-Mer** (p157). From Morondava you can fly, sail or drive (if you're brave) down to Toliara (p115) in the south. Alternatively, you can fly or drive back to Antananarivo (p70).

The wild west route is about 630km, encompassing tarmac, river and dirt roads. Leaving out Parc National des Tsingy de Bemaraha will reduce it to about a week.

TAILORED TRIPS

BEACH ODYSSEY

The dizzying variety of perfect beaches and coral-fringed islands of Madagascar and the Comoros means that unless you're prepared to take several internal flights or spend months travelling, you'll have to be selective.

Begin in **Mayotte** (p255), where the charms lie almost entirely underwater, with several diving companies available to help you discover them. Snorkel with sea turtles, then island-hop to the hidden bays and rocky islets of the **Parc Marin de Mohéli** (p248). Continue to **Grande Comore** (p235) to relax on the white sands of the beaches at Itsandra or Mitsamiouli. **Anjouan** (p249) offers less in the way of beaches than the other Comoros islands, but is still worth a visit for the chance to swim in the perfect bay of **Moya** (p254).

A flight or perhaps a passing yacht can take you to **Nosy Be** (p160) and its outlying islands, which provide at least a week's worth of diving, sailing, fishing or simply lazing on beaches that are fit for the most discerning castaway.

The beach odyssey needn't end there – you can always head from Nosy Be to **Diego Suarez** (p175) and set off eastwards, ticking off the beaches at **Sambava** (p226), **Antalaha** (p225) and **Nosy Mangabe** (p219), with perhaps a spot of whale-watching on your way to **Île Sainte Marie** (p206).

BIODIVERSITY TOUR

A good cross-section of Madagascar's biodiversity is accessible along or near RN7 between Tana and Toliara, although most is found in the rainforests of the eastern seaboard. This itinerary provides a snapshot of what's available.

Beginning in **Toliara** (p115), seek out some of the amazing birds in the spiny forest behind **Ifaty** (p124), then visit the fascinating botanic garden at **Arboretum d'Antsokay** (p127). From there, head north to the mountains, stopping at **Parc National Zombitse-Vohibasia** (p124) before the long drive to **Parc National de Ranomafana** (p103). Spend at least two days looking for birds and lemurs along the trails in this beautiful rainforest park, and take a guided walk to watch nocturnal species.

From Ranomafana, continue via Antananarivo to **Parc National d'Andasibe-Mantadia** (p192) to observe indris and other lemur species, plus more stunning birds, chameleons, plants and insects.

If time permits, other worthwhile options are to cut across from Antsirabe to **Morondava** (p153) for the dry western deciduous forest at the **Réserve Forestière de Kirindy** (p156), the best place to see the elusive *fosa*; fly to **Fort Dauphin** (p130) and visit **Parc National d'Andohahela** (p136), or **Réserve Privée de Berenty** (p136) for some excellent wildlife photo opportunities; and drive to **Station Forestière d'Ampijoroa** (our favourite; p147) for a superb ecotourism experience with a great variety of lemurs, waterbirds and crocodiles.

History
MADAGASCAR

ARRIVALS FROM ASIA & EUROPE

Considering that humans evolved on the African continent just across the Mozambique Channel, their arrival in Madagascar was comparatively late and by a rather circuitous route. Anthropological and ethnographical clues indicate that Indo-Malayan seafarers may have colonised the island after migrating in a single voyage, stopping en route at various points in the Indian Ocean. Their coastal craft possibly worked their way along the shores of India, Arabia and East Africa, trading as they went, before finally arriving in Madagascar. Linguistic clues also support this theory, as elements of Sanskrit have been identified in the Malagasy language.

These first settlers brought with them the food crops of their homelands, such as rice, and even today the island's glassy tiers of paddy fields resemble the landscape of Southeast Asia. This Asian way of life was tempered over the years by contact with Arabic and African traders, who plied the seas of the region with their cargoes of silks, spices and slaves. Gradually the Asian culture of the new settlers was subsumed into a series of geographically defined kingdoms, which in turn gave rise to many different Malagasy tribes.

Marco Polo was the first European to report the existence of a 'great red island', which he named Madagascar, after possibly having confused it with Mogadishu in Somalia. But Arab cartographers, who at the time were way ahead of their European counterparts, had long known the island as Gezirat Al-Komor, meaning 'island of the moon' (a name later transferred to the Comoros). It wasn't until 1500 that the first Europeans set foot on Madagascar, when a fleet of Portuguese vessels arrived. As Portugal's political and military power waned over the ensuing centuries, the Dutch and British tried to establish permanent bases at various points around the Madagascar coast, only to be defeated by disease and less-than-friendly locals who suspected them of being slave traders.

More successful were the efforts of buccaneers from Britain, France, North America and elsewhere, who for several decades from the end of the 17th century onwards made Madagascar an Indian Ocean base from which they attacked merchant ships on their way to and from Europe via the Cape of Good Hope. The pirates allegedly buried copious amounts of treasure and certainly contributed generously to the local gene pool.

A History of Madagascar, by Mervyn Brown, is the most up-to-date and authoritative work on the islands' history.

Flags, lists of kings and queens, and the chance to listen to Madagascar's national anthem are all at www.worldstatesmen .org/Madagascar.htm.

TIMELINE Madagascar

2nd century AD	1500	late 18th century
Madagascar is settled by Indo-Malayans who migrate by sea from the distant shores of Indonesia and Malaysia. They bring with them agricultural, linguistic and cultural traits. Most present-day Malagasy are descended from these settlers.	Portuguese sailors under the command of Diego Dias become the first Europeans to set foot on Madagascar; Dias names the island Ilha de São Lourenço, but as Portuguese influence wanes the name is forgotten.	Merina chief Ramboasalama assumes the throne at Ambohimanga and with the help of European arms traders and military advisors unifies the various Merina peoples into a powerful kingdom.

'NO FRONTIER BUT THE SEA'

As Malagasy trade with Europe grew during the 18th century, several rival kingdoms began to vie for dominance. The Menabe people under Andriamisara I founded a capital on the banks of the Sakalava River, from which the modern-day Sakalava tribe took its name. Meanwhile on the east coast, Ratsimilaho – the son of an English pirate and a Malagasy princess – succeeded in unifying rival tribes into a people that became known as the Betsimisaraka. In central Madagascar a certain Chief Ramboasalama took the snappy name Andrianampoinimerinandriantsimitoviaminandriampanjaka (Andrianampoinimerina for short), meaning 'Hope of Imerina', and unified the Merina into a powerful kingdom that soon came to dominate much of Madagascar.

In 1810 Andrianampoinimerina was succeeded by his equally ambitious son Radama I, who organised a highly trained army that conquered Boina (the main Sakalava kingdom in northwestern Madagascar), the Betsimisaraka peoples to the east, the Betsileo to the south and the kingdom of Antakàrana in the far north, whose warrior princes preferred suicide or exile to surrender. Unable to take the Sakalava kingdom of Menabe by force, Radama prudently married Princess Rasalimo, daughter of the Menabe king, thereby fulfilling a vow made by his father that the Merina kingdom would have no frontier but the sea.

King Andrianampoinimerina gave his soldiers charms made from crocodile teeth filled with magic herbs to protect them from the bullets of their Sakalava enemies.

His empire-building complete, Radama I set about courting European powers, especially Great Britain. British missionary influence followed; the London Missionary Society (LMS) soon arrived with a contingent of Welsh missionaries, many of whom died from fever when they reached Madagascar. Undaunted, the survivors set about converting the Merina court to Christianity and set up several schools around the country. By 1835 the Bible had been printed in Malagasy.

In 1828 Radama died at the tender age of 36. His successor was his widow Ranavalona I, who may well have done away with him herself, and she promptly set about reversing Radama's policies. Those who refused to abandon Christianity were hurled over the cliffs outside the Rova in Antananarivo (p77). During her 33 years in power Ranavalona elevated torture and execution to new plateaus of inventiveness. Boiling water was poured over victims tied to stakes in pits, while some condemned prisoners were sawn in half or had their arms and legs chopped off and were sewn up into sacks for a lingering death. She was said to be sexually insatiable and had a stream of lovers, many of whom were put to death in their turn.

Criminal suspects under Queen Ranavalona I were forced to drink a strong poison. If they vomited profusely enough, they were declared innocent. Most died.

FRENCH CONQUEST & COLONIALISM

One of the few Europeans Queen Ranavalona tolerated was a French engineer, Jean Laborde, who built her summer palace and began Madagascar's industrial revolution with his huge factory complex at Lac Mantasoa. In 1861 Queen Ranavalona died, understandably unlamented by what remained of her subjects.

1817	1828	1861
Radama I enters into diplomatic relations with Great Britain, beginning a period of British aid and influence that remained strong until well into the 19th century. Missionaries convert the Merina court to Christianity.	Ranavalona I becomes queen, commencing a 33-year genocide of her people, killing perhaps 25% of them. She reverses Radama's policies, declares Christianity illegal and denounces European influence, isolating Madagascar from the world.	Ranavalona dies and Radama II becomes king, abolishing forced labour and reinstating freedom of religion. Missionary activity begins to expand once more and Christianity becomes the predominant religion of Madagascar.

She was succeeded by her son Radama II, who thankfully rescinded most of his mother's policies and welcomed back the Europeans.

After Radama II had been in power for a year a mysterious plague killed thousands of people in Antananarivo. The malady was attributed to the ancestors' discontent over the new king's relations with foreign powers and the growing influence of outsiders in Madagascar. In May 1862, Radama II was assassinated, strangled by a silken cord to avoid the *fady* (taboo) over the shedding of royal blood.

Flashman's Lady, by George Macdonald Fraser, is the fictional account of how a Victorian poltroon became entwined with Queen Ranavalona, and includes plenty of colourful detail on life at her court.

Rainilaiarivony, the king's assassin, took the post of prime minister and married Radama's widow, who took the title Rasoherina I. Any ideas the queen might have had of emulating her powerful predecessor were quickly quashed when the prime minister issued an edict stating that she could act only with the consent of her ministers – effectively leaving the real power to her husband.

Rasoherina survived until 1868 and was succeeded by Ranavalona II, who died in 1883 and was succeeded by Ranavalona III. Prime Minister Rainilaiarivony married both succeeding queens and became the principal power behind the throne, building a magnificent residence for himself in Antananarivo (p78).

By the late 19th century British interest in Madagascar had begun to wane and French influence increased. This turned to outright aggression in 1883 when French warships occupied major ports and forced the Malagasy government to sign a treaty declaring the island a French protectorate.

Further demands ensued, and in 1894 the French accused the Merina government of tyranny and demanded the capitulation of Queen Ranavalona III. When she rejected their demands a French army marched on Antananarivo, taking the capital in September 1895.

On 6 August 1896 Madagascar was officially declared a French colony. General Joseph Gallieni, the first governor-general, attempted to destroy the power of the Merina by suppressing the Malagasy language and all British influence, declaring French the official language. In 1897 Queen Ranavalona III was sent into exile in Algeria and the Merina monarchy was abolished.

MALAGASY NATIONALISM & INDEPENDENCE

In the early part of the 20th century Madagascar's new rulers abolished slavery, although it was replaced with an almost equally exploitative system of taxes, which resulted in forced labour for anyone who could not pay. Land was expropriated by foreign settlers, and a coffee-based import and export economy developed. With economic growth and an expanding education system a new Malagasy elite began to emerge, and resentment of the colonial presence grew in all levels of society. Several nationalist movements evolved among the Merina and Betsileo tribes, and strikes and demonstrations became more frequent.

Nationalist leader Jean Ralaimongo shared a room in Paris with the young Ho Chi Minh.

Nationalist leader Jean Ralaimongo began the Malagasy independence movement in the 1930s, but his campaign was cut short by the outbreak of WWII.

1896	1930s	1947
Madagascar becomes a French colony; Governor-General Joseph Gallieni declares French the official language and sets about destroying the power of the Merina and removing all British influence.	A Malagasy independence movement begins to gather momentum, fuelled by resentment of the French colonials by a growing, educated middle class and led by Nationalist leader, Jean Ralaimongo.	A rebellion led by Joseph Raseta and Joseph Ravoahangy is brutally suppressed by the French using Senegalese troops; tens of thousands of Malagasy are killed in the struggle and the rebellion's leaders are sent into exile.

During the first half of WWII the French in Madagascar came under the authority of the pro-Nazi Vichy government. But the Allies, fearing the Japanese could use Madagascar as a base to attack shipping, launched a seaborne attack and captured the town of Diego Suarez (p175). Antananarivo and other major towns also fell to the British after months of fighting but were handed back to the Free French (those who fought on the side of the Allies in WWII) of General de Gaulle in 1943.

Postwar Madagascar experienced a nationalist backlash, with resentment towards the French culminating in a rebellion in March 1947. The rebellion was eventually subdued after an estimated 80,000 to 90,000 Malagasy were killed. Its leaders, Joseph Raseta and Joseph Ravoahangy, were sent into exile. During the 1950s nationalist political parties were formed, the most notable being the Parti Social Démocrate (PSD) of Philibert Tsiranana, and reforms in 1956 paved the way to independence.

On 14 October 1958 the Malagasy Republic was proclaimed, becoming an autonomous state within the French Community. After a period of provisional government a constitution was adopted in 1959 and full independence was achieved on 26 June 1960, with Tsiranana the country's first president.

The colonists retained an economic advantage through Tsiranana, who referred to *les colons* as 'the 19th tribe'. But his government's continued ties with France, combined with a period of economic decline, contributed to the president's increasing unpopularity. After an uprising in southern Madagascar was brutally repressed in 1971, and a massive antigovernment uprising in the capital in 1972, Tsiranana was forced to resign and hand over power to his army commander, General Gabriel Ramantsoa.

Tabataba (The Spreading of Rumours), directed by Raymond Rajaonarivelo, is a film set in a small village near Manakara during the bloody 1947 rebellion against French rule.

THE 'THIRD REPUBLIC'

In February 1975 after several coup attempts, General Ramantsoa was forced to step down and was replaced by Colonel Richard Ratsimandrava, who was assassinated within a week of taking office. The rebel army officers who had announced the military takeover were quickly routed by officers loyal to Ramantsoa, and a new government headed by Admiral Didier Ratsiraka, a former foreign minister, came to power.

Not surprisingly, by this time French expats had begun to leave the country in droves, taking with them their skills, money and technology. Ratsiraka attempted radical political and social reforms in the late 1970s, severing all ties with France and courting favour with former Soviet-bloc nations. Following the example of Chinese leader Mao Zhedong, Ratsiraka even compiled a 'red book' of government policies and theories.

In March 1989 Ratsiraka's dubious election for a third seven-year term sparked riots and 1991 was marked by widespread demonstrations demanding the president's resignation. From May 1991 to January 1992, the government, economy and transportation systems ground to a halt in general strikes and riots, and protests left dozens dead.

26 June 1960	1975	1991
Madagascar gains full independence from France in a peaceful transition; Philibert Tsirinana is elected president, though in effect the French still run the country, controlling trade and financial institutions, and maintaining military bases.	General Gabriel Ramantsoa steps down after coup attempts; his followers appoint Admiral Didier Ratsiraka as leader. Ratsiraka adopts Soviet-style ideology and severs ties with France, leading to economic decline.	Further economic decline ignites widespread strikes and protests; the so-called 'Third Republic' calls for free elections but Ratsiraka refuses to step down. Opposition leader Albert Zafy is eventually elected president.

Check out www
.metmuseum.org/toah
/hd/madg_1/hd_madg
_1.htm for information
on Merina history from
the Metropolitan
Museum of Art in New
York.

In late October 1991, an agreement was signed with opposition politicians in preparation for popular elections and the birth of the so-called 'Third Republic'. However, Ratsiraka still refused to step down. In July 1992 there was an attempted civilian coup, but the rebels failed to gain popular support and were forced to surrender.

Civil unrest leading up to the first round of elections culminated in the blockading of the capital and the bombing of a railway bridge between Toamasina and Antananarivo. For weeks, the capital was without petrol and transportation was disrupted.

The first round of elections, which remained remarkably peaceful, resulted in victory for opposition candidate Professor Albert Zafy, ending Ratsiraka's first 17 years in power. But after years of communist-style dictatorship and economic mismanagement, Zafy's government found it difficult to ignite the economy and gain the trust of the people. Zafy was accused of money laundering and dealings with drug traffickers.

After trying to sack his prime minister the 70-year-old Zafy was unexpectedly impeached by his parliament in July 1996 for abuse of authority. New presidential elections were called in November 1996 and to the surprise of everyone, including international monitors, Ratsiraka (who had been in exile in France for the previous 19 months) won. Appealing for Madagascar to become a 'humanist and ecological republic', he took office once again in February 1997.

REFORM & A NEW OPTIMISM

Self-made millionaire Marc Ravalomanana began his path to success by pedalling around his hometown on a bicycle selling pots of homemade yogurt. By the time he became mayor of Antananarivo in 1999, his company, Tiko, was the biggest producer of dairy products in Madagascar and he was able to give away his yogurt to supporters on the streets. On election, he started to clean up the capital and won huge popularity.

In 2001 Ravalomanana announced his candidacy for the presidency of Madagascar under the banner of his TIM party (which stands in Malagasy for 'I Love Madagascar'). Using his business skills to court foreign investment, he pushed for rapid economic development and promised to stamp out government corruption, reduce poverty and repair Madagascar's badly maintained infrastructure.

Ravalomanana claimed outright victory in presidential elections in December 2001. But there was just one snag – so did Didier Ratsiraka. A bitter six-month struggle for power ensued, with both men insisting they were the rightfully elected leader of the country; there were accusations of vote-rigging by both sides. As Ravalomanana swore himself in as president, Ratsiraka declared a state of emergency and imposed martial law. As protests by supporters of both sides grew violent, Ratsiraka and several of his provincial governors set up an alternative capital in Toamasina.

1996	2001	2006
Among widespread accusations of criminal activities, President Zafy is impeached for abuse of power and general elections are called. Ratsiraka is returned to power and becomes president again in 1997.	Former yogurt peddler Marc Ravalomanana claims victory in presidential elections. Ratsiraka declares martial law and violent protests ensue; world opinion swings behind Ravalomanana, who is declared the winner after a six-month showdown.	Marc Ravalomanana is swept to office for a second term as president. Encouraging economic growth leads the World Bank to wipe US$20 billion from Madagascar's national debt; Unesco grants Madagascar a third World Heritage site.

The military eventually swung towards Ravalomanana, tipping the balance of power, and in April 2002 the Malagasy High Constitutional Court declared Ravalomanana the outright winner. By August Ravalomanana's administration had received endorsement from the UN, then won a convincing majority in elections for the National Assembly. Ratsiraka refused to accept that the game was over but left for exile in France anyway.

Ravalomanana quickly set about his reform agenda, introducing a new currency (the ariary) and repairing major road networks throughout the country. Foreign investors were cheered by a major hike in economic growth, and wooed by laws providing tax breaks and allowing foreigners to own land on the island. The World Bank issued the new government with a US$30 million credit to help fight poverty.

Ravalomanana won a second term in office in 2006, and in April 2007 a referendum endorsed constitutional reforms that will increase presidential powers and make English an official language. 'Madagascar is ready for take-off', Ravalomanana once told a press conference. For the moment, most people seem to share his belief, and the consensus is that the country is further than expected down the road to economic recovery.

THE COMOROS

Ancient seafarers traditionally hugged the coastline of continents and used island chains as stepping stones to colonise new lands. The Comorian chain formed a feasible route to Madagascar and it is thus probable that the earliest inhabitants of the Comoros islands were the same Indo-Malayan seafarers who first reached Madagascar about 2000 years ago. But for the same reason – the islands' proximity to Africa and established trade routes – further waves of immigrants settled the islands, including the Shirazis (Persians), who appeared in the Comoros in the 15th and 16th centuries.

The only comprehensive history of the islands in English is Malyn Newitt's *The Comoro Islands: Struggle Against Dependency in the Indian Ocean.*

The name Gezirat Al-Komor was used by medieval Arab cartographers to describe Madagascar, and at some point the name came to refer to the Comoros themselves. During the heyday of the Swahili civilisation, the Comoros became a major marketplace for goods such as spices, hides, weapons and precious metals. Many of the sailing dhows that landed in the Comoros' harbours also brought men, women and children captured from as far away as Zambia. Some of these slaves escaped or managed to buy their freedom, remaining on the islands to add an African element to the Arabic origin of today's Comorians.

The first reliable European accounts of the Comoros came from the Portuguese travellers Diego Dias and Ferdinand Soares, but until the mid-19th century Malagasy pirates, rather than European explorers, caused the most disruption to Comorian life. Pirate raids were common, with some Comorian women preferring suicide to capture and slavery. During this time the number

TIMELINE Comoros

2nd century AD	15th century	late 19th century
The Comoros are settled by the same Indo-Malayans who eventually went on to colonise Madagascar; in a relatively short time traces of their Asian ancestry are subsumed by African, Arab and Shirazi (Persian) immigrants.	The Comoros become part of a network of Islamic sultanates set up by the Shirazis along the western edge of the east coast of Africa, absorbing Swahili trade, architecture and culture.	One by one Comorian sultans willingly allow France to annexe the islands in return for protection or aid. French planters and traders prosper under France's relaxed attitude to slavery.

of sultans mushroomed at an alarming rate and at one stage there were no fewer than 12 sultans on the island of Grande Comore alone. Inter-sultanate squabbling and even war was a regular occurrence. This situation was exploited by the French, who during the late 19th century were jostling the other European superpower – Great Britain – for a strategic advantage in the region.

In 1830 a Malagasy prince, Ramanetaka, staged a coup on Mohéli, which left him in power as sultan. The French tried to gain a foothold in Mohéli by sending a governess to educate his young daughter, Fatima I. The ruse failed but Fatima began an affair with Joseph François Lambert, a French trader and adventurer from Mauritius. Lambert set up great plantations on Mohéli but by 1867 the affair had begun to wane. Fatima abdicated and fled the Comoros with a French gendarme, opening the way for the island to become a French protectorate.

COUPS & COUNTER-COUPS

'In 1908 Grande Comore was formally annexed, giving France a strategic base to balance the British presence on Zanzibar'

Meanwhile on Mayotte, Sultan Adriansouli ceded the island to the French in exchange for protection from his rivals. In May 1843 the island was transformed from a sultanate into a French planters' and slaveholders' haven, then a full colony of France. The ambitious sultan Saïd Ali of Grande Comore was even more forthright: in 1881 he formed a coalition with the French to oust the previous incumbent and take over as the island's *tibe* (grand sultan). And on Anjouan, Sultan Abdallah III ran into problems when at the behest of the British he agreed to halt slavery. Anjouan's landowners, who depended on slaves to farm their plantations, revolted. In April 1886 the ageing sultan turned to France, which had a more relaxed approach to slavery, and signed the treaty making the island a French protectorate. In 1908 Grande Comore was formally annexed, giving France a strategic base to balance the British presence on Zanzibar, and in 1912 Anjouan joined the rest of the Comoros as a full colony of France.

In a referendum held in 1974 the voters of Grande Comore, Anjouan and Mohéli voted for independence; Mayotte elected to stay under French rule. A few months later Ahmed Abdallah Abderemane of Grande Comore announced a unilateral declaration of independence and the formation of the Federal Islamic Republic of the Comoros, which consisted of Grande Comore, Anjouan and Mohéli. France intervened on behalf of Mayotte and the Comoros' transition to independence went ahead without Mayotte. In December 1975 France recognised the new government then stood back and waited for the fireworks.

In January 1976 Abderemane was overthrown in a mercenary-engineered coup by Ali Soilih, who imposed a form of Maoist-Marxist socialism and ruled using a private army that beat and robbed its way around Grande Comore under the euphemistic title of Jeunesse Révolutionnaire (Revolutionary Youth). Soilih spent long spells in his palace smoking marijuana and drinking whisky in the company of young women. Meanwhile on Mayotte a whopping 99% of the population voted to stay with France, not surprisingly.

1974	1976	1978
Ahmed Abdallah Abderemane announces a unilateral declaration of independence and the formation of the Federal Islamic Republic of the Comoros, comprised of Grande Comore, Mohéli and Anjouan; Mayotte votes to stay with France.	Ali Soilih seizes power after a coup and unsuccessfully tries to turn the Comoros into a secular, socialist republic; 99% of Mayotte's population votes to remain part of France.	Soilih is toppled in a coup by French mercenaries led by Bob Denard, setting in train nearly 20 years of further coups and counter-coups, including one by Denard himself; Denard is eventually packed off to France.

Relief came for Grande Comore when a band of French mercenaries led by Bob Denard landed at dawn on 13 May 1978. Within a few hours the army had surrendered and people took to the streets to celebrate. Ali Soilih was shot while 'trying to escape' and Ahmed Abdallah Abderemane was reinstated as president.

PLUS ÇA CHANGE...

Ahmed Abdallah was re-elected in March 1987, but allegations of fraud by the government resulted in numerous arrests, tortures and killings. In 1989 Abdallah was shot by his presidential guard in his palace. Bob Denard seized control but was quickly forced to surrender and then deported.

In 1990 Saïd Mohamed Djohar was declared winner of the Comoros' first free presidential elections since independence in 1975. For a while it looked as though things would improve, but his administration was dissolved and a referendum about whether he should continue to rule was held in 1992. Djohar was re-elected but Denard and his mercenaries returned in 1995 and packed the unpopular president off to Réunion. France sent 600 commandoes who forced the mercenaries to surrender and Denard was once again bound for Paris.

Mohammed Taki Abdul Karim was elected as president in December 1996. But after years of 'humiliation' by France and the Moroni-based government, Mohéli and Anjouan declared themselves autonomous republics. Taki ordered an invasion of Anjouan, but the government's forces were routed by the Anjouan militia. In 1997 self-elected president Ibrahim declared Anjouan's full independence from the federal government in Grande Comore. Almost immediately guerrilla war broke out between Ibrahim's supporters and those who wanted Anjouan to remain part of the federation.

Grande Comore also seemed to dissolve into anarchy. President Taki died suddenly in November 1998 and an interim government was appointed. On 30 April 1999 yet another military coup, this time staged by Colonel Azali Assoumani, ousted Grande Comore's interim government. Assoumani promised to reunite the islands as l'Union des Comores with a new constitution. In April 2002 elections were held for the four presidential roles; Assoumani declared himself the winner of the Union elections, and each island elected its own president. But it's just like old times again: with four presidents and only three islands, political and administrative confusion reigns and businessmen protest that they don't know which government to pay their taxes to! Only Anjouan rejected attempts to bring the island back into the Federal Republic until 2001, when a new 'military committee' led by Major Mohamed Bacar seized power.

The UN periodically calls on France to hand Mayotte back to l'Union des Comores but plans are afoot to change the island's status to a full *département d'outre mer* (overseas department), which would bring even closer administrative links with France.

Browse news stories about Madagascar and the Comoros with a humanitarian perspective at www.irinnews.org.

1999	April 2002	May 2006
A military coup staged by Colonel Azali Assoumani ousts the Grande Comore's interim government. Assoumani starts a process of reconciliation with Anjouan and Mohéli and promises a return to civilian rule.	Presidential elections are held in the Comoros; Assoumani declares himself the winner and president of l'Union des Comores; Grande Comore, Anjouan and Mohéli elect their own island presidents.	Ahmed Abdallah Sambi, a businessman and Islamic moderate educated in the Middle East, is elected as the second island president, taking over from President Azali Assoumani.

The Culture

THE NATIONAL PSYCHE
Madagascar

On arrival in Madagascar your first impression is likely to be of a polite but rather reserved, even distant, people. This may come as a surprise if you've already experienced the confidence and ebullience of Africans. But regarding the Malagasy as Africans is a big no-no. As far as the citizens of *La Grande Île* are concerned, they are just that – an island people, by implication far superior to the 'primitive' Africans. When the French colonised Madagascar they used Senegalese troops in some of their military operations, and to this day many Malagasy regard black Africans as nothing more than dangerous brutes.

In reality, the apparent timidity you'll encounter is a reflection of *Fihavanana*, which means 'conciliation' or 'brotherhood'; it stresses avoidance of confrontation and achievement of compromise in all walks of life. Most Malagasy seem reserved in everyday conversation, but in their culture it is unseemly to discuss some subjects. For example, it is considered tactless to air personal problems, even with close friends. Likewise, searching or indiscreet questions are avoided at all costs. *Fihavanana* is enshrined in Malagasy society, but it masks a fierce pride in the superiority of Malagasy culture, which is on the increase. Marc Ravalomanana's government has declared its aim of breaking the French cultural influence on the country and restoring Malagasy language and traditions.

If you see a young Malagasy man wearing a comb in his hair, he's advertising his search for a wife.

Politeness in general is very important to the Malagasy, and impatience or pushy behaviour is regarded as shocking. Passengers arriving for a flight place their tickets in a neat row on the check-in desk before patiently awaiting their turn. Similarly, bank customers arrange their papers in strict order along the counter while queuing, with no jostling or cheating tolerated. Indeed, customers may take the opportunity to catch up with friends, and someone further back in the queue will invariably call them when their turn arrives. As a foreigner you *may* be waved to the front of a bank queue – especially if, for example, a farmer clutching a shoebox full of old Malagasy francs is ahead of you – but never assume you will be given preferential treatment.

Nonetheless, the welcoming of strangers and the traditions of hospitality are held sacred throughout Madagascar. It is considered a household duty to offer food and water to a guest, no matter how poor the inhabitants are themselves. All over the country you'll come across a version of the same legend about the villagers who refused a cup of water to a mysterious stranger, only to be punished by having their village immolated.

Sexually, Malagasy society is fairly liberated; in some parts of the country young women are quite forward with sexual advances to men, including foreigners. Among the Malagasy, marriage is a pretty relaxed institution and divorce is common. Children are seen as the primary purpose of marriage, and essential to happiness and security. The idea that some people might choose not to have children is greeted with embarrassed disbelief. Women are seen – by themselves, anyway – as the most dynamic force in Malagasy society; wives are regarded as the head of the domestic sphere even if they also go out to work.

The family is the central tenet of Malagasy life, and includes not only distant cousins but also departed ancestors. Even urban, modern Malagasy, who reject the belief that ancestors have magic powers, regard those who are no longer alive as full members of the family. At *Famadihana* (literally, 'the turning of the bones') exhumation ceremonies, it's not unusual to see people lining up for a family photograph with the shroud-wrapped bodies of dead family members laid out neatly in the foreground.

The Comoros

A greater contrast could not be imagined than the Comorians, who bear little resemblance to the Malagasy on any level. For the most part they are outgoing, extroverted and emotional, ready to discuss their problems, life stories or political opinions at the drop of a *kofia* (embroidered skull cap). The people of Mayotte are a notable exception to this generalisation, and appear on first acquaintance to be rather stand-offish and surly. A succession of ever less competent governments has left Comorians with a healthy scepticism about politicians; most realise that they must rely on themselves to get ahead but, perhaps understandably, corruption and sharp business practices are rife.

The Comoros are Islamic states, where family values are strictly enshrined, and life revolves around the mosque and religious events such as the fast of Ramadan. Society is strictly divided, with the upper classes defined as those who have made a Grand Mariage (an elaborate wedding ceremony) or completed the pilgrimage to Mecca. Comorians generally regard themselves as African, holding close ties with fellow Muslims in Kenya and Zanzibar. In general they mistrust the Malagasy, whose pirates hounded the islands for centuries. Resentments also run high between Comorians from the different islands, with occasional outbreaks of inter-ethnic violence.

The colours of the Malagasy flag represent the red of royal blood, the white of the people and the green of the forest.

LIFESTYLE
Madagascar

The Malagasy home is the centre of the extended family, ancestors included. It is always furnished with care and attention, regardless of how poor the householder may be. Custom dictates that furniture, doors and windows should all be aligned according to astrological principles and placed in specific parts of the building.

In many areas it's considered disgusting to have a toilet inside the house, or to defecate inside a building at all, even if it's a purpose-built latrine. Health workers in Madagascar are trying to change this tradition because open-air toilets carry a higher risk of disease.

Personal adornment and fashion are hugely important to the Malagasy. This is partly influenced by the French colonists, but men and women alike take great care with their appearance. Hats, the most beloved of all fashion items, are worn cocked jauntily over one eye or with the brims demurely turned down to shade the face. It's not unusual to see swaggering young men sporting the sort of floral straw hat that Westerners associate with old ladies at garden parties! The influence of French culture has remained strong since independence: the French language continues to be widely spoken; it's not uncommon to see village women carrying a baguette in a traditional woven raffia shopping bag; and teenage boys play *boules* in the dusty streets of rural towns, avoiding the Citroen 2CVs and Renault 4s buzzing past.

Most Malagasy still believe life is largely governed by the forces of nature. It's still common to find sacred offerings left at the base of baobab trees, beside forest waterfalls or in front of royal tombs. Family outings to a beautiful

---

FADY

Fady is the name given to a system of local taboos designed to respect the ancestors. *Fady* can take innumerable forms and varies widely from village to village. It may be *fady* to whistle on a particular stretch of beach, to walk past a sacred tree, to eat pork or to swim in a certain river.

Although foreigners and other outsiders are normally exempt from *fady* (or are excused for breaking them), the taboos should be respected. The best thing to do is to ask locals for information, and to be particularly careful in the vicinity of tombs or burial sites.

MALAGASY PROVERBS

■ He who refuses to buy a lid for the pot will eat badly cooked rice.

■ Other people's children cause your nostrils to flare.

■ Done in by his own trade like a water merchant in the rain.

---

spot of family or tribal significance are a popular leisure activity and are usually accompanied by a picnic.

Concepts of time and date also have a great influence on Malagasy lifestyle. For example, Malagasy strongly believe in *vintana* (destiny), which influences the dates of parties held to mark circumcisions, marriages or reburials. Friday, which is associated with nobility, is considered a good day to hold a celebration.

In tourist hotspots such as Nosy Be and Diego Suarez it is common to see European men with beautiful young Malagasy girls on their arm. Foreign men may find the sexually liberated Malagasy women hard to resist, but prostitution is rampant in some major centres and HIV/AIDS is on the rise in Madagascar (see opposite). In recent years several arrests have been made on grounds related to sex tourism and the abuse of minors.

The Comoros

Islamic culture has led to the adoption of many aspects of Arab dress and custom in the Comoros. For example, men wear long, white robes known in Swahili as *kanzus*, often accompanied by embroidered skullcaps called *kofias*. Women cover their heads when walking outside the home.

Excellent articles on Comorian culture and literature can be found at www.comores-online.com/accueilgb.htm – even if it's all in French.

Homes are often extremely colourful, decorated with luridly patterned fabrics and elaborate gold-and-black plastic furniture. A picture of the holy mosque at Mecca nearly always has pride of place. The homes of those Comorians who've made the pilgrimage to Mecca usually feature a large photo of the pilgrim standing outside the mosque. Shoes are always left outside the house, as walking on the floor would render it unclean for prayer. Toilet paper is not used – instead a bucket of water or hosepipe is provided for the same purpose.

The centre of local life is the village or town square, known as the *bangwe*, where men spend many hours sitting in the shade of trees, discussing religious or political matters, drinking strong Arabic coffee and playing dominos or traditional board games.

ECONOMY

Both Madagascar and Comoros rank on the UN's register of the world's 50 poorest countries. Madagascar's economy is mainly subsistence agriculture, with rice, cassava, bananas and beans as some of the main food crops. The principal cash crops are coffee, vanilla, sugarcane, cloves and cocoa, with coffee, vanilla and sugar earning a substantial percentage of foreign exchange. There is a small amount of manufacturing, largely restricted to agricultural products and textiles, with some oil refining; and despite the recent sapphire boom the country is relatively poor in mineral resources. After years of socialist mismanagement the country has gone from being a major producer of rice in the 1960s to importing rice for subsistence today. Most foreign trade is with France, Japan and the USA, and Madagascar relies heavily on aid from international agencies.

Even after independence French companies have dominated the Comorian economy, diverting most of their profits overseas and investing little in the islands' infrastructure. As a consequence food crops have declined and the islands have become increasingly dependent on food imports, especially rice.

Foreign aid is generally minuscule but has seen steady improvement in public health, education and sustainable agriculture. France receives most of the Comoros' exports, which include vanilla, ylang-ylang and cloves; imports mainly consist of rice, meat, petroleum and building materials.

POPULATION

Madagascar's population is one of the fastest-growing in the region and is growing at a rate of about 3% annually. The island shares one culture and linguistically is remarkably homogeneous.

Malagasy people are officially divided into 18 tribes, whose boundaries are roughly based on old kingdoms. Tribal divisions are still evident between ancient enemies such as the Merina and the Sakalava. Also important is the distinction between Merina highlanders and so-called *côtiers*. Literally, *côtiers* refers to those from the coast, but really means any non-Merina groups.

Forty-five percent of the population of Madagascar is under 14.

The main ethnic groups are Merina, who make up 27% of the population, Betsimisaraka (15%), Betsileo (12%), Tsimihety (7%), Sakalava (6%), Antaisaka (5%) and Antandroy (5%); a number of smaller groups makes up the remainder.

In the Comoros the main ethnic groupings are not usually emphasised, but they include the Antalote, Cafre, Makoa, Oimatsaha and Sakalava (who are the descendents of Malagasy pirates).

HEALTH

Since Madagascar's first HIV/AIDS case was diagnosed in 1987, the disease's incidence has increased both as a percentage of population and in real figures. In January 2007, 39,000 people were estimated to be affected in Madagascar. Fortunately, these figures are still comparatively low compared with much of sub-Saharan Africa. In Madagascar HIV/AIDS is spread mainly through heterosexual sex; women account for more than half of the adult victims.

SPORT

Malagasy are of course soccer mad, although the national team has yet to make the World Cup finals. Madagascar participated in the Olympic Games for the first time in 1964 and has entered a team in nearly every Olympics since then, although it is still to win a medal. Malagasy athletes compete mainly in track and field events, but in 2006 an alpine skiing team was sent to the Winter Olympics for the first time.

RELIGION

Traditional Malagasy culture is rooted in reverence and respect for one's ancestors. Among most tribes, this is manifested in a complex system of *fady* (taboos) and burial rites, the best known of which is the ceremonial exhumation and reburial known as *Famadihana* (see boxed text, p37).

Traditional Malagasy religion has been shaped by diverse influences. The funeral rites of many tribes, for example, have Austronesian roots, while the status of cattle is thought to have African roots and belief in *vintana* may originate with Islamic cosmology.

About half of Madagascar's population adheres to traditional beliefs, while the efforts of proselytising Europeans mean that the other half now worship at Catholic and Protestant churches. A small proportion, mainly on the west coast, is Muslim. In recent years, Christian revival meetings held in venues such as sports stadiums and town halls have become popular, with charismatic preachers and lots of singing and dancing. Even among Christians, there is generally great respect and reverence for traditional rituals.

Comorian people are overwhelmingly Muslim.

LE GRAND MARIAGE

The major events in any Comorian village or town are the immense and overblown wedding ceremonies known as Grands Mariages. The most elaborate sometimes require three years of planning and can plunge the bridegroom into debt for the rest of his life.

Although revolutionist Ali Soilih and his juvenile delinquents (see p30) tried to do away with the Grand Mariage, most Comorian men still aspire to one. Economic factors, however, have dictated that few these days can afford to foot the bill.

A Grand Mariage is almost always arranged between an older, wealthy man and a young bride, often selected when she is still just a child. Not only must the man pay for the elaborate two- to nine-day *toirab* (public festivities), which involve catering for the entire village, but he must also present his fiancée with a huge dowry of gold jewellery, which she is entitled to keep in the event of a divorce.

All this entitles him to wear a special *m'ruma* (sash), which signifies his status as a *wandru wadzima* (*grand notable* in French). Only *grands notables* may participate in village councils held in the *bangwe* (village or town square).

If you hope to attend a *toirab*, your chances will be best in July and August. Just wait around looking curious about what's happening; you're sure to be invited, or in fact forced, to join in. Bring some kind of present (a small amount of money is best) and don't take photos unless invited.

ARTS
Literature

The earliest Malagasy literature dates from historical records produced in the mid-19th century. Modern poetry and literature first began to flourish in the 1930s and 1940s. The best-known figure was the poet Jean-Joseph Rabearivelo, who committed suicide in 1947 at the age of 36 – reputedly after the colonial administration decided to send a group of basket-weavers to France to represent the colony instead of him. Modern-day literary figures include Jean Ndema, Rakotonaivo, Rainifihina Jessé and Emilson D Andriamalala. Nearly all their works are published in French or Malagasy.

Haiteny: The Traditional Poetry of Madagascar, by Leonard Fox, has translations of beautiful Merina poems charting love, revenge and sexuality.

The first Comorian literature was in the form of folk tales and histories laid down in Arabic by princes, sultans and aristocrats. A lot of Comorian literature is in Shimasiwa (the Comorian dialect), but some writers to look out for are Aboubacar Said Salim, Said-Ahmed Sast and Abdou Salam Baco.

Oral Traditions

Hira gasy are popular music, dancing and storytelling spectacles held in the central highlands of Madagascar. Brightly clad troupes of 25 performers compete for prizes for the best costumes or the most exciting spectacle. An important part of *hira gasy* is *kabary*, in which an orator delivers a series of proverbs using allegory, double entendre, metaphor and simile. The speaker continues for as long as possible while avoiding direct contact with the subject at hand. Unfortunately, unless you have fluent Malagasy, you're unlikely to agree with the proverb that says: 'While listening to a *kabary* well spoken, one fails to notice the fleas that bite one'.

Over the Lip of the World: Among the Storytellers of Madagascar, by Colleen J McElroy, is a journey through Malagasy oral traditions and myths.

More visitor-friendly are the songs and acrobatic dances that follow the *kabary*. Dancers are dressed in oddly old-fashioned European-style gowns called *malabary*, and women also wear the traditional *lamba* (scarf). The themes are upbeat, extolling the virtues of honesty and encouraging young people to respect their parents. The competition winner is decided by the audience.

Most Comorian literature also derives from oral traditions, which have been passed down through the generations in the form of *hali* (folk tales). *Hali* are similar to fables and normally end with a moral.

Music

Most traditional Malagasy music revolves around favourite dance rhythms: the *salegy* of the Sakalava tribe, with both Indonesian and Kenyan influences; the African *watsa watsa*; the *tsapika*, which originated in the south; and the *sigaoma*, which is similar to South African music.

Apart from at special events such as the Donia festival in Nosy Be (see boxed text, p163), traditional Malagasy music can be hard to find and is often restricted to rural areas. The music you'll hear blasting out of tinny radios and rocking the local discos is usually a cheesy blend of guitar rock, rough-and-ready rap and hip-hop, and soulful ballads. Love songs with catchy choruses are the nation's favourite, and singers such as national treasure Poopy (yes, that's her real name) keep the syrup coming with a stream of identikit but irritatingly catchy hits.

The most widely played traditional wind instrument is the *kiloloka*, a whistle-like length of bamboo capable of only one note. Melodies are played by a group of musicians, in a manner similar to a bell ensemble. The tubular instrument you'll see on sale at tourist shops and craft markets is a *valiha*, which has 28 strings of varying lengths stretched around a tubular wooden sound box; it resembles a bassoon but is played more like a harp. It has fallen out of favour in Madagascar but is still played in Malaysia and Indonesia, which suggests that it was brought to Madagascar by the earliest settlers of the island.

Other well-known contemporary Malagasy pop groups and singers include Jaojoby, Tiana, Mahaleo, Dama (who was popular enough to get elected to parliament in 1993) and Jerry Marcos, a master of *salegy*. Malagasy groups that have toured internationally, mainly in France and the UK, include Njava and Tarika. The best place to see live performances is at the bigger venues in Antananarivo – look in the newspapers on Friday for event details (p86).

There is a remarkably wide range of musical styles in the Comoros, which have absorbed cultural and musical influences from East Africa, the Middle East, Madagascar and southern India. Contemporary Comorian artists often mix traditional sounds with reggae or rap backbeats in collaboration with European producers. Traditional instruments include gongs, drums, tambourines, rattles, oboes, zithers and five-stringed lutes.

Check out the latest from the Malagasy music scene at www.madanight .com. The site is mostly in French, but there are lots of articles and band interviews.

Voices from Madagascar: An Anthology of Contemporary Francophone Literature, edited by Jacques Bourgeacq and Liliane Ramarosoa, contains Malagasy writing in French and English.

FAMADIHANA

On the crest of a hill a grove of pine trees whispers gently. In the shade, trestle tables are spread with sticky sweetmeats and bowls of steaming rice. A band plays a rollicking, upbeat tune as the stone door of a family tomb is opened. Old ladies wait at the entrance, faces dignified under their straw hats. Middle-aged men are getting stuck into lethal homemade rum, dancing jerkily to the rhythms of the band.

One by one the corpses are brought out of the tomb, wrapped in straw mats and danced above the heads of a joyful throng. The bodies are re-wrapped in pristine white burial *lambas* (scarves), sprayed with perfume and meticulously labelled by name with felt-tip pens. A period of quiet follows, with family members holding the bodies on their laps in silent communication, weeping but happy at the same time. The air is charged with emotion. Then the bodies are danced one more time around the tomb, a few traditional verses are read out and the stone is sealed with mud for another seven years.

Famadihana ceremonies take place every year between June and September in the *hauts plateaux* (highlands) region from Antananarivo south to Ambositra. These days it's generally OK to attend one, as long as your visit is arranged through a hotel or local tour company (p285). On no account should you visit without an invitation and never take photos unless specific permission has been granted.

RESPONSIBLE TOURISM TIP

Resist the urge to hand out money or gifts to those cute children in the villages and towns of Madagascar. Rather than helping them, you will be teaching them to beg from every new traveller they see. If you want to do something to aid those you meet, donate money to the local school or clinic instead.

Architecture

Each region of Madagascar has its own architectural style and building materials. The Merina and Betsileo of the *hauts plateaux* (highlands) live in distinctive red-brick houses that are warm on cold nights. The typical Merina home is a tall, narrow affair with small windows and brick pillars in the front supporting open verandas. The Betsileo areas dispense with the pillars and trim their houses with elaborately carved wood. Coastal homes are generally constructed of lighter local materials, including cactus and raffia palm.

The interesting film *Quand les Étoiles Rencontrent la Mer* (When the Stars Meet the Sea), directed by the Malagasy Raymond Rajaonarivelo, is the story of a young boy born during a solar eclipse.

In the independent Comoros (but not Mayotte), Swahili architectural traditions are superbly preserved. The old Arab towns in Moroni (p239) and Mutsamudu (p252) are laid out haphazardly with mazelike narrow streets. Townhouses are tall and narrow, with internal balconies running around a central courtyard and an open cooking area at the back. Traditionally doors are elaborately carved with Islamic lettering or abstract motifs, and sometimes inlaid with brass studs. Mosques, particularly those used in Friday prayers, are splendid, glittering, white affairs with high, elegant minarets and rows of galleries around the outside. They are often built using funds from Islamic organisations in the Middle East.

Textile Arts

See http://africa .si.edu/exhibits/malagasy for a good overview of traditional Malagasy textile arts, with historical context and information on materials used.

Textiles have always played a huge part in Malagasy society, with some types of cloth even being imbued, it is believed, with supernatural powers. The Merina used cocoons collected from the wild silkworm to make highly valued textiles called *lamba mena* (red silk). The silks were woven in many colour and pattern combinations, and in the past had strong links with royal prestige, expressed by the colour red. Worn by the aristocracy in life and death, *lamba mena* were also used in burial and reburial ceremonies.

These days ancestral materials such as *lamba mena* are combined with modern textiles such as lycra, or 'found objects' such as shells or even computer circuit boards. Ask at the Centre Culturel Albert Camus (p74) in Antananarivo for details of textile exhibitions.

Theatre & Dance

In addition to *hira gasy* (p36), the best place to see traditional dance performances is at the Donia, the arts festival held every year in Nosy Be (see boxed text, p163). The Centre Culturel Albert Camus (p74) in Antananarivo is the best place to see theatre and dance performances in the capital. In the provinces, the various branches of the Alliance Francaise can usually provide information on local events.

In the Comoros, dancing forms an integral part of every Muslim festival. One of the most popular is the *mougodro*, a circular dance with African and Malagasy origins in which men, women and children all participate.

On Mayotte, the most popular dance is the *wadaha* (or *danse de pilon*) in which women and young girls dance in a circle around a mortar filled with rice, to the rhythm of drums, guitars and popular songs, simulating the pulverisation of the rice with pestles. It also serves as a pre-nuptial dance. Contact the Comité du Tourisme (p260) in Mayotte for details of performances.

Food & Drink

Food is taken very seriously in Madagascar, where French, Chinese and Indian influences have blended with local eating traditions into an exciting and often mouth-watering cuisine. Regional variations are common, with a great variety of fruits, vegetables and seafood dictating local tastes and recipes. Much the same applies in the Comoros, which also has Swahili and African influences.

The most interesting Malagasy food is served up in private homes, so if you're hoping to sample some of the unique local dishes you're probably best off making friends with hospitable local cooks. But if you don't manage to inveigle your way into a Malagasy home, rest assured that restaurants in towns right across the country normally serve excellent French cuisine to suit all budgets, from simple zebu *steack frites* (steak and chips) to *paté de foie gras* (goose liver paté) and *magret de canard* (duck fillet). Western staples such as pizza and pasta are easy to find, too. In the Comoros, restaurants are few and far between, but those that do exist serve up delicious local dishes.

STAPLES & SPECIALITIES
Rice
Eating rice three times a day is so ingrained in Malagasy culture that people sometimes claim they can't sleep if they haven't eaten rice that day. If you don't like rice then brace yourself, because the average Malagasy considers a bowl of rice a perfectly valid meal in itself. Indeed, in rural areas rice is often accompanied only by a bowl of warm water with a couple of cabbage leaves floating in it (this 'soup' is known as *ro*).

However, most travellers will find that the Malagasy staple is served up with a stew made from *hen'omby* (boiled beef), *hen'andrano* (fish), *hen'akoho* (chicken or duck) or vegetables, with a few spices added to give it flavour. A common side dish is *brêdes* (boiled greens) in water.

The most common alternative to rice is a steaming bowl of *mi sao* (fried noodles with vegetables or meat) or a satisfying *soupe chinoise* (clear noodle soup with fish, chicken or vegetables) – dishes that show the Asian origins of the Malagasy. Poorer rural communities supplement their rice diet with starchy roots such as manioc or corn. In the Comoros, cassava (*mhogo* in Swahili) replaces rice as the staple food. It looks like boiled potatoes and tastes like nothing at all.

The growth of a rice plant is described in Malagasy using the same words as those for a woman becoming pregnant and giving birth.

Meat
Zebu cattle not only provide status, transport and a handy means of obtaining a wife in Madagascar, they are also well known for their excellent meat. Zebu beef in stews or zebu steak, if cooked well, is hailed by carnivores as succulent and delicious. Some eateries specialise in zebu meat and we found zebu shasliks particularly tasty nearly everywhere we tried them. Lower-quality beef is often cut into small pieces, simmered until done, shredded, then roasted until it is browned. Pork is sometimes available in Chinese restaurants, but it's *fady* (taboo) to eat pork in many parts of Madagascar, and entirely forbidden in the Muslim Comoros. Stringy chicken or goat is standard fare at *hotelys* (small roadside places that serve basic meals).

A 2002 survey conducted by the Food and Agricultural Organization of the UN estimated that Madagascar had 11 million cattle, almost two million sheep and goats and 21 million chickens.

Fish
Lovers of seafood are in for a treat in coastal Malagasy towns and everywhere in the Comoros, for every *resto* (restaurant) menu features freshly caught fish

of the day and usually lists a variety of fresh lobster, prawn or squid dishes as well. Seafood prices are so low that all but those on the tightest budgets can gorge themselves at whim on these 'fruits of the sea'. The freshwater crayfish caught and sold around Ranomafana make a delicious and unusual variation away from the sea. Hotel restaurants in the area often feature these on their menus, or you can buy these *ecrévisses* ready-boiled and salted from roadside vendors or as a snack during the Fianarantsoa–Manakara train trip in the dry season.

If you decide to buy your fish from local fishermen while staying near the coast, make sure you find out when the catch is landed. This varies from place to place and could determine whether your dinner is straight out of the ocean or has been sitting in the sun all day.

Fruit

Mangoes, lychees, bananas of all shapes and sizes, and even strawberries are available in various parts of Madagascar. Likewise fresh juice is on sale everywhere in Madagascar and the Comoros. Bear in mind that the juice in cheaper restaurants will be diluted with untreated water. For a delicious thirst-quencher near the beach, split open a young coconut and drink the vitamin-packed juice inside.

Breakfast

Rice is traditionally eaten for breakfast everywhere in Madagascar, but *petit déjeuner* is the great failing of French cuisine. Those used to something substantial to start the day may not take kindly to the slice of stale bread and coffee invariably served up in the morning. If you're staying in more upmarket accommodation you may be offered the option of eggs. You'll eventually get used to it, but if not console yourself by planning lunch – the main meal of the day.

Comorians prefer to start the day with *supu* – an oily meat broth with shreds of beef floating in it, plus the odd knuckle of cartilage. The general form is to buy this from the market and carry it home in a plastic bag.

Snacks

A tip: don't give out sweets to the children who beg for them – without access to dentists, their teeth will rot. Try giving them chewable fruit-flavoured vitamins instead.

One of the first things you'll notice on arriving in Madagascar is the dizzying variety of patisserie. Presumably a legacy of the French, sticky cakes, croissants, pastries and meringues are on sale in even the most humble of cafés. In the bigger cities, the concoctions on offer at glitzier *salons de thé* (tearooms) would rival the snootiest Parisian *boulangerie* (bakery). Baguettes can be bought everywhere in Madagascar and the Comoros.

Savoury snacks include the ubiquitous samosas (called *sambos* and nearly always filled with minced meat), small doughnuts called *mofo menakely,* and *masikita* (skewers threaded with grilled beef). The odd, log-like thing you'll see sold in glass boxes on the pavements of Antananarivo and elsewhere is *koba,* a concoction made from peanuts, rice and sugar, wrapped tightly in banana leaves, baked and sold in slices. More pleasure for the sweet of tooth lies in Roberts chocolate, so good that even nonchocoholics may be converted.

President Ravalomanana's Tiko company ferries little pots of yogurt and sachets of flavoured milk to the remotest corners of the island. Homemade yogurt is also available in glass pots in even the humblest *hotely*.

DRINKS

Most Malagasy like to accompany a rice meal with a drink of rice water. This brown, smoky concoction, known as *ranovola,* and often jokingly referred to as 'whisky malgache', is made from boiling water in the pot containing the burnt rice residue. It is definitely an acquired taste.

Excellent coffee is usually served at the end of the meal in French restaurants, but if you drink it white you'll have to learn to love condensed milk. In the Comoros, tea is spiced with lemongrass or ginger, and coffee is served syrupy and black in tiny Arabic-style cups.

The most popular local-brand Malagasy beers are Three Horses Beer (known as THB) and Gold, which is slightly stronger and more flavoursome. The most common import brand is Castle from South Africa.

However, Madagascar's speciality is rum. Most bars and restaurants have an array of glass flasks behind the bar filled with *rhum arrangé* – rum in which a variety of fruits and spices have been left to steep. Nearly all of them have an alcohol content that will blow your socks off.

Madagascar's small wine industry is centred on Fianarantsoa (p105). You'll probably want to try a glass out of curiosity, but unfortunately it's pretty ghastly stuff and you're unlikely to repeat the experience. Still, hats off to the Swiss vignerons who have tried to establish the industry and you might consider taking a bottle home as a souvenir. Imported French and South African wine is served in better restaurants in Madagascar, but only in the most upmarket, Westernised restaurants in the Comoros. On Mayotte, all wine, beer and spirits are imported from France.

VEGETARIANS & VEGANS

Fish-eating 'vegetarians' should have no problems in either Madagascar or Comoros. French restaurants rarely cater for vegetarians, but small local *hotelys* in Madagascar can usually whip up some noodles, soup or rice and greens. Protein could be a problem for vegans, as beans are not as widely available in Madagascar as they may be elsewhere.

For recipes and presentation tips check out www .sas.upenn.edu/African_ Studies/Cookbook /Madagascar.html.

In the Comoros, vegetable dishes are harder to find, but beans are back on the menu – don't miss the delicious Swahili red-bean-and-coconut stew known as *maharagwe*. If you eat eggs, omelettes are available almost everywhere. Neither Malagasy nor Comorians find vegetarianism very difficult to understand and they are often more than happy to cater for special diets if you are polite and give them enough notice. Restaurants that are especially good for vegetarians are mentioned in our listings.

CELEBRATIONS & CUSTOMS

A Malagasy proverb says 'the food which is prepared has no master'. In other words, celebrating in Madagascar or the Comoros means eating big. Weddings, funerals, circumcisions and reburials are preceded by days of

---

DOS & DON'TS

■ Do bring a present (a small amount of money or a bottle of rum) if you're invited to a Malagasy celebration. Women should wear modest clothes.

■ Do check before eating pork in rural Madagascar – in some places it's *fady* (taboo).

■ Do hold your wrist with the opposite hand when passing food or drinks to a Malagasy – they will be impressed with your manners.

■ Do offer to pay for food consumed in villages while trekking or visiting.

■ Don't eat or pass food with your left hand in the Comoros – the left hand is considered unclean in Muslim societies.

■ Don't drink alcohol in the street, public places or most hotel restaurants in the Comoros.

■ Don't eat, drink or smoke in public in daylight hours during the fast of Ramadan in the Comoros.

TRAVEL YOUR TASTEBUDS

Look out for these on your culinary travels in Madagascar:

Achards Hot pickled vegetable curry used as a relish.

Betsa-betsa Fermented sugar-cane juice.

Kitoza Dried beef strips charcoaled and often served with cornmeal mush for breakfast.

Punch coco Sickly but delicious alcoholic drink made from sweetened coconut milk.

Ravitoto Bitter-tasting, dark-green cassava leaves, often added to pork dishes.

Tapia Small red berries that taste similar to dates.

We Dare You...

Only for the brave of heart and mouth:

Locusts When a locust storm attacks, the locals retaliate by catching and frying the crop-eating critters.

Pimente malgache The hottest flavour of food.

Sakay Red-hot pepper mixed with ginger and garlic paste; thankfully served on the side, not in the food.

Toaka gasy Illegal and dangerous home-brewed rum, served in plastic buckets.

---

boiling up food in cauldrons big enough to fall into. Extended family, friends and often passers-by, too, are invited to share the food, which is usually a stew made of chicken, several salads and, of course, a mountain of rice.

The squeamish are advised not to turn up at a venue the day before a party – you're likely to be greeted by the sight of dozens of trussed zebu cattle having their throats slit before being butchered to feed the expected guests. At Malagasy parties, copious quantities of home-brewed rum are consumed, and helpless drunkenness is entirely expected.

Ma Cuisine Malgache (Karibo Safako), by Angeline Espagne-Ravo, contains the best collection of Malagasy recipes in French.

A true Malagasy or Comorian serves up a meal without any fancy preliminaries such as cocktails or hors d'oeuvres. In Madagascar heavier dishes with rich sauces are kept for Sunday, celebrations or holidays. Light dishes such as greens boiled in water or peas are served to aid digestion the day after a particularly heavy meal.

When drinking in Madagascar, it's customary to pour a little on the ground first as an offering to the ancestors.

Comorians politely say 'bismillah' (thanks to Allah) before starting their meal. The food is heaped together on the plate and eaten with a spoon, although many Comorians prefer to eat with their hands. Meals in more traditional households are eaten sitting on mats on the floor. Cooking is done outside the house in an open courtyard.

WHERE TO EAT & DRINK

The least expensive places in Madagascar and the Comoros are street stalls (which are not found everywhere) and *hotelys*, small informal restaurants serving basic meals. These are sometimes called *gargottes* in French and are found in every city and town. They are your best bet for fast food during the day, but they're rarely open much past 7.30pm. Standards of hygiene vary widely and none would be likely to pass a food safety test in the West. For tips on how to avoid health problems with food, see the Health chapter (p286).

The next step up from *hotelys* are *salons de thé*, tearooms that offer a variety of pastries, cakes, ice cream and other snacks, and sometimes sandwiches and light meals as well. All serve tea and coffee. Most close at about 6pm; a few close at lunchtime, too.

Lastly, there are restaurants *(restos)*, which range from modest to top-end establishments and serve French, Indian or Chinese cuisine with a few Malagasy dishes thrown in. Most offer a *menu du jour* (three-course set menu), or a *plat du jour* (daily special), sometimes just called a *speciale*. Most hotel dining rooms offer a set three-course (or more) dinner known as a *table d'hôte*. Prices for these are usually around Ar15,000 to Ar25,000. For à la carte menus, the average price of a main course is Ar10,000.

EAT YOUR WORDS

Menus in Madagascar and the Comoros are almost exclusively in French, even in the cheapest roadside restaurants. In Madagascar at least, we have found the brusque reputation of Gallic waiters to be greatly exaggerated. But to help you avoid puzzled stares we suggest brushing up on your ordering skills and learning some basic French food jargon, which we've listed below. For further pronunciation guidelines, see p293.

The African Cookbook, by Bea Sandler, has some good recipes from Madagascar.

Useful Phrases

What's the speciality here?
Quelle est la spécialité ici?	kel ay la spay·sya·lee·tay ees·ee

I'd like a local speciality.
J'aimerais une spécialité régionale.	zhay·mer·ray ewn spay·sya·lee·tay ray·zhyo·nal

I'd like to order the ...
Je voudrais commander ...	zher voo·dray ko·mon·day

well done
bien cuit	bee·en kwee

The bill, please.
La note, s'il vous plaît.	la not seel voo play

I'm vegetarian.
Je suis végétarien/végétarienne. (m/f)	zher swee vay·zhay·ta·ryun/vay·zhay·ta·ryen

I don't eat ...	*Je ne mange pas de ...*	zher ner monzh pa de ...
meat	*viande*	vyond
fish	*poisson*	pwa·son
seafood	*fruits de mer*	frwee der mair

Food Glossary

BASICS

beurre	bur	butter
oeufs	erf	eggs
pain	pun	bread
poivre	pwav·re	pepper
riz	ree	rice
sel	sel	salt
sucre	sew·krer	sugar

MEAT

bœuf	berf	beef
canard	ka·nar	duck
porc	por	pork
poulet	poo·lay	chicken
saignant	say·nyo	rare (steak)

SEAFOOD

crevettes	kre·vet	prawns
langouste	long·goost	lobster

VEGETABLES

haricots	a·ri·ko	beans
oignons	on·yon	onions
pomme de terre	pom·der·tair	potato

SPECIALITIES

archards	ar·char	hot, pickled vegetable curry
grillades	gree·yard	grilled meats
mi sao	mee·sow	stir-fried noodles with meat or vegetables
poulet au gingembre	poo·lay o zhan·zhom bre	chicken with ginger
ro	ro	a leaf-based broth
soupe chinoise	soop·sheen·waaz	Chinese noodle soup
steack frites	stek freet	steak and chips
zebu au poivre vert	ze·bu o pwav·re vair	beef steak with green-pepper sauce

Environment

THE LAND

Madagascar is the world's fourth-largest island, after Greenland, Papua New Guinea and Borneo. It has remarkable landscapes, wildlife and vegetation, which an understanding of its ancient origins will help explain. What is now the island of Madagascar was once sandwiched between Africa and India as part of the supercontinent Gondwana, a vast ancient landmass that also included Antarctica, South America and Australasia. Gondwana began to break apart about 180 million years ago, but Madagascar remained joined to Africa at the 'hip' – in the region of modern East Africa – for another 20 million years. About 88 million years ago the eastern half of Madagascar broke off, moving northward to eventually become India, by which time modern Madagascar had drifted to its present position. Since then, Madagascar has remained at its present size and shape, isolated from the rest of the world.

Madagascar measures 1600km on its longest axis, aligned roughly northeast to southwest, and 570km from east to west at its widest point. Almost the entire island is in the tropics, albeit well south of the equator, and only the southern tip protrudes below the Tropic of Capricorn. The 5000km-long coastline features many long, sweeping sandy beaches with coral reefs and atolls offshore in some areas, and is dotted with several small islands, including Nosy Be to the northwest and Île Sainte Marie off the northeast corner.

A chain of mountains runs down the eastern seaboard, forming a steep escarpment and trapping moisture that helps create the island's rainforests, which are rich in biodiversity. There is no modern volcanic activity on the island, although it previously occurred in the central highlands; there are extinct volcanoes at Parc National de Montagne d'Ambre (p184), the Ankaratra massif and Lac Itasy, west of Antananarivo. The island's highest point is 2876m Maromokotro, an extinct volcanic peak in the Tsaratanana massif, followed by the 2658m Pic Imarivolanitra (formerly known as Pic Boby) in Parc National d'Andringitra.

Madagascar is tipping east very slowly, and the entire west coast contains mostly marine fossil deposits. Going east from the western coastline, limestone is replaced by sandstone which rises into majestic formations in places such as Parc National de l'Isalo (p122). Sapphire deposits found recently near the park have prompted a rush of fortune-seekers and the sudden growth of boom towns easily seen from Route Nationale 7 (RN7). Further east are deposits of minerals and semiprecious stones, such as jasper, agate, zircon, rose and smoky quartz, moonstone, tourmaline, morganite beryl and amethyst, although few precious stones and minerals are found in commercially viable quantities.

Northern and western Madagascar host impressive limestone karst formations – jagged, eroded limestone rocks that contain caves, potholes, underground rivers and forested canyons rich in wildlife such as crocodiles, lemurs, birds and bats. Karst is known locally as *tsingy*, and is protected within one of Madagascar's three World Heritage sites, Parc National des Tsingy de Bemaraha (p151), as well as in the Réserve Spéciale de l'Ankàrana (p186).

All four of the Comoros' islands are volcanic in origin. Grand Comore is geologically the youngest of the archipelago, and hosts the world's largest active cone, Mt Karthala – a gigantic, steaming time bomb that could go off at any time. All four islands have a rugged hinterland dominated by their peaks, with coastlines fringed by beaches, old lava flows and coral reefs with some fine diving.

The Institute for the Conservation of Tropical Environments (ICTE) at http://icte.bio.sunysb .edu, part of the Stony Brook University site, has photos of rainforest wildlife and natural history details, as well as information on research and tourist opportunities in southeastern Madagascar.

Lords and Lemurs, by Alison Jolly, is a history of the Réserve Privée de Berenty that skilfully weaves together the stories of the spiny desert Tandroy people, three generations of French plantation owners, lemurs and lemur-watchers.

WILDLIFE

Madagascar's 80-million-year isolation created an explosion of plants and animals found nowhere else on earth. When Gondwana broke apart many of the large animals we know today had yet to evolve, but Madagascar took with it a cargo of primitive forms that were then common to both land masses. Thus, when humans first arrived the island supported hippopotami, aardvarks and giant flightless birds similar to modern African forms such as the ostrich. Modern primates had not yet evolved, but Madagascar's world-famous lemurs were probably descended from common ancestors akin to Africa's bushbabies. With the arrival of humans many of the larger forms were wiped out and over the last thousand years 16 species of lemur, plus tortoises, the hippopotami and giant aardvarks, the world's largest bird (the 3m-high elephant bird *Aepyornis*) and two species of eagle have become extinct at human hands. Continued habitat degradation threatens many more species and the conservation of Madagascar's wildlife is now a worldwide priority.

For more information, see the Wildlife section (p49).

Animals

MAMMALS

Madagascar's wildlife is so little known that as recently as 1986 a new species of lemur was discovered, the golden bamboo lemur, and new bird species were discovered in 1995 (Cryptic Warbler) and 1997 (Red-shouldered Vanga).

Madagascar's best-known mammals are the lemurs, of which there are about 70 living species and subspecies. A further 16 – mostly giant – species are known from subfossil deposits; the tragedy is that these remains point to a unique lemur megafauna that died out perhaps only a few hundred years ago. Among those wiped out were gorilla-sized, indri-like species as well as many forms recognisably akin to living species.

Modern lemurs are divided into five families: the nocturnal woolly lemurs or avahis, the beautifully marked sifakas and indris (of which only one species is extant), all well known for their leaping abilities; a family of small, nocturnal species that includes dwarf and mouse lemurs, the world's smallest primates; the 'true' lemurs, such as the ring-tailed and ruffed lemurs, a family that also includes the bamboo lemurs; the sportive lemurs; and, most remarkable of all, the bizarre, nocturnal aye-aye, which extracts grubs from under bark with a long, bony finger. The best places to view lemurs are the national parks of Ranomafana (p103), d'Andasibe-Mantadia (p192) and de Montagne d'Ambre (p184), Station Forestière d'Ampijoroa (p147) and Réserve Forestière de Kirindy (p156). Although it is somewhat contrived, Réserve Privée de Berenty (p136) offers some outstanding lemur photo opportunities.

Nick Garbutt's *Mammals of Madagascar* is a comprehensive guide to mammals – lemurs, carnivores, tenrecs and bats – that live on the island. It is illustrated with superb photos and is now available in paperback.

Madagascar also has many species of small mammal, such as bats, including flying foxes, and rodents, including giant jumping rats, red-forest rats and tuft-tailed forest mice. Although they are not nearly so well known or spectacular as the lemurs, tenrecs also demonstrate how the island's wildlife has taken some remarkable evolutionary turns. These small, primitive mammals are related to shrews and have radiated to fill a similar niche as tiny hunters of the leaf litter. Among their diverse forms are shrew tenrecs, the hedgehog-like spiny tenrecs and even an otter-like aquatic species.

There are six species of carnivore – all are mongooses and civets – including the ring-tailed mongoose, the fanaloka and the puma-like, lemur-eating *fosa*. Offshore, migratory humpback whales provide a spectacle in July and August at sites such as Ifaty (p124) and Île Ste Marie (p206).

BIRDS

Madagascar's birdlife does not attain the mindboggling richness of Africa, but it makes up for it with five endemic families and the highest proportion of endemic birds of any country on earth: of the 209 breeding species, 51% are endemic. A large percentage of birds are forest-dwelling and therefore under pressure from land clearing. Fortunately, there is an excellent system of national parks and reserves, and bird-watchers stimulate local economies near these reserves by paying for accommodation and the services of skilled naturalist guides.

Among Madagascar's unique bird families are the *mesites* – skulking, babbler-like birds thought to be related to rails; the spectacular ground-rollers, including a roadrunner-like species unique to the spiny forests; the tiny, iridescent *asities*, similar to sunbirds and filling a similar niche; and the *vangas*, which have taken several strange twists as they evolved to fill various forest niches.

Birds of the Indian Ocean Islands, by Ian Sinclair and Olivier Langrand, is an excellent field guide to all of Madagascar's birds.

As with birds nearly everywhere, each habitat has a suite of speciality species adapted to particular niches, plus more generalised species that can survive in many habitats, and there are a number of predators and nocturnal species as well. Most species are resident (ie nonmigratory), although a few are seasonal migrants to East Africa. Waterbirds are rather poorly represented in Madagascar because there are comparatively few large bodies of water; some of the best concentrations are on the west coast near Station Forestière d'Ampijoroa (p147). The richest habitat by far for birds (and all other terrestrial life forms) is the rainforest of the eastern seaboard, although many of these species are rare and poorly known. The dry forests of southern and southwest Madagascar are also rich in birds, including some unique and highly endangered species.

REPTILES & AMPHIBIANS

There are 346 reptile species on Madagascar, including most of the world's chameleons, ranging from the largest – Parson's chameleon, which grows to around 60cm – to the smallest, the dwarf chameleons of the genus Brookesia. If you take a guided walk in many of the excellent national parks, your guides will almost certainly point out a few of these amazing lizards, as well as other interesting species such as the bizarre leaf-tailed geckos and bright-green day geckos. Amazingly, the verdant forests support not a single snake species harmful to people; among the many beautiful snakes are the Madagascar boa and leaf-nosed snake. In contrast, the Nile crocodile is just as dangerous here as it is in Africa and it kills people every year. Madagascar also supports several species of tortoise, some of which, including the radiated tortoise, are highly endangered.

Madagascar has the world's smallest chameleon – smaller than your thumb.

Madagascar also has over 200 species of frog, including the bright-red tomato frog and iridescent brightly coloured Malagasy poison frogs *(Mantella)*.

FISH

Most of the freshwater fish are endemic and include colourful rainbow fish, cichlids that can often grow to a large size and the swamp fish. Freshwater

---

GOING, GOING... BACK AGAIN!

The last century saw several Madagascan bird species pushed perilously close to the brink of extinction. Waterbirds have fared particularly badly: the Alaotra Grebe has not been seen since the late 1980s and all three of the country's endemic duck species are rare. One, the Madagascar Pochard, was last seen in 1994 when a female was rescued by a conservation worker from a fisherman's net on Lac Alaotra. The rescuer kept the bird alive in a bath in the hope that a mate would be found, but it succumbed and the Madagascar Pochard was presumed extinct. But in 2006 the unthinkable happened: nine adult Madagascar Pochards were discovered with young on a remote lake in the Alaotra basin in northern Madagascar. Although the bird is seemingly back from the dead, there is no room for complacency and the exact location of the birds is a well-kept secret until effective conservation measures can be put in place.

fish are one of the most endangered groups of animal on Madagascar, owing to silting of rivers through erosion and runoff.

The region's most amazing fish story concerns the coelacanth, a marine species that was known only from ancient fossils until a living specimen was hauled up by a fisherman in 1938. It has since been shown to be quite common in the deep oceanic trenches near the Comoros.

Plants

The rosy periwinkle – a flower endemic to Madagascar – has been a source of alkaloids that are 99% effective in the treatment of some forms of leukaemia.

Madagascar's plants are no less interesting than its animals and its flora is incredibly diverse. About 6000 species are known to science, including the bizarre octopus trees, several species of baobab and a pretty flower that is used to treat leukaemia.

The island's vegetation can be divided into three parallel north–south zones, each supporting unique communities of plants and animals: the hot, arid west consists of dry spiny desert or deciduous forest; the central plateau (known as the *hauts plateaux*) has now been mostly deforested; and the wettest part of the country, the eastern seaboard, supports extensive tracts of rainforest. Mangrove forests grow in suitable sites along the coast, particularly near large estuaries. All of these habitats have suffered extensive disturbance at human hands.

The spiny desert is truly extraordinary: dense tangles of cactus-like octopus trees festooned with needle-sharp spines are interspersed with baobabs whose bulbous trunks store water, allowing them to survive the dry season. The baobabs' large, bright flowers are filled with copious amounts of nectar, often sipped by fork-marked lemurs. About 60 species of aloe occur in Madagascar and many dot the spiny desert landscape. Excellent stands of spiny desert flora can be easily seen at Réserve Privée de Berenty (p136) and Réserve Spéciale de Beza-Mahafaly (p129), and in the hinterland of Ifaty near Toliara. The excellent Arboretum d'Antsokay (p127) near Toliara makes a fine introduction to Madagascar's dry country plants.

Incredible as it seems, the vast areas of blond grassland of the *hauts plateaux* are actually the result of clear felling by humans, long before Europeans arrived with their advanced technology. The boundary of the sole remaining patch of natural forest, at Parc National Zombitse-Vohibasia (p124), stands in forlorn contrast to the degraded countryside surrounding it. Growing among the crags and crevices of Parc National de l'Isalo (p122) are nine species of *Pachypodia* including a tall species with large fragrant yellow-white blossoms, and the diminutive elephant-foot species that nestle in cliff crevices on the sandstone massif.

Madagascar's eastern rainforests once covered the entire eastern seaboard and still support the island's highest biodiversity, most of which is found nowhere else on earth. Giant forest trees are festooned with vines, orchids and bird's-nest ferns (home to tree frogs and day geckos); and provide the fruits, flowers and leaves that lemurs thrive on. Most trees flower from September to November with fruits abundant when the rains come from November to March. Throughout the forests are more than 10 species of endemic bamboo, with three species of bamboo lemurs that eat them. Tree-like screw palms *(Pandanus)* are abundant in rainforest swamps; villagers harvest the leaves to weave mats, vests and hats.

There are 1000 species of orchid in Madagascar, more than in all of Africa; most bloom from November to March. More than 60 species of pitcher plants *(Nepenthes)* are found in swampy parts of rainforests, and can be seen at Ranomafana. Insects are attracted to the nectar of these carnivorous

(Continued on page 65)

WILDLIFE

When Madagascar broke away from Africa some 90 million years ago, its cargo of primitive animals evolved in some novel directions, free from the pressures felt on other land masses, such as human hunters. The result is some of the world's most amazing biodiversity – and thanks to a great network of reserves and excellent local naturalist guides, Madagascar is also one of the world's great ecotourism destinations. Lemurs are the main attraction for most nature-lovers, but the island also offers superb bird-watching and a host of smaller animals that could keep you occupied for several trips.

Typical Lemurs

Evolutionary forces pushed and pulled ancestral lemurs into myriad shapes and sizes that today range from the tiny mouse lemurs to the giant indri. 'Typical' lemurs are long-tailed, monkeylike animals with a rather catlike face, prominent ears and prehensile hands with separate digits ('fingers'). Most are arboreal (living and feeding in trees) and active by day. Most lemurs in this family are highly social – foraging, sleeping and moving in family groups or extended troops. Troop composition can vary, but in some species females dominate.

④ Crowned Lemur

Length 75-85cm, including 41-49cm tail; weight 1.1-1.3kg A sexually dichromatic species (ie males and females have different coloration) that occurs in dry deciduous forest and rainforest in northern Madagascar. Habituated troops can be seen at Réserve Spéciale de l'Ankàrana (p186).

① Ring-tailed Lemur

Length 95-110cm, including 56-62cm tail; weight 2.3-3.5kg This is the most terrestrial and sociable of all lemurs, foraging in groups of 13 to 15 animals for fruit, flowers, leaves and other vegetation in spiny and dry deciduous forest. Habituated troops live at Réserve Privée de Berenty (p136).

② Black-and-white Ruffed Lemur

Length 110-120cm, including 60-65cm tail; weight 3.1-3.6kg This species' social behaviour is complex: in some areas males and females appear to occupy exclusive territories, but at other sites mixed social groups occur. It is inquisitive and easily seen at Parc National d'Andasibe-Mantadia (p192).

③ Red Ruffed Lemur

Length 100-120cm, including 60-65cm tail; weight 3.3-3.6kg Like other ruffed lemurs, this species eats primarily fruit, is highly vocal and sometimes hangs by its hind feet while feeding. It is found only in lowland primary rainforest on the Masaola Peninsula (p223).

⑤ Common Brown Lemur

Length 100cm, including 41-51cm tail; weight 2-3kg Groups of this species vary from three to 12 individuals. It is active during the day but may be partly nocturnal during the dry season. Common at Parc National d'Andasibe-Mantadia (p192) and introduced to the Comoros.

⑥ Mongoose Lemur

Length 75-83cm, including 45-48cm tail; weight 1.1-1.6kg Mongoose lemurs live in pairs with their offspring. They tend to be more secretive than other 'typical' lemurs, but can be readily seen at Station Forestière d'Ampijoroa (p147). This is one of only two lemur species found in the Comoros.

⑦ Black Lemur

Length 90-110cm, including 51-65cm tail; weight 2-2.9kg Males are totally dark brown or black, while females vary from golden brown to rich chestnut with flamboyant white ear and cheek tufts. Restricted to northwestern rainforests but easily seen in Réserve Naturelle Intégrale de Lokobe (p167) on Nosy Be, and on Nosy Komba.

Sifakas

The family that includes the nine species of sifaka also includes the indri, largest of the living lemurs, and the nocturnal *avahis* or woolly lemurs. Sifakas, also known as *simponas*, are active by day and generally cling vertically to trunks. They are prodigious leapers that can move rapidly by propelling themselves from tree to tree with elongated back legs. Many species are attractively marked and easily seen at national parks where troops have been habituated.

❸ Decken's Sifaka
Length 92-110cm, including 50-60cm tail; weight 3-4.5kg Little is known about this sifaka, but it is protected by a strong local *fady* (taboo) and can readily be seen even in the middle of towns within its range in western Madagascar. It lives in troops of six to 10 individuals and is common along the main tourist trails in Parc National des Tsingy de Bemaraha (p151).

❶ Milne-Edwards' Sifaka
Length 83-100cm, including 41-47cm tail; weight 5-6.5kg This rainforest sifaka is arboreal and restricted to the southern half of the eastern seaboard. Habituated troops can be readily seen at Parc National de Ranomafana (p103), which forms the core of its range. As with many lemur species, the female is dominant and is resident in the troop (males often migrate between troops). Troops number three to nine individuals.

❷ Verreaux's Sifaka
Length 90-110cm, including 50-60cm tail; weight 3-3.5kg This beautiful lemur is one of the smallest sifakas and often features in tourist promotions because it makes balletic bounds across clearings, leaping sideways on its strong back legs while holding its forelegs above its head. This species is restricted to dry deciduous forest in the south and southwest, and leaps between spiny forest trees without apparent harm. It is easily seen at Réserve Privée de Berenty (p136).

❹ Coquerel's Sifaka
Length 93-110cm, including 50-60cm tail; weight 3.7-4.3kg This is another attractive sifaka that is active during the day, commonly travelling in groups of four or five. It feeds mainly on mature leaves and buds during the dry season, switching to young leaves, flowers and fruits in the wetter months. It is restricted to dry deciduous forest in Madagascar's northwest. Troops can be seen fairly easily at Station Forestière d'Ampijoroa (p147).

❺ Diademed Sifaka
Length 94-105cm, including 44-50cm tail; weight 6-8.5kg Arguably the most beautiful of all lemurs, this striking species is the largest sifaka and is almost as large as the indri. Troops number eight or more and are composed of both males and females. It is widely distributed on the eastern seaboard but best seen at Parc National d'Andasibe-Mantadia (p192), where habituated troops share the rainforest with indris and black-and-white ruffed lemurs.

Nocturnal Lemurs & Indri

Approximately half of all lemur species are nocturnal. Nocturnal species belong to several families, but are included together here as they are typically less colourful than diurnal species and generally not as easy to observe. The nocturnal species are the smallest of all lemurs, and include mouse lemurs (the smallest of all primates), dwarf lemurs and sportive lemurs; the aye-aye is classified in its own family and even among lemurs stands out for its uniqueness. Nocturnal lemurs typically shelter in tree hollows during the day and may use the same roosting site day after day.

Milne-Edwards' Sportive Lemur

Length 54-58cm, including 27-29cm tail; weight 1kg
Long, powerful back legs enable the eight species of sportive lemur to leap from tree to tree, balanced by a long tail. They sleep during the day in holes in trees and emerge after dark to feed. This species lives in dry deciduous forest in the west and northwest and can generally be seen at Station Forestière d'Ampijoroa (p147). *Fosas* are a major predator, pulling the lemurs from their sleeping quarters.

Grey Mouse Lemur

Length 25-28cm, including 13-14cm tail; weight 58-67g Like most mouse lemurs, this species can be very common in suitable habitats, which include deciduous dry forest, spiny forest and secondary forest. It is typically active in the lower tree layers, although it moves very quickly and often retires from torchlight soon after being spotted. Mouse lemurs eat insects, fruit, flowers and other small animals, and are preyed upon by forest owls.

Western Avahi

Length 59-68cm, including 32-37cm tail; weight 0.9-1.3kg The two species of *avahi* have dense fur that gives them a 'woolly' appearance and the alternative name woolly lemurs. Their diet consists of a large variety of leaves and buds, and families huddle together during the day in dense foliage in the canopy. *Avahis* are restricted to dry deciduous forests in western and northwest Madagascar. Commonly seen at night at Station Forestière d'Ampijoroa (p147).

Aye-aye

Length 74-90cm, including 44-53cm tail; weight 2.5-2.6kg With its shaggy, grizzled coat, bright orange eyes, leathery batlike ears and long, dextrous fingers, the aye-aye is a strange-looking animal and the subject of much superstition. The middle digit of each forehand is elongated, and is used to probe crevices for insect larvae and other morsels. Aye-ayes are difficult to see but widely distributed in rainforests and dry deciduous forests.

Indri

Length 69-77cm, including 5cm tail; weight 6-9.5kg Known locally as *babakoto*, the indri is actually a member of the sifaka family. It is the largest of living lemurs and also has the largest voice: its territorial calls can travel 3km through the forest. It can leap up to 10m between tree trunks, and travels in family groups of two to six while foraging chiefly for leaves. Habituated troops can be seen at Parc National d'Andasibe-Mantadia (p192) and, like many vegetarians, spend hours a day resting.

Other Mammals

Although lemurs are the undoubted highlight, Madagascar has many other types of native land mammal, including eight predators (although most of these are nocturnal and difficult to see); dozens of bats and rodents; and tenrecs – primitive, shrewlike animals that have evolved into at least two dozen forms, including spiny and aquatic species. Tenrecs provide further examples of how a few species stranded on the Madagascan landmass as it drifted away from Africa evolved into numerous forms to fill vacant niches – in their case, as small predators of the leaf litter.

1 Hedgehog Tenrec

Length 16-22cm, including 1.5cm tail; weight 180-270g Hedgehog tenrecs are nocturnal and forage by sniffing out insects and their larvae and fallen fruit among leaf litter (although they can also climb). During the day they shelter in tunnels under logs or tree roots. They are found in many habitats, including leafy parts of Antananarivo, and are usually seen on nocturnal walks in Parc National de Montagne d'Ambre (p184) and Réserve Privée de Berenty (p136).

2 Madagascar Flying Fox

Length 23-27cm; wingspan 1-1.2m; weight 0.5-0.75kg Flying foxes roost upside down in big, noisy colonies, like most bats, but use trees rather than caves as roosting sites. Colonies can number up to 1000 individuals and great flocks take to the wing at dusk, fanning out across the countryside to feed on fruit. A colony of this species is a permanent fixture at Réserve Privée de Berenty (p136).

3 Ring-tailed Mongoose

Length 60-70cm, including 27-32cm tail; weight 0.7-1kg This attractive mongoose is widespread and active by day, and is therefore probably the easiest carnivore to spot. It is largely terrestrial but can also climb well. Family parties communicate with high-pitched whistles as they forage for small animals, including reptiles, birds and eggs, insects, rodents and even small lemurs. Generally seen at Parc National de Ranomafana (p103) and Réserve Spéciale de l'Ankàrana (p186).

4 Fosa

Length 140-170cm, including 70-90cm tail; weight 5-10kg The legendary *fosa* is a solitary and elusive predator of lemurs and other animals. It is extremely agile and catlike, although it is not a true cat, even descending trees head first. It is reputed to follow troops of lemurs for days, climbing trees to pick them off as they sleep at night. *Fosas* were the villains in the animated film *Madagascar*.

5 Fanaloka

Length 61-70cm, including 21-25cm tail; weight 1.5-2kg Also known as the Malagasy or striped civet, the nocturnal, foxlike *fanaloka* is found in eastern and northern rainforests. It hunts mostly on the ground but can climb well, eating rodents, birds and other animals. During the day it sleeps in tree hollows and under logs. It is regularly seen on night walks at Parc National de Ranomafana (p103).

6 Giant Jumping Rat

Length 54-58cm, including 21-24cm tail; weight 1.1-1.3kg Madagascar's largest rodent is strictly nocturnal. Pairs live in burrows with their offspring, foraging for seeds and fallen fruit after dark. They generally move on all fours but also hop on their hind legs. It is found in a relatively small area of dry deciduous forest in western Madagascar, although it was formerly more widespread, and is regularly encountered at Réserve Forestière de Kirindy (p156).

Birds of Open Country

Madagascar's bird life is unusual for much the same reason its mammals are unique, ie several ancient families evolved in isolation and today more than 80% of Madagascar's birds are endemic. Unique families include the *mesites* – furtive, ground-loving birds related to rails; *asities*, which are tiny iridescent birds similar to sunbirds; the colourful ground-rollers; and the high-flying cuckoo-rollers. Many of Madagascar's birds are now rare or endangered and others have become extinct within the last 100 years or so. About 20 bird species are endemic to the Comoros and many are clearly descended from Malagasy species that have spread to the archipelago.

④ Giant Coua
Length 62cm Couas are largely terrestrial, pheasantlike birds, although they can fly to escape predators. They feed on small animals such as lizards, including chameleons, and insects. The stately giant coua is easily seen at Réserve Privée de Berenty (p136).

⑤ Madagascar Scops Owl
Length 22-24cm Like many owls, scops owls are usually difficult to find during the day, although guides in national parks will often know of a regular roost. This species is common in most forested habitats.

⑥ Madagascar Kingfisher
Length 15cm A flash of orange usually gives this bird away when it dives into water after small fish and tadpoles. Otherwise, it sits still for long periods and could be overlooked, although it is common near fresh water all over Madagascar.

① Madagascar Crested Ibis
Length 50cm Many ibises feed in marshes, but this species is a forest bird found in both rainforest and dry deciduous forest. It is shy and difficult to see but is common at Station Forestière d'Ampijoroa (p147) and Parc National d'Andasibe-Mantadia (p192).

② Madagascar Kestrel
Length 25-30cm Madagascar has comparatively few birds of prey but this is probably the most common. It is often seen hovering over grasslands near highways before pouncing on prey such as rodents, lizards and insects.

③ Long-tailed Ground-roller
Length 47-52cm Perhaps the most amazing ground-roller of all, the long-tailed ground-roller is restricted to the spiny forest of the southwest. It resembles a colourful roadrunner, complete with long, barred tail and cocky, upright stance.

⑦ Madagascar Hoopoe
Length 32cm In flight these extraordinary birds show their stripes to best advantage and look like a huge butterfly. Its crest can be fanned but normally lies flat. It is common throughout the island, especially in dry deciduous forest.

⑧ Madagascar Bee-eater
Length 23-31cm Best seen in full sunlight, loose flocks of these graceful birds forage for flying insects over open country. They nest in hollows in river banks and road cuttings. Some individuals migrate to East Africa annually.

Rainforest Birds

Madagascar's rainforests support the island's highest bird diversity; birding in this environment can be both challenging and extremely rewarding. You'll have to watch your footing while craning your neck to look into the canopy. Long quiet spells can be suddenly broken by a frenetic 'wave' of feeding birds as they move through the forest. Such bird waves can be composed of a dozen or more different species that will have you scrabbling through your field guide trying to identify them before they disappear among the foliage. A few of the more common and interesting rainforest birds are described here.

5

6

1 Blue Vanga

Length 16cm This stunning *vanga* is unmistakable and common in most forest types over most of the island. In bird feeding parties it is often conspicuous, travelling in pairs or small groups.

2 Nelicourvi Weaver

Length 15cm Most weavers are associated with grasslands but this is a rainforest species that often associates with flocks of greenbuls while foraging in the forest. Females also have a yellow head but lack the striking black 'mask' of the males.

3 White-headed Vanga

Length 20cm A robust *vanga* found in many forest types, including rainforest, throughout the island. Only males are black-and-white, females being greyish, but both sexes have a stout hooked bill. Commonly joins other species in mixed feeding flocks in rainforests.

4 Helmet Vanga

Length 29cm Looks like no other bird – its extraordinary, bright-blue bill is incongruously large, almost toucanlike, and thought to act as a resonator when birds call in the forest. Restricted to intact rainforests of the Masoala Peninsula (p223).

5 Pitta-like Ground-roller

Length 26cm Ground-rollers hop rapidly over the forest floor; all but one species is confined to the eastern rainforests, where they are most easily found when males are calling in September and October. This stunning species is relatively common at Parc National d'Andasibe-Mantadia (p192).

6 Madagascar Paradise-flycatcher

Length 18-30cm Females of this large, active rainforest flycatcher are rufous with a black head, but males sport 12cm tail streamers and may be rufous, white or black, or a combination of all three. Common at Parc National de Ranomafana (p103).

6

Reptiles, Amphibians & Fish

Madagascar's reptiles have also taken some fascinating evolutionary turns. Most famous of these are the chameleons, including the largest and smallest species known. Chameleons have some amazing adaptations for hunting insects in the trees, including the ability to change colour; eyes that can swivel independently of each other on raised cones to watch for enemies and prey simultaneously; and a sticky tongue that shoots out to catch prey. Several species of sea turtle nest on suitable beaches and Madagascar is also home to some 200 species of frog.

8

1 Parson's Chameleon

Length up to 40cm, rarely 69cm (males); females smaller
The world's largest chameleon, this species
is endemic to Madagascar, where it inhabits
rainforests, typically in or near the canopy of
narrow ravines. Males have a massive casque
(helmetlike structure) and two blunt 'horns'.

2 Pygmy Leaf Chameleon

Length 28mm (males) to 33mm (females) This is
possibly the smallest of all lizards and is
found on Nosy Be, where it hunts among
leaf litter and on low branches. Leaf (or
stump-tailed) chameleons resemble dead
leaves and have only a partly prehensile tail.

3 Giant Day Gecko

Length up to 28cm Day geckos may be seen
clinging to tree trunks in rainforests, where
they hunt insects and other small animals
among foliage. Males bob their head and
wave their tail to show dominance to rivals
or to attract mates.

4 Nile Crocodile

Length up to 5m Madagascar's crocs are on
average smaller than their African counterparts, but they are every bit as dangerous.
They are found in freshwater habitats,
including the Canal des Pangalanes, and
a population lives in the cave system of
Réserve Spéciale de l'Ankàrana (p186).

5 Radiated Tortoise

Length 40cm; weight 15kg This striking tortoise
is confined to the dry forests of southern
Madagascar, where it is endangered due
to hunting. It is the subject of an intensive
conservation programme and is being bred
in captivity at Arboretum d'Antsokay (p127).

6 Tomato Frog

Length 6cm (males) to 10.5cm (females) This striking frog is restricted to northwestern Madagascar and endangered because of the pet
trade. Females are larger and brighter than
males and both sexes exude sticky mucus
when threatened by a predator.

7 Coelacanth

Length 1.8m; weight 95kg These deep-sea fish
were known only from 65-million-year-old
fossils until 1938, when a live coelacanth
was caught by a fisherman near Anjouan. It
is now known to be quite common in deep
trenches off the Comoros.

8 Madagascar Tree Boa

Length up to 2m Most boas are arboreal but
this iridescent snake – also known as the
rainbow boa – hunts largely on the ground,
killing its prey by constriction. It preys on
rodents, including the giant jumping rat,
and gives birth to live young. Rainbow boas
are found all over the island but especially
in rainforests.

Insects & Other Invertebrates

When Charles Darwin was shown a Malagasy orchid with an extraordinarily long nectar spur, he concluded that it had coevolved with an insect that could pollinate it. Sure enough, 40 years later a hawk-moth was discovered in Madagascar's rainforests with a 30cm proboscis – long enough to pollinate the unusual orchid – and yet another of the great man's predictions was confirmed. Madagascar's forests support thousands of such fascinating and unusual invertebrates. Most are insignificant, but you will almost certainly encounter clouds of brilliant butterflies, huge moths and bizarre beetles.

❶ Flatid Leaf Bug

Looking at first glance like clusters of tiny flowers, these are actually colonies of adult bugs that have evolved to look like fuchsia flowers as protection against predators. Their young, known as nymphs, look like pieces of lace or lichen attached to branches.

❷ Giraffe-necked Weevil

Length 2.5cm This bizarre little beetle is quite common in Parc National de Ranomafana (p103) and Parc National d'Andasibe-Mantadia (p192). It is found only on the small tree Dichaetanthera cordifolia. Females lay a single egg on a leaf then roll it into a tube to protect the growing larva, which feeds on the leaf. Only the males have the long 'neck'.

❸ Comet Moth

Wingspan up to 22.5cm; tails 20cm These spectacular silk moths are native to Madagascar. Females are larger than males and lay 120 to 170 eggs on leaves of trees belonging to the mango family. The large cocoon has holes that act as drainage so the pupa inside doesn't become waterlogged during downpours. Males have huge antennae that can detect female pheromones from several kilometres away.

(Continued from page 48)

plants, but are trapped by downward-pointing spines along the inside of the 'pitcher' and are eventually dissolved and absorbed by the plant.

Fine stands of rainforest can still be seen in the national parks of Ranomafana (p103), d'Andasibe-Mantadia (p192), de Montagne d'Ambre (p184) and de Marojejy (p227).

Dry, deciduous forest can best be seen in the national park of d'Ankarafantsika and its d'Ampijoroa forest reserve (p147), and the Réserve Forestière de Kirindy (p156). This forest contains giant baobabs, but no palms or ferns. Travellers should not miss the majestic Avenue du Baobab (p156) on the way to Réserve Forestière de Kirindy, which has stands of thousand-year-old baobabs.

NATIONAL PARKS

The environmental movement in Madagascar began in earnest in 1985 with an international conference of scientists, funding organisations and Malagasy government officials. Biologists had long known that Madagascar was an oasis of amazing creatures and plants, but the clear felling and burning of forests all over the island were threatening these treasures. Concerned international donors and the Malagasy government joined together to plan a major conservation programme.

Madagascar Living Edens, by Andrew Young, is a series of breathtaking images of Madagascar's special wildlife. The predator/prey interactions give this film the suspense of a thriller.

By 1989 Madagascar had the world's first country-wide Environmental Action Plan, which offered a blueprint for biodiversity action for the next 20 years. The first step was to create a national park system, called the Association Nationale pour la Gestion des Aires Protégées (Angap; National Association for the Management of Protected Areas), and then set Angap to work on creating new parks and training new staff.

Since then much has changed: in 1985 there were two national parks in Madagascar and today there are over 14, with more in the pipeline. During the first five years of the Environmental Action Plan, five sites were chosen as integrated conservation and development projects. The national parks were officially mapped and registered, and teams were trained to work in them. Villages were courted with sustainable alternatives to forest destruction, such as bee-keeping, fish farming and tree farming.

In the late 1990s focus shifted from national parks to a more regional approach. This broader view started biological, botanical and anthropological surveys in vast stretches of wilderness connecting the parks, especially concentrating on the southern forest corridor between Ranomafana and d'Andringitra, and the northern forest corridor connecting Mantadia with Zahamena. This included mapping with Geographic Information Systems (GIS) and setting up ecological monitoring.

At the World's Park Conference in 2003 President Ravalomanana announced a bold plan to expand protected areas by three times. At the time only 10% of Madagascar was covered with natural vegetation and 3% of the country was protected in national parks, classified forests or natural reserves.

The Duke University Primate Center website at www.duke.edu /web/primate has great photos and up-to-date natural-history facts about lemurs, including details on the release of black-and-white ruffed lemurs back into the wild in Madagascar.

In 2007 the new government's plan to nominate more World Heritage sites culminated in the declaration of the Rainforests of the Antsiranana World Heritage site, which encompasses six rainforest national parks on the eastern seaboard. Madagascar's only other World Heritage sites are currently Parc National des Tsingy de Bemaraha (p151) and Royal Hill of Ambohimanga (p90).

NATIONAL PARKS & RESERVES

Park	Features	Activities	Wildlife	Best Time to Visit	Page
Parc National d'Andasibe-Mantadia	spectacular pristine forest, excellent local guides, well-marked trails	walking, night-walking, lemur-watching, bird-watching	habituated lemurs, including indris, diademed sifakas, black-and-white ruffed lemurs; superb bird-watching with ground-rollers, bird waves	Sep-Nov	p192
Parc National d'Andringitra	rugged granite peaks with great trails and scenery	hiking, climbing	high-altitude ring-tailed lemurs, held sacred by local people	dry season	p110
Parc National d'Ankarafantsika (Station Forestière d'Ampijoroa)	western dry deciduous forest surrounding a lily-covered lake, knowledgeable guides	excellent walking, lake cruises	mongoose lemurs, Coquerel's sifakas, brown lemurs, waterbirds, fishing eagles, crocodiles	May-Nov	p147
Parc National de l'Isalo	rugged sandstone mountains, gorges with cool pools, great sunsets	hiking, swimming, photography	Verreaux's sifakas, ring-tailed lemurs	Apr-Oct	p122
Parc National de Mananara-Nord	Unesco biosphere reserve, remote park with primary rainforest plus coral reefs	hiking, experiencing local village culture	aye-ayes, hairy-eared dwarf lemurs, tomato frogs, chameleons	dry season	p216
Parc National de Marojejy	remote mountainous peaks covered with lush rainforest, canyon with magnificent cliffs	overnight camping, hiking	silky sifakas, helmeted vangas, large malachite-green millipedes	Apr-May Sep-Dec	p227
Parc National de Masoala	Madagascar's largest national park, rainforest intact from mountaintop to sea level, fishing villages	hiking, snorkelling, swimming, lemur-watching, bird-watching, whale-watching in the blissfully blue Baie d'Antongil	unique birds, aye-ayes, red-ruffed lemurs	Sep-Nov	p223
Parc National de Montagne d'Ambre	lush rainforest on an extinct volcano, spectacular waterfall, old French botanic garden, great views	hiking, lemur-watching, bird-watching	crowned lemurs, Sanford's lemurs, Amber Mountain rock thrushes	dry season	p184

People & Wildlife

Enlightened conservationists know that sequestering natural areas is only part of the solution to preserving biodiversity, and that for conservation programmes to succeed in poor developing nations the goodwill of people in and around protected areas must be sought. From the very beginning of Madagascar's environmental movement, the needs of the people living in and around the parks were incorporated into park management plans, and 50% of park admission fees from tourists are returned to villagers that live around the parks. This money is used to build wells, buy vegetable seeds,

Park	Features	Activities	Wildlife	Best Time to Visit	Page
Parc National de Ranomafana	pristine rainforest watershed straddling mountain streams	great walking, lemur-watching, bird-watching	three species of bamboo lemurs, including golden bamboo lemurs, nine other lemur species, rainforest birds such as ground-rollers, brown mesites, crested ibises & Henst's goshawks	dry season	p103
Parc National des Tsingy de Bemaraha	World Heritage site protecting limestone *tsingy* & forested canyons	rock-climbing, hiking, camping	Decken's sifakas, brown lemurs, fishing eagles	Apr-Nov	p151
Parc National Zombitse-Vohibasia	last remnant of forest in the sea of *hauts-plateaux* (highlands) grasslands, excellent guides	hiking, lemur-watching, bird-watching	red-tailed sportive lemurs, Madagascar cuckoo-rollers, Appert's greenbuls, chameleons, day geckos	Apr-Oct	p124
Réserve de Nosy Mangabe	rainforest-covered island wildlife geckos, whales	hiking, camping, spotlighting for fronted brown lemurs, leaf-tailed offshore	best place to observe aye-ayes, white-	Jul-Sep	p219
Réserve Privée de Berenty	remnant gallery forest & spiny desert in a sea of sisal, great local culture museum	hiking, lemur-watching, photography	ring-tailed lemurs, brown lemurs, Verreaux's sifakas, giant couas	Apr-Oct	p136
Réserve Spéciale de Beza-Mahafaly	spiny desert, gallery forest	lemur-watching, photography	ring-tailed lemurs, Verreaux's sifakas	Apr-Sep	p129
Réserve Spéciale de l'Ankàrana	eroded limestone pinnacles, canyons & bat caves, subterranean streams with crocodiles	hiking, caving, lemur-watching, bird-watching	crowned lemurs, Sanford's lemurs, fishing eagles nesting on cliffs, dry-forest bird life, ring-tailed mongooses	dry season	p186

help with tree nurseries, rebuild schools and build small dams to facilitate paddy, rather than hillside, rice cultivation. By visiting a national park, you are economically helping village residents.

Ecotourism has fostered employment opportunities in villages around major national parks, such as Mantadia, Ranomafana and Zombitse-Vohibasia. Bird-watchers in particular are usually keen to see as many of the endemic species as possible and are willing to pay well above the odds for the privilege. This has created its own set of problems but in general the demand for skilled naturalist guides creates well-paid opportunities for Malagasy people in such areas.

Biodiversity Research & Parks

Most of the research on the unique animals and plants of Madagascar occurs in national parks. In 2003 an international Malagasy research and training centre called Centre ValBio was inaugurated adjacent to Parc National de Ranomafana (p103). It is mostly funded by universities from Europe and the USA, and researchers from all over the world visit to take advantage of its modern facilities. Stop in to have lunch, chat with the scientists, see a slide show of the staff's ongoing research and hear about the latest biodiversity findings.

In *Zoboomafoo: Leapin' Lemurs*, Chris and Martin Kratt have created the first wildlife series specifically for viewing by children. A leaping sifaka takes you on an adventure explaining why you should save the lemurs of Madagascar.

ENVIRONMENTAL ISSUES

Madagascar's incredible evolutionary trajectory ground to a halt some 1500 years ago with the arrival of humans. The arrival of people in previously uninhabited lands all over the world has invariably heralded an 'extinction event', whereby large animals are quickly wiped out, followed by varying degrees of ecological change before an area becomes uninhabitable or an equilibrium is reached. Owing to their unique and often fragile ecologies, islands are particularly hard hit; the human impact on Madagascar was devastating.

People, like all biological organisms, must eat, and first to fall were the large ground-dwelling animals that provided an abundant source of ready protein. Wildlife that has evolved without human contact is said to be 'naive', and often lacks the defences or even reflexes to escape human hunters. Madagascar's populations of giant lemurs, aardvarks, hippos and large flightless birds probably fed humans for several centuries, but the end was inevitable and all that remains today are bleached bones and thousands of crushed *Aepyornis* eggs.

Common tenrec mothers can give birth to 25 infants at one time, the most of any mammal in the world.

The other major environmental factor is habitat destruction; forest clearing goes on even today and as humans encroach on once seemingly limitless parcels of land the animal inhabitants suffer. Erosion, exacerbated by deforestation, is now one of the country's most serious problems, and has given rise to the description of Madagascar as the 'great red island'. In the most dramatic cases, the ground has slumped, leaving eroded landslides of red soil, which now scar most of the highlands and have turned rivers red. When you fly over the country, you can see the red, silted waters of the rivers pouring the soil of Madagascar into the sea. Soil erosion is a major threat to freshwater fish, many of which are on the brink of extinction.

Malagasy soils are old and fragile, and cannot survive the annual burning that occurs across the island. Fire is also used in political protest, its meaning going far beyond agricultural use. You will see the effect of deforestation everywhere; much of it has occurred within the last thousand years. Within a decade of a forest being slashed and burned, it becomes irretrievable. The savannah wasteland of the *hauts plateaux* is covered with an invasive, sun-loving grass, and almost no endemic plants or animals can exist in this 'novel' environment, which covers more than 80% of the island. People also have a tough time living on this fragile landscape, with no fertile soil and polluted water, so it is in everyone's best interest to help people and wildlife live in harmony.

The conservation efforts of the 1990s slowed the devastation of natural resources, and satellite photos suggest most park boundaries have been preserved from slash-and-burn methods. The government has seen that its future depends on preserving and marketing its natural resources – and this bodes well for Madagascar's future.

Madagascar

ANDREW MACCOLL

Antananarivo

Antananarivo is a bustling place with activity on every corner. Here people flood the streets, walking down the middle lanes between traffic, knocking on taxi windows, selling everything you can imagine – fruit, sunglasses, flowers, cell phones, calculators, bamboo, even live animals. Pollution from all the automobiles is nearly unbearable, and you're bound to have an itch in your throat before too long. Motorcycles whizz by, slicing through the seemingly endless sea of cars and bodies, moving in every direction. Stalls selling every kind of goods imaginable line the thoroughfares, their wares squeezed into the tiniest nooks and crannies and sometimes spilling out into traffic. You can find everything: fresh produce, raw meat, embroidered linen, electronics, tin matchbox-style replicas of taxis and rickshaws, leather goods and handicrafts.

At first glance Madagascar's capital city resembles a Mediterranean hill town, with its highest point 2643m above sea level. But most of Antananarivo, also known as 'Tana', sits at around 1400m. Regardless of the altitude, walking here can be a leg-burner. Exploring the rich cultural, historical and architectural sites by foot is easy, providing you're willing to climb hundreds of ancient stone steps and mingle into the city's fray. Most people only spend a couple of days in Tana, getting over jetlag before they travel on to other regions. But before you decide on where to go next, give at least three days to experience this crumbling hillside capital city like none other. You won't be disappointed.

HIGHLIGHTS

- Sampling real Malagasy life, hill views and a dose of history around the **Rova** (p77)
- Tackling the country's best range of international and gourmet cuisine in the many fine **restaurants** (p83)
- Soaking up the ambience as you soak in the baths at **Balnéoforme Colbert** (p79)
- Shopping for hard-fought bargains at one of Tana's hectic, eclectic **markets** (p79)
- Saying 'so much for the city' and striking out into the surrounding **highlands** (p89)

Highlands ★

Antananarivo ★

POPULATION: 1.2 million ■ HIGHEST POINT: 2643m ■ PRINCIPAL TRIBE: Merina

HISTORY

The area that is now Antananarivo was originally known as Analamanga (Blue Forest), and is believed to have been populated by the Vazimba, mysterious ancestors of today's Malagasy. In 1610 a Merina king named Andrianjaka conquered the region, stationed a garrison of 1000 men to defend his new settlement, and renamed it Antananarivo, 'Place of 1000 Warriors'.

In the late 18th century, Andrianampoinimerina, the warrior king, moved his capital from Ambohimanga to Antananarivo, which became the most powerful of all the Merina kingdoms. For the next century, Antananarivo was the capital of the Merina monarchs and the base from which they carried out their conquest of the rest of Madagascar.

Tana remained the seat of government during the colonial era, and it was the French who gave the city centre its present form, building two great staircases and draining swamps and paddy fields to create present-day Analakely. In May 1929, the city was the site of the first major demonstration against the colonialists.

Today Antananarivo province is Madagascar's political and economic centre, and has a total population of about four million. Madagascar's president, Marc Ravalomanana, hails from Tana and served as the city's mayor before his presidency.

ORIENTATION

Ivato airport lies 12km from Antananarivo, and the journey there or back can take up to 45 minutes during rush hour.

Central Antananarivo can be roughly divided into two sections: the Haute-Ville (upper town) and Basse-Ville (lower town). The centre of Basse-Ville and the commercial district is the multi-laned Ave de l'Indépendance, which runs southeast from the train station through the crowded main market area of Analakely, with a steep staircase leading to Place de l'Indépendance in the rather quieter Haute-Ville. Another staircase, directly opposite, leads to the busy district of Ambondrona, where several hotels are located. Narrow streets lead further uphill to the Rova (royal palace). Down the other side of the hill from Haute-Ville is the heart-shaped Lac Anosy (Lake Anosy). Tana's outer districts go on for miles, so allow yourself plenty of time if you're visiting somewhere in the suburbs.

Finding your way around central Tana isn't always easy either – street signs are rare and contradictory, and most streets have interchangeable French and Malagasy names, neither of which are generally known to locals.

Maps

Both Edicom and FTM publish detailed plans of the city centre and suburbs, sold at bookshops or the Ortana tourist office (p75),

---

ANTANANARIVO IN...

Two Days

Start your day the French way with coffee and croissants at any of the city's cafés before visiting the **Musée d'Art et d'Archéologie** (p78) and exploring the Haute-Ville. After high tea in **Patisserie Colbert** (p85), take a taxi up to the **Rova** (p77) and the **Musée Andafivaratra** (p78). Sunset is perfect for drinks and traditional Malagasy music at the **Grill du Rova** (p83), followed by dinner at **La Varangue** (p84).

The next morning, walk round **Lac Anosy** (p76), stopping to admire the flower market and barbers' stalls, then squeeze your way in to the market of **Analakely** (p79) for some hectic browsing and bargaining. After lunch at a local *hotely*, visit an exhibition at the **Centre Culturel Albert Camus** (p74), then have a traditional Malagasy banquet at **Chez Mariette** (p84).

Four Days

Follow the two-day itinerary, then head out to **Ilafy** (p90) and the **royal palace** (p90) at Ambohimanga for a taste of Merina history. Back in town, sample one of Tana's more exotic restaurants to put you in the mood for drinking and dancing at **Pandora Station** or **Le Bus** (p86).

The next day, spend the morning shopping at the **Marché Artisanale la Digue** (p87) in La Digue, then relax those muscles with a spa treatment at the fabulous **Balnéoforme Colbert** (p79).

ANTANANARIVO

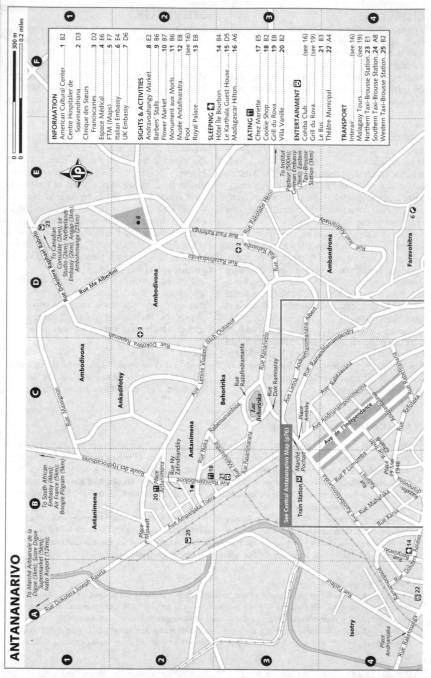

0   300 m
0   0.2 miles

INFORMATION	
American Cultural Center........	1 B2
Centre Hospitalier de	
Soavinandriana......................	2 D3
Clinique des Sœurs	
Franciscaines.........................	3 D2
Espace Médical.......................	4 E6
FTM (Maps).............................	5 F7
Italian Embassy......................	6 E4
UK Embassy............................	7 D6

SIGHTS & ACTIVITIES	
Andravoahangy Market..........	8 E2
Barbers' Stalls........................	9 B6
Flower Market........................	10 B7
Monument aux Morts............	11 B6
Musée Andafivaratra..............	12 E8
Pool..	(see 16)
Royal Palace...........................	13 E8

SLEEPING	
Hôtel Île Bourbon..................	14 B4
Le Karthala Guest House........	15 D5
Madagascar Hilton.................	16 A6

EATING	
Chez Mariette........................	17 E5
Cookie Shop...........................	18 B2
Grill du Rova..........................	19 E8
Villa Vanille...........................	20 B2

ENTERTAINMENT	
Cohiba Club............................	(see 16)
Grill du Rova..........................	(see 19)
Le Bus....................................	21 B3
Théâtre Municipal..................	22 A4

TRANSPORT	
Interair...................................	(see 16)
Malagasy Tours......................	(see 19)
Northern Taxi-Brousse Station.	23 E1
Southern Taxi-Brousse Station.	24 A8
Western Taxi-Brousse Station.	25 B2

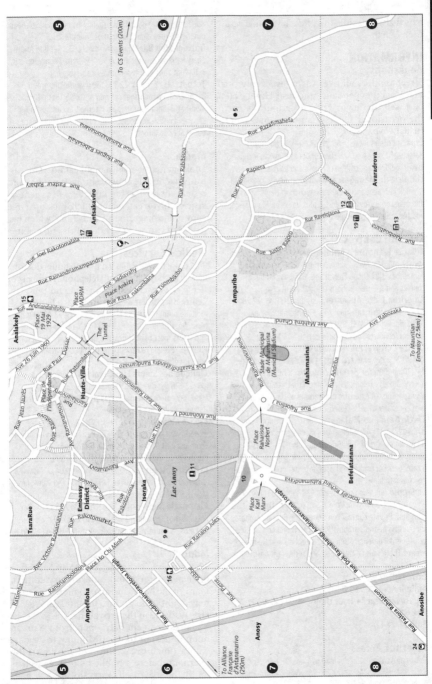

which also offers its own free, but rather less useful, map.

INFORMATION
Bookshops
Street vendors all over town, especially on Place de l'Indépendance and near Hôtel Colbert, sell the major French periodicals and the occasional English-language magazine (usually *Newsweek*).

Espace Loisirs (Map p76; ☎ 032 07 034 84; Rue Ratsimilaho) The best selection of books in town, including French guidebooks, children's books and novels.

Librairie de Madagascar (Map p76; ☎ 22 224 54; 38 Ave de l'Indépendance) A good selection of newspapers and magazines (mostly French), plus books on Madagascar and the Indian Ocean region.

Cultural Centres
Alliance Francaise d'Antananarivo (off Map pp72-3; ☎ 22 211 07; www.alliancefr.mg; Rue Seimad, Andavamamba; ▣) Offers French and Malagasy language courses and sponsors various cultural events.

American Cultural Center (Map pp72-3; ☎ 22 200 89; ramanantth@state.gov; 7 Rue Rainizanabololona; ☺ 2-5pm Tue & Wed, 8.30am-12.30pm Thu) Occasional lectures, concerts and exhibitions.

Centre Culturel Albert Camus (CCAC/CCF; Map p76; ☎ 22 213 75; www.ccac.mg; 14 Ave de l'Indépendance; ☺ 10am-6pm Tue-Sat) The centre has a multimedia library and an exhibition hall, offers French courses and also sponsors an extensive programme of concerts, dance, film and other events. Closed Thursday morning.

Cercle Germano-Malagasy (Goethe-Zentrum; Map p76; ☎ 22 214 42; biblio@cgm-mada.de; Escalier Ranavalona; ☺ 8am-5.30pm Mon-Sat; ▣) Offers a library with German magazines and newspapers, as well as a café, German language classes, internet access, concerts and German films.

Le Studio (off Map pp72-3; ☎ 033 11 968 33; Ivandry; ☺ 10.30am-8pm Mon, Wed & Sat, to 10pm Thu-Fri, 2.30-6pm Sun) Private cultural centre near the Russian Embassy specialising in photography (Pierrot Men etc) and applied arts, plus documentary and film screenings and themed events. There's also a craft shop and restaurant onsite.

Emergency
Ambulance (☎ 22 357 53)
Espace Médical 24-hour clinic (☎ 22 625 66)
Fire (☎ 18)
Police (☎ 17)

Internet Access
Cyberpaositra Analakely (Map p76; Ave 26 Juin 1960); Haute-Ville (Map p76; ☎ 22 296 76; www.paositra.mg;

Rue Ratsimilaho) Both Tana's main post offices have cheap internet centres charging Ar30 per minute.

Outcool Web Bar (Map p76; ☎ 22 553 77; Rue Andrianary Ratianarivo; per min Ar38; ☺ 9am-11pm Mon-Sat, 3.30-9pm Sun) Also functions as a sociable bar.

Teknet (Map p76; ☎ 22 313 59; www.teknetgroup .com; Ave Ramanantsoa; per min Ar40; ☺ 8am-10pm Mon-Sat, 3-8pm Sun) Prepaid internet, fax and printing services, English keyboards. Also operates a Cyberspace outlet at Ivato airport.

Media
Look out for the English publication *Madagascar News* on sale at bookshops. It has bar and restaurant listings for Tana, as well as general articles. If you can read French, pick up a free copy of the magazine *Sortir à Tana*, which has details of clubs, bars, restaurants and events.

Medical Services
The daily newspapers list out-of-hours doctors, as well as the location and telephone numbers of dentists, duty chemists and other hospitals.

Centre Hospitalier de Soavinandriana (Hôpital Militaire d'Antananarivo; Map pp72-3; ☎ 22 403 41; Rue Moss, Soavinandriana; ☺ 24hr) Has X-ray equipment and stocks most basic drugs and medicines. The hospital employs several French doctors. Requires payment in advance of treatment.

Clinique des Sœurs Franciscaines (Map pp72-3; ☎ 22 235 54; Rue Dokotera Rajaonah, Ankadifotsy) Has X-ray equipment and is well run and relatively clean. Requires payment in advance.

Espace Médical (Map pp72-3; ☎ 22 794 38; esmed@wanadoo.mg; 65 Bis Rue Pasteur Rabary) A private clinic just east of the city, with laboratory and X-ray capabilities and several French-trained doctors.

Institut Pasteur (off Map pp72-3; ☎ 22 412 72; www .pasteur.mg; Ambatofotsikely, Avaradoha; ☺ 9am-5pm Mon-Fri) The best place for lab tests.

Pharmacie Metropole (Map p76; ☎ 22 200 25; Rue Ratsimilaho; ☺ 8am-noon Mon-Sat) One of Tana's best and most convenient pharmacies, near the Hôtel Colbert.

Money
The bureaux de change at Ivato airport often offer better rates and quicker service than many of the banks in Tana, so there's no need to wait until you get into the city. An ATM is also available in the arrivals hall.

Banks are generally open from 8am to noon and 3pm to 6pm Monday to Friday, with a lunch break, and are closed on the afternoon before a public holiday as well as on the holiday itself. Virtually all now have reliable ATMs (Visa only), though some may not operate outside banking hours.

Some more upmarket hotels change cash and travellers cheques for their guests. The Madagascar Hilton has a 24-hour ATM.

Bank of Africa (BOA) Basse-Ville (Map p76; Ave de l'Indépendance); Haute-Ville (Map p76; ☎ 22 202 51; Place de l'Indépendance) Changes travellers cheques and gives cash advances on MasterCard as well as Visa.

BFV-SG Basse-Ville (Map p76; Ave de l'Indépendance); Haute-Ville (Map p76; ☎ 22 206 91; Ave Ramanantsoa) Travellers cheques, Visa advances and Western Union transfers.

BMOI (Map p76; ☎ 22 346 09; Place de l'Indépendance) Changes travellers cheques.

BNI-CL (Map p76; ☎ 22 228 00; 74 Ave 26 Juin 1960) Travellers cheques and Visa advances. There's also an ATM on Place 19 Mai 1946.

Socimad Bureau de Change (Map p76; ☎ 22 643 20; Rue Radama I; ◷ 8am-noon & 2-5pm Mon-Fri, 8-11.15am Sat) Changes travellers cheques, and does advances on Visa cards. Also has a 24-hour office at the airport.

UCB (Map p76; ☎ 22 272 62; Rue des 77 Parlementaires Français) Changes travellers cheques and gives fairly rapid cash advances on both Visa and MasterCard.

Post & Telephone

There are public telephones for domestic and international calls at both post offices as well as plenty dotted around town. You can buy phonecards from any shop or kiosk.

Post Office (Paositra) Basse-Ville (Map p76; Ave 26 Juin 1960; ◷ Mon-Fri); Haute-Ville (main post office; Map p76; ☎ 22 296 76; www.paositra.mg; Rue Ratsimilaho; ◷ 7am-5pm Mon-Fri, 8-11am Sat) Tana's two main post offices.

Tourist Information

Maison de Sainte Marie (Map p76; ☎ 24 265 02; Rue Ramandriamapandry) Information, transport and reservations for Île Sainte Marie, on the east coast (see p206). The office is shared with MadaBus (p87).

Office National de Tourism (ONTM; Map p76; ☎ 22 660 85; www.madagascar-tourisme.com; 3 Rue Elysée Ravelomanantsoa) Limited amounts of countrywide information.

Ortana (Map p76; ☎ 24 304 84; ortana2006@yahoo .fr; Escalier Ranavalona) New, helpful regional tourist office with keen staff and plenty of brochures on local and national destinations.

Travel Agencies

For Tana-based tour operators offering trips within Madagascar, see the full listings on p285. For international and general travel services such as air tickets and package holidays, try the following agencies:

Dodo Travel & Tours (Map p76; ☎ 22 690 36; www .dodotraveltour.com; Rue Elysée Ravelomanantsoa)

Islanders (Map p76; ☎ 22 640 23; 44 Rue Ratsimilaho)

Transcontinents (Map p76; ☎ 22 223 98; transco@dts .mg; 10 Ave de l'Indépendance)

Voyages Bourdon (Map p76; ☎ 22 296 96; voyagesbourdon@simicro.mg; 15 Rue Patrice Lumumba, cnr Rue Radama I)

DANGERS & ANNOYANCES

Antananarivo is safer than many developing-world capitals, and if you take standard precautions, you shouldn't have any difficulties. Public transport isn't safe at night, especially between the town and the airport. Even in the centre it's a good idea to take taxis; if you do walk, go in a group, and remember that much of the city has no streetlights. During the day, keep an eye out for pickpockets in markets, on public transport and in other crowded areas.

Persistent street vendors selling postcards, newspapers, cigarettes, vanilla or other souvenirs can also be a pain, especially around Place de l'Indépendance and the best-known hotels – ignore them or give a single firm 'no' and they should give up more quickly.

Police checks on foreigners, whether on foot or in taxis, are not uncommon in Tana at night. Bear in mind that you are required to carry ID with you at all times; if you don't have it chances are you'll be asked for a *cadeau* ('present', ie bribe) rather than being marched down to the police station, but either way it's better to keep your passport on you, suitably concealed of course.

As an added environmental hazard, you may experience headaches or throat irritation for the first few days in Tana, particularly if you are prone to respiratory allergies or asthma. This is due in part to the altitude and in part to the city's polluted air.

Scams

On arrival at Ivato airport you're very likely to be approached by one or more freelance guides, who promise to arrange transport or tours to other parts of the country, particularly the popular Tsiribihina River trip. Some travellers have found this a convenient way of departing quickly without lengthy shopping around; however, even with a signed

ANTANANARIVO

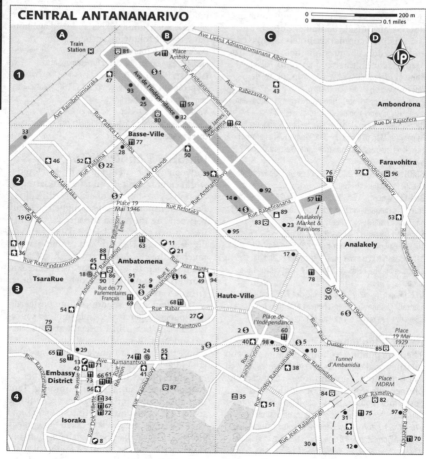

CENTRAL ANTANANARIVO

0   200 m
0   0.1 miles

contract you have few guarantees, and some readers have reported incidents of 'guides' simply taking the money and disappearing. The only sure way to avoid this is to book in advance with official tour operators, which is often more expensive. See p285 for tips on how to organise your trip.

See also p271 for scams to do with the new currency.

SIGHTS & ACTIVITIES
If your knees can withstand the long flights of stairs and steep, sloping streets, central Tana is a good place to explore on foot. Walking around the Haute-Ville or the streets around Ave de l'Indépendance, you'll come across plenty of little cameos of Malagasy life, such

as women selling embroidered tablecloths spread out on the sidewalks, men hawking rubber stamps from improvised stalls on the steps, or taxi drivers sharing a hunk of peanut cake bought from a roadside kiosk. Most of the attractive old buildings are in Haute-Ville, which is quieter and easier to stroll around than the hectic, exhaust-fume-ridden Basse-Ville.

Lac Anosy
Antananarivo's lake (Map pp72–3) lies in the southern part of town, an easy downhill walk from Haute-Ville. In the early morning you may see flocks of white cattle egrets roosting in the nearby trees. The lake is at its most beautiful in October, when the jacaranda trees

are covered in purple blossom. On an island, connected to the shore by a causeway, stands a large white angel on a plinth, the Monument aux Morts (Monument to the Dead), a WWI memorial erected by the French. There's a daily flower market just opposite the end of the causeway and a neat little row of barbers' stalls on the southern shore. On sunny weekend afternoons, the paths around the lake fill up with strolling couples and families; however, they can also attract hawkers, loiterers and less savoury types, so avoid wandering here on your own at quiet times and definitely at night.

The Rova, Avaradrova & Andohalo

The **Rova** (Palais de la Reine; Map pp72-3; Rue Ramboatiana), or royal palace, is the imposing structure that crowns the highest hill overlooking Lac

Anosy. Gutted in a fire in 1995, it is still under restoration and was not open to the public at time of research. If it has reopened when you visit, remember that it is *fady* (taboo) to point your finger directly at the royal tombs or the palace itself.

Even with the palace closed, the adjacent districts of Avaradrova and Andohalo are fine places to stroll around for an hour or two, with stunning views on all sides, plaques detailing the significance of some interesting historical buildings and a sense of real local life around you. See our Walking Tour (p79) for more details.

Freelance guides often hang around the Rova entrance and offer their services for walks around the area, including commentary on the exhibits in the nearby Musée Andafivaratra. They usually speak good English and are full of trivia about the palace, local buildings and the history of the city. Make sure you negotiate a price in advance, otherwise they will spin the tour out for over two hours, then emotionally blackmail you into paying an extortionate fee of €30 or more once it's finished! Around Ar5000 per person is a perfectly generous price.

To get to the Rova from the centre of Antananarivo, it's a stiff 4km walk or an easy taxi ride (around Ar3000). Minibuses 103, 134 and 190 will also take you there, if you can work out the routes!

Musée Andafivaratra

Housed in a magnificent pink baroque palace, a few hundred metres downhill from the Rova, the **Andafivaratra museum** (Map pp72-3; admission Ar3000; ☯ 10am-5pm Sat-Thu) is filled with furniture, portraits and memorabilia from the age of the Merina kings and queens. The building was the former home of Prime Minister Rainilaiarivony, the power behind the throne of the three queens he married in succession. Even with the Rova closed, the museum provides ample reason to visit the old royal quarter, particularly by illuminating some of the colourful characters that drove Madagascan history: mad Queen Ranavalona I, dumpy in a coral silk crinoline, scowls out from her oil painting like a psychotic Queen Victoria, while Jean Laborde, the French adventurer presumed to be her lover, glowers from beneath his beard in the black-and-white photograph next to it. There's also a huge gilt throne, the Merina crown jewels, coats of chain mail and, surprisingly, tiny military uniforms belonging to former monarchs. Explanations of the exhibits are in English as well as French.

In the museum's rear courtyard, you'll find a collection of wooden huts in the traditional styles of each of Madagascar's five regions, constructed for a visit from former French president Jacques Chirac.

Musée d'Art et d'Archéologie

Smaller than the Musée Andafivaratra, but still worth popping into, the **Musée d'Art et d'Archéologie** (Map p76; ☎ 22 210 47; Rue Dok Villette; admission by donation; ☯ noon-5pm Tue-Fri) in the Haute-Ville gives an overview of archaeological digs around the island, including displays of grave decorations from the south (known as *aloalo* – see the boxed text, p130), an extensive exhibition of musical instruments and a few talismans and objects used for sorcery.

THE ROVA

When the Rova (pronounced 'roova') does finally reopen, a visit here is thoroughly recommended, as there are few other places in Madagascar that better represent the turbulent and often bloody history of the Merina royal dynasty.

The palace gate is protected by a carved eagle, the symbol of military force, and a phallus, the symbol of circumcision and thus nobility. Inside the gate are royal tombs in the form of wooden huts. The French moved the remains of Merina kings and queens from the Rova when they took over the city in 1845, an act that is still considered to be profane by the Malagasy. Today the remains are back, and the townspeople still visit them to ask for blessings.

The palace itself, known as Manjakamiadana (A Fine Place to Rule), was designed for Queen Ranavalona I by a Scottish missionary named James Cameron. The outer structure, built in 1867 for Ranavalona II, was made of stone, with a wooden roof and interior. Crows still wheel around the satellite aerials that flank the towers of the palace – the birds were considered sacred by the Merina royal family, having apparently warned one king of an impending attack.

Beside the imposing stone structure is a replica of a Malagasy palace in the old style. This was built to resemble the palace of King Andrianampoinimerina, who founded the Merina kingdom. It looks like a black wood hut, with a tiny, raised doorway. The royal bed is situated in the sacred northwest corner of the hut. The simple furniture inside is aligned according to astrological rules. The king supposedly hid in the rafters when visitors arrived, signalling whether the guest was welcome by dropping pebbles onto his wife's head.

Whether the palace is open or not, the best time to visit the area is towards the end of the afternoon, so you can wander the streets then enjoy the spectacular colours of the sunset with the city spread out below.

Markets

For Shakespeare, all the world was a stage; for Antananarivo it seems that all the world's a market, which must make at least half the population hawkers. Everywhere you look vendors tout their wares from stalls, carts and inverted cardboard boxes, or simply wander the streets looking hopeful.

The main official market is found in the 'pavilions' at **Analakely** (Map p76). It's a packed, teeming place, selling clothes, household items, dodgy VCDs and every food product you could imagine, plus a few things you probably couldn't – look out for the shop(s) selling '100% organic bat guano'. The smaller **Marché Communal de Petit Vitesse** (Map p76), west of the train station, sells more or less the same goods.

Another highlight is the colourful **flower market** (Map pp72–3), held daily on the southeastern edge of Lac Anosy. For souvenirs, the **Marché Artisanale de La Digue** (see p87) is Tana's best-known craft market. There's another, smaller market at **Andravoahangy** (Map pp72–3), about 1.5km northeast of the northern end of Ave de l'Indépendance.

Spas, Salons & Pools

For a truly indulgent experience, try **Balnéoforme Colbert** (Map p76; ☎ 22 625 71; Hôtel Colbert, 29 Rue Printsy Ratsimamanga; ☺ 1-9pm Mon-Sat, 10am-6pm Sun), a fantastic spa with a mosaic swimming pool and Turkish bath. A variety of stunningly decorated treatment rooms offer body wraps, bubble baths and every kind of massage imaginable – relaxing, slimming, water, ying-yang… It's not cheap, but it is worth it, especially if you've just arrived back in Tana after some hard trekking.

As well as selling local oils and bath, spa and spice products, **BioAroma** (Map p76; ☎ 22 326 30; bioaroma@simicro.mg; 54 Ave Ramanantsoa; ☺ 8am-6pm Mon-Fri, 9am-5pm Sat, 9am-noon Sun), surely Tana's most aromatic shop, hands out full-body massages from Ar28,000, plus a comprehensive range of facials, body masks, reiki and other esoteric treatments, including the 'gravity sheet' (hanging by the feet to stretch the spine). A handy leaflet explains (in English) each treatment and which ones may be painful!

The state-approved natural health chain **Homeopharma** (Map p76; ☎ 22 269 34; www.madagascar-homeopharma.com; Rue Ranavalona III; ☺ 8am-6pm Mon-Fri, 9am-5pm Sat) has outlets all over Tana and throughout the country; many, such as the Haute-Ville branch, offer massages and other treatments. You can even arrange themed tours, with emphasis on health and wellbeing amid the tourist spots.

The **spa** at Le Royal Palissandre (p83) is another good spot, and the Madagascar Hilton (p83) has a 25m **pool** (admission Ar10,000; ☺ Mon-Fri summer only) as well as spa and exercise facilities.

WALKING TOUR

Tana offers numerous opportunities for interesting walks, but this one takes in many of the city's major sights (see Map p80). For details of longer walks in and around Tana, look for the useful booklet *Cheminements Touristiques et Culturels D'Antananarivo*, published by the Mission de Coopération et d'Action Culturelle, in local bookshops.

To begin your tour, hail a taxi to the starting point – the magnificent **Rova (1**; p77). The palace is not currently open to the public, but you can take the path around the outside, with or without a guide, to explore the surrounding area.

A few hundred metres downhill from the palace, past the remaining classical pillars of the former Palais de Justice (law courts), is the **Musée Andafivaratra (2**; opposite), housed in the magnificent palace of the former prime minister. From here, wend your way down to the twin-towered **Andohalo Cathedral (3)**, which was built on the spot where Queen Ranavalona liked to throw Christian martyrs from the cliffs. Nearby you'll find the reconstruction of Jean Laborde's house, which served as Madagascar's first French consulate.

Stroll at leisure through the lanes to reach Rue Ratsimilaho, the main artery of the lively Haute-Ville. After the pretty garden on Place de l'Indépendance, head down Rue Rainilaiarivony to have a look at the **President's Palace (4)**, with its sentry boxes painted red and green to match the Malagasy flag. Continuing down Ave Ramanantsoa and Ave Rainitsarovy (watch out for white cattle egrets in the trees on the left), you'll reach **Lac Anosy (5)**. Turn right and circumambulate the lake, passing rows of **barbers' shops (6)** on the southern side, then end your tour with a look at the **flower market (7)** and a stroll over the causeway to the **Monument aux Morts (8)** in the centre. From here, you can once again see the Rova, perched on the hilltop in its scaffolding cage, a world away from the bustle around you.

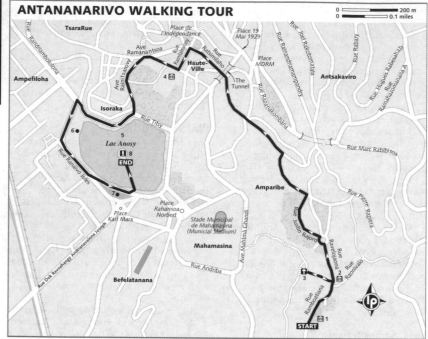

ANTANANARIVO WALKING TOUR

COURSES
As well as French and Malagasy language courses, dance lessons are a popular pastime for locals and visitors alike. Besides classes at the main cultural centres (see p74), you could try traditional and ballroom dancing at the Ministry of Culture & Tourism centre **CEMDLAC** (Map p76; 6 Ave de l'Indépendance).

TOURS
Many tour operators here can offer city tours and day trips around Antananarivo, but **Tany Mena Tours** (Map p76; ☎ 22 326 27; tany menatours@simicro.mg; Ave de l'Indépendance) is the only company that really specialises in them. The catalogue has a whole range of fascinating themed walks and excursions with a cultural emphasis, led by genuine experts such as historians or anthropologists (some English-speaking). A half-day guided tour of Tana, taking in the palace of Ambohimanga (see p90), costs €23 per person in a group of three to five; other possibilities include craft workshops, visiting animist sacred sites and a two-day trip into the highlands (€100 per person).

For a full list of companies offering tours around Madagascar, see p285.

SLEEPING
Antananarivo has an excellent selection of accommodation, but the best places tend to be booked solid during peak season (Christmas, summer and French school holidays), so it's a good idea to make bookings in advance. Only the top-range hotels have lifts, and many of the lower-priced places have very steep stairs. Not many establishments could be viewed as child-friendly – things such as childcare and highchairs are only available in the very upmarket hotels.

Prices for midrange and top-end hotels are often quoted in euros, but you can always pay in ariary, and sometimes in US dollars. Many smarter hotels will also take Visa credit cards. A *vignette* (tourist tax) of Ar600 to Ar4000 per night is added to all prices here.

Budget
Hôtel Moonlight (Map p76; ☎ 22 268 70; hasinaherizo@yahoo.fr; Rue Rainandriamapandry; r Ar13,000-30,000) Far and away the cheapest decent option

in town; the creaky wood floors and flock wallpaper simply add character to this budget stalwart. The 2nd-floor rooms are the priciest and biggest, with unimpressive private bathrooms, and there's a communal terrace. There aren't many restaurants in the surrounding area, so you'll probably want to take a taxi across town in the evenings if you stay here.

ourpick Hôtel Isoraka (Map p76; ☎ 22 335 81; saka@malagasy.com; 11 Ave Ramanantsoa; r Ar18,000-40,000) Recently acquired and revamped by the owners of the Sakamanga (p82), the Isoraka remains a popular, friendly budget choice and the best value in town. The pricier rooms are arguably even nicer than the Saka's, with TV, phone, private bathroom and linen bathrobes! The only downside is its small size and lack of extra facilities such as a restaurant, hardly a hardship given its central location.

Hôtel Le Jean Laborde (Map p76; ☎ 22 330 45; labordehotel@hotmail.com; 3 Rue de Russie; r Ar25,000-55,000) This dim and cosy bar-restaurant is favoured by French expats for its convincing taste of home, and it does a good impersonation of a country pension, decking out its rooms in wooden floors and furniture (not to mention green walls and pink corridors). The cheaper rooms share a toilet, while the most expensive has TV, phone and even its own salon, complete with three-piece suite.

Chez Francis (Map p76; ☎ 22 613 65; francis vacheresse@yahoo.fr; Rue Rainandriamapandry; r Ar29,000-43,000) Not far from the Moonlight, Chez Francis is split over two buildings – it's worth stretching the pennies to go for the newer pastel-painted annexe, which has tiled floors, TVs and shared balconies. Most rooms have their own shower cubicle, but toilets are shared. Meals are available by arrangement.

Midrange

Hôtel Shalimar (Map p76; ☎ 22 640 03; yascom@ wanadoo.mg; Rue Mahafaka; r Ar30,000-60,000; ⌘) Having started life as a reputable Indian restaurant, the Shalimar has branched out (or rather, up) to offer accommodation over four floors of mostly spacious rooms with TV, Disney mirrors and the occasional nod to its Asian heritage. There's a travel agency on site and an open upstairs terrace, as well as a second, more basic branch of the restaurant near Hotel Sakamanga.

Merina Lodge (Map p76; ☎ 24 522 33; merina lodge@wanadoo.mg; Impasse OSTIE, off Rue Andrianary Ratianarivo; r Ar30,000-63,000) Quite transparently in-

tended to rival the Sakamanga, this endearing new establishment makes a pretty good fist of its attempt at competition, tricking out its rooms almost entirely in wood – including the bathrooms! It's quiet, friendly and a good choice, though it lacks the Saka's extra facilities. You may also get the chance to play football with local kids in the small alley that leads to it.

Hôtel-Restaurant Shanghai (Map p76; ☎ 22 314 72; shangai@malagasy.com; 4 Rue Rainitovo; r Ar35,000-36,000) Uninspiring yet thoroughly acceptable for the price, this hotel in the embassy quarter is a little musty but has a nice front courtyard. The Chinese owners seem a little stressed at times, perhaps from the strains of coordinating the very reasonable restaurant (mains Ar3800 to Ar8000), where the menu features that Oriental classic, frogs' legs.

Hôtel Île Bourbon (Map pp72-3; ☎ 22 279 42; 12 Rue Benyowski; r Ar37,000) Tucked away round a corner, this eccentrically laid-out old house is run by a former resident of Réunion, giving a slightly different Indian Ocean flavour to the carpeted white rooms with their big local paintings. There's live music in the restaurant in the evenings, and creole cuisine to go with it (mains Ar8400 to Ar28,000), plus plenty of exotic rums – try the 'aphrodisiac' mixture if you're feeling frisky!

Hôtel White Palace (Map p76; ☎ 22 664 59; 101 Rue de Liége; r Ar37,000-59,000, apt Ar76,000; ⌘) A good-value business option not far from the Anjary, with rooms divided into three categories, plus studio 'apartments' for up to three people. Book in advance to arrange airport transfers (Ar30,000). Breakfast is included.

Anjary Hôtel (Map p76; ☎ 22 244 09; www.anjary -hotel.com; 89 Rue de Liége; r Ar39,000; ⌘ ⌘) Seven storeys of smallish but comfortable Western business-style rooms, with good facilities including a travel agency, gym, sauna and massage centre, *salon de thé* and the 'exotic terrace' Indian restaurant (no alcohol). A new annexe across the road offers even more rooms and a snack bar. The slightly dubious Basse-Ville location may be off-putting for solo travellers.

Le Karthala Guest House (Map pp72-3; ☎ 22 248 95; le_karthala@yahoo.fr; 48 Rue Andriandahifotsy; r incl breakfast Ar41,000) A very friendly, family-run B&B with a pretty garden courtyard and colourful terrace. The spacious rooms are packed with wood for maximum character, and even have funky swing doors into the skylit bathrooms. The top-floor rooms, right under the roof, share a bathroom, though the price is the same.

Le Cactus Vert (Map p76; ☎ 22 624 41; lecactus vert@wanadoo.mg; 15 Rue Radama I; r Ar60,000-74,000) This rather attractive building stands out immediately from its busy Basse-Ville surroundings, and the effect is no less appealing inside, flaunting a wide palette of greens, plenty of wood and a distinctly Wild West feel (the saloon doors to the bathrooms are a great touch). There's also a handy bar and restaurant on site.

our pick **Hôtel Sakamanga** (Map p76; ☎ 22 358 09; www.sakamanga.com; Rue Andrianary Ratianarivo; r Ar65,000-235,000; ⛶ 🖳) A perennial favourite with those in the know, the Sakamanga attracts travellers at all points on the budget scale, setting store by a friendly atmosphere, varied rooms, characterful décor and beyond-comprehensive services. The intriguingly mazy layout leads to a garden and café-bar-library, with enough cased artefacts in the corridors to open a mini museum, and the upstairs restaurant (opposite) is an institution in its own right. Some tours are on offer, although reports of these vary, or you can seek out your own group on the online message board, http://sakamanga.boardin globe.com. Reserve well in advance, as the Saka is almost always full – as a result, it's the only vaguely cheap hotel to have a permanent gaggle of street vendors outside!

Radama Hôtel (Map p76; ☎ 22 319 27; radama@simicro .mg; 22 Ave Ramanantsoa; r Ar80,000; ⛶ 🖳) According to its brochure the Radama goes for 'charm and authenticity', and you do indeed get a sense of the Malagasy personal touch in the friendly service and polished dark-wood environment. The larger doubles, with balconies and bathtubs, are particularly good value. On the ground floor, the red-hued restaurant does a good line in local cuisine (mains Ar6000 to Ar9000), and traditional music can be arranged.

Hôtel Raphia (Map p76; ☎ 22 253 13; hotelraphia@ wanadoo.mg; Rue Ranavalona III; s/d/tr €16/18/20, with shared bathroom €13/15/17) This family-run Haute-Ville option comprises an eccentric but appealing selection of wood-clad rooms with a traditional feel to them. Half- and full-board rates are also available, catered for in the hotel's semi-open terrace pizza restaurant to take full advantage of the hillside location.

Karibotel (Map p76; ☎ 22 665 54; karibotel@wanadoo .mg; 26 Ave de l'Indépendance; r €25-29) Very central

and perfectly comfortable, but not particularly exciting. The cheapest rooms share toilets, the priciest have balconies. If you're planning a wedding or other big event, ask about the Domaine Manerinerina permanent marquee, 12km from town.

Résidence Lapasoa (Map p76; ☎ 22 611 40; www .lapasoa.com; 15 Rue de la Réunion; s/d/ste €35/38/50) Beautifully decorated enough to have a top-end air, the spacious rooms here boast wooden floors, TV, minibar and four-poster beds. There's a very friendly, family atmosphere, and it's in a nice quiet location just next to the Musée d'Art et d'Archéologie. The Lapasoa is also a good place to get information on quality arts and crafts, which may explain why itinerant souvenir sellers tend to hang around outside. A 'family' room sleeping up to five people costs €58. The same owners run the superb Kudéta restaurant (p84) next door.

Top End

our pick **La Varangue** (Map p76; ☎ 22 273 97; varangue@ simicro.mg; 17 Rue Printsy Ratsimamanga; r Ar145,000-168,000, ste Ar190,000; ⛶) Tana's only genuine luxury boutique hotel, the Swiss-run Varangue is discreetly set down a steep lane next to the President's Palace. The seven spacious rooms come in two categories – the cheaper ones have modern décor, the more expensive ones are beautifully furnished in dark wood with rustic-style furniture, rich fabrics and balconies overlooking the city. Vintage cars and wooden pirogues help set the tone outside as well. Book in advance to get a room; even if you don't manage a room, the world-renowned restaurant (p84) is well worth a visit.

Hôtel du Louvre (Map p76; ☎ 22 390 00; www.hotel -du-louvre.com; 4 Place de l'Indépendance; r €71-105; ⛶ 🖳) A new and very convenient hotel next to the Shoprite supermarket in the Haute-Ville, with traditional wooden floors and Malagasy art giving way to a more modern laminate style in the rooms. Rates include breakfast, served in a pleasant open courtyard space. Jetsetters may like to note that the hotel also houses the Consulate of Monaco.

Hôtel de France (Map p76; ☎ 22 213 04; www.siceh -hotels.com; 34 Ave de l'Indépendance; r incl breakfast €75-85; ⛶ 🖳) One of two three-star places along Ave de l'Indépendance run by the Siceh agency, it's kitted out in uniform sub-Ikea painted fittings and pastel shades, with a good French restaurant, ground-floor café and a truly big terrace.

ANTANANARIVO

Hôtel Tana Plaza (Map p76; ☎ 22 218 65; www
.siceh-hotels.com; 2 Ave de l'Indépendance; r incl breakfast €75-
100; ☒ ☐) The second Siceh hotel is broadly
similar to its sibling, with marginally nicer
but smaller rooms. Both hotels are popular
with package tours.

Hôtel Colbert (Map p76; ☎ 22 202 02; resa
.colbert@wanadoo.mg; Rue Printsy Ratsimamanga; r €115-330;
☒ ☐ ☲) The bizarre maroon tower at the
heart of this luxury hillside hotel belies the
distinguished history of Tana's most prestig-
ious address, originally founded as a handful
of rooms above a café in 1928. A touch of
colonial grandeur remains, particularly in the
marble-clad lobby and the extravagant spa
(p79), but the rooms don't always live up to
these benchmarks – opt for the new Carayon
wing, impeccably styled despite being more
modern. Luckily the hotel facilities are uni-
formly excellent, encompassing three restaurants, two bars, a patisserie, business centre,
travel agency, hair salon, perfume shop and
a small slot-machine casino. The reception
staff speak impeccable English and are a mine
of information on anything and everything
in Tana.

Le Royal Palissandre (Map p76; ☎ 22 605 60; www
.hotel-palissandre.com; 13 Rue Andrianahifotsy; r incl breakfast €117-156; ☒ ☐ ☲) Another good top-end
choice, up the steps behind the Analakely
market, the Royal Palissandre offers a well-
balanced blend of smart facilities, modern
comforts and traditional style, fully kitted
out with handmade rosewood furniture and
balcony views. Internet access and use of the
gym, spa and terrace pool are free for guests,
though treatments such as massages are extra
(from Ar50,000).

Madagascar Hilton (Map pp72-3; ☎ 22 260 60;
madagascar.hilton.com; Rue Pierre Stibbe, Anosy; r €150-
275; ☒ ☐ ☲) In a massive skyscraper just
south of Lac Anosy, the Hilton offers exactly
what you'd expect – smallish but comfortable
rooms, business centre, travel agency, casino,
spa, patisserie, shops, three restaurants, several bars and a nightclub. There's also a pool,
gym and tennis court for the energetic, and
it's one of the only hotels in the country with
no-smoking rooms and full disabled access.

EATING & DRINKING
In addition to the hotel restaurants mentioned above, Tana is well served by eateries, from cheap-and-cheerful local *hotelys* to
sumptuous *salons de thé* and sublime French

temples of *gastronomie*. For a comprehensive
list of restaurants, including some detailed
reviews and maps, look for the *Guide des
Tables Antananarivo* (Ar20,000), a handy
annual mini-directory available in Tana
bookshops.

Restaurants
MALAGASY & INDIAN OCEAN
Impala (Map p76; ☎ 032 04 092 67; Ave Ramanantsoa;
mains Ar5000-16,000; ☺ lunch & dinner) Taking its
cue from the other side of the Mozambique
Channel, this brand-new 1st-floor restaurant
has a distinctly African flavour in both dishes
and décor. The main courses are a bit more
French-tinted, though if you're inspired by the
safari trappings and animal-print ceilings you
could demand the 'lion's portion', a massive
500g steak!

Le Caf'Art (Map p76; ☎ 033 11 435 03; Rue Ranavalona
III; mains Ar7000-14,000; ☺ lunch & dinner) A friendly
little brick-terrace bistro in the Haute-Ville,
serving pizza and Malagasy food; the best
seats are in the garden courtyard overlooking
the city's steep bits. Incidentally, the name is
a sly French pun: it's pronounced the same as
cafard, which means cockroach!

Restaurant Sakamanga (Map p76; ☎ 22 358 09; Rue
Andrianary Ratianarivo; mains Ar7200-14,500; ☺ breakfast, lunch & dinner) Tana's favourite hotel is also
home to one of Tana's favourite restaurants,
striking the perfect balance between gastro
French and straightforward local cooking,
with personable service to boot. Set menus
may come in even cheaper than the dishes,
and a lunchtime buffet is also available in the
luscious garden. It may be worth reserving if
you're in a group, though you can always sit
in the cosy bar sampling rums until a table's
free.

Grill du Rova (Map pp72-3; ☎ 22 627 24; Rue Ramboatiana, Avaradrova; mains Ar8000-15,000; ☺ lunch &
dinner Mon-Sat, lunch Sun) A well-established and
stylish restaurant/cabaret on the hillside just
below the Rova (the clue's in the name). The
menu features French and Malagasy dishes,
while the cabaret showcases local jazz and
traditional music (see above).

Villa Vanille (Map pp72-3; ☎ 22 205 15; Place Antanimena; mains Ar10,000-30,000; ☺ lunch & dinner) Another
classy establishment outside the centre, in
an old colonial villa, with nightly music performed by bands from all across the Indian
Ocean islands. The cooking is similarly eclectic, though as you'd expect from the name, the

region's most famous and flavoursome orchid features heavily.

Chez Mariette (Map pp72-3; ☎ 22 216 02; 11 Rue Joel Rakotomalala; meals Ar44,000; ☯ dinner only, by reservation) A truly unique gastronomic opportunity: superchef Mariette Andrianjaka has cooked for notables as diverse as Paloma Picasso and Prince Albert of Monaco during her long career, and has even had a collection of her recipes published by Unesco. These days she entertains guests in her magnificent 19th-century villa, preparing elaborate six-course set meals based on *haiti* cuisine, the traditional banquets once served to Merina royalty. These might include anything from carp to eel or goose, accompanied by myriad vegetable and rice dishes. At the end of the meal, the boss herself emerges to do the rounds and explain her techniques. Advance reservation is required, preferably in groups of four or more.

FRENCH

Chez Sucett's (Map p76; ☎ 22 261 00; 23 Rue Raveloary; mains from Ar5000; ☯ lunch & dinner) From the outside, the red glow and 'Private' sign give Sucett's the air of a slightly seedy cabaret, but there's little of ill repute here: venture through the door and you'll find plenty of budget-conscious travellers and keen eaters tucking into the French and creole cuisine amid the inevitable male expats and their 'companions'. In short, it's exactly what local journalists have in mind when they call Isoraka 'Tana's Montmartre'.

Le Petit Verdot (Map p76; ☎ 22 392 34; 27 Rue Rahamefy; mains Ar7000-9000; ☯ lunch & dinner Mon-Fri, lunch Sat & Sun) Capturing just a little of the culinary essence of Bordeaux, this tiny red-brick bistro goes for a homely atmosphere and hearty rustic food, plus a very good selection of imported wines and cheeses.

La Boussole (Map p76; ☎ 22 358 10; 21 Rue Dr Villette; mains Ar8000-11,000; ☯ lunch & dinner Mon-Fri, dinner Sat & Sun) The 'Compass', an attractive, lively bar-restaurant, has funky décor and live bands on Thursdays. The restaurant serves mainly French brasserie-style dishes, while the bar whips out more prosaic snacks such as burgers and the like. Once you've finished browsing the menu, have a look round the varying art for sale on the walls.

Le Rossini (Map p76; ☎ 22 342 44; Ave Ramanantsoa; mains Ar8000-15,000; ☯ lunch & dinner) You might not expect a visit to Madagascar to widen your knowledge of France, but this rarefied dining room should at least educate your palate: it specialises in cuisine from the southwest Perigourdin region, a distinctive variant of the better-known traditions, using lots of duck and foie gras. Despite the Italian name, it's widely regarded as one of the best French restaurants in the city.

Le Lounge'Art (Map p76; ☎ 22 612 42; Rue des 77 Parlementaires Français; mains Ar10,000-17,000; ☯ lunch & dinner) Perfect for indecisive diners, the menu here only features a handful of options, changing daily according to seasonal produce and whim. The local chefs have been well-schooled in European techniques by the French owners, and can cater for individual demands (if you ask nicely, of course). On a hot day, wander down the long leafy 'tunnel' for a drink on the agreeable front terrace.

Kudéta (Map p76; ☎ 22 281 54; 15 Rue de la Réunion; Ar11,800-20,000; ☯ breakfast, lunch & dinner) Playing on the region's reputation for political instability may not be very PC, but it really would take a *coup d'état* to unseat this superbly stylish bar-restaurant from its position at the pinnacle of the Tana eating scene. The menu makes imaginative use of local ingredients, creating a sophisticated fusion cuisine that suits the chic ethnic décor perfectly and tastes sensational too. The sleek dining room is almost always packed with fashionable folk, so book ahead at weekends.

our pick La Varangue (Map p76; ☎ 22 273 97; varangue@simicro.mg; 17 Rue Printsy Ratsimamanga; mains Ar17,000-26,000; ☯ lunch & dinner Mon-Sat) Currently the best address in the city for real gourmet cuisine, La Varangue has achieved a fantastic reputation thanks to kitchen maestro (and chocolate specialist) Lalaina Ravelomanana, who was recently voted among the world's top five chefs. The menu is concise but painstakingly constructed, and features a great-value three-course set meal at Ar25,000, not to mention a Ar66,000 gastronomic taster menu that we're reliably informed would cost you five times as much anywhere in Europe. Light music is played in the elegant dining room, or you can venture out onto the terrace, which overlooks the hotel's charming garden. La Varangue is a near-mandatory Tana dining experience.

MEDITERRANEAN & INTERNATIONAL

Le Chalet des Roses (Map p76; ☎ 22 642 33; 13 Rue Rabary; grills Ar6000-12,000; ☯ lunch & dinner Mon-Sat, dinner Sun)

Down by the embassy district, this is a sunny, pretty balcony bistro serving unambitious but tasty pizza, pasta and salads.

Nerone (Map p76; ☎ 22 231 18; Rue Ranavalona III; mains Ar8500-15,000; ☽ lunch & dinner Mon-Sat, dinner Sun) A very high-quality restaurant in the Haute-Ville, with authentic specials, exquisite pasta, good wine and mock-Roman décor. It's probably the best Italian experience you'll have in Madagascar, even if your tastes are more De Niro than Nero.

L'Indigo (Map p76; ☎ 24 220 52; Rue Raveloary; mains Ar9000-15,500; ☽ lunch & dinner) The theme's Tex-Mex, the music's Latin, the owner's Algerian and the menu hits everything from tacos to teriyaki, but this colourful restaurant seems none the worse for its ethnic identity crisis, attracting a multinational clientele. In fact the selection of world cuisine is among its high points: where else could you find souvlaki, meze, Jamaican curry and tequila prawns all on the same table?

Le Sud (Map p76; ☎ 22 310 22; 23 Rue Dr Villette; mains Ar10,000-15,000; ☽ lunch & dinner) 'The South' here refers not to the Med, which does influence the menu, but to the southern region of Madagascar itself, which provides much of the model for the interior design. If eating modern international cuisine in a replica spiny desert seems just too weird, this orangey-red restaurant-grill-café-concert has live music most evenings to distract you.

ASIAN

Dun Huang (Map p76; ☎ 22 669 65; 1 Rue James Adrianisa; mains Ar4000-10,000; ☽ lunch & dinner) An unremarkable but handy Chinese eatery just off Ave de l'Indépendance, good for the usual soups and standards.

Grand Orient (Map p76; ☎ 22 202 88; 4 Place Ambiky; mains Ar4000-12,000; ☽ lunch & dinner Mon-Sat) The oldest Chinese restaurant in town, near the station, combines Chinese and Malagasy cooking in relatively upmarket surrounds, rising above the bustle outside with true zen poise.

Arirang (Map p76; ☎ 24 271 33; Ave Ramanantsoa; mains Ar5000-10,000; ☽ lunch & dinner) Korean cuisine makes its Malagasy debut, apparently with some success given the numbers of Seoul brothers who frequent this bright dining room. The menu looks thoroughly authentic, a perfect excuse to experiment with lesser-known dishes such as *sensun gas, dongas* or a two-person *kimchi*.

Cafés & Salons de Thé

Tana's many French-style patisseries, cafés and *salons de thé* serve pastries, cream cakes, hot drinks, breakfasts and, in many cases, wonderful ice cream.

Cookie Shop (Map pp72-3; ☎ 032 07 142 99; Ave Rainizanabolone; snacks from Ar100; ☽ breakfast & lunch Mon-Sat) Strategically sited near the American cultural centre, this bright, sparky café does its bit for the international community by furnishing bagels and sweet treats to a loyal following of cookie-crunchin' US expats, aid workers and Peace Corps volunteers.

Blanche Neige (Map p76; ☎ 22 206 59; 15 Ave de l'Indépendance; cakes from Ar400; ☽ breakfast Tue-Sun) 'Snow White' is one of central Tana's most popular cafés, whether you want a hearty set breakfast (Ar2700 to Ar4800), cake, ice cream or a Belgian waffle.

Honey Salon de Thé (Map p76; ☎ 22 621 67; 13 Ave de l'Indépendance; cakes from Ar500; ☽ breakfast Wed-Mon) Just next door to Blanche neige, sweet sweet Honey puts more emphasis on its patisserie selection, presenting its treats almost as beautifully as a jewellery store.

Patisserie Colbert (Map p76; Hôtel Colbert, Rue Printsy Ratsimamanga; cakes from Ar2000; ☽ breakfast & lunch) The Colbert's lavish patisserie is the last word in sumptuous confectionery – listen hard and you'll hear the forlorn cries of abandoned diets.

Quick Eats

The cheapest meals in town are provided by various food stalls around town, which serve rice with chicken or zebu, samosas, *soupe chinoise* (Chinese noodle soup), *mi sao* (stir-fried noodles) and other local dishes from around Ar300 per portion; try the western end of Ave Ramanantsoa or around the market at Analakely. Get there early – many places stop serving by about 8pm.

Tropique Snack (Map p76; Ave 26 Juin 1960; dishes from Ar1500; ☽ breakfast & lunch) Opposite the Analakely market, this little canteen serves up all the usuals, with plenty of mirrors for those who like to watch themselves eat.

Saka Express (Map p76; ☎ 24 334 39; Rue Andrianary Ratianarivo; mains Ar2700-10,000; ☽ breakfast, lunch & dinner Mon-Sat, lunch & dinner Sun) The Hôtel Sakamanga's snack cafeteria and takeaway outlet specialises in pizza and sandwiches.

Resto-Snack Zédéa (Map p76; ☎ 032 02 084 73; Ave Rabezavana; mains Ar3500-5000; ☽ breakfast, lunch & dinner) An unusually intimate café in the busy market

ANTANANARIVO

area, wooing foreigners as much as locals with a comprehensive menu of Malagasy, Western and 'exotic' dishes such as Thai pork.

Mad'Delices (Map p76; ☎ 22 226 41; 28 Ave Grandidier; dishes Ar3600-5000; ☺ breakfast, lunch & dinner) Right opposite the Hotel Isoraka, this is a convenient spot for a fresh-baked breakfast, and also turns out pizza, steak and a variety of local and European dishes the rest of the day.

Buffet du Jardin (Map p76; ☎ 22 338 87; Place de l'Indépendance) Now under new management, this long-standing snack stop and bar has undergone substantial renovation, but will have to work to stay the city's favourite (ie only) 24-hour eatery.

Self-Catering

Antananarivo has several well-stocked supermarkets and plenty of smaller food shops and kiosks. There are also a handful of hypermarkets in the outer suburbs, such as the vast Score Digue (off Map pp72–3) to the north of town. You can pick up cheaper vegetables, meat and fish at the Analakely market (Map p76); look out for the little white 'Sahamadio' jeeps selling homemade condiments, preserves and other local produce.

Shoprite Analakely (Map p76; ☎ 22 360 89; Ave Andrianampoinimerina); Haute-Ville (Map p76; ☎ 22 357 09; Rue Ratsimilaho; ☺ 8.30am-7.30pm Mon-Sat) Reliable central supermarket outlets stocking mainly imported goods.

TAF le Gourmet (Map p76; ☎ 22 215 42; Rue Patrice Lumumba) Established in 1945, this is a smart shop for locally produced coffee and tea and other fancy goods such as chocolate.

Epicerie Hediard (Map p76; ☎ 22 283 70; 14 Rue Jean Jaurès) This prestige Parisian deli sells the finest luxury imported goods, from tea to wine and cheese, and holds regular free tastings in its small café section.

ENTERTAINMENT

To find out what is going on and where, buy any of the three national daily newspapers, *Midi Madagasikara, Madagascar Tribune* and *L'Express de Madagascar*, all of which have advertisements for upcoming events, particularly in the Friday issue. Posters around town also give plenty of notice of forthcoming concerts.

Hira Gasy

The traditional Malagasy performance of acrobatics, music and speeches, *hira gasy* (p36) events are held most Sunday afternoons in the villages around Antananarivo. Check newspapers for details.

Music & Theatre

Centre Culturel Albert Camus (CCAC; Map p76; ☎ 22 213 75; 14 Ave de l'Indépendance) Antananarivo's foremost cultural venue holds regular concerts, theatre events, dance performances, art exhibitions and film screenings.

Théâtre Municipal (Teatro Munisipaly; Map pp72-3; 4 Rue Hector Berlioz) This old theatre, in the Isotry district southwest of the train station, holds Malagasy theatre and dance performances, as well as some concerts.

Théâtre de Verdure Antsahamanitra (Map p76; Ave Rainitsarovy) On the northeastern edge of the lake, the amphitheatre here has occasional pop concerts, known as *spectacles*, featuring artists from the Malagasy charts. Tickets are generally very cheap.

Grill du Rova (Map pp72-3; ☎ 22 627 24; Rue Ramboatiana, Avaradrova) This popular restaurant has regular music recitals, including a piano bar on Friday, traditional performances from noon to sunset every Sunday, and improvised musical soirées on the first and third Wednesday of each month.

Hôtel Le Glacier (Map p76; ☎ 22 202 60; Ave 26 Juin 1960) The slightly disreputable bar here has cabaret, bands and traditional music performances at weekends, just don't mind the prostitutes that frequent the establishment.

A number of old cinemas also sometimes serve as gig venues; the **Ritz** (Map p76; Rue Paul Dussac & Ave 26 Juin 1960) is the largest.

Nightclubs

Tana has a reasonable selection of nightclubs, most of which start late and stay open as long as there's a crowd; admission may be charged at weekends. Music policy is a familiar mix of commercial dance, US hip-hop and R&B, Malagasy chart hits and French soft-rock anthems. Many places are packed with prostitutes, so unaccompanied guys in particular can expect a bit of unsolicited attention.

Pandora Station (Map p76; ☎ 22 377 48; Rue Rabobalahy; ☺ Tue-Sun) Enter through the giant mouth to access this surreal UV-saturated underworld of quasi-Aztec décor, trouser-wearing stools and strange-brand spirits. Snacks and pizzas are also served.

Le Bus (Map pp72-3; ☎ 22 691 00; Ave Rainizanabolone; admission Ar5000; ☺ from 10.30pm Thu-Sat) Tana's biggest, flashiest club space, designed in a modern style with the DJ spinning recent tunes from his lofty winged booth above the dance floor.

Cohiba Club (Map pp72-3; Madagascar Hilton, Rue Pierre Stibbe, Anosy; admission Ar10,000; 🕑 from 10pm Thu-Sat) The Hilton's house nightclub has an eclectic music policy, including Indian and other theme nights, though high prices make it a bit of a posing palace.

Guru Club (Map p76; ☎ 24 301 61; Rue Ramelina; 🕑 from 6pm) More of a lounge feel than the bigger clubs, with dance music and occasional fashion nights.

Bar Mojo (Map p76; ☎ 22 254 59; Rue Rakotomahefa; 🕑 from 6pm) A finger-snappingly cool music space with regular poetry-slam and reggae-dancehall nights amid the DJs and bands.

SHOPPING

Marché Artisanale de La Digue (off Map pp72-3; La Digue; 🕑 9am-5pm Mon-Sat) The most popular place to pick up art and crafts is the Marché Artisanale in the suburb of La Digue, about 3km out of town on a bend in the Ivato airport road. Artisans and middlemen from all over the country sell their products here; popular souvenirs include embroidered tablecloths, brightly coloured raffia baskets, recycled metal models, wooden carvings and of course big bundles of vanilla. Bargaining is essential – bring your hardest nose! A taxi (around Ar14,000) is the easiest way to get here and back with your purchases.

Gemstone Market (Marché des Pierres; Map p76; Gare de Soarano; 🕑 Sat & Sun twice monthly) If you're looking to buy precious stones, this regular outdoor market in the train-station parking lot brings together suppliers from around the island in a secure environment, with verifiable stones and export licensing available on site.

For trekking, camping gear and the like, try **CS Events** (off Map pp72-3; ☎ 22 413 82; www.csevents -madagascar.com; Rte du Mausolée, Andrainarivo), near the eastern taxi-brousse station, which has a wide selection of international branded products.

You will find plenty of arts, crafts, T-shirts, coffee and spices in the souvenir shops in central Tana. Good outlets include the following:

Baobab Company (Map p76; ☎ 22 691 08; Rue Ranavalona III) Universally popular T-shirts and clothes; there's another branch on Rue Andrianary Ratianarivo.

Le Flamant Rose (Map p76; ☎ 22 557 76; 45 Ave de l'Indépendance; 🕑 9am-6pm) Craft souvenirs, raffia items and embroidery.

Les Jocondes (Map p76; ☎ 22 384 68; Rue Andrianary Ratianarivo; 🕑 9am-5pm) Elegant wooden sculptures by resident French artist Jean-Jacques Teiten.

Roses & Baobab (Map p76; ☎ 24 104 25; Rue des 77 Parlementaires Français; 🕑 9am-6pm) Local paintings and wood carvings, plus *salon de thé*.

GETTING THERE & AWAY
Air

For details of flights from Ivato airport, see p276 for international routes and p280 for domestic services. The following airlines have offices in Tana:

Air Austral/Air Mauritius (ARIO; Map p76; ☎ 22 359 90; www.airaustral.com; Rue des 77 Parlementaires Français)

Air France (off Map pp72-3; ☎ 23 230 01; www.airfrance .com; Tour Zital, Rte des Hydrocarbures, Ankorondrano)

Air Madagascar (Map p76; ☎ 22 222 22; www .airmadagascar.com; 31 Ave de l'Indépendance)

Corsair (Map p76; ☎ 22 633 36; www.corsair.fr; 1 Rue Rainitovo Antsahavola)

Interair (Map pp72-3; ☎ 22 224 06; www.interair.co.za; Madagascar Hilton, Rue Pierre Stibbe, Anosy)

Bus

MadaBus (Map p76; ☎ 24 222 72; www.madabus.com; Rue Ramandriamapandry) is an innovative new concern that runs comfortable hop-on hop-off services along Madagascar's principal tourist routes, the RN7 (Route du Sud) to Toliara (Ar135,000) and the eastern road to Tamatave (Ar68,000), with optional activities, connections to destinations such as Île Sainte Marie, and complete tour packages also available. Buses run three times weekly on each route from April to January; tickets are valid for two months. The Tana staff speak good English and are incredibly helpful for all kinds of queries.

Car & Motorcycle

Car-rental agencies in Tana all handle rentals for use throughout the country, and drivers are generally obligatory. Rates shown are for short hires with unlimited mileage, not including petrol.

Budget (Map p76; ☎ 22 611 11; budget.rent_a _car@simicro.mg; 4 Ave de l'Indépendance; per day from Ar106,000)

Hertz (Map p76; ☎ 22 229 61; somada@sicam.mg; 17 Rue Rabefiraisana; per day from Ar107,380)

Sixt (Map p76; ☎ 22 621 50; sixtintermad@simcro.mg; 2 bis Rue Rahamefy; per day from Ar102,190) Self-drive only.

ANTANANARIVO

Transpost (Map p76; ☎ 22 302 27; Rue Ratsimilaho; 4WD per day from Ar115,000) Good-value agency run by the post office.

You can also hire cars through the larger hotels in Tana, and through most of the tour operators listed on p285. See p282 for general information on car rentals and rates.

Taxi-Brousse

Taxis-brousses leave from Tana to almost everywhere in Madagascar; for most regional destinations you can just turn up and be on a bus within an hour or so. Check times if you plan to take one of the daily connections to Mahajanga or Toliara, or any other long-distance national route. For more details, see the specific destination chapters.

There are four main taxi-brousse stations (gares routières), all crammed chaotically with minibuses, cars and coaches. A taxi to any of them should cost around Ar6000.

Eastern taxi-brousse station (Gare Routière de l'Est; off Map pp72–3; Ampasampito) About 3.5km to the northeast of the town centre. Taxis-brousses and taxis-be (big taxis) to Lac Mantasoa (Ar4000) and Moramanga (Ar6000).

Northern taxi-brousse station (Gare Routière du Nord; Map pp72–3; Ambodivona) About 2km northeast of the city centre, this station has transport to Toamasina (Ar20,000), Mahajanga (Ar32,000) and Diego Suarez (Ar73,000).

Southern taxi-brousse station (Gare Routière du Sud; Map pp72–3; Anosibe) About 1.5km southwest of Lac Anosy. Provides transport to all points south, as well

as some points on the east and west coasts. There are regular departures to Antsirabe (Ar10000), Fianarantsoa (Ar21,000), Morondava (Ar32,000), Manakara (Ar36,000), Toliara (Ar38,000) and Fort Dauphin (Ar78,000).

Western taxi-brousse station (Gare Routière de l'Ouest; Map pp72–3; Antanimena) About 300m north of Soarano train station. Has taxis-brousses to Ivato (Ar15,000) and the airport.

Train

There are no passenger trains presently operating from Antananarivo's Gare de Soarano. However, plans to reopen the line to Toamasina via Andasibe appear to be progressing gradually, so enquire when you arrive.

GETTING AROUND

Most restaurants and hotels are within a short distance of each other, so it's usually no problem to walk, except at night, when it's a good idea to take a taxi if you're going any distance. For places in the suburbs, a taxi is almost invariably the easiest option.

To/From the Airport

Ivato airport is 12km from the city centre. Taxis to or from the city centre should cost around Ar20,000, although this depends on the time of day and your bargaining skills – ignore the 'official' price lists brandished by drivers at arrivals! A taxi-brousse from Ivato village, just outside the airport, costs Ar3000 to town, but don't do this at night – it's not safe. The taxi-brousse station is about 2km

---

THE MERINA

The region surrounding Antananarivo is known as Imerina (Land of the Merina Tribe). Today the Merina tend to be among the most well-educated and Westernised of the Malagasy tribes. They are also among the most Christianised, though great importance is still placed on *Famadihana*: traditional reburial ceremonies (see p37).

Merina hierarchy is based on a three-tier caste system, largely dependent on skin colour. The *andriana*, or nobles (generally fairer-skinned and with pronounced Asiatic rather than African features, reflecting their Indonesian ancestry), comprise the upper echelon, while the *hova*, or commoners, make up the middle class. The remainder – descendants of former slaves – are the *andevo* (workers), although this term is now generally avoided for tact's sake.

The first Merina kingdoms were established around the 16th century, and by the late 19th century the Merina were the dominant tribe in Madagascar. Ordinary Merina citizens customarily worked as administrators, shopkeepers, teachers and traders. Their position was enhanced by the choice of Antananarivo as the seat of the French colonial government, and by the establishment of an education system there.

Today, the Merina still fill many of the same jobs, and remain at the forefront of public life: on his election in 2002, President Marc Ravalomanana became the first Merina national leader since the abolition of the monarchy.

from the airport, and the taxis-brousses come into the western taxi-brousse station (see opposite).

Bus

A few large buses and dozens of minibuses meander around Antananarivo and the outlying suburbs; the standard fare is Ar400. Most begin and end around Ave de l'Indépendance in the centre of town; they'll only stop at official bus stops, though it's not always obvious where these are. Try to avoid the peak periods, from around 7am to 8.30am and 5pm to 6.30pm. As in any crowded setting, beware of pickpockets in the crush. Given the traffic and narrow, steep roads, it is often quicker to walk to places nearby. It's generally much easier to take a taxi if you don't know the area in which your destination is located.

Car & Motorcycle

Hiring a car to drive yourself around Antananarivo's traffic chaos is very nerve-wracking, and it's unlikely to be worth the hassle because of the relatively high risk of damage to the vehicle through minor accidents or vandalism.

For a listing of some rental agencies in the capital, see p87.

Taxi

At times there appear to be more taxis than people on the streets of Antananarivo, so you will never have much difficultly finding one, even late at night. The ubiquitous Citroën 2CVs and Renault 4s tend to be cheaper than normal sedans. Taxis caught outside upmarket hotels are the most expensive. Fares are negotiable, so ask at your hotel for the going rate, and always agree on the price before getting in the car; trips around town should cost Ar3000 to Ar6000, often depending on whether the journey is downhill or uphill! Night prices are more expensive.

AROUND ANTANANARIVO

The highlands around Antananarivo are often ignored by travellers pushing on to other regions, but the whole area is perfect day-trip country if you have a bit of time to spare. Keen cyclists could easily tour all of the 12 sacred hills surrounding the city, and even a brief excursion offers plenty of spectacular views and an insight into the history and culture of the Merina people.

IVATO

About 13km from Antananarivo is the village-suburb of Ivato, where the international airport is located. If you're staying here or killing time between flights, pay a visit to the newly revamped **Croq Farm** (☎ 22 030 71; www.reptel.mg; admission Ar6000; 9am-5pm), a commercial breeding and trading enterprise that offers the chance to see various species of lemur, chameleons and even the rare fossa, Madagascar's biggest predator, alongside the enormous resident crocodiles. If you're feeling guilty about dining on croc in the park restaurant or eyeing that scaly handbag in the shop, you can buy a nice lump of meat and help feed the hand that bites you... The park's about 3km from the airport; a taxi costs around Ar8000 return.

Sleeping & Eating

If you want to avoid paying taxi fares to and from the city, there are some modest hotels in and around Ivato, most offering free airport transfers for guests.

Le Manoir Rouge (☎ 24 576 96; www.manoirrouge.com; dm Ar10,000, r Ar21,000-30,000) It's almost worth packing up early just to stay a night or two at this amiable backpacker-friendly guesthouse, a scant 700m from the airport. The varied rooms (most with shared bathroom) sleep up to six people, or 16 in the dorm, and there's a grassy garden where you can camp for Ar5000. Excellent meals and bike hire are available, and the brisk owner can help with all sorts of inquiries, particularly regarding local excursions.

Auberge du Cheval Blanc (☎ 22 446 46; www.cheval-blanc-madagascar.com; r Ar32,000;) The white rooms here are quite plain, but it's a clean, smart establishment perfectly placed for the airport. There's a restaurant and a pretty garden, and it takes credit cards (5% fee).

Getting There & Away

A taxi from the airport to Ivato will cost Ar10,000 and from Ivato village to Antananarivo should be around Ar15,000. Taxis-brousses into Antananarivo leave every 20 minutes from the Ivato taxi-brousse station and cost Ar4000, or you may be able to grab a minibus along the main road for Ar500.

ILAFY

Originally called Ambohitrahanga, Ilafy was founded around the turn of the 17th century on a sacred hilltop, and was used as a country residence by the Merina royal family. The wooden residence was redesigned in the 1830s by Ranavalona I and was used as a hunting lodge by Radama II, who is buried in a modest tomb in the small grounds. It is now an **ethnographic museum** (admission Ar3000; ☺ 9am-noon & 2-5pm Tue-Sun) illustrating tribal life around Madagascar, with exhibits including model tombs, hunting and fishing tools, modern wooden carvings and information about magic and religious rituals.

Ilafy lies 12km from Antananarivo just east of the road leading to Ambohimanga. To get there from Antananarivo, either take a taxi or find a taxi-brousse headed for Ambohimanga from the eastern taxi-brousse station. Some taxis aren't able to make it up the steep dirt road to the museum, so you may need to walk the last stretch. Minibus No 192 from Tana (Ar400) stops 1km from the residence.

AMBOHIMANGA

Ambohimanga ('blue hill' or 'beautiful hill') was the original capital of the Merina royal family. Even after the seat of government was shifted to Antananarivo for political reasons, Ambohimanga remained a sacred site, and was off-limits to foreigners for many years. The entire hill was Unesco-listed in 2001 as 'the most significant symbol of the cultural identity of the people of Madagascar'.

The entrance to Ambohimanga village is marked by a large traditional gateway, one of the seven gateways to the eyrie-like hilltop. To one side is a large, flat, round stone. At the first sign of threat to the village, the stone would be rolled by up to 40 slaves, sealing off the gate.

Sights

A few hundred metres uphill from Ambohimanga village is the **Rova**, the fortress-palace of the all-powerful Merina king Andrianampoinimerina. These days it's still under renovation and closed to visitors but walks in the surrounding forest are possible, as is imagining the former grandeur of the palace.

Slaves were once sacrificed on the rock inside the palace's entrance, and the many pilgrims who come to ask the blessings of the royal ancestors sometimes still slaughter animals in the same spot. The fortress was constructed using cement made from egg whites – 16 million eggs were required to build the outer wall alone. Inside the wall stands the wooden summer palace of the queens of Madagascar, constructed by the French engineer Jean Laborde in 1870. It's been beautifully restored and painted in blue and red, and has original European-style furniture inside. The dining room is lined with mirrors, which allowed the queen to check that no-one was sneakily poisoning her food.

Next door, in a striking contrast to the elegance of its neighbour, is the blackened wood hut that was the pre-colonial king's palace, dating from 1788. The central pole is made from a single trunk of sacred *palissandre* (rosewood), which was reportedly carried from the east coast by 2000 slaves, 100 of whom died in the process. The top of the pole is carved to show a pair of women's breasts, a symbol of the king's polygamy and thus power. Behind it are the open-air baths where the king performed his royal ablutions once a year, in the company of his 12 wives and diverse honoured guests. Afterwards his bathwater was considered sacred and was delivered to waiting supplicants.

Follow the steps round past the palace compound for amazing views back towards Tana. On your way back out, look out for the *pierre griffée* (scratched stone), once used for legal proceedings, oaths of allegiance and a form of trial by ordeal involving bull's blood.

Getting There & Away

Ambohimanga is 21km north of Antananarivo, and easily visited as a day trip. Taxis-brousses leave throughout the day from the eastern taxi-brousse station (Ar600, one hour). From the village, you'll need to walk 1km up the hill to the Rova. Charter taxis from Antananarivo cost around Ar50,000 for the return trip, including a visit to Ilafy and waiting time.

ANJOZOROBE

Few tourists venture into this northeastern corner of the highlands, 90km from Tana, but now there's at least one good reason to explore it: **Soa Camp** (☎ in Antananarivo 22 530 70; www.boogie-pilgrim.net; packages from Ar25,500 per person), a simple but comfortable tented eco-camp set in a small private reserve in the middle of the

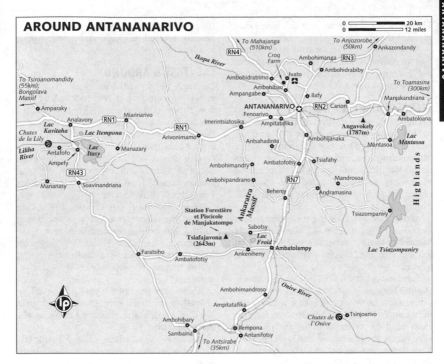

AROUND ANTANANARIVO

66,500-hectare Anjozorobe forest corridor. The area is a major biodiversity hotspot, and one of the biggest surviving swathes of rainforest in the plateau region. As well as forest walks and mountain biking, the camp works with **Mad'Arbres** (☎ in Antananarivo 22 417 54; www .madarbres.com) to offer tree-climbing activities, designed to awaken your inner lemur… Bookings are through Boogie Pilgrim in Antananarivo (see p285).

LAC MANTASOA
This 2000-hectare artificial lake, which was built in 1837, is a good place for fishing, sailing and picnicking, and has become a popular weekend retreat for Antananarivo residents.

In 1833, three years before the surrounding land was flooded, the Frenchman Jean Laborde built a country palace for Queen Ranavalona I, as well as carpentry and gunsmith shops, a munitions factory, an iron forge and a foundry. The primary aim was to supply the monarch with swords, arms and ammunition. Most of this now lies underwater, but Laborde's **home** and his **grave** in the

local cemetery can still be seen, along with the closed **munitions factory**.

Mantasoa village lies about 60km east of Antananarivo, about an hour south of the RN2. The lake lies around 3km southeast of Mantasoa village; follow the main path through the village.

Direct taxis-brousses go from Antananarivo's eastern station to Mantasoa village (about Ar4000). Start early from Antananarivo for a day trip, and leave the lake by about 2pm.

ANTSAHADINTA
Antsahadinta (Forest of Leeches), founded by King Andriamangarira in 1725, is one of the most remote and best preserved hilltop villages around Antananarivo. The **Rova**, or royal precincts, contain several terraced tombs and a well-maintained garden. As you enter the settlement, the large tomb on your right belongs to Queen Rabodozafimanjaka, one of King Andrianampoinimerina's 12 wives. Accused of disloyalty, she had to undergo an ordeal with tanguin, a strong poison, and no one today is certain whether she survived it.

There is a small **museum** near the tomb that explains the whole story (in French).

Antsahadinta is 14km southwest of Antananarivo. As the road is in bad condition and public transport is scarce, the best options are to walk or hire a vehicle.

AMBATOLAMPY & AROUND

A charming and very typical plateau town, Ambatolampy lies on both the RN7 and the railway line, 68km south of Antananarivo. The surrounding area, including the forestry station at **Manjakatompo** (admission Ar5000), is a good place to do some walking and bird-watching among the picturesque forests and hills of the Ankaratra Massif.

About 2km south of the town centre and 1km east of the main road, the **Musée de la Nature** (☎ 42 492 64; admission Ar5000; ☒ 8am-5pm) has an extensive collection of butterflies and insects.

Manja Ranch (☎ 033 11 993 70; bijouxline@yahoo.fr; r Ar10,000, bungalows Ar25,000) has pretty rooms and a peaceful setting just south of town near the museum. You can camp here for free, but you must eat at the restaurant. The ranch is about 1km east of the main road and is signposted. There are sometimes horses for hire to explore the surrounding area.

Camping is possible at Manjakatompo with your own tent and supplies.

To get to Manjakatompo, taxis-brousses from Ambatolampy to Ankeniheny, 1km from the station entrance, make the trip Monday, Wednesday and Thursday only (Ar8000).

It's possible to hire a local driver to take you here for around Ar15,000 and a day's notice in advance.

LAC ITASY & AROUND

Lac Itasy (45 sq km) was formed when the valley surrounding it was blocked by lava flow about 8000 years ago. Although the area has been completely deforested and none of the original vegetation remains, the volcanic domes that rise above the landscape have a certain beauty of their own. Itasy has been declared a site of interest by the WWF, and a large area of land has been allocated for research into bird species.

There are good possibilities for hiking around the lakeshore (except in the boggy south), but crocodiles and bilharzia make swimming a bad idea. The crater lake of **Lac Andranotoraha**, about 5km south of Ampefy, is also alleged to contain a Loch Ness–style monster!

About 5km west of Ampefy, in the village of **Antafofo**, the Liliha River plunges more than 20m. In French, the falls are known as the **Chutes de la Lily**.

Lac Itasy lies near the village of Ampefy, 120km west of Antananarivo and south of Analavory (which lies along the RN1). To get here, take a taxi-brousse headed for Tsiroanomandidy from Antananarivo and get off in Analavory. From there, wait for another taxi-brousse heading south, or hitch or walk south along the RN43 for about 7km to Ampefy.

Central Madagascar

Driving the thousand odd kilometres between Antananarivo and Toliara on the famous Route Nationale 7 (RN7; Route du Sud) takes you straight through Central Madagascar, where the scenery is as stimulating and surreal as the culture. The RN7 might be Madagascar's busiest highway (not to mention tourist trail), but to the barefoot Bara herdsmen, walking from as far as Toliara with nothing but a stick and the clothes on their back, it's just a footpath useful for herding hundreds of zebu to market in Antananarivo.

Some parts of Central Madagascar feel as far removed from the conventional vision of Africa as possible. Glassy, terraced rice paddies juxtaposed against cool, misty mountains and thick-walled red huts constructed from crimson soil, make you think you've been transported to Southeast Asia. Meanwhile the expanses of green rolling hills and golden fields dotted with medieval villages and tidy rows of grapes look European. Hit a city, however, and you slam back into chaotic Africa. Brightly painted *pousses-pousses* (rickshaws), their drivers hustling hard for fares, compete with zebu carts and overpacked buses for space along rutted streets where touts hawk everything from price-guns to strawberries.

To really experience Central Madagascar's chameleonlike ability to change, you'll have to get out of your car. There is fantastic trekking through cloud forests and volcanic craters in the region's stunning national parks, home to vegetation and animals (lots of lemurs) found nowhere else on earth. For a more cultural experience, spend three days trekking through Betsileo villages. Central Madagascar is also famous for its beautiful handicrafts. Best of all, it's one of the cheapest, and easiest, places to travel in Madagascar.

HIGHLIGHTS

- Walking through cloud forests and tracking lemurs in **Parc National de Ranomafana** (p103)

- Summiting Madagascar's second-highest mountain, Pic Imarivolanitra, in spectacular **Parc National d'Andringitra** (p110)

- Checking out intricate woodcarvings by Zafimaniry artisans in the **villages** (p102) around Ambositra

- Supporting home-grown tourism by visiting the community-run **Anja Reserve** (p110), where lemurs are plentiful

- Riding Madagascar's only rails on a **train ride** (p108) through the countryside from Fianarantsoa

- HIGHEST POINT: 2643m
- PRINCIPAL TRIBES: Betsileo, Merina

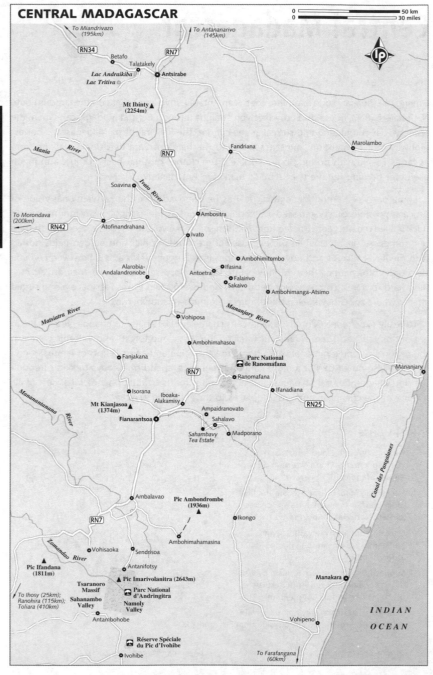

CENTRAL MADAGASCAR

CENTRAL MADAGASCAR

0   50 km
0   30 miles

To Miandrivazo
(195km)

To Antananarivo
(145km)

RN34

Betafo
Talatakely

RN7

Lac Andraikiba
Lac Tritiva

Antsirabe

Mt Ibinty
(2254m)

Mania   River

RN7

Fandriana

Marolambo

Soavina

Ivato River

To Morondava
(200km)

RN42

Ambositra

Atofinandrahana

Ivato

Ambohimitombo

Alarobia-
Andalandronobe

Ifasina
Antoetra   Falairivo
Sakaivo

Ambohimanga-Atsimo

Matsiatra   River

Mananjary River

Vohiposa

Ambohimahasoa

Fanjakana

Parc National
de Ranomafana

Mananantanana   River

RN7

Ranomafana

Mananjary

Isorana   Iboaka-
Alakamisy

Ifanadiana

RN25

Mt Kianjasoa
(1374m)

Fianarantsoa

Ampaidranovato

Sahalavo

Sahambavy
Tea Estate

Madporano

Ambalavao

Pic Ambondrombe
(1936m)

Ikongo

Zomandao   River

RN7

Ambohimahamasina

Vohisaoka   Sendrisoa

Pic Ifandana
(1811m)

Antanifotsy

Manakara

To Ihosy (25km);
Ranohira (115km);
Toliara (410km)

Tsaranoro
Massif

Pic Imarivolanitra (2643m)

Parc National
d'Andringitra

Sahanambo
Valley

Namoly
Valley

Canal des Pangalanes

Antambohobe

INDIAN

Vohipeno

OCEAN

Réserve Spéciale
du Pic d'Ivohibe

Ivohibe

To Farafangana
(60km)

Getting There & Around

Traversing the RN7, either by taxi-brousse (mostly minibuses now) or rental car, is one of the most popular, and easy, journeys in the country. Nearly all of Central Madagascar's towns and attractions lie on, or just off, this highway, one of Madagascar's few. The RN7 is paved, well maintained and relatively fast.

Taxis-brousses regularly ply the road between the capital and the coast; some go direct from Antananarivo to Toliara (Ar25,000, 24 hours with an overnight stop in Fianarantsoa). If you have the cash, this trip is best done by private vehicle. It costs more, but allows you to tailor your own trip and stop when something catches your eye. Locally owned cars (which nearly always come with a driver) can be hired in Antananarivo, Toliara and Fianarantsoa, and sometimes in the smaller cities in between (ask at hotels or the bus station). The thousand or so kilometre drive from Antananarivo to Toliara takes at least three days, but many require you rent for at least five days – or pay a lot more. The longer you hire for, the cheaper the rate. Expect to pay between Ar75,000 and Ar125,000 per day for a five-day rental, with price entirely dependent on your bartering skills and whether the driver has much business at the moment. You will also have to pay for all the petrol, including for the return trip, regardless of whether you return. Most drivers also charge an extra day's fare for their return trip. When we made the journey, petrol cost Ar300,000 return from Antananarivo to Toliara. **Roger Felix** (☎ 032 077 3330, 22 328 09), based in Antananarivo, is a recommended driver to hire. He does the trip in a big white minibus, which he even lets you sleep in if you don't want to pay for a hotel. Roger is honest, friendly and knows the region well. He speaks a bit of English, and has all the necessary government permits to carry tourists.

Most people drive this route one way from Antananarivo to the south, which means dozens of empty vehicles head north each day. If you happen to be going to Antananarivo, or somewhere along the way, you may be able to score a comfortable direct ride north pretty cheaply. Unless you negotiate for a whole regional tour (which should still be cheaper from this direction, as nearly all the drivers live in Antananarivo), your driver may pick up locals and other travellers along the way, but the ride is usually less crowded than taxis-brousses.

The airport in Toliara is a good place to check for available rentals. Arrive right before a flight arrives or departs – drivers often drop their clients at the airport then wait around in hopes of finding another fare.

Once in the central highlands it's easy to get between cities by local taxis-brousses (they make more stops than the direct ones). These are cheap, crowded and depart when full from the town station.

From Fianarantsoa, a passenger train goes to Manakara on the east coast (p231) – it's a popular and worthwhile trip.

ANTSIRABE
pop 159,000

There seems to be a *pousse-pousse* (rickshaw) for every person in Antsirabe (ant-sira-*bay*), a bustling city where the look and attitude is classic highland Madagascar. The urban oasis in a rural desert is an almost elegant place where the fresh air, cool climate (nights can be freezing) and therapeutic springs led Norwegian missionaries to build a health retreat in the late 1800s. When the French came to town, Antsirabe became a chic spa getaway for wealthy colonists wanting to escape Antananarivo's hustle.

Today, the city thumps to a uniquely Malagasy beat – it's colourful, chaotic, cluttered, gritty and poor. Brightly painted rickshaws crowd wide palm-lined boulevards, their drivers hustling hard for enough fares to feed their families, and gangs of scraggly children and young mothers with furrowed brows beg on the streets.

If you're looking for Madagascan art, Antsirabe is definitely worth the three-hour drive from Antananarivo. The town has numerous artisan workshops with quality handicrafts – in some cases the attention to detail on even the smallest metal bicycle is truly amazing. To check out these places, help the community and gain a uniquely Madagascan experience, visit the shops with a *pousse-pousse* tour – these start from as little as Ar400 for one stop, but we'd suggest paying a bit more. On the activities front, Antsirabe is the best place to find a tour operator for a three-day run down the Tsiribihina River in Western Madagascar.

Orientation

North of the cathedral is an area of long wide boulevards and colonial-era buildings, plus banks, the post office and several hotels and

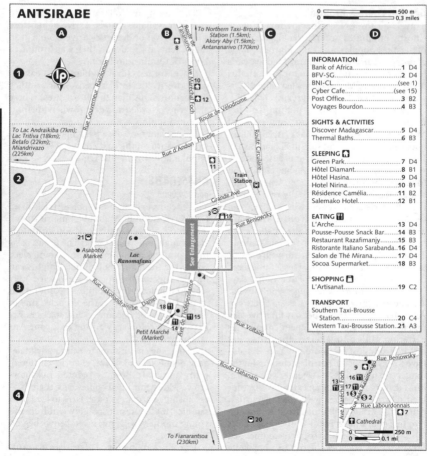

ANTSIRABE

INFORMATION	
Bank of Africa	1 D4
BFV-SG	2 D4
BNI-CL	(see 1)
Cyber Cafe	(see 15)
Post Office	3 B2
Voyages Bourdon	4 B3

SIGHTS & ACTIVITIES	
Discover Madagascar	5 D4
Thermal Baths	6 B3

SLEEPING	
Green Park	7 D4
Hôtel Diamant	8 B1
Hôtel Hasina	9 D4
Hotel Nirina	10 B1
Résidence Camélia	11 B2
Salemako Hotel	12 B1

EATING	
L'Arche	13 D4
Pousse-Pousse Snack Bar	14 B3
Restaurant Razafimanjy	15 B3
Ristorante Italiano Sarabanda	16 D4
Salon de Thé Mirana	17 D4
Socoa Supermarket	18 B3

SHOPPING	
L'Artisanat	19 C2

TRANSPORT	
Southern Taxi-Brousse Station	20 C4
Western Taxi-Brousse Station	21 A3

restaurants. The dusty and bustling lower-lying part of the town contains the southern taxi-brousse station and the market.

Information
The big banks all have ATMs that accept international cards these days. They also change money. Choices include the Bank of Africa, on the eastern side of Rue Jean Ralaimongo, BNI-CL next door, and BFV-SG, which is opposite. The post office is near the train station, and there is a card phone nearby.

Cyber Cafe (Rue Jean Ralaimongo; per min Ar30; ☺ 8am-midnight) Attached to Restaurant Razafimanjy, this internet café stays open late.

Voyages Bourdon (☎ 44 484 60; Ave de L'Indépendance) This travel agency can assist with booking

Air Madagascar flights for other parts of Madagascar (there are no flights to or from Antsirabe). It can also arrange car rental.

Sights & Activities
Saturday is market day in Antsirabe, and it's worth a wander around the town's two big markets, Asabotsy Market and Petit Marché. The town also has numerous handicraft shops and is a good place to stock up on gifts for the folks back home. The Norwegian built **thermal baths** still exist, but are so dirty you wouldn't want to swim.

FAMADIHANA
Famadihana (literally, the 'turning of the bones') is the name given to the traditional

exhumations of dead ancestors by the Betsileo and Merina people. *Famadihana* are joyous and intense occasions, which occur in each family roughly every seven years. Amid feasting, drinking, music and dancing, the bodies of the dead are disinterred from the family tomb, wrapped in bamboo mats, and carried and danced around the tomb. The bodies are then re-shrouded and reburied.

Famadihana ceremonies occur in the region around Antsirabe between July and September only. Local tour operators or *pousse-pousse* men can help you find one and arrange an invitation. If you receive an invite, it's polite to bring a bottle of rum as a gift for the host family, and to ask before taking pictures. Foreigners are generally warmly welcomed, and most people find that the experience, far from being morbid, is moving and fascinating. For more information, see the boxed text, p37.

Tours

Antsirabe is the best place to pick up a tour down the Tsiribihina River (p149) in Western Madagascar. Most float trips departing from Antsirabe (transport included) are combined with a visit to Parc National des Tsingy de Bemaraha (p151) and last around seven days. You can also organise shorter excursions to Parc National de Ranomafana (p103) or to the Zafimaniry villages, near Ambositra (p100). Besides the places listed here, nearly every hotel in town offers some kind of excursion.

Discover Madagascar (☎ 032 40 322 50; discovermad@yahoo.com; Rue Jean Ralaimongo) In the Hôtel Baobab, this company has a good reputation. Guide Désiré speaks impeccable English and runs a variety of trips, including the popular Tsiribihina River and Tsingy de Bemaraha combo – which includes a transfer by zebu cart.

L'Arche (☎ 032 12 591 52; robinsoncruso20032000@yahoo.fr; Ave Maréchal Foch) Guides Laza and Robinson Crusoe (yes, that's his real name) are based in the L'Arche restaurant and do trips down the Tsiribihina River and to Tsingy de Bemaraha, together or separately. They can also organise car hire. Laza speaks better English than Robinson.

Mr Raherison (☎ 033 11 662 72; laicriri@yahoo.fr; Hôtel Hasina) Affiliated with Hôtel Hasina, this guide runs Tsiribihina River descents. The hotel can provide information, but contact Mr Raherison directly for booking and prices.

Roadhouse Tours (☎ 44 492 26; www.madagascar-info.de) A German-run outfit that does Tsiribihina River descents, hikes around the Zafimaniry villages near Ambositra, and excursions around the whole country.

Sleeping

Winter nights in Antsirabe are bitterly cold, and none of the hotels have heat. Bring enough warm clothes.

Green Park (☎ 032 07 535 81; Rue Labourdonnais; camping per tent Ar5000, r Ar25,000) This place has a beautiful garden and picnic ground. There are three excellent round rooms, very prettily decorated, all with hot water and balconies. Green Park is often full.

Akory Aby (☎ 032 40 878 73; akoryaby@messagerie.net; s/d Ar12,000/16,000; 🖳) Just outside town, this is a new guesthouse run by a friendly Frenchman who speaks a bit of English. It has five rooms for now, although there are plans to expand (and also to build a snack bar), with shared bathrooms. Room 1 is the best and biggest, but all are spacious, colourful and great value. There is a rooftop deck and cheap internet (just Ar20 per min). It's across from the northern taxi-brousse station.

Hôtel Diamant (☎ 44 488 40; diamant@madawel.com; Rte de Tananarive; s/d Ar17,000/28,000; 🖳) A big

BE WARNED: IT'S COLD OUT HERE

If you're coming from the beaches and it's July or August, get ready for quite a shock – a cold shock that is – when you hit the central highlands. The climate in the *hauts plateaux* (highlands) is cool, with crisp air and clear blue skies during much of the year. In the winter it can seem downright freezing.

None of the hotels have heating and many are extremely drafty, so nights can be particularly punishing if you're not prepared. If you are coming through this area in winter – and everyone driving the RN7 (Route de Sud) will spend at least a few nights here (it's impossible to do in one day) – pack a pair of lightweight moisture-wicking long underwear (top and bottom) with you. These will keep you warm under your clothes during the day, and you can sleep in them at night. A light sleeping bag is also good – some places only provide one blanket. Rain gear is not really necessary, but you will want long pants and shirts and a light jacket, especially if you plan on trekking (camping can get really, really cold).

POUSSE! POUSSE!

Brightly painted and sporting racy names such as 'Air France' and 'Zidane', *pousses-pousses* (literally, 'push-push') are the Malagasy version of the rickshaws found in Asia. Hundreds of them fill the wide avenues of Antsirabe and cluster like oversized prams in front of the post office and the market. Passengers and freight vary – from haughty teenage girls, reclining like queens, to newly slaughtered cows, heads lolling and hoofs protruding.

When it rains, the price doubles and a sheet of plastic is pulled over the *pousse-pousse* as a makeshift hood. Most *pousse-pousse* men – who are also sources of information about almost anything in Antsirabe – rent their vehicles, and have to make a certain number of rides a day just to break even. In pursuit of their goal, they hound pedestrians relentlessly with whistles, hisses and cries of '*pousse!*'. Rides cost Ar400 per person.

Chinese-style edifice in the exhaust-fume-ridden northern part of town. The rooms, though, are peaceful, wood-floored and good value. Mattresses are firm, and each bedspread has a different pattern. The restaurant (Chinese dishes Ar5000), café and disco on site are all very tacky, but civilised and extremely popular.

Salemako Hotel (☎ 44 495 88; salemakojulia@yahoo.fr; Ave Maréchal Foch; r Ar24,000-38,000) Horse lovers looking to ride will be happy here: there are equines on the property and horseback rides start at Ar16,000 for one hour. Rooms are in a lumbering old mansion with sweeping ceilings and a grand dark-wood lobby with a stained-glass window. Rooms are massive, but a bit drafty and quite sparse in the decoration department.

Hôtel Hasina (☎ 44 485 56; Ave de L'Indépendance; r from Ar29,000) Right in the village centre, Hôtel Hasina is the best value in town. Rooms get great sunlight streaming through big windows and dappling the lovely hardwood floors. Beds are good, with mattresses neither too soft nor hard. There is a small table and chairs, and some rooms have balconies. The owner speaks excellent English; tours are organised.

Hotel Nirina (☎ 44 486 69; Ave Maréchal Foch; r incl breakfast Ar30,000) The five rooms at this family-run and friendly place are rather small and come with shared bath. The exterior, however, is lovely, with grapes growing in the well-maintained yard. Excursions can be arranged. No English is spoken.

Résidence Camélia (☎ 44 488 44; camelia@simicro.mg; Ave de L'Indépendance; r Ar52,000-85,000) A very genteel little guesthouse with a tranquil shady garden, it offers rooms in various shapes, sizes and prices. The nicest come with lovely curtains, bright colour schemes and rugs to keep your feet warm.

Eating

In the lower end of town, and in the area just south of the cathedral, are numerous places serving inexpensive Malagasy food and other meals.

Pousse-Pousse Snack Bar (rice dishes Ar1200; ☯ lunch & dinner Thu-Tue) Near the market, this is one of the better places for really inexpensive Malagasy food.

Salon de Thé Mirina (Rue Jean Ralaimongo; mains Ar2000-5000; ☯ breakfast & lunch Tue-Sun) An unassuming little tin-fronted restaurant that makes a great pit stop on your way out of town in the morning. It serves a number of breakfast options, as well as pastries, ice cream and snacks come midday.

our pick Restaurant Razafimanjy (☎ 020 44 483 53; Rue Jean Ralaimongo; mains Ar3000-5000; ☯ lunch & dinner) This locally recommended place (you see a lot of couples dining with their drivers) cooks Malagasy-seasoned Chinese food with excellent results. The menu is very long, with meat, chicken and seafood cooked dozens of different ways. There are also a number of vegetarian choices. The stir-fried Chinese noodles we ate here were the best we found in the country. There is cabaret at night, and the attached internet café stays open until midnight.

Ristorante Italiano Sarabanda (☎ 032 44 17 307; mains Ar6000-8000; ☯ lunch & dinner) A small pizza joint with just a handful of tables, including a few out front, that does about a dozen different combinations of cheese, sauce, topping and dough. It is nicely laid out with colourful woven tablemats and deep-red walls adorned with local art. The wood-oven pizzas are delicious and big enough to share.

L'Arche (☎ 032 02 479 25; mains Ar6000-9000; ☯ lunch & dinner Mon-Sat) This long-established place serves homely French favourites and pizzas to expats, river guides and tourists – a Tsiribihina River company is based out of the bar. L'Arche grooves after dark on nights when reggae and traditional Malagasy bands rock the place.

The best-stocked supermarket is **Socoa**, behind the Petit Marché.

Shopping

There are several shops in town selling carvings and Antaimoro paper. One to try is **L'Artisanat** (Ave de L'Indépendance), which is near the post office. You might also be approached in the street to buy gemstones – not a good idea unless you're an expert.

Getting There & Away

Antsirabe is 170km south of Antananarivo. There are three taxi-brousse stations: the northern one for transport to Antananarivo (Ar7000, four hours) and all points north; one in the southern end of town for transport to Ambositra (Ar5000, two hours), Fianarantsoa (Ar10,000, five hours), Miandrivazo (Ar10,000, five hours) and Morondava (Ar15,000, 15 hours); and another one on the western edge of town for transport to nearby villages.

Getting Around

Antsirabe can be easily negotiated on foot, but there are also a few taxis that can be chartered for getting around town and to destinations in the surrounding area, or you can take the bus.

Car rental can be arranged through **Voyages Bourdon** (☎ 44 484 60) and a guide called **Omega** (☎ 032 04 912 46), who can be found at L'Arche restaurant. Prices are around Ar90,000 per day for a 2WD vehicle, not including petrol.

The *pousse-pousse*, or rickshaw, is the main form of local transport in Antsirabe. The standard fare for town rides is about Ar400.

AROUND ANTSIRABE
Lac Andraikiba & Lac Tritiva

In the hills west of Antsirabe are two volcanic lakes, both easy day trips from town. **Lac Andraikiba**, the larger of the two, lies 7km west of Antsirabe off the Morondava road (RN34). In the 19th century, it was a favourite retreat of Queen Ranavalona II; today it is dirty with sewage, although it's possible to walk around the shores of the lake. According to tradition, Lac Andraikiba is haunted by the ghost of a pregnant girl who drowned during a swimming competition with another girl for the prize of marriage to a Merina potentate. Villagers say that each day at dawn she may be seen resting for a few minutes on a rock by the lakeshore.

The turquoise **Lac Tritiva**, which lies in the hills about 18km southwest of Antsirabe, is smaller and more picturesque than Lac Andraikiba, and makes a better excursion. It is said that the lake's water level inexplicably falls during the rainy season and rises in the dry season. An easy walk circles the lake. To enter the area around Lac Tritiva you'll need to pay a Ar2500 fee, which will also get you

---

SOS CHILDREN'S VILLAGE IN ANTSIRABE

SOS Children is a charity that cares for more than 60,000 orphaned and abandoned children in 123 countries. Sponsors and individual donors around the world support the charity, which provides children with a new family in a village environment. The charity also provides education for more than 100,000 children and funds programmes that assist vulnerable families to stay together. A children's village was opened in Antsirabe in 2003 with 12 family houses. The village also has a nursery, a school and a medical centre, which are shared with the local community.

In 2007 the family of Tom Parkinson, who died during the writing of this book, set up the Tom Parkinson Memorial Fund in his memory. Donations to the fund have gone towards the construction of an Asama classroom at the SOS school in Antsirabe. Asama classes are for teenagers who never attended school or dropped out of primary school because their parents couldn't afford to send them. The classes are aimed at helping young people to earn their primary school certificate within a year, which will give them the chance to obtain higher paid employment and better support themselves and their families. The Memorial Fund will continue to support the costs of Asama classes at the school. If you'd like to make a donation to the fund, visit www.soschildrensvillages.org.uk.

a couple of kids to guide you (while trying to sell you polished stones).

As with Lac Andraikiba, a tragic legend surrounds Lac Tritiva. The waters are supposedly haunted by two star-crossed lovers who leapt from the cliff's edge when they were refused permission to marry. Their spirit is said to live on in two intertwined thorn trees above the lake. In accordance with local *fady* (taboos), you shouldn't bring pork to the region and should not swim in the lake.

Camping is possible at both lakes; village accommodation can also be arranged. Taxis-brousses go from Antsirabe to Talatakely, on the northeastern side of Lac Andraikiba; the lake is 1km south of the main road.

Betafo

The Merina town of Betafo (the name means 'many roofs') is 22km west of Antsirabe. As well as the roofs in question, the village has numerous arcades and intricate wrought-iron trimmings, plus amazing views over the surrounding rice paddies. There's an imposing **Catholic church** behind the taxi-brousse station with some modern stained glass inside.

The interesting old town is dominated by **Lac Tatamarina**, a crater lake. A short circular road at the northern end of the lake passes a **cemetery** with tombs of local kings.

From the lake, follow the signs for the 5km return walk through often-muddy fields to the **Chutes d'Antafofo** – a two-tiered, 20m waterfall slicing through basalt rock.

There are no hotels in Betafo, but basic meals are available at *hotelys* (small roadside place that serve basic meals).

Buses and taxis-brousses to Betafo leave Antsirabe throughout the day from the western taxi-brousse station.

AMBOSITRA

pop 28,000

High on a plateau surrounded by misty green peaks, the lively village of Ambositra (am-*boo*-sh-tr) boasts as much fresh mountain air as you can gulp. It is the arts-and-crafts capital of Madagascar – in between the tall red-brick Betsileo houses lining crooked streets are over 25 artisans' shops, selling woodcarvings, raffia baskets, polished stones, *marqueterie* (objects inlaid with coloured woods) and paintings. The souvenirs here are cheaper than those in Antananarivo, and the atmosphere in the shops less high-pressure.

Orientation & Information

Coming into town from the north, Rue du Commerce (the main road) passes the market area before it forks. To the left, it continues through a congested area towards the banks and the southern taxi-brousse station. The right fork leads to the quieter upper part of town, with a church and the post office.

BNI-CL in the town centre changes cash and travellers cheques and does advances on Visa cards. It also has an ATM. There's a BTM-BOA branch too.

Sights & Activities

There are many good walks from Ambositra through the nearby villages, where you can see the artisans at work in their homes, working the wood with homemade tools or spreading brightly dyed raffia out in the sun to dry. At the western edge of town is a **Benedictine monastery**, where the monks and nuns sell postcards, cheese and jam in a small **shop** (☿ until 6pm).

Tours

For visits to the Zafimaniry villages or local beauty spots contact the **Maison des Guides** (☎ 47 714 48; guides per day Ar20,000), a guide co-operative which has a small office next to the Grand Hôtel.

Alternatively, ask at the Grand Hôtel or Prestige Hôtel for François Nirina, a highly respected guide, who organises trips around Ambositra and may also be able to hire out mountain bikes and arrange adventurous tours further a field.

Sleeping

Winter nights are beyond chilly here; make sure your hotel provides blankets. We came, unprepared, in winter, and froze our arses off. Ambositra is severely lacking in independent restaurants – be prepared to eat where you sleep.

Prestige Hôtel (☎ 47 711 35; Rue du Commerce; camping Ar5000, r Ar20,000) A simple and very good-value hotel. There's a wide choice of rooms with very comfortable beds, and a lovely little garden with a nice view. Breakfast is served for an extra Ar3000. It's also one of the few hotels in town that allow you to camp.

Hotel-Restaurant Jonathan (☎ 47 713 289; r Ar21,000-30,000) This new hotel must be doing something right, because they were full when we stopped by. The 10 rooms feel pretty modern with TV and decent mattresses – the

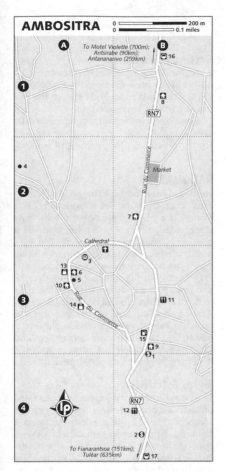

AMBOSITRA

To Motel Violette (700m);
Antsirabe (90km);
Antananarivo (259km)

RN7

Rue du Commerce

Market

Cathedral

Rue du Commerce

RN7

To Fianarantsoa (151km);
Tuléar (635km)

ourpick **Hotel Sokela De La Mania** (☎ 47 711 95; r Ar27,000-35,000) On the outskirts of town, this very peaceful place has fabulous views, especially at sunset. Rooms are in a big white colonial building and offer lots of space and light with huge windows – get one facing out onto the rice paddies. There is an onsite restaurant serving simple meals (Ar2000 to Ar7000) including cold sandwiches. It can be very cold and drafty at night.

Eating

L'Oasis (☎ 47 713 01; mains from Ar1000; ☺ breakfast & lunch) To stock up on fresh bread and other basic groceries for the long taxi-brousse ride south, head to this little place just north of the southern station. It also does a few hot Chinese dishes if you want to sit down.

Hotely Tanamasoandro (Hotely Gasy; ☎ 47 713 65; mains from Ar2400; ☺ lunch & dinner) This unpretentious local favourite is very popular for both its ambiance and huge portions. The restaurant's interior is a strange mix of Malagasy and Scottish themes, but it's very attractive.

Getting There & Away

Transport to points north, including Antsirabe (Ar5000, two hours) and Antananarivo (Ar7000, five hours), departs from the far northern end of town, about 2km north of the fork and down a small staircase from Rue

cheapest share baths. The restaurant (mains Ar3000 to Ar8000) is a good choice even if the hotel is full. It serves a big selection of pizzas, meats, Malagasy dishes and breakfasts.

Motel Violette (☎ 47 610 84; Rue du Commerce; r Ar24,000, bungalows Ar41,000) At the north end of town near the taxi-brousse station, this place has a comfortable setup. Rooms are very simple, but have good bathrooms and some have views. The on-site restaurant (mains Ar3000 to Ar9000) serves good French and Malagasy food.

Hôtel Mania (☎ 47 710 21; r from Ar25,000) Tucked away in a leafy, gated courtyard in the centre of town, it has big, clean rooms with a peach colour scheme and spotless marble bathrooms.

du Commerce, where you'll find a whole lot of taxis-brousses lined up on the side of the road. Departures for Fianarantsoa (Ar6000, four hours) and other points south are from the southern taxi-brousse station, just south of L'Oasis restaurant.

ANTOETRA & AROUND

The cluster of villages southeast of Ambositra is a Unesco World Heritage site inhabited by the **Zafimaniry people**, a subgroup of the Betsileo who are known for their woodcarving. Many of their homes are works of art, with shutters and walls carved into geometric designs.

The main village is Antoetra, which is linked with other villages higher on the massif by a good system of walking tracks. Sadly, Antoetra has been marred by deforestation and tourism – you can expect bare hillsides, mud and very persistent souvenir sellers.

You're most likely to enjoy a visit to this area if you do a trek of at least three days, which will allow you to get far enough off the beaten track to experience real village life, watch skilled woodcarvers at work and enjoy the surrounding hills and forests.

All tours must start in Antoetra, where you'll need to pay a 'community fee' of Ar3000 at the mayor's office in the centre of the village. The best villages to visit are **Sakaivo** (five hours' walk from Antoetra), **Falairivo**, the highest of the villages (two hours from Sakaivo), and **Antetezandrota** (one hour from Sakaivo).

For all the villages, except Antoetra, you will need to visit with a guide, who can help you communicate with the locals and instruct you in local *fady*. Guides can be arranged in Ambositra (p100) or Antsirabe (p97). Expect to pay around Ar25,000 per day for an English-speaking guide, a bit less for a French speaker.

The best times to visit are the months of May, June and September. During the rainy season the paths get very muddy and some become impassable.

Sleeping & Eating

There is no lodging in Antoetra, but you can usually arrange camping. Get permission first from the mayor – you have to see him anyway to arrange the permit. **Camping** (Ar1500) or superbasic **hut accommodation** (Ar10,000) can normally be arranged at the other villages.

You will need to be self-sufficient with food and water as nothing is available in the villages. Tours arranged in Ambositra sometimes include basic meals.

Getting There & Away

Antoetra lies about 40km southeast of Ambositra. Taxis-brousses travel weekly (departing at 6am on Wednesday) between the two towns (Ar5000, two hours).

None of the other villages are served by taxis-brousses, but they can all be reached from Antoetra via the network of walking trails.

RANOMAFANA

Nestled in the hills next to the rushing Namorana River, the village of Ranomafana (Hot Water) is a friendly place. For a long time it served as a thermal bath centre and was a popular spot during the colonial era. Today it's mostly used as a jumping-off point for visiting Parc National de Ranomafana, which is just 7km away. With more sleeping options than the park, many people choose to spend the night in this tiny village. The market is huge, both in size and popularity, and worth a wander. Look for sweet juicy strawberries and bright woven basket. Streets are filled with lots of dogs and kids and lots of people just sitting around, but it's a friendly place that's not intimidating.

Sights & Activities

The **thermal baths** for which the town is named are across a bridge, behind the now-defunct Hôtel Station Thermale. The baths are in a beautiful setting, but they are still a bit dingy – although they're cleaner than the ones at Antsirabe. Some people don't mind a little algae and dirt in their mineral water, and if you are that type you'll probably like the rustic feel here. Plus the water is supposed to cure various ailments, including rheumatism, asthma, stomach ailments and sterility. Just below the baths is a deliciously warm, and much cleaner, **swimming pool** to float on your back and admire the forested hills. Village women also offer **massage** (Ar12,000 per 30 min) here.

On the road out of the village, about 400m towards the park, is the grandly titled **Environmental Interpretation Centre** (admission free; ☺ daily), which has explanations of forest biodiversity in French and English, plus a small gift shop.

Sleeping & Eating

Note that sleeping places are strung out along the main road, quite a long walk from each other. Ranomafana doesn't have any Western-style restaurants outside its hotels, so check the menu where you're thinking of staying to see if it will suffice. Walking at night is not recommended – there are no street lights and it gets very, very dark.

Hôtel Manja (bungalows Ar18,000, r Ar38,000, mains Ar5000) Bungalows here are small weathered affairs that have seen their share of wet seasons. But they are clean, relatively comfortable and much better value than the rooms, which are nothing special. The hotel's best asset is the gigantic wooden restaurant with a porch overlooking the river. It serves tasty, inexpensive Malagasy meals. This is also a good choice if you arrive late at night off the taxi-brousse from Manakara or Mananjary – it's easy to spot in the dark, and there's always someone around to let you in. Look for the hotel about 500m before town as you arrive from the east.

Hôtel Domaine Nature (☎ 75 750 25; desmada@ malagasy.com; r Ar40,000, mains Ar12,000) This very charming hotel, 4km out of the village on the road to the park, has rustic bungalows on stilts and fantastic views of the forest and waterfalls. Be warned, however, that there are a lot of steps to climb.

our pick Ihary Hotel (☎ 75 523 02; bungalows from Ar42,000, mains from Ar5000) We loved Ihary's tranquil thatched-roof bungalows right on the river – snag the one closest to the water and let its babble lull you into slumber. Bungalows are small, but very tidy and breezy with lots of windows. The restaurant serves good food and even has a few pool tables. Ihary fills fast; book ahead.

Centrest Hotel (☎ 75 523 02; r Ar62,000, mains from Ar6000) In a great hillside location on the edge of town, Centrest is the most upmarket option in the village. Rooms are big and spotless and sit off stone pathways that meander through a lush tropical garden filled with local flowers and trees. Even if you're not staying, the restaurant is worth visiting. It serves a big menu, including yummy pastas and veg options. Malagasy dishes and seafood are also plentiful. Guests can visit the hotel's private reserve at Mahakajy, 9km away, which has chameleons and 80 species of orchid. English is spoken.

Getting There & Away

Taxis-brousses go daily from Ranomafana to Fianarantsoa (Ar5000, three hours) and Manakara or Mananjary (Ar20,000, six hours). If you're arriving from either place, let the driver know if you want to get off at the park entrance rather than in the village. Taxis-brousses from Manakara usually arrive in Ranomafana in the middle of the night.

Chartering a taxi from Fianarantsoa for a day visit to Ranomafana costs about Ar100,000.

PARC NATIONAL DE RANOMAFANA

Trekking through Parc National de Ranomafana's 40,000 hectares of misty and magical cloud forest is a soul-soothing experience. The air always feels fresh and cool (it can rain anytime), and the scenery is spectacular. The landscape consists of odd-shaped rolling hills, thick with dark-green vegetation, and numerous small streams that turn into waterfalls as they plummet off slate-grey rocks and into the rushing Namorona River below. Ranomafana was set up in 1986 to protect two species of rare lemur – the golden bamboo lemur and

---

THE BETSILEO

The Betsileo, Madagascar's third-largest tribe, inhabit the *hauts plateaux* area around Fianarantsoa and Ambalavao. They only began viewing themselves as a nation after being invaded and conquered by the Merina in the early 19th century.

The Betsileo are renowned throughout Madagascar for their rice-cultivation techniques – they manage three harvests a year instead of the usual two, and their lands are marked by beautiful terracing and vivid shades of green in the rice paddy fields. Betsileo herdsmen are famous for their trilby hats and the blankets they wear slung in a debonair fashion around their shoulders. Betsileo houses are distinctively tall and square, constructed from bricks as red as the earth of the roads.

As well as the *Famadihana* (reburial ceremony), which was adopted from the Merina after the unification of Madagascar, an important Betsileo belief centres on *hasina,* a force that is believed to flow from the land through the ancestors into the society of the living. Skilled traditional practitioners are thought to be able to manipulate *hasina* to achieve cures and other positive effects. The reverse of *hasina* is *hera,* which can result in illness and misfortune.

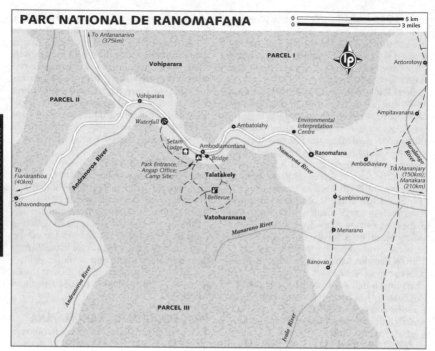

PARC NATIONAL DE RANOMAFANA

the greater bamboo lemur. Today it's one of Madagascar's most popular parks, with fabulous forest walks, lemur-spotting and excellent tourist facilities, including a posh new resort and a well-organised info centre.

Information

The park entrance, the Angap reception, information centre, the campsite and Setam Lodge are all in the tiny village of Ambodiamontana, about 7km west of Ranomafana village.

Entrance permits, available at reception, cost Ar25,000 per person for one day, and Ar40,000 for three days; 50% of this park fee goes to local people for use in community projects. Taking a guide is compulsory. Two-hour circuits cost Ar15,000 (up to four people) during the day and Ar20,000 after dark. Multiday treks are Ar60,000 per day. Guides speak English, French, Italian and German, and should be booked through reception.

The best time to visit is during the drier July to November season. However, the park can get very crowded during this time, particularly in July and early August. Temperatures range from 20°C to 25°C during the day and regularly drop as low as 10°C at night.

Wildlife

Parc National de Ranomafana is home to 29 mammal species, including 12 species of lemur. On a typical day's walk, you are likely to see red-bellied lemurs, diademed sifakas and red-fronted lemurs. With luck, you may also see a golden bamboo lemur. This species was first discovered in 1986; Ranomafana is one of its two known habitats.

Even rarer is the broad-nosed gentle lemur, which was thought to be extinct until it was rediscovered in Ranomafana in 1972; it was observed again in the late 1980s, and is very occasionally seen by visitors to the park.

Night visits to the park involve a trip to a clearing where bait is set to attract woolly, mouse and sportive lemurs, as well as the striped civet (*Fossa fossana*). Baiting wildlife for tourist observation is a controversial practice, and for some visitors the whole experience can seem rather contrived and artificial.

Not to be confused with *F. fossana*, the much larger fosa (*Cryptoprocta ferox*), a puma-like creature and the largest of Madagascar's predators, is the bane of local farmers, who blame it for night raids on stock and other mischief. The *fosa* is rarely sighted.

The park's bird life is also rich, with more than 100 species. Of these, 68 species are endemic to Madagascar. The forests abound with geckos, chameleons and frogs.

Although most visitors come for the animals, the plant life is just as impressive, with orchids, tree ferns, palms, mosses and stands of giant bamboo.

Hiking

There are three major walking trails that go through the park. The short **Ala Mando trail** (Petit Circuit) takes a leisurely two hours up and back and heads as far as the lookout at Bellevue, with lemur-spotting along the way. The **night walk** follows the same route, ending up in the Place du Nuit to see the nocturnal lemurs and the civet. The three- to four-hour **Moyen Circuit** goes a bit further in its search for lemurs.

Multiday treks not only allow you to spend a night in the forest, they also take you deeper into the park and away from the crowds.

Sleeping & Eating

Angap has a set of **campsites** (per tent Ar2000) at the entrance to the park, but you will need your own tent. Camping elsewhere in the park is only allowed on the guided treks organised through Angap. Again, you'll need a tent.

ourpick **Setam Lodge** (☎ 22 234 31; www.setam -madagascar.com; r Ar112,000) If you want to splash out in this region, there's no better setting to do so than this luxurious new place. Perched on a hill about 500m into the park from the entrance and up a steep set of stairs, it blends beautifully into its surroundings. Staying at this eco-lodge allows you to experience Ranomafana's magic by day (it runs its own walking tours) without sacrificing comfort come night. The spotless rooms are entered through carved wood doors and include enormous beds with real duvets, white walls adorned with artistic photos and, best of all, space heaters for freezing winter nights! The restaurant has huge windows featuring fabulous cloud-forest views. It serves breakfast (Ar7000 to Ar9000) and a set three-course meal at lunch and dinner (Ar20,000). Guests are encouraged to book online, where you'll also find the best deals.

Getting There & Away

The park entrance is 7km west of Ranomafana village on the main road. Getting to and from the park by taxi-brousse is now organised and easy. Buses to towns on the eastern coast stop by the entrance around noon each day to pick up and drop off passengers. About 20 taxis-brousses heading west to Fianarantsoa (Ar5000, three hours) stop here between 7.30am and noon. These buses will stop in Ranomafana village if you ask.

Hitching is also pretty easy – dozens of tourist rental cars head to and from the park every day.

FIANARANTSOA

pop 138,000
Madagascar's second-largest city, Fianarantsoa, is nothing to write home about. Although it resembles Antananarivo with its hillside location, steep cluttered streets and pollution, it lacks most of the capital city's charm. If you're travelling the RN7 by chartered car, however, you will almost certainly spend the night here, as the central location of Fianarantsoa (or Fianar as it's often called) makes it an ideal overnight rest stop. Wander the chaotic old town's narrow streets, crammed with touts and vendors and sleeping dogs, and stop for a drink at a little *hotely* along the way. Or visit one of Fianar's popular markets, where mamas draped in bright sarongs shop for kiddie clothes and veggies with a squawking chicken tucked nonchalantly under one arm.

Orientation

Fianarantsoa is divided into three parts. Basse-Ville (Lower Town), to the north, is a busy, chaotic area with the main post office and the train and taxi-brousse stations. Up from Basse-Ville is Nouvelle Ville (New Town), the business area with the banks and several hotels. Further south and uphill is Haute-Ville (Upper Town), which has cobbled streets, a more peaceful atmosphere, numerous church spires and wide views across Lac Anosy and the surrounding rice paddies.

Information

Fianar has many banks with ATMs that also change currency and do Visa card cash advances.

Angap (☎ 75 512 74; angapfnr@dts.mg) Can provide information and permits for the parks near Fianarantsoa. Permits can also be purchased at the parks themselves.

CENTRAL MADAGASCAR

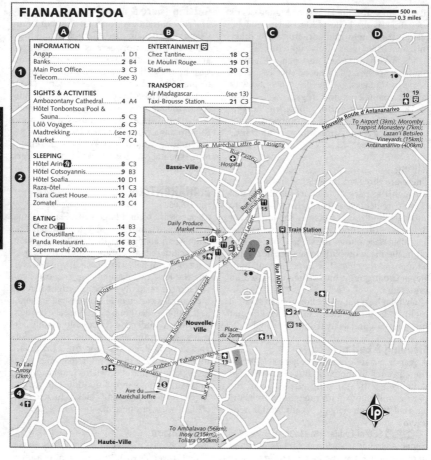

FIANARANTSOA

INFORMATION
Angap	**1** D1
Banks	**2** B4
Main Post Office	**3** C3
Telecom	(see 3)

SIGHTS & ACTIVITIES
Ambozontany Cathedral	**4** A4
Hôtel Tonbontsoa Pool & Sauna	**5** C3
Lôlô Voyages	**6** C3
Madtrekking	(see 12)
Market	**7** C4

SLEEPING
Hôtel Arin	**8** C3
Hôtel Cotsoyannis	**9** B3
Hôtel Soafia	**10** D1
Raza-ôtel	**11** C3
Tsara Guest House	**12** A4
Zomatel	**13** C4

EATING
Chez Do	**14** B3
Le Croustillant	**15** C2
Panda Restaurant	**16** B3
Supermarché 2000	**17** C3

ENTERTAINMENT
Chez Tantine	**18** C3
Le Moulin Rouge	**19** D1
Stadium	**20** C3

TRANSPORT
Air Madagascar	(see 13)
Taxi-Brousse Station	**21** C3

Main Post Office & Telecom Office (internet access per min Ar50; 7am-9pm Mon-Sat) Opposite the train station.

Sights & Activities

The oldest and most attractive part of town is **Haute-Ville** (known as Tanana Ambony in Malagasy). A stroll (or climb) around the cobbled streets here offers great views of the surrounding countryside. In the centre of Haute-Ville, and dominating the skyline, is the imposing **Ambozontany cathedral**, which dates back to 1890.

Fianar is a market town, with at least one small market open every day. Fianar's largest market is the weekly **Zoma**, where you'll find everything from beef sausages to party hats. It's held on Friday along Araben'ny Fahaleo-

vantena, and is hugely popular with locals who come as much to catch up on the week's events as to purchase dinner.

In hot weather, head for the large **pool** (admission Ar15,000) at the Hôtel Tonbontsoa. There's also a **sauna** (per hr Ar20,000) for sweating out Fianar's pollution.

Tours

Several hotels and tour operators can organise excursions to Parc National de Ranomafana, Ambalavao and the Sahambavy Tea Estate. It is also possible to arrange walking tours to the many picturesque Betsileo villages surrounding Fianarantsoa.

Tsara Guest House, Hôtel Cotsoyannis and some other hotels in Fianarantsoa will hold your luggage while you visit Parc National de Ranomafana or go trekking.

The Ranomafana treks advertised in Fianarantsoa focus on the Tanala villages in the area surrounding Parc National de Ranomafana. These multiday treks can be tough going, especially in the rainy season, when you will spend a lot of time slogging through rice paddies and dense patches of forest. You will need good shoes and long trousers to dissuade the leeches.

Places that organise treks and excursions include:

Hôtel Arinofy (☎ 75 506 38) This hotel organises treks and homestays in the Betsileo villages around Fianarantsoa.

Le Maison des Guides (☎ 75 517 30) This new company is a village initiative that's well worth supporting. It specialises in mountain and village treks with an emphasis on community tourism.

Lôlô Voyages (☎ 75 519 80; lolovoyages@dts.mg) This recommended guide specialises in treks and hikes in the Tanala villages around Parc National de Ranomafana. He also can arrange excursions to nearby attractions, pirogue excursions on the Matsiatra River (Ar150,000 for two days), and private transport between Fianarantsoa and Antananarivo that stops at points of interest along the way.

Madtrekking (☎ 75 502 06; mad.trekking@wanadoo .mg; Rue Philibert Tsiranana) This excellent company affiliated with Tsara Guest House (its office is right next door) offers a wide variety of excursions, including trekking in Parc National de Ranomafana, day hikes through villages around Fianarantsoa and pirogue excursions on the Matsiatra River. It can also hire out 4WDs, with driver, for around Ar150,000 per day.

Sleeping

Hôtel Arinofy (☎ 75 506 38; camping/s/d Ar12,000/ 15,000/19,000) Northeast of the taxi-brousse station in a quiet area, this is a friendly local guesthouse that also organises community tourism in the villages around Fianarantsoa. It has a variety of rooms at different prices and allows camping (tents provided in the price) when rooms are full. The restaurant serves Malagasy dishes (from Ar4000), and there's a kitchen (rare) for self-caterers. Cars can be hired.

Raza-ôtel (☎ 75 519 15; d Ar17,600-24,600, mains from Ar6000) Set back from the main street in a quiet courtyard off a side road, this is a charming and nicely decorated family-run guesthouse. There are just four rustic rooms, unfortunately with saggy mattresses, but the restaurant and bar area are super-cosy with lots of comfortable seating. You need to order in advance for evening meals – the restaurant closes if it doesn't have any customers.

Hôtel Cotsoyannis (☎ 75 514 72; cotso@malagasy .com; d from Ar29,000, mains from Ar6000) 'Le Cotso' has a garden courtyard and rustic, simple and attractive rooms that are great value for money. There's also a cosy restaurant with a log fire and good pizzas and crepes, which are its speciality. It also runs Camp Catta, a rock-climbing hotel just outside Parc National d'Andringitra on the Tsaranoro Massif (see p112).

Tsara Guest House (☎ 75 502 06; www.tsaraguest.com; Rue Philibert Tsiranana; r Ar35,000-111,000, mains Ar5000-15,000) Wildly popular, this orange-painted converted church enjoys a reputation as one of the best guesthouses in Madagascar. The public area décor is excellent – a roaring fire and bright-red walls in the reception area, a glass-walled restaurant serving delicious food, and a charming outdoor terrace with great views. Prices vary considerably here. The cheapest rooms, with shared bathrooms, seem a bit overpriced, as do the midrange 'chambres comfortable', but you are paying for the ambiance more than the amenities. The most expensive rooms are quite posh, however, and fairly priced – one has a king bed. English is spoken, and excursions can be arranged. Advance bookings are recommended.

our pick Zomatel (☎ 75 507 97; www.zomatel -madagascar.com; Araben'ny Fahaleovantena; r from Ar45,000, mains Ar5000-13,000; 🏊 💻) If you just want a good night's sleep in a comfortable Western-style business hotel, head to Zomatel. The mattresses are fantastic – no sagging here – and beds have soft duvets. Set back from the road in a gated complex, the hotel also has a formal restaurant, internet centre and low-key pizzeria with pool tables. It's also where you'll find the Air Madagascar office.

Hôtel Soafia (☎ 75 503 53; soafia@simicro.mg; Nouvelle Route d'Antananarivo; r from Ar45,000, mains from Ar7000; 🏊) Surely a contender for the weirdest hotel in Madagascar – an enormous Chinese-style palace, fitted out like a kitsch 1970s theme park, plastic pagodas and all. There's an equally large swimming pool, a vast, empty restaurant, a travel agency, a 'dance club' and an arcade of shops. Labyrinthine corridors lead to rooms fitted out haphazardly with gilt trimmings, some with bathrooms you could play football in. The prices are reasonable for the facilities, so lovers of the surreal might want to stay here for sheer novelty value.

CENTRAL MADAGASCAR

Eating

For excellent French cuisine visit the restaurant at the Tsara Guest House. Hôtel Cotsoyannis' restaurant is famed for its wood-fired pizzas and crepes. **Supermarché 2000**, in Basse-Ville, is the best-stocked place for self-caterers.

Le Croustillant (☎ 75 920 13; mains Ar3000-6000; ☺ breakfast, lunch & dinner) The service can be very slow, but it's worth the wait – our stir-fried seafood noodles were about as fresh as you can get. The small and unpretentious restaurant has a large menu that includes everything from omelettes to pasta. The Chinese dishes are particularly good.

Chez Dom (☎ 75 512 33; Rue Ramanana; mains from Ar5000; ☺ lunch & dinner; ⌨) A smoky backpacker café with internet access and a bar specialising in local rum. Freelance guides, available for excursions and treks, loiter here.

Panda Restaurant (☎ 75 505 69; Rue Ramanana; mains from Ar6000; ☺ lunch & dinner Mon-Sat) If your ultimate fantasy involves dining on sautéed bat while staring at murals of copulating pandas painted on a restaurant wall, fulfil it here. Definitely a top contender for Madagascar's strangest eating establishment, Panda serves an eclectic menu that includes bat, pigeon, frog and wild duck. It also does excellent Chinese. Ring ahead if you're absolutely craving bat or pigeon, as they are not always available.

Entertainment

On Sunday afternoon, spirited games of football (soccer) are played at the **stadium** (off Ave du Général Leclerc), near the train station. There are also occasional beer festivals here, attended by university students from as far away as Antananarivo. Look out for posters around town.

For dancing, try **Le Moulin Rouge** at the northeastern end of town, which plays everything from Malagasy to Euro-pop. **Chez Tantine**, by the taxi-brousse station, is also fun and attracts a lively Malagasy crowd.

Getting There & Away

AIR

Air Madagascar (☎ 75 507 97; Araben'ny Fahaleovantena) flies once weekly between Fianarantsoa and Antananarivo; look for the booking agent in the complex behind the Zomatel. The Fianarantsoa airport is 3km northeast of the city.

TAXI-BROUSSE & MINIBUS

Frequent taxis-brousses connect Fianarantsoa with Ambositra (Ar5000, three hours),

Antsirabe (Ar7000, about seven hours) and Antananarivo (Ar10,000, nine to 10 hours).

Minibuses also go daily to Ambalavao (Ar400, two hours), Ihosy (Ar7000, four hours), Ranohira (Ar9000, seven hours) and on to Toliara (Ar12,000, 11 hours). Departures from Fianarantsoa are at around 5pm, arriving in Toliara at about 4am the next day. If you're heading east there are multiple vehicles daily between Fianarantsoa and Ranomafana (Ar5000, three hours), Mananjary (Ar8000, eight hours) and Manakara (Ar10,000, 10 hours). It's no longer possible to go from Fianarantsoa straight to Fort Dauphin (Taolagnaro) as the road is impassable – you have to go to Toliara first.

TRAIN

Fianarantsoa is connected to Manakara on the eastern coast by Madagascar's only functioning passenger train service, the FCE *(Fianarantsoa–Côte Est)*. The train leaves Fianar early each morning and chugs on lines built in the 1930s through plantations and past hills and waterfalls, reaching Manakara around seven hours later. It takes about an hour longer in the other direction as the train has to go uphill. Despite its antiquity and unreliability, the train is still an economic lifeline for the people of the inland villages, who use it to transport their cargoes of bananas and coffee to be sold and exported.

Departures from Fianarantsoa are scheduled for Tuesday, Wednesday, Thursday, Saturday and Sunday at 7am, and from Manakara on Monday, Wednesday, Thursday, Friday and Sunday at 7am, although there are frequent delays and cancellations. Tickets cost Ar25,000/16,000 in 1st/2nd class.

No advance reservations are taken – simply arrive at the station about an hour before departure. The only actual difference between 1st and 2nd class is that the seats and windows are bigger, and it's less crowded. First class is generally only used by tourists, while 2nd class is packed with a noisy and friendly crowd of Malagasy, all leaning out of the windows at each tiny station to haggle with hordes of vendors balancing baskets of bananas, crayfish or fresh bread on their heads.

For the best views of the cliffs, misty valleys and waterfalls en route, sit on the north side of the train (ie the left side when going from Fianarantsoa to Manakara). However, the most impressive waterfall is on the right as you go towards Manakara, just after Madporano, about two hours from Fianarantsoa. Bring water, and, if you're making the journey in winter, plenty of warm clothes – it's often freezing early in the morning, when some of the best views can be hidden by fog.

For a more detailed history of the railway and the regions through which it passes, pick up a booklet called *The FCE: A Traveler's Guide* by Karen Schoonmaker Freudenberger. It's available in English and French for Ar7500 at the station or at the reception of the Zomatel hotel.

Getting Around

Taxis to the airport, 3km to the northeast, should cost between Ar2500 and Ar5000 depending on the time of day and the driver's willingness to barter!

Taxis charge Ar1500 per person for rides within Fianarantsoa. Villages and destinations in the surrounding area are served by *buxi* (minivans), which have route numbers marked in their front window. The fare to all destinations is Ar800; departures are from the taxi-brousse station.

AROUND FIANARANTSOA

Home to vineyards, tea estates and quaint medieval-style villages, the area around Fianarantsoa feels a lot like Europe. It is also considerably more attractive than the town itself and is well worth visiting.

Heading south from Fianarantsoa the landscape changes dramatically. Gone are the deep crimsons of the north, replaced instead by huge golden savannas punctuated by giant boulders.

Vineyards

Wine production in the area around Fianarantsoa began in the 1970s, with technical expertise and funding from a Swiss corporation. Today, Fianarantsoa is Madagascar's wine-making centre. Several of the largest vineyards lie northwest of town along the route to Isorana, or northeast along the road to Ambositra.

The most popular and accessible vineyard is **Lazan'i Betsileo** (☎ 75 516 24), about 15km north of Fianarantsoa. If you're visiting on your own, ring in advance.

About 7km outside Fianarantsoa is the **Maromby Trappist monastery** (admission Ar1000), where you can observe the wine-making process and taste the wine. To get here, take *buxi* No 24 (Ar500) towards Vohipeno and ask the

driver to drop you off at the junction, from where the monastery is about a 2km walk.

You can easily charter a taxi from Fianarantsoa for transport to either vineyard (or both). This should cost between Ar30,000 and Ar50,000 return.

Sahambavy Tea Estate

The **Sahambavy Tea Estate** (admission Ar7500; ⏱ 7.30am-3.30pm Mon-Fri) produces high-quality tea for export and a lesser grade for local consumption. It lies near the village of Ampaidranovato, about 15km east of Fianarantsoa and along the rail line towards Manakara. A visit includes a tour of the tea-processing factory and ends with a tea-tasting.

Organised day excursions can be arranged in Fianarantsoa for about Ar75,000, including the entry fee. To visit on your own, take a taxi-brousse heading towards Sahalavo to the signposted turn-off, from where you will need to walk about 1km. Alternatively take the train to Sahambavy station (the second stop after Fianar) and walk about 500m from there.

The only place to stay around here is the **Lake Hôtel** (☎ 75 518 73; r from Ar25,000, set dinners Ar10,00). It's a well-run Chinese establishment near the station.

AMBALAVAO

pop 25,000

Ambalavao (New Valley) is one of the most beautiful towns in the *hauts plateaux*. The brightly painted buildings of the main street look a bit like gingerbread houses with their steeply tiled roofs and carved, weathered wooden balconies. Outside, women sit in the clear highland sunlight, spinning silk or kneading dough, little raffia hats perched on their heads and blankets around their shoulders. Every Tuesday and Wednesday, the town plays host to the largest zebu market in the country, with tough, wizened herdsmen walking from as far away as Toliara to sell their cattle.

The World Wide Fund for Nature (WWF) and the **Parc National d'Andringitra office** (☎ 75 340 81) is on the northern edge of town, opposite Ambalavao's only petrol station. The office can provide information on the park and assist with transport and guides.

If you're looking for gifts made from wild silk and a chance to visit a silk workshop look for a shop called **Nathocéane** on the main street.

CENTRAL MADAGASCAR

Sights

FABRIQUE DE PAPIER ANTAIMORO

The **Fabrique de Papier Antaimoro** (Antaimoro Paper Factory; ☎ 75 340 01; admission free; 🕙 7.30-11.30am & 1-5pm) lies behind the Hôtel Aux Bougainvillées. You can see the women of the factory making paper from scratch. They start with the bark of the *avoha* bush, which is first boiled in water to form a pulp, then it is pounded, spread out over cotton cloth on wooden frames and left in the sun to dry. Once it's almost dry, fresh flowers are pressed into it. It is then left to dry again, after which the paper is removed from the frames and made into cards, envelopes and picture frames, all of which are for sale.

ANJA RESERVE

Readers love this small village **reserve** (admission Ar7000), about 7km from Ambalavao, that features a semi-tame colony of ring-tailed lemurs and some Betsileo tombs in a small patch of forest. Not only do you get great lemur close-ups, the reserve is a total community initiative. A local guide named Adrien started the park about a decade ago to promote regional tourism, create jobs and teach villagers the importance of conservation.

The reserve's relatively small size (although the terrain is tough going – lots of rock scrambles and bush walking) means you pretty much have a 100% chance of spotting a lemur. Its popularity has put it on the tour circuits, however, and you are likely to find yourself bumping into other groups of tourists on your hike. Guides are mandatory and cost Ar10,000 per person for two hours.

Besides managing the reserve, Adrien runs two-night **tours** (☎ 032 48 479 30; adrientrek@yahoo .fr; trips Ar100,000) in Parc National d'Andringitra that can focus on either rock-climbing or hiking. Rates include guide, entrance fees, food, transfers and all equipment. Adrien's tours are very fairly priced, and he speaks excellent English and comes well recommended – Tom Parkinson spent a few days trekking with him while researching this guidebook. Adrien is based at the Hôtel Aux Bougainvillées.

To get to the reserve, you can make a day's walk of it, or catch a taxi-brousse towards Ihosy and ask to be dropped at the office of the reserve. If you've chartered a vehicle, most include a stop here on their RN7 (Route de Sud) itinerary.

Sleeping & Eating

There are around half a dozen hotels, of varying quality in town, if this place is full.

Hôtel Aux Bougainvillées (☎ 75 340 01; ragon@ wanadoo.mg; r Ar40,000-60,000, mains around Ar10,000) On the grounds of the paper factory, this hotel has a bit of character. The rooms are comfortable and clean, but only the more expensive have hot water and private bathrooms. There's a decent restaurant, which is popular with tour groups at lunch. If you need information, look for Adrien, the well-respected guide based at the hotel part-time.

Getting There & Away

Ambalavao lies 56km south of Fianarantsoa. The town has direct taxi-brousse connections with Fianarantsoa (Ar3000, 1½ hours), Ihosy (Ar5000, two hours) and Ilakaka (Ar6000, five hours). For destinations further north, you'll have to go to Fianarantsoa first.

PARC NATIONAL D'ANDRINGITRA

The beautiful Parc National d'Andringitra (an-*dring*-itr) is a paradise for walkers and climbers. It has spectacular views of huge granite peaks towering above the Namoly and Sahanambo Valleys, 100km of well-developed hiking trails and the opportunity to climb Pic Imarivolanitra, which at 2643m is Madagascar's second-highest peak. The roads into the park are no less spectacular, surrounded on all sides by the glittering mud and symmetrical patterns of thousands of paddy fields.

The areas around the northern part of the park (where the main tourism area is located) are primarily inhabited by the rice-cultivating Betsileo, while the largest group in the south is the cattle-herding Bara. Andringitra is administered in partnership with the local communities, who can be visited in the villages bordering the park – ask your guide to arrange a trip, or inquire at the WWF *gîte* near the park entrance.

Information

The **WWF/Angap office** (☎ 75 340 81) in Ambalavao can provide information on the park and on weather conditions, verify camping-ground availability, and help find guides.

The main entrance to the park, and the most common starting point for treks, is in the Namoly Valley on Andringitra's eastern side. There is another entrance at the Sahanambo Valley on the park's western border.

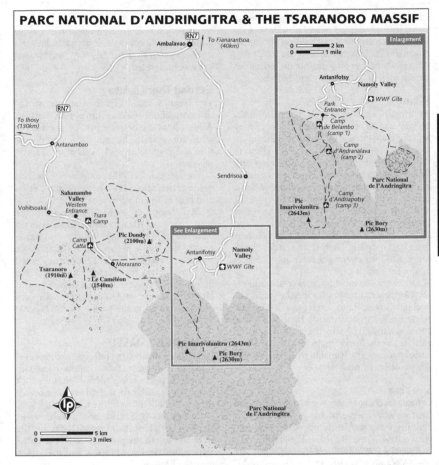

PARC NATIONAL D'ANDRINGITRA & THE TSARANORO MASSIF

When visiting the park, you will need to be self-sufficient with both food and water. It's also important to respect local *fady*, which are taken seriously in this area. There is a *fady* that pork should not be consumed in the valley or near the sacred waterfalls, and another that no boats should cross the Zomandao River. Your guide can help you with others. Andringitra is a 'pack it in – pack it out' park, so you'll need to take all rubbish from your visit out with you.

Temperatures in Andringitra drop as low as -7°C at night during the winter months of June and July, while daytime highs in December and January reach 25°C. You will definitely need extra warm clothing and a good sleeping bag if camping during the winter. Afternoon mists are common, and you should be prepared for

bad weather at any time of year. The park is officially closed in January and February when heavy rains make access difficult.

Permits (Ar10,000 for three days) can be arranged at both the Namoly Valley and Sahanambo Valley entrances.

Local guides can be arranged at either entrance gate and are required for all hikes. Fees start at Ar10,000 and are dependent on how far you want to hike.

Wildlife

Fourteen lemur species have been identified in Andringitra – more than in any other park in Madagascar – but sightings by visitors are rare since most of their habitat is outside the tourism zone. Among Andringitra's lemur

CENTRAL MADAGASCAR

species is an ecotype of *Lemur catta* (ring-tailed lemur) adapted to living in the mountains, which has been sighted on the upper reaches of Pic Imarivolanitra. The park's rich flora includes over 30 species of orchid, which bloom mainly in February and March.

Hiking

Andringitra's 100km of trails traverse a variety of habitats and offer fantastic trekking. There are four main circuits catering to various abilities. One of the most popular is the climb to the summit of Pic Imarivolanitra (2643m). There is now a natural trail up the mountain, which makes the summit accessible to most visitors with no technical climbing skills, although you'll need a reasonable degree of fitness for the hike. The circuit takes about 12 hours, so it's best to allow at least two days from start to finish. There is a beautiful camping ground for overnight stays about 3.5km before the summit.

Other circuits include the easy Asaramanitra (6km, about four hours) and the scenic Diavolana (13km, six to seven hours). The best route for lemur-spotting is Imaitso (14km, about eight hours) which goes through the eastern forests. Pocket maps and details of the various routes are available from the WWF/Angap office in Ambalavao.

Sleeping

Camping grounds (camping per tent Ar5000) The park has four wilderness camping grounds, all with running water and flush toilets. Tents can be rented from some of the local guides.

WWF gîte (☎ 75 340 81; s/d Ar13,000/20,000) The *gîte*, in Namoly, is outside the park bounda-ries about 6km from the start of the trails. It offers very simple accommodation in a lodge with a lobby fireplace, communal toilets and a self-catering kitchen. Advance reservations are recommended.

Getting There & Away

The Namoly Valley entrance lies east of Andringitra, about 100km south of Fianarantsoa. Allow about 2½ hours from Fianarantsoa in a private vehicle. The road is in good condition and negotiable with 2WD at most times of year.

The Sahanambo Valley entrance to the west of the park is about 110km from Fianarantsoa and four hours in a private vehicle.

Taxis-brousses go to Namoly from the western side of the market in Ambalavao on Thursday. On other days you can find transport to the village of Sendrisoa, 17km before Namoly, then walk in. For Sahanambo, you'll have to get a taxi-brousse to Vohisaoka, 15km before the entrance. Alternatively, you can charter a vehicle in Ambalavao for the very scenic drive up to the park (about Ar75,000 per day).

TSARANORO MASSIF

Just outside the western boundary of Parc National d'Andringitra is the Tsaranoro massif. It has an approximately 800m-high sheer rock face considered by rock climbers to be one of the most challenging in the world.

Camp Catta (☎ 75 505 68; www.campcatta.com; tent per person €7-11, bungalow per person €17-53), on the western edge of the park, is run by the Hôtel Cotsoyannis in Fianarantsoa, and specialises in rock climbing.

Southern Madagascar

Hot, weird and wild, Southern Madagascar is a cinematographer's wet dream. Filled with the world's most exotic flora and surreal landscapes, the countryside looks like no other place on earth. This is the Madagascar of the Discovery Channel, and the country's most visited region. It's a mixed-up land where unreal forests of long-limbed spiny succulents compete with baobabs sporting trunks tattooed with psychedelic red and yellow swirls for the title of trippiest attraction. It's also home to some fabulous national parks for trekking, including popular Parc National de l'Isalo, and beautiful deserted beaches with excellent snorkelling around pristine reefs.

The bustling port of Toliara (Tuléar) is worlds apart from the rural countryside. Bedecked in bougainvillea and jacaranda and filled with narrow corridors ripe with the smells of salty ocean water and fresh baguettes, it also has a hint of ethnic spice in the often-gritty air. The wide boulevards here are home to both Arab and French architecture, with elaborate domed mosques sitting next to crumbling, whitewashed colonial buildings.

For a real adventure, head to the southeast, where you'll find Madagascar at its most wild and real. Travel here is rough, and takes a lot of time and patience – roads are often nothing more than dirt tracks, and tourism facilities are pretty nonexistent. But the area is rich in history, and steeped with legends of shipwrecked sailors, rogue spice traders and colonies of pirates. Two oceans collide outside Fort Dauphin (Taolagnaro), home to Madagascar's best surfing, but sadly the town has been taken over by titanium mines and is of little interest to tourists.

SOUTHERN MADAGASCAR

HIGHLIGHTS

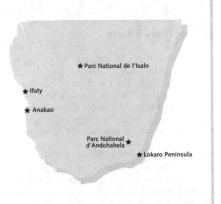

- Trekking through the giant boulders of **Parc National de l'Isalo** (p122) and looking for lemurs

- Diving in the pristine, turquoise waters off **Anakao** (p127)

- Spending a few days away from it all on the gorgeous white-sand beaches of **Ifaty** (p124)

- Walking in the bizarre spiny forest in **Parc National d'Andohahela** (p136), home to a forest of spiny cactus-like trees

- Camping in the rainforests or on the beaches around **Lokaro Peninsula** (p134)

★ Parc National de l'Isalo

★ Ifaty

★ Anakao

Parc National ★
d'Andohahela

★ Lokaro Peninsula

■ HIGHEST POINT: 1964m	■ PRINCIPAL TRIBES: Antaisaka, Antandroy, Bara, Mahafaly, Vezo

SOUTHERN MADAGASCAR

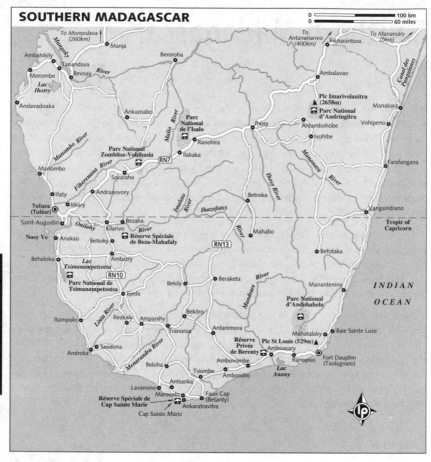

Getting There & Away

The quickest and easiest options for arriving in southern Madagascar are a flight on Air Madagascar or a road trip down the 'Route du Sud' – the Route Nationale 7 (RN7) from Antananarivo. You can also take the **MadaBus** (☎ 32 42 089 69; www.madabus .com), which has coach lines running between the major cities, is a comfortable way to travel, and is less expensive than flying or hiring a private vehicle. Some sample fares are: Antananarivo–Antsirabe (Ar25,000), Antsirabe–Fianarantsoa (Ar36,000) and Fianarantsoa–Toliara (Ar75,000). Check the MadaBus counter at Office Regional du Tourisme, next to the Central Market (Marché Central) in Toliara.

AIR

Air Madagascar flies daily from Antananarivo to Toliara (one hour) and Fort Dauphin (about two hours). Both cost around Ar550,000, depending on seat availability.

BUS & TAXI-BROUSSE

The RN7 between Antananarivo and Toliara is well served by minibus and the higher-capacity *camions-brousses* (large trucks). The total journey time between the two towns is about 24 hours; but most people do the journey in stages, taking in attractions such as the impressive Parc National de l'Isalo on the way. Off the RN7, the roads are poorly maintained and public transport is scarce. You can try hitching on a passing truck, but you could spend a week waiting on the side of the road for some kind of ride.

Getting Around

Once you've arrived, transport in southern Madagascar is tricky. But by bus, taxi-brousse, *taxi-be* (big taxi), *pousse-pousse* (rickshaw) or zebu-drawn cart plus patience, you'll be able to follow an itinerary with little trouble. Many of the roads, particularly between Fort Dauphin and Toliara, are in a very bad state and are only negotiable by 4WD vehicles.

BUS & TAXI-BROUSSE

Numerous taxis-brousses (bush taxis) and buses ply the route between Toliara and Antananarivo, stopping at all the major towns. Off this route, possibilities are more limited. *Camions-brousses* do the extremely arduous 30-hour trip between Toliara and Fort Dauphin daily, and go north up the coast from Toliara to Morondava. Around each major town *taxis-be* serve the outlying villages, but long-distance routes off the RN7 are rarely well served by public transport. See the individual town sections for specific details.

CAR

For lovers of 4WD adventures, the south offers plenty of possibilities – the road from Toliara to Fort Dauphin passes through a diverse countryside, which is appreciated better in your own car. Likewise the trip from Toliara to Morondava, taking in some beautiful beaches, is possible in a 4WD during the dry season. You can hire 4WD vehicles in Toliara and Fort Dauphin, or rent one in Antananarivo and drive it south.

Motorcycles are available for hire in Toliara – see p119 for details.

TOLIARA (TULÉAR)

pop 115,000

Slightly grimy and definitely sweltering against the humid backdrop of the Tropic of Capricorn, the 'white city', so-called by central highlanders because of the light-coloured buildings, is becoming southern Madagascar's leading town. The approaching views are outstanding: you can see vast sand dunes which run along the coast. Here, you witness a convergence of the savannah, the bush and the grassy plains, meeting with little monotony. It's a sizzling, dusty place, bustling with brightly painted *pousses-pousses*, refuse-strewn alleys, and dishevelled archi-

tectural remnants from the French colonial facelift – all slipping into heat-drenched languor between midday and 3pm. The city has broad avenues flanked by tamarind and flame trees, sandy crowded alleys concealing narrow corridors and colonial-era buildings ending abruptly in a wall of rubble. Toliara is the end point for those travelling the RN7, and you may very well end up spending a few days here waiting for transport elsewhere (remember: *mora mora* or 'slowly, slowly'). If you have a little extra time, however, and are looking for a good-value and up-and-coming beach destination, try the southern beaches around Ifaty. They see fewer crowds than up north, and are starting to gain attention as an upmarket romantic getaway destination. It's also a good stopping point if you're starting the long trek to Fort Dauphin by road – you can stock up on supplies.

Orientation

Toliara's airport, Ankorangia, lies 7km to the east, along the congested main road from the taxi-brousse station. Blvd Gallieni leads into the town centre about 1km to the west where most banks, hotels, markets and businesses are located. From here Ave de France leads down past the post office to the port.

Information

The BNI-CL, BFV-SG and Bank of Africa all have branches that change cash and travellers' cheques plus ATMs. BNI-CL does cash advances on Visa cards; Bank of Africa can advance money on MasterCard. Socimad, next to the mosque, changes cash and travellers cheques for slightly better rates than the banks, and does advances on Visa cards.

Angap (☷ 7am-4pm Mon-Fri, 7am-noon & 2-4pm Sat & Sun)

Centre Hospital Regional (CHR; ☎ 94 418 55; Rue G Campistron; ☷ 24hr) Has urgent medical care and medicine, and performs surgery.

CyberM@ki (per 1hr Ar18,000; ☷ 8am-6pm Mon-Sat) Surf the web at high speed or burn CDs (Ar2700).

Cyber Paositra (per min Ar50; ☷ 8am-8pm Mon-Fri, limited hrs Sat) Behind the post office in the Agate shop; covers basic email needs with a reliable connection.

Office Regional du Tourisme (☎ 94 446 05; 2nd fl Chamber de Commerce, Blvd Gallieni; www.tulear-tourism .com) Sells maps of the RN7 (Route de Sud) and has other useful information.

Post Office (Blvd Gallieni)

Telecom (Blvd Gallieni) Has card phones.

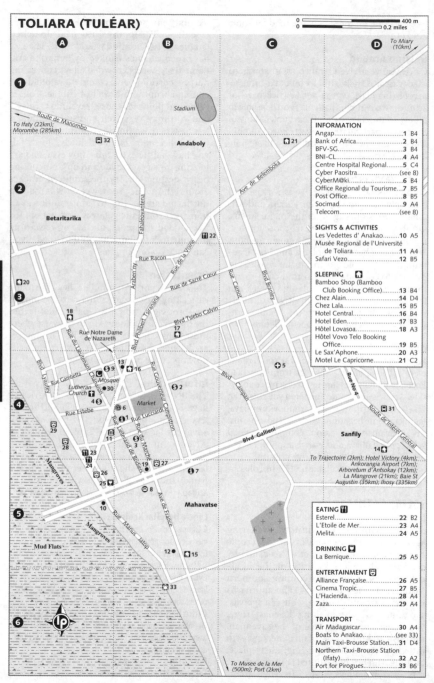

TOLIARA (TULÉAR)

0 ——————— 400 m
0 ——————— 0.2 miles

SOUTHERN MADAGASCAR

To Miary (10km)

Route de Manombo
To Ifaty (22km); Morombe (285km)

Stadium

Andaboly

Betaritarika

Fahaleovantena

Arabeny

Rue Racon

Rue de la Voirie

Rue de Sacré Coeur

Rue Carnot

Blvd Philibert Tsiranana

Blvd Bramley

Blvd Tsiebo Calvin

Ave de Betemboka

Rue du Lieutenant Charton

Rue Notre Dame de Nazareth

Blvd Lyautey

Rue Gambetta

Mosque

Lutheran Church

Rue Estebe

Market

Blvd Campan

Rue Couvenur Campistron

Rue Lucciardi

Rue du Marché

Rue Léonard de Brales

Blvd Gallieni

Sanfily

Route de l'intérêt Général

Rue No 4

Mangroves

Mangroves

Mud Flats

Rue Marius Jutop

Mahavatse

Rue de France

Ave de France

To Trajectoire (2km); Hôtel Victory (4km); Ankorangia Airport (7km); Arboretum d'Antsokay (12km); La Mangrove (21km); Baie St Augustin (35km); Ihosy (335km)

To Musee de la Mer (500m); Port (2km)

INFORMATION
Angap	1	B4
Bank of Africa	2	B4
BFV-SG	3	B4
BNI-CL	4	A4
Centre Hospital Regional	5	C4
Cyber Paositra	(see 8)	
CyberM@ki	6	B4
Office Regional du Tourisme	7	B5
Post Office	8	B5
Socimad	9	A4
Telecom	(see 8)	

SIGHTS & ACTIVITIES
Les Vedettes d' Anakao	10	A5
Musée Regional de l'Université de Toliara	11	A4
Safari Vezo	12	B5

SLEEPING ⛺
Bamboo Shop (Bamboo Club Booking Office)	13	B4
Chez Alain	14	D4
Chez Lala	15	B5
Hotel Central	16	B4
Hotel Eden	17	B3
Hôtel Lovasoa	18	A3
Hôtel Vovo Telo Booking Office	19	B5
Le Sax'Aphone	20	A3
Motel Le Capricorne	21	C2

EATING 🍴
Esterel	22	B2
L'Etoile de Mer	23	A4
Melita	24	A5

DRINKING 🍷
La Bernique	25	A5

ENTERTAINMENT 🎭
Alliance Française	26	A5
Cinema Tropic	27	B5
L'Hacienda	28	A4
Zaza	29	A4

TRANSPORT
Air Madagascar	30	A4
Boats to Anakao	(see 33)	
Main Taxi-Brousse Station	31	D4
Northern Taxi-Brousse Station (Ifaty)	32	A2
Port for Pirogues	33	B6

Sights

A few blocks southwest of the market, the **Musée Regional de l'Université de Toliara** (admission Ar2300; 8-11.30am & 2.30-5.30pm Mon-Fri) has undergone a recent renovation and features exhibits on local culture, an egg from the pre-historic elephant bird *Aepyornis*, and other oddities including a freaky ancient mask with real human teeth.

Only really worth a visit for sea-lovers, the **Musée de la Mer** (Ocean Museum; admission Ar2000; 8am-noon & 3-5pm Mon-Fri, 8am-noon Sat) has displays of pickled sea life, coral and shells, including a rare coelacanth. It's near the end of the road that leads to the port.

Tours

The following places can organise all kinds of excursions to attractions in the surrounding area.

Chez Alain (☎ 94 415 27; www.chez-alain.net in French; Sans Fil) Down a small lane near the main taxi-brousse station, they have information on tours and activities plus mountain bikes to rent.

Les Vedettes d' Anakao (☎ 94 437 21; vedettes@tulear-tourisme.com; Mahavatse 2) Formerly Compagnie du Sud, has 4WDs for hire and can help get you started on your own adventure.

Motel Le Capricorne (☎ 94 431 66; capric@dts.mg; Ave de Belemboka) Visits to the remarkable Réserve Privée de Berenty west of Fort Dauphin can be arranged here.

Safari Vezo (☎ 94 413 81; safarivezo@netclub.mg; Ave de France) Does boat transfers (Ar100,000) and excursions to Anakao and Nosy Ve.

Trajectoire (☎ 94 433 00; www.trajectoire.it in French & Italian; Rte de l'Aéroport) Specialises in motorbike and quad hire and off-the-beaten-path cycling, trekking and camping excursions in southern Madagascar.

Sleeping

BUDGET

Hôtel Lovasoa (☎ 94 480 39; r with shared/private bathroom Ar13,000/15,000) Generally acceptable and basic rooms with fans but no nets set around a shady courtyard and garden.

Hotel Central (☎ 94 428 84; r with shared/private bathroom Ar14,000/22,000) Conveniently located in the centre of town near the market and museum, Hotel Central has enormous, breezy rooms with balconies, but no restaurant.

Chez Lala (☎ 94 434 17; Ave de France; r from Ar30,000;) This laid-back and genial guesthouse has parquet-tiled rooms in the main block and smaller but still cosy rooms near the garden. A TV lounge, great espresso and loads of info make this quiet place popular, especially with

budget-conscious travellers. It also rents bicycles and quads, and does transfers to Ifaty and St Augustin (Ar100,000).

Chez Alain (☎ 94 415 27; c.alain@wanadoo.mg; Sans Fil; r from Ar30,000) A Toliara institution, Chez Alain is very comfortable and boasts uncomplicated and peaceful bungalows in the garden, a convivial bar and an excellent restaurant. They rent mountain bikes, and the dive centre **L' Ancre Bleu** (chez.alain@simicro.mg) is also located here.

MIDRANGE & TOP END

Le Sax'Aphone (☎ 94 440 88; saxaphone@simicro.mg; Besakoa; r Ar20,000-38,000, bungalows Ar45,000) This tranquil French-run B&B has three rooms in the main house and a couple of bungalows in the garden. There's a restaurant, piano bar and friendly atmosphere, plus it has the best mattresses in town – plush, supportive things from Switzerland. English and German is spoken and there is a TV lounge with over 200 CDs to satisfy your musical whims.

Hotel Victory (☎ 94 440 64; www.hotelvictory.net; Rte de l'Aeroport; d Ar49,000-109,000;) This upmarket hotel has a big pool that feels great after a long day on the road. Set back from the chaotic main road, Victory creates a physical and mental reprieve that allows you to enjoy relaxing with a beer, eating in the lovely restaurant or sleeping soundly in clean and comfortable surroundings. Transfers from the airport are free.

Hotel Eden (☎ 94 415 66; eden.hotel@yahoo.fr; r from Ar52,000;) Rooms at this modern, well run and well located hotel have TV, phone, minibar and safe. The hotel offers free airport transfers, has a restaurant and can arrange activities.

Motel Le Capricorne (☎ 94 426 20; capric@dts.mg; Ave de Belemboka; s/d Ar61,000/69,000; mains Ar8000;) Le Capricorne, 1.5km northeast of the town centre, is clean, well-maintained and popular with package tour groups. It's comfortable and spacious, with a whitewashed courtyard restaurant and a casino. The helpful, English-speaking staff organises excursions and transfers to Ifaty and Anakao.

Eating

French food is very popular and found all over town. The cheapest places to eat are the food stalls near the market. A level up, and also inexpensive, are several *salons de thé* (tea rooms) in the centre of town, which do breakfasts and milkshakes, and usually pastries.

Chez Alain (☎ 94 415 27; Sans Fil; mains Ar7000-9000; lunch & dinner) Chez Alain's restaurant has long sustained a reputation around the city for serving excellent French cuisine, especially seafood. Attached to the hotel of the same name, it fills quickly at meal times.

Le Sax'Aphone (☎ 94 440 88; Besakoa; mains Ar7000-10,000; ☺ breakfast, lunch & dinner) This is a jovial spot in a lovely garden behind an iron gate at the hotel of the same name. It serves a small menu, which changes daily but usually includes some kind of pasta and fish. At night proprietor Alain often plays old jazz hits on the piano.

L'Etoile de Mer (☎ 94 428 07; Blvd Lyautey; mains Ar7000-11,000; ☺ lunch & dinner Mon-Sat) Dishing up good Afghan and Indian food as well as some of the best pizzas in Toliara, this place has been around forever and garnered a good reputation. Try the great fresh seafood.

Esterel (☎ 32 04 697 75; Voirie; mains Ar8000-12,000; ☺ lunch & dinner Mon-Sat) Esterel specialises in French cuisine and offers pasta, pizza and seafood as well as delicious chocolate pudding on the attractive open-air terrace.

Melita (☎ 33 11 598 82; Blvd Lyautey; dishes Ar9000-13,000; ☺ lunch & dinner) This smart restaurant serves European and Malagasy food, and concocts every cocktail imaginable. There's a great breeze from the tables at the clean terrace bar, and the small menu includes pasta and fish along with a variety of meat dishes.

Drinking & Entertainment

Alliance Francaise (Blvd Lyautey) has schedules of cultural events and French newspapers and magazines. French and occasional subtitled English films are shown at **Cinema Tropic** (admission Ar2000).

Popular drinking hang-outs in town include **La Bernique** (☎ 032 02 606 55; Blvd Gallieni; tapas Ar7000; ☺ Mon-Sat), which has an extensive assortment of malt whiskies, and the bar at Chez Alain.

The main nightclubs in town are **Zaza** (Blvd Lyautey) and the huge Mexican-style **L'Hacienda** (Blvd Lyautey), which both get going about midnight. Young Malagasy girls and middle-aged *vazaha* (foreign) men are the main customers at both, but the environment is generally OK.

Getting There & Away

AIR

Air Madagascar (☎ 94 415 85, 94 422 33) has an office northwest of the market. It flies from Antananarivo to Toliara (Ar550,000, one hour) daily, from Toliara to Fort Dauphin (Ar600,000, one hour) about three times a week, and heads occasionally to Morondava (Ar800,000, 1½ hours) via Morombe.

BOAT

For scheduled boat transfers from Toliara to points south such as St Augustin, Anakao and Beheloka, contact **La Compagnie du Sud** (☎ 94 437 21; www.compagniedusud.com in French), which does transfers from Ar80,000 per person. Departures can be cancelled, however, if there's not enough passengers. It has an office in the pirogue port south of the post office.

You can also find pirogues (local cargo boats) at this port that run along the coast to the north and south. Allow plenty of time (three to four days to Morombe), and bring water and food.

HITCHING

It's relatively easy to hitch a lift from Toliara to Antananarivo as many tourist vehicles and supply trucks from Antananarivo return to the capital empty. Expect to pay a bit more than the taxi-brousse fare. The best places to ask are the major hotels.

TAXI-BROUSSE

The main taxi-brousse station, which handles transport to Antananarivo, Fianarantsoa and Fort Dauphin, is in the far eastern part of town along the main road.

Taxis-brousses leave very early every day for Antananarivo, arriving in Fianarantsoa around 5pm, and Antananarivo at about 5am the next day. Desinations and fares include Ranohira (Ar16,000), Ihosy (Ar18,000), Fianarantsoa (Ar24,000) and Antananarivo (Ar35,000). Fares on smaller and slightly faster minibuses are from Ar5000 higher. Vehicles to Antananarivo usually fill up quickly, so get to the station early or book a seat the afternoon before.

A *camion-brousse* leaves daily for Fort Dauphin (Ar35,000), via Betioky, Ampanihy and Ambovombe, taking 30 to 60 hours depending on breakdowns and road conditions.

Transport along the sand road north to Ifaty (Ar3000, one to three hours) and Manombo departs from the northern taxi-brousse station on Route de Manombo. There are a few trucks daily to both destinations, generally departing between 6am and early afternoon.

A taxi-brousse leaves for Morondava a few times weekly (Ar60,000, two days). The road is very rough, and you will need to change vehicles in Beyoay and overnight in Manja on the way.

Taxis-brousses also connect Toliara with St Augustin (Ar4000, two hours) via a good sealed road once a day Tuesday to Saturday. Departures are at noon from Toliara and

2am from St Augustin. There's a taxi-brousse every Thursday to Beheloka and Itampolo (12 hours).

Getting Around

TO/FROM THE AIRPORT

A taxi between Ankorangia Airport and the centre of town costs a standard Ar15,000 and many hotels in Toliara and Ifaty do airport transfers.

BICYCLE

Chez Alain (☎ 94 415 27; c.alain@wanadoo.mg; Sans Fil) Rents out bicycles.

Chez Lala (☎ 94 434 17; Ave de France) Bicycles can be rented or you can arrange motorcycle or quad hire here.

CAR & MOTORCYCLE

Most tour companies listed on p117 hire 4WD cars for excursions around Toliara. Prices start at Ar150,000 per day without fuel. **Trajectoire** (☎ 94 433 00; www.trajectoire.it; Rte de l'Aéroport) hires out motorcycles from Ar140,000 per day without petrol, and quad bikes from Ar153,000 per day.

POUSSE-POUSSE

Standard rates for *pousse-pousse* rides start at about Ar500.

TAXI

For rides within town, taxis charge a standard rate of Ar2000 per person, but can climb as high as Ar15,000 at night. Don't be afraid to barter when you believe the price is unfair.

EAST OF TOLIARA

Ihosy

Ihosy, pronounced *ee*-oosh, is a quiet town of average size functioning mostly as a stopping point for travellers heading south on the RN7. It's also the traditional capital of the polygamous and warlike Bara tribe. The Bara have a distinctly close relationship with cattle, often placing a higher value on zebu than on their wives. It wasn't until French colonial times that the Bara finally ceased resistance to Merina rule. Among Bara, a man's true worth is judged by the number of zebu he owns, with cattle-rustling being a time-honoured rite of passage into manhood. Ihosy is most striking in October when the jacarandas are blooming. You may find yourself overnighting in Ihosy between taxi-brousse and private-hire journeys going to north or south Madagascar.

If you need accommodation, try **Relais Bara** (☎ 75 800 17; r Ar10,000-30,000), near the roundabout, **Hôtel Nirina** (r Ar10,000), which is near the taxi-brousse station, or **Chez Evah** (☎ 32 4323 829; r Ar12,000), 400m down the road to Toliara on the right. Ihosy is a transport junction where the RN13 from Fort Dauphin meets the RN7, which connects Antananarivo and Toliara. Taxisbrousses regularly ply the good 216km road between Ihosy and Fianarantsoa (Ar13,000, four to five hours), and between Ihosy and Toliara (Ar18,000, five to six hours).

Daily taxis-brousses travel along the very rough road to Fort Dauphin (Ar45,000, 36 hours), via Ambovombe.

Ranohira

The small town of Ranohira provides a convenient base for exploring Parc National de l'Isalo and is the nearest significant settlement to Ilakaka, a once sleepy, now bustling town at the centre of the sapphire trade. Acres of waving yellow grass stretch skyward all around the town, randomly broken up by towering rock massifs. At sunset or sunrise, the whole vista unfurls with an unearthly red and pink glow.

Angap (🕒 7am-4pm Mon-Fri, 7am-noon & 2-4pm Sat & Sun) is next to Hotel Berny, 100m from the centre of town.

ACTIVITIES

The focus of activity in Ranohira is trekking in nearby Parc National de l'Isalo. The best trekking option for budget travellers is undoubtedly **Momo Trek** (☎ 75 801 77). Debonair Momo runs an extremely efficient operation involving porters, equipment (tents, mattresses, sleeping bags and even pillows) and food from his base in the village. You choose your route and your menu, and Momo will organise everything else, including the appointment of one of the Angap guides. The only extras you pay for are your park permit (Ar40,000 for three days), camp-site fee (Ar10,000 per night) and drinks.

Prices vary according to the size of the group – a two-day, three-night trek will cost around Ar65,000 per person for two people, Ar72,000 for four or more. Such is Momo's popularity that you'll usually have no trouble finding other trekkers to share the costs.

Alternatively you can arrange a trek yourself; basic supplies are available in the village and several of the Angap guides can hire out

SOUTHERN MADAGASCAR

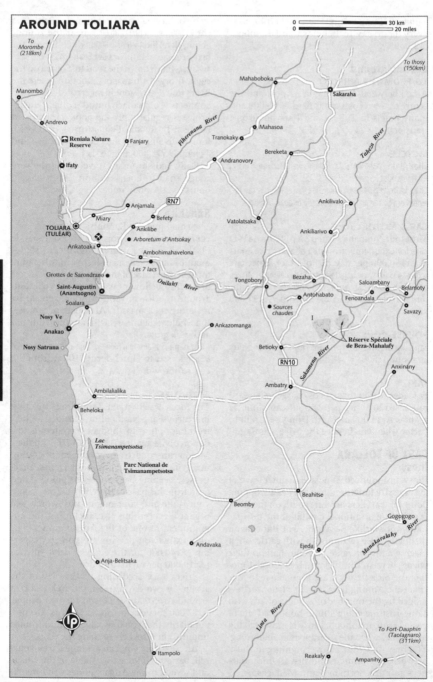

AROUND TOLIARA

0 ————— 30 km
0 ————— 20 miles

To Morombe (218km)

To Ihosy (150km)

Manombo

Andrevo

Reniala Nature Reserve

Fanjary

Ifaty

Mahaboboka

Sakaraha

Mahasoa

Tranokaky

Berereta

Andranovory

Fiherenana River

Tahezi River

Anjamala

RN7

Befety

Miary

Ankilibe

Arboretum d'Antsokay

TOLIARA (TULÉAR)

Ankatoaka

Ambohimahavelona

Les 7 lacs

Grottes de Sarondrano

Saint-Augustin (Anantsogno)

Soalara

Nosy Ve

Anakao

Nosy Satrana

Ankazomanga

Ambilalialika

Beheloka

Lac Tsimanampetsotsa

Parc National de Tsimanampetsotsa

Vatolatsaka

Ankilivalo

Ankiliarivo

Tongobory

Bezaha

Saloambany

Belamoty

Antohabato

Fenoandala

Savazy

Sources chaudes

Betioky

RN10

I

II

Réserve Spéciale de Beza-Mahalafy

Onilahy River

Sakamena River

Ambatry

Anxinany

Beomby

Beahitse

Gogogogo

Monakaralahy River

Andavaka

Ejeda

Anja-Belitsaka

Linta River

To Fort-Dauphin (Taolagnaro) (311km)

Itampolo

Reakaly

Ampanihy

LP

ZEBU

Together with the lemur, the chameleon and the *ravinala* (travellers' palm), the zebu (Malagasy cow) is one of the most identifiable symbols of Madagascar. Zebu indicate wealth and status, and are sacrificed during ceremonies, yoked in pairs to wooden-wheeled *charettes* (carts) or chased in herds around rice fields to break up the earth for planting. Zebu are herded (and rustled) in vast numbers by the Bara and other southern tribes. According to tradition, a young Bara man must prove himself by stealing zebu in order to be considered a desirable marriage partner. Being imprisoned for zebu-rustling only enhances his appeal in the eyes of his prospective bride and her family.

Zebu have large wobbling humps on their backs and flaps of loose skin dangling lugubriously from their throats. The flap of skin increases surface area and thereby allows better regulation of heat, and the hump stores fat in case of famine. These physical advantages make zebu particularly hardy and well adapted to their often harsh living conditions.

---

tents and equipment. See p122 for details of guide fees.

SLEEPING & EATING

Chez Momo (☎ 75 801 77; camping/bungalows Ar10,000/25,000) The base for Momo's trekking outfit has Bara-style huts, a friendly bar with a dining room and basic bungalows with outside (cold) showers. It's also a good place to pitch a tent for the night.

Motel Isalo (☎ 22 330 82; r from Ar25,000, mains Ar7000) On the north side of the main road about 2km east of Ranohira, this is a tranquil place with rows of stone bungalows and great views. It has comfortable rooms with attractive mosaic bathrooms plus a restaurant.

Hôtel l'Orchidée de l'Isalo (☎ 75 801 78; r Ar25,000-45,000) L'Orchidée is a very relaxing option in the middle of the village with a nice restaurant. Marble floors, stone walls and nicer bathrooms style out the newer rooms while cheaper ones are older and a bit worse for wear.

Hôtel Berny (☎ 75 801 76; d with shared/private bathroom Ar35,000/50,000, larger r Ar100,000) Hôtel Berny is a wonderful brick-clad establishment with a cosy fireplace that's near the Angap office. The best rooms are inside a little chateau around the garden where pet lemurs and tourists can play freely. It has spacious rooms and bathrooms, lots of hot water and a restaurant, and is ideal after an exhausting trek.

Isalo Ranch (☎ in Antananarivo 24 319 02; www.isalo -ranch.com; BP 3, 313 Ranohira; d with shared/private bathroom Ar40,000/64,000, tr Ar80,000; ☻) A comfortable midrange place with gorgeous views. It has 19 bright, cheerful and attractively decorated bungalows spread around a garden. It's 5km south of Ranohira on the way to the park. A taxi-brousse from Ilakaka can drop you

off. The owner is the brother of celebrated photographer Pierrot Man, and the place is popular with German tourists.

Le Relais de la Reine (in Antananarivo ☎ 22 336 23; www.3dmadagascar.com/relaisdelareine; d from Ar150,000, mains Ar28,000; ☻) About 10km southwest of Ranohira, Le Relais de la Reine sits on the edge of Isalo and is one of the most magnificently located hotels in Madagascar. Its plainchic rooms and pool are sculpted around natural rock formations, with a skilfully decorated bar, restaurant and sun terrace in the main building. There's also an equestrian centre on site for sunset gallops across the savannah. The hotel organises treks and car excursions in the surrounding area. It doesn't accept credit cards, and booking ahead is mandatory.

GETTING THERE & AWAY

For travel from Ranohira to Ilakaka, the best options are to catch a passing taxi-brousse, hitch or take a *taxi-ville* (Ar15,000). From there, taxis-brousses leave every morning and afternoon for Toliara and Ambalavao (Ar20,000, six hours), and sometimes continue to Fianarantsoa. You may also be lucky enough to find a taxi-brousse travelling between Toliara and Antananarivo with an empty seat. One or two direct taxis-brousses each morning connect Ranohira with Ihosy, 91km to the east (Ar18,000, two hours). You can always ask around in the hotels to see if any empty tourist vehicles are going back to Antananarivo – Chez Momo is a good place to start.

Public transport from Toliara generally arrives in Ranohira between 10am and 1pm, while vehicles from the north usually arrive before 10am.

SOUTHERN MADAGASCAR

Parc National de l'Isalo

Parc National de l'Isalo (ish-*ah*-loo) covers 81,540 hectares of the eroded Jurassic sandstone massif of the same name. It's a marvel of evolutionary processes, with an unearthly, sometimes eerie landscape that's home to endemic plants and ringtail, brown and sifaka lemurs, as well as sacred Bara burial sites. Its flaxen plains are dotted with serrated grins of stratified rock reaching to the terracotta horizon. Its interior boasts valleys, waterfalls and canyons. You won't be alone in admiring l'Isalo's beauty, however – it's one of Madagascar's most popular national parks. If you want to get away from other visitors, you'll need to do a trek further into the park, which could mean several days of hiking. Alternatively, some of the park can be explored easily by car. The entry fee for l'Isalo is Ar25,000 per person.

Numerous local *fady* (taboos) are in effect in l'Isalo and should be respected while trekking. L'Isalo's rocky cliffs and ridges often shelter concealed Sakalava tombs – remember that it's *fady* and disrespectful to point at tombs with your finger outstretched.

A local tradition requires placing a stone on existing burial markers to ask for the fulfilment of wishes and safe passage. It's said that if your wish comes true, you should return to the site to say thank you. The best time to visit l'Isalo is in the dry season between April and October.

Outside the park, south of town and between Isalo Ranch and La Relais de la Reine is **La Maison d'Isalo** (admission free; ⏰ 7am-6pm). It features an interactive eco-museum that's kid-friendly, with information about the people living around the park and wildlife biodiversity, plus commentary in English, French, and Malagasy. Photos, poems and paintings here illustrate the area's cultural significance, and there's a shuttle available from town.

INFORMATION

Park permits cost Ar25,000 for one day and Ar40,000 for three, and are available from Angap (p119) in Ranohira; staff speak English. Built into the park tariff, 50% of admission fees go to local independent projects promoting sustainability and conservation.

Official guides are required in the park, and can also be arranged at Angap – their names and competence levels are on display. Many speak English, and some speak German and Italian. Guide fees vary depending on the length and routing of your hike, but range from about Ar25,000 to Ar100,000 per group (up to four people) per day.

WILDLIFE

Although animal life isn't the park's most prominent feature, there are some interesting lemur species to watch out for, including grey mouse, ring-tailed and brown lemurs, and Verreaux's sifaka. The best place for lemur-spotting is the aptly named Canyon des Singes. There are more than 50 bird species, including the endemic Benson's rock thrush, a small grey bird with a vivid scarlet breast.

Most vegetated areas of the park are covered with dry grassland or sparse, low deciduous woodland. Near streams and in the lush pockets of rainforest in the deeper canyons, there are ferns, pandanus and feathery palm trees. At ground level in drier areas, look for the yellow flowering *Pachypodium rosulatum* (especially beautiful in September and October), which

---

TOP THREE ISALO EXPERIENCES

Isalo is so packed with adventures it's sometimes hard to figure out the must-dos; here are three of our favourites.

Canyon des Singes (Canyon des Makis) Lose yourself as the sun is blotted out when you enter the Canyon des Singes, meaning literally 'canyon of monkeys'. It's a fun day-walk from Ranohira, but it's better to stay overnight and leave time for proper exploration and wildlife viewing.

Canyon des Singes to Piscine Naturelle Be prepared for a long walk, but the geography along the way is spectacular, with obscured canyons, colourful mountain ranges and strange flora in addition to the likelihood of seeing sifakas and ringtail lemurs.

Piscine Naturelle At Piscine Naturelle, swimming under the pandanus trees gives you a lush tropical umbrella overhead while a tumbling waterfall pours into a deep green pool. Score! A natural stone cave overlooking the falls is fun to explore and the water is great for swimming. You'll appreciate this natural amenity after the long hot trip over the massif from Canyon des Singes.

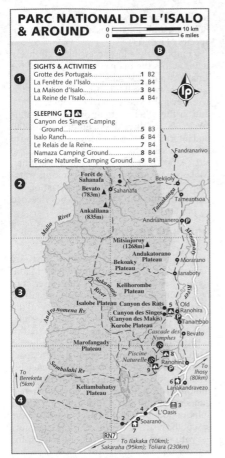

PARC NATIONAL DE L'ISALO & AROUND

0   10 km
0   6 miles

SIGHTS & ACTIVITIES
Grotte des Portugais.................1 B2
La Fenêtre de l'Isalo................2 B4
La Maison d'Isalo...................3 B4
La Reine de l'Isalo..................4 B4

SLEEPING
Canyon des Singes Camping
  Ground...........................5 B3
Isalo Ranch........................6 B4
Le Relais de la Reine...............7 B4
Namaza Camping Ground...........8 B4
Piscine Naturelle Camping Ground...9 B4

resembles a miniature, almost spherical baobab tree, and is often called 'elephant's foot'.

Unfortunately, fires are an ongoing problem and large swathes of l'Isalo are subject to intentional (illegal) and accidental burning. Poaching and hunting are also rampant, much to the detriment of the local ecology.

HIKING

There are several trails to follow in the park, all starting and finishing at Ranohira. A map of all the current routes is on display at Angap (p119) in Ranohira. On all of the hikes, carry plenty of water and a Steripen or purification tablets for streams and rivers. There's little shade on l'Isalo's wide plains, so bring a hat and sunscreen. You will need to be self-

sufficient with food which you can usually get in town. All distances quoted in this section are from Ranohira.

Piscine Naturelle is a gorgeous natural swimming pool, fed by a waterfall; see the boxed text, opposite. There's a well-kept camping ground (Ar5000 per person).

Other popular day hikes include **Canyon des Rats**, 9km one-way on foot (about two hours), or 16km by car and then 1km on foot. In **Canyon des Singes** (Canyon des Makis) you will have a good chance of seeing sifakas or ring-tailed lemurs leaping through the trees.

You can hike (or scramble) from the peaceful camping ground near the dried-up river **Namaza** through deep gorges full of thick vegetation to a high waterfall called **Cascade des Nymphes**. The gorges in this area are excellent for bird-watching, and there's a good chance of seeing ring-tailed lemurs. If camping at Namaza, try not to use too much firewood.

The **Grotte des Portugais** at the far northern end of the park is a cave about 30m long and 3m high, filled with animal droppings. The surrounding views are wonderful, and this part of the park sees far fewer visitors than the south. In the nearby **Forêt de Sahanafa** are natural water sources and four species of lemur, nocturnal and diurnal.

Trekking to the Grotte des Portugais is more of an expedition than visiting other park attractions, as there is no direct access from Ranohira over the massif. The trip begins with a 33km walk along the front range of l'Isalo to the villages of Tameantsoa and Bekijoly. From Bekijoly, a track heads 19km west to the cave. The return trip from Ranohira takes five days on foot.

Alternatively, if you have your own transport, you can drive to the village of Andriamanero, 20km north of Ranohira, from where it's a two- to three-day trek to Grotte des Portugais and back.

CAR CIRCUITS

If you prefer to explore l'Isalo by vehicle, Angap has a half-day car circuit starting near La Maison d'Isalo and ending up at the canyons, passing several of l'Isalo's most striking geological formations and offering the chance to see the traditional life of the cattle-raising Bara tribe who live on the park's borders. The guide fee for this circuit is Ar25,000 per car.

The rock formation known as the **La Reine de l'Isalo** (Queen of Isalo) lies 10km southwest of Ranohira. As you are heading south, look for the rock about 10m from the road on the left. The stone is said to resemble a seated queen, and appears to some people to move as they pass by.

La Fenêtre de l'Isalo is a natural rock 'window' that lies southwest of Ranohira about 4km from Soarano. It is covered with green and orange lichen, and affords vistas over the plain. It's best viewed from below in the afternoon sun.

SLEEPING

There are several camp sites in and near the park – including those near Canyon des Singes (Canyon des Makis), Piscine Naturelle and Namaza. They have varying facilities, but the best equipped, at Piscine Naturelle, has showers, toilets, sheltered dining tables and a big cooking area. Camping elsewhere in the park is possible if you are going on a longer trek, but you'll need to obtain permission from the Angap office.

If you don't want to camp, the hotels are for the most part located to the south of the park in the small town of Ranohira, which serves as a great base for visiting l'Isalo. Two of the top-end places listed in Ranohira are actually just outside l'Isalo's boundries and make great getaways if you're willing to splurge. See p119 for more info on Ranohira.

GETTING THERE & AWAY

The beginning of various hikes in the Parc National de l'Isalo can be reached from Ranohira on foot or in a vehicle.

Ilakaka

Several years ago, Ilakaka boomed from a tiny village to the epicenter of the sapphire trade. Today, tourist buses drive through with windows up while gem dealers swagger under the weight of briefcases handcuffed to their wrists and guns on their hips. Dealers in shiny suits mingle with soiled miners and blasé prostitutes on the dilapidated main street. On the outskirts of town, eagles fly over scoured earth left by the open sapphire mines. South of Ilakaka is a gigantic casino surrounded by dusty plains.

Ilakaka is also a major taxi-brousse hub, and you may end up waiting some time here; if you need to stay there are a few motels in the centre of town.

Parc National Zombitse-Vohibasia

The 36,852-hectare Parc National Zombitse-Vohibasia protects a variety of flora and fauna, including various species of sunbird, greenbul, *coua* and *vanga*. It is also home to eight species of lemur.

Zombitse, the most accessible section, extends across the main road northeast of the small town of Sakaraha, 75km from Ilakaka. There are two walking circuits in Zombitse, with several more under development here and in the other parts of the park. Permits (Ar15,000 for three days), guides (Ar20,000) and information can be obtained at the Angap offices in Sakaraha or Toliara. There's a camp site (Ar5000) at Zombitse, but no facilities. Make sure to bring all the drinking water you will need. It's 150km northeast of Toliara along the RN7. The area is best reached by private vehicle

NORTH OF TOLIARA
Ifaty

Ifaty is the collective name given to two dusty fishing villages – Ifaty/Mangily and Madio Rano – between which are strung a series of beach bungalow hotels. Ifaty is more visited than Anakao to the south of Toliara, and the beach is narrower and rockier, but the snorkelling is good. Diving, especially for sharks, is better here than further south. In July and August, you may see migrating whales pass nearby through the Mozambique Channel. Inland, a dry desert leads into sparsely scrubbed mountains with much of the terrain parched and several salt flats dousing the air with a sulphury odour. The Reniala Nature Reserve east of the beach is an otherworldly spiny forest with good bird-watching and a must for wandering through ancient baobabs.

There is nowhere in Ifaty to change money, and remember when choosing a hotel that the only sandy beaches are located to the north of Ifaty/Mangily.

ACTIVITIES

The 35m coral reef running offshore along the coastline offers decent diving. While some sections of the reef are dead or damaged, it attracts a wide variety of fish. Most notable are the various species of shark, which are best viewed near a break in the reef known as the Northern Pass. At both the full moon and the new moon, Ifaty experiences sharp tidal variations, so diving trips and other activities must be timed accordingly.

Dive prices are fairly standard, averaging about Ar120,000 for a *baptême* (first-time dive)

and Ar200,000 for a night dive; snorkelling costs around Ar35,000. Most places also offer multi-dive or lodging and diving packages. The main dive centres and water-sports operators are listed here; some are closed in May.

Bamboo Club (☎ 032 04 004 427; www.bamboo-club .com in French) The northern end of Mangily; offers PADI open-water certification courses, has all the water sports and does excursions to the baobab forest.

Lakana Vezo (☎ 032 04 858 60) Runs diver certification courses with a choice of various dive packages, plus windsurfing and deep-sea fishing.

Le Grand Bleu (☎ 032 02 621 38; hotelvovotelo@ simicro.mg) Located next door to Hôtel Vovo Telo, but not part of its setup. It's very highly recommended by readers and arranges standard diving packages and introduction dives for beginners. English-speaking.

SLEEPING & EATING

Many hotels in Ifaty have a booking and information office in Toliara. During the July to August high season, it's worth making reservations in advance.

Ifaty's hotels are spread out over several kilometres of beach and most are about 1km to 1.5km in from the road, so if you're arriving by taxi-brousse and want to shop around, plan on a lot of walking or negotiate for the driver to make stops. Here's a sampling of what's on offer.

Chez Alex (☎ 32 04 098 29; r from Ar14,000) Budget travellers should check out these inexpensive beachfront bungalows with shared bathrooms and a restaurant. It organises pirogue snorkelling trips.

La Voile Rouge (☎ 032 04 311 42; lavoilerouge@ wanadoo.mg; r with shared/private bathroom Ar35,000/60,000) A friendly budget beach hangout with lots of character and a nice restaurant and bar. Right on the beach, a lagoon sits nearby for swimming at low tide.

Hôtel Vovo Telo (☎ 032 02 621 48; hotelvovotelo@ simicro.mg; r Ar42,000, mains Ar15,000) This small but lively and friendly midrange hotel and restaurant, right in Mangily village, has hammocks, excellent French food, horse riding and diving next door. There's a booking office opposite the post office in Toliara.

Lakana Vezo (☎ 94 426 20; lakanavezo@wanadoo.mg; d incl breakfast Ar72,000) Book through the Motel le Capricorne (p117) in Toliara. Lakana Vezo features roomy and well-decorated bungalows with fans, access to a good beach, and a diving and water sports centre on site. Club Nautique, perhaps the best in Ifaty, can organise powerboat excursions to Anakao and Nosy Ve.

Bamboo Club (☎ 32 04 004 27; www.bamboo-club .com; r Ar81,000-150,000, mains Ar20,000) This place caters mostly to divers, but is well set up and comfortable, with bungalows on the beach, a small swimming pool, plus a dive school on site. The booking office is in the Bamboo Shop (bamboo.club@moov.mg) in Toliara. There's an excellent terrace restaurant serving Indian Ocean specialties for an après-dive meal.

Nautilus (☎ 94 418 74; nautilus@wanadoo.mg; r Ar140,000-245,000; ▨) An upmarket hotel with a dive centre and ultramodern rooms shaped like nautilus shells plus a great seafood restaurant all within spitting distance of the beach.

our pick **Hôtel Le Paradisier** (☎ 94 429 14; www .paradisier.com in French; r Ar170,000, set dinner Ar30,000) Entering the luxurious Paradisier, you can't miss the ceiling hole hovering above a tropical mini-jungle lobby that opens into a sea-facing courtyard and dining room. Looking seaward from the stone path, it's hard to determine where the shimmering infinity pool ends and the ocean begins. The rooms here are in two-storey loft-style chalets with a raised third chamber on top. Airy, chic interiors with modern bathrooms, natural hardwood

---

DETOUR: RENIALA NATURE RESERVE

Feathered-friend lovers won't want to miss a visit to **Reniala Nature Reserve** (☎ 94 417 56; admission Ar8500; camp sites Ar6000, bungalows Ar11,000; ☷ 8am-6pm summer, 8am-5pm winter), a birder's paradise 500m north of Mangily with hundreds of species calling it home. Experience an otherworldly landscape of barbed plants and rare species that have adapted enough to thrive in the reserve's harsh natural environment. Close to the sea, in a thorny forest of baobab trees and succulents, Reniala is small at just 45 hectares, but it has a floristic and faunistic wealth that includes more than one thousand species. It is also a good habitat to view Madagascar's tortoises and different reptile species. The reserve is just 27km from Toliara; look for it at the end of Mangily village. To really experience the stillness, and wildness, of this dehydrated habitat, spend the night. There are simple bungalows and also camping sites.

accents and a 180-degree view of sunny beach-front from the front door or balcony make this our favourite. See turquoise water rising out of a deeper blue, eventually encroaching onto the sandy beach as you dine in the mod-ish glass-front restaurant. Water sports and whale-watching (in season) are also on offer. It's a good place to unwind and enjoy five-star organisation, beach and surf activities, and unexpected comfort in a windswept desert of barbed flora.

GETTING THERE & AWAY

Ifaty village lies 22km north of Toliara along a sandy pot-holed road. Several taxis-brousses leave daily from the northern taxi-brousse sta-tion in Toliara, usually between 6am and early afternoon; the trip costs Ar19,000 and takes one to two hours. You can get out at Ifaty, Mangily or Madio Rano villages, or along the road in between, although many of the hotels are around 1km from the road – just tell the driver where you'd like to be dropped. Trans-fers provided by the hotels for their clients cost around Ar27,000 per person, while taxis in Toliara charge around Ar60,000.

Travel to Andavadoaka and points north can also be done by boat (see below).

Andavadoaka

The tiny beachside village of Andavadoaka is fast becoming popular with tourists who come for the pristine beaches, schools of many fish species and relative remoteness. Andava-doaka lies about two-thirds of the way along the coast between Ifaty and Morombe. A reef runs offshore and excellent diving is possible. The area's main attraction is its quiet beaches, plentiful marine life and laid-back pace.

Coco Beach (☎ 22 427 01; bungalows Ar13,000, mains Ar7000) has traditional, brightly painted bun-galows and basic but inexpensive meals. Book through Hôtel Baobab (right).

Laguna Blu Resort (www.lagunabluresort.com in Ital-ian; r Ar265,000) is an upmarket Italian package-tour resort with an on-site dive centre; it does excursions into the surrounding area.

Access is possible via boat from both Ifaty and Morombe. From Ifaty, allow about five hours with a speedboat run by a tour operator, or several days via local pirogue (Ar100,000). Boat access is sometimes restricted during the rainy months of January and February.

There is no regular taxi-brousse service from either Morombe or Ifaty. If driving with

your own vehicle, inquire first about road conditions. Coco Beach is run by the same people as Hôtel Baobab (below), and often it's possible to hitch a lift with a supply vehicle running between the two.

Morombe

Morombe (Vast Beach) is a spread-out seaside fishing village about halfway between Toliara and Morondava. As road access is very dif-ficult, it is seldom visited by tourists, and it's less appealing as a destination than the villages to the north and south of it, but it makes a useful stop if you're driving.

The best hotel in town is probably **Hôtel Baobab** (☎ 22 427 01; r Ar28,000; 🐞), which is south of town and has concrete sea-view bungalows – plus staff can help arrange ex-cursions in the area.

For inexpensive lodging try the basic **Hôtel Croix du Sud** (r Ar8000) which is comfortable, with hot water. Hôtel Croix du Sud and Hôtel Baobab both have good restaurants.

Air Madagascar flights link Morombe a few times weekly with Morondava (Ar135,000) and Toliara (Ar150,000).

By land, Morombe lies about 285km north of Toliara along a rough and sandy road. There are usually several vehicles weekly direct to Morombe from both Toliara (Ar25,000) and Morondava (Ar35,000); allow about 18 hours from Toliara and 12 hours from Morondava. You can also try to find a pirogue to take you from either Ifaty or Morondava (Ar150,000), a journey of several days for which you'll need all your own food and water.

SOUTH OF TOLIARA

Along the shoreline south of Toliara a string of rather unspoilt Vezo fishing villages, inter-spersed with some of the most pristine white beaches in Madagascar, offers less touristy resorts than those to the north, even if they're a little harder to get to. Anakao, Nosy Ve and, further south, Beheloka and Itampolo are the area's main attractions. The tide doesn't go out as far in the southern beaches, making swimming possible for most of the day.

If you're just heading to the southern beaches such as Anakao or Beheloka for a few days, your best bet is to take a boat transfer from Toliara (Ar65,000).

To travel by road through the spectacu-larly arid landscapes between Toliara and Fort Dauphin you will need either a good 4WD vehicle or the willingness to put comfort (and any sightseeing) aside and spend two to three days squashed into the back of a lorry. There are two routes: most travellers and all public transport follow the inland RN10 via Betioky and Ampanihy. Simple accommodation is available in both places.

During the dry season between May and late October it is possible, and often faster, to take the coastal route via Beheloka, Itampolo and Saodona. You will need your own 4WD for this as there is no regular taxi-brousse traffic, and you'll have to ford at least two rivers (which is impossible in the rainy season).

If you are travelling to Fort Dauphin by *camion-brousse*, a few things are worth noting. Firstly, the vehicles that pass the towns en route are often full, so if you're planning on doing the journey in stages, you could spend a lot of time waiting for a seat. Secondly, there's nowhere along the way to pick up provisions, so stock up on some basics in either Toliara or Fort Dauphin. If you will be riding in the back of the truck, bring along a scarf and pullover for the dust by day and the cool wind by night.

Arboretum d'Antsokay

This interesting private garden, also known as **Auberge de la Table** (☎ 032 02 600 15; admission incl tour Ar8500, r Ar16,000, mains Ar10,000; ◷ 7am-8.30pm), was established by a Swiss botanist and has close to 900 species of plants, with 90% endemic to the region. It's a must if you're interested in the flora of southern Madagascar. An English-speaking guide is included in the price. Simple bungalows are available if you want to stay the night, and the restaurant specialises in goat's cheese.

The arboretum lies about 12km southeast of Toliara, just a few hundred metres from the main road. To get here, catch any bus or taxi-brousse from the centre of Toliara heading towards Befety and ask to be dropped off, or charter a taxi. You can also walk from the junction to St Augustin (2km).

St Augustin

An intrepid group of English puritans arrived in the bay at St Augustin in March 1645, eager to start a new colony like the one in Virginia and spurred onwards by reports of the fertility of the soil and the benevolence of the locals. Sadly for the puritans, the soil proved unfruitful and the locals weren't as benign as

reported – they had begun to equate foreigners with slavery. Disease and starvation took a heavy toll, and only 12 of the 140 settlers ever returned to England. Baie St Augustin was left to become a haunt of pirates.

Today, St Augustin, with its little white church spire contrasting against the cliffs behind it, still has a lost, end-of-the-world feel. There's a lagoon for swimming, and several good hikes are possible from the village; 4km to the north are the **Grottes de Sarondrano**, two caves filled with fresh, translucent blue water. Nearby are several springs and a natural swimming pool – ask in the village for someone to show you the way and instruct you as to local *fady*.

About 5km from the main road and easily accessible by public transport is **Hotel Melody Beach** (☎ 032 02 167 57; moukar@wanadoo.mg; r Ar28,000), which has bungalows overlooking the beach and is a good place to stay if you plan on heading to Baie St Augustin or Anakao.

In St Augustin village proper, try **Longo Mamy** (☎ 032 04 344 64; r A12,000) which has simple but comfortable bungalows facing the bay. Meals can be arranged and feature Malagasy dishes. Inquire at Longo Mamy about excursions to the rivers, springs and caves around the village.

About 10km from Toliara on the way to St Augustin is **La Mangrove** (☎ 94 415 27; www.chez alain.net; r from Ar25,000, meals Ar9000), run by Chez Alain (p117). There's no beach, but the jetty is a relaxing spot for sunset drinks. Camping is possible and there are some good walks in the area – you can spot lemurs in a nearby cave. You can also organise boat trips to Nosy Ve and Anakao here (Ar10,000 each way).

St Augustin lies about 35km south of Toliara along a good road; the two towns are connected Monday to Saturday by taxi-brousse (Ar6000). Boat transfers (Ar45,000, two hours) can be arranged from Toliara.

Anakao & Nosy Ve

The petite but pleasantly bustling Vezo fishing villages of Anakao A and Anakao B are blessed with an entrancing semi-circle of white-sand beach, a slice of turquoise water and a fringe of emerald-green vegetation. An assortment of guesthouses on either side of the villages are perfect for recuperating from a tough journey, doing a bit of diving or admiring the hundreds of brightly painted pirogues rocked gently by breaking waves. Very serious divers, however, consider the diving slightly better at Ifaty to the north, especially for seeing sharks.

Most of Anakao's dive sites are around the nearby island of Nosy Ve, a former haunt of pirates. Today, it is visited mainly by those interested in exploring the offshore reef and by fishermen from Anakao. There's a Marine Reserve fee (Ar2000) to visit the island. Offshore about 7km south of Anakao is the island of **Nosy Satrana**, which offers some excellent additional dive sites.

In between the second Anakao village and **La Reserve** is a headland with a big **Vezo cemetery**. Aepyornis eggshell fragments can be seen on the dunes around here. Should you find any, remember it's illegal to collect them.

There is nowhere to change money in Anakao, so be sure you have cash – either ariary or euros. At the time of research, the lack of fresh water was a major problem in Anakao and only Le Prince Anakao had running water, which was not always reliable.

TOURS
The tour companies listed on p117 offer trips to Anakao, starting from about Ar50,000 per person. For diving, boat transfers or whale watching, try **Safari Vezo** (☎ 94 413 81; safarivezo@netclub.mg; Ave de France) in Toliara.

SLEEPING & EATING
Anakao villages and the surrounding beaches have several very relaxed and well-run beach hotels, some of which have booking offices in Toliara.

Chez Emile (☎ 032 04 023 76; r Ar16,000, mains Ar10,000) Right behind the village, Chez Emile's economical and basic rooms are breezy and quiet, and quite a long way inland among the dunes. The beach restaurant, with a view of the fishing boats, is the best place to eat traditionally prepared seafood and hang with locals at the friendly bar. Rooms are clean, with bucket showers and outside long-drop toilets; some have electricity.

Longo Vezo (☎ 94 437 64; longovezo@simicro.mg; r from Ar27,000, transfers Ar40,000) The well-appointed bungalows here are discreetly hidden among the sand dunes, with bucket showers, verandas and solar-powered electricity. Guests dine together in the evenings, so there's a relaxed and outgoing atmosphere. There's also a dive centre on site, with CMAS certified instruction. Dives cost Ar120,000, while certification courses cost around Ar800,000. Snorkelling, surfing, whale-watching or 4WD day trips can also be organised. It's peaceful, unpretentious

and definitely one of the best options in Anakao. Book through the office at the pirogue port in Toliara.

Safari Vezo (☎ 94 413 81; safarivezo@netclub.mg; d with shared/private bathroom A34,000/61,000, set menu Ar25,000) Nearer to the village, this long-established place is more gregarious and lively than the hotels to the north. The bungalows are strung out for miles along the beach, with terraces and bucket showers. The restaurant has a maritime theme, draped in fishing nets with gingham tablecloths, and a menu that specialises in seafood. Diving can be organised here, too.

Hotel La Reserve (☎ 032 02 141 55; quad@dts.mg; r Ar37,000, mains 9000) Endeavour the 45-minute walk or quick pirogue ride to reach this gem just around the headland from Anakao and you'll be rewarded. The sand here stretches uninterrupted and uninhabited for miles. La Reserve occupies a prime location, and is comfortable, well run and friendly. Guests dine together with the French proprietors in the evenings. The clean and updated wooden bungalows are perched on stilts, with solar power and stunning views. This is the beach, and the hotel, to go for surfing in the area. The staff can also organise 4WD trips along the coast, whale-watching tours and fishing tours.

Le Prince Anakao (☎ 94 439 57; anakao@simicro.mg; r from Ar72,000) This hotel has more of a resort feel than its two neighbours. Bungalows here are very comfy with modern bathrooms, but do not have hot water or mosquito nets. Cheaper rooms are available in the second row back from the beach. The hotel has an office at the pirogue port in Toliara. It's about a 15-minute walk from here to the village of Anakao.

GETTING THERE & AWAY
Anakao lies about 22km south of St Augustin. Safari Vezo and **Compagnie du Sud** (☎ 94 437 21; www.compagniedusud.com in French) offer transfers via motorboat from Toliara for about Ar50,000 per person – one way. If you are booking a hotel in advance, most provide transfers for around the same price, which may include a mixture of road and sea travel. Alternatively, ask around at the pirogue port in Toliara for local transport, or get the taxi-brousse to St Augustin and try to find a pirogue from there (Ar45,000).

Beheloka
This modest fishing village makes a convenient and relaxing stop if you are following the coastal route south from Toliara. For

information and bookings check with Chez Alain (p117) in Toliara. **Chez Bernard/La Canne à Sucre** (☎ 94 437 21; compagniedusud@yahoo.fr; camping/d Ar9000/44,000, set dinner Ar7500) provides simple but decent bungalows.

The main Angap office is in Toliara (p119) but there is a smaller branch here – really just a little building a few kilometers before the park's entrance – where you can also purchase tickets and arrange guides.

Taxis-brousses go to Beheloka from Toliara on Thursday (Ar22,000, 12 hours). With your own vehicle, head southeast from Toliara along the RN7 for 70km to Andranovory, then turn south on to the RN10 towards Betioky and Ambatry. About 8km south of Ambatry, turn right onto a track heading west about 75km to Beheloka. Allow up to 12 hours from Toliara. **Compagnie du Sud** (☎ 94 437 21; www.compagniedusud .com in French) offers boat transfers from Toliara to Beheloka for Ar50,000/80,000 one way/return per person provided there are enough passengers. Boats leave at 7am and 3pm daily.

Parc National de Tsimanampetsotsa

The centrepiece of this 43,200-hectare park is the large, shallow **Lac Tsimanampetsotsa** and the sacred **Grotte de Mitoho** on the northeastern rim. The waters of the Mitoho cave are eerily opaque and pale, inhabited only by a species of blind white fish. The park supports more than 70 bird species, including thousands of pink flamingos, and a healthy population of ring-tailed lemurs as well as the park's symbol, the Grandidier's mongoose. There's a Ar10,000 permit fee to visit the park.

There are two camping grounds in the reserve but you will need to be completely self-sufficient with food and water. Angap in Toliara (p119) or Beheloka can provide guides and hire camping equipment. Several hotels in Anakao arrange day trips to the park by 4WD.

The northern part of the lake begins 7km inland from the coast and about 10km southeast of Beheloka. There is a very rough track from Beheloka to the lake and cave. It's also possible to reach the lake by hiring a pirogue or boat down the coast from Anakao to the village of Etoetse, and then hiking inland.

Réserve Spéciale de Beza-Mahafaly

This remote reserve consists of two particular types of forest, spiny and riverine forest, situated 3km apart. During the dry season, the rivers are just a trickle, but when it rains they can flood and submerge the entire area. Lemur species found at the reserve include ring-tailed, fat-tailed dwarf, mouse and sportive lemurs, all of which are very easily viewed. Other prevalent mammals are the rare large-eared tenrec, the fossa (Madagascar's largest carnivore) plus Verreaux's sifakas. For information regarding the reserve, visit the Angap office in Toliara (p119).

Accommodation is available in Betioky, the nearest major town to the reserve. For camping, you'll need to be self-sufficient with food. To get to Beza-Mahafaly without your own transport, you need to get to Betioky (easy by taxis-brousse from Toliara) and then walk or take a zebu cart the 17km to the reserve.

Itampolo

Itampolo is a lobster fishing village 95km south of Beheloka, an additional stop on the hard 4WD trip towards Fort Dauphin or a boat ride south from Anakao. Another Chez Alain enterprise, **Gite d' Etape Sud-Sud** (☎ 94 415 27; c.alain@wanadoo.mg; camping Ar10,000, r from Ar25,000, set dinner Ar18,000) has accommodation overlooking the bay and a nice restaurant.

Taxis-brousses (Ar30,000, 15 hours) go from Toliara to Itampolo on Thursday and return on Saturday. It's also possible to reach Itampolo from Beheloka on the sand road along the coast (about 100km); allow at least two hours by 4WD.

To continue south from Itampolo along the coastal road, travel about 45km along a rough track to the Linta River, which you will need to drive through (only possible during the dry season). From Saodona, on the river's eastern bank, there is an arduous roadway for about 85km to the northeast, where you join the RN10 at Ampanihy. Allow almost a full day for the stretch from Saodona to Ampanihy, and check the state of the road and river levels before setting out.

Ampanihy

Ampanihy (place of bats) is famed for its mohair carpets, has a few amenities and is a good place to break the journey between Toliara and Fort Dauphin. Nearby are imposing stands of spiny forest and several walking trails, as well as numerous Mahafaly burial sites. For walks, it's best to go with a guide; ask at your hotel.

About 20km northwest of Ampanihy, near the village of Reakaly, is a gigantic **baobab**, considered to be one of the largest and oldest still standing. There are not many taxis in town, but it is fairly easy to hitch a lift out to the tree.

Hôtel Angora (d Ar19,000) is the most comfortable place to stay the night, with decent rooms, camping possibilities in the garden and a restaurant.

Ampanihy lies about 285km from Toliara and 225km from Ambovombe. Most days there is a direct vehicle from Ampanihy to Toliara. There is also frequent transport between Ampanihy and Betioky. Vehicles from Toliara to Fort Dauphin are often full when they pass through Ampanihy, so heading east you may need to wait a day or two for a vacant seat.

The road is particularly bad between Ampanihy and Tranoroa to the east; the 40km trip can take over three hours. If you have your own vehicle, it's often faster to turn northeast at Tranoroa towards Bekitro, from where there is a track heading southeast to Antanimora on the RN13 (which rejoins the RN10 at Ambovombe).

FORT DAUPHIN (TAOLAGNARO)
pop 42,944

Fort Dauphin (its rarely used Malagasy name is Taolagnaro) was just starting to become a popular stop on the tourist trail; then a group of rich foreign companies decided to extract titanium from the soil outside town, and ruined it all. Sure, Fort Dauphin had always been remote and windy and often looked as if it had been hit by a grenade (or more likely a cyclone), with craters in the streets, decaying buildings and too much flying dust. But the city also was blessed with good surfing and a gorgeous location along a curved sandy bay dotted with half-sunk shipwrecks.

All that changed when a couple of South African and Canadian companies had the grand idea to mine titanium. Not only is the mining destroying the fragile bay, it's also wreaking havoc on the tourist industry. The huge influx of foreign workers needing a place to sleep means nearly all of Fort Dauphin's hotels are fully booked for an entire year straight. Don't arrive without a reservation or you will be sleeping on the street.

If you can get out of town, however, and are looking for tough travel in beautiful surroundings, then it may be worth stopping off here. A number of excellent ecotourism projects make it relatively easy to get off the mining track and enjoy the lush, semi-tropical landscapes, stands of spiny forest and wild beaches of this corner of Madagascar.

Fort Dauphin was one of the original French territories in Madagascar. In 1643 the Société Française de l'Orient founded a settlement on a peninsula 35km to the south of the present-day town. The colonists constructed Fort Flacourt and named the surrounding settlement Fort Dauphin, after the six-year-old prince who was to become Louis XIV. The colony survived until 1674 when, facing war with the local inhabitants and constant attacks of disease, it was abandoned. Some years later, the French returned in the form of slave traders who used Fort Dauphin as a port. At the end of the 19th century it was incorporated into the united French colony of Madagascar.

TOMB ART

The Mahafaly and Antandroy people of southern Madagascar are renowned for their intricate tomb art, the most colourful and skilfully decorated on the island. Tombs, which are constructed by the community, can take up to a year to complete. The huge monoliths, some of which can be 15 sq m, are painted with scenes from the life of the deceased, and frequently adorned by *aloalo* – wooden posts carved with curved geometric figures. These can be family scenes or events from daily life, such as games, transport, work or sex. Carving *aloalo* has become an art form in itself, and representations of *aloalo* can be found all over Madagascar.

Each stage in a tomb's construction is marked by ceremonies and the sacrifice of zebu, and the finished tombs are also adorned with zebu skulls, corresponding to the number of cattle sacrificed upon that person's death. Very important figures in Mahafaly or Antandroy society may merit as many as 100 bovine victims, but the majority of the tombs are adorned with 10 or fewer. Sadly, many of the tombs in southern Madagascar have been desecrated and robbed in the past, and are now off-limits to visitors, but some are still visible by the side of the road as you drive around the region. Remember not to point at the tomb with your finger – it's a sign of disrespect to the deceased.

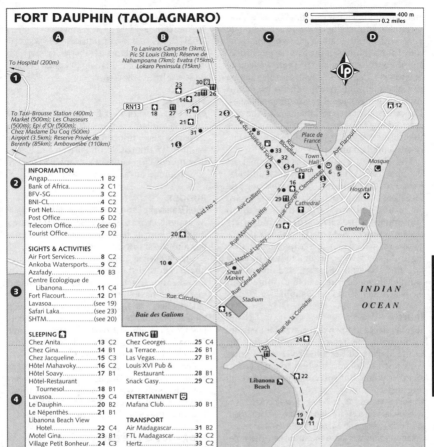

FORT DAUPHIN (TAOLAGNARO)

INFORMATION
Angap...................1 B2
Bank of Africa.............2 C1
BFV-SG....................3 C2
BNI-CL....................4 C2
Fort Net..................5 D2
Post Office...............6 D2
Telecom Office.........(see 6)
Tourist Office............7 D2

SIGHTS & ACTIVITIES
Air Fort Services.........8 C2
Ankoba Watersports.......9 C2
Azafady..................10 B3
Centre Ecologique de
  Libanona...............11 C4
Fort Flacourt............12 D1
Lavasoa...............(see 19)
Safari Laka...........(see 23)
SHTM..................(see 20)

SLEEPING
Chez Anita...............13 C2
Chez Gina................14 B1
Chez Jacqueline..........15 C3
Hôtel Mahavoky...........16 C2
Hôtel Soavy..............17 B1
Hôtel-Restaurant
  Tournesol..............18 B1
Lavasoa..................19 C4
Le Dauphin...............20 B2
Le Népenthès.............21 B1
Libanona Beach View
  Hotel..................22 C4
Motel Gina...............23 B1
Village Petit Bonheur....24 C3

EATING
Chez Georges.............25 C4
La Terrace...............26 B1
Las Vegas................27 B1
Louis XVI Pub &
  Restaurant.............28 B1
Snack Gasy...............29 C2

ENTERTAINMENT
Mafana Club..............30 B1

TRANSPORT
Air Madagascar...........31 B2
FTL Madagascar...........32 C2
Hertz....................33 C2

Fort Dauphin enjoys one of the sunniest and least humid climates on the east coast, although winds can be strong at any time of year, particularly between September and December. June and July tend to be rainy, with the short dry season beginning around August or September.

Information
Angap office (☎ 92 212 68) Up a hill about 1km west of Ave du Maréchal Foch; has information about Parc National d'Andohahela and other areas of interest. The WWF office is also here.
Bank of Africa (BOA; Ave du Maréchal Foch) Changes cash and travellers cheques, and gives advances on MasterCard.
BFV-SG (Ave du Maréchal Foch) Changes cash and travellers cheques, and gives advances on Visa cards.

BNI-CL (Ave Flacourt) Changes cash and travellers cheques.
Fort Net (per min Ar50; ☼ Mon-Sat 8-7pm) Internet café around the corner from the post office, with a reliable connection.
Post Office (Ave Flacourt)
Telecom (Ave Flacourt) The area code for Fort Dauphin is 92.
Tourist Office (☎ 032 02 846 34; www.fort-dauphin.com; Rue Realy Abel) Tons of information about the region, including a list of tour operators and excursions. Helpful tourism maps illustrate all the main attractions in the area.

Sights & Activities
On Fort Dauphin's northeastern tip is **Fort Flacourt** (admission Ar5000; ☼ 8-11am & 2-5pm Mon-Sat, 2-6pm Sun), built by the French in 1643. Today,

little remains but a few cannons. To see what is left, and to admire the view, you can negotiate a 'fee' with a soldier at the gate who will show you around. Photos of the fort are permitted, but not of the barracks. The **Centre Ecologique de Libanona** (☎ 92 217 54; www.andrewleestrust.org .uk) was established to help educate locals and visiting scientists about environmental issues. The centre is located in Libanona on the cliff overlooking Libanona beach, and makes for an informative visit if you're interested in environmentalism and speak French.

The cleanest and prettiest beach in Fort Dauphin itself is at **Libanona**, on the southwestern side of the peninsula. The beach along **Baie des Galions** to the north of Libanona is the place for surfing and windsurfing (late August to May only). To hire surfboards or windsurfers call in to **Ankoba Watersports** (☎ 92 215 15; www .ankoba.com), which can also help organise diving and fishing trips. From late June or early July until about mid-September, dolphins and humpback whales are visible offshore from the beaches around Fort Dauphin.

Tours

Several places in town that can organise tours throughout the region, including to Cap Sainte Marie and Réserve Privée de Berenty. For most excursions, it's best to get a group together yourself if you are interested in cutting costs.

Air Fort Services (☎ 92 212 24; www.airfortservices .com; Ave du Maréchal Foch) This company, which also has an office in Toliara, rents a variety of vehicles, arranges a variety of excursions in the southeast, and runs Réserve de Nahampoana (p134).

Azafady (☎ 92 212 65; www.madagascar.co.uk) Azafady isn't a tour operator, but a volunteer organisation working on community tourism projects around Fort Dauphin. It runs several well-equipped camping grounds in village, beach and forest sites in the region and can provide transport, camping equipment and guides to independent travellers who want to experience local life and nature while helping village communities. If you're interested in staying longer in Madagascar, ask the staff about volunteering opportunities.

Lavasoa (☎ 92 21 175; lavasoa.free.fr in French) This quality operator located at the Lavasoa hotel in Libanona offers trips to little-known spots throughout the region. Boat and 4WD rental can also be arranged. It has a camp site on the Lokaro Peninsula and offers boat transfers there for Ar105,000 per person.

Safari Laka (☎ 92 212 66; www.safarilaka.com) A reliable outfit based at Motel Gina with a variety of excursions

to the surrounding area, including a good day trip to the rainforest at Enato and the Lokaro Peninsula.

SHTM (☎ 92 212 38; www.fortdauphinhotel-link.com) An upmarket company based at Le Dauphin, catering mainly to package tours. SHTM is the only option for visiting Réserve Privée de Berenty.

Sleeping

Now that most of Fort Dauphin's remaining hotels (a tourism crisis in 2002 forced many to close and never re-open) are booked solid for months at a time by South African and Canadian mining companies, it's essential to reserve your room in advance if you want to stay.

BUDGET

Hôtel Mahavoky (☎ 032 07 990 79; Ave du Maréchal Foch; r with shared bathroom Ar18,000-20,000) This renovated budget favourite has panoramic views of the bay and the shipwrecks dotting the coast.

Chez Jacqueline (☎ 92 217 68; r Ar19,000) Jacqueline has cute little bungalows and is handy for Libanona beach. The rooms are small and breezy and have hot water.

Motel Gina (☎ 92 212 66; motelgina2005@yahoo.fr; bungalows Ar24,000-77,000) Airy wooden slatted cottages, each sleeping three to four people, have full bathtubs, stone inner walls and thatched roofs, and are set in a verdant garden.

Chez Anita (☎ 92 213 22; anita@fort-dauphin.com; bungalows Ar25,000-38,000) Rather worse for wear, but still comfy, A-frame bungalows arranged around a quiet garden. Chez Anita is on a small lane near the cathedral and has a restaurant.

MIDRANGE & TOP END

Hôtel-Restaurant Tournesol (☎ 92 216 71; r from Ar31,000) Very clean, bright and good-value bungalows sitting behind an attractive restaurant plus wonderful views of Pic St Louis.

Le Népenthès (☎ 92 210 61; nepenthes@fort-dauphin.com; off Ave du Maréchal Foch; r Ar37,000-56,000) The chalet-style cottages with wooden roofs are clean, have hot water and are situated on spacious grounds. You can arrange transport and guides to Lokaro/Evatra through reception.

Hôtel Soavy (☎ 92 213 59; www.soavy.com; r Ar38,000-75,000) The best rooms here are airy, decked out in bright colours and have TV, hot water and mosquito nets. Smaller rooms are simpler, but just as clean and bright. There are more basic rooms without hot water for Ar24,000.

Village Petit Bonheur (☎ 92 212 60; villagepetitbon heur@fortnet.net; r Ar61,000; mains Ar8500) Knowledgeable management, stunning sea views and spacious, tiled rooms with balconies make this another superb option near Libanona beach. The owner rents out 4WD vehicles, not including driver and petrol.

Lavasoa (☎ 92 211 75; www.lavasoa.com in French; r/bungalow Ar95,000/122,000) Overlooking Libanona beach, this friendly guesthouse has delightfully planned bungalows in a superb location on the edge of a cliff. All are wooden-floored and gaily painted, with awesome views; some rooms have a mezzanine level. The hotel runs a tour company and also Pirate Camp (p135) on the Lokaro Peninsula. Book in advance as this place is very popular. There's a small canteen on site which serves breakfast.

Libanona Beach View Hotel (☎ 033 12 510 46; libanonabeachview@fortnet.net; ste incl breakfast Ar96,000) This slick upmarket hotel with self-catering facilities is the new kid on the block, but aims to make an attractive impression on visitors to Fort Dauphin. The views of Libanona beach and Pic St Louis in the distance are amazing and the English-speaking staff very helpful in deciding what activity to pursue.

Le Dauphin (☎ 92 212 38, 033 11 300 28; r Ar165,000-260,000) Traditionally the most upmarket hotel in Fort Dauphin, this is the flagship of the de Heaulme hotel empire and the headquarters of SHTM tours, who book tours to Réserve Privée de Berenty. It's clean, bright and comfortable rather than mega-luxurious.

Eating

Les Chasseurs (mains Ar5000-12,000; ☯ lunch & dinner) Near the taxi-brousse station, this friendly neighbourhood institution has seafood, grills, pasta and pizzas.

La Terrace (mains Ar7000-22,000; ☯ lunch & dinner) With great views of Baie Dauphine (Shipwreck Bay), this classy outdoor restaurant/café has excellent meals with views second to none. It has a fully stocked bar catering to your cocktail whims while you stare at the sunset silhouette on the bay.

Chez Georges (Le Local; ☎ 033 12 515 14; mains Ar8500-11,000; ☯ breakfast, lunch & dinner) This popular local eatery enjoys a laid-back surf atmosphere in a hut overlooking Libanona beach. Catch-of-the-day fish and dressed crab are recurrent specialities. Good things really do come to those who wait. As popular as it is, we suggest getting there early, ordering, then going for a swim while it's prepared.

Louis XIV Pub & Restaurant (☎ 033 142 8421; mains Ar11,000; ☯ lunch & dinner) This cheerful establishment serves up standard pub grub plus a few specialties on an al fresco patio and is a fun place to meet other travellers or just chill out and listen to live music in the evenings.

Las Vegas (mains Ar13,000; ☯ breakfast, lunch & dinner) A popular local place with Malagasy dishes, seafood and pizzas early in the evenings, and traditional music and dancing later on.

Several of the hotels in town also have respectable restaurants, including Chez Néné at Motel Gina, Chez Anita and Village Petit Bonheur, which specialises in Malagasy dishes.

There are a few cheap *hotelys* near the taxi-brousse station and around the market. **Chez Madame du Coq** and **Epi d'Or** are two of the better ones, serving pastries, salads and genuine espresso alongside the usual sundries. **Snack Gasy**, near the cathedral, is a vegetarian-friendly, authentic Malagasy canteen that's perfect for a cheap meal and a cold THB.

Entertainment

For a bit of decadent nightlife, try the disco at **Mafana Club** (men Ar10,000, women free; ☯ 5pm-4am Wed-Sun). Get your party on at Fort Dauphin's recently pimped-out nightclub that's fast becoming known as the place to get your swerve on. You'll shake to a mix of Malagasy and Western music, especially on busier Friday and Saturday nights. The interior décor is swanky and the deck looks out over Baie Dauphine. Las Vegas features regular Malagasy music and reggae shows.

Getting There & Away

AIR

Air Madagascar flies daily between Fort Dauphin and Antananarivo (Ar565,000, two hours), and several times weekly between Fort Dauphin and Toliara (Ar486,000, one hour). Smaller twin-engine otter planes also sometimes fly up the east coast from Fort Dauphin to Farafangana, Manakara and Mananjary; all flights to these destinations cost Ar325,000. Bear in mind that flights are often full to any destination in this region, so booking ahead is certainly advised.

Air Madagascar (☎ 92 211 22) is just off Ave du Maréchal Foch, on a hill up from the Bank of Africa.

CAR

Cars are available for hire to do the trip to Toliara at Village Petit Bonheur, near Libanona beach, which has 4WD vehicles for around

Ar150,000 (plus petrol) for the total trip. Drivers are Ar28,000 extra.

TAXI-BROUSSE

Fort Dauphin's taxi-brousse station is in Tanambao, in the northwestern part of town along the road leading to the airport. Roads from Fort Dauphin are rough in all directions, except for the short sealed stretch to Ambovombe (Ar2000, two hours).

Taxis-brousse travel from Fort Dauphin to Toliara (Ar30,000, two days) daily. This is a very rough trip, so it's best to break up the journey and spend some time exploring the various towns and nature reserves along the way. Taxis-brousse stop at Amboasary (Ar10,000 two hours), Ampanihy (Ar20,000, one day) and Betioky (Ar40,000, two days).

To Ihosy (Ar30,000, 36 hours), Fianarantsoa (Ar45,000, about 60 hours, dry season only) and Antananarivo (Ar50,000, three days), the route goes via Ambovombe and then north along the RN13. Heading towards Ihosy and Fianarantsoa, it's not feasible to break the trip until Ihosy, as it is difficult to get onward transport from the smaller villages along the way. The roads are appalling and facilities almost nonexistent, so this isn't a trip for the faint-hearted.

Getting Around

The airport is 4km west of town. Taxis to/from the centre cost around Ar10,000 per person.

You'll need a 4WD to visit most attractions around Fort Dauphin. Rentals cost between Ar125,000 and Ar175,000 (depending on your bartering skills and demand). The rate includes a driver and unlimited kilometres, but you'll usually have to pay for petrol yourself. Make sure to ask whether petrol is included when negotiating, and if it is not, try for a lower daily rate. It is usually possible. Places that rent 4WDs include Air Fort Services and Lavasoa hotel.

Next to the Jovenna petrol station near the town centre you'll find a branch of **Hertz** (☎ 032 05 416 75). The company rents cars for Ar155,000 per day plus fuel and an extra Ar15,000 for a driver.

FTL Madagascar (☎ 92 213 26; www.ftl.mu) is across from the BFV-SG bank and rents bicycles starting at Ar15,000 per day along with motorcycles starting from Ar105,000 per day.

Taxis within town, including to the taxi-brousse station, cost Ar1800 per person.

AROUND FORT DAUPHIN

The tour operators listed on p132 can arrange trips to the following places and other places close to Fort Dauphin. You can organise trips yourself by taxi-brousse to destinations along the sealed Fort Dauphin–Ambovombe road. Elsewhere, the roads are sandy and/or muddy and public transport is infrequent, so hiking, pirogues or a tour may be your only options.

Pic St Louis

The summit of the Pic St Louis (529m), which you can see around 3km north of Fort Dauphin, offers good views of the town and coast including as far as Baie Sainte Luce. From the base, allow 1½ to three hours for the ascent and 1½ hours for the descent. A dawn climb is ideal, before the going gets too hot or windy. You'll need a guide to show you the way – ask in town or contact one of the tour agencies (p132).

Réserve de Nahampoana

This small **forest reserve** (admission incl guide Ar34,000; ☾ sunrise-sunset) offers a short walking circuit to see lemurs, tortoises, crocodiles, birds and a variety of plants endemic to southern Madagascar. It's a good place to visit if you want to see (and stroke) tame lemurs and don't have the time or the money to visit the Reserve Privée de Berenty.

Nahampoana also makes a peaceful place to stay if you don't want to be in among the noise and dust of Fort Dauphin itself. There are **rooms** (r Ar75,000) and a small **restaurant** (mains Ar5000-9000). If you stay the night you can do walks in the forest after dark to see the tiny *Microcebus* (mouse lemur).

The reserve is 7km north of Fort Dauphin. Visits can be organised with **Air Fort Services** (p132) or other travel agencies for about Ar55,000 including the entry fee, or you can charter a taxi or a pirogue.

Evatra & Lokaro Peninsula

Lokaro Peninsula is a spectacular and well-preserved area of inland waterways, green hills, barrier beaches and natural swimming holes. It lies about 15km northeast of Fort Dauphin along the coast, or about 40km by road.

Day excursions offered by travel agencies in Fort Dauphin cost about Ar235,000 per person for a group of three. Most begin with a 3km drive from Fort Dauphin to the shore of Lac Lanirano then continue by boat to Lac Ambavarano. On the northeastern end of this lake

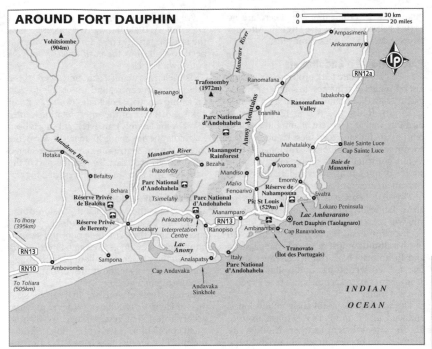

is the tiny fishing village of Evatra, from where it is about 20 minutes on foot over the hills to a good beach. Once at Evatra, you can arrange a pirogue to visit nearby Lokaro Island, or just stay and explore the peninsula itself, which has numerous opportunities for swimming, canoeing, snorkelling and walking. To reach the Lokaro area by road, you'll need a 4WD; allow about two hours from Fort Dauphin.

To reach Lokaro independently, follow the above route, hiring a pirogue from locals, or head northeast on foot from the customs post at the harbour in Fort Dauphin along the eastern beach for about 15km. On foot, it will take a full day; you will need to be self-sufficient with food and water and do not go alone. It's better to do this walk in a group, as there are high incidents of assaults and robberies along this beach.

Once on the peninsula, options include **Pirate Camp** (bungalows Ar51,000), run by Lavasoa in Fort Dauphin, which also has a camp site and hires equipment; or the Azafady camp site, where the profits go to benefit the local community. Azafady can facilitate the pirogue journey, provisions and gear if you want to stay here, or you can arrange things yourself

and just use the site. Contact Azafady (p132) or the Lavasoa hotel (p133) in Fort Dauphin to organise excursions to the peninsula.

Baie Sainte Luce

Baie Sainte Luce was the original site of the first French colony in Madagascar, established in 1642. It was abandoned by the settlers when they built Fort Dauphin a year later. It's a relaxing spot with a slice of unspoilt humid coastal rainforest running almost all the way down to a curved sandy beach. It's often possible to see lemurs in the forest.

The Azafady camp site here is right on the edge of the forest, and guides from the village of Sainte Luce are available to show you the lemurs, flying foxes and crocodiles that inhabit the area. Consult the list pinned up at the camp site for details of possible excursions and prices. It's best to contact Azafady in Fort Dauphin (p132) to let the villagers know you're coming and check the camp site is available.

If you have a vehicle, drive 35km north of Fort Dauphin to the village of Mahatalaky (three hours by taxi-brousse) then continue 4km further and turn right; from there, it's

SOUTHERN MADAGASCAR

10km down to the camp site. There are no taxis-brousses on the last stretch. Alternatively, ask Azafady about transport.

Parc National d'Andohahela

This 76,020-hectare park protects some of the last remnants of rainforest in southern Madagascar, as well as spiny forest and 13 species of lemurs. It also boasts over 120 species of birds, as well as a variety of amphibians and reptiles, including crocodiles. Its boundaries encompass the Trafonomby, Andohahela and Vohidagoro mountains, the last of which is the source of numerous rivers and an important catchment area for the surrounding region.

The park is divided into four 'parcels' or areas: Tsimelahy, in a transitional zone where you will see a variety of vegetation including *Pachypodium* and baobab; Malio, made up of low-altitude rainforest; and Mangatsiaka and Ihazofotsy, both characterised by spiny forest. Each section has trail walking; walks range from two to six hours and take in pools and waterfalls.

The whole park is still fairly undeveloped and wild, and requires a 4WD to get around, but for self-sufficient campers it offers the chance to immerse yourself in the landscape of the area without the rather contrived atmosphere and high prices of the Reserve Privée de Berenty.

Drop into Angap (p131) in Fort Dauphin before your visit to the park, as facilities are still being developed and some notice may be needed to organise porters and guides.

The park's well-organised **interpretation centre** lies along the RN13 at Ankazofotsy, about 40km west of Fort Dauphin. You can buy entry permits (Ar25,000 per day) and hire guides (from Ar7000) here – but again these may need to be arranged in advance (and are mandatory to take). Guides speak English as well as French.

Even if you don't have time to spend in the park it's worth visiting the interpretation centre. Built with the help of the WWF and American Peace Corps volunteers, the centre teaches locals and tourists the importance of preserving native forests and waterways for future generations. Exhibits are clearly labelled in Malagasy, English and French.

Camp sites in each parcel cost Ar8000 (except for the less developed camp site at Malio, which costs Ar5000). Cooking and washing facilities are available, but you will need to be self-sufficient with equipment and food.

All taxis-brousses heading west from Fort Dauphin (Ar10,000) towards Amboasary pass the interpretation centre. From here, you will need to walk into the park unless you have your own vehicle.

Tsimelahy is about 13km northwest of the interpretation centre, and is possible to visit on a long day trip. For Malio, which is about 15km northeast of the interpretation centre (4WD vehicles only), an overnight stay is best. Ihazofotsy begins about 30km northwest of the interpretation centre and can only be reached on foot or by zebu cart. To visit this part of the park you will need to stay at least one night.

Réserve Privée de Berenty

This place is the Madagascan version of the grand old East African safari-lodge experience – minus the swimming pool and swanky bungalows. You do get to watch tame lemurs frolic in the garden or walk in peace through quiet forest trials without the constant companionship of a guide.

Berenty was established in 1936 by sisal planter Henri de Heaulme in order to preserve gallery forest. The reserve, together with its small companion reserve of Bealoka, 7km to the north, contains nearly one-third of the remaining tamarind (or kily) gallery forest in Madagascar, nestled between the arms of a former oxbow lake on the Mandrare River.

The reserve is now managed by de Heaulme's son Jean de Heaulme. In the decades since its founding, the Berenty's relative ease of access has attracted numerous researchers, and in 1985 the WWF awarded Jean de Heaulme the Getty prize for nature conservation.

Berenty was first opened to tourists in the early 1980s and has since become one of Madagascar's most visited reserves. It's a very colonial, slightly surreal place at first sight, with the endless, spiky rows of the de Heaulme sisal plantation stretching away on all sides, and white picket fences neatly dividing the bright-red roads that surround the bungalows. It's very popular with pre-booked package tours.

Berenty isn't all sugary sweet; it's got a bit of controversy surrounding it. Some of the reserve's early practices – feeding bananas to lemurs, sweeping leaf debris off forest tracks – led to environmental problems, and some visitors complain that the whole experience is contrived, ecologically unsound and overpriced. Adventurous and mobile visitors with enough time to visit Madagascar's other wilder parks (nearby Andohahela, for example) will likely find Berenty a disappointment.

Other travellers love it. For visitors with little time or limited mobility, Berenty offers a chance to experience the magic of the forest, observe lemurs up-close (Berenty's photo opportunities are second to none), and get an insight into the Antandroy culture of the region with a visit to the excellent **anthropological museum** on site.

Some of Berenty's early practices have been stopped, and teams have begun to remove non-endemic plant invaders such as sisal, raketa and the rubber vine from the forest.

INFORMATION

Berenty can only be visited on a tour organised by **SHTM** (☎ 92 212 38; fax 92 211 32; Fort Dauphin; half-board €64). If you are coming from Toliara, you can make arrangements through **Motel Le Capricorn** (☎ 94 426 20; capric@dts.mg; Toliara).

Berenty also charge a compulsory transfer fee of €200 for one or two people, or €85 per person for a group of three or more.

The trails are easy to follow and guides are not required. In fact, one of Berenty's main attractions is the chance to wander in the forest alone. However, a good guide can help you with spotting wildlife, particularly on night walks in the spiny desert.

WILDLIFE

The Berenty forest contains over 115 plant species, providing habitat for a variety of wildlife. The 200-hectare forest, which is dominated by the tamarind, is enclosed by spiny desert, sisal plantations and the Mandrare River.

Most visitors come to see the lemurs, of which the ring-tailed are the most prominent. Many animals still have memories of unrestrained banana-feeding by tourists, and in the compound it's not unusual to see visitors being besieged by hopeful animals.

One of the best times to visit Berenty is late September/October, just after the young are born. In late September, the baby ring-tailed lemurs are clinging to their mother's undercarriage, but after a couple of weeks they climb onto her back and cling as she goes about her daily business. Males are normally relegated to the sidelines and, except during breeding season in April or May, are largely exempted from the ring-tailed lemurs' social life.

Berenty's other stars are the Verreaux's sifakas, graceful white lemurs that line up carefully along the patches of open ground around the bungalows before crossing with wild and comical two-footed leaps. Also present in the forest are troupes of red-fronted brown lemurs, which scamper along the ground uttering soft grunting calls rather like furry pigs. This species was transplanted to Berenty from western Madagascar. At night, walking in the moonlit, silvery spiny forest, you might see two species of nocturnal lemur: the sportive lemur (*Lepilemur*) and the grey mouse lemur, whose eyes flash red in the beams of the torch.

Berenty is also good for bird-watching, with 83 bird species, nine of which are birds of prey. The most abundant is the Madagascan buzzard *(Buteo brachypterous)*. Others to watch for are the Madagascan coucal, the Madagascan paradise flycatcher, six species of *vanga* and four species of *coua*.

There are 26 species of reptile, including two species of chameleon, the radiated tortoise and the rare Madagascan spider tortoise.

The best times for walks along the forest paths are between about 5am and 6am, in the late afternoon, and just after dark. Although the sifakas and ring-tailed lemurs are habituated to visitors, you'll find the nocturnal lemurs and smaller creatures are still skittish.

SLEEPING & EATING

You definitely need to remember you are paying for the experience of walking freely through a magical forest reserve, because at €64 per room (including a meal), plus all the transfer fees, this place can start to feel overpriced pretty damn fast.

There are 12 new bungalows with relatively consistent hot water that are clean and comfortable. The six older bungalows are dingy, with cold water. Electricity is turned out every night at 10pm, and without a fan to circulate air the bungalows can get very hot, especially the old ones.

Set meals cost about Ar15,000. The food is average and there is nothing whatsoever for vegetarians. In high season the reserve can get very busy, so it's best to book in advance.

GETTING THERE & AWAY

Berenty is situated about 80km west of Fort Dauphin and approximately 10km northwest of Amboasary. There's no way of getting there apart from on the expensive compulsory

SOUTHERN MADAGASCAR

transfers organised by SHTM in Fort Dauphin. If you arrive in your own vehicle, you are most likely to be refused entry.

AMBOVOMBE
pop 57,500

Driving into the dusty and not particularly interesting town of Ambovombe will gladden the hearts of those who've arrived overland from Toliara – the town is connected to Fort Dauphin by 110km of relatively good sealed road. On Monday the town holds a zebu market, the biggest in the south, from dawn until midmorning.

Few travellers stay in Ambovombe because the area is easily accessible from Fort Dauphin. If you do want to overnight here, try the clean **Hôtel L'Oasis** (☎ 92 700 16; r Ar15,000).

Taxis-brousses run frequently along the good sealed road between Ambovombe and Fort Dauphin (Ar2000, three hours). All traffic towards Toliara also passes through Ambovombe, so finding a lift westward is generally not difficult. Ambovombe is the junction for the rugged trip along the RN13 to and from Ihosy.

RÉSERVE SPÉCIALE DE CAP SAINTE MARIE & FAUX CAP

Madagascar's southernmost tip, Cap Sainte Marie (known in Malagasy as Tanjon'ny Vohimena), is a stark and windswept place where you'll feel you've travelled to the end of the earth. To protect 14 species of bird and two rare species of tortoise, the surrounding area has been set aside as a special reserve. There's the chance to walk on beaches strewn with *Aepyornis* eggshell fragments. Between July and November, you may be able to spot some migrating whales offshore.

There is little human development at the cape other than a religious statue, a lighthouse and the former lighthouse-keeper's house. At the village of Marovato, about 35km southwest of Tsiombe and about 15km northeast of Cap Sainte Marie, is a small Angap station marking the entrance to the reserve area. Guides can be arranged here for Ar15,000.

East of Cap Sainte Marie along the coast is Faux Cap (Betanty), which offers good views,

but little else. There is no direct road access between the two points. **Tsiombe**, 30km north on the RN10, is the closest major town to Faux Cap and a good place to break the taxi-brousse journey between Ampanihy and Fort Dauphin.

There is no accommodation at Cap Sainte Marie. Camping is allowed but, because of the strong winds, it is usually not feasible unless you set up your tent next to or inside the lighthouse-keeper's house. There's no charge, but you will need to request permission at the Angap office in Marovato. You'll also need to be self-sufficient with equipment, water and food.

Most travellers visit Cap Sainte Marie as an excursion from **Lavanono**, 30km to the west (about a two-hour journey by 4WD). The best accommodation option in the Lavanono area is **Libertalia** (madalibertalia@yahoo.fr; bungalows Ar25,000, mains from Ar5000), which also runs tours. It offers five solar-powered bungalows in stone buildings that are simple but not uncomfortable. The surroundings are the best part – there are beautiful views. The restaurant serves the usual mix of Malagasy and French food, but it's good, and the beers are cold. Cap Sainte Marie trips cost Ar140,000 per person, while canoe and kayak rental is available for Ar14,000 per hour.

Cap Sainte Marie, just over 200km from Fort Dauphin, is difficult to reach unless you take a tour, have access to a mountain bike or a good 4WD, or have plenty of time at your disposal. Tours are best arranged in Fort Dauphin (p132). Allow about half a day between Fort Dauphin and Tsiombe if travelling by 4WD and another few hours from Tsiombe to Lavanono.

To reach the region on your own, take a taxi-brousse as far as Beloha, from where there is very sporadic transport south to Lavanono. From Lavanono you will need to walk (about 30km) southeast to Cap Sainte Marie. Cap Sainte Marie is also accessible on foot from Marovato. Alternatively, take a taxi-brousse to Tsiombe, from where it is a hot 30km walk to Faux Cap. Once off the RN10, there is no regular public transport on any of these routes. Between May and November you may be lucky and get a lift with a lobster truck.

Western Madagascar

The 'wild west' attracts two types of cowboys – those in search of tough travel in rough country and ones looking to charter a private plane to the ultimate hidden paradise.

Madagascar's hard-to-reach western region – divided in two, with no roads linking the south and north – looks like it fell off another planet. It is pockmarked with trippy natural attractions. You can swim in a bottomless bowl of tomato bisque lapping against a deserted white-sand beach in the south – the ocean along the coast north of Morondava is a brick-red colour highlighted with a range of muddy browns (the odd colouring is, sadly, a direct effect of deforestation and erosion, which cause lateritic soils to leach into the water). Or to really blow your mind, walk the celebrated Avenue du Baobab, just outside Morondava, staring up at a line of giant trees more than one thousand years old.

In the national parks, forests of bizarre looking *tsingy* (karst) rise in spikes and crippled spires and create the kind of landscapes described in sci-fi novels. With thousands of acres of dry, deciduous forests, they are havens for hikers and cyclists. River rats can get their fix with a float trip down the Tsiribihina River, while scuba and sun lovers can spend days exploring uninhabited islands and diving in the coral reefs off the southwest coast near Bel-Sur-Mer.

Western Madagascar is also attracting a growing number of travelling lovebirds who fly in specifically to stay at the romantic, often luxurious, vaguely safari-style hideaways on secluded far-north beaches.

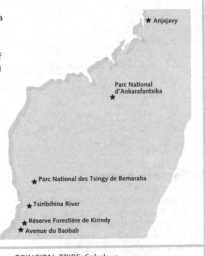

HIGHLIGHTS

- Floating down the **Tsiribihina River** (p149) in a wooden pirogue (dugout canoe) and camping on sandbanks at night under a million stars
- Climbing among the soaring stone pinnacles of **Parc National des Tsingy de Bemaraha** (p151)
- Splashing out at Madagascar's exclusive fly-in beach resort, the remote and romantic **Anjajavy** (boxed text, p150), which doubles as a wildlife reserve
- Contemplating creation while spying on copulating tortoises or searching out the jumping rat in the **Réserve Forestière de Kirindy** (p156) and the **Parc National d'Ankarafantsika** (p147)
- Toasting with a cold beer and watching the sunset among the giant trees of **Avenue du Baobab** (p156), outside Morondava

★ Anjajavy

Parc National d'Ankarafantsika ★

★ Parc National des Tsingy de Bemaraha

★ Tsiribihina River

★ Réserve Forestière de Kirindy
★ Avenue du Baobab

WESTERN MADAGASCAR

| ■ HIGHEST POINT: 850m | ■ PRINCIPAL TRIBE: Sakalava |

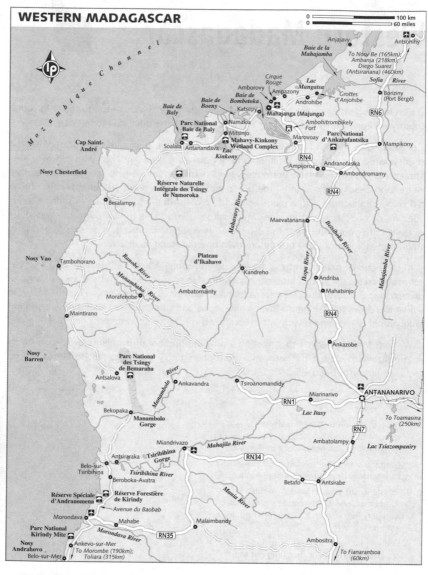

WESTERN MADAGASCAR

0 — 100 km
0 — 60 miles

Anjajavy

Antsohihy

Baie de la
Mahajamba

To Nosy Be (165km);
Ambanja (218km);
Diego Suarez
(Antsiranana) (460km)

Cirque
Rouge

Amborovy

Lac
Mangatsa

Sofia   River

Ampazony

Androhibe

Grottes
d'Anjohibe

Boriziny
(Port Bergé)

Baie de
Boeny

Baie de
Bombetoka

Katsepy

RN6

Baie de
Baly

Namakia

Mahajanga (Majunga)

Ambohitrombikely
Fort

Parc National
Baie de Baly

Mitsinjo

Mahavy-Kinkony
Wetland Complex

Marovoay

Parc National
d'Ankarafantsika

Mampikony

Cap Saint-
André

Soalala

Antanandava

Lac
Kinkony

RN4

Andranofasika

Ampijoroa

Ambondromamy

Nosy Chesterfield

Réserve Naturelle
Intégrale des Tsingy
de Namoroka

RN4

Besalampy

Maevatanana

Nosy Vao

Tambohorano

Plateau
d'Ikahavo

Kandreho

Andriba

Mahatsinjo

Ambatomainty

Morafenobe

RN4

Maintirano

Ankazobe

Nosy
Barren

Parc National
des Tsingy
de Bemaraha

Antsalova

Ankavandra

Tsiroanomandidy

ANTANANARIVO

RN1

Miarinarivo

Bekopaka

Manambolo
Gorge

Lac Itasy

To Toamasina
(250km)

RN7

Miandrivazo

Mahajilo River

Ambatolampy

Lac Tsiazompaniry

Antsiraraka

Tsiribihina
Gorge

RN34

Belo-sur-
Tsiribihina

Tsiribihina River

Beroboka-Avatra

Betafo

Antsirabe

Réserve Spéciale
d'Andranomena

Réserve Forestière
de Kirindy

Avenue du Baobab

Morondava

Mahabe

Malaimbandy

Parc National
Kirindy Mite

Ambositra

Nosy
Andrahovo

Ankevo-sur-Mer

Belo-sur-Mer

To Morombe (190km);
Toliara (315km)

RN35

Morondava River

Mozambique Channel

Mahavavy River

Ranobe River

Manambaho River

Manambolo River

Ikopa River

Betsiboka River

Mahajamba River

Mania River

To Fianarantsoa
(60km)

Getting There & Away

With the exception of the well-maintained Route Nationale 4 (RN4) between Antananarivo and Mahajanga, the roads in this region are poor (although slowly improving) and transport outside cities can be tough. The only way to get from Morondava in the south and Mahajanga in the north by road is to backtrack through Antananarivo. The road between Antananarivo and Morondava is in bad condition, especially during the rainy season, and the trip takes at least two days. The road north to Mahajanga is a pleasure to drive. The 560km stretch of pavement is one of Madagascar's easiest road journeys and takes only 10 hours.

Flying is your best option for fast travel. Air Madagascar has regular flights to the large towns, plus twin-engine otters servicing the smaller villages. The fly-in resorts on the north coast use private charters.

MAHAJANGA (MAJUNGA)

pop 162,969

Mahajanga is a sprawling and somnolent port town with a palm-lined seaside promenade, wide avenues, shady arcades and walls draped with gorgeous bougainvillea. It is sometimes also known as Majunga.

With its large Muslim and Indian populations, and historical connections with Africa, Mahajanga is one of the country's more colourful and ethnically diverse places, similar in atmosphere to many places on the East African coast. The women wrap themselves in the brightly coloured cotton wraps seen in the Comoros, Zanzibar and Mombasa, and there are some Swahili-style carved doorways amid the crumbling buildings in the town's older part.

North and south of Mahajanga are white-sand beaches, although some are not suitable for swimming due to sharks and strong currents. It's best to ask at the hotels, tour companies or even bars in Mahajanga to get the scoop on what's safe and what's not (currents change, as do shark patterns) before diving in anywhere around here.

HISTORY

Mahajanga became established in the 18th century as a trade crossroads between Madagascar, the East African coast and the Middle East. Swahili and Indian traders settled in the town, resulting in a thriving commerce in cattle, slaves, arms and spices from the Orient and the Middle East.

When Merina king Radama I overthrew the Sakalava people, Mahajanga's inhabitants rioted and set one section of the town on fire. Because of the capital's strategic location, the French selected it as the base of operations in 1895 for their expeditionary forces, which would turn Madagascar into a French protectorate.

ORIENTATION

Most hotels and restaurants are in the older part of town, as far as Rue du Colonel Barre in the east, with the port to the south and the bay to the west. Running beside the bay is a palm-lined promenade known as La Corniche.

At the intersection of Ave de France and La Corniche is an enormous baobab tree, thought to be well over 700 years old. It is considered *fady* (taboo) to touch it.

INFORMATION

Bank of Africa (BOA; cnr Rue Georges V & Rue Nicolas II) Changes money, ATM.
BFV-SG (Rue du Maréchal Joffre) Changes money, ATM.
BNI-CL (Rue du Maréchal Joffre) Opposite the Hôtel de France. Changes money, ATM.
Espace Medical (☎ 62 241 75; ⏱ 24hr) The best place for medical treatment.
Kaotry Le Baobab (Rue Georges V; per min Ar30) Next to Anjary Hotel, this new cybercafé has fast connections and serves cold drinks. Best of all, it's air-conditioned!
Post Office (Rue du Colonel Barre) Opposite the cathedral. The Telecom office is here too, and there are also card-phones in town.

SIGHTS & ACTIVITIES

Preserved fish and dinosaur bones are on show at the **Mozea Akiba** (Akiba Museum; ☎ 62 236 85; University of Mahajanga; admission Ar2500; ⏱ 9-11am & 3-5pm Tue-Fri, 3-5pm Sat & Sun). It also has a few small displays including photographs and explanations (some are in English) about the Grottes d'Anjohibe, the Parc National d'Ankarafantsika and Cirque Rouge.

Fort Rova (Ave du Rova), at the end of Rue du Maréchal Joffre, was built in 1824 by King Radama I and extensively damaged during the French-Malagasy wars of the late 19th century. The Rova offers good views over the city and bay.

If you want to sunbathe in style, or perhaps train for the next Olympic games, there is no better stop than the absolutely massive 50m **swimming pool** (nonguests per day Ar10,000) at La Piscine Hôtel (p144). The hotel is one of Mahajanga's most swanky, so reading on the sun-loungers, sipping cocktails out of coconuts or floating, arms extended, in the sparkling cold water all feel especially sweet if you've been roughing it for a while.

TOURS

Several hotels and tour operators can assist with organising excursions to nearby attractions such as Cirque Rouge (Ar75,000), Grottes d'Anjohibe (Ar300,000), Ampijoroa (Ar100,000) and Katsepy (Ar280,000). Prices

WESTERN MADAGASCAR

MAHAJANGA (MAJUNGA)

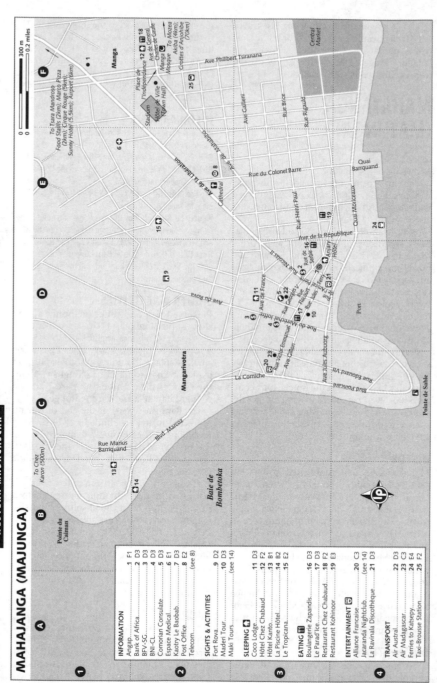

SAKALAVA EROTICA

The western part of Madagascar has traditionally been the area with the strongest African influence. The language of the dark-skinned western peoples contains many words taken from African languages. The dominant tribe in the area is the Sakalava, who venerate the relics not of their own personal ancestors, but of their ancient royal families. This belief, plus the use of spirit mediums to communicate with dead royalty, also has an African base.

The Sakalava are perhaps best known for covering the tombs of their dead with elaborate, erotic carvings, often depicting oral sex or other acts considered *fady* (taboo) in life. Although Sakalava tombs were once visible throughout the entire western region, today consider yourself very lucky if you're given the chance to see one of the copulating couples carved onto the old wood. Thanks to a group of people – mostly art dealers without morals – who purchased the poached erotica from unscrupulous relic-hunters and sold it, nearly all western Madagascar's sacred tombs had been pillaged to the point of destruction by the 1980s.

Following this desecration, the Sakalava now (understandably) keep the location of burial grounds still containing intact tombs top secret. It's important to respect their privacy. If you are lucky enough to be invited to visit a Sakalava tomb, please keep your hands to yourself and take only photos.

---

quoted are per person per day for a group of four. Cars can be hired for about Ar120,000 – it's cheaper to charter a taxi. Try the following places if you'd like to organise a tour:

Maderi Tour (☎ 62 032 34; www.maderi-tour.com in French; Rue Jules Ferry) Catamaran sailing trips as far north as Nosy Be, plus 4WD excursions and longer trips around Madagascar. It has just opened the Antsanitia Beach Resort (p149), an hour north of town, that's getting good reviews.

Maki Tours (☎ 032 400 3400; makitours@wanadoo.mg; La Piscine Hôtel) An upmarket company that runs 4WD day trips as well as longer, tailored holidays around the region. It also rents cars.

SLEEPING
Budget

Hôtel Kanto (☎ 62 229 78; Rue Marrius Barriquand; r from Ar10,000, mains from Ar2500; ⚡) A good-value and peaceful option up a hill behind La Piscine Hôtel about 2km north of town. There's a view of the sea from the garden terrace, and the rooms (no nets) are simple but clean. The restaurant (open Monday to Saturday) serves good Malagasy dishes.

Chez Karon (☎ 62 226 94; r from Ar15,000; ⚡) It's on the ocean, but the beach here has been almost entirely eroded. Still, travellers give it good marks for basic, but clean rooms, friendly hosts and good food at the onsite restaurant. Fishing and, more strangely, wild-boar-hunting excursions are arranged.

Hôtel Chez Chabaud (☎ 62 233 27; nico@wanadoo.mg; off Ave de Général Charles de Gaulle; r Ar15,000-30,000, mains Ar8000-22,000; ⚡) This hotel opposite the well-regarded restaurant of the same name has 18

rooms of varying size and comfort. Both the hotel and restaurant are run by two friendly French sisters who speak good English.

Midrange & Top End

Coco Lodge (☎ 62 230 23; www.coco-lodge.com in French; Ave de France; r from Ar65,000; ⚡ ⚡) A very chic and well-designed little hotel with pretty pink buildings built around a small pool and bar. There's also a casino on site. It is excellent value for Mahajanga and attracts travellers from all over the world.

Le Tropicana (☎ 62 220 69; www.hotel-majunga.com; Rue Administrateur; r Ar65,000-75,000, mains from Ar10,000; ⚡) A set of rustic bungalows in a lush garden that are small, but full of character (and often full of guests – reserve ahead). The restaurant puts an exotic spin on French fare, infusing local spices into classic dishes with great results. The caged lemurs in the garden were a real downer, however, and hopefully will be freed – we're not the first visitors to complain.

Sunny Hotel (☎ 62 235 87; rasseta@dts.mg; r Ar150,000, mains from Ar15,000; ⚡ ⚡) This hotel is back in good graces after releasing its resident lemurs from the cages they were once cruelly confined to – lots of travellers complained. The animals now live free in nearby trees. Outside of town near the airport, Sunny is a good choice if you don't care much about seeing Mahajanga, have ariary to burn and want a classy crash pad while waiting for a flight out. You'll pay for its quiet locale and poshness, but rooms are comfortable and spacious with satellite TV. Plus there is a big pool, tennis courts and even a fitness centre. The restaurant serves excellent food; excursions and car hire are arranged.

La Piscine Hôtel (☎ 62 241 72/3/4; piscinehotel@dts .mg; Blvd Marcoz; r Ar150,000; ⧓ ⧉) One of Mahajanga's most upmarket hotels is chiefly famous for its fantastic Olympic-sized 50m-long swimming pool. There are also great sea views, a terrace restaurant, a casino and a nightclub at this French-owned place. The rooms are luxurious, with satellite TV and telephone, although without the amenities they would feel quite overpriced. The hotel has its own tour company for excursions.

EATING

Mahajanga has loads of Indian restaurants. The least expensive places to eat are the tiny food stalls set up in the late afternoon along La Corniche. For more cheap eats, head north to the suburb of Tsara Mandroso, on Route de l'Aéroport, where hundreds of brightly coloured shops and cafés are packed together along the side of the road. Besides the places listed here, you'll find many of the hotels we've listed have quality restaurants.

Boulangerie Zapandis (☎ 62 221 36; Rue de Serbie; snacks & coffee Ar1000-5000; ⧖ 6am-noon & 4-7pm, closed Tue & Sun) A true French patisserie serving wonderful cakes, pastries, croissants and creamy ice cream. Locals stop in to pick up crispy loaves of French bread in the morning, and usually end up lingering, chatting with friends over juice and real espresso.

Le Parad'Ice (☎ 62 231 34; Rue du Maréchal Joffre; mains Ar2500-10,000; ⧖ 7am-2pm & 5-9pm Mon-Sat, 5-9pm Sun) Some say it serves the best ice cream in Madagascar, with lots of fruit flavours – the passionfruit has been recommended. Just down the road from Air Mad's office, it is also known for great breakfasts and a menu of burgers, grills and sandwiches. There's a bar.

Restaurant Kohinoor (Rue Henri Garnier; mains Ar5000-15,000; ⧖ lunch & dinner) Serving great Indian food amid super-kitsch décor, this small place is popular with expats, tourists and vegetarians – it does a veggie special every day. Carnivores will dig the delicious curries, many with a coconut-milk base.

Marco Pizza (☎ 032 40 032 02; pizza from Ar10,000; ⧖ lunch & dinner) American Peace Corps volunteers frequent this pizza joint, where they sure know how to make a delicious pie. The cook and owner is a friendly Frenchman who personally tends to each guest. You wash your pizza down with a cocktail or try some homemade ice cream for dessert. It's a few kilometres from the centre.

ENTERTAINMENT

Mahajanga's main socialising spot is the seafront promenade, La Corniche, which fills up at sunset with people out for a stroll.

Popular nightspots in town include **Jacaranda Nightclub** (admission Ar2500; ⧖ Thu-Sat) at La Piscine Hôtel and **La Ravinala Discothèque** (admission Ar2500) at Hôtel Le Ravinala.

Alliance Francaise (☎ 62 225 52; afmajunga@dts .mg; cnr La Corniche & Rue Victor Emmanuel) has a programme of films, exhibitions and concerts.

GETTING THERE & AWAY
Air

Air Madagascar (☎ 62 224 21; Rue Victor Emmanuel) flies several times weekly to Nosy Be (Ar288,000) and Antananarivo (Ar200,000) and once a week to Diego Suarez (Ar330,000). There are also twice-weekly flights on **Air Austral** (☎ 62 223 91; Rue Georges V) between Mahajanga and Dzaoudzi (Mayotte) for about €350 one way.

Boat

The MSL ferry **Jean Pierre Calloch** (☎ 62 226 86), which leaves weekly for Nosy Be, and takes around 20 hours, is a far better alternative than the cargo ships that also sporadically go there; see p164 for more details. See opposite for details about ferry trips to Katsepy.

Bus & Taxi-Brousse

Transport between Mahajanga and Antananarivo by road is very easy – it's one of the best maintained highways in the country. To travel in luxury book online with **Transport Première Class** (firstclass@mel-wanadoo.mg), which runs comfortable buses between the two cities (Ar69,000, 10 hours). These sit just two people to a row – as opposed to the average five or six in the traditional taxi-brousse – and include a packed lunch in the price.

The taxi-brousse station is east of town along the two-lane Ave Philibert Tsiranana. Vehicles go daily to Antananarivo (Ar15,000, 12 to 15 hours, daily) and to Diego Suarez (from Ar50,000, 36 hours) at least three times per week. The road is rough – particularly the 218km between Antsohihy and Ambanja. Apart from Antsohihy, there are few good places to break the trip. If you do decide to disembark en route, you may find yourself waiting several days for onward transport. For Nosy Be, you will need to change vehicles in Ambanja.

In the dry season it's possible to go as far south as Soalala, Besalampy and perhaps even Maintirano, but the trip is long and difficult, and transport is scarce. To continue further south towards Morondava, you will need to either take one of Air Madagascar's small twin-engine planes or backtrack via Antsirabe.

GETTING AROUND
To/From the Airport
The airport is 6km northeast of town, and taxis cost Ar10,000 per trip, although you may be able to barter the price lower. You can also catch a taxi-brousse from the road outside the airport to the station in town for Ar1000.

Car
As in most places in Madagascar, the least expensive car hire means chartering a taxi (for day trips) or hiring a car from a local who also drives. Any of the upmarket hotels or tour companies in Mahajanga can arrange 4WD rental. Expect to pay around Ar150,000 per day for 4WD rentals and around Ar70,000 for a regular car. Petrol is extra.

Taxi
Shared taxis around town charge Ar800 per ride. The standard rate for charter taxis is Ar1500 per ride (Ar3000 to Mozea Akiba) in town.

AROUND MAHAJANGA

While Mahajanga may not be the most interesting place in the world, the areas to its north, south, east and west do have some fabulous attractions.

Travel outside Mahajanga can be tough. Many roads are in notoriously bad condition, or in the case of the fly-in resort area, totally nonexistent.

WEST OF MAHAJANGA
There are a few places to check out west of town. It is also one of the more easy-to-reach areas.

Katsepy
Katsepy (kah-tsep) is a small, sleepy fishing village across the estuary from Mahajanga

MASONJOANY

In many areas of western and northern Madagascar, you will see women with their faces painted white. This facial mask, known as *masonjoany*, is supposed to protect skin from the sun, make it softer and suppler and remove blemishes. It's applied during the day and usually removed at night.

Masonjoany is made by grinding a branch from a tree of the same name against a stone with a small amount of water to form a paste. The *masonjoany* tradition persists in the Comoros, where the paste is made from ground sandalwood and coloured a startling canary yellow.

with a couple of swimmable beaches. It's also a good starting point for organising adventures to remote wildlife conservation areas southwest of Mahajanga.

It's worth a day visit solely to dine at **Chez Mme Chabaud** (☎ 62 233 27; r Ar25,000-50,000, mains from Ar7000; ☼ lunch & dinner). The family-run restaurant and small hotel has been serving tasty dishes for three decades now. Although the original matron has passed away, her two daughters (who also run Mahajanga's respected Restaurant Chez Chabaud) are doing an excellent job of continuing their mother's dining legacy. If you want to spend the night, there are rooms. Tours can be arranged.

A ferry (Ar2250, one hour) runs twice daily from the ferry dock in Mahajanga to Katsepy. It departs at 7.30am and 3pm Monday to Saturday. From Katsepy, the ferry leaves at 9am and 4.30pm.

Mahavy-Kinkony Wetland Complex
The brand new Mahavy-Kinkony Wetland Complex, which only gained government protection status in 2007, is the result of several semiprotected areas merging into one. Now covering 268,236 hectares, it incorporates a diverse and fragile ecosystem consisting of marine bays, river and river delta, and 22 lakes, including Madagascar's second-largest, Lac Kinkony. The preserve is also home to dry deciduous and gallery forest, savannah, marshland, mangrove, caves and lots of wildlife. Decken's sifakas and mongoose lemur are just two of the nine species of lemur identified here. Nine must be Mahavy's lucky number – nine species of bat (one of which has yet to

be fully described and recorded) also call the place home.

The bats and lemurs are cool, but most people come here for the birds. There are 143 species, and the park is the only place where all of western Madagascar's species of waterfowl can be seen in the same location – on the shores of Lac Kinkony. If you're interested in watching birds mate, visit between July and September.

Sleeping options are still quite limited. The gateway town of **Namakia**, about 75km southwest of Mahajanga, and the village of **Mitsinjo**, nearby, both boast a few small hotels.

Kaeloper Jean Cesar (Mitsinjo; r Ar10,000) has very basic rooms with shared facilities. Meals (Ar2500 to Ar5000) are available, but must be ordered in advance. Otherwise there are a few nearby *hotelys* serving Malagasy cuisine for cheap. Ask about camping in the fenced garden if you have your own equipment.

To get to the reserve you'll have to drive on a rougher-than-hell road (we're not even sure if you can call it a road) from Katsepy. It's probably easier not to attempt it in your own vehicle – join a tour out of Katsepy (see Chez Mme Chaubaud, p145) or Mahajanga (p141). It's a pretty drive at least; the rugged track leads past amazing *tsingy* scenery that keeps you mesmerised for hours.

EAST OF MAHAJANGA

To see the best attractions in this harsh region, you'll need to visit in a 4WD during the dry season. Otherwise access may be impossible.

Grottes d'Anjohibe

Some of the most impressive caverns in Madagascar are the remote Zohin' Andranoboka (Big Caves), which are also referred to as the Grottes d'Anjohibe (Anjohibe Caves), after a nearby village.

A series of subterranean rooms and galleries adorned with stalactites, stalagmites and other cave decorations (although many have been damaged by tourists) wind underneath two small hills. The most extensive section of cave stretches over 5km.

The route to the Grottes d'Anjohibe is passable only between April and October. With a 4WD vehicle, follow the main road southeast from Mahajanga for 10km, then turn northeast on a seasonal track, which leads 63km to the caves.

Sporadic taxis-brousses will go as far as Androhibe, about 15km before the caves, from

where you will need to walk. Guides can be arranged at Androhibe or at Anjohibe.

Cirque Rouge

The Cirque Rouge is one of western Madagascar's famous naturally bizarre sights. This amphitheatre of eroded rock is tinted in a rainbow hue of colours including red, pink, green and grey. A stand of *ravinala* palms surrounding a freshwater spring decorates one end. The best time to visit is from May to November.

A charter taxi will cost between Ar20,000 and Ar50,000 for the return trip from Mahajanga. Otherwise, it is a 45-minute walk from Amborovy village via a ravine heading inland from the coast. If you want to ask your taxi to drop you off and pick you up later, two hours should be plenty of time.

Lac Mangatsa

The tiny Lac Mangatsa (also known as Lac Sacré) is about 50km northeast of Mahajanga, near the sea. Locals come here to give thanks or to petition the help of the Boina royal ancestors, reincarnated in the form of the immense *tilapia* fish (freshwater perch) that inhabit the lake's clear waters.

Strict *fady* prohibits fishing and bathing, but feeding the fish is allowed. The surrounding green belt harbours wildflowers and interesting lizards, chameleons and spiders, all of which are also protected by *fady*. The best time to visit is from May to October.

There is no public transport to the lake; you will need to walk or charter a taxi. From the Mahajanga airport, go west 1km along the sealed road, then turn right on to a rough track and continue for 11km northeast to the lake. Local *fady* are taken seriously here, and it's best to visit with a guide. Organised tours from Mahajanga cost about Ar100,000/55,000 per person for a day/half-day trip.

SOUTH OF MAHAJANGA

This area is home to Parc National d'Ankarafantsika, one of the more interesting natural attractions in the Mahajanga region.

Ambohitrombikely Fort

Southeast of Mahajanga, in the midst of a very dense forest, are the ruins of the 19th-century Ambohitrombikely fort, built by the Merina. The surrounding area is littered with cannons, cannonballs, cooking utensils and other implements.

To get here, take a taxi-brousse or private vehicle along the road towards Marovoay, and then arrange a guide locally. There is a small display about the fort at the Mozea Akiba in Mahajanga.

Parc National d'Ankarafantsika

Probably the most interesting trip out of Mahajanga is to Parc National d'Ankarafantsika (130,026 hectares), which contains the only fully protected example of dry western deciduous forest in Madagascar. At the park headquarters (in the area known as **Station Forestière d'Ampijoroa**) is a fascinating breeding centre for two threatened tortoise species, the flat-tailed tortoise *(Pyxis planicauda)* and the very rare ploughshare tortoise *(Geochelone yniphora)*, as well as the only Malagasy endemic turtle, the *rere (Erymnochelys madagascariensis)*. This centre is jointly run by the Malagasy government and the Durrell Wildlife Conservation Trust.

ORIENTATION & INFORMATION

The reserve is 120km from Mahajanga and straddles the RN4. It takes two hours to reach by private vehicle, a bit longer by taxi-brousse.

The headquarters and visitor centre are in the town of **Ampijoroa**.

The driest time to visit d'Ankarafantsika is between May and November, but October and November can get very hot. Wildlife viewing is often better during the early part of the December-to-April wet season, when rainfall is still relatively light.

Park permits cost Ar10,000 for one day and Ar20,000 for three; these can be bought at the **Angap office** (☎ 62 226 56) in Mahajanga or at the Angap office in Ampijoroa. Guides (compulsory) can also be arranged at Ampijoroa. Many speak English, so ask. Guides charge Ar10,000 per group (up to five) for a walking tour. You should tip a little extra at the end if they've impressed you as the guides are usually quite poor and most are very well informed and enjoyable.

To appreciate the park fully you'll need at least two days.

WILDLIFE

Parc National d'Ankarafantsika is home to eight lemur species, many easily seen, including Coquerel's sifaka and the recently

---

SURVIVAL OF THE FITTEST

The ploughshare tortoise is currently being reintroduced to its native habitat around Soalala, southwest of Mahajanga. The tortoise's vulnerability comes in part from its unusual mating habits – in order to mate with the female, the male tortoise must become aroused by fighting with other males. Males fight by locking together the front of their shells, which are shaped like a plough, before trying to tip each other over. If no other males are available to fight with, the male is unable to copulate and thus numbers drop, leading to even fewer males and a further decline in population. More details on the ploughshare's bizarre sexual habits can be found in the book *The Aye-Aye and I* by Gerald Durrell, whose estate runs the Durrell Wildlife Conservation Trust.

This trust operates **Project Angonaka** in the Parc National d'Ankarafantsika. It is one of Madagascar's most successful captive tortoise breeding projects. Although it took many years of trial and error in the sex-therapy department, the world's rarest tortoise is now breeding here so successfully that it's being reintroduced in greater numbers each year to the Baie de Baly area – the tortoises' home before the poachers killed them off. Sadly, the poaching problem hasn't been entirely eradicated. Even the breeding project isn't immune to theft – security was visibly strengthened after the theft of a large number of ploughshare tortoises a decade ago. Overall results have been positive, however, with more than 150 captive bred turtles released into lakes around d'Ankarafantsika. The Durrell project has had such success with the ploughshare that it's expanded its breeding programme to other turtles, including the rare, super-endangered big-headed/side-necked turtle living only in Madagascar's western lakes.

Park rangers can point you in the direction of the fenced-off area, but because of the extra security it takes to ensure the safety of these very rare species, the facility is not open to the public at this moment. You can get close enough, however, to glimpse the tortoises through a chain-link fence. Still if you're interested in seeing the Durrell project from afar, ask at the park headquarters.

WESTERN MADAGASCAR

discovered *Microcebus ravelobensis*. You're also likely to see brown lemurs and four nocturnal species: sportive, woolly, grey mouse and fat-tailed dwarf lemurs. More elusive is the rare mongoose lemur, which is observed almost exclusively here. The best chances of seeing one are at the onset of the wet season, when this lemur is active during the day. Other mammals include two species of tenrecs and the grey long-tailed mouse *(Macrotarsomys ingens)*, which is found only in d'Ankarafantsika's higher elevations.

D'Ankarafantsika is also one of Madagascar's finest bird-watching venues, with 129 species recorded, including the rare Madagascan fish eagle and the raucous sickle-bill vanga. There are over 70 species of reptiles, including small iguanas, a rare species of leaf-tailed gecko *(Uroplatus guentheri)* and the rhinoceros chameleon *(Chamaeleo rhinoceratus)* – the male sports a large bulblike proboscis.

Vegetation consists of low and scrubby deciduous forest with pockets of such dryland plants as aloe and *Pachypodium* (or 'elephant's foot') plus baobabs and orchids.

ACTIVITIES

Hiking is the name of the game here. In the last five years a lot of effort has been put into upgrading the trail system, which now includes six trails. Each offers opportunities to spot different types of animals, plants and birds. The Circuit Coquereli takes between 1½ and three hours and is a good choice for first-time visitors. The walk is easy, so you have plenty of energy to look for sifakas and brown lemurs.

If you're sleeping over, try a **night walk**. These usually depart around 7pm and take 1½ hours. The nocturnal walks cover easy terrain and are an essential highlight of a park visit. This is the only time you will have a chance to spot the mouse lemur. It is also easier to spot chameleons after dark.

SLEEPING & EATING

Options are getting better around here each year.

Gîte d'Ampijoroa (☎ 62 226 56; angapmjg@wanadoo .mg; r from Ar20,000), at the park headquarters, offers fairly small rooms with communal facilities. Mattresses are of good quality and you get a mosquito net. It also has a few slightly more upmarket bungalows, with private bathrooms, on the shores of Lac Ravelobe. Meals and drinks can be arranged with advance notice.

There is a big Angap-run **camp ground** in the park itself. Regular **tent sites** (Ar6000) include access to showers, eating shelters and water points. Tents can be rented for Ar10,000. If you want to camp without cramping your style, try renting a **luxury safari tent** (Ar25,000). It sits on a wooden platform and you can hire a mattress for an extra Ar4000.

The **Ambodimanga camp site** (tent platforms Ar4000; bungalows around Ar30,000), about 700m before the park entrance on your left-hand side coming from Mahajanga, is a community-run project with two bungalows and more than a dozen sheltered tent platforms, but you'll need your own tent.

GETTING THERE & AWAY

The entrance to the park is just off the RN4 about 114km southeast of Mahajanga and 455km from Antananarivo. To get here, catch a taxi-brousse towards Andranofasika. These depart Mahajanga early in the morning. Ask to be dropped off at Ampijoroa, 4km before Andranofasika, where you'll find the park headquarters and visitor centre.

NORTH OF MAHAJANGA

To really taste the 'wild west', you'll want to go north towards Nosy Be. Although the 642km stretch of road is slowly being improved thanks to some EU funding, it's still far from easy in parts.

The road is decent for the first 153km from Mahajanga to **Ambondromamy**, the town just past the Parc National d'Ankarafantsika, but starts to deteriorate rapidly afterwards. It is in bad shape by the time you hit **Boriziny** (Port Bergé), a popular overnight stop, especially with taxi-brousse. From Boriziny, a marginally better road winds north to **Antsohihy**, the main town with an airport, and a large missionary and educational presence. Allow anywhere from 20 to 35 hours between Mahajanga and Antsohihy.

If you've had enough of bumping around in a taxi-brousse, there are a few weekly flights connecting Antsohihy with Nosy Be, Antananarivo and Mahajanga; the Air Madagascar office is at Hôtel Biaina.

From Antsohihy north to **Ambanja** the road is rough and quite impassable in the wet season. It can take 10 to 15 hours or more to do the 218km stretch in the dry. Once in Ambanja, it's easy to find taxis-brousses to Ankify or Antsahampano and catch the boats across to Nosy Be. Make sure to ask for a

WESTERN MADAGASCAR

speedboat; if you've just done this journey by taxi-brousse you'll deserve one.

Luckily you can rest up for the journey before it really begins. The newest place to sleep in this area is also the coolest. Located just an hour north of Mahajanga on a pretty beach, **Antsanitia Beach Resort** (☎ 62 023 34; www .antsanitia.com; bungalows Ar80,000-120,000; ☒) already has a great reputation. Travellers are raving about the idyllic location and fantastic amenities. Check out the big blue pool surrounded by an open-air polished wood bar and excellent restaurant. The thatched bungalows are spacious with gorgeous wood-planked interiors and huge windows. The eco-responsible hotel also gets our thumbs up for the community enhancement projects it runs in the local village. To get here from Mahajanga, stop by Maderi Tour (p143) and arrange a transfer.

TSIRIBIHINA RIVER REGION

This region, between Antsirabe and Morondava, is home to the beautiful Tsiribihina River and spectacular Parc National des Tsingy de Bemaraha, a Unesco World Heritage site. Tours of the park are often combined with float trips down the Tsiribihina River. Most tour companies are based in Antsirabe; see the list on p97.

TSIRIBIHINA RIVER

Even though it's become Madagascar's favourite organised tour, drifting leisurely down the Tsiribihina (Tsi-ree-been) River in a traditional wooden pirogue remains a Zen experience. The air is silent except for the plunk of the local *piroguier*'s paddle splashing against the dark curtain of water. Lemurs hop from treetop to treetop and fish swim alongside your boat. Floating down the 146km stretch of river allows you to experience Madagascar from a new perspective; you have access to areas so remote they can only be reached by boat. The scenery is beautiful and varied, and the route takes you through the striking Tsiribihina Gorge and past stretches of deciduous forest. Lunch is taken in the shade of giant trees on the river banks or next to cascading waterfalls, and camp is made each night on the flat white sandbanks in the shallows.

Bring along a hat and/or umbrella, sun cream, mosquito repellent, rain protection, plenty of drinking water, and a bird book if you're at all interested – the bird-watching along the river is fantastic and not many guides know all the species.

The trip begins in Miandrivazo and ends in the village of Belo-sur-Tsiribihina. The main time for river descents is from April to November. During the rainy season, nights are spent in villages rather than on the sandbanks.

Unfortunately the huge influx of tourists now making this tour means the river is no longer as pristine as it once was. Travellers have noted piles of only half-buried human faeces and trash at campgrounds, and the sheer number of boats running this stretch of river means you'll likely hit a pirogue traffic jam at some point. During peak tourist season (June to August) the whole three-day trip can feel a bit more like a water-park ride than a wilderness adventure. To avoid the bulk of crowds, visit during the shoulder season between wet and dry.

The trash and improper burial of human waste are real issues in this fragile ecosystem. The natural balance is being damaged by too much traffic already, and if travellers and guides don't do more to clean up their waste, the problem will only be exacerbated in the future. Take responsibility for yourself, don't litter and make sure to bury any waste in a hole at least 15cm deep and 30m from the river.

Tours

Miandrivazo and Antsirabe are generally the easiest places to organise river descents. A standard trip includes a guide and *piroguiers*, boats, food and water, tents, transport to and from the river, and the first and last night's hotel accommodation. Bargain hard, discuss your menu in advance and try to examine the camping equipment before you pay. Organised tours cost from €95 to €155 per person for a three-day trip with a group of four people. The price depends on whether your tour departs from Antsirabe (220km away) or Miandrivazo and the type of boat you take.

Many companies, particularly the ones in Antsirabe, combine the river descent with a visit to the Parc National des Tsingy de Bemaraha. These trips cost around €300 and last seven days.

SLEEPING IN STYLE: MADAGASCAR'S HOT NEW FLY-IN CRIBS

When you spend US$3000 on an airline ticket to get to an exotic sounding island, it's not crazy to want to spend some of your trip staying somewhere that feels as luxurious and paradise-like as the name Madagascar suggests.

Now you can. For those of you tired of the crowded resort scene and looking for something truly off the radar – we're talking big cocktail-party bragging rights here – than Madagascar's fly-in resorts are your answer. The vibe out here is Robinson Crusoe meets the celebrity homes featured on MTV's *Cribs*.

Grab a map of the coast between Mahajanga and Nosy Be and you'll see just how empty the northern part of this indented coastline is. This is a land void of roads, of houses, of anything really … except for three fly-in resorts. Each is unique, and about as close to paradise as one finds in Madagascar, especially if you are here on honeymoon (or any sort of romantic getaway).

Lodge des Terres Blances (☎ 261 320 433 820; www.lodgeterresblanches.com; r per person all-inclusive €110) This place is so remote only a bush pilot could find it, which is exactly what happened. Owned by former bush pilot Jacky Cauvin, this is the least posh and most reasonably priced of the three resorts. There are six basic, but comfortable, bungalows in a gorgeous location – a white beach backed by lush forests that are home to lemur and geckos. Pampering is kept to the minimum – guests all dine together at a big table in the evening (vegetarians won't like it here), electricity runs off a generator (but it's pretty reliable) and guests can help themselves to snacks and drinks at any time from the fridge. It's a simple place that's popular with sports fishermen and French holidaymakers. Jacky, who speaks perfect English, can arrange drop-offs for picnic hikes or boat trips to hidden coves and baobab-rich islands. He is also full of facts about Sakalava culture and Malagasy animals and plants. Get him talking after a couple of post-sunset tumblers of the delicious house rum. The lodge, about 100km north of Mahajanga, can be reached via plane (€170) or boat (€120) transfers.

Getting There & Away

Tour operators in Morondava or Antananarivo can arrange vehicle transfer to Miandrivazo (about Ar150,000 plus fuel one way from Antananarivo). Alternatively, you can fly or take a taxi-brousse.

MIANDRIVAZO

pop 16,026

Miandrivazo (Mee-an-dree-vaaz), which lies along the main road, Route Nationale 34 (RN34), between Antsirabe and Morondava, enjoys the dubious honour of being the hottest place in Madagascar. It also is the starting point for canoe tours down the Tsiribihina River to Belo-sur-Tsiribihina on the coast. Unless you're looking to join one of the popular pirogue trips, there's really no reason to stop in Miandrivazo.

Even though Miandrivazo is the starting point for the river trips, most tour operators are based in Antsirabe (see p97), 220km away in Central Madagascar along a good road. Tours booked out of Antsirabe include transport to Miandrivazo, which takes about three hours.

If you haven't pre-booked, or you're coming from a direction that makes it easier to go to straight to Miandrivazo, it's not hard to arrange river trips here. It may even work out cheaper – if you deal directly with the local pirogue owners you may be able to score a three-day trip for as little as Ar200,000 per person. The hotel listed here also runs excursions. These include meals and equipment, and usually a night at the hotel afterwards. Three-day trips cost between €90 and €155 per person, depending on the season and what type of boat you choose.

Chez La Reine Rasalimo (☎ 95 924 38; r & bungalows from Ar25,000) is the town's most upmarket sleeping choice, although it's still pretty inexpensive. It has cool and spacious bungalows and a restaurant serving good French and Malagasy food for about Ar10,000. It's on the edge of town with good hill views.

Air Madagascar flies weekly to Miandrivazo from Mahajanga (Ar240,000), Morondava (Ar110,000) and Antananarivo (Ar125,000).

There are daily taxis-brousses to Antananarivo (Ar20,000, 10 hours), Antsirabe (Ar10,000, six hours) and Morondava

La Maison de Marovas-Be (☎ 870 761 291 717; www.marovasabe.com; per person all-inclusive €150; ☛) The Moramba Bay location is not quite as pretty as the other two lodges: the surrounding forest has suffered serious slash-and-burn scars and the water isn't quite as clean and clear. The hotel, however, makes up for a lack of gorgeous surrounds with superb architecture and amenities. The resort is tastefully laid out with three suites and six pimped-out rooms, all with balconies. The swimming pool is a stunner. The owners are involved in reforestation projects for local forests, and guests can contribute by planting a tree. Air transfers cost another €300 per person return from Antananarivo or €150 from Mahajanga.

Anjajavy (in Paris ☎ 33 1 44 69 15 03; www.anjajavy.com; per person all-inclusive from €190; ☒ ☐ ☛) A world-class Relais Chateau property, Anjajavy is more than just a posh beach resort. It's also an environment saver. The resort leases 450-hectares of native dry deciduous forest (disappearing rapidly throughout Madagascar thanks to rampant clear-cutting by locals too poor to care) adjacent to it, and protects the land as a nature preserve. Take a walk for some amazing wildlife viewing. Coquerel's sifakas, brown lemurs and grey-headed lovebirds are just a few of the strange sounding and looking members of the animal and reptile kingdoms that call this place home. At times the forest grows right up and over the *tsingy* spires poking out of the rich earth.

Back at the resort, the 25 villas, made from polished rosewood, feature fine linens and plenty of space. The hotel is completely eco-friendly and also involved in enrichment projects benefiting the local village. Free activities offered to guests include guided hikes to a cave where you'll see the skulls of extinct lemurs embedded in the walls, and snorkelling trips to surrounding coral reefs. Or take lessons in water-skiing, windsurfing and catamaran sailing. If you'd rather relax, the big square pool sits flush to a strip of flawless white sand beyond which a deep blue ocean beckons. Massages are available for €20 per hour. A three-day minimum is required, but you'd be happier staying for five or seven. The resort is perfect for honeymooners. Anjajavy can only be reached by private plane. Air transfers are pricey at €475 return from Morondava.

(Ar15,000, eight hours). Road conditions are good. Taxis coming from Antananarivo reach Miandrivazo at night.

BELO-SUR-TSIRIBIHINA
pop 16,250
Belo-sur-Tsiribihina, lost in the marshes and mangroves of the Tsiribihina Delta, is a starting point for excursions to Parc National des Tsingy de Bemaraha. It's often referred to as 'Belo', and is not to be confused with the coastal village of Belo-sur-Mer, which lies further south.

In an endearing colonial-style building, **Hôtel du Menabe** (☎ 22 209 20; r Ar15,000) has some rather magnificent rooms with huge double beds – check out a few. Each comes with a fan and mozzie net. Located in the village centre, it also has a restaurant known for good zebu and tilapia filets.

Mad Zebu (☎ 032 40 387 15; mains Ar6000-12,000), on the main road about 250m down from Hôtel du Menabe, is a very clean restaurant serving simple meals. Sit out on the terrace and watch village life sweep by. Air Madagascar has an agent here.

Camions-brousses (large trucks) run at least once daily between Belo-sur-Tsiribihina and Morondava (Ar10,000, four hours). Departures are usually in the morning from the ferry crossing outside Belo. In the wet season, the road gets muddy and the trip can take six hours; hitching a ride with a private 4WD is a better idea. *Camions-brousses* also go to Bekopaka (for Parc National des Tsingy de Bemaraha) daily in the dry season. The trip takes about five hours.

PARC NATIONAL DES TSINGY DE BEMARAHA
Parc National des Tsingy de Bemaraha is a Unesco World Heritage site and, at 66,630 hectares, is one of the largest and most spectacular protected areas in Madagascar.

The highlight is the jagged, limestone pinnacles, known as *tsingy*. Formed over centuries by the movement of wind and water, and often towering several hundred metres into the air, they are quite a sight. Walkways and bridges allow visitors to climb on top of the smaller areas of *tsingy* (known as Petits Tsingy), while ropes and climbing equipment are needed to negotiate the larger pinnacles.

WESTERN MADAGASCAR

PARC NATIONAL DES TSINGY DE BEMARAHA & AROUND

The maze-like *tsingy* (known as Grands Tsingy) once gave shelter to the mysterious Vazimba, the first inhabitants of Madagascar, and the deep caves between them served as the venue for their ancient spiritual cults. Fragments of Vazimba pottery can still be found hidden in crevices between the rocks.

The park also has about 90 species of birds, eight species of reptiles, and 11 species of lemurs, including Decken's sifaka.

Information

Entry permits can be arranged at **Angap** (☎ 22 013 96; www.tsingy-madagascar.com; per day Ar25,000) at the park entrance on the north bank of the Manambolo River, near the ferry crossing at Bekopaka. Guides are compulsory and cost between Ar6000 and Ar30,000 per group of up to five, depending on the length of the hike you choose. Many guides speak English, and can be arranged through Angap.

Activities & Tours

Much of the walking in the *tsingy* area of the park is pretty strenuous – gaps between the rocks are very narrow, bridges are high and the caves under the pinnacles are cramped and dark. Anyone with a low level of fitness or vertigo might find exploring the *tsingy* difficult.

The area can only be visited between April and November; for much of the year rain makes it inaccessible. For both the Petits Tsingy and Grands Tsingy, bring good shoes, plenty of water and a torch for the numerous caves you'll be exploring. When in the park, remember that it's *fady* to smoke, go to the toilet outside designated areas, or point at the *tsingy* with your finger outstretched.

The Petits Tsingy, in the southern end of the park near the village of Bekopaka, is the most accessible section of the park. The much larger Grands Tsingy to the north is more difficult to reach, but more impressive. Near the park office are numerous walks including the Andadoany and Ankeligoa circuits, which both lead to the Petits Tsingy. Visits to Grands Tsingy are generally done partially by way of car. If you don't have a car, one possibility is to walk from Bekopaka north towards Grands Tsingy, set up camp, explore the area (with a guide from Bekopaka), and then walk back to Bekopaka the next day.

Given the difficulties of access, most travellers visit des Tsingy de Bemaraha as part of an organised tour. This way your transport is provided, and tours can be tailored to your interest and fitness level. Organised park tours usually last three days, but can go longer if you want to spend time around Grands Tsingy. Trips cost between €75 and €150 and start and finish in Belo-sur-Tsiribihina or Morondava.

Sleeping & Eating

Angap camping ground (tent pitch Ar2500) This camp site, with showers and toilets, is near the park office.

Hôtel Relais des Tsingy (☎ 95 523 18; bungalows Ar60,000-82,000; ☽ mid-Apr–mid-Nov) The most upmarket option around the park, it has big, round bungalows made from natural materials. The hotel is about 2km from the ferry crossing. Half-board (breakfast and dinner) is compulsory and costs Ar25,000 per person.

Getting There & Away

The park entrance, camp site and Petits Tsingy section are on the north side of the Manambolo River ferry crossing near Bekopaka, about 80km of very rough road north of Belo-sur-Tsiribihina. The Grands Tsingy section lies 20km further north. Reaching the park on your own is possible, but an organised tour is much easier.

In the dry season, there are *camions-brousses* three times a week from Morondava (Ar20,000, two days) to the Manambolo River ferry crossing via Belo-sur-Tsiribihina. Organised tours include 4WD transport to the park entrance. From the park entrance, the main way to reach the Grands Tsingy is by 4WD. It's a hot four-hour walk, so bring enough water if you hike it. Rates for a chartered 4WD from Morondava to the park usually average about Ar150,000 to Ar200,000 per day.

MORONDAVA

pop 31,500

Morondava is a laid-back seaside town with sandy streets and gently decaying clapboard houses. Many people come here just to see the magnificent Avenue du Baobab right outside town. The giant trees, some a thousand years old, stand regal guard in an almost straight line along a rich earthen path that's a joy to walk down. Morondava is also a good place to organise a visit to Parc National des Tsingy de Bemaraha further north.

Tranquil mangrove swamps, which can be explored by pirogue, are found on Morondava's southern edge. There is good birding in here, including opportunities to observe kingfishers, egrets and other birds. There are decent beaches to the south and north, although the city's beachfront has been pretty much eroded away.

The area around Morondava was once the epicentre of the Sakalava kingdom, and home to burial grounds with erotically carved tombs for which the tribe is famous. Sadly, nearly all the sacred tombs have been destroyed. They were pillaged to the point of destruction (see the boxed text on p143 for more) decades ago.

ORIENTATION

The main town, with the market, shops and hotels, stretches along Rue de L'Indépendance and Rue Principale. To the southwest is the peninsula of Nosy Kely, with numerous bungalows and beach resorts. It's bordered to the west by the sea and the east by a mangrove swamp. To reach Nosy Kely, follow Rue de L'Indépendance to its terminus and then go left.

INFORMATION

The Bank of Africa, just south of the main road on the eastern edge of town, and the BFV-SG, at the western edge of town just off the beach road, are just two of many banks that change money and have ATMs.

For internet access check out **Cybercenter** (per min Ar100; ☿ Mon-Sat) on the end of Rue Principale, facing the Mada Bar.

BEACHES

The beach at Nosy Kely is fairly attractive, although it has also suffered severe erosion over the last decade. Check out the southern end for the most sand. Strong currents prevent swimming in many areas, and views are marred by concrete pilings.

Much better is quiet Betania beach at the southern end of the peninsula. There is now one place to stay, but even if you don't, it makes a good day trip. To get to the beach arrange transport with a pirogue captain (about Ar1500).

TOURS

The following places can organise excursions to Belo-sur-Mer, Parc National des Tsingy de Bemaraha, Tsiribihina River and Réserve Forestière de Kirindy, or through the mangrove swamps, as well as deep-sea fishing trips and diving excursions.

Baobab Tours (☎ 95 520 12; Baobab Café) This respected, upmarket, agency specialises in deep-sea fishing and diving trips; it also organises reliable trips to Parc National des Tsingy de Bemaraha, Belo-sur-Mer and boat trips up and down the coast.

Chez Maggie (La Masandro; ☎ 95 523 47; www .chezmaggie.com) This American-owned hotel doubles as a tour company running excursions to the Avenue du Baobab, Réserve Forestière de Kirindy, *tsingy* and national parks. It also owns a 42ft catamaran for charter, and does sea transfers to Belo and Toliara. Chez Maggie is an agent for Remote Rivers (www.remoteriver.com), which runs sustainable-travel-focused trips down the little-explored Mangoky, Mahavavy and Manambolo Rivers.

Book accommodation online at lonelyplanet.com

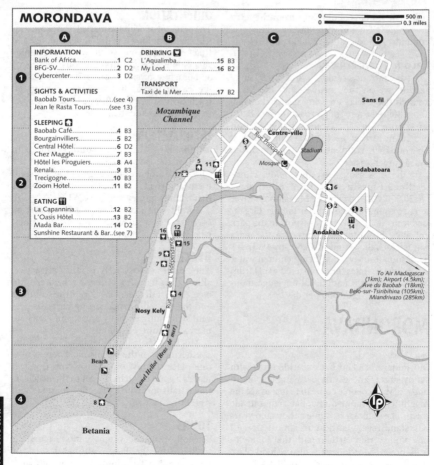

MORONDAVA

0 ___ 500 m
0 ___ 0.3 miles

INFORMATION		
Bank of Africa	1	C2
BFG-SV	2	D2
Cybercenter	3	D2

SIGHTS & ACTIVITIES		
Baobab Tours	(see 4)	
Jean le Rasta Tours	(see 13)	

SLEEPING 🏠		
Baobab Café	4	B3
Bourgainvilliers	5	B2
Central Hôtel	6	D2
Chez Maggie	7	B3
Hôtel les Piroguiers	8	A4
Renala	9	B3
Trecicogne	10	B3
Zoom Hotel	11	B2

EATING 🍴		
La Capannina	12	B2
L'Oasis Hôtel	13	B2
Mada Bar	14	D2
Sunshine Restaurant & Bar	(see 7)	

DRINKING 🍷		
L'Aqualimba	15	B3
My Lord	16	B2

TRANSPORT		
Taxi de la Mer	17	B2

Mozambique Channel

Sans fil

Centre-ville

Rue Principale

Stadium

Mosque

Andabatoara

Andakabe

Rue de l'Indépendance

To Air Madagascar (1km); Airport (4.5km); Ave du Baobab (18km); Belo-sur-Tsiribihina (105km); Miandrivazo (285km)

Nosy Kely

Canal Hellot (Bras de mer)

Beach

Betania

WESTERN MADAGASCAR

Jean le Rasta Tours (☎ 95 527 81, 032 04 931 60; L'Oasis Hôtel) Charismatic Jean le Rasta, or Rasta Jean, speaks English, is reliable and owns a 4WD. He runs, or organises, a range of tours including to Parc National des Tsingy de Bemaraha and Réserve Forestière de Kirindy, and transfers to Belo-sur-Mer or further south down the coast. Look for him at the grungy backpacker dive, L'Oasis.

SLEEPING

There are several hotels in the centre of town, but most travellers opt for the beach at Nosy Kely. Many places offer discounts in the low season.

Town

Central Hôtel (☎ 95 520 81; r incl breakfast from Ar12,000) An old-school cheapie, Central is right on the

main road. The good-value, clean and cool rooms on the 2nd floor come with fans and hot showers. There is no restaurant.

Zoom Hotel (☎ 95 920 59; r from Ar15,000; 🖳) Rooms at this new place are clean, good value and ensuite – two even have air-con. It is near the popular L'Oasis, which is known for its good eating, drinking and tours.

Beach

Almost all the beachfront places have restaurants. The following is just a selection of what's on offer.

Trecicogne (☎ 95 520 69; trecicogne@dts.mg; r Ar10,000-25,000, mains from Ar5000) A very pretty guesthouse right at the end of Nosy Kely peninsula, with a veranda overlooking the mangrove canal. The newly built wooden rooms have very clean bathrooms. The restaurant serves good food and tours are arranged.

Bougainvilliers (☎ 95 521 63; bol_nd@yahoo.fr; r Ar25,000-65,000) This place has a range of rooms at various prices. The more expensive ones come with ensuites, air-con and hot water. Manager Francois Vahiko is the head of the Morondava Guide Association and provides assistance in arranging tours. The restaurant serves great food.

Hôtel les Piroguiers (☎ 95 526 19; piroguiers@yahoo .fr; bungalows from Ar30,000) Across the river on Betania beach, which is much prettier than Nosy Kely, this is a delightful find. The bungalows are simple but clean, and sit on stilts. The atmosphere is that of a tranquil fishing village with a twist – this village is famous for its very large, sun-loving pigs. To reach the hotel, take a pirogue taxi or motorboat.

Renala (Au Sable d'Or; ☎ 95 520 89; r & bungalows from Ar65,000; 🖳) This well-maintained place offers a choice between bungalows and hotel rooms – the latter are the cheapest air-con rooms in the area. The 13 solid-wood bungalows come with tiled floors and telephones. There's an attractive two-storey restaurant. It's on the beach at Nosy Kely.

Chez Maggie (La Masandro; ☎ 95 523 47; www.chez maggie.com; r Ar75,000-100,000; mains Ar17,000; 🖳) The blue-and-white painted two-storey bungalows here are stylishly decorated and have their own sitting area. Owned by a friendly American named Gary, it's well organised and up to Western standards. Gary loves to chat, which makes it a good choice for solo travellers, or anyone starved for English conversation. There is a great restaurant, a small pool and beachfront location. Organised excursions are available.

Baobab Café (☎ 95 520 12; www.baobab.mg; r from Ar80,000, mains Ar12,000-28,000; 🖳 🖳) Morondava's most upmarket option has very smart and stylish rooms with fridge and TV. Twin rooms have two double beds, and there's a pool, snooker table and game room and a tour agency for excursions and fishing trips. It's on the river on the east side of Nosy Kely – don't get a room overlooking the river, as these can be smelly.

EATING & DRINKING
Apart from the hotel restaurants, there are numerous small Malagasy *hotelys* along the main road and near the beach. Cheap eats and a good atmosphere can be had at Bar le Jamaica on the beach and Drugstore Restaurant in town.

Mada Bar (mains Ar2000-15,000; 🕑 lunch & dinner) Fresh fruit juice, excellent ice creams and pizzas are all the specialities at this little place with a full menu and relaxed ambiance. It's also great at multitasking – kayaks and motorbikes are available for rent.

L'Oasis Hôtel (☎ 95 522 22; Rte de Batalege; mains Ar5000-12,000) Presided over by an affable local guy called Jean le Rasta, or Rasta Jean, the bar and restaurant at this hotel is definitely engaging. There is live music, including drums and reggae performed by Rasta Jean and other local musicians. The food is great.

La Capannina (☎ 95 520 69; mains from Ar8000; 🕑 lunch & dinner Thu-Tue) Run by an Italian and Malagasy couple, this place serves yummy, and consistently reliable, Italian food – think lots of pastas and different sauces. Sit outside on the attractive terrace; look for La Capannini on the beach road.

our pick **Sunshine Restaurant & Bar** (☎ 95 523 47; Chez Maggie; breakfast Ar9000, mains Ar17,000; 🕑 breakfast, lunch & dinner) Chez Maggie's thatched-roof restaurant, with fabulous sunset views of the Mozambique Channel, offers a rotating daily menu of fresh-caught fish and seafood, delicious cheese and lots of fresh fruits and veggies. Barbecue jumbo shrimp, and anything with crab, are the house specialities. The bar has a wide selection of scotch, whiskey and delicious homemade coco rum. It's a good place to settle in for a night of drinking.

Other happening spots to imbibe come dark include the bar at L'Oasis Hôtel; **L'Aqualimba**, which is a big open venue that sometimes hosts live shows; and the divey disco with our all-time favourite bar name, **My Lord** (🕑 Tue-Sun).

GETTING THERE & AROUND
Taxis between town and the airport cost Ar10,000, while shared taxis in town cost Ar1500.

Air
Air Madagascar flies several times weekly between Morondava and Antananarivo (Ar225,000), Toliara (Ar200,000) and Morombe (Ar180,000). The Air Madagascar office is on the road to the airport.

Boat
Morondava is connected with the villages to the south by pirogues. Wooden cargo boats (without engines) depart weekly for

Morombe. Facilities on most boats are very basic; bring sun protection and all the food and water you will need.

The Taxi de la Mer (Ar50,000, 2½ hours) is a newish ferry running twice a week between Morondava and Belo-Sur-Mer.

Taxi-Brousse

Morondava is 700km from Antananarivo, but the road is in quite bad condition. Driving takes between 12 and 17 hours.

The tarmac is in fairly good shape until you reach Miandrivazo, when it becomes a tough-as-nails, grating 120km drive to Malaimbandy that can take six hours alone. The final bit to Antananarivo is also in very poor condition, although you won't mind so much as the scenery is so gorgeous. Rice paddies are framed by huge baobabs, and if you arrive in Antananarivo in early morning, the soft light turning the Mediterranean-style hill-town's buildings a glowing golden, is heavenly. You can rent a car and driver in Morondava for the trip – ask around at the hotels and taxi-brousse stands.

Taking a taxi-brousse to Antananarivo (Ar30,000, 18 hours) is a cheaper, although almost unbearably uncomfortable option, due to the length of the trip. Still these are reliable, leaving Morondava around noon and arriving in Antananarivo around 6am the next morning. Taxis-brousses also run to Morondava and Antsirabe (via Miandrivazo); they take about 15 hours and cost Ar20,000. Vehicles depart daily between about noon and 2pm, arriving in Antsirabe early the next morning.

To Toliara (Ar35,000) there are *camions-brousses* three times weekly during the dry season, departing Morondava around noon and taking two days along a rough road. Vehicles to Belo-sur-Tsiribihina depart once or twice every morning (Ar10,000, five hours).

AROUND MORONDAVA

AVENUE DU BAOBAB

One of the most photographed spots in Madagascar is the avenue of *Adansonia grandidieri* baobabs on either side of the road about 15km north of Morondava, along the road to Belo-sur-Tsiribihina. The best times to visit are at sunset and sunrise, when the colours of the trees change and the long shadows are most pronounced. The trees here are as old as one thousand years; it's the kind of awesome sight

that stays planted pleasantly in your memory for a lifetime.

A great way to explore Avenue du Baobab is via a guided quad-bike tour with **Loc' Découverte** (☎ 032 04 70 619; tours Ar150,000), based in Morondava. A taxi from town costs about Ar30,000 return.

RÉSERVE FORESTIÈRE DE KIRINDY

The Réserve Forestière de Kirindy, 60km northeast of Morondava, covers about 12,500 hectares and was established in the late 1970s as an experiment in sustainable logging and forest management. Today it's still mostly visited by researchers, but travellers who spend a few days here could be rewarded with a glimpse of the *fosa* (*Cryptoprocta felix*). Madagascar's largest predator – not to be confused with the fossa – is an elusive puma-like creature. The best time to spot a *fosa* is in October. If you don't get to see the *fosa*, you might be lucky enough to see one of Madagascar's most charming rodents, the giant jumping rat.

Information

Entry permits to the reserve cost Ar25,000, paid at the entrance. There are no official guides, but a few *pisteurs* (untrained guides who mostly speak Malagasy only) are available just to show the way to the best sites for viewing wildlife. A list of the trees you'll see en route is available at the park entrance.

Wildlife

In addition to the *fosa*, the reserve supports six species of lemurs, mainly nocturnal, including the fat-tailed lemur and the tiny mouse lemur (*Microcebus myoxinus*), believed to be the world's smallest primate. There are also 45 bird species and 32 reptile species, including the rare Madagascan flat-tailed tortoise (*Pyxis planicauda*). Other creatures include the giant jumping rat, and several tenrec and mongoose species. Keep in mind that some animals hibernate during the winter months of June to August. For the best chance of seeing the *fosa*, a stay of at least three nights is needed.

Sleeping & Eating

Choose from camping (Ar10,000), dorms (Ar15,000) or bungalows (Ar20,000 to Ar40,000). All are located at the reserve's headquarters, where you'll also find a small restaurant serving simple meals and cold beer.

WESTERN MADAGASCAR

There are 12 bungalows, but the four new ones are most comfortable, with shared flush toilets (as opposed to long-drops). Dorm beds come with mozzie nets, sheets and blankets. Electricity can be sporadic. Bring a good torch.

Getting There & Away

Kirindy is about 60km northeast of Morondava, signposted off the Belo-sur-Tsiribihina road. The reserve can be easily reached by taxi-brousse; ask drivers on the route between Morondava and Belo-sur-Tsiribihina to let you off at the entrance to the road down to the reserve. From the main road, it's a 5km walk to the entrance.

PARC NATIONAL KIRINDY MITE & RÉSERVE SPÉCIALE D'ANDRANOMENA

Not to be confused with the much more popular Réserve Forestière de Kirindy, the new **Parc National Kirindy Mite** (per day Ar10,000) lets you really get off the beaten track. Even though it's located just 34km south of Morondava, this ultra-wild and isolated park saw only 70 visitors in 2006! One hurdle to visiting is the complete lack of infrastructure – to stay you need to be a totally self-sufficient camper. Keen birders will dig this place. There are numerous opportunities to spot rare birds on a littoral lake and nearby sand dunes.

Réserve Spéciale d'Andranomena is around 30km to the northeast of the Morondava, and also very remote with no visitor facilities. There is excellent bird-watching on a seasonal (wet) lake close to many impressive baobabs, and you can camp.

At the moment both these parks are really only a destination for keen naturalists, but if you're interested in visiting, drop into the very helpful **Angap office** (☎ 95 524 20) in Morondava.

BELO-SUR-MER

Belo-sur-Mer is an attractive seaside village on the edge of a small but picturesque lagoon.

The village is a regional ship-building centre and huge cargo vessels are still constructed on the beach in the same manner they were made two centuries ago.

Belo-Sur-Mer's star attraction is a string of seven gorgeous **coral-fringed islands**, some semi-submerged, off its coast. They're little known and seldom visited; you can live the whole Robinson Crusoe smash-a-coconut-with-your-bare-hands fantasy on a couple of these islands for a day. Diving is particularly good thanks to the proximity of a deep passage through the Canal de Mozambique – you get to see some really big fish, deep-water critters like the octopus and even sea turtles.

To reach the islands, charter a pirogue for a day. Day trips cost around Ar65,000 if you barter, or check out the offerings at L'Ecolodge du Menabe's dive school. For certified divers, the two-dive deal for Ar130,000 (as opposed to one dive at Ar100,000) is the best value. Novices can be baptised by sea – introductory dives cost Ar110,000. Those just wishing to snorkel can tag along for about half-price.

In addition to its dive school, **L'Ecolodge du Menabe** (☎ 871 763 963 816; www.menabelo.com; r from Ar35,000, set dinner Ar25,000) is also one of the village's best hotels. It is well managed and has eight rooms in a peaceful garden. The restaurant serves good food, but is restrictive with an expensive fixed three-course menu.

Access to Belo-sur-Mer is by 4WD (from May to November) or boat. There are taxis-brousses between Belo-sur-Mer and Morondava, but the route is sometimes blocked. It's also possible to arrange transport with local pirogue captains. Allow plenty of time – the trip often takes more than a day – and bring all the water and food you may need. It is much easier to arrange a motorboat transfer with one of the hotels or tour operators in Morondava (p153). These do the trip in around 2½ hours, which makes it more worthwhile.

Northern Madagascar

If you're unable to decide between an over-easy beach vacation or a 'lace up your boots and forge a new trail' kind of holiday, you'll dig travel in Northern Madagascar.

White-sand beaches, air perfumed with ylang-ylang and vanilla, snorkelling in a sea of emerald, mangrove swamps and centuries-old baobabs are all hallmarks of Madagascar's most interesting, diverse and, at times, disparaged region. Villages of simple homes made from sticks sit flush with the lux new tourist resorts.

The eclectic region is split into two distinct parts. Nosy Be is Madagascar's premiere kick-back-and-relax beach destination. The island is as swanky (and expensive) as the country gets, with a number of posh resorts (although they're not exactly Bora Bora luxury-wise). Overall it's a charming place, with gorgeous water and delicious seafood, where it's very easy to lose track of time for a week or so.

The Diego Suarez area is Madagascar's best-kept secret, and especially appealing to those seeking paradise lost – it sees far fewer visitors. Here you'll find two national parks still so wild that four new species of lemur were discovered in 2006 alone! There are kilometres of hiking trails through psychedelic forests of spindly red rocks and past trees with tumours shaped like giant squid growing off their sides. On the coast, palm-fringed sandy shores, sparkling sapphire water and an emerald sea keep beach bums smiling for days. Diego is the place to go if you want to race quad-bikes over dunes or try kitesurfing in one of the three beautiful bays framing the city.

HIGHLIGHTS

- Enjoying rum punch and grilled lobster under the palm trees at Chez Loulou, and catching another amazing sunset on Nosy Be's **Andilana beach** (p171)

- Indulging in a little adventure – either via quad-bike or kite-board – and checking out the brilliant scenery around **Diego Suarez** (p175)

- Taking solitary walks in the dappled rainforest of **Parc National de Montagne d'Ambre** (p184)

- Discovering spires of ruby-red *tsingy* and nearly a dozen species of lemur in the wild **Réserve Spéciale de l'Ankàrana** (p186)

- Uncovering the underwater world while diving off **Nosy Komba** (p172)

■ HIGHEST POINT: 1785m   ■ PRINCIPAL TRIBE: Antakàrana

NORTHERN MADAGASCAR

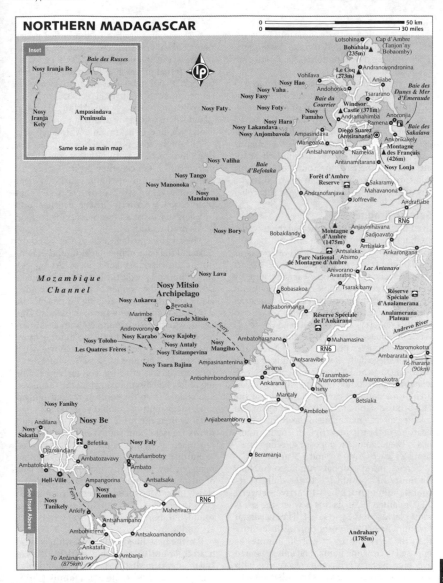

Getting There & Away

Air Madagascar (☎ 82 211 93; Ave Sourcouf, Diego Suarez) flies between Nosy Be and Milan (€871) twice a week; it also has flights from Nosy Be to Antananarivo (Ar304,600), Réunion (Ar600,000) and Diego Suarez (Ar132,000) three times a week. From Diego Suarez there are daily flights to Antananarivo (Ar304,600) and regular flights to Sambava (Ar192,000),

Toamasina (Ar525,600) and Mahajanga (Ar288,000). Remember, if you fly Air Madagascar into the country you are eligible for a 50% discount on domestic flights – bring your outbound tickets to the Air Mad office. Note that ticket prices fluctuate wildly in Madagascar, and are dependent on the cost of petrol, as well occupancy, so use these rates only as a guide.

Sailing yachts regularly come into Nosy Be, and many are prepared to take passengers. Their principal destination is the Comorian island of Mayotte.

The road journey from Diego Suarez to Antananarivo is a long and arduous one, particularly if you elect to do it by taxi-brousse (bush taxi; Ar60,000, at least two days). The worst patch of road is the 200km of the Route Nationale 6 (RN6) south of Ambanja. To Mahajanga (Ar55,000, 36 hours), expect a similarly arduous ride. To the east, the route to Ambilobe takes around two hours, followed by at least a day of potholes before you arrive at Iharana.

Getting Around

Even though the road is sealed all the way, the six-hour minibus ride from Ankify (the port for boats to Nosy Be) to Diego Suarez is as hard on the arse as it is on the attitude. Expect vehicles to be filled to triple capacity, and try to move as little as possible or you'll likely end up with someone's body part across your face! The good news is the route from Nosy Be to Ankify (via ferry) then on to Diego (by road) is one of Madagascar's most organised; numerous taxis-brousses ply the route between the port and Diego daily. If you're coming or going between Diego and Nosy Be you can purchase a boat/minibus combo ticket (Ar40,000). If you aren't on a combo ticket, just show up at the taxi-brousse stand in Ankify at about 9am and ask for a direct – make sure to clarify this before boarding or the trip may triple in length – minibus to Diego; going the opposite direction taxis-brousses leave Diego around 5.30am.

Ferries and speedboats run between Nosy Be and Ankify multiple times daily year-round, although it's best to arrive between 7.30am and 8.30am as this is when the sea is most placid and the trip safest. The speedboat (around Ar20,000) costs only a little more than the ferry and takes just 30 minutes as opposed to two long hours. The only reason to ever take the ferry is if you have a vehicle with you. Don't expect life-vests on either vessel.

NOSY BE

pop 40,000

Despite being Madagascar's number-one beach destination, attracting thousands of sunscreen-slathered tourists from across the globe year round, Nosy Be and its surrounding islands

(p172) remain paradise in the buff. Luxury doesn't always mean electricity or even a good mattress, but it's this exact lack of 21st-century fluff that makes it so appealing in the first place. With only one super-pimp package resort (aimed squarely at the Italian charter market), Nosy Be is refreshingly void of bling. This is an island where you can read a trashy novel in the sand without ever hearing the whir of jet-skis.

Although Nosy Be's beaches (and resorts) don't look as fantasy-fulfilling as some in the Caribbean or Greece, they do win points for tranquillity, gorgeous light, sparkling clear turquoise water (void of the seaweed that plagues many Eastern African beaches) and excellent al fresco restaurants serving seafood feasts on the sand.

The air is scented with ylang-ylang and vanilla and the pace of life is as slow and drawn-out as the island's killer sunsets. As the sky turns pink and purple the last rays of sun make silhouettes of the wooden pirogues and women clad in bright sarongs walking home with the day's catch in buckets on their heads. This event, which starts around 5.45pm and manages to stretch on for nearly an hour, is more intense and captivating than any movie you'll ever see. And as most of Nosy Be's infrastructure is on its western edge, you can witness the big yellow ball disappearing into the shadowed sea straight from the comfort of your bungalow's saggy mattress should you choose.

Nosy Be is the most expensive destination in Madagascar, and rooms can cost twice as much here as on the mainland. Still, compared to Europe or North America, prices remain relatively low and many visitors find the lack of major development and *mora mora* (slowly slowly) lifestyle worth the few extra euros it costs to get here. The climate is sunny all year round, but there's a risk of cyclones in February and March.

For the best-hued water and whitest sand head as far north as possible. With its fields of sugarcane, rum distilleries and single-gauge railway, inland Nosy Be has a faintly Caribbean atmosphere. If you can drag yourself away from the beach there are some beautiful out-of-the-way corners to explore.

History

Nosy Be's first inhabitants are believed to have been 15th-century Swahili and Indian traders. Later, the island served as a magnet for refugees, merchants and settlers of all descriptions.

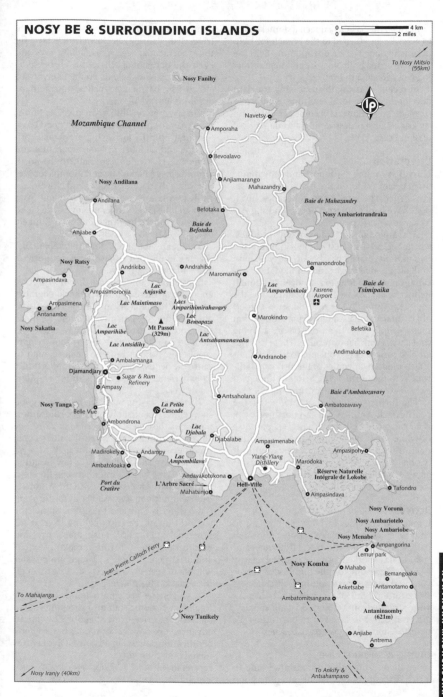

NOSY BE & SURROUNDING ISLANDS

0 — 4 km
0 — 2 miles

To Nosy Mitsio (55km)

Nosy Fanihy

Mozambique Channel

Navetsy

Amporaha

Bevoalavo

Anjiamarango
Mahazandry

Baie de Mahazandry

Nosy Andilana

Andilana

Befotaka

Nosy Ambariotrandraka

Anjiabe

Baie de Befotaka

Nosy Ratsy

Andrikibo

Andrahibo

Bemanondrobe

Ampasindava

Maromanify

Lac Amparihinkola

Baie de Tsimipaika

Ampasimoronjia

Lac Anjavibe

Fasrene Airport

Ampasimena

Lac Maintimaso

Lacs Amparihimirahavary

Marokindro

Antanambe

Lac Bemapaza

Befetika

Nosy Sakatia

Lac Amparihibe

▲ Mt Passot (329m)

Lac Antsahamanavaka

Andimakabo

Lac Antsidihy

Andranobe

Ambalamanga

Djamandjary

Sugar & Rum Refinery

Ampasy

Antsaholana

Baie d'Ambatozavavy

Ambatozavavy

Nosy Tanga

La Petite Cascade

Belle Vue

Ambondrona

Lac Djabala

Djabalabe

Ampasimenabe

Ampasipohy

Madirokely

Andampy

Lac Ampombilava

Ylang-Ylang Distillery

Marodoka

Réserve Naturelle Intégrale de Lokobe

Ambatoloaka

Andavakotokona

Port du Cratère

L'Arbre Sacré

Hell-Ville

Ampasindava

Tafondro

Mahatsinjo

Nosy Vorona

Nosy Ambariotelo

Nosy Ambariobe

Nosy Menabe

Ampangorina

Lemur park

Jean Pierre Calloch Ferry

Nosy Komba

Mahabo

Bemangoaka

To Mahajanga

Anketsabe

Antamotamo

Ambatomitsangana

Antaninaomby (621m)

Nosy Tanikely

Anjiabe

Antrema

Nosy Iranjy (40km)

To Ankify & Antsahampano

In 1839, the Sakalava queen Tsiomeko fled to Nosy Be and turned to the French for help in resisting her Merina enemies. In 1841, the Sakalava ceded both Nosy Be and neighbouring Nosy Komba to France.

In recent years, with increasing tourism development and local environmental pressures, deforestation has become a problem on the island, as has destruction and damage of offshore coral reefs.

Orientation

Nosy Be's capital, main port and only major town is Hell-Ville, on the island's southeastern corner. There are no good beaches, but it does have banks, internet access and the Air Madagascar office.

Ambatoloaka and Madirokely beaches, which begin 10km west of Hell-Ville, are the two most developed beaches on Nosy Be, and both offer a wide range of accommodation and eating options catering to all budgets. Although neither beach is Nosy Be's most attractive, the more expensive hotels here do such a good job at international and local promotion that many people book them out before arriving (not always with happy results). These beaches are also convenient if you need to be near Hell-Ville's modern amenities or the airport. Madirokely, to the north, is the better of these two (which are really one joint strip of sand).

The further north you go, the better the beaches get. Andilana, at the northwest tip, is by far Nosy Be's crown jewel. A paradise of white sand, swaying palms and the most postcard-worthy turquoise water around, it is one of Nosy Be's least developed parts. It appeals to honeymooners and couples looking for romantic tranquillity.

Activities

Organised activities in Nosy Be are still in relative infancy. To really get off the beaten path, charter a boat with a local fisherman and spend a day snorkelling and exploring nearby islands. Depending on the number of people you have and your bargaining skills, charters start at around Ar75,000 per person. To live out your stranded-on-a-deserted-island fantasy, ask your driver to take you to the northeast's deserted, and wildly gorgeous, beaches.

DIVING & SNORKELLING

Nosy Be and the other islands are home to a rich diversity of marine life and offer good diving and snorkelling. Boxfish, surgeonfish, triggerfish, damselfish, clown fish, yellow-fin tuna, barracuda, eagle rays, manta rays and even the occasional whale can all be spotted. Around Nosy Sakatia you're likely to see clown fish, barracuda, turtles, and perhaps dolphins and whale sharks.

On average, visibility on dives is about 15m year-round – much more on good days. The best months for diving are from April to June and October to November. July and August can be windy, especially to the north around Nosy Mitsio. The best months for seeing whale sharks are October and November; while manta rays seem more prevalent from April to June and October to November. Good spots for snorkelling include Nosy Tanikely and Nosy Mitsio.

Prices are about €37 for a baptême (first dive), €35/65 for one/two with equipment, and €40 for a night dive.

You should understand that if you have an accident there is no hyperbaric chamber anywhere in Madagascar. You will have to be air-lifted out to Mauritius or Réunion; make sure you have insurance. If you're at all worried, do an introductory dive (even if you're certified) as these don't go deep enough to cause the bends, but still offer the opportunity to experience Madagascar's unique underwater world.

If you are staying in Andilana there is good snorkelling just offshore on the northernmost portion of the beach. You need to go early – be back by around 11am when the tides come in, otherwise the return swim may be a bit treacherous. The reef is just a few hundred metres off the beach. Enter between the steps leading up to Au Belvedere and the Andilana Resort and it's an easy wade out to the point – the water is only chest deep for all but the last portion of the trip, making it great for novices. With big ocean fish, manta rays and even turtles, not to mention moving conchs and bright coral, there's enough underwater wildlife to keep even experts smiling through their mask. Plus it's free.

Dive courses are conducted in French or English with some staff also speaking Italian or German. Prices start at about €225 for an advanced open-water course; it's best to book certification courses in advance. Dive centres include the following.

Forever Dive (☎ 032 07 125 65; forever.dive@simicro .mg; Madirokely) A smaller operator, Forever Dive is run by the friendly Sylvia and offers intro and double dives at slightly lower prices, and doesn't charge more for solo divers.

Océane's Dream (☎ 86 614 26, 032 07 127 82; oceand@wanadoo.mg; Ambatoloaka) One of the most well-established and recommended operators on the island offers single and introductory dives along with catamaran-based diving cruises to Nosy Mitsio, Nosy Iranja and Nosy Radama for €550 per person. A minimum of two people (previous certification required) is needed. It also does CMAS dive courses.

Tropical Diving (☎ 032 07 127 90; Madirokely) Offers a good range of PADI courses and a variety of diving excursions to the islands; it's inside the Coco Plage Hotel.

FISHING
The best months for fishing are from March to June and October to December. For sailfish, the season runs from June to October. Fishing excursions aren't cheap – expect to pay at least €400 per day per boat, including equipment, for a maximum of four people. Fishing operators include the following.

International Fisching Club (☎ 86 614 29; hotel .espadon@malagasy.com; Hôtel L'Espadon, Ambatoloaka)
Le Grand Bleu (☎ 86 634 08; www.legrandbleunosybe .com in French; Le Grand Bleu Hotel, Ampasimoronjia)

OTHER ACTIVITIES
Riding a quad or a motorbike across sand, through water or along a dusty red dirt track is becoming a popular way to spend a Nosy Be afternoon, and many midrange and top-end resorts now offer the sport on their activity menu. There are a few good operators in the Andilana area, including **Le Grand Bleu** (☎ 86 920 23; www .legrandbleunosybe.com; Le Grand Bleu Hotel, Ampasimoronjia). This hotel just south of Andilana proper rents two-person quad bikes and Yamaha 400 motorbikes for Ar171,000 per three hours (pay only Ar121,500 if you're riding solo). The hotel also offers old fashioned water-skiing for Ar67,500 per person (minimum of two people), and rents sea kayaks (half/full day Ar37,800/48,600) and snorkelling equipment (Ar10,800 per day). Excursions to snorkelling favourite Nosy Fanny cost Ar94,500 per person including lunch and equipment.

On Andilana beach, **Quad Run** (☎ 86 921 51) rents two person quad bikes for €40 per day; get info at **Kokóa Surf, Sun & Fun** (☎ 86 921 122; www.kokoa-nosybe.com; Andilana Beach) on the beach between Chez Loulou and the souvenir stalls. Owned by Roberto Moreni, who also speaks English, it is a first-class company geared pri-

THE DONIA

Every June, Nosy Be holds a week-long music festival known as the Donia. Groups from Madagascar and neighbouring islands perform at venues in various parts of the island, with attendant carnival, sporting events and seminars. For French-language information, go to http://perso.wanadoo .fr/jbemizik/donia.htm.

marily to the Italian market. It also teaches the arts of kitesurfing (per hour €30) and windsurfing (per hour €15). Although prices are a bit steeper than elsewhere, Roberto's clients don't seem to mind paying for the personalised service – many return year after year.

Tours
Naturally, Nosy Be is home to dozens of tour companies, some specialising in multi-day dive or snorkel cruises around the various islands, while others simply provide interisland transport or day excursions. Many dive operators also organise boat excursions. In addition to the contacts listed here, touts sell trips directly to hotel guests and sunbathers on the beach. Although not everyone is happy with these trips in local wooden pirogues, most people return quite satisfied, if a little tomato coloured – take plenty of sunscreen! If you know how to barter, these excursions can work out to be significantly cheaper – a day of snorkelling around Nosy Be's sister islands, with stops for lunch and sunbathing, should cost between Ar75,000Ar and AR100,000.

Organised operators include the following:
Daniel (☎ 032 04 069 59; Hell-Ville) A long-established operator offering glass-bottomed catamaran day cruises to Nosy Komba and Nosy Tanikely. Rates are Ar80,000 per person including a slap-up lunch and free rum (but excluding other drinks) and transport to and from your hotel. Snorkelling equipment can be hired for Ar10,000. The *Daniel* departs daily at about 8.30am from the port in Hell-Ville, returning in the late afternoon. The boat can drop you off at Nosy Komba and/or Nosy Tanikely, and pick you up one or more days later for no extra cost. A minibus to the port departs Ambatoloaka at 8am daily from Location Jeunesse on the main street. Sailing time is about 45 minutes from Hell-Ville to Nosy Komba, about one hour from Nosy Komba to Nosy Tanikely, and about one hour from Nosy Tanikely back to Hell-Ville.
Island Quest (☎ 86 615 52; www.islandquest.co.za) Check out the pimp website at this well-organised South

African company. Trips are based aboard the luxury catamaran *Bossi*, which sleeps up to eight people. This operator offers four- and five-day island cruises; diving and fishing can also be arranged. Book well in advance as it fills fast. Rates start at around €200 per person per day, including meals (but not booze; you can bring your own, however), dives and fishing.

Jungle Village (☎ 86 93 102; www.nosybe-jungle village.com; Ampasipohy) A beach bungalow operation that also runs tours around northern Madagascar. These include visits to nearby islands and trekking in the parks near Diego Suarez. Trips start at €431 per person for seven nights; prices are dependent on the class of accommodation you choose to stay in on the road.

Kokóa Surf, Sun & Fun (☎ 86 921 122; www .kokoa-nosybe.com; Andilana beach) Rents luxury villas in Andilana, and runs camping trips to nearby Nosy Iranja (€175 per person). Customised private transport and tours around Madagascar are also arranged – an option for getting to Diego Suarez in style if the planes are full.

Libertalia Aventure (☎ 86 925 41; www .libertalia-aventure.com; Andilana) With a slick brochure, this upmarket and eco-friendly company specialises in adventures across Northern Madagascar. Trips from Nosy Be last between two and 12 nights and include everything from tours tailored specifically towards mountain-biking, trekking or sailing. Two-night sailing trips to islands around Nosy Be start at €75 per person per day. Rates include meals and lodging. In Andilana, head to Chez Loulou restaurant to book directly – boats leave from here anyway.

MadaVoile (Blue Planet, Escapades; ☎ 86 616 37, 86 620 80; www.madavoile.com in French; Ambatoloaka) Three names, one reliable operator. It offers a wide range of land- and sea-based tours including trips around the islands, and to Réserve Spéciale de l'Ankàrana and Parc National de Montagne d'Ambre. English and German are spoken.

Getting There & Away

AIR

Air Madagascar (☎ 86 613 60; Rte de l'Ouest, Hell-Ville) flights link Nosy Be's Fasrene Airport with Antananarivo every day (Ar304,600), often via Mahajanga (Ar288,000) or Diego Suarez (Ar132,000). Flights also go to Sambava and Dzaoudzi in Mayotte. There are also international flights to Milan and Réunion.

Air Austral (☎ 86 612 40) and **Air Mauritius** (☎ 86 612 40), both in Hell-Ville, can book regular flights to Mayotte, Réunion and Mauritius.

BOAT

Nosy Be is best reached from the mainland port of Ankify by small speedboat (Ar20,000,

30 minutes). These depart in both directions starting around 7.30am. The channel crossing is best undertaken in the morning, before the afternoon tides make the sea rough. Two ferries also make the crossing, but unless you have your car with you (both take vehicles) there's no reason to take these as they are much slower.

If you're travelling with a vehicle, the **Fivondronana Ferry** (☎ 032 02 358 40) leaves Nosy Be for Anstahampano port, near Ambanja, daily. Departure times vary according to the high tide, and the journey takes about two hours. Passenger tickets cost Ar15,000. You can buy tickets at the port or at the office on the main street.

Cargo boats still travel between Nosy Be and Mahajanga, and less frequently between Nosy Be and Diego Suarez. The trips take anywhere from 24 to 72 hours and is very uncomfortable. Check the blackboard outside the Auximad office at the port in Hell-Ville as departures are irregular.

Most of the private yachts passing through Nosy Be are bound for Mayotte (the passage costs about €300). The best place to ask is at Nandipo bar in Hell-Ville. The yachting season runs between August and November.

TAXI-BROUSSE

It's a long, hard ride by taxi-brousse between Diego Suarez and Ankify, the port from which boats depart to Nosy Be. See p160 for the scoop on the journey.

Getting Around

The main road on Nosy Be, between the airport and Andilana via Ambatoloaka is sealed, flat and fast and almost all hotels sit just yards off it. Internal roads are generally rougher and hillier.

TO/FROM THE AIRPORT

Nosy Be's Fasrene Airport is on the island's east side, about 12km from Hell-Ville. The taxi fare from the airport to Hell-Ville is around Ar15,000. It is about Ar30,000 to Ambatoloaka and Ar40,000 to Andilana – and nearly 50km to the northwest.

CAR & MOTORCYCLE

Most tour operators and upmarket hotels arrange car hire. Regular cars cost about Ar100,000 per day with a driver; the price does not include petrol. Expect to pay about

€85 per day for a 4WD with a driver, although a 4WD is not really necessary.

Nosy Red Cars (☎ 032 07 946 46) in Ambatoloaka hire out groovy little red beach buggies (only for use on designated main roads) for €50 per day with the first 50km included. **Location Jeunesse** (☎ 86 614 08), in Ambatoloaka, rents out Honda 250cc motorcycles (Ar40,000 per day), scooters (Ar30,000 per day) and mountain bikes (Ar15,000 per day) that are sometimes in mediocre condition. Be sure to check your contract and the condition of the bike very carefully before parting with any money.

TAXI & TAXI-BROUSSE

Shared-taxi fares are Ar1000 between Hell-Ville and Ambatoloaka (20 to 30 minutes), and Ar2000 between Hell-Ville and Andilana (45 minutes). Elsewhere on the island, public transport is scarce. Your best chance for catching a taxi-brousse from Andilana into Hell-Ville is in the parking lot behind Chez Loulou. Although taxis-brousses can be scarce during the week, on Sundays there are dozens lined up to transport the groups of Malagasy, couples and families that come from all over the island to picnic, dance, drink beer, swim and socialise before the working week starts again.

A charter between Hell-Ville and Ambatoloaka costs Ar10,000, to Andilana it's Ar30,000. Short hops around Hell-Ville cost Ar1800 per trip.

HELL-VILLE

Despite the off-putting moniker (named for Admiral de Hell, a French governor of Réunion), Nosy Be's main town is anything but hellish. Rather, it's an upbeat, if rather dishevelled, place where frangipani and bougainvillea frame crumbling ruins of old colonial buildings, sidewalk cafés bustle with backpack-touting tourists sipping strong espresso, and expats gather at everyone's favourite bar, Nandipo, for a gossip and wood-oven pizza. After a long stay in the bush, or at one of Nosy Be's isolated beach resorts, Hell-Ville is a good place to catch up on world affairs and get a plate of pasta. If you are planning on catching the speedboat to the mainland, it may be worth spending the night here too. Not only are hotels cheaper than elsewhere in Nosy Be, you'll be just minutes away from the port where boats depart (and it's easy to find combo tickets to Diego Suarez from touts around town; just don't pay until the morning when you get a ticket at the

port). For information about getting to and from Hell-Ville, see opposite.

Orientation & Information

Hell-Ville is relatively compact, with most restaurants and shops clustered in the centre square. Hotels are spread along the main road, Blvd de l'Indépendance. The port is at the extreme southeast corner of town.

INTERNET ACCESS

Cyber Café – Impressions Photos (☎ 032 41 325 49; per min Ar100; ☼ 8am-noon & 3-6pm Mon-Fri, 8am-noon Sat) Across the street from the Oasis Café, it is a bit hard to spot. Climb two flights of stairs on the left side of the building behind the big souvenir shop and follow the signs.

MEDICAL SERVICES

Unless it's a true emergency, go to the hospitals in Antananarivo, which are much better. French is the primary language, although some doctors speak English and Italian.
Hôpital Principal (☎ 86 613 95) Emergency facilities.

MONEY

All the major banks, including Bank of Africa (BOA), BFV-SG and BNI-CL, have branches in Hell-Ville equipped with modern ATMs accepting international cards. The banks also change money and travellers cheques and do credit-card advances – note they all shut down between noon and 3pm every day.

POST & TELEPHONE

The **post office** and **Telecom office** are on the corner of Blvd de l'Indépendance and Rue Passot. There are several card phones in town.

Sleeping

It's probably worth staying here your last night if you're planning to leave Nosy Be by speedboat early the next day – the port is just down the street from the centre and you'll pay less to sleep here.

Hôtel Plantation (☎ 86 614 38; Rue du Docteur Manceau; r Ar20,000-32,000; ☒) In a beautiful old colonial mansion, this is a charming little place where rooms come with sea-facing balconies. The cheaper rooms have fans, the most expensive air-con. The quaint little bar is perfect for sundowners, while the restaurant serves high-class French cuisine (set three-course menu Ar26,000).

Hôtel Belle Vue (☎ 86 513 84; r from Ar22,000; ☒) It works for a night, although all but the most

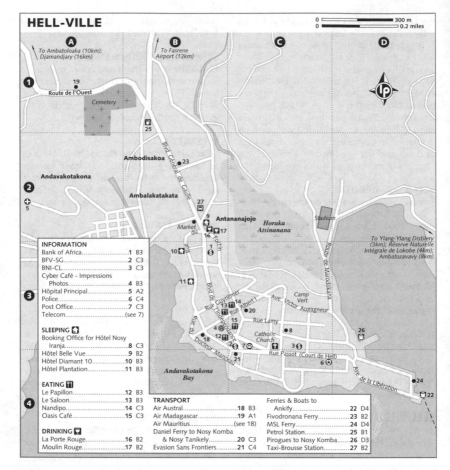

HELL-VILLE

0   300 m
0   0.2 miles

INFORMATION	
Bank of Africa	1 B3
BFV-SG	2 C3
BNI-CL	3 C3
Cyber Café - Impressions Photos	4 B3
Hôpital Principal	5 A2
Police	6 C4
Post Office	7 C3
Telecom	(see 7)

SLEEPING	
Booking Office for Hôtel Nosy Iranja	8 C3
Hôtel Belle Vue	9 B2
Hôtel Diamant 10	10 B3
Hôtel Plantation	11 B3

EATING	
Le Papillon	12 B3
Le Saloon	13 B3
Nandipo	14 C3
Oasis Café	15 C3

DRINKING	
La Porte Rouge	16 B2
Moulin Rouge	17 B2

TRANSPORT	
Air Austral	18 B3
Air Madagascar	19 A1
Air Mauritius	(see 18)
Daniel Ferry to Nosy Komba & Nosy Tanikely	20 C3
Evasion Sans Frontiers	21 C4
Ferries & Boats to Ankify	22 D4
Fivodronana Ferry	23 B2
MSL Ferry	24 D4
Petrol Station	25 B1
Pirogues to Nosy Komba	26 D3
Taxi-Brousse Station	27 B2

expensive rooms are very small and have no hot water or mozzie nets. Mattresses are made from very soft foam, but there's air-con and it's only a five-minute walk to the best restaurants in Hell-Ville. If you're interested in checking out the local dance scene, this might be your pick as it's only a stumble away from a popular cabaret. If you want to sleep it can be very loud, but the bar is good about shutting off the music by 11pm. Breakfast is served for an extra fee.

Hôtel Diamant 10 (☎ 86 614 48; 660405 Rue Docteur Manceau; r Ar50,000; 🗙) Near the centre, this bright painted place is one of the town's most upmarket. It has a sort of Miami Art Deco look – lots of glass and pastels. It definitely stands out amid the ruins of its neighbours! Rooms have mod tile floors, satellite TV, safes, minibars and

sea views and are pretty comfortable. There is a big rooftop terrace where you can pop up to watch the sunset. Bring a few beers.

Eating & Drinking

After eating the same shrimp or calamari dish for a week straight, Hell-Ville's eating options will seem like culinary heaven. Besides the places listed here, a couple of the hotels have restaurants.

Oasis Café (☎ 86 611 57; mains Ar6000-12,000; ☽ breakfast, lunch & dinner) Oasis' sidewalk seating is the hottest dining property in town. The menu includes everything from pesto pasta to warm panini sandwiches, burgers and pizza. Plus there's a choice of Western-style breakfasts with eggs, bacon and the works. Oasis also sells delicious pastries and ice creams and, best of all, real espresso drinks.

Le Saloon (☎ 86 921 77; mains Ar7500-9000; ☺ lunch & dinner) A wannabe cowboy bar with the Malagasy interpretation of Western US art, Le Saloon is nevertheless a pleasant spot offering daily *plats du jour* and an à la carte menu of grilled meats, seafood, spaghetti dishes and, of course, fresh *poisson*. The indoor and outdoor seating fills quickly at lunch and dinner.

Le Papillon (☎ 86 615 82; mains Ar8000-15,000; ☺ lunch & dinner Mon-Sat) For Italian food – lots of pasta dishes, served with real parmesan cheese, along with pizzas and seafood – and even a few Chinese plates, Le Papillon is probably the best bet in Hell-Ville. It's a cool and breezy place located in a crumbling old colonial house.

Nandipo (mains Ar11,000-13,000; ☺ breakfast, lunch & dinner) This is the yachtsmen and expat hangout of choice, where many regulars get stuck into the beer by 9am. It also serves excellent wood-oven pizzas, spontaneous live music and the best ambiance in town. Sit inside amid the cluttered wooden bar and high tables or outside in the garden. Either way the conversation often centres on finding a berth on a boat headed for Mayotte or the islands near Nosy Be.

La Porte Rouge (☎ 85 513 84) Next to the Hôtel Belle Vue, La Porte Rouge is a very social watering hole popular with the Malagasy locals. The ambiance is animated and amiable, and there's plenty of dancing and even a cabaret. Nearly cater-corner to La Porte Rouge is **Moulin Rouge**, which offers the same scene.

MT PASSOT & CRATER LAKES

Mt Passot (329m), Nosy Be's loftiest point, lies about 15km north of Hell-Ville (somewhat further by road). It's a good spot for watching the sunset or admiring the view. Some of the larger hotels arrange sunset minibus tours to the summit of Mt Passot, or you can hire a taxi to the top and walk back down (8km)

to Djamandjary. You can also get here by mountain bike or motorcycle.

RÉSERVE NATURELLE INTÉGRALE DE LOKOBE

The Réserve Naturelle Intégrale de Lokobe protects most of Nosy Be's remaining endemic vegetation. The reserve is home to the black lemur and several other lemur species. Other wildlife includes the boa constrictor and the giant (but harmless) Madagascan hog-nosed snakes, identified by intricate checkerboard markings.

You will need a guide to walk around in Lokobe, which can be arranged at Jungle Village. There is also a fee of Ar1000 per person payable to the village chief, who will approach you with a 'ticket'. Tours with a recommended guide called Jean Robert can be arranged by most of the hotels on the island for around Ar40,000.

A jack-of-all trades resort, **Jungle Village** (☎ 86 93 102; www.nosybe-junglevillage.com; r €32, bungalows from €45, set dinner €12) is in the tiny village of Ampasipohy, in the north of the reserve. The beach bungalows come in different sizes and are made from local materials – lots of thatch. Each comes with a net and outside sitting area. Travellers on a budget can grab one of the slightly cheaper hotel rooms. With lounge chairs (with padding!) in the sand and all sorts of excursions on offer, this is a good place to just kick back and relax. Full board is offered for an extra €22 per person per night. To reach Jungle Village, take a taxi to the village of Ambatozavavy. From here you can walk to the reserve at low tide in about 40 minutes; just follow the curve of the beach, or go via pirogue (about Ar30,000).

AMBATOLOAKA

Nosy Be's southernmost beach is one of the island's most popular and touristy, but far from its best. Despite its less than model look –

YLANG-YLANG

The low, gnarled ylang-ylang (e-lang-e-lang) tree is seen in plantations all over Nosy Be. Its scented green or yellow flowers are distilled to make oil, which is exported to the West for perfume. The trees are pruned into low and rather grotesque shapes to make picking the flowers easier.

The large **ylang-ylang distillery** (admission free; ☺ 8am-3.30pm Mon-Fri, 7.30am-2.30pm Sat) is about 3km east of Hell-Ville. You can see the ylang-ylang being distilled on Monday, Wednesday and Friday only.

To reach the distillery head east from Hell-Ville along the Route de Marodokany for 3km. All taxi drivers know where the place is. A fare should cost about Ar5000.

crumbling buildings and massive earthen pot-holes sit next to new luxury resorts with shim-mering swimming pools – Ambatoloaka boasts great variety. Sleeping choices range from Nosy Be's cheapest beach digs to some of the island's more exclusive hotels. Numerous restaurants within walking distance keep your stomach from getting bored – that's a real concern in more remote beaches where dining can be lim-ited to just one restaurant and self-catering is near impossible. If you're a beach connoisseur, you can always stay here and grab a taxi north to Andilana (see p171) for a day trip.

The beach, which merges with Madirokely, is a long swath of honey coloured sand that meets a ribbon of deep blue water flecked with turquoise and sapphire. Locals often gather on the sand for a game of pick-up soccer at lunchtime, manoeuvring their homemade ball around the tourists sunbathing on bright Madagascar-made sarongs.

On the downside, Ambatoloaka can seem straight-up sleazy. Its hotels are favourite haunts of old French men who come to seduce, and then usually leave, the poor, desperate and un-educated young Malagasy women who venture here from country villages in hopes of a better life with a Western man. Sadly, this version of their dream rarely comes true. Although you see signs in stores and hotels around the country condemning the use of children as sex slaves, in Ambatoloaka the problem is still obviously illustrated in the hotels and restaurants.

Orientation

Ambatoloaka sits in front of the tiny fishing village of the same name, about 10km west of Hell-Ville. Many taxi drivers will try to steer you here if you don't give them a location on the way from the airport. For car rentals, ring **Location Jeunesse** (☎ 86 614 08) or ask at your hotel. Be sure to check your car over for damage before signing the contract.

Sleeping

Places are often full, so it's best to reserve in ad-vance, but only agree to one night at first. This way you can make sure it's what you're looking for *after* seeing it. The following is just a selec-tion of many Ambatoloaka hotels. Lots of places quote in euros and some actually, preposter-ously, penalise you for using the local currency by tacking on extra 'conversion' fees.

Authentique, Chez Aly (☎ 86 616 42; bungalows from Ar15,000) By far the cheapest digs on this beach,

you really do get what you pay for at Chez Aly – don't expect any sort of luxuries. The plain wooden bungalows are set back a way from the beach and can't be described as anything other than rudimentary. Still it is ultra-cheap and sits next to the most popular beachfront restaurant in the neighbourhood, Chez An-geline, which is worth the splurge.

Le Coucher du Soleil (☎ 86 616 20; coucherdusoleil@ wanadoo.mg; d from Ar36,000) This Swiss-run budget hotel is the best value in its price bracket. The setting is lovely, and there are good sunset photo ops. It has spotless comfortable bunga-lows, each with a four-poster bed, mosquito net and terrace. Breakfast is available. The hotel is about five minutes' walk from the beach. Look for it about 200m above the main road on a hill. It's signposted.

Hotel La Residence d'Ambatoloaka (☎ 032 02 579 48; r Ar72,000, mains Ar6000-20,000; 🍴) This place was full when we stopped by, and guests said the block of 12 bungalow rooms behind the beachfront restaurant were simple but satisfy-ing – although the place seemed quite popular with single foreign men and their lady friends. Regardless of whether you stay the restaurant is a good bet for vegetarian and pasta options, and of course loads of fresh seafood.

Hôtel Benjamin (☎ 86 92 764; www.hotelbenjamin -nosybe.com; r €34) Situated in a great little garden and quiet location back from the road (look for it behind Coco Plage) this is one of the best deals for simple sleeping. The wooden bunga-lows are nothing fancy, but each comes with a stylish petite veranda. Some even have ham-mocks (although none have hot water). If you're planning a family reunion or just have a lot of friends, you can rent the villa. It sleeps up to 18 people in four bedrooms and has a kitchen and private pool! It costs €220 per night.

Hôtel Gerard et Francine (☎ 86 061 05; www.hotelger ardetfrancine.com; r incl breakfast from €40) A beautifully decorated family guesthouse with bright-yellow walls, wooden floors and a veranda overlooking the beach. The rooms come in all shapes and sizes – some are in the main house and some in the garden. The hotel uses solar power, which is not only good for the environment; it also means the lights stay on when Nosy Be's power clicks off, which was pretty often when we were there. It's best to make advance reservations, as this place is often full.

Coco Plage (☎ 032 07 769 64; coco.plage@simicro.mg; r €47-75; 🍴 🛏) If you're interested in diving, this could be a good choice. The long established Tropical Diving (see p163) is based here. There are 12 renovated, and tasteful, rooms with beach views and another six facing a pretty garden. You can also organise fishing trips and the Karibo Restaurant is very popular.

Hôtel L'Espadon (☎ 86 614 28; hotel.espadon@malagasy .com; r from €75; 🞂) Ambatoloaka's most upmarket option is comfortable and quite popular. Rooms feature giant original paintings of fish, and are large, tiled affairs with white walls and wooden shutters. Satellite TV and minibars in each room, along with beds, umbrellas and drink service on the sand, all lend a resort vibe. The glassed-in restaurant is handy, and usually crowded, specialising in Malagasy and Asian-influenced seafood dishes.

Eating

Besides the places listed here, check the sleeping listings as some hotels have restaurants.

Chez Mama (mains Ar5000-15,000; 🕒 lunch & dinner) For a true Malagasy eating experience, try Chez Mama, located on a little alley before Hotel La Résidence. It serves heaped plates of fresh fish and calamari along with local staples such as zebu and rice. Half portions are available.

La Saladerie (☎ 86 614 52; mains Ar6500-20,000; 🕒 lunch & dinner Mon-Sat) This is a smart terrace restaurant and bar with great sea views that serves healthy salads, grilled fish and Italian food. It's a good place to head for a sunset cocktail.

Baobab Kafe (mains Ar8000-13,000; 🕒 lunch & dinner) This aptly named café has the best décor in town – it's done up as a shrine to Madagascar's baobab tree, complete with photos and sculptures. It serves a small menu of mostly seafood, fish and zebu, along with cheaper snacks (burgers and sandwiches), kids plates and plenty of cocktail choices. It's popular with both *vazaha* (foreigners) and Malagasy. Look for it in front of Hotel La Résidence.

Chez Angeline (mains Ar8000-22,000; 🕒 lunch & dinner) In the centre of the village, Chez Angeline is the best restaurant on this beach. The small but very good French-influenced menu includes sumptuous zebu steak and succulent prawns. The ambiance is animated at night, and there is a very good assortment of local rums at the bar.

Karibo Restaurant (mains Ar9000-18,000; 🕒 lunch & dinner) If you're craving a bit of Italian food, this place at the Coco Plage hotel will satisfy your craving. It isn't your grandmother's kitchen in Bologna, but it does a decent selection of pastas –

including a spicy lobster sauce with spaghetti – and pizzas. Meat lovers can have zebu.

Drinking & Entertainment

Djembe Disco (admission Ar2000) is Nosy Be's favourite nightclub, located at the end of the village on the road leading to Madirokely town. It's the place to be seen in the evenings – popular with local couples, expats and single foreign men looking for love. Besides a dance floor, Djembe features pool tables and pictures of poker playing dogs on the walls. At Ar5000 per beer, and Ar3000 for water, it's a bit pricy. But then again, isn't that the truth about clubs the world over?

MADIROKELY

Madirokely beach is basically a northern extension of Ambatoloaka – there's no visual distinction between the two. It is the prettier half, however, and a bit more tranquil. Madirokely appeals to divers, with a couple of well-established scuba clubs located here and some decent diving in the vicinity.

Just because it's a bit less developed than Ambatoloaka, don't expect it to be less crowded. Madirokely still sees plenty of tourists, many of whom come on prebooked package holidays from Europe and places can fill fast. Don't worry too much if you can't snag a room. Madirokely and Ambatoloaka interlock, so it is very easy to sleep on one and chill or eat on the other.

Sleeping

There are a couple of good places to stay here, although not all are on the water.

Le Grand Large (☎ 86 615 84; r Ar50,000-75,000, mains Ar8000-15,000; 🞂) Located right on the beach in the village, this little guesthouse has smallish (but not bad-value, especially considering the location) rooms in a variety of prices according to view and size. All have a bathroom with hot water. The unpretentious and relaxed bar-restaurant faces the sea and serves mostly seafood dishes with a French flavour. There are occasional barbecues on the terrace overlooking the beach. Rates drop in the low season.

L'Heure Bleue (☎ 86 614 21; www.heurebleue.com; bungalows €75-85; 🞂) On a hill overlooking the village and away from the noise, this pretty little hotel has a terrace with great views and a gorgeous swimming pool. The bungalows are made of polished wood and come with smart linen bedclothes and giant sliding glass doors opening onto balconies with distant ocean views and armchairs for private sunbathing.

Le Marlin Club (☎ 86 613 15; marlin.club@simicro.mg; s/d €120/240; ❄) The rooms and bungalows are very classy at this chi-chi Italian-run hotel with brass nautical lamps and wooden floors. The bar and restaurant, however, are a bit tacky. There's a snack bar on the beach, and facilities for water sports, diving and fishing excursions.

Eating

Remember, it's almost as easy to eat in Ambatoloaka, which has many more choices.

La Caméléon (☎ 032 04 311 80; mains Ar10,000-25,000; ☟ lunch & dinner) An unpretentious little place, this restaurant at the extreme western edge of the beach serves a variety of pizzas, snacks and seafood and zebu mains. It also has a few rooms for rent.

Tsimanin Kafé (☎ 032 04 016 00; mains Ar15,000-40,000; ☟ lunch & dinner Thu-Sat, lunch only Mon & Tue, closed Wed) You'll be tempted to eat many courses in this attractive wooden restaurant on the beach that offers the complete gastronomic French dining experience. Tsimanin has been around long enough to garner a stellar rep with visiting French gourmets for its sophisticated fresh fare. Expect lobster profiteroles, prawns in oyster sauce, local foie gras and fish prepared Malagasy style, plus a few lighter lunch dishes. Unfortunately there is not much for vegetarians, but there's an extensive wine list.

AMBONDRONA & BELLE VUE

You can see shadows of the mainland hills across the navy- and turquoise-specked sea at the quiet beach of Ambondrona. On a small bay just north of Madirokely, it's more tranquil than its southern neighbour, with an almost blissfully lost vibe.

To get here by road, follow the pavement north to the sugar-cane railway then turn left at the first drivable track and follow it down towards the water. It's hard to reach by public transport; your best bet is to take a taxi, or rent a bicycle or car to get around.

Just north of Ambondrona is a beach known as Belle Vue. From here northwards, the beaches and villages on a whole are quieter and more attractive than at Ambatoloaka and Madirokely.

Sleeping

Tsara Loky (☎ 86 610 22; d from Ar20,000, mains Ar5000-15,000) This local place right on the beach has

a good restaurant (order in advance) and a variety of rooms and bungalows – the best have bathrooms and hammocks outside, the cheapest are basic rooms in the main house.

Domaine de Manga Be (☎ 86 616 30; urslinder@wanadoo.mg; r Ar48,000-240,000) A rather stylish and original self-catering complex aimed predominantly at families. The beautifully decorated studio apartments, villas, rooms and bungalows come in all shapes and price ranges, but all have kitchens or kitchenettes, nets and fans. If you pay a supplement you can hire an apartment with a cook to prepare your meals.

Nosy Be Hôtel (☎ 86 614 06; www.nosybehotel.com; r from €75; ❄ ☞) Rooms are colourful and almost eccentric at this luxury eco-conscious hotel – think yellow walls and bright-blue bedspreads. The hotel sits in a lush garden on the edge of the beach; don't miss the fantastic pool facing the ocean. There is an on-site dive centre, and quadbike and island-hopping trips can be arranged. Readers give it good feedback (it attracts a lot of prebooked European tourists), especially in regards to wheelchair accessibility.

DJAMANDJARY

Unlike other villages on Nosy Be, Djamandjary (dza-*man*-dzar) does not seem particularly concerned with attracting tourists, and despite being the island's second-largest community it holds little interest to travellers. Hotels are some distance from the centre, and this is OK as the town and the beach in front of it are pretty filthy. Head left from town along the sand, and it gets increasingly nicer.

Sleeping

The recommended sleeping options here are both upmarket.

Orangea (☎ 032 04 200 85, 86 061 98; www.orangea-nosybe.com in French; bungalows from €65; ☞) Sweeping lawns lead down to the brightly coloured restaurant and pool deck at this cheerful, classy place that is very popular with families. The whitewashed and orange-painted bungalows contain cushions made from African fabrics, and have hot water in the bathrooms. The cheapest bungalows have only fans, while more expensive options come with air-con. Breakfast is served for an extra €5. An excellent sleeping choice; it's often full, so reserve in advance.

Vanila Hôtel (☎ 86 615 23; vanilahotel@simicro.mg; d incl breakfast €116; ❄ ☞ ▣) This top-end beach hotel is designed to blend into the environs with a thatched roof and lots of open-air lounges. At night the lovely garden is lit by flame torches and the entire place emits a warm atmosphere day or night. Rooms are charming and there are two bars and a restaurant. Rent bikes for Ar20,000 per day, or arrange a sailing or diving trip. The hotel caters more to couples and families than tour groups. Low-season rates drop by about €30.

AMPASIMORONJIA

Ampasimoronjia is the next village up from Djamandjary. There are several hotels between here and Andilana, to the north. Please note the area is quite isolated – be prepared to eat where you sleep or shell out bucks to call a taxi to take you to dinner. If you are looking for a romantic get-away-from-it-all experience, then a few of the places listed below will appeal. If you yearn for company, you'll be happier further south.

Sleeping & Eating

There are a number of places to stay just off the main road, but they are very spread out.

Le Relais (☎ 86 615 10; r Ar15,000-30,000) This is a no-frills but friendly backpacker-style place, about five minutes' walk from the beach. There's a funky bar with a ping-pong table, and meals can be arranged. It also has bikes and boats for hire. The cheapest rooms share bathrooms.

Corail Noir (☎ 86 634 47; www.corailnoirhotel.com; s/d from €42/63; 🕿 🖳) One of Nosy Be's newer luxury resorts, this large place sits right on the beach. The pool overlooks the ocean, as do views from many rooms – although the water here is only average looking. Still, padded sun chairs and drinks served from coconuts in the sand are pretty enticing, as are the plush rooms with safe, minibar, telephone and satellite TV. Check with your travel agent or online for promotions, as it sometimes runs deals.

Chanty Beach (☎ 86 614 73; www.chantybeachhotel .com; r & bungalows incl breakfast €55-90) This German-run place is a charming, if slightly staid, white colonial-style guesthouse in a neat garden on the beach. Some of the clean bungalows have their own kitchenette, and there's a small restaurant/bar serving mostly seafood. Half-board is available. Activities include sailing trips and boat rentals. Diving and island excursions can be arranged. There is snorkelling nearby.

ourpick Le Grand Bleu (☎ 86 634 08; www.legrand bleunosybe.com; d with breakfast from Ar150,000; 🕿 🖳) On a hill overlooking the sea, Le Grand Bleu has spectacular views from its terrace restau-rant where you can curl up on a pillowed chair and read a book or chow on wood-fired pizza. The bungalows are very pretty, with blue-and-white walls, wood floors, four-poster beds with mosquito net and a minibar. The star attraction is the dazzling infinity pool perched on a hill overlooking the ocean far below. Le Grand Bleu has half- and full-board options. All sorts of excursions and activities are offered, or just grab a sea kayak and hit the ocean. The secluded location makes it popular with honeymooners.

La Table d' Alexander (☎ 033 142 4722; mains Ar10,000-25,000; 🕒 lunch & dinner) In a fantastic location right on the beach, this place gets good marks for its French and Malagasy-influenced seafood dishes. It is at the extreme northern edge of Ampasimoronjia, and is an inexpensive taxi ride from Andilana.

ANDILANA

Far and away Nosy Be's best beach, Andilana, at the island's northwest tip, also offers its best sunsets – the big yellow ball seems to sink directly in front of you and the ensuing bleed from orange to pink to purple before a long fade to velvet is mesmerising. The beach itself is a long stretch of pearly white sand, the water true turquoise and clear as gin. Placid and warm, it's perfect for floating under a big, sunny and blue Madagascan sky.

With the exception of one pimped-out new luxury resort, Andilana is nearly void of large-scale development. Tourism infrastructure is limited to a handful of small guesthouses, a few guys selling lobsters on the side of the road, and a strip of stalls on the southern end of the beach, where villagers sell local crafts (check out the exceptional raffia beach bags woven with bright blocky patterns).

Andilana ignites on Sundays when French expats and Malagasy from around Nosy Be come for a lazy day in the sun. Gossiping gaggles of women, dressed in bright sarongs and with sunflowers painted on their faces, lay out picnics for their families on a shaded bit of sand. Young lovers and groups of teen-age girls giggle and scream as they splash about in the warm blue sea, and old men sip bottles of THB beer as they lean against the trunks of the coconut palms. Chez Loulou is right on the water and famous for its Sunday brunch, which is always packed. The seafood feast is accompanied by live music, and afterwards everyone lingers for beer, dancing and seemingly spontaneous Malagasy jam sessions on the drums and guitar.

Andilana is a pretty mellow place, but if you need to release tension go get a **massage**. Given on an open-air terrace just off the beach, the one-hour sessions are wonderfully relaxing and cost just Ar25,000. The massages are an initiative of the village women, so getting one puts money straight into local pockets.

If you just want to spend the afternoon by the pool and eat, then it may be worth forking out the €30 to do so at the swanky new Hotel Andilana Beach, which caters almost exclusively to Italian package tourists. Morning and afternoon packages allow you to spend half a day by the giant, blue pool and eat one free meal – a buffet lunch or dinner. The morning package gives you more sun time (dinner packages don't let you arrive before 3pm, and the sun sets by 6pm). Soft drinks are free all day, but booze is extra.

Sleeping & Eating

Options for both slumber and chow are skimpy here.

Chez Eugénie (☎ 86 92 353; chezeugenie.nosybe .madagascar@gmail.com; r incl breakfast €35, set menu Ar25,000) There are just five rooms at this little hotel and restaurant owned by a French and Malagasy couple. Abodes are small, but impressive, with firm mattresses and high-quality linens. It is a good choice for couples as rooms have one bed and the atmosphere is intimate. The French owner speaks some English, and takes clients on canoe and snorkelling excursions when he has time. The restaurant does three-course set menus that rotate daily. Everything is cooked fresh and no frozen ingredients are used – this also means choices are limited. Chez Eugénie is set a few hundred metres back from the beach in the village just before the turn-off for Au Belvedere.

ourpick **Au Belvedere** (☎ 86 928 08; belvedere andilana@yahoo.fr; r incl breakfast Ar125,000) We couldn't get enough of the sunsets and tranquillity here. Perched on a bluff overlooking the beach, this is a small and simple hotel – there are no TVs, minibars or fridges. But it's the lack of mod amenities that makes Belvedere so damn charming in the first place. The decent-sized rooms each come with a front porch – complete with sun chairs and tables – overlooking the ocean. Big wooden slatted doors and windows offer great ventilation, but don't keep the bugs out (mozzie nets over the four-poster beds do

that job). The front doors swing open wide enough to let you watch the sunset from bed. Keep the doors open a crack at night to let the ocean sounds lull you to sleep. If you stay a week, ask for a 10% discount.

Hotel Andilana Beach (www.nosybe.com; full-board per person from €134; ❄ ⟲ ⊑) Andilana's swankiest, actually its only, all-inclusive resort (including alcohol) is in a quiet cove on the headland from the main beach. Rooms are turned out exactly the way a fashion-conscious Italian crowd would demand, and that's exactly who this hotel caters to. Even though the clientele is nearly exclusively Italian (lots of couples), anyone can stay as long as they book online. There is no booking phone number, and walk-ins aren't welcome. Use the website or a travel agency. The hotel also boasts a few restaurants, poolside bars, a fabulous lobby and a slick disco – guests only.

Chez Loulou (set menu Ar25,000, mains Ar15,000; ❄ lunch & dinner) As one of only two restaurants in Andilana, it's a good thing Chez Loulou is so good. Right on the beach, with tables in the sand, this casual restaurant and bar serves sumptuous seafood – we especially liked the shrimp with ginger sauce. You can choose from a set-price three-course meal or order just a main course off the menu. If you want to linger after dessert at lunch, grab a sun chair and an ice-cold THB and kick back with a good book. On Sunday, Chez Loulou organises a delicious seafood buffet lunch (all you can eat for Ar50,000) famous for its lobster.

ISLANDS OFF NOSY BE

If you're looking for the full barefoot, Robinson Crusoe experience, and can afford more than €50 per night, it is well worth heading out to one of the smaller and less-visited islets surrounding Nosy Be. Some of the resorts are fabulous, offering world-class pampering, and the tranquillity can't be beaten. If you're on a tighter budget take a day-trip by pirogue to check out the palm-fringed white beaches and excellent snorkelling.

NOSY KOMBA

The most visited (and visible) of the islands around Nosy Be, Nosy Komba rises off the ocean floor midway between the mainland and Nosy Be. Most people visit Nosy Komba on an organised tour from Nosy Be (see p163).

Alternatively you can hire a pirogue or motorboat at the port in Hell-Ville for around Ar10,000 to Ar20,000.

Boats land at **Ampangorina**, where there is an interesting craft market – look for the big multi-coloured raffia bags or striped baobab trees. If you just want to spend time sunbathing ask your pirogue operator to take you straight to **Anjiabe beach**, on the southwest coast.

Resting your head on Nosy Komba's shores is possible, although paradise here is far from free. **Jardin Vanille** (☎ 032 07 127 97; jardinvanille@wanadoo.mg; half/full-board per person €45/54) offers a number of cute and comfortable Malagasy-style bungalows perfectly located on Nosy Komba's best beach, Anjiabe. The restaurant serves a rotating, and very fine, menu and overlooks the sea. Jardin Vanille is popular with French tourists, so book ahead. Numerous excursions can be arranged, including snorkelling, diving and fishing trips, and Nosy Be transfers.

For total luxury, you'll want to visit **Tsara Komba** (☎ 033 14 823 20; www.tsarakomba.com; half/full board per person from €90/104; Anjiabe), which only offers full- or half-board options. With just three rooms and a suite it's about as exclusive, and secluded, as you get. The polished wooden rooms come with king-sized beds and a porch looking out onto the sea. The al fresco restaurant, also facing the water, serves fine food and even better views – at dusk passing pirogues blaze golden from the sun's dying rays. Transfers and all the usual excursions can be arranged.

If you've just popped over for the day and need kibble, try little **Chez Yolande** (☎ 032 04 787 29; mains Ar7000-20,000; ☽ lunch & dinner) in Ampangorina, facing the sea. It serves lots of yummy seafood dishes with local sauces and a selection of light snacks.

NOSY TANIKELY

Nosy Tanikely is 10km west of Nosy Komba. It is an officially protected marine reserve and one of the better remaining snorkelling and diving sites in the area, with coral, numerous fish and the occasional sea turtle. Snorkelling equipment can be hired near the picnic area for Ar5000.

Camping is possible, but you'll need to bring everything with you. If you're having lunch on the beach, make sure your operator takes all its rubbish away when you leave.

Most organised day tours combine Nosy Tanikely with Nosy Komba, using the beach on Nosy Tanikely for a lunchtime picnic.

NOSY SAKATIA

At just 3 sq km, Nosy Sakatia, just off the west coast of Nosy Be, is quiet and tiny. It offers the opportunity to wander along forest tracks, see baobabs, fruit bats and chameleons and do some diving.

Stay at **Sakatia Passions** (☎ 86 614 62; www.saka tia-passions.com in French; d incl breakfast from €60; ☒) over a weekend so you can partake in the Sunday seafood buffet (not a bad deal at €14), which is absolutely massive and accompanied by live music. The 12 bungalows, nestled in a coconut plantation just behind the ocean, are done up with dark polished wood and rough-hewn porches; all have sea views. The friendly eco-resort also helps fund a school for poor village children – ask how you can get involved. Sailing, fishing and diving trips can all be arranged. Couples looking for the rustic, yet still romantic, honeymoon, or families wanting to teach their children about giving back to the community, will find this place appealing. Solo travellers and party people may want to steer clear – it's very isolated. Meals cost €14 and usually include a fish, seafood or meat main, appetizer, and desert.

To get to Sakatia Passions, you need to go to Chanty Beach hotel in Ampasimoronjia, and radio across for a boat transfer.

NOSY MITSIO

Divers, listen up: this one's for you. Nosy Mitsio is a small and beautiful archipelago about 55km northeast of Nosy Be where the main attraction is its excellent and still relatively virgin dive sites. Nosy Mitsio is also home to picture perfect-beaches – you know, the white-sand, bathtub-warm translucent turquoise sea and no-people variety.

Best of all, Nosy Mitsio offers one more hour of sunlight per day than mainland Madagascar! To get here you cross a time zone; Nosy Mitsio is one hour ahead, but not far enough west for it to matter light-wise, meaning it gets dark an hour later here than on Nosy Be.

There is a beach **camp site** on the southwestern side of Grande Mitsio, but you'll need your own supplies.

If you've got the cash, Nosy Mitsio is one of the premier addresses in all of Madagascar to drop your swanky anchor, as the very swish and back-to-basics **Hôtel Tsara Bajina** (☎ 86 612 49; www.tsarabanjina.com; full board per person around €150) is here. You won't find TVs, phones or even newspapers, just true Zen relaxation in a posh

NORTHERN MADAGASCAR

but personable environment. You can tell a lot of thought was put into decorating the 21 bungalows, which feature mosquito-net canopies over tasteful wood-frame beds, striped pillows and quality linen. Each has a private terrace overlooking the sea. Snorkelling, sailing and water-skiing are included in the price. Most people come to dive, and the attached PADI-certified club will help you explore Mitsio's famous coral reefs. Boat transfers from Nosy Be cost another €64.

Tropical Diving (☎ 032 07 127 90; www.tropical -diving.com) and **Le Marlin Club** (☎ 86 613 15; marlin .club@simicro.mg), both in Madirokely on Nosy Be, can organise multiday camping and diving trips to Nosy Mitsio.

The trip between Nosy Be and Nosy Mitsio takes about four to six hours. Most of the dive and tour operators on p162 can arrange transfers to the islands.

NOSY IRANJA

Nosy Iranja, southwest of Nosy Be, actually consists of two islands: the larger and inhabited Nosy Iranja Be (about 200 hectares) and the smaller Nosy Iranja Kely (13 hectares). The islands are connected by a 1.5km-long sand bar, negotiable on foot at low tide. Sea turtles regularly lay their eggs on the beaches.

The luxurious **Hôtel Nosy Iranja** (☎ 86 616 90; iranja@simicro.mg; bungalows from €175; 😂), on Nosy Iranja Kely, has chic hexagonal bungalows with decks, hammocks and easy chairs. Inside a four-poster bed, CD player and a wood-and-stone bathroom await. Naturally, an array of excursions can be arranged. Helicopter transfers and a gym are also at your disposal. There's a three-night minimum stay at the hotel, which needs to be booked in advance – ring or email.

The trip from Nosy Be to Nosy Iranja takes about two hours in a speedboat, and longer in slower vessels. The tour and dive companies on p163 offer trips here.

SOUTHEAST OF NOSY BE

AMBANJA

Ambanja is a small, tree-lined town on the Sambirano River, and the junction for overland travel to and from Nosy Be. Madagascar's first vanilla capital is a long way from being a tourist capital, although locals are trying. There are possibilities for biking tours and overnight pirogue float trips (just ask around –

it wasn't very organised when we were there) and the chance to experience rural northern Madagascan life.

If you want to spend the night, try **Chez Patricia** (r from Ar10,00). It's the best place to stay, and has a restaurant.

From Ambanja there is daily transport to Ankify (Ar10,000, from three hours), where you'll find the ferry to Nosy Be. Taxis-brousses also go to Diego Suarez (Ar10,000, from three hours) in the northeast.

The road between Ambanja and Antananarivo is now paved all the way and in relatively good condition. By taxi-brousse the trip takes 24 hours; if you have a vehicle it's about 16 hours.

ANKIFY

The small town of Ankify is the main port for boats and ferries between the Malagasy coast and Nosy Be. If you do the crossing from Nosy Be too late, and can't find a minibus to Diego Suarez, you will need to spend the night. The last taxi-brousse for Diego leaves around 11am as no one wants to drive after dark.

Le Baobab (☎ 033 07 208 87; baobabankify@wanadoo .mg; r Ar60,000), about 500m from the ferry landing, is where you'll want to sleep. It offers quaint round bungalows, views across to Nosy Be and a small restaurant.

Getting There & Away

The road between Ankify (where ferries depart to Nosy Be) and Diego Suarez to the northeast is well sealed and serviced by dozens of sardine-packed taxis-brousses every day. It is never hard to catch a ride if you need to get across the top of the island, but beware it is an arse-numbing six-hour journey (Ar30,000) even in a 'direct' minibus. In Madagascar, direct doesn't mean the minibus doesn't stop, it just stays stopped only long enough to fill itself beyond bursting every time someone disembarks along the way! Most people only see this area through the smudged glass of their speeding taxi-brousse, and there is little reason to stop. If you do, however, there are a few towns in this largely unpopulated, and very poor, northern central region. Nondirect taxis-brousses often stop for lunch in Ambanja, which can last for hours.

For more transport details to and from Ankify see the Nosy Be transport section on p164.

DIEGO SUAREZ & AROUND

It's still the country's undug tourism sapphire, but don't expect the Diego Suarez area to stay this way forever. The regional tourism board is working hard to get the place on the world's adventure map, and we guess it won't take long. This region pretty much sells itself. With two bodies of water – the Canal de Mozambique and the Indian Ocean – that sparkle the colour of Madagascar's famous sapphire, swaying coconut palms, white-sand beaches and a lack of sprawling resorts, this region is perfect for those in search of a private beach paradise.

And the region has a lot more than beaches. It's also rich in other natural wonders – from forests of red rock *tsingy* (karst, or limestone pinnacles) to hike, to two national parks so diverse and undiscovered that new lemur species are still identified in them each year.

Beside the town of Diego Suarez, which is the main hub of activity but not necessarily the most beautiful place to stay, there are three gorgeous bays with a scattering of accommodation options for all budgets. You can stay in a honeymoon suite with a round bed and private balcony at a gorgeous hillside resort, or in rough traditional bungalows smack in the poor fishing village of Ramena. Some find the latter a bit too uncomfortable, while others see it as an opportunity to experience local life. The choice is always yours.

Regardless of where you choose to slumber, there's plenty of activities to keep you from getting restless. Try snorkelling in the Emerald Sea, where you can walk out to the fish, then dip your head into the sparkling clean water and have a real look. The Diego Suarez region is also ground zero for Madagascar's burgeoning adventure-sports industry. For now kite-boarding and quad- and dirt-biking on dunes and homemade tracks are the two major activities. In Diego, you can organise tours and excursions to anywhere in northeastern Madagascar, and both the parks and beaches are near enough to be visited on a day trip from town.

DIEGO SUAREZ (ANTSIRANANA)
pop 74,500

Diego is far from the prettiest spot in the region, but its central location – almost equidistant from the beaches and national parks – makes it a good place to anchor oneself. Plus its wide streets, old colonial buildings and generally sleepy feel give it a languid, genteel air only experienced in the tropics. This is a slow-moving place where nearly everything shuts for most of the afternoon, and the residents still indulge in long afternoon naps. Recently, however, Diego has picked up a bit of steam – a little too much for the tastes of some locals – as an increasingly popular port of call for cruise ships. On days when the big boats anchor, Diego's usually quiet restaurants and shops become packed with loud crowds jabbering in a dozen different languages.

There are no beaches in Diego itself, but there are plenty of very good ones in the vicinity. The town is cheaper than Nosy Be, and offers sporty travellers lots of opportunities to explore the surf and turf.

Orientation

Diego is a sprawling place, but relatively easy to get around. Most places of interest for travellers are around Rue Colbert, on or near which most hotels, restaurants and offices are located. South of Place du 14 Octobre are taxi-brousse stations and the market.

Information

There are banks with ATMs and money-changing facilities up and down Rue Colbert, including Bank of Africa (BOA), BFV-SG, BMOI and BNI-CL.

Angap (☎ 82 213 20) Tourist information about 2km south of town on the airport road; can provide limited information on both Parc National de Montagne d'Ambre and the Réserve Spéciale de l'Ankàrana.

Housseni.com (☎ 82 22 505; Av Tollendal; per min Ar25) The fastest internet option in town is located in the Ny Havana building opposite the petrol station.

Post Office (Place Foch)

Telecom Office (Place Foch) There are also card phones scattered around town.

Tourism Board (www.office-tourisme-diego-suarez .com) Check out the new official city tourism board website for regional info.

Activities & Tours

Jump your quad-bike over a small dune ditch, climb a mountain, visit the national parks or head out to the Baie de Sakalava to try your hand at windsurfing: Diego and the surrounding region offers it all.

If you just want to spend the afternoon by the pool, Le Grand Hotel (see Sleeping) lets

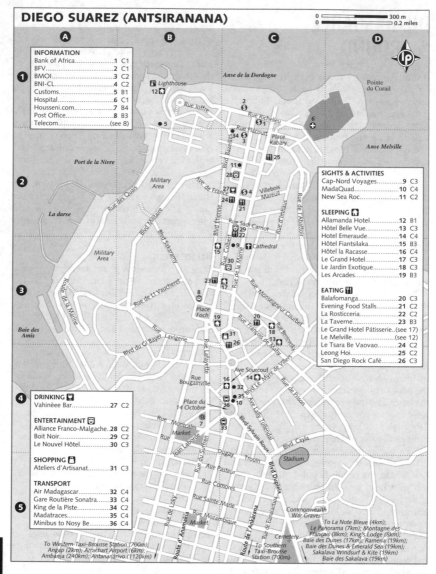

DIEGO SUAREZ (ANTSIRANANA)

INFORMATION
Bank of Africa...................1 C1
BFV..................................2 C1
BMOI...............................3 C2
BNI-CL............................4 C2
Customs..........................5 B1
Hospital..........................6 C1
Housseni.com.................7 B4
Post Office......................8 B3
Telecom.....................(see 8)

SIGHTS & ACTIVITIES
Cap-Nord Voyages.............9 C3
MadaQuad.......................10 C4
New Sea Roc....................11 C2

SLEEPING
Allamanda Hotel..............12 B1
Hôtel Belle Vue................13 C3
Hotel Emeraude...............14 C4
Hôtel Fiantsilaka..............15 B3
Hôtel la Racasse..............16 C4
Le Grand Hotel.................17 C3
Le Jardin Exotique............18 C3
Les Arcades.....................19 B3

EATING
Balafomanga....................20 C3
Evening Food Stalls..........21 C2
La Rosticceria..................22 C2
La Taverne.......................23 B3
Le Grand Hotel Pâtisserie..(see 17)
Le Melville...................(see 12)
Le Tsara Be Vaovao..........24 C2
Leong Hoi........................25 C2
San Diego Rock Café........26 C3

DRINKING
Vahinèee Bar....................27 C2

ENTERTAINMENT
Alliance Franco-Malgache.28 C2
Boit Noir..........................29 C2
Le Nouvel Hôtel...............30 C3

SHOPPING
Ateliers d'Artisanat..........31 C3

TRANSPORT
Air Madagascar................32 C4
Gare Routière Sonatra......33 C4
King de la Piste................34 C4
Madatraces......................35 C4
Minibus to Nosy Be..........36 C4

NORTHERN MADAGASCAR

you use its sparkling blue **swimming pool** for an entrance fee of Ar10,000 per day – not a bad deal, especially when it's super-hot out and you just want to relax in a bit of luxury (there's even a swim-up bar).

The following companies, mostly based in Diego town, offer a variety of regional tours or day-long adrenalin-pumping excursions.

Cap-Nord Voyages (☎ 82 255 06; cap.nord.voyages@ wanadoo.mg; Hôtel Colbert, 51 Rue Colbert) Offers excursions to Montagne d'Ambre and l'Ankàrana, plus car hire. It can do day trips to l'Ankàrana, followed by a drop-off at Ankify for Nosy Be.

Evasion Sans Frontiers (☎ 82 230 61; esf .diego@wanadoo.mg) This well-respected company runs day trips to the magnificent Réserve Spéciale de l'Ankarana (see p186), about 70km southwest of Diego, home to Madagascar's most famous fiery red *tsingy*. The full-day trip (€50) includes lunch. The walking here is not technical – you can get right up to the *tsingy* in a vehicle, so this trip works well for folks of all ages and fitness levels. Evasion does comfortable transfers (no overpacked minibuses here) between Diego and Ankify (€20), but you need to book in advance. Quad-biking and windsurfing can also be arranged.

King de la Piste (☎ 82 225 99; www.kingdelapiste .de) A German-run company based at King's Lodge, 8km south of Diego on the road to Ramena; it organises trips to l'Ankàrana and Montagne d'Ambre. It has its own camp sites in l'Ankàrana and two hotels on the outskirts of Diego. It also does car hire, including some no-frills budget rentals. It is a good first contact for all activities.

MadaQuad (☎ 032 408 8814; www.madaquad.net; 9 Ave Sourcouf) One of Diego's top quad-biking companies, it runs a variety of guided tours that visit the red *tsingy*, three bays, Windsor Castle and surrounding beaches and dunes. Guided trip options for two-person quads include half-day (driver/passenger Ar170,000/45,000), full-day (driver/passenger Ar270,000/100,000) and overnight camping (driver/passenger Ar650,000/250,000). The camping trip includes an Emerald Sea snorkelling stop.

New Sea Roc (☎ 82 218 54 or 032 02 32 57; 26 Rue Colbert) Offering rock-climbing expeditions and equipment, New Sea Roc specialises in climbing and camping trips (€40 per person per day) on the Nosy Hara archipelago offshore. Now a protected area, the marine park is three hours from Diego. New Sea Roc also offers fishing, snorkelling and trekking excursions. The eco-friendly company was invaluable in the successful campaign to convince the provincial government to turn Montagne de Français into a protected wilderness area.

Sakalava Windsurf & Kite (☎ 032 04 512 39; Baie de Sakalava) Next to the bungalows on the main beach at Sakalava, this is the place to come for windsurfing. Lessons are offered, and there is equipment rental if you already know what you're doing.

Sleeping
BUDGET
Budget travellers will dig Diego – there are plenty of cheap choices. Reserve in advance if you have your heart set on a particular room.

Hôtel Belle Vue (Chez Layec; ☎ 82 210 21; belle vuedie@blueline.mg; 35 Rue François de Mahy; d Ar12,000-20,000) A lively hotel that's good for linking up with other travellers – there's a noticeboard for tours. Rooms are simple, but all come with fan and net. The cheapest rooms share baths, but even these have hot water.

Hôtel Fiantsilaka (☎ 82 223 48; 13 Blvd Étienne; r Ar15,000-35,000; ⚡) The rooms here are fairly old with saggy mattresses, but travellers say it's good value for money. It's clean, central and the owners are friendly. There's an upstairs restaurant with Chinese and Malagasy dishes.

Les Arcades (☎ 82 231 04; arcades@blueline.mg; Place Foch; r Ar16,000-42,000, mains Ar6000-11,000; ⚡ 🖳) The eight rooms here have long been popular with French backpackers in the know: they're cheap, you can grub at the attached restaurant and you can check your email. Rooms are all a bit dingy with cheap mattresses that look like an elephant slept on them. The best rooms are numbers 2 and 8. These come with air-con and chaise lounges. The restaurant serves grills, burgers and interesting dishes like Egyptian kofta. At night it doubles as a lively bar. English is spoken.

LIBERTALIA

The first mention of the Pirate Republic of Libertalia was in a 1726 story by Daniel Defoe. According to Defoe, Libertalia was founded around the Baie des Français by Captain Misson, a French adventurer with a Robin Hood bent who sailed the seas freeing slaves and avoiding bloodshed whenever possible. He teamed up with a defrocked Dominican priest, Father Caraccioli, to set up a communist Utopia.

They began building with the help of 300 Comorians (who were a 'gift' from the Sultan of Anjouan) as well as assorted African slaves, and British, French, Dutch and Portuguese pirates. A parliament was formed, a printing press was started, crops were planted, stock was reared and a new international language was established.

All seemed to be going well until the Malagasy people living around the 'International Republic of Libertalia' descended en masse from the hills and massacred the Libertalian population. Caraccioli was killed, but Misson escaped. His eventual fate remains a mystery.

As yet, there is no physical evidence of Libertalia, and some historians have relegated it to the realms of fantasy. Sceptics argue that Robinson Crusoe's creator could easily have invented a pirate republic.

NORTHERN MADAGASCAR

MIDRANGE

This is only a sampling of the midrange options in town; there are many more – just take a walk down Rue Colbert.

Hôtel la Racasse (☎ 82 223 64; Ave Sourcouf; d from Ar45,000; ⚒) Rooms here are good value (although check it out before booking, as some are still a bit shabby), and relatively comfortable, with lots of space. Even the cheapest rooms have private bathrooms, and the best come with safes, TV, air-con and private sitting areas. The restaurant on the 1st floor is convenient – it opens early and closes later than most. Plus it has a ping-pong table.

ourpick Le Jardin Exotique (☎ 82 219 33; r Ar50,000-70,000; ⚒) Check out a few rooms at this quirky, good-value, almost-boutique hotel, before deciding on one. Some are much larger and lighter than others. All come with parquet floors, four-poster beds, mozzie nets and a bold and creative paint job. The cheapest just have fans, but no less character. Mattresses are good and firm, and some rooms are real doubles (that's one bed, boys and girls). The rooftop terrace has picnic tables and the views over the light-green sea are particularly awesome at sunset (bring a few cold beers up with you – there's a fridge in all the rooms). The garden area, with its marble statues and flowers, is wonderful – as erotic as it is exotic.

TOP END

Two luxury hotels have opened in Diego in the last three years. Both are recommended.

Hotel Emeraude (☎ 82 225 44; www.hotelemeraude -diego.com; cnr Rue Rigult & Rue Gauche; s/d/ste Ar80,000/ 100,000/150,000; ⚒) Classy, comfortable and centrally located, Emeraude is a relatively new colonial-style hotel with 18 fabulously spacious rooms featuring satellite TV and minibar. Each room is a bit different, but all have lovely bedspreads, polished-wood furniture, elegant curtains and local art on freshly painted walls. The suites are great, with slick bathrooms kitted out with Jacuzzis. Land and sea excursions can be arranged; airport transfers are free. The on-site restaurant, Le Jongue, specialises in Vietnamese. For its price range (you'd be surprised at the number of lesser hotels on Rue Colbert that charge more), it's very good value.

Le Grand Hotel (☎ 82 230 63; www.grand-hotel-diego .com; Rue Colbert; r Ar237,500; ⚒ 🖥 🍷) This hotel lives up to its moniker. One of Diego's two new luxury establishments, Le Grand is smack in the middle of town and offers 66 rooms and suites. All are large and posh with satellite TVs, plush chairs and modern polished-wood bed frames. The lobby area, with a TV lounge, shops and a restaurant, opens up to a great terrace. Here you'll find the large sparkling clean pool surrounded by lounge chairs, tables and umbrellas. You can grab a drink from the swim-up bar or sunbathe on a wooden island in the middle of the pool. Nonguests can buy day pool passes for Ar10,000. The checked marble spa and big airy fitness centre are two assets.

Allamanda Hotel (☎ 82 210 33; www.hotels-diego .com; Rue Richelieu; d €95; ⚒ 🖥 🍷) The other swanky new place is just steps from the sea – the long pool offers great ocean views – and has all the luxuries you would expect from a top-end hotel. The exterior of the building itself is a bit bland and boxy, but the really big rooms are supercomfy and come with mod art and low lighting, and sometimes balconies. The restaurant has a stellar reputation.

Eating

Diego has dozens of Western-style snack bars, ice-cream parlours and diners. The following is just a selection of what's on offer. In the early evenings, there are good street-food stands along Rue Colbert. **Leong Hoi** (Rue de la Marne) is a well-stocked supermarket.

Le Grand Hotel Pâtisserie (Le Grand Hotel; mains Ar600-Ar2500; ⏲ 6.30am-12.30pm & 3.30-9pm) Everyone in Diego comes here in the morning for crispy loaves of fresh-baked French baguettes, but tourists not partaking in a picnic can also enjoy this delightful little patisserie attached to the Grand Hotel. It's a great choice for an economical and light breakfast. Besides a dizzying variety of wonderful gelato and pastries (fancy a real Napoleon?), it also serves espresso drinks and snacks such as baby-sized pizzas.

San Diego Rock Café (☎ 82 219 88; Ave Tollendal; mains Ar6000-15,000 ⏲ 6am-midnight) This new joint is the funkiest eatery in Diego, and it serves food continuously from open to close. There is a Betty Boop theme and lots of artistic renderings on the walls. Chairs and tables are shiny metal, and an entire menu page is devoted to Western-style breakfasts! There's another page equally loyal to dessert. If you don't want eggs or frozen dairy, there are also pizzas, burgers and fries, Malagasy curries, fish soups and grilled shrimps. The friendly owner had plans to start a small hotel; check in with her if you're looking for a place to slumber.

La Taverne (☎ 032 02 212 83; Rue Colbert; mains Ar8000-12,000; 🕑 lunch & dinner) Choose from old leather couches inside or sidewalk seating out. The place serves lots of pizzas and fills up at meal times. The décor includes old French beer posters and murals of famous African jazz stars.

Balafomanga (☎ 82 228 94; 18 Rue Louis Brunet; mains Ar9000-20,000; 🕑 lunch & dinner) We loved how accommodating this place was when it came to making up your own versions of its mains – we enjoyed the grilled calamari appetizer with parsley and garlic paired with spaghetti. The big menu offers a bit of everything, although the delicious food definitely has a big French and Malagasy influence. It's a funky dining environment – Chinese lanterns cast a green glow on the multicoloured walls and tablecloths. A faux flame burns in a dangling cast-iron pot, and rows of home-brewed fruit-flavoured rum sit in big plastic pots on the low-lit bar.

our pick **La Rosticceria** (☎ 82 236 22; 47 Rue Colbert; larosticceria@wannadoo.mg; mains Ar12,500-14,000; 🕑 noon-10.30pm Mon-Sat) Mmmm, this Italian restaurant has a fantastic selection of risottos, gnocchi, lasagne and fresh-made tagliatelle and spaghettis with pesto, cream, meat or seafood sauces. The ambiance is as delicious as the food. Inside there is a nautical theme, with intricately carved wooden vessels and old maps for decoration. Outside tables sit on the sidewalk. Save room for coffee and dessert – both the real espresso and the creamy gelato are marvellous. There are six rooms for rent upstairs (Ar72,000) per room. These have big beds, Asian lampshades and Malagasy art decorating white walls – they are quite lovely.

Le Tsara Be Vaovao (☎ 032 04 940 97; 36 Rue Colbert; mains Ar14,000-22,000; 🕑 lunch & dinner) This locally recommended restaurant takes its food seriously. The place specialises in Malagasy and French fusion, and incorporates many local spices and fresh ingredients into its wood-fire cooking. Besides serving all manner of zebu steaks, grilled to order, it does a selection of French favourites like fois gras and grilled duck. There are a few pasta dishes as well, but not much for vegetarians.

Le Melville (☎ 82 210 33; www.hotels-diego.com; Allamanda Hotel, Rue Richelieu; mains Ar15,000-40,000; 🕑 breakfast, lunch & dinner) Even if you can't afford to stay at the Allamanda, it's worth coming to its restaurant for the excellent seafood and fish. We met more than one travelling couple that recommended the place for its romantic atmosphere – it's right on the water with a fabulous patio that's particularly alluring at sunset. The food is fresh, high quality and infused with regional spices and flavours.

Drinking & Entertainment

Diego has a heck of a lot more nightlife than most Madagascan cities – you can actually do a little club crawl of your own now down Rue Colbert!

Vahinée Bar (Rue Colbert) A local favourite that's perfect for an après-dinner drink. The food is okay – try the noodle soup – but most people stop by for cocktails. The atmosphere is good, and there's often live music. Look for the bar opposite the BNI-CL bank. It opens early and closes late.

Boit Noir (Rue Colbert) This is a very popular disco that attracts a chic crowd and a lot fewer prostitutes than other Diego clubs. There's plenty of dirty dancing, however, and people dress to impress.

Le Nouvel Hôtel (Rue Colbert) Diego's most popular seedy nightclub is a real dive; it's dark and dingy and usually packed with an oft-raunchy crowd of sailors and their entourage of lady friends. In the day, it becomes the domain of sad-looking, hard-drinking locals downing a breakfast pint.

Alliance Franco-Malgache (☎ 82 210 31; afdiego@wanadoo.mg; Rue Colbert; 🕑 8.30-11.30am & 3-7.30pm Tue-Sat, 3-7.30pm Mon) The Alliance is housed in a magnificently restored Art Deco–style building, which is worth a look on its own. There are regular art exhibitions here, along with film screenings and concerts. The library has French books and magazines. Stop by for the latest programme of events.

Shopping

Wander down Rue Colbert as new shops open here each season. Check out **Ateliers d'Artisanat** (☎ 82 293 85; Rue Colbert), which has a huge selection of handicrafts and art-work from all over Madagascar. You will also find women selling Madagascan art at the taxi-brousse stations.

Getting There & Away

AIR

Air Madagascar (☎ 82 211 93; Ave Sourcouf) links Diego with Antananarivo (Ar304,600) daily and has regular flights to Sambava (Ar192,000), Toamasina (Ar525,600) and Mahajanga (Ar288,000).

BOAT
There is no scheduled passenger service from Diego. However, cargo boats, which often accept passengers, travel regularly to and from coastal towns, including Mahajanga and Sambava. There are no set schedules, and sometimes these inexplicably stop running for a while, so you will need to inquire at the port.

TAXI-BROUSSE
Diego Suarez has three taxi-brousse stations. Most transport departs from the southern taxi-brousse station along Route de l'Ankàrana. Vehicles heading for destinations west and north, including Ramena (Ar2000, one hour) and Joffreville (for Parc National de Montagne d'Ambre; Ar3000, one hour), depart from the western taxi-brousse station along Route de la Pyrotechnie. Vehicles for Ambanja and Nosy Be (Ar30,000, six hours), Mahajanga (Ar60,000, 36 hours) and Antananarivo (Ar70,000, two days) depart from the Gare Routière Sonatra, near the Rex cinema. For Iharana, Sambava and other destinations on the northeast coast, it's quicker to get a taxi-brousse to the junction town of Ambilobe and change to a vehicle heading east. It's possible to travel from Diego to Sambava in one long day, although taxis-brousses usually take longer. In the rainy season this route can take several days.

Most people get to Nosy Be via a direct minibus and boat combo. The entire trip costs only Ar40,000 and you'll find touts in town selling tickets (or you can head directly to the taxi-brousse rack). Your bus should not leave before 5.30am, if the person selling the ticket says it does, it's not legit; we know of one couple that got sold a 'direct' minibus and boat combo, but were picked up from their hotel at 3.30am and were driven around Diego's suburbs hunting for clients for three hours before the bus finally departed.

No matter what type of minibus you end up in, expect it to be filled to capacity times three. If this doesn't appeal to you, and you don't want to fly, pay a bit more and go with **Evasion Sans Frontiers** (☎ 82 230 61; esf.diego@wanadoo.mg), which does the trip in a luxury, air-con minibus. The journey costs €20, including boat transfer to the island, and must be booked in advance by ringing the office.

Getting Around
Diego's Arrachart Airport is 6km south of the town centre. Taxis charge Ar10,000 to

get there. Otherwise, you can walk out to the main road and catch a taxi-brousse into town (Ar2000). If you want to get out to the beaches, you can hire a taxi for the trip – make sure the driver waits (don't pay everything up front) or you may be stranded for quite some time. A round trip to either the Baie de Sakalava or Ramena should cost Ar60,000, but you'll have to barter. Around town taxis are Ar1800.

King de la Piste (p177) and Cap-Nord Voyages (p176) can organise 4WD rental for around Ar100,000; the petrol costs extra.

NOSY LONJA
The small island of Nosy Lonja in the middle of the Baie des Français is known in French as Pain de Sucre (Sugar Loaf) for its supposed resemblance to the much larger Sugar Loaf Mountain in Rio de Janeiro harbour in Brazil. It's off limits to foreigners and considered sacred by the Malagasy, who use it for *fijoroana* (ceremonies in which they invoke the ancestors).

ROAD TO RAMENA
Some of the region's best sleeping options, especially for couples and families, are on the road between Diego Suarez and Ramena beach. There's also plenty to do activities-wise. If you want to take a hike, head to **Montagne des Français** (admission Ar25,000) named in memory of the Malagasy and French forces killed in 1942 in Allied resistance to the pro-German Vichy French forces. It is a small and still relatively attractive wild place about 8km from Diego. Unfortunately it's facing environmental degradation problems that the government has done little to stop despite the park's new status as a protected wilderness area (see boxed text, p182).

The start of the trail is just before King's Lodge (see Sleeping). It is a hot, two hour climb to the summit, but it's worth it. Along the way you'll pass interesting dry forest vegetation, caves, a fort's remains and abundant bird life. There are chances for rock-climbing and great views across the bay.

Sleeping
The following places offer their own tours and excursions, and some even run free daytime shuttles into Diego Suarez.

King's Lodge (☎ 82 225 99; Rte de Ramena; www .kingdelapiste.de; r €30) The simplest sleeping option in this area, King's attracts lots of hikers who come to climb Montagne des Français. The German owner also runs the Parc Botanique des Mille Baobabs (see boxed text, p182) and is almost fanatically enthusiastic about ecotourism. He can provide very helpful and detailed info about the region's flora and fauna, as well as climbing and hiking routes up the mountain. The rooms are very clean, with mozzie nets and fans. Most are really breezy, which keeps them cool despite the lack of air-con. You can swim off the beach near the front.

Le Panorama (☎ 82 225 99; Rte de Ramena; www .kingdelapiste.de; r €50; 🛰 🛋) This is a true country boutique joint with an absolutely gorgeous pool that has a small waterfall and lovely thick padding on the sun chairs around it. The 12 bungalows have thatched roofs and redbrick-and-stone walls. Inside you'll find a breezy space with white-washed walls and wooden beams on the ceiling; there's more local wood on the dark-polished floors and matching four-poster beds. There is a large open-air restaurant, and the lodge is very eco-friendly. Excursions can be arranged.

our pick Hôtel La Note Bleue (☎ 032 07 666 26; www.diego-hotel.com; s/d €98/115, honeymoon suite €238; 🛰 🛋 💻) This is the best splash-out option in the region, a luxury hotel with character. The owner, who speaks excellent English among five other languages, has owned hotels around the world and knows how to run a tidy ship. Rooms are gorgeous. Each is huge and has a giant balcony with a swing and fabulous sea views. Honeymooners should reserve the honeymoon suite. It is absolutely enormous and feels like you are staying in a millionaire's private home – think marble statues in the bathroom and a round bed, a giant living room with a flatscreen TV, a Jacuzzi, and an enormous private patio looking straight out to Nosy Lonja that's breathtaking come sunset. There is a restaurant with fabulous food and house rum, a huge pool with two waterslides (the hotel is very kid-friendly), an open-air gym and a spa offering massage. La Note Bleue has its own dock, and boat, and runs loads of watery excursions as well as land tours. It also rents quad-bikes, motorcycles and bicycles. It's a luxury experience made personable; look for it 3km from town.

RAMENA

The beach in front of this poor fishing village is a tiny palm-fringed spot 18km northeast of Diego Suarez. Boats crowd the small stretch of golden sand, and you'll find plenty of women touting massages and men selling fishing trips on the beach. Chickens and children run free on the sandy, garbage-strewn village streets that front the beach, and if you come looking for a hotel you'll likely have a posse of advisors before you even reach the place. But your posse will be friendly, and sure they want to make a buck off you, but they're not intimidating. In fact, there's something appealing about the whole down-home Malagasy fishing-village vibe this place so strongly emits. Plus the water – a turquoise and cerulean sea flecked with white caps set against a pale baby-blue sky – is freaking gorgeous. And it might not be long before Ramena really cleans up its act; the place is growing quickly, and its hotels are gaining a rep as good alternatives to city sleeping.

Sleeping & Eating

Try to book ahead during French school holidays when many places fill ultra-quick.

Badamera (☎ 032 07 733 50; r from Ar20,000) A few hundred metres up a hill from the beach, this popular and laid-back budget place has a shabby air, but a stylish terrace and restaurant that gets good reviews for its food. The rooms and bungalows are basic and hot (no fans), but they're clean and come with nets. Though the surrounding area is pretty scruffy, the beach isn't far away.

Villa Palm Beach (☎ 032 02 409 04; palmbeach@ netcourrier.com; r Ar26,000-56,000; 🛰) A clean and homely pension just down the hill from Badamera, it offers well-kept rooms in a family house. Accommodation is very simple, with nets, fans and wood floors, but it still feels nice and there are sea views. There are now a few more expensive rooms with air-con and newer furnishings.

La Case en Falafy (Chez Bruno; ☎ 032 02 674 33; bungalows Ar30,000; 🛋) It's away from the beach a bit, but this is a convivial place with a bar, good pool and open-air restaurant. The thatched-roof bungalows sit in a nice garden. Try for one at the back of the property – they are a bit more spread out and quiet. Tours and excursions can be arranged here.

Restaurant L'Émeraude (☎ 032 07 725 95; set menu Ar40,000; 😋 lunch & dinner Wed-Mon) This rather smart restaurant on the beach has a great reputation for its excellent food and Saturday-night disco. To find it walk down the road to the beach from Fihary Hotel and turn left at the pier. It's the first restaurant you'll see.

NORTHERN MADAGASCAR

SAVING MADAGASCAR ONE BAOBAB AT A TIME

York Pareik is one of a small, but growing, group of global citizens practicing homegrown eco-tourism. The long-time Diego Suarez area resident (Pareik originally hails from Germany) is a local hotelier and a one-man conservation promotion machine. Pareik, through sheer will and stubbornness (and, let's face it, a hell of a lot more money than most Madagascans make in a lifetime) is actually making headway in saving Madagascar's unique northern ecosystem one baobab at a time.

Pareik created the **Parc Botanique des Mille Baobabs** (admission €3) in 2002 in part to help stop baobab poaching on Montagne des Français. Although the mountain is supposedly now an officially protected wilderness area, the government is doing little to stop poor locals from razing baobabs to grow rice or burying and burning garbage in the park's fragile ecosystem. Parc Botanique des Mille Baobabs sits at the front of Montagne des Français, on land Pareik leased from the government using money he raised through German lenders. Since he doubts the government will do anything to stop the poaching, Pareik hopes to change it himself by educating locals about the importance of sustainable living. His goal isn't to keep the locals out of the park, he says, but to educate them on why it's so destructive to cut down the baobab trees. He has signs in both French and the local dialect, and he brings in groups of schoolchildren to teach them about ecotourism. Locals do not pay the same entrance fee as foreigners.

'Really, my purpose in creating the park was only partly to protect the ecosystem here, it was also for education purposes. I want to teach the locals, and the tourists, about the importance of

Getting There & Away

Taxis-brousses make several runs between Diego Suarez and Ramena (Ar2000) each day – although you may have to wait a while to get back. Chartering a taxi is an easier option, but will cost about Ar60,000 return.

BAIE DES SAKALAVA

On the eastern side of the peninsula that juts into the bay east of Diego is the up-and-coming Baie des Sakalava, which has a more beautiful beach than Ramena and a more remote atmosphere – it's not smack in the middle of a village.

You'll find a water-sports centre at the **Hôtel-Club de Sakalava** (☎ 032 04 512 39; www.sakalava.com; bungalows Ar25,000), which offers kitesurfing and windsurfing lessons and equipment rental. The place also arranges fishing and excursions, and mountain-bike, 4WD and boat rental. There are seven bungalows here, but unless you're taking lessons with the club, it can be hard to snag one – you'll often be told the place is full even if it's not.

Another larger and much swankier hotel is being planned for this beach. When it's complete – which could be years away – it will likely bring a lot of tourists.

To get here, head to Ankorikakely village, 13km from Diego along the main road, then walk or hitch another 5km from the signposted turn-off. It's very easy to hire a taxi from Diego to get here and back – make sure your driver doesn't abandon you, however – for around Ar60,000.

BAIE DES DUNES & MER D'ÉMERAUDE (EMERALD SEA)

Wild and free, the **Baie des Dunes** is our favourite bay in the area. Located north of the Baie des Sakalava, it offers the most remote beaches of them all. The white sand slopes gently into the brilliant coloured water, and you'll often have the place to yourself. The beach is guarded by a rusting military installation with a long-forgotten gun emplacement. Near its crumbling stone buildings an old lighthouse stands proud and a tapestry of white-flecked waves crash into jagged rocks below. To the left of the beach you'll find a small reef and a number pools before the ocean floor drops steeply and takes you into excellent snorkelling territory – definitely bring a mask, tube and fins.

More good snorkelling is to be found on the opposite side of the headland in the uber-gorgeous **Mer d'Émeraude** – literally a translucent Emerald Sea. To get to Mer d'Émeraude, you'll have to charter a fishing boat from Ramena or arrange a trip with one of the hotels. Much of the sea sits on a bit of a sandbar, which means you can wade slowly into schools of brightly coloured fish. Just keep your flippers on please, so you don't muck up and touch the relatively virgin coral.

NORTHERN MADAGASCAR

protecting the environment. It is only through education that the nature will be saved,' Pareik says as he sits on a weathered wooden bench starring out over the mangrove swamp to the sea

The mangrove-tree roots, knotted and criss-crossed like the veins on an old man's arthritic hand, rise in curved arches from the sandy swamp. The swamp is part of Pareik's conservation area. So is a circular 3km walking trail with resting points that also offer big signs with detailed information about native plants and creatures – you can find chameleons, geckos and hedgehogs in these dusty hills. The park features flora and fauna native only to northern Madagascar, including five of Madagascar's seven species of baobabs.

When he started the park five years ago, Pareik planted 5000 baobabs on the property. He says he'll never see them grow over 10ft – he won't live that long. Baobabs, which are entirely reliant on water for growth, seem to be the slowest-growing trees on earth. Even though Pareik planted the trees five years ago, some only reached our knees, while others only topped our ankles.

'Baobabs don't flower until they are 100 years old,' Pareik says. 'They grow so slow; that's why it's so harmful if they are cut down because you cut one of those big trees they have out (in western Madagascar) down and you'll have to wait a thousand years for another to grow to its size.'

There are eight species of baobab in the world, and six of these are found only in Madagascar (the seventh is indigenous to eastern African as well, and the eighth species is found only in northern Australia). Northern Madagascar is home to five species of baobab.

The Parc Botanique des Mille Baobabs is adjacent to King's Lodge (see p180).

The Baie des Dunes and Emerald Sea can be reached by vehicle or foot. Both are included on organised tours from Diego; see p175. Or you can charter a taxi from Diego, Ramena or the Baie des Sakalava to take you there. The cost is anywhere from Ar30,000 to Ar100,000 depending on your starting point. Note that to reach the Baie des Dunes you have to pass through a military base, and you will need to purchase a permit (Ar2000) from one of the sentries at the main gate.

You can walk from Baie des Sakalava to Baie des Dunes in about two hours, passing mangroves and interesting rock pools.

WINDSOR CASTLE

This 391m-high rock formation lies about 2km north of the village of Andramahimba, northwest of Diego Suarez. It served as a French fort and lookout, and was taken by the occupying British in 1942. A decaying stairway leads to the top, with good views over the **Baie du Courrier**.

Windsor Castle can only be accessed by 4WD vehicle. Follow the route west along the bay for 20km and turn north at Antsahampano. At the 32km point from Diego Suarez (which is 12km beyond Antsahampano), turn west down a track and continue for a further 5km.

Organised tours from Diego Suarez cost about Ar50,000 per person with a group of four.

JOFFREVILLE

Its name evokes images of colonial pomp, and indeed, Joffreville, established in 1902, was once a pleasure resort for the French military. Today it's little more than a small village with battered signs and plenty of small shacks. Still the place manages to retain a relaxing country ambiance and there are excellent views of the surrounding bays from all sides. It is also home to several excellent hotels. Most people use the town as a jumping off point to visit the fabulous and adjacent Parc National de Montagne d'Ambre.

Sleeping & Eating

The village store sells a few basics, but if you plan on camping in the park you'll need to get food and other supplies in Diego. All the hotels do meals of varying standards.

Auberge Sakay Tany (☎ 032 04 281 22; www.sakay -tany.com; r from Ar25,000, set dinner Ar20,000) A simple, quaint guesthouse with lots of character. The four rustic rooms in the main house are painted a cheery yellow. Some share baths, but there are now a few private bathrooms. The garden area is particularly nice, with a thatched dining area and a swing.

Nature Lodge (☎ 032 07 123 06; www.naturelodge -ambre.com; d €60, dinner €15) Almost as beautiful as Le Domaine de Fontenay, and considerably cheaper, this newer hotel has wooden safari-lodge-style cottages with chic interiors and

NORTHERN MADAGASCAR

amazing views, and a well-decorated thatched dining room and bar. The food is excellent.

Le Domaine de Fontenay (☎ 033 11 345 81; www .lefontenay-madagascar.com; r €120) This luxurious and charming hotel is one of Madagascar's best. It has eight very chic bungalows with stone floors, huge wood-and-marble bathrooms and four-poster beds. The restaurant in the old farmhouse features a chimney designed by Gustave Eiffel, of the Tower fame. It also has an orchid garden, giant tortoises and a private nature reserve with lemurs, reptiles, birds and great views over Diego's bay. English is spoken.

Getting There & Away
It is easy to catch a taxi-brousse to Joffreville (Ar3000, two hours) from Diego. Buses depart frequently from Diego's western taxi-brousse station.

You can also hire a taxi from Diego Suarez for the day from about Ar100,000 round trip, including waiting time or a trip to the Park National de Montagne d'Ambre, 4km away.

PARC NATIONAL DE MONTAGNE D'AMBRE
Wander blissfully through sun-dappled dry forests and stop at a misty waterfall, where you can return the stares of lemurs laughing at you from high above the treetops, in the 18,200 hectares of Parc National de Montagne d'Ambre. A prominent volcanic massif, it is one of northern Madagascar's most visited natural attractions. A new road through the park means tourist development is no longer limited to the northern area of the park – a small pass through the *tsingy* has been created and it is now popular to do a three-day trek from the park's eastern edge to its western boundary (there are built-in rest spots along the way, and you can rent tents at the eastern entrance). With taxis-brousses delivering you right to the gate, there's really no excuse not to visit – the wildlife is phenomenal. Once at the gate, it is easy to pick up a guide (now required) to lead you around. Let them know how much time you have – three days is the most you really need in this park – and where you'd like to trek. If you can only spare a day, visits are easily arranged from Diego. Note that hiking in the extreme southern reaches is still quite difficult, although it can be arranged.

Information
Angap (◷ 8am-4pm), at the park entrance a few kilometres southwest of Joffreville, can help

with information, permits (per day Ar25,000) and guides (per day €10 or €15), which are compulsory. The office also distributes a leaflet with a map of the self-guided trails and some information about the park.

Wildlife
Of the nearly a dozen species of lemurs found in the park, the most notable are the crowned lemur and Sanford's lemur. Others include the rufous mouse lemur, the dwarf and northern sportive lemurs, the aye-aye and the local Montagne d'Ambre fork-marked lemur. Among other mammals, the ring-tailed mongoose is probably the most frequently observed.

Reptile and amphibian life here includes frogs, geckos, chameleons and snakes. Some chameleons to watch for are the fairly common blue-nose chameleon (*Chamaeleo boettgeri*) and the stump-tailed chameleon.

Among the park's more than 70 species of birds are the crested wood ibis (*Lophotibis cristata*) and the malachite kingfisher (*Alcedo vintsioides*).

Hiking
It takes three days to hike from the eastern to western entrances along the new **cross-park road**, which is about the maximum amount of time you need in Montagne d'Ambre anyway. The hike is mildly strenuous, and passes through some really trippy scenery – mushrooms grow off the edges of trees and ring-tailed mongooses wander freely, and you pass *tsingy* mazes where lemurs leap from rock to rock and chameleons and geckos chill in the dark crevices between.

Other signposted walking trails in the northern part of the park take in the **Petit Lac**, a small crater lake also known as Lac de la Coupe Verte, and **Cascade Antankarana**, a beautiful waterfall flowing into a tranquil pool surrounded by fern-covered cliffs. Nearby is the path known as **Jardin Botanique**, a forest track lined by orchids, palms, lianas and bromeliads. Not far away, another trail leads to the small **Cascade Sacrée**, a sacred waterfall where locals often make offerings.

A longer track leads to the viewpoint over **Cascade Antomboka**, a narrow waterfall, which plunges 80m into a forest grotto. From the viewpoint there is a steep and slippery descent to the base of the cascade where you are likely to see butterflies and, with luck, crowned lemurs.

PARC NATIONAL DE MONTAGNE D'AMBRE

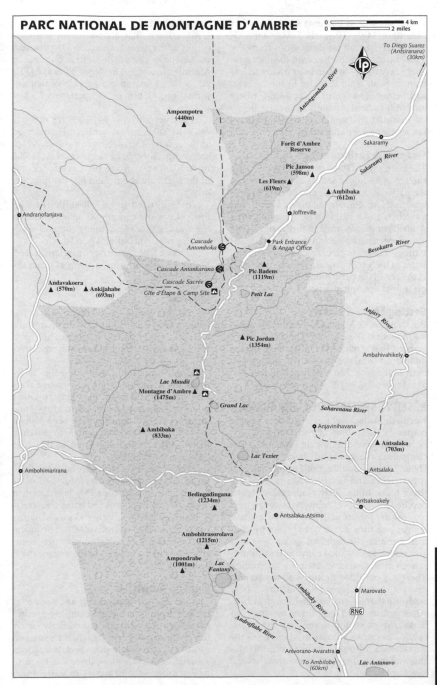

The summit of **Montagne d'Ambre** (Amber Mountain; 1475m) is reached via an approximately 11km trail heading south from the park entrance. From the camp site it's a relatively easy three- to four-hour hike, and less than an hour from the base to the summit. Just below the summit is **Lac Maudit**, where local *fady* (taboo) prohibits swimming. Below the summit to the southeast is the larger **Grand Lac**, where you are allowed to camp.

Sleeping & Eating

The park's **gîte d'étape** (dm Ar12,000) and camp site are in an idyllic setting about 3km from the park entrance, at the end of an avenue of towering South American pines. The *gîte* has a kitchen and a sitting area. Camping costs Ar5000 per person under a shelter or Ar1000 outside; tents can be hired at the park entrances. There are picnic tables, showers and water at the site. There are several camp sites in the rest of the park, which have no facilities; get info at the Angap office.

Getting There & Away

Parc National de Montagne d'Ambre lies about 40km south of Diego Suarez. The park entrance is about 4km southwest of Joffreville along the main road – taxis-brousses will deliver you right to the gate. Taxis in Diego will take you here for around Ar100,000 round trip.

RÉSERVE SPÉCIALE DE L'ANKÀRANA

Northern Madagascar's most precious reserve comes in the colour of ruby. The 18,225-hectare Réserve Spéciale de l'Ankàrana encompasses the beautiful Ankàrana Massif about 100km southwest of Diego Suarez. It is a striking and undeveloped fantasyland that's home to uniquely Madagascan sights: psychedelic forests of ruby-red *tsingy* sit next to semi-dry forests where nocturnal sportive lemurs pop their heads out of holes by your feet. Running through and under the *tsingy* are hidden forest-filled canyons and subterranean rivers, some containing crocodiles. There are bat-filled grottos and mysterious caves steeped in legend and history, where traditional rites are still held and *fady* is strictly observed. Don't touch anything or make any noise and never have sex in the caves. The massif is considered sacred to the Antakàrana, who took refuge from the Merina among its *tsingy* and caves, where several kings are buried.

Information

L'Ankàrana is managed by Angap, which has offices at the main entrance in Mahamasina, in Ambilobe and at the western entrance at Matsaborimanga. The **Angap office** (☎ 82 213 20) in Diego Suarez can provide general information. All offices are open from 7.30am to 4pm.

Entry permits cost Ar25,000 for one day or Ar40,000 for three and can be arranged at the reserve entrance, as can guides, which are compulsory. Fees range from Ar15,000 to Ar30,000 per group per circuit. Fees for night walks are about Ar12,000 per hour per group.

You will need to be self-sufficient with food, water and camping supplies (although there are now some camping supplies available for hire), including a good torch.

As most lakes and rivers here are sacred, bathing or swimming in them is generally not permitted.

Wildlife

On the high dry *tsingy*, succulents such as *Euphorbia* and *Pachypodium* predominate, while the sheltered intervening canyons are filled with leafy cassias, figs, baobabs and other trees typical of dry deciduous forest.

Of the area's more than 10 species of lemurs, the most numerous are crowned, Sanford's and northern sportive lemurs. Other mammals include tenrecs and ring-tailed mongooses. (Mongooses have been known to visit camping grounds at night in search of food – don't try to touch them, as they may be infected with rabies.)

Over 90 species of birds have been identified in the reserve, including the orange-and-white kingfisher, crested coua, Madagascan fish eagle, crested wood ibis and banded kestrel.

Fourteen of Madagascar's 33 species of bats live here, as well as numerous chameleon and gecko species, and some (albeit rarely seen) crocodiles living in rivers in the underground caves.

Sights & Activities

The route to the **Grands Tsingy** and the pretty **Lac Vert** from Andriafabe camping ground passes through forest, and usually offers the chance to see lemurs, chameleons and some of l'Ankàrana's rich vegetation. From Andriafabe, most groups drive the 16km to Anilotra then walk for about two hours. A sec-

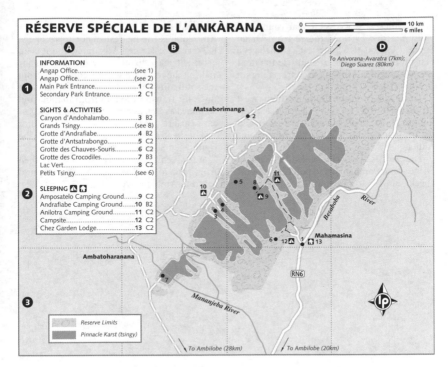

RÉSERVE SPÉCIALE DE L'ANKÀRANA

0   10 km
0   6 miles

INFORMATION
Angap Office.............................(see 1)
Angap Office.............................(see 2)
Main Park Entrance....................**1** C2
Secondary Park Entrance...........**2** C1

SIGHTS & ACTIVITIES
Canyon d'Andohalambo...............**3** B2
Grands Tsingy............................(see 8)
Grotte d'Andrafiabe....................**4** B2
Grotte d'Antsatrabongo...............**5** C2
Grotte des Chauves-Souris...........**6** C2
Grotte des Crocodiles..................**7** B3
Lac Vert...................................**8** C2
Petits Tsingy.............................(see 6)

SLEEPING
Amposatelo Camping Ground......**9** C2
Andrafiabe Camping Ground.....**10** B2
Anilotra Camping Ground.........**11** C2
Campsite.................................**12** C2
Chez Garden Lodge..................**13** C2

To Anivorana-Avaratra (7km);
Diego Suarez (80km)

Matsaborimanga

Betahoha River

Mahamasina

Ambatoharanana

Mananjeba River

To Ambilobe (28km)   To Ambilobe (20km)

Reserve Limits

Pinnacle Karst (tsingy)

ond circuit from Andrafiabe camping ground (around three to four hours) takes in the **Grotte d'Andrafiabe** and some canyons.

Easily reached on foot from the main entrance is the impressive **Grotte des Chauves-Souris** (Cave of Bats) with superb stalactites, stalagmites and other interesting formations, and thousands of bats hanging from the walls. Nearby is a small viewpoint from where you can look over the **Petits Tsingy**.

The **Grotte des Crocodiles** (Cave of Crocodiles) is in the far southwestern corner of the reserve and is accessible by 4WD from Ambilobe. To reach the cave, turn off the road before Ambatoharanana village. You are far more likely to see lemurs and chameleons here than crocodiles.

In order to really begin to explore l'Ankàrana's attractions, you will need to allow at least three days, including one day each way for transport from Diego Suarez. Bring water and sun protection, as walking in the reserve can get very hot.

Sleeping & Eating

In the park you have a choice of **camping** (Ar2000) or staying in a **bungalow** (Ar6000). The latter are

very basic but are clean and come with nets. Camping grounds in the reserve include one about 3km from Mahamasina near the Petits Tsingy and Grotte des Chauves-Souris; Andrafiabe on the western edge of the reserve near Andrafiabe village; and Anilotra in the centre of the reserve near the Grands Tsingy. Anilotra is unpopular with campers, as there's no water source here, but lots of mosquitoes. Watch out for scorpions at all of the camping grounds.

Outside the park, near Mahamasina, **Chez Garden Lodge** (☎ 033 114 5905; bungalows Ar8000) offers basic bungalows in a better setting than those in the park – the garden is really nice, plus there is a bar. Speaking of Mahamasina, the village is very poor and the school is always accepting donations. If you are interested in contributing, ask at the Angap office on your way in.

Getting There & Away

Mahamasina village is approximately 100km southwest of Diego Suarez and about 40km north of Ambilobe (Ar1000) along Route Nationale 6 (RN6). The main reserve entrance

NORTHERN MADAGASCAR

at Mahamasina is accessible year-round and easily reached by taxi-brousse from Diego Suarez (Ar6000, two hours). It's easy to get a taxi-brousse at the end of your trip to either Diego Suarez or Ambanja (for travelling on to Nosy Be).

To reach Matsaborimanga, turn west off the RN6 road on to a rough track a few kilometres south of Anivorana-Avaratra and continue for about 35km to the reserve entrance.

The park is also well covered by many of Diego's tour companies and hotel excursions; check out p175 for more info.

AMBILOBE

Ambilobe is the nearest major town to the Réserve Spéciale de l'Ankàrana, and it is an excellent place to stock up on supplies for visiting the reserve if you are coming in from the south on your own. It is also the junction town for transport to and from Iharana and Sambava as well as other towns on Madagascar's eastern coast.

The best accommodation option is the signposted **Hôtel de l'Ankàrana** (r Ar20,000).

A few vehicles go early every day between Ambilobe and Diego Suarez, Iharana and south to Ambanja (Ar5000).

Eastern Madagascar

Pirates aren't stupid. They figured out how juicy Eastern Madagascar's treasures were and looted its coastline centuries before the rest of us caught on. A couple of hundred years later the real pirates are gone and the secret is out: there's plenty of leftover booty in the form of dazzling pearl beaches, sparkling sapphire water and lush jade rainforests.

Travel in large parts of Eastern Madagascar isn't easy in anyone's book, but you can't say it's not an adventure. In fact, for some just the lure of trying to get around is enough reason to come. Author Tom Parkinson 'spent weeks researching via canoe and foot, it was the only way to get around...but he said it was a highlight of his trip', his mother wrote to us after his death.

Periodically ravished by cyclones, infrastructure along the wild and rugged long eastern coastline is poor at best. In the course of your travels, transport here will usually include riding in a zebu cart, long hikes through thick forest, and chugging along the region's multiple waterways in a flat-bottomed boat. It's not for everyone, but if you're bored of the easy travel life, this coast should get your blood pumping again.

Not everywhere along the Vanilla/Pirate/Cyclone (it goes by all three) Coast is hard to reach. The well-surfaced road between Antananarivo and Toamasina is one of Madagascar's most travelled, with most folk flocking in this direction to see (and hear) the indri, Madagascar's biggest lemur, in Parc National d'Andasibe-Mantadia. Further north the beautiful Île Sainte Marie is also easy to reach, and the island's palm-fringed beaches and turquoise water are beginning to edge out Nosy Be's as a sun-worshipper's favourite paradise.

HIGHLIGHTS

- Lying out in the sun, swimming in the sea or looking for whales on gorgeous, and accessible, **Île Sainte Marie** (p206)

- Trekking through one of Madagascar's best rainforests on the **Masoala Peninsula** (p223)

- Exploring the otherworldly, Jurassic Park–like scenery at **Réserve de Nosy Mangabe** (p219) while on a mission to find its golden beach

- Experiencing Madagascar at its most watery remote, boating down the **Canal des Pangalanes** (p228), where you're unlikely to see any other foreigners

- Listening for the eerie wail of the indri at popular **Parc National d'Andasibe-Mantadia** (p192), not far from Antananarivo

Réserve de ★ ★Masoala Peninsula
Nosy Mangabe

★ Île Sainte Marie

Parc National
d'Andasibe-Mantadia
★

Canal des Pangalanes ★

- HIGHEST POINT: 1785m
- PRINCIPAL TRIBES: Antaimoro, Betsimisaraka, Tsimihety

Getting There & Away

AIR

Air Madagascar has flights from Antananarivo to Toamasina (€80, one hour) daily, and several times a week from Antananarivo to Île Sainte Marie (€209, 1½ hours). You can also fly into Sambava or Antalaha, but these flights are scheduled less frequently. Air Madagascar also operates regional flights direct from Réunion to Toamasina.

Air Austral flies from Toamasina to Réunion, continuing to Mauritius.

BOAT

Toamasina is linked to Mauritius and Réunion by a passenger boat that departs approximately every two weeks. For more information, see p202.

Cargo boats from Diego Suarez occasionally round the Masoala Peninsula as far as Maroantsetra, but they are few and far between and facilities are minimal.

LAND

The twisting, turning Route Nationale 2 (RN2) from Antananarivo to Toamasina is well served by taxis-brousses and buses.

Coming from the south, travel by road is only possible with plenty of time and patience, and even then you'll only get as far as Mananara, 225km south of Toamasina. From the north, the road stops after Antalaha, where you may have to don your walking boots, flag down a passing cargo boat or, quickest of all, buy an air ticket.

Getting Around

AIR

Air Madagascar makes small plane hops up and down the northeast coast from Toamasina and Antananarivo, stopping at Maroantsetra (€128 from Toamasina) and Antalaha. Several weekly flights connect Île Sainte Marie to Toamasina (€80).

BOAT

From rusty-bottomed canal barges to overloaded cargo vessels, boats figure highly on the transport map of the east.

The French-built Canal des Pangalanes, which runs from Farafangana to Toamasina, is silted up and impassable in places but is definitely the main thoroughfare of the region. Regular cargo vessels and motorboats ply the most visited northern waters between

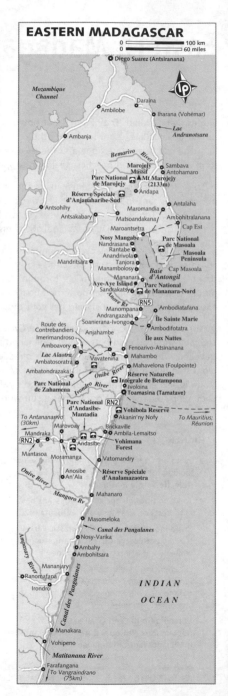

Ambila-Lemaitso and Toamasina. For more details, see p228.

Boats replace taxis-brousses as the main form of public transport for the coastal towns north of Soanierana-Ivongo. Few of the boats have any passenger facilities, however, and none has fixed schedules – it's simply a matter of hanging around the ports and waiting for something to arrive that's going your way. Several ferries a day, some equipped with such luxuries as seats and lifejackets, do the run across from the mainland to Île Sainte Marie. See p209 for details.

BUS & TAXI-BROUSSE
From the towns on the RN2, you'll be able to find onward transport to places like Andasibe and Ambatondrazaka, although once off the RN2 the roads are generally poor.

North of Toamasina, taxis-brousses continue daily as far as Soanierana-Ivongo, from where you catch the boat to Île Sainte Marie. Taxis-brousses are usually prevented from travelling further north due to collapsed bridges and enormous potholes. Likewise, no taxis-brousses go south from Toamasina, but further down the coast the towns of Mananjary, Manakara and Farafangana are linked by regular, if rickety, vehicles.

TRAIN
The once-famous passenger train between Antananarivo and Toamasina is currently suspended, but a limited service has restarted between Andasibe and Brickaville. Ask locally or in Antananarivo for the latest news.

The only other trains in the region are the cargo engines that run along the single-gauge railway linking some of the villages on the Canal des Pangalanes. These are supposedly forbidden from taking passengers, but if you're lucky you might be able to talk your way on board.

ANTANANARIVO TO TOAMASINA

MORAMANGA
pop 24,000
The market town of Moramanga lies along the Antananarivo–Toamasina road, 115km east of Antananarivo and 30km west of Andasibe. It's hardly a tourist town, but you'll have to stop here if you're heading to or from

Parc National d'Andasibe-Mantadia on public transport.

The BNI-CL and BFV-SG banks have branches with ATMs on the main road.

If you have a bit of time to kill between taxis, the **Musée de la Gendarmerie** (Police Museum; ☎ 56 821 39; Camp Tristany; admission Ar3000; ☽ 9-11am & 2-5pm Sat & Sun, other times by appointment), about 1km southwest of the market, exhibits cannons, police uniforms, a vintage taxi-brousse and, strangely, an enormous bunch of dried marijuana.

Sleeping & Eating
Motel-Restaurant Rindra (☎ 56 821 53; r with shared bathroom Ar10,000-17,000) On the single main road. Offers simple, spacious rooms with wood floors and furniture, plus some balconies and a popular restaurant. Note that there are just two communal bathrooms for all the rooms.

Hotel Nadia (☎ 56 822 43; s/d/tr Ar10,000/ 14,000/20,000) Another basic budget option in the middle of the busy market – it's serviceable and has a cafeteria, but could be cleaner.

Hôtel Restaurant Espace Diamant (☎ 56 823 76; r Ar25,000-36,000, with shared bathroom Ar20,000) A short walk west of the *gare routière*, it has the best standards in town, with new tiled rooms, big beds and a big restaurant. Staff seem refreshingly eager to please!

Le Coq d'Or (☎ 56 820 45; mains from Ar2000; ☽ lunch & dinner Mon-Sat, lunch Sun) A neat painted café on the main road, serving *soupe chinoise*, fried chicken and other Malagasy meals.

La Flore Orientale (☎ 56 820 20; mains from Ar3000; ☽ lunch & dinner) A big yellow Chinese restaurant with an extensive menu, right by the market.

La Sirène Dorée (mains from Ar3000; ☽ breakfast, lunch & dinner) Just a tad smarter than its rivals, with mirrored windows concealing restaurant, pizzeria, patisserie and *salon de thé*.

Getting There & Away
Taxis-brousses leave regularly from Antananarivo's eastern taxi-brousse station for Moramanga (Ar5000, 2¾ hours). There are direct taxi-brousse connections from Moramanga to Andasibe (Ar2000, 1½ hours) every few hours.

To get to Toamasina (Ar11,000, five to seven hours), you may need to wait until a vehicle coming from Antananarivo arrives with space.

A limited passenger-train service has now started running along with the freight services, shuttling one tiny carriage from Moramanga to Brickaville and back, via Andasibe, every Tuesday and Saturday (Ar3500). It's slow and not particularly practical, as the station is some distance from the town centre.

PARC NATIONAL D'ANDASIBE-MANTADIA & AROUND

One of the most popular attractions in Madagascar, thanks to its unique wildlife and convenient location near Tana, this 12,810-hectare park encompasses two distinct areas: the smaller Réserve Spéciale d'Analamazaotra (sometimes referred to as Périnet, its French colonial-era name), in the south by Andasibe, and the much larger Parc National de Mantadia, to the north. There are also several small private reserves near Andasibe.

The landscape in both sections consists of beautiful primary forest studded with lakes, but the real draw is the rare indri, Madagascar's largest lemur. The wondrous indri has been described as looking like 'a four-year-old child in a panda suit' and is famous for its eerie wailing cry, which sounds like something between a fire engine and Pavarotti in pain – hearing it through the early-morning mist is a truly affecting experience. Indris can be heard calling almost daily in the Réserve Spéciale d'Analamazaotra, mainly early in the morning and at dusk.

As it's easiest to access, d'Analamazaotra gets the most visitors, and tends to fill up during July and September, Madagascar's tourist high season. The best times to visit are from September to January and in May. During the winter months of June to October, the park can get very cold, so bring enough warm clothing with you. If the weather has been wet (which it often is), watch out for leeches on the trails.

INFORMATION

Opening hours for both d'Analamazaotra and Mantadia are 6am to 4pm, plus night visits by arrangement. Entry permits (one/two/three days Ar25,000/37,000/40,000) allow access to both parks, and can be purchased at the main entrance to d'Analamazaotra, near Andasibe. Guides gather here from around 6.30am waiting for clients; it's worth following your instincts and being a bit selective, as some of the less qualified guides show very little effort or enthusiasm. A list of official Angap-approved guides is displayed at the reception, with details of their skills and qualifications, and fixed guide fees (valid for groups of up to three people) are shown on a board outside. You can also contact the **Association des Guides d'Analamazaotra** (☎ 56 832 35; assoguiand@yahoo.fr; ⏲ 7am-5pm) at the Angap office to arrange your circuit.

All of the guides speak French and some also speak English, German, Spanish, Italian or Japanese, though not always sufficiently well to explain the park properly – check before setting out. Don't hire guides who approach you in Andasibe or Moramanga, as they may not actually have authorisation to enter the park.

Most travellers stay in or near the very charming village of Andasibe (see p195). The closest hotel to Mantadia is Vakôna Forest

---

THE LEGEND OF BABAKOTO

The indri is known in Malagasy as *babakoto*, meaning 'Father of Koto'. The word *indri* actually means 'look up there', and was mistaken for the animal's name by a European explorer being shown the *babakoto* by locals.

Tradition relates that the *babakoto* got its name when a young boy named Koto climbed a tree in the forest in search of honey. Koto disturbed a bee's nest and, stung all over, released his grip on the branches. He was saved from falling to the ground by an indri, which caught him in its arms, and thus earned its name.

An alternative version of the legend has young Koto venturing into the forest to look for food. When he fails to return, his father goes out to look for him, but he, too, never comes back. Eventually the villagers send out a search party, but all they can find is two indris crying mournfully from a tree; seeing their strangely human appearance, the villagers decide the missing pair must somehow have been turned into lemurs, and name the creature *babakoto* in honour of the father who searched so faithfully for his son.

Whichever story you prefer, it's still *fady* (taboo) for villagers here to kill or eat indris, which has played a considerable part in their continued survival.

Lodge. You can **camp** (tent sites Ar5000) behind the Angap office at the main park entrance.

WILDLIFE

In d'Analamazaotra, there are about 60 family groups of two or five indris; their cry, which can be heard up to 3km away, is used mainly to define a particular group's territory, though there are also distinct mating and alarm calls. Indris are active on and off throughout the day, beginning about an hour after daybreak, which is usually the best time to see them. Despite the incredible cacophony of sound that comes out of the forest, each individual only calls for about four or five minutes per day.

Indris eat complex carbohydrates, and therefore need to spend much of their day in a sedentary manner digesting their food. They spend most of their time high in the forest canopy, feeding, sleeping and sunning themselves. Their powerful hind legs make them capable of 10m horizontal leaps from tree to tree, perfectly balanced despite their stumplike tail. Indris are also very sensitive to any change in environment, which is the main reason for their endangered status – not only does deforestation threaten their habitat, but no indri has ever survived in captivity, as they simply stop eating and die.

The indris are very much the stars of the show, but you may also see woolly lemurs, grey bamboo lemurs, red-fronted lemurs, black-and-white ruffed lemurs and diademed sifakas. In 2005 the Goodman's mouse lemur was discovered here and identified as a distinct species. Eleven species of tenrec, the immense and colourful Parson's chameleon and seven other chameleon species are also found here. Over 100 bird species have been identified in the park, together with 20 species of amphibian. The park is also home to the endemic palm tree *Ravenea louvelii,* found nowhere else on the island.

Réserve Spéciale d'Analamazaotra

The entrance to d'Analamazaotra is 2km along a sealed road from Andasibe. Because the reserve is small, most of it can be covered in short walks. The best time for seeing (and hearing) indris is early in the morning, from 7am to 11am.

Before you begin exploring, it is worth visiting the interpretation centre at the park reception, which has a display on indris and information about the park.

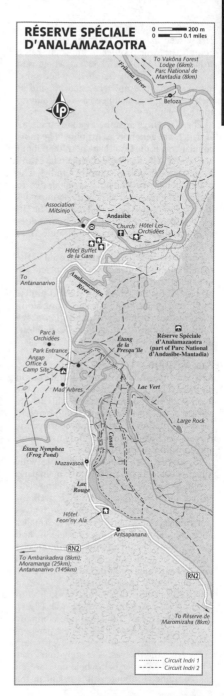

D'Analamazaotra has two small lakes, **Lac Vert** (Green Lake) and **Lac Rouge** (Red Lake). Behind the Angap office is the small **Parc à Orchidées** (7.30am-noon & 2-5.30pm), which is at its most attractive in October; by late summer it's almost completely dried up, and as there's no signage you need a good guide to appreciate it fully.

There are three organised walking trails, all of which are generally easy going. The most popular trail is the **Circuit Indri 1** (Ar4000, about two hours), which includes the main lakes and the territory of a single family of indris. The slightly longer **Circuit Indri 2** (Ar8000, two to four hours) visits the lakes and encompasses the patches of two separate families. The **Circuit Aventure** (Ar12,000, up to six hours) does all of the above, plus some moderately more strenuous walking.

Night walks (Ar8000) take place along the road on the perimeter of the reserve, and are not permitted in the forest itself. You will probably be able to see tenrecs and mouse and dwarf lemurs on this walk – bring along a strong torch (flashlight), and discourage your guide if they try to take an illegal detour into the woods.

Parc Mitsinjo

Based at the d'Analamazaotra forest station on the Andasibe road, about 150m from the Réserve Spéciale d'Analamazaotra, this private park (56 832 33; mitsinjo@hotmail.com; 7am-5pm & 6.30-9pm) is run by local guides, who formed the Association Mitsinjo to promote conservation and community tourism.

It's a great idea to add Mitsinjo to your itinerary before or after visiting the main park: the guides here are very friendly and knowledgeable, and here you can do a night walk inside the actual forest (Ar12,000), which gives you a much better chance of seeing the smaller nocturnal lemurs, sleeping chameleons and rare leaf-tailed lizards. Standard daytime circuits start at Ar15,000, going up to Ar35,000 for two four-hour walks on consecutive days, and there's no separate entry fee.

The Association Mitsinjo also works in conjunction with **Mad'Arbres** (032 43 105 48; www .madarbres.com), a fantastic adventure company that lets you get a completely new perspective on the forest: an indri's-eye view from up in the trees themselves! A canopy tour costs Ar50,000/80,000 per half/whole day, or you can combine climbing with a circuit in the

park for Ar80,000. Camping (Ar5000) and pirogue trips (Ar10,000) are also available, and the whole set-up is highly recommended.

For information, the Association Mitsinjo also runs a small handicrafts shop in Andasibe itself, opposite the post office.

Parc National de Mantadia

The Parc National de Mantadia (10,000 hectares), about 17km north of d'Analamazaotra, was created primarily to protect the indris. It also hosts two species of lemur not found in d'Analamazaotra: the diademed sifaka and the black-and-white ruffed lemur. The park, a quiet, beautiful area with numerous waterfalls, is undeveloped and seldom visited compared with its popular neighbour to the south, so if you're here in high season it's well worth the detour to escape the crowds.

Established circuits include **Circuit Rianasoa** (Ar4000, one hour), **Circuit Chute Sacrée** (Ar8000, about 1½ hours) and **Circuit Tsakoka** (Ar12,000, about three hours). For more of a challenge, you can also embark on an Adventure Circuit of two to three days, camping in the park. Guides, information and tickets can all be obtained at the main park entrance near Andasibe. You'll need all your own camping equipment if you're planning to stay the night; the Angap **camp site** (tent sites free), just outside the park, has no facilities.

To get to Mantadia from the main park entrance, you will most likely need your own vehicle or bicycle. Transport can usually be arranged with park staff, or sometimes through guides and local hotels.

Réserve de Maromizaha

This 10,000-hectare ecotourism reserve, about 8km southeast of the Parc National d'Andasibe-Mantadia, offers good camping, numerous walking tracks, stands of rainforest and panoramic views. The area is also home to 11 lemur species, although you probably won't see many of them. They include diademed sifakas and black-and-white ruffed lemurs, both of which are also found at Mantadia. Visits here can be organised with the guides at Parc National d'Andasibe-Mantadia. The reserve is accessible from the park gate via an easy trail. No permit is necessary.

Vohimana Forest

Established as a private reserve in 2001, this crucial forest corridor links Andasibe-

Mantadia with the forests of the south, and is administered by the NGO **Man and the Environment** (MATE; ☎ in Antananarivo 22 674 90; www.mate.mg), which is developing it as an ecotourism site in conjunction with their conservation work. At present facilities include around 20km of walking trails, three picnic areas and a botanical garden, and local guides have been trained in some interesting specialist circuits highlighting medicinal plants and 'agricultural rock-climbing'. Contact MATE for all details on access, tariffs and facilities; volunteer placements are also available.

ANDASIBE

Andasibe (an-da-see-*bay*) is a muddy former logging village that makes a convenient base for visiting both the Réserve Spéciale d'Analamazaotra and Parc National de Mantadia. It's also a charming little place in its own right, surrounded by forest, straddling a river and bisected by a railway line that is slowly regaining regular traffic. The only concrete buildings are the station, the post office and a couple of churches, and you won't find any banking facilities here.

Sleeping & Eating

Hôtel Les Orchidées (☎ 56 832 05; s/d/tr with shared bathroom Ar12,000/15,000/20,000) Housed in a wooden building right in the centre of the village, this well-signposted guesthouse has basic wooden rooms with mosquito nets. Good-value Malagasy meals (mains Ar2000 to Ar4100) are available at the restaurant, a few doors down.

Hôtel Buffet de la Gare (☎ 56 832 08; r Ar23,600-35,400, bungalows Ar35,400-64,900) Not just for train-spotters – this Andasibe institution is housed in the declining but still impressive 1938 station building (enter via the platform!), and has berthed visiting wildlife luminaries from Gerald Durrell to Sir David Attenborough. The main building retains some nostalgic character, but really you want to choo-choo your way to one of the smart new bungalows opposite or 500m up the road, where you'll find unusual luxuries such as stone hearths and log fires.

Hôtel Feon'ny Ala (☎ 56 832 02; bungalows Ar38,000-64,900) Whoever named this charming garden hotel 'Song of the Forest' was pretty much on the money – the site is virtually part of the forest, so close that you can hear the indris doing their vocal exercises. The thatched bungalows are rather close together but very

comfortable, with hot showers. A couple of basic bungalows with shared bathroom are also available (Ar17,700). The restaurant does good evening meals and can provide picnic lunches for walkers. It's a handy 300m from the RN2 Andasibe junction, but about 1.5km south of the entrance to the park.

OUR PICK **Vakôna Forest Lodge** (☎ in Antananarivo 22 213 94; www.hotel-vakona.com; r from €60; ⚓) How many hotels do you know that come with their own lake? This little piece of paradise is Andasibe's most upmarket hotel, and quite possibly one of the best in Madagascar. The beautiful gardens are set in a 'forest' of eucalyptus trees, centred on the lake, where the main island holds a beautiful glass-walled restaurant with sun deck and log fire. Once you get over the setting, the facilities are pretty astounding too: the grounds encompass a zoo and crocodile farm, lemur sanctuary and equestrian centre (Ar9000 per hour), plus squash court, pool table and table tennis if you prefer your sports competitive. Should you happen to find time to visit your room, you'll discover terracotta-coloured bungalows resplendent with wood floors, whitewashed walls, big bathrooms, minibar and terrace. Vakôna is on the road between Andasibe village and the Parc National de Mantadia; to get here you will need to have your own vehicle, arrange transfers with the hotel (Ar15,000) or try to hitch a lift.

Getting There & Away

From Antananarivo, the best way to reach Andasibe is to take a taxi-brousse to Moramanga, where you'll find direct taxis-brousses to Andasibe which can drop you at your hotel of choice. Otherwise, you can take any taxi-brousse along the RN2 to the Andasibe junction, from where you'll need to walk or hitch the 3km to the village itself.

Reaching Toamasina from Andasibe can be tricky. There are two direct taxis-brousses a day (Ar11,000, up to six hours) to Toamasina, but they're often full, so it's worth asking at your hotel about making a reservation (Ar4000) if you're on a tight schedule. Solo travellers may be able to find a vehicle with a free seat on the main road at the Andasibe junction, but expect a long wait and a fare of anything between Ar7500 and Ar12,000. If you can't start early, you may be better off going to Moramanga and catching a vehicle there.

In theory you could also charter a taxi from Antananarivo and visit as a long day trip, though this is unlikely to be much cheaper than hiring a car for the day. Allow at least three hours each way, and keep in mind that to arrive early enough to hear the indris, you'll have to leave by 6am.

The tiny Moramanga–Brickaville passenger train passes through Andasibe every Tuesday and Saturday (Ar3500).

LAC ALAOTRA

The area around Lac Alaotra, Madagascar's largest body of water, is a centre of biodiversity, supporting 74 species of water birds, including two unique species, the Madagascar pochard and the Alaotran little grebe, and animals such as the Alaotran gentle lemur (entertainingly known as *hapalémur Brando* in French).

Sadly, Lac Alaotra also exemplifies the environmental damage that affects many parts of Madagascar, with the gentle lemur critically endangered and the two endemic bird species most likely extinct. Population growth, hunting, burning and clearance of marshes, overfishing, pollution from pesticides and invasion by introduced plants and fish have all contributed to the degradation, as seen in the red-tinged waters of the 20,000-hectare lake itself.

The good news is that steps are being taken to restore the ecological balance. The Durrell Wildlife Conservation Trust has led a six-year project to raise awareness of the value of the marshes, foster pride in the Alaotran gentle lemur and encourage commitment to wise use of the wetlands. As a result, in 2003 the government added Alaotra to the international Ramsar list of important wetlands, making it one of just three protected wetland sites in Madagascar.

At a local level, fishermen have agreed to limited mesh sizes and a closed season, while marsh clearance is being reduced and new marshes planted. With fish stocks increasing and lemur populations recovering, it's now hopeful that the effects of environmental degradation here can be repaired, if not reversed.

Vehicle access to Alaotra is tricky due to limited infrastructure. One of the few places where the road meets the lake is at Andreba, on the east of the lake (accessible by taxi-brousse from Ambatondrazaka), where there is a **lemur reserve**. Ask for the *responsable*, who will organise a canoe and a guide. It's best to visit in the early morning for the best chances of sightings.

PARC NATIONAL DE ZAHAMENA

West of Fenoarivo-Atsinanana is the 41,402-hectare **Parc National de Zahamena** (admission Ar10,000). Still in the development stage, Zahamena protects important areas of rainforest, 13 species of lemur and 61 endemic bird species.

The park is managed by Angap with support from Conservation International; for information, contact the **park office** (☎ 57 300 33) in town. There are some basic camp sites in the park and simple local accommodation in the nearby village of Vavatenina. You will need to be self-sufficient with food, water and equipment. Depending on road conditions it may be easier to reach Zahamena from Ambatondrazaka (opposite).

LAC ALAOTRA & PARC NATIONAL DE ZAHAMENA

BONE IDOL

In the last few years, nearly 1000 ancestral tombs in the Ambatondrazaka region have been broken into by thieves intent on stealing human bones. Although the thieves themselves have often been caught and sentenced, the reason behind the crimes remains mysterious. The unknown traffickers, who have so far evaded capture, offer as much as US$4000 for a kilogram of bones.

The thefts of the bones, which are regarded as sacred, have caused widespread distress among families of the region, and wild rumours abound as to what they could be wanted for, with suggested culprits ranging from foreign mafiosos to desperate AIDS victims convinced the bones could cure them. No convincing theory has yet been raised, however, and the thefts continue.

AMBATONDRAZAKA

pop 35,000

Ambatondrazaka is the nearest major town to Lac Alaotra, out on a tricky road well away from the major tourist routes. It's a sprawling place surrounded by rice fields, which have replaced most of the area's original forest cover – if you pass over the region by air, look out for the striking erosion gullies that striate the battered countryside.

Hôtel Voahirana (☎ 54 812 08; r Ar12,000), near the market, has clean rooms and a reasonable restaurant, and can help organise excursions and treks in the region. **Hôtel Max** (☎ 54 813 86; r Ar15,000-25,000, with shared bathroom Ar10,000), near the train station, is more comfortable, with TVs and hot water in the more expensive rooms.

A taxi-brousse runs most days on the rough road between Moramanga and Ambatondrazaka (Ar9000, four to six hours). Direct taxis also depart many times weekly from Antananarivo's eastern taxi-brousse station (Ar11,000).

From Ambatondrazaka, there is usually at least one vehicle daily to Imerimandroso (Ar2000, one to two hours).

Air Madagascar no longer serves Ambatondrazaka.

ROUTE DES CONTREBANDIERS

The Route des Contrebandiers (Smugglers' Path) is a muddy and slippery five- to six-day trek connecting Imerimandroso (50km north of Ambatondrazaka on the eastern edge of Lac Alaotra) with the village of Anjahambe (about 35km to the west of Mahambo). Historically, the Route des Contrebandiers was used by smugglers bringing goods from Réunion and Mauritius into the Merina highlands.

Today, few travellers attempt the trek, primarily because access is difficult and the going is tough. If you do attempt it, you'll need camping gear, including a waterproof groundsheet, although some villages along the way have small, very basic hotels. You'll also need to be self-sufficient with food; water is available, but a good filter is essential. Seek out a guide from the Hôtel Voahirana in Ambatondrazaka.

BRICKAVILLE

Brickaville, reached by train (Ar3500) or taxi-brousse (Ar6000, three hours) from Moramanga or taxi-brousse from Toamasina (Ar5000, three hours), is an old sugarcane-growing town on the RN2 between Antananarivo and Toamasina. The town itself is little more than a string of buildings along the road, with a couple of basic hotels and *hotelys* near the diminutive station, but it's possible to start trips on the southern Canal des Pangalanes (p228) from here.

TOAMASINA (TAMATAVE)

pop 174,000

Mada's second city, Toamasina (often still known by its French name Tamatave) was developed as a resort during colonial times. Photographs from a hundred years ago show French holidaymakers posing in long bathing costumes in front of wooden beach huts. These days, the town is a popular holiday destination among the more affluent Malagasy. Every Sunday, come rain or shine, the town's fashionable youth gather on the seafront to promenade, flirt and ride around in high-wheeled *pousses-pousses* (rickshaws).

Despite its reputation as a pleasure resort, first impressions of the town are not edifying, especially if you arrive during one of the frequent downpours. Once-grand colonial buildings, now covered in mould, line the streets.

But despite this atmosphere of decay, Toamasina is a vibrant and important town, a centre of commerce for the east and one of the country's major ports. It's also a convenient

EASTERN MADAGASCAR

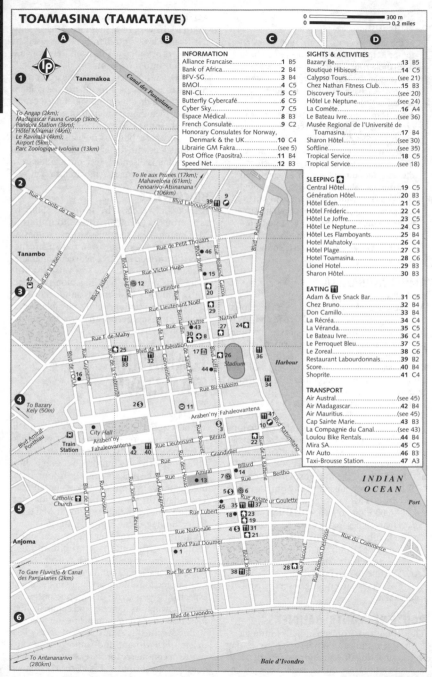

TOAMASINA (TAMATAVE)

0   300 m
0   0.2 miles

INFORMATION
Alliance Francaise..........................1 B5
Bank of Africa................................2 B4
BFV-SG...3 B4
BMOI..4 C5
BNI-CL..5 C5
Butterfly Cybercafé........................6 C5
Cyber Sky......................................7 C5
Espace Médical..............................8 B3
French Consulate............................9 C2
Honorary Consulates for Norway,
    Denmark & the UK..................10 C4
Librairie GM Fakra....................(see 5)
Post Office (Paositra)...................11 B4
Speed Net....................................12 B3

SIGHTS & ACTIVITIES
Bazary Be.....................................13 B5
Boutique Hibiscus.........................14 C5
Calypso Tours...........................(see 21)
Chez Nathan Fitness Club.............15 B3
Discovery Tours........................(see 20)
Hôtel Le Neptune......................(see 24)
La Comète....................................16 A4
Le Bateau Ivre...........................(see 36)
Musée Regional de l'Université de
    Toamasina..............................17 B4
Sharon Hôtel.............................(see 30)
Softline......................................(see 35)
Tropical Service...........................18 C5
Tropical Service........................(see 18)

SLEEPING
Central Hôtel...............................19 C5
Génération Hôtel.........................20 B3
Hôtel Eden..................................21 C5
Hôtel Fréderic..............................22 C4
Hôtel Le Joffre.............................23 C5
Hôtel Le Neptune.........................24 C3
Hôtel Les Flamboyants..................25 B4
Hotel Mahatoky...........................26 C4
Hôtel Plage..................................27 C3
Hotel Toamasina..........................28 C6
Lionel Hotel.................................29 B3
Sharon Hôtel...............................30 B3

EATING
Adam & Eve Snack Bar.................31 C5
Chez Bruno..................................32 B4
Don Camillo.................................33 B4
La Récréa.....................................34 C4
La Véranda...................................35 C5
Le Bateau Ivre..............................36 C4
Le Perroquet Bleu.........................37 C5
Le Zoreal.....................................38 C6
Restaurant Labourdonnais.............39 B2
Score...40 B4
Shoprite......................................41 C4

TRANSPORT
Air Austral.................................(see 45)
Air Madagascar...........................42 B4
Air Mauritius.............................(see 45)
Cap Sainte Marie.........................43 B3
La Compagnie du Canal..............(see 43)
Loulou Bike Rentals......................44 B4
Mira SA.......................................45 C5
Mr Auto......................................46 B3
Taxi-Brousse Station.....................47 A3

spot to break the journey between Antananarivo and Île Sainte Marie, or to organise a trip down the Canal des Pangalanes.

HISTORY

The origin of the Malagasy name Toamasina is disputed. One theory states that it was derived from the 16th-century Portuguese name São Tomás (St Thomas), while another attributes it to King Radama I's first visit to the ocean in 1817, when it's said that the king knelt to taste the water and said 'Toa masina' – 'It is salty!'

Thanks to its importance as a commercial port and slaving centre, Toamasina was one of the first major targets of the European colonial powers; the British captured the town in 1811, but then ceded it to France in 1816 as part of the Treaty of Paris. The new owners promptly burned everything and left the remains to the increasingly powerful Merina until 1883, when the city was taken to allow the establishment of a French protectorate in the region. Civil unrest obliged the French to retake the city in 1894, and it remained an official territory right up to independence.

During the political strife in 2002, the Toamasina region was one of the centres of support for former president Didier Ratsiraka, whose family originated in the area. Militant factions blockaded the RN2, cutting the main fuel supply lines to Antananarivo. The blockades were removed by force, but not before a thriving black-market trade in petrol had sprung up.

ORIENTATION

Central Toamasina operates on a slightly irregular rectangular grid system bounded by the north–south streets Blvd Augagneur and Blvd Joffre (the main commercial street, with many of the town's shops and hotels). The waterfront road Blvd Ratsimilaho runs roughly parallel to them for much of its length. Araben'ny Fahaleovantena (or Ave Poincaré) is the main east–west thoroughfare, connecting the waterfront with the train station.

INFORMATION
Bookshops
Librairie GM Fakra (Rue Joffre; ✖ Tue-Sun, afternoon Mon) Some English newspapers and magazines, plus maps of the region and postcards.

Cultural Centres
Alliance Française (☎ 53 334 94; aftamatave@dts.mg; Blvd Paul Doumer) French film screenings a few times a

week, plus the usual exhibitions, concerts, language, music and dance classes.

Internet Access
Butterfly Cybercafé (☎ 033 02 088 72; Blvd Joffre; per hr Ar1800)
Cyber Sky (Blvd Joffre; per min Ar30; ✖ 8am-8pm Mon-Sat)
Speed Net (☎ 53 916 03; Blvd Augagneur; per min Ar15)

Medical Services
Espace Médical (☎ 53 315 66; Blvd de la Libération; ✖ 24hr)

Money
The main banks in the centre all have Visa ATMs. There are numerous moneychangers around Blvd Joffre; Hôtel Le Neptune may change travellers cheques outside of normal banking hours.
Bank of Africa (BOA; Blvd Augagneur)
BFV-SG (Cnr Blvd Joffre & Araben'ny Fahaleovantena)
BMOI (Blvd Joffre)
BNI-CL (Blvd Joffre)

Post & Telephone
Mastercom (☎ 033 14 977 60; Blvd Joffre) International calls for around Ar600 per minute, plus bureau de change.
Post Office (Paositra) (☎ 53 323 99; Araben'ny Fahaleovantena) Main post office. There are cardphones here and around town. Also offers internet.

Tourist Information
Angap (☎ 53 327 07; Rte d'Ivoloina) General information about national parks in the region, a few kilometres out of town on the road to the airport.
Madagascar Fauna Group (☎ 53 308 42; mfgmad@ dts.mg; Rte de l'Aéroport) Information on the Parc Zoologique Ivoloina (p203) and related conservation programmes.

TOURS

The following companies can assist with car hire, excursions down the Canal des Pangalanes, air packages to Île Sainte Marie and trips to Parc Zoologique Ivoloina, Mahambo and the beach resorts north along the coast. You could also ask about visiting the Île aux Prunes, a tiny island 16km northeast of town, with its unusual 1932 lighthouse.
Boutique Hibiscus (☎ 53 334 03; Blvd Joffre) A half-day trip on the canal costs Ar150,000 per boat.
Calypso Tours (☎ 53 312 90; www.calypsotour .freesurf.fr; Hôtel Eden, Blvd Joffre) A budget tour company

offering day trips on the Canal des Pangalanes for Ar60,000 per person.

Discovery Tours (☎ 032 02 456 75; fidelysco@yahoo .fr; Génération Hôtel, Blvd Joffre) Tours on the Canal des Pangalanes for Ar60,000 per person per day.

La Comète (☎ 53 339 53; cometetam@yahoo.fr; Blvd de l'OUA) Speedboat transfers for six to 10 people to hotels on the Canal des Pangalanes.

Softline (☎ 53 329 75; softline@dts.mg; 20 Blvd Joffre) Trips on the Canal des Pangalanes for Ar60,000 per person per day; also offers bike and scooter hire.

Tropical Service (☎ 53 336 79; www.croisiere -madagascar.com; 23 Blvd Joffre) Top-end local tours, cruises, car hire, transfers and travel services.

SIGHTS & ACTIVITIES
Musée Regional de l'Université de Toamasina

The small **University Museum** (admission by donation; ☉ 9am-4pm Tue-Sun) constitutes barely 2½ rooms of farming tools, fishing implements, archaeological finds and tribal charms, along with poster displays on deforestation and local conservation projects. Some of the captioning is in English, including translations of some typically cryptic Malagasy proverbs.

Markets

Toamasina's colourful **Bazary Be** (Big Market) sells fruit, vegetables, spices, handicrafts and beautiful bouquets of flowers (should you feel the need to brighten up your hotel room). The **Bazary Kely** (Little Market) sells fish and produce in the ruins of a commercial complex on Blvd de la Fidelité, west of the train station.

Swimming & Sports

Hôtel Miramar (opposite) and Hôtel Le Neptune (opposite) both have swimming pools charging Ar2000 to Ar3000 for nonguests. Le Bateau Ivre (p202) offers free swimming if you eat there, or charges Ar2000 if you don't. The Sharon Hôtel (opposite) has its own fitness centre and luxury beauty salon; if you want a cheaper gym or cardio workout, try **Chez Nathan Fitness Club** (☎ 032 02 721 15; Blvd Joffre; per day from Ar6000; ☉ 8am-8pm Mon-Sat), opposite the Génération Hôtel.

SLEEPING

As befits its status as a holiday town, Toamasina is fairly well equipped with hotels, although they're mostly faded and overpriced. There are lots of mosquitoes in Toamasina, so opt for a hotel with nets, or bring your own.

Budget

Hotel Mahatoky (☎ 53 300 21; Blvd de la Liberté; r Ar8000-15,000) If you just need a crash pad before getting an early taxi-brousse, this little maroon place by the *gare routière* should do the job. It's very basic, but you do get mosquito nets and surprisingly good-looking showers in the better rooms (the cheapest share a bathroom and squat toilet).

Hôtel Eden (☎ 53 312 90; calypsotour@netcourrier.com; Blvd Joffre; r with shared/private bathroom Ar13,000/15,000) The simple but functional rooms at this popular 1st-floor backpackers' hotel towards the busier end of Blvd Joffre have fans but no nets. Calypso Tours is based here, so it's a good place to organise tours on the Canal des Pangalanes, if you can get the staff to cheer up a bit.

Le Ravinala (☎ 53 308 83; fgbaril@wanadoo.mg; Rte de l'Aéroport; r with shared/private bathroom Ar15,200/17,200) Funky polished bamboo furniture makes this friendly beach guesthouse an attractive option, though it's a long way from the centre so you'll have to take taxis or get to know the minibus routes. There's an attached restaurant, open Wednesday to Monday.

Lionel Hotel (☎ 032 02 543 56; cnr Blvd Joffre & Rue Lt Noël; r Ar16,000-30,000, with shared bathroom Ar12,000-15,000; ☒) A good-value option a couple of blocks from the waterfront, offering tiled rooms with nets, hot water, a communal lounge area and optional TV (Ar1400 per day). Prices may be quoted in Fmg, so check carefully before paying!

Hôtel Plage (☎ 53 320 90; hotel_plage@simicro.mg; Blvd de la Libération; r Ar17,000-28,000, with shared bathroom Ar14,000-15,000) Even Toamasina's pushy *pousse-pousse* men don't rate this big central block: the huge, bare lobby leads onto dim rooms with big saggy beds and wire on the windows for an extra prison feel. It's only really a back-up if other places are full. Sailors and prostitutes tend to frequent the bar-disco.

Midrange

Génération Hôtel (☎ 53 321 05; generationhotel@wanadoo .mg; Blvd Joffre; r Ar22,900-53,900; ☒) Cheery pinks and yellows enliven the good range of rooms here, which also get the benefit of rugs and slightly period-effect furniture. The English-speaking staff are helpful and friendly, and the terrace restaurant is well-liked locally. The hotel also has an annexe in Mahavelona (p204), on the coast north of town.

Hôtel Fréderic (☎ 53 347 40; Rue Lt Bérard; r Ar26,900-34,900; ☒) This fading block on a quiet corner, formerly the Capricorne (if they haven't managed to change the signs yet), has a mixture of tiled and parquet rooms with some fridges but no nets. Terrace rooms 101 and 102 are easily the best seats in the house. A pizza restaurant and cabaret/piano bar complete the picture.

Hôtel Les Flamboyants (☎ 53 323 50; Blvd de la Libération; r with fan/air-con Ar28,000/32,000; 🍴) The first port of call for many expats, foreign residents and regional businessmen, Les Flamboyants has plenty of space over several floors, with personable staff, small TVs, nets and individual boilers for hot water. It's an easy distance from the *gare routière* and has its own big Chinese-themed restaurant at ground level.

Hôtel Miramar (☎ 53 332 15; www.miramar-hotel-tamatave.com; Blvd Ratsimilaho, Salazamay; r Ar30,000-50,000, bungalows Ar70,000-74,000; 🍴 💻) A slightly faded upmarket establishment with a scout-camp air, on the beach about 4km north of town. The multicoloured bungalows, some split into separate rooms, are scattered around the quiet garden and have little sitting areas outside, but no mosquito nets. The hotel is also the local American Express travel service representative, and runs the Hôtel Betty Plage (p215) on Île Sainte Marie. Be careful when walking on the beach, as there have been reports of muggings in the area.

Hôtel Le Joffre (☎ 53 323 90; www.tamatave-hotel-joffre.com; 18 Blvd Joffre; r Ar30,000-90,000; 🍴 💻) As you'd expect from anywhere named after a mustachioed old-school general, the Joffre commands some remnants of colonial charm, particularly on the trellised café terrace, perfect for an evening beer. Once inside, however, the rooms are plain and functional rather than luxurious; all have nets, TV and phone, and some have a balcony overlooking the road. The hotel is often full of tour groups in high season, so it's best to book in advance. Like many other places, it also has a sister hotel up the coast, Le Grand Bleu (p204) at Mahavelona.

Hotel Toamasina (☎ 53 335 49; www.hotel-tamatave.com; 13 Rue de la Colonne; r Ar33,900-55,000, ste Ar47,960-55,880; 🍴) This endearingly quirky guest-house-hotel is a nice little find, tucked away to the south of town a short walk from the busy main streets. The rooms are a mixed bag of shapes, sizes and styles; the suites in particular are good value, rejoicing in animal-print armchairs, satellite TV, VCR, phone, safe and fridge. There's a hair salon and a small souvenir shop on site, as well as the very reasonable Pousse-Pousse restaurant.

Central Hôtel (☎ 53 340 86; www.central-hotel-tamatave.com; Blvd Joffre; r Ar35,200-50,000; 🍴) The Central, a whiteish four-storey block, has smart rooms with balconies, elegant beds, four-poster mosquito nets and orange stripey bedspreads, plus phone and TV. Its excellent restaurant, La Véranda (below), is just up the street.

Top End
Neither of Toamasina's top-end hotels is particularly amazing; they offer little in the way of character and only a few extra facilities to separate them from the midrange options.

Hôtel Le Neptune (☎ 53 322 26; neptune@wanadoo.mg; Blvd Ratsimilaho; d/tr Ar64,000/74,000; 🍴 💻) Relishing its plum location opposite the seafront, the Neptune has a sundeck, casino, slot machines and a disco (open Monday to Saturday). The smart but not overplush rooms have new bathrooms, old-fashioned balconies, TV, minibar and white linen, but no mosquito nets. For once the sea-view rooms aren't where you want to be, as they get the karaoke noise from the outdoor bar! Rates were discounted at research time due to renovations, so don't be surprised if they've risen considerably by the time you arrive.

Sharon Hôtel (☎ 53 304 20; sharonhotel@wanadoo.mg; Blvd de la Libération; r Ar184,000, ste Ar312,000; 🍴 💻) Toamasina's most modern and upmarket option. The spotless contemporary style here does much to warrant its four-star rating, furnished in fake walnut with blue walls, red carpets and gilt trimmings. The huge suite comes with its own whirlpool bath as well as all the standard equipment like TV, phone and minibar. There's a pool, sauna, spa (massages Ar20,000) and gym on site, and a pizzeria in the courtyard to supplement the main restaurant. Visa cards accepted.

EATING
Chez Bruno (☎ 53 333 78; Blvd de la Libération; snacks from Ar500; 🕐 breakfast & lunch) A handy patisserie café near Hôtel Les Flamboyants, known for its above-average coffee.

Adam & Eve Snack Bar (☎ 53 334 56; Blvd Joffre; mains from Ar2000; 🕐 breakfast, lunch & dinner Tue-Sun) One of the most popular budget options on Blvd Joffre, the open bar and terrace of this cheap-eats Eden have a loyal following for their Malagasy dishes, juice, ice cream and crêpes.

La Véranda (☎ 53 334 35; off Blvd Joffre; mains Ar4000-9000; 🕐 lunch & dinner Mon-Sat) If you've just returned from Île Sainte Marie, you may find yourself dining with most of your flying companions here – this is the terrace of choice for the vast majority of French expats and visitors thanks to its wide-ranging menu and very reasonable prices. The three-course set menu (Ar13,000) changes daily, and is usually far too tempting to let you settle for a light meal.

Le Zoréol (☎ 53 332 36; 11 Blvd Joffre; mains Ar5000-8000; ☺ lunch & dinner) This a fairly typical expat-run bar, with free pool tables, Beaujolais Nouveau and lots of rum, but also offers pizza, pasta and Réunionnaise cuisine (zoréol is a common nickname for French residents of this other Indian Ocean island). On Wednesday and Sunday it's only open in the evening.

Don Camillo (☎ 032 07 668 10; Blvd de la Libération; pizzas Ar5000-9000; ☺ lunch & dinner) We're not convinced the staff are Italian, but in most other respects Don Camillo delivers the authentic thin'n'crispy goods to a thoroughly edible standard. Takeaway is also available, though it'll cost you an extra Ar1000 for the box.

Le Perroquet Bleu (☎ 032 40 270 55; Rue Lubert; mains Ar6000-14,000; ☺ breakfast, lunch & dinner) Another friendly wood-clad restaurant with a barlike feel to it, serving up all kinds of French and regional dishes. The eponymous blue parrot is still just about clinging to its perch, though it's a scraggy shadow of its former self if the oil-painting portrait on the wall is anything to go by.

La Récréa (Blvd Ratsimilaho; mains Ar6000-15,000; ☺ lunch & dinner) Toamasina waterfront's latest arrival is a fantastically conceived thatched edifice combining restaurant, cocktail bar and souvenir shop, with stylish all-bamboo furniture and fixtures, pool tables, seating spilling out towards the beach and even an old light aircraft outside. The menu covers Malagasy, Italian, French fusion and even fondue.

Restaurant Labourdonnais (☎ 53 350 67; Blvd Labourdonnais; mains Ar6000-16,000; ☺ lunch & dinner Mon-Sat) Next door to the French consulate, this unflashy green-and-white establishment sits discreetly in its walled compound, providing refined creole cuisine for the regular dining diplomats.

Le Bateau Ivre (☎ 53 302 94; Blvd Ratsimilaho; mains Ar7000-16,000; ☺ lunch & dinner; 🐕) Next to La Récréa, the 'Drunken Boat' assures its own popularity with a 25m swimming pool (open from 9am) and boisterous live music in the evenings, plus a seafood-oriented menu. It's a great place for kids, but the pool gets packed at weekends.

Self-caterers and treat-seekers should try the **Score** (Araben'ny Fahaleovantena; ☺ 8.30am-1pm & 2.30-7pm Mon-Sat, 8.30am-12.30pm Sun) or **Shoprite** (Araben'ny Fahaleovantena) supermarkets.

ENTERTAINMENT

Toamasina's nightlife tends towards the dodgier end of the scale, particularly when large groups of foreign sailors come through on shore leave. Most of the restaurants listed under Eating also function as respectable bars if you just want a few quiet drinks.

The most popular nightspot in the town centre is the disco and casino at **Hôtel Le Neptune** (☺ Mon-Sat); see p201. Further out towards the airport, there's **Pandora Station** (Rte de l'Aéroport; ☺ Tue-Sat), which also has pool tables and a snack bar, and **Bar Code** (Rte de l'Aéroport), a similar bar-club with food and karaoke. If you're feeling brave try **L'Univers** (Blvd Joffre; ☺ 24hr), a 'gritty' all-hours locals' bar with a pétanque pitch.

GETTING THERE & AWAY
Air

Air Madagascar (☎ 53 323 56; Araben'ny Fahaleovantena) flies at least once daily between Toamasina and Antananarivo (Ar203,000), sometimes via Île Sainte Marie (Ar163,000). Other services connect Toamasina with Sambava (Ar203,000, weekly), Maroantsetra (Ar163,000, three weekly) and Antalaha (Ar203,000, twice weekly). Be warned that during the vanilla season (June to October), the planes that fly up and down the northeast coast can be full.

Air Madagascar and **Air Austral** (☎ 53 312 43; 1 Rue Lattre de Tassigny) each have two weekly flights to St-Denis on Réunion (from Ar974,700).

Boat

Boat travel is generally slow and uncomfortable, but is often the only option when roads on the northeast coast are impassable. Bear in mind, however, that weather conditions can make sea voyages dangerous, particularly around the cyclone season (December to March); always check forecasts and ask local advice before travelling. Standards vary widely; cabins are sometimes available, but on most boats you can expect to be bedding down on deck, and you will need to bring your own food and water.

Cargo boats leave from Toamasina for Île Sainte Marie, Mananara, Antalaha, Antsiranana and Taolagnaro, although you generally have to wait to find one that accepts passengers. Fares and schedules vary wildly, so you'll need to ask around regularly in the port area, and be prepared to wait at least several days. **Mira SA** (☎ 53 349 28; sa.mira@wanadoo.mg; 79 Blvd Joffre) is one company with an office in town, and has roughly monthly boats heading north and south; a ticket to Iharana or Manakara will cost you Ar60,000, while Nosy Be and Toliara come in at Ar100,000.

The luxury cruise liner *MS Mauritius Trochetia* leaves Toamasina for Réunion and Mauritius approximately every two weeks. One-way fares to Réunion are €210/177 for a 1st-/2nd-class cabin (based on two people sharing), and €247/227 to Mauritius. More expensive deluxe cabins are also available. For tickets, go to **Tropical Service** (☎ 53 336 79; 23 Blvd Joffre), near the Hotel Joffre.

If you're heading to Île Sainte Marie, the boat company **Cap Sainte Marie** (☎ 53 351 48; cap-sainte -marie@wanadoo.mg; Rue Maitre Nativel; ☻ 6-7am & 10am-5pm Mon-Sat, to noon Sun) has an office in Toamasina and runs daily bus transfers to meet their shuttle at Soanierana-Ivongo (€60 return). Sharing the same office, **La Compagnie du Canal** (☎ 032 02 183 87; compagnieducanal@wanadoo.mg) has daily services to Manambato (€50) via Ankanin'ny Nofy (€35), on the Canal des Pangalanes.

Taxi-Brousse
The taxi-brousse station at the northwestern edge of town serves Antananarivo as well as points north as far as Soanierana-Ivongo (Ar8000, four hours) and south as far as Mahanaro. Minibuses and coaches run along the RN2 throughout the day to Moramanga (Ar12,000, five to seven hours) and Antananarivo (Ar13,000 to Ar15,000, at least seven hours). It is best to leave early to ensure that you reach your destination during daylight.

Three weekly MadaBus services run between Toamasina and Antananarivo (€25), calling at Brickaville and Andasibe. For tickets and/or connections to Île Sainte Marie, go to the Cap Sainte Marie office.

If road conditions permit, you may be able to find a *camion-brousse* (truck) or similar large vehicle heading towards Mananara or Maroantsetra (Ar70,000, two to three days). See p206 for more details on this route.

Train
There was no regular train service to or from Toamasina at time of research. Plans are afoot to reinstate passenger services eventually, so inquire at the Toamasina or Antananarivo stations for an update.

GETTING AROUND
Taxis between town and the airport (5km north of town) should cost around Ar7000,

though drivers will demand Ar10,000 at arrivals. Taxi rides within town are Ar2000.

Some local minibuses shuttle passengers around town for Ar300, if you can work out the routes; service No 4 goes to the Bazar Kely and the port.

With its wide, flat avenues, Toamasina is ideal for cycling. For bike rental try **Loulou Bike Rentals** (☎ 032 04 414 83; Blvd Joffre; per day Ar8000; ☻ 7.30am-6pm), opposite the stadium.

To hire a car locally, look for posters offering private rentals in restaurants around town, or ask at an agency such as Tropical Service (p200; per day from €42) or **Mr Auto** (☎ 53 305 38; Blvd Joffre; per day from Ar70,000). Prices may rise if you want to take the vehicle beyond Mahavelona.

Pousse-pousse drivers charge from Ar500 per trip within the town centre. The 'drivers' seem fairly friendly but are very persistent and have a reputation for hassle, particularly at night.

NORTH OF TOAMASINA

PARC ZOOLOGIQUE IVOLOINA
The **Parc Zoologique Ivoloina** (☎ 53 012 17; www .seemadagascar.com; admission Ar10,000; ☻ 9am-5pm) is a conservation-friendly and very well-run zoo and botanical garden set on a lovely lake just north of Toamasina. The Madagascar Fauna Group, a worldwide association of zoos and conservation organisations, has set up an education centre, captive breeding programmes for endangered species and a halfway house for animals being reintroduced into the wild. It's not just a tourist attraction but also a key site for raising local awareness of wildlife and conservation issues – around 70% of an estimated 14,000 annual visitors are Malagasy nationals.

The zoo's beautiful grounds cover 282 hectares and contain more than 100 lemurs from a dozen different species, including the aye-aye, as well as chameleons, radiated tortoises, tree boas and tomato frogs. There are both caged and semi-wild lemurs; feeding is not permitted (though you may still see locals turning up with a bunch of bananas to tempt the wild ones down for photo ops). As part of the reintroduction programme, 13 captive-bred ruffed lemurs were recently released into the wild at the MFG's nearby Réserve Naturelle Intégrale de Betampona.

The botanical garden contains more than 75 species of native and exotic plants, and there is a model farm on site designed to demonstrate sustainable agricultural methods. Four walking trails of between 500m and 2.5km give you the opportunity to explore the park thoroughly; the 'Puzzle Trail' is ideal for kids, with a leaflet giving questions and clues to follow, and on the first Saturday of every month there is a 4km guided walk at 8am (Ar12,000). It is also possible to hire a pirogue for a turn around the lake (Ar2000), or to picnic on the shores. A kiosk by the lake sells the admission tickets, explanatory booklets in English, French or Malagasy, and a small selection of drinks and snacks.

For detailed information on Ivoloina, and on how your local zoo can support conservation efforts in Madagascar, stop by the office of the **Madagascar Fauna Group** (☎ 53 308 42; www .savethelemur.org; Rte de l'Aéroport), 4km north of central Toamasina.

Ivoloina's **camp site** (tent sites Ar4000), in a pretty spot next to the lake, has toilets, showers and sheltered picnic tables.

Parc Zoologique Ivoloina is 13km north of Toamasina. A charter taxi from town costs around Ar30,000; taxis-brousses to Ivoloina village (Ar1500) leave every hour or two. From Ivoloina village it's a scenic 4km walk to the park entrance. Tour companies in Toamasina charge about Ar75,000 per vehicle.

MAHAVELONA (FOULPOINTE)

Mahavelona, more commonly known as Foulpointe (fool-*pwant*), is a small, nondescript coastal town near some white-sand beaches. There are sharks offshore; swimming anywhere away from the hotel area, which is protected by a reef, is risky. The best beaches are at the southern end of town, which has acquired a distinctly resorty air, with a hatful of tourist hotels and overpriced restaurants attracting attendant posses of hawkers, kids and fishermen proposing souvenirs, boat trips, snorkelling or beach barbecues. Bargain hard before taking up any of these offers.

Ruins of the 19th-century Merina **Fort Manda**, built for Radama I, are about 500m north of Mahavelona. Its walls, which are 8m high and 6m thick in places, are made from coral, sand and eggs, similar to the material used in the walls of Ambohimanga (p90), near Antananarivo.

Sleeping & Eating

Pension Colargol (Chez Mamabako; ☎ 57 220 26; bungalows with shared bathroom Ar7000-20,000) You couldn't get much further from the image of a seaside re-

sort: this collection of very basic, shabby shacks behind the Manda Beach Hôtel has no beach access, overlooks a slightly swampy stream and doesn't offer meals. However, at these prices the farmyard atmosphere and genuine family welcome may just sway budget hardliners.

Génération Hôtel Annexe (☎ 57 220 22; www.gen eration-hotel-foulpointe.com; r Ar17,900-37,900, bungalows Ar29,900-59,900) Under the same management as Génération Hôtel in Toamasina, this garden site towards the southern end of the strip offers a choice between standard concrete rooms and nicer thatched bungalows, some two-tier models sleeping up to six people. It's not directly on the beach but the big terraced restaurant is only 20m away.

Le Grand Bleu (☎ 57 220 06; www.hotel-grandbleu.com; bungalows s/d Ar35,000/40,000, r Ar40,000-46,000;) The 'Big Blue' has a similar set-up to the Génération, with two main differences: the complex fronts directly onto the beach, and here it's the rooms that come better equipped, though if you're any judge of character you'll forego air-con for the subtler breezes of the cute wickerwork bungalows. Pirogue trips and other activities are organised here. Bookings can be made through the Hôtel Joffre (p201) in Toamasina.

Manda Beach Hôtel (☎ 57 220 00; www.mandabeach -hotel.com; r Ar38,000-57,000, bungalows Ar67,000;) Mahavelona's most upmarket option, about 100m south of Le Grand Bleu. The thatched beachside cabins here have polished wooden walls, sundecks and ethnic-printed bedcovers. If you opt for one of the underwhelming row of rooms, make sure you at least get one that faces towards the sea! The hotel's stretch of beach is the best you'll find, and it has a pool table and tennis courts in the grounds. Direct transfers here from Toamasina airport cost Ar53,000 for up to three people.

Getting There & Away

Mahavelona lies 58km north of Toamasina. Minibuses depart from the Toamasina taxi-brousse station daily, generally in the mornings (Ar4000, 1½ hours). For short hops, such as to Mahambo or Fenoarivo-Atsinanana, you can try flagging down just about any vehicle going in the right direction; hotel vehicles may be able to take you all the way to Toamasina, but you'll have to pay at least the equivalent of the taxi-brousse fare.

Several vehicles daily pass Mahavelona on their way between Toamasina and Soanierana-Ivongo. Heading south, the time they pass Mahavelona depends on what time the ferry from Île Sainte Marie arrives at Soanierana-Ivongo. Heading north, wait by the road side before 9am to get there in time for the best boats.

MAHAMBO

Mahambo is a coastal village with a safe swimming beach and luxuriant vegetation that comes right down to the shore in some places. For the moment it's much quieter and generally more enticing than Mahavelona, primarily because it's further from the main road, and while facilities are already expanding it should still be some time before resort life starts to take over in the same way.

Halfway down the long track between the main road and the village you'll find **Quad Evasion** (☎ 032 04 011 96), a new venture with a vast litter of quads, scooters and bikes for hire. They're all great ways to explore the area if you're staying for a while; a basic pushbike costs Ar25,000 per day, while quads go for Ar100,000. You can also take a complete quad package, including guide and drinks, for €60 per day.

Sleeping & Eating

Le Zanatany (☎ 57 301 35; bungalows from Ar12,000) Resplendent in its bright-blue paint job, this little restaurant in the centre of the village also has the cheapest rooms you'll find here.

Ylang-Ylang (☎ 57 300 08; mamitina@wanadoo.mg; bungalows Ar20,000-25,000) If you can't be on the beach, then this wonderfully scented garden site is a fine substitute. The bungalows all come with veranda, nets and nice linen, but the split-level raffia versions have the edge over the standard wood'n'brick models. The meals are near Foulpointe prices though (mains Ar12,000 to Ar40,000).

Le Dola (☎ 57 300 50; bungalows Ar25,000-50,000) A short distance past La Pirogue, Le Dola enjoys an equally good beach position but is a much less sophisticated operation, offering simple thatched concrete huts with nets and scrappy bathrooms. It can seem a bit deserted at times, which may explain why the restaurant's such good value (mains Ar2000 to Ar6000).

La Pirogue (☎ 57 301 71; www.pirogue-hotel.com; r Ar50,000-75,000, bungalows Ar55,000-112,500) One of the best accommodation options on the whole east coast, imaginatively designed with actual pirogues built into the fabric of the charming wooden bungalows! Even the rear-facing rooms muster up plenty of character, with nets and hot water, and the food's excellent (mains Ar5400 to Ar18,000), especially if you do a full seafood barbecue. It's right on a small bay, and a whole host of boat-based activities are on offer, such as deep-sea fishing (€280 per boat), whale safaris (€30 to €50 per person) and of course pirogue trips (€12 per hour). Bungalow rates rise by up to 20% in high season (July to August, Christmas and Easter); if you're hesitating at the price, bear in mind that 5% of profits are donated to a local charity.

Getting There & Away

Mahambo is 30km north of Mahavelona (Ar2500) and about 90km from Toamasina (Ar6000). Coming here, ask the driver to drop you at the intersection (you'll see the hotel signs), then walk about 2km down the sandy track heading east. For information on travel along the coast north of Toamasina, see p206.

FENOARIVO-ATSINANANA

The bustling clove-scented town of Fenoarivo-Atsinanana (usually referred to as just Fenoarivo, which means 'Thousand Warriors', or Fénérive-Est) was the first capital of the Betsimisaraka. It was here in the early 1700s that the founder, Ratsimilaho, united the tribe and proclaimed himself king. Ratsimilaho's modest **tomb** is on a tiny lemur-inhabited island just offshore, opposite a popular local swimming area known as the **piscine**; a pirogue across should cost around Ar3000 (negotiable).

About 3km south of Fenoarivo is Vohimasina, the ruins of an old **pirate fort** with triangular water wells; it's not signposted so you'll need local help to find it. You can also visit a nearby **clove factory**.

The town is the major population centre along the coast road, and has a post office, a lively market, a card phone and a Bank of Africa branch. Visitor facilities aren't really up to the standard of its coastal neighbours, and it's better for a brief day trip than an extended stay.

Sleeping & Eating

Le Girofla d'Or (☎ 57 300 42; r with shared bathroom Ar13,000-17,000) In the centre of town, near the taxi-brousse stop and not far from the market, the 'Golden Clove' has basic rooms with nets and a dusty restaurant serving Malagasy food.

Hôtel Belle Rose (☎ 57 300 38; r Ar16,000-28,000) About 500m from the centre on the road leading to the hospital, this is a bit more comfortable than the other options but is some distance from the beach.

Le Girofla Beach (☎ 57 300 42; r Ar17,000-19,000, with shared bathroom Ar15,000-17,000) The Girofla's seaside annexe overlooks a rocky patch of beach about 1.5km east of town. It's a nice site, with thatched brick-weave bungalows, but standards aren't great and the bathrooms are distinctly grotty. The turn-off is signposted; follow the road past the piscine to reach the hotel.

Getting There & Away

Fenoarivo is about 15km north of Mahambo, and is serviced by taxis-brousses on the Toamasina to Soanierana-Ivongo route. You can ask to be dropped at the beach turn-off or in the centre of town.

SOANIERANA-IVONGO

Soanierana-Ivongo is a small town notable primarily as a port for boats to and from Île Sainte Marie. If the pronunciation of the name defeats you, you can get away with referring to it as 'Sierra-Ivongo'.

There are no really good accommodation options, so it's best to try to time your travels to avoid having to stay overnight. If you do stay, the obvious place is **Hôtel Les Escales** (☎ 032 43 174 63; bungalows with shared bathroom Ar10,000), right next to the boat jetty. Les Escales is also the place to come for boat and taxi-brousse information and tickets, although the touts will be sure to find you as soon as you step out of your vehicle anyway. There is a restaurant here – order well in advance as meals can take hours to cook.

If you're heading to Île Sainte Marie it's best to get here as early as possible to have your pick of the boat companies. Departures vary according to the tides; for full information on boat connections to and from the island, see p209.

Taxis-brousses head to Soanierana-Ivongo from Toamasina (Ar8000, three to four hours) departing from around 6am every morning. However, they are not necessarily coordinated with boat departures. Returning to Toamasina, vehicles wait for the arrivals from Île Sainte Marie.

The road from Soanierana-Ivongo north to Mananara is dignified with the name Route Nationale 5 (RN5). However, for much of its length it's still no more than a collection of deep potholes joined together with either dust or mud, depending on the season. There are six major river crossings en route, served by ferries and/or fragile bridges. Assuming there are any taxis-brousses running, and that nothing else goes wrong (a big assumption), you can expect to cover the 127km in about two days, including an overnight stop.

There have been several instances of taxis-brousses overturning along this route or falling through weak bridges. In all of Madagascar's rough, tough journeys, this one particularly stands out – so it's only to be attempted by the seriously masochistic or truly desperate. Should this describe you, you can expect to be quoted about Ar40,000 for the journey. Private vehicles attempting the route will charge about the same for a lift.

The only other way to get up the coast from Soanierana-Ivongo is to take a boat across to Île Sainte Marie, then look for another boat for the onward journey.

MANOMPANA

This small coastal village 38km north of Soanierana-Ivongo is becoming an increasingly popular stop for alternative tours from Toamasina, skipping the busier resort spots in favour of rural isolation. Nearby attractions include the scenic Point Tintingue, the protected Ambodiriana forest and the even smaller fishing village of Antanambe. A French charity has also set up an education and cultural centre here, staffed partly by volunteers.

As yet there are few facilities, and public transport is limited, but with a bit of time it should certainly be possible to come here independently. **Tropical Service** (☎ 53 336 79; www.croisiere -madagascar.com) in Toamasina is the main operator for organised trips, charging €255 for a four-day package (€352 including Antanambe).

ÎLE SAINTE MARIE

Said to resemble a mildly pregnant woman lying down, the slender 57km-long island of Île Sainte Marie lies 8km off the coast. It's been popular with Europeans ever since the days when it was inhabited by pirates, and even now its Malagasy name, Nosy Boraha, is rarely used. The pirates are gone, of course, but the island is still a favourite spot for expats and tourists, and beach hotels take up much of the western coastline. Despite this, Île Sainte Marie has avoided some of the resort excesses of Nosy Be and still retains considerable charm, particularly in the remoter beaches and the small villages that dot the lush agricultural interior.

While there's plenty of scope for sunbathing and beach-bumming, Île Sainte Marie rewards the active type, and its rugged interior is a particularly good place for hiking, cycling or motorcycling. Water sports are on offer everywhere, and between July and September the waters around the island play host to migrating humpback whales, a major attraction for visitors (see right).

Rain can be expected year-round on Île Sainte Marie, although the weather is usually least wet from late August to late November. Between December and March, the island is subject to violent cyclones.

Because it sees so many foreign visitors, prices are slightly higher on Île Sainte Marie than on the mainland.

History

The Malagasy name of the island, Nosy Boraha, is thought by some European sources to mean 'Island of Ibrahim' or 'Island of Abraham', a name perhaps bestowed by early Arabic or Jewish settlers. Though this is theoretically possible, local lore traces it to the legend of a fisherman named Boraha who was saved from drowning by a whale in an echo of the biblical story of Jonah. The commonly used French name, Île Sainte Marie, is indisputably derived from Santa Maria, the name originally given to it by 16th-century Portuguese sailors.

French settlers attempted to found a colony on Île Sainte Marie in the 1640s, but were thwarted by strong tropical fevers, which killed most of the pioneers. From then on the island became the hideout of a motley international band of English, Portuguese, French and American pirates. Presumably the hardened buccaneers had stronger constitutions and lower standards than the sheltered settlers – either that or the rich pickings from silk-laden ships passing en route to India made the profits worth the privations.

Around this time, according to the popular story, a Frenchman named Jean-Onésime Filet (known as 'La Bigorne', or 'The Horned') was shipwrecked on a beach here while fleeing the repercussions of an affair with the wife of a fellow officer. One of the local women who found him and restored him to health was none other than Princess Betia or Bety, the daughter of Betsimisaraka king Ratsimilaho (himself the son of an English pirate). Bety and La Bigorne were married, and in July 1750, after the death of her father, Bety ceded the island to France. In fact it's unlikely that Filet played any role in the process, which was probably orches-trated by the French commercial agent Gosse, but whatever the reality, in 1752 the local population revolted and massacred the French settlers, exiling Bety to Mauritius and returning control of the island to the Betsimisaraka. In 1818 the French returned, eventually turning the island into a penal colony. In recognition of Princess Bety's magnanimous gift to France, the independence agreement of 1960 allowed the inhabitants of Île Sainte Marie to choose between French and Malagasy nationality. Although the majority chose Malagasy, many retain French names.

Activities

DIVING & SNORKELLING

Île Sainte Marie may not have all the coral it once did, but it still offers some decent diving. The season runs from July to January; the best time is from October to December. Dive centres are often closed between February and May.

Some popular diving sites are found around the two shipwrecks in the far north and along the eastern coast, offshore from Sahasifotra. Snorkelling gear is also widely available at the various beach hotels. There are three independent dive centres on the island.

Il Balenottero (Map p212; ☎ 57 400 36; www .ilbalenottero.com; Ambodifotatra) Dives €30, PADI/SSI courses €350. Also offers whale-watching, yacht cruises and fishing trips.

Le Lémurien Palmé (Map p212; ☎ 57 040 15; www .lemurien-palme.com; Ambodifotatra) Dives €35, try dives €42. Also offers whale-watching and motorcycle hire.

Mahery-Be (Map p208; ☎ 57 401 48; maherybe@wanadoo.mg) On the coast road south of Mahavelo. Dives €30, try dives €40, courses from €275. Also offers whale-watching, fishing and boat hire.

FISHING

The best season for deep-sea fishing is between late September and March/April. Il Balenottero, Mahery-Be, Le Maningory hotel and some other upper-end hotels organise game fishing expeditions, including boat hire, drinks and equipment.

WHALE-WATCHING

Every year from July to September, several hundred humpback whales swim through the waters off Île Sainte Marie, with many staying in the Baie d'Antongil to the north to give birth or to look for mates. During this time, virtually everywhere on Île Sainte Marie offers 'whale safaris' around the island; the dive centres

EASTERN MADAGASCAR

ÎLE SAINTE MARIE

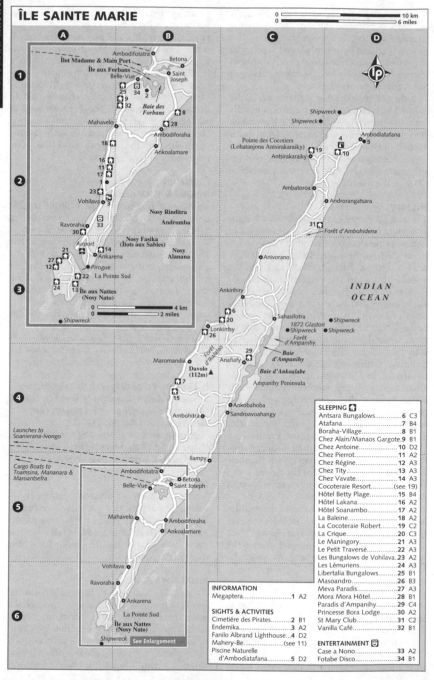

0   10 km
0   6 miles

Ambodifotatra
Îlot Madame & Main Port
Île aux Forbans
Belle-Vue
Betona
Saint Joseph
25 34
9   2
32
Baie des Forbans
8
Mahavelo
28
Ambodiforaha
Ankoalamare
18
16
11
17
1
23
Vohilava   3
Nosy Rinditra
Andromba
Ravoraha
30   33
Nosy Fasika
(Îlots aux Sables)
Nosy Alanana
Airport
21   14
Ankarena
27
12   Pirogue
22 La Pointe Sud
24   13 Île aux Nattes
(Nosy Nato)
Shipwreck

Ambodifotatra
Betona
Shipwreck
Shipwreck
Pointe des Cocotiers
(Lohatanjona Antsirakaraiky)
Antsirakaraiky
4   Ambodiatafana
5
19
10
Ambatoroa
Androrangatsara
31   Forêt d'Ambohidena
Anivorano
Ankirihiry
Sahasifotra
1872 Glaston   Shipwreck
Shipwreck   Shipwreck
Forêt d'Ampanihy
Baie d'Ampanihy
Anafiafy   29
Baie d'Ankoalabe
Ampanihy Peninsula
Ankobahoba
Sandroavoahangy
6
20
Lonkintsy
26
Forêt d'Ikalalao
Maromandia
Davolo (112m)
7
15
Ambohitra

INDIAN OCEAN

0   4 km
0   2 miles

Launches to Soanierana-Ivongo

Cargo Boats to Toamsina, Mananara & Maroantsefra

Ilampy
Ambodifotatra
Belle-Vue   Betona
Saint Joseph
Mahavelo
Ambodiforaha
Ankoalamare
Vohilava
Ravoraha
Ankarena
La Pointe Sud
Île aux Nattes
(Nosy Nato)
Shipwreck   See Enlargement

INFORMATION
Megaptera...........................1 A2

SIGHTS & ACTIVITIES
Cimetiére des Pirates..........2 B1
Endemika.............................3 A2
Fanilo Albrand Lighthouse...4 D2
Mahery-Be.....................(see 11)
Piscine Naturelle
  d'Ambodiatafana..............5 D2

SLEEPING
Antsara Bungalows..............6 C3
Atafana................................7 B4
Boraha-Village....................8 B1
Chez Alain/Manaos Gargote.9 B1
Chez Antoine.....................10 D2
Chez Pierrot......................11 A2
Chez Régine.......................12 A3
Chez Tity...........................13 A3
Chez Vavate.......................14 A3
Cocoteraie Resort..........(see 19)
Hôtel Betty Plage..............15 B4
Hôtel Lakana.....................16 A2
Hôtel Soanambo................17 A2
La Baleine..........................18 A2
La Cocoteraie Robert.........19 C2
La Crique...........................20 C3
Le Maningory.....................21 A3
Le Petit Traversé...............22 A3
Les Bungalows de Vohilava..23 A2
Les Lémuriens...................24 A3
Libertalia Bungalows.........25 B1
Masoandro.........................26 B3
Meva Paradis.....................27 A3
Mora Mora Hôtel...............28 B1
Paradis d'Ampanihy...........29 C4
Princesse Bora Lodge.........30 A2
St Mary Club.....................31 C2
Vanilla Café.......................32 B1

ENTERTAINMENT
Case a Nono......................33 A2
Fotabe Disco.....................34 B1

THE PIRATE KINGDOM

By the early 18th century, Île Sainte Marie had become the headquarters of the world's pirates. At one stage the pirate population of Madagascar numbered close to 1000. English and French naval policing had slowed profits in the once-lucrative Caribbean to a trickle, so Madagascar, and Île Sainte Marie in particular, was an ideal base from which to ambush traders sailing around the Cape of Good Hope between Europe and the Far East.

One of history's most infamous pirates, Captain Kidd, arrived on the island after a long siege on the high seas, and was supposedly buried here after his execution in London. The wreck of his ship, the *Adventure,* was discovered by divers in 2000 at the entrance to Baie des Forbans, but much of Kidd's treasure has never been found...

The pirates frequently took up with local women, and their offspring came to be known as Zanimalata (Children of Mulattos). Of these, it was Ratsimilaho, the son of Malagasy princess Antavaratra Rahena and English pirate Thomas White, who would have the greatest impact on Madagascar. Ratsimilaho was leader of the Zanimalata and, thanks to a number of military victories, he became founder and chief of the unified Betsimisaraka, feared throughout the region as ruthless and very successful pirates and fighters. Even today they're still the second most influential tribal group in Madagascar, after the highland Merina.

---

and shuttle-boat companies are good places to start, as hotels without their own boats often arrange trips through them anyway. Getting to see these amazing creatures close up can be a real highlight of a visit to Madagascar.

The standard price is €30 per person for a half-day trip, including lunch, though some local operators may go as low as €21. Be sure the boat is seaworthy before handing over your money, don't go out in bad weather, and make sure your captain doesn't try to take you too close to the whales (300m is the official limit). Budget travellers take note: if you really can't afford an excursion, you have a slim chance of seeing a distant tail on the boat trip to or from the mainland!

For more details about the whales, see the boxed text, p222. If you speak sufficient French, look out for the *Petit guide pratique à l'usage des observateurs des baleines à bosse à Madagascar* (Ar5000), on sale at some hotels, or visit the office of **Megaptera** (Map p208; www.megaptera.org), an international whale conservation body, on the south coast road near Vohilava.

Tours

There are few independent tour operators on Île Sainte Marie apart from the dive centres, but most midrange and top-end hotels organise tours around the island by 4WD, pirogue or boat, including day excursions to Île aux Nattes, Pointe des Cocotiers at the north of the island, and Baie d'Ampanihy. Prices vary according to group size and where you start your tour.

Adventure company **Madaventure** (☎ 032 04 782 37; www.madaventure.com) has a base in Ambodifotatra and offers multiday quad and beach-buggy tours of the island, as well as individual vehicle hire.

Festivals & Events

Île Sainte Marie has a pretty active calendar of parties, exhibitions, sports competitions and the like, especially in summer – look out for the posters scattered around Ambodifotatra and elsewhere. **Festival des Baleines** (Zagnaharibe), the Festival of the Whales, is the year's main cultural happening, held on the Îlot Madame over five days in late August/early September. Events include exhibitions, talks, craft sales, concerts and the Miss Zagnaharibe beauty contest.

Getting There & Away

AIR

Air Madagascar (☎ 57 400 46; Bombodifotatra) flies daily between Île Sainte Marie and Antananarivo (Ar280,300) and six times weekly to Toamasina (Ar163,000). Flights to Mananara, Maroantsetra and destinations further north usually involve a stopover at Toamasina. Flights up the northeast coast are often full; in the vanilla season (June to October) book as far in advance as possible, and reconfirm all bookings.

BOAT

From Soanierana-Ivongo, several boat companies run *vedettes* (shuttles) to Ambodifotatra's harbour. The fastest and most reliable is **Cap Sainte Marie** (☎ 57 404 06; www.cap-sainte-marie.com), which has daily morning departures (€24, one hour). Boats leave Ambodifotatra at 6am and Soanierana at 10am, connecting in each direction with the company's direct Toamasina minibus (€11, three hours).

The **Princesse Saphira** (☎ 032 04 681 86) is a similar fast service, or there are a couple of cheaper, slower boats such as the *Rozina IV* and the *Magnifique*, which leave later and cost around Ar25,000 (two hours).

Don't be fooled by the regularity of the crossings: this can be a dangerous route, especially between June and August when water levels are low, and while most journeys pass without incident, there was a fatal accident as recently as 2006. Sailings should be cancelled in bad weather or rough seas; if in doubt about conditions, it's best to wait until the weather is better before attempting the crossing and to choose one of the more seaworthy boats.

All the launches have offices by the ports in Ambodifotatra and Soanierana-Ivongo. Before sailing out to the island, passengers are required to go to the police station in Soanierana-Ivongo to register. There's a fair bit of spray on the boats, so it's worth bringing something waterproof to protect you and your luggage.

Many travellers choose to fly one way between Antananarivo and Île Sainte Marie and then travel the other way overland, stopping off at a few places along the way. You can travel by road and sea between Toamasina and Île Sainte Marie via Soanierana-Ivongo in one day if you get an early start.

Cargo boats also sail between Île Sainte Marie and Mananara, Maroantsetra and Toamasina. There are no set schedules; inquire at the port on Îlot Madame. Departures from Île Sainte Marie are often in the evening or at night, depending on the tides, and you'll probably have to wait at least a few days for something to turn up. For more information, see the individual town sections.

Getting Around

Apart from the stretch of tarmac between La Crique and Belle-Vue, most roads on Île Sainte Marie are in bad condition, often comprising little more than rocky, muddy or sandy tracks.

TO/FROM THE AIRPORT

The airport is located at the southern tip of the island, 13km south of Ambodifotatra. Hotel transfer prices range from Ar2000 to Ar30,000 one way, depending on distance and hotel.

If you can find one, taxis-brousses usually charge Ar3000 between the airport and Ambodifotatra. A private taxi costs Ar18,000. Allow plenty of time – it can take a good half hour or so to travel down the bumpy road.

BICYCLE

Île Sainte Marie is ideal for mountain bikes, although some of the steeper roads at the northern end of the island (particularly the road north of Lonkintsy) are too rutted and rough to be enjoyable, particularly in the rainy season, when they can become very slippery.

Virtually every hotel and all kinds of other places have bikes of varying quality for hire. The going rate is around Ar7000 per day.

BOAT

The dive centres (p207), boat companies (p209) and some of the upper-end hotels can usually help arrange private boat rental for transfers, excursions or fishing trips. Prices start at around €225 per day for a boat for up to four people.

Inexpensive pirogue trips along the coast, or to Île aux Forbans or Île aux Nattes, can easily be arranged with locals.

CAR & MOTORCYCLE

A couple of top-end hotels rent out cars with drivers for expeditions around the island, although this is seldom the best way to get around. Try Hôtel Soanambo (p214) in the south of the island, or the Boraha-Village (p216). Rates are around Ar100,000 per day for a 4WD.

Hiring a motorcycle or quad is a much better way of getting around the island and off the beaten track. Many of the roads are heavily potholed, so you'll need to be a fairly confident rider to negotiate them safely; if you're hesitant there'll usually be someone who can do the driving for you for no extra charge.

The easiest place to pick up some wheels is from the guys who set up in front of the Bank of Africa in Ambodifotatra every day; the going rate is Ar50,000 for a trail bike. Several other shops and stalls in town, along with the majority of the mid- to upper-end beach hotels, also have fleets of motorbikes, scooters, quads and bicycles for hire.

TAXI & TAXI-BROUSSE

There are a few taxis-brousses on Île Sainte Marie. Most run along the route between the airport and Ambodifotatra (Ar3000); a few travel north along the road from Ambodifotatra up as far as Ankirihiry and La Crique (Ar2500). Elsewhere on the island, they are few and far between. At night there's no service at all, although a couple of minibuses known as *ramassages* may run at weekends to ferry passengers to the nightclubs.

Private taxis are more common, though disproportionately expensive, and usually hang out by the harbour in Ambodifotatra; you have a reasonable chance of flagging one down along the airport road, but anywhere else you may have to get your hotel to phone for it. Tariffs are fixed and posted at the tourist office and hotel receptions: it's Ar18,000 to La Pointe, Ar 20,000 to Ambodiforaha and Ar30,000 to La Crique, or Ar100,000 for a full day's hire.

AMBODIFOTATRA

Ambodifotatra (am-bodi-*foot*-atr) is Île Sainte Marie's only town and has all the island's practical facilities. It's really just a string of buildings around the harbour about a quarter of the way up the island's single main road, with no major attractions of its own, but if you haven't preplanned your stay you'll find everything you need to organise yourself here.

Information

The **Bank of Africa** (BOA; Map p212; Arabe La Bigorne) and BFV-SG (Map p212) handle cash, travellers cheques and card advances, though the latter may take a couple of hours. Both have Visa ATMs. Outside banking hours, local traders may be willing to change euros or dollars at mainland rates – ask around.

The post office (Map p212) is in the upper part of Ambodifotatra, just south of the main part of town. There's a Telma (Map p212) telephone office on the main street.

Internet access is available at **Cyber Corsaire** (Map p212; ☎ 57 403 59; Arabe La Bigorne; per hr Ar7200; 8am-noon & 2.30-6.30 Mon-Fri, 9am-noon Sat), on the main road.

Ambodifotatra now has an excellent tourist office, the **Office Régional du Tourisme** (ORT; Map p212; ☎ 032 40 084 43; Arabe La Bigorne), run by the dynamic young M Orpheu, who speaks fluent English, helps organise many of the island's regular events and knows just about everything that goes on here. Brochures, leaflets and a full accommodation list are available.

Sights

Sites of interest in the town itself include Madagascar's oldest **Catholic church** (Map p212), which dates from 1857 and was a gift to the island from Empress Eugénie of France. Near the post office you'll also find a granite **fort** (1753; Map p212), which is still a military facility and closed to the public.

Just south of the fort is the **tomb of Sylvain Roux** (Map p212), France's first commercial attaché on the east coast of Madagascar and a pivotal figure in French colonial expansion. At the northern end of town is the **tomb of François Albrand** (Map p212), a French military commander of the island who died in 1826 at 31. If you read French, the rather melancholy epitaph may just shame you into phoning home.

A **market** (Map p212) is held daily in the town centre.

CIMETIÈRE DES PIRATES

This appropriately eerie and overgrown pirate cemetery (Map p208) is located beside Baie des Forbans, about a 10-minute walk southeast of the causeway. There's not a whole lot of solid evidence that the faded gravestones really do belong to brigands, though one does bear a recognisable skull and crossbones. The large black tomb in the centre of the plot is supposedly the last resting place of William Kidd, buried in an upright position as a symbolic punishment for his crimes; sadly the brass plaque confirming this was stolen some time ago.

Guides hang around the turn-off to the cemetery to collect the 'community tax' entrance fee (Ar2000), show you the way and provide a commentary on the graves. They can be helpful in deciphering and explaining the very worn inscriptions, but be sure to negotiate the fee first – the usual starting price is an exorbitant Ar15,000 per couple, but Ar3000 to Ar5000 per person is ample.

Access to the cemetery is via an isolated foot track, which crosses several tidal creeks, slippery stones and logs. The cemetery can only be reached on foot at low tide, but it may be possible to get here by pirogue – signs on the path give a phone number for pick-ups, or ask at your hotel.

ÎLE AUX FORBANS

This small island (Map p208), located opposite the cemetery in Baie des Forbans, is the site of the ruins of an ancient **gateway**. Its significance is unknown, but it is thought to have been a pirate landmark or lookout post.

EASTERN MADAGASCAR

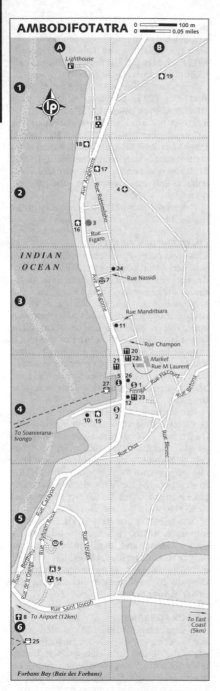

AMBODIFOTATRA

0 —————— 100 m
0 —————— 0.05 miles

INDIAN
OCEAN

To Soanierana-
Ivongo

To Airport (12km)

To East
Coast
(5km)

Forbans Bay (Baie des Forbans)

INFORMATION
Bank of Africa...1 B4
BVF-SG...2 B4
Cyber Corsaire..3 A2
Hospital..4 B2
Office Régional du Tourisme.........................5 B4
Post Office..6 A5
Telma (Telephone Office).............................7 A3

SIGHTS & ACTIVITIES
Catholic Church... 8 A6
Fort...9 A5
Il Balenottero...10 A4
Le Lemurien Palmé.....................................11 B3
Market..12 B4
Tomb of François Albrand...........................13 A1
Tomb of Sylvain Roux................................ 14 A6

SLEEPING
Hôtel Zinnia..15 A4
La Banane...16 A2
La Bigorne...17 A2
Le Drakkar..18 A2
Les Palmiers...19 B1

EATING
Chan Kan..20 B3
Choco Pain...21 B4
Food Stalls..22 B4
Restaurant William Kid...............................23 B4

TRANSPORT
Air Madagascar...24 B3
Cargo Boats to Mananara, Maroantsetra &
    Toamasina..25 A6
Offices for Boats to Soanierana-Ivongo.......26 B4
Small Boat Harbour.....................................27 A4

ÎLOT MADAME

This tiny island at the entrance to Baie des Forbans is connected by two causeways to Ambodifotatra to the north and Belle-Vue, in the south. The island served as the fortified administration centre of the French East India Company until it was taken over by local government offices. It has a deep harbour for larger cargo boats and yachts, and also houses the **Centre Culturel Reine Bety** (☎ 032 02 507 94; admission Ar2000; ☽ 7.30am-5.30pm Mon-Sat), which contains a small museum.

Sleeping & Eating

Unless you're on a tight budget, waiting for a boat or allergic to sand, there is no great reason to stay in Ambodifotatra, where there is no beach. Note that restaurants here close relatively early, often by 9pm.

Le Drakkar (Map p212; ☎ 57 400 22; bungalows with shared bathroom Ar10,000; r Ar13,000-18,000) A colonial-looking old house that has a rather Caribbean air to it. It's a bit scruffy, but charming, with rum, soul music, kids and dogs everywhere. The bungalows behind the house are quite simple, but perfectly clean and adequate. The restaurant serves cheap seafood. An interesting option if you're on a budget.

La Banane (Map p212; ☎ 032 02 280 26; Arabe La Bigorne; dm Ar10,000, r with shared bathroom Ar18,000) A manky double and a spartan six-bed room above a much nicer bar-restaurant, listed here purely because it's one of the few dormitories in the whole of Madagascar.

Hôtel Zinnia (Map p212; ☎ 57 400 09; r with shared bathroom Ar12,000-15,000) Few-frills accommodation right by the harbour (and next to the noisy electricity substation). The bungalows behind the main house here are rather basic, but have their own bathrooms. The rooms upstairs above the restaurant are big and well decorated, sharing a bathroom with hot water.

Les Palmiers (Map p212; ☎ 57 402 34; bungalows Ar15,000) A little compound with smart, good-value bungalows with a fan and net, up a path from the centre of town. There's cold water only in the bathrooms.

La Bigorne (Map p212; ☎ 57 401 23; Arabe Angleterre; bungalows Ar20,000-33,000) The best choice in town. Very well-maintained polished dark-wood bungalows with a good French restaurant have fans, but no nets. There's a dining terrace (mains Ar7000 to Ar19,000) on the wooden veranda in the garden.

Restaurant William Kid (Map p212; ☎ 57 400 72; mains Ar6000-16,000; ☺ breakfast, lunch & dinner) If the good Captain was still aboard he'd probably have whoever misspelled his name keelhauled, although the flattery of being painted as Johnny Depp might soften the blow. Either way, this prime spot opposite the harbour does fine juices, breakfasts and all the usual Franco-Malagasy staples for piratical appetites.

For the cheapest eats on the island, try the food stalls that appear in the market area around 6pm daily. Self-caterers can investigate **Choco Pain** (☎ 57 400 28) and its adjoining supermarket, near the harbour, for pastries, cheese and imported items, or **Chan Kan** (☎ 57 400 06), opposite, for general groceries, although supplies at both are fairly limited.

SOUTH OF AMBODIFOTATRA

About halfway down the southern road, just before Vohilava, **Endemika** (admission Ar10,000; ☺ 8am-noon & 2-5pm Mon-Sat) is a small private zoo and botanical garden showcasing some of the island's indigenous flora and fauna.

Ankarena, the southeastern tip of Île Sainte Marie, has a fine stretch of peaceful reef-protected beach and a deep **cave** in the base of the cliffs, which is home to hundreds of bats. The cave has given rise to several pirate legends, most of which concern hidden treasure. To reach Ankarena, walk across the small hill to the east of the airport.

Sleeping & Eating

Most of the island's hotels are along the strip between Ambodifotatra and the airport; wherever you arrive you can expect to be met by touts proposing one or other of the midrange rivals. The beach is narrower here, but still white and beautiful, and staying close to the town and airport will save you spending time and money on transfers to remoter parts of the island. Another advantage is that the hotels are close enough together for ease of evening dining.

The smaller and better-value bungalow complexes in the south and around the island have limited space and are frequently booked out during the high season (mid-December to mid-January, April to May, and July to October), as well as on weekends and Malagasy holidays, so it's worth making reservations at these times. Reduced rates are usually available in the low season.

BUDGET

Chez Alain/Manaos Gargote (Map p208; postal address BP 515, Île Sainte Marie; camping/d Ar8000/16,000) This budget camp site also has reed bungalows with no electricity. About 3.5km south of Ambodifotatra. Malagasy meals can be arranged.

La Baleine (Map p208; ☎ 57 401 34; lantoualbert@ wandadoo.mg; bungalows with shared/private bathroom Ar10,000/20,000, with hot water Ar25,000) A bit more comfortable than Chez Alain, but still fairly simple – although the bungalows here have nets. Restaurant meals and internet access available.

Chez Vavate (Map p208; ☎ 57 401 15; r Ar18,000) A slightly eccentric set-up at the top of a hill overlooking the airport. Neat bungalows have good sea views, and there's a beach at the bottom of a steep path. Snorkelling is possible nearby.

Vanilla Café (Map p208; ☎ 032 07 09 050; d Ar20,000) A small place near Chez Alain/Manaos Gargote, which has basic bungalows with shower and shared toilet. There's a good beach here.

Chez Pierrot (Map p208; ☎ 57 401 43; r Ar20,600) Spick-and-span bungalows with bright bedcovers are arranged in a neat garden with cropped lawns next to the sea. Each bungalow has its own deckchairs, and hammocks are strung here and there in the shade. Good value.

EASTERN MADAGASCAR

MIDRANGE & TOP END

Libertalia Bungalows (Map p208; ☎ 57 403 03; www
.lelibertalia.com; d Ar54,000) About 2.5km south of
Ambodifotatra, this is one of the classiest midrange choices on the island. The setting and
beach are lovely, there's snorkelling off a private
jetty, and the bright blue-and-white bungalows
have fans and mosquito nets. It's a small place
on a small beach, but it's friendly and very well
maintained. Excursions and rental bikes can
be arranged.

Les Bungalows de Vohilava (Map p208; ☎ 57 402 50;
www.vohilava.com; r Ar62,000) The rooms here are
absolutely enormous, with a similarly huge
attached sitting room and terraces with ham-
mock. It's a low-key and very relaxed place, with
a bar, a good beach and some pet tortoises. You
can hire bikes, motorcycles and kayaks. The
restaurant does snacks and evening meals.

Hôtel Soanambo (Map p208; ☎ 57 401 37; hsm@dts
.mg; s/d €32/42, dinner €12; P ⊠ ⧖) One of Île
Sainte Marie's most upmarket complexes,
with rows of whitewashed bungalows strung
along a narrow beach. The cheaper bungalows, although very well decorated, are small
for the price. Bigger, plusher bungalows with
TV and telephone, and 'condos' with a sitting area, are also available. There's a pool
and sundeck, a pontoon for swimming at
low tide, tennis courts and car/motorcycle/
mountain-bike hire. It's very comfortable,
but a bit 'resorty', and often full with package tours.

Hôtel Lakana (Map p208; ☎ 57 401 32; http://taniko
.free.fr/lakana/hotel_eng.htm; r €33) This is a well-
regarded but perhaps slightly overpriced hotel
with a set of bungalows on stilts over the sea
(each has its own bathroom back on land)
and smarter rooms (with inside bathrooms)
clustered together in the garden. There's a
shop, restaurant and bar on site. Various excursions can be arranged, along with bike, car
and motorcycle hire.

Princesse Bora Lodge (Map p208; ☎ 57 040 03;
www.princesse-bora.com; d half board per person low/high
/whale-watching season Ar230,000/270,000/310,000) The
most luxurious of the lot. The huge round
bungalows have a fan, net, safe, suspended
wooden bed, enamel bathroom, terrace
and balcony. You even get a little footbath
outside for washing the sand off your feet!
Some two-storey family bungalows are also
available. The beach has comfortable sun
beds and an outdoor shower, but there's
no pool. The restaurant is quite expensive,

naturally. The hotel organises conservation-
friendly whale-watching trips in conjunction
with an organisation called **Megaptera** (www
.megaptera.org). There is also a wide range of watersports, diving and excursions on offer.

Entertainment

The main nightlife spots are Fotabe Disco (Map
p208), about 1.5km south of Ambodifotatra, and
Case a Nono (Map p208), near the airport.

NORTH OF AMBODIFOTATRA

The west coast north of Ambodifotatra also has
some good beaches. The hotels here are further
apart and a little bit harder to access. North
of La Crique, the road is abysmal, so you're
better off going by boat. The **Piscine Naturelle
d'Ambodiatafana** (Map p208; admission Ar2000) is a natural swimming hole at the northeastern tip of the
island, formed by a series of hollow basins in
the coastal rocks, which are filled by the high
tide. To reach them, walk 8km northeast along
the main track from Ambatoroa on the west
coast. Access with a motorcycle or mountain
bike is possible, although it's tough going.

Southwest of Ambodiatafana and along the
same access track is the **Fanilo Albrand lighthouse**
(Map p208). From the ridge, it's sometimes possible to see Maroantsetra and Baie d'Antongil.

Sleeping

BUDGET

Chez Antoine (Map p208; r with shared/private bathroom
Ar10,000/20,000) This well-established and fun local
place in the far north offers good value if you
don't mind being miles off the beaten track and
not being on the beach. Antoine can also cook a
slap-up lunch for those on their way to Piscine
Naturelle d'Ambodiatafana. Very peaceful.

Antsara Bungalows (Map p208; ☎ 57 401 59; r Ar10,000-
40,000) On the other side of the road from a
rather swampy looking beach, this charming
old wooden building on stilts has bungalows
up the hill behind it, plus a few down by the
water. Room facilities vary widely, from barely
functional huts to rooms with bathrooms and
hot water.

WARNING

Many areas of the coast north and south
of Ambodifotatra are home to sea urchins.
Check locally before going swimming and
always wear something on your feet.

MIDRANGE & TOP END

Hôtel Betty Plage (Map p208; ☎ 57 400 66; bettyplage@yahoo.fr; bungalows Ar30,000-80,000) This good-value hotel is the base for the Lemurien Palmé dive operation. The bungalows are smart and spacious, with mosquito nets, and the beach is narrow but sandy. It's a very comfortable place to base yourself if you're planning lots of diving.

Atafana (Map p208; ☎ 032 04 637 81; bungalows Ar40,000-60,000) A very friendly and welcoming family-run place. The bamboo bungalows are fairly simple for the price, with four-poster beds with mosquito nets and spacious bathrooms. The more expensive rooms have a little sitting area as well. This is a great spot to watch the sunset, and swimming is possible even at low tide. Family bungalows for five people are also available. The food is better value than the rooms; half-board options are available.

La Cocoteraie Robert (Map p208; ☎ 57 401 70; s/d €14/16) This established hotel has wooden bungalows with big, clean bathrooms in a gorgeous spot among the palm trees. The beach here is one of the best on the island. The downside is that it's rather difficult to get to – you have to call the hotel for a boat transfer from La Crique or the airport. There are some bikes for hire.

La Crique (Map p208; ☎ 57 401 60; bungalows €21) La Crique's rooms have mosquito nets and verandas with deckchairs from which you can look out to sea over a rose garden. The shared bathrooms only have cold-water showers. There's a terraced restaurant. Airport transfers are available, or you can get here by taxi-brousse from Ambodifotatra; ask to be dropped at the top of the rutted track that leads down to the hotel.

Cocoteraie Resort (Map p208; ☎ 57 401 73; soanamb.tan@simicro.mg; s/d €47/68, dinner €12) Next door to La Cocoteraie Robert, this is a much more upmarket place on the same fantastic beach. The bungalows are painted a rather gaudy yellow and green, but are very well constructed and decorated. The hotel is managed by the same people as Soanambo in the south, and has the same rather resorty feel to it. Excursions and watersports are all on offer. Airport transfers (€25 per person) combine boat and car.

Masoandro (Map p208; ☎ 57 040 05; masoandro@simicro.mg; r half board per person €53) Masoandro, near Lonkintsy, is definitely the most chic of Île Sainte Marie's hotels – the interiors of the main building and bungalows are decorated in a stunning ethnic style that brings in many elements of traditional Malagasy design. The beautifully simple bedrooms have polished wood floors, cream cotton bedcovers and murals on the walls. Steps run down to a sandy bay beach from the hotel.

ÎLE AUX NATTES

Also known as Nosy Nato, Île aux Nattes is off the southern tip of Île Sainte Marie. It's got just about everything you could want in a tropical island – curving white beaches, turquoise sea, a lush green interior and a good range of cheap and chilled-out guesthouses, plus one upmarket hotel. Access is via pirogue, leaving from the beach just southwest of the airport runway. You can swim or walk across the narrow channel at low tide; the water is about chest height. If you're heading around to the southern tip of the island, a pirogue transfer should cost about Ar7000.

The island itself can be explored on foot in less than three hours – but why hurry? Better to stay a night – or several nights – and adjust to the feeling of sand between the toes.

Sleeping

The places following don't have telephone numbers and many of them are located on nameless streets; asking around is your best bet.

Chez Tity (Map p208; r Ar24,000) This is a friendly local place, popular with backpackers, with a bit more character than the rest. Some of the simple huts have their own deck on stilts over the sea. The beach is quite narrow here. Snorkelling equipment and pirogues can be hired.

Chez Régine (Map p208; r Ar24,000) Some readers have highly recommended this simple, inexpensive guesthouse in a peaceful spot on the west coast of the island. The food is very good, but order several hours in advance.

Le Petit Traversé (Map p208; ☎ 57 402 54; r Ar40,000) A simple and overpriced option, but it's got a good beach and is opposite the airport, so you can get off the plane and be up to your neck in turquoise sea soon afterwards. No hot water.

Meva Paradis (Map p208; ☎ 032 022 07 80; r €20, bungalows €30) Recently taken over by new owners, this hotel sits in manicured gardens on the west coast. Full-board and long-stay options are available. The beach is excellent, and the bungalows in particular are very comfortable.

Le Maningory (Map p208; ☎ 032 709 005; per person half board s/d/tr €63/46/42) The most upmarket option on Nosy Nato sits on a lovely beach in the northwest of the island. The smart bungalows, made of bamboo and wood and set slightly back from the beach, have verandas, draped mosquito nets and hot water, while the deck bar/restaurant has easy chairs and *foosball* (table football). It's rustic, tasteful and incredibly relaxing. Excursions, fishing and diving can be arranged. Rates include breakfast and transfers. If you get a pirogue here from the airport beach, the hotel will pay the boatman.

NORTHEAST COAST

The wildest and least visited part of the island, the northeast coast can be reached via the cross-island road just outside Ambodifotatra. It's a good hike or bike across, but makes for a bumpy car ride. The sand on the east coast beaches is *not* firm enough for motorcycles and the bush is too thick to ride in. The road to the southern hotels is surfaced, so access is easy.

The **Ampanihy Peninsula** offers relative isolation and a beautiful stretch of sand. It is separated from the mainland by the narrow Baie d'Ampanihy. The easiest access to the peninsula is by pirogue from the village of Anafiafy, followed by a five-minute walk across the peninsula's narrowest point to the beach.

Paradis d'Ampanihy (Map p208; fax 57 402 78, addressed to Hélène; r with shared/private bathroom Ar12,000/20,000) The place to stay if you want to spend time on the Ampanihy Peninsula. The restaurant's speciality is dishes with coconut sauce. There are guides for visiting the nearby forest.

Mora Mora Hôtel (Map p208; ☎ 57 401 14; www.mora mora.info; bungalows €35-50) This slightly overpriced hotel has a glass-walled restaurant on stilts with a sea view and lots of books – a good place to while away some time if you're here when it's raining. Two of the rooms are on a pontoon over the ocean, and share a bathroom. There's almost no beach, so you swim off the jetty. The hotel is about 5km southeast of Ambodifotatra; there are two access roads (both signposted).

St Mary Club (Map p208; ☎ 57 040 08; www.stmaryclub .it; r €60, bungalow €70-85; P ☒) An Italian-run luxury hotel right up on the northeast tip of the island. There's a swimming pool, a huge lounge/dining room, and big, smart bungalows with safes and air-con.

Boraha-Village (Map p208; ☎ 57 400 71; www.boraha .com; s/d half board €70/90) An excellent and very well-run upmarket hotel, with fantastic food and personal service. The smart bungalows have big sliding doors, safes, verandas and bright, tasteful décor. There's a huge range of imaginative 4WD and boat excursions on offer, plus fish-

ing, a cookery school and massages. The hotel also runs a tour of the Canal des Pangalanes, concentrating on the behind-the-scenes life of the villages. Guides speak English.

THE VANILLA COAST

Once north of Soanierana-Ivongo, you're into the remote northeast corner of Madagascar, centre of the vanilla industry.

The recent vanilla boom has led to a new prosperity in the northeast, with many peasant farmers abandoning other crops such as coffee to grow more vanilla. More money, however, has not led to more development, and the infrastructure in the northeast remains very limited, with no roads to speak of and not much in the way of telephone services. People in this area are much more interested in vanilla than tourism, so guides, porters and competent hotel staff are hard to find in some places.

PARC NATIONAL DE MANANARA-NORD

The very remote Parc National de Mananara-Nord (23,000 hectares) encompasses some of the last remaining lowland rainforest in Madagascar. An additional 1000 hectares of offshore islets and their surrounding reefs are protected as a marine national park. The largest of these islets is Nosy Atafana, southeast of Mananara town.

Mananara-Nord is the only known habitat of the hairy-eared dwarf lemur, but lemurs are not the main attraction in the park, and are not always seen by visitors. The park also protects indris, diademed sifakas, brown lemurs, ruffed lemurs and aye-ayes, as well as a variety of geckos (including the endemic uroplatus and day geckos), and dugong, whales and offshore reef life. The area's primary appeal – apart from its forest – is the opportunity to get to know a remote area of Madagascar and experience rural Malagasy life. The park is still in an early stage of development, so the staff ask that travellers give them advanced warning of their visit via the Angap offices in Antananarivo, Maroantsetra or Mananara. Turning up in the park unannounced is not encouraged.

Information

Entry permits for Mananara-Nord (including Nosy Atafana) cost Ar15,000 for three days. Guide fees range from Ar10,000/15,000 per

PARC NATIONAL DE MANANARA-NORD

0 — 4 km
0 — 2 miles

SIGHTS & ACTIVITIES
Aye-Aye Island.......1 B2

SLEEPING
Camp Site..............2 B2
Gîte....................3 B2
Hut.....................4 B2
Tanymarina...........5 B3

half/full day to Ar45,000 for four days. Porter fees are the same. Guides in the park are still inexperienced and not employed full-time, so to get a good one, and make sure he's available, you'll need to contact the Angap offices in Antananarivo, Maroantsetra or Mananara in advance. The best English-speaking guide is Luther.

The only topographical maps of the area are those put out by FTM (p270). These are not available in Mananara, so you will need to purchase it in advance in Antananarivo. A rudimentary map of the park is available from Angap in Mananara.

Hiking

Two circuits are available in Parc National de Mananara-Nord, although others are in the pipeline for the future. The circuits both start at Sarasota, about 2.5km south of Mananara. From here you head north along the sparsely travelled coastal road, then west towards the forest of Vintana Sud (four hours). After spending the night at the village of Partook, on the edge of the forest, continue southeast the next day to return to Sahasoa.

The second circuit available in the park is a trip by boat to Nosy Atafana. You can of course combine the circuits by doing the walk and then the boat trip afterwards, or vice versa. For any trip in the park, you'll need to be self-sufficient with food and water. A limited amount of camping equipment is for hire in the park office at Sahasoa.

Hiking in the park is fairly hard going, so you'll need to be fit to attempt a trek here.

Sleeping & Eating

In Antanambe, **Tanymarina** (Chez Grondin; r from Ar20,000) has rooms and chalets. There is a restaurant here, plus a boat for visits to Nosy Atafana.

There are **gîtes** (r or camping Ar8000) run by the park in Sahasoa and Antanambe. Both have rooms, a camp site, shower and toilets.

In Marotoko village, at the edge of the forest of Ivontaka Sud, there is a hut where you can stay overnight and some rivers nearby for washing. On Nosy Atafana there is a camp site with a water supply; bungalows are planned.

Getting There & Away

The park's remoteness makes it very hard to get to. For visits to Nosy Atafana, you can hire a boat from Mananara or Antanambe. Boat transfers to Nosy Atafana take about 2½ to three hours (one way) from Mananara, and about 30 minutes from Sahasoa. However, boats (Ar250,000) are expensive. The park is planning to buy a boat of its own, which will bring the cost down considerably. If you go to Nosy Atafana from Mananara, you'll need to call into Sahasoa on the way to pick up your guide (this must be arranged in advance with the park office in Mananara).

For visits to Ivontaka Sud, you'll need to get to Sahasoa – five hours in a 4WD, six hours by bike, or a long day on foot.

NOSY ATAFANA NATIONAL MARINE PARK

Nosy Atafana, offshore to the southeast of Mananara town, consists of three islands and the surrounding coral reef. As well as good **snorkelling**, it offers the chance to observe a unique **coastal forest** not found on the mainland.

Nosy Atafana is easily visited on a day trip from Mananara. It's possible to walk between the three islands at low tide.

VANILLA

The vanilla plant was introduced to Madagascar from Mexico by French plantation owners, who named it *vanille* (*lavanila* in Malagasy), from the Spanish *vainilla* or 'little pod'. It is a type of climbing orchid, *Vanila planifolia*, which attaches itself to trees. The vanilla seeds grow inside a long pod hanging from the plant and each pod contains thousands of seeds, which are collected and cured in factories. Dark-brown or black pods are the most desirable because of their stronger aroma.

Madagascar is one of the world's largest producers of vanilla, which – together with other spices such as cloves and pepper, and essences such as ylang-ylang – traditionally has accounted for about one-third of the country's exports. It grows most abundantly in the northeastern parts of the country, particularly on the northeast coast where the hot and wet climate is ideally suited for its cultivation.

Cyclone Hudah, which destroyed more than 20% of Madagascar's vanilla crop in 2000, caused a shortage of supply, a huge escalation in price – in 2003, a kilo of vanilla was changing hands for as much as FMg2,000,000 (Ar400,000) – and a subsequent increase in vanilla-related crime, including thefts and even murders.

MANANARA
pop 33,000

Mananara is a small and very out-of-the-way town set in an attractive clove- and vanilla-producing area at the southern entrance to Baie d'Antongil. The coast south of Mananara is particularly striking, with small, isolated fishing villages and little else – certainly not any serviceable roads. Mananara has seen big social changes of late, as the price of vanilla has soared. As a result, large shiny 4WD cars bump up and down the potholed streets. Auctions are hosted at the Saturday-evening parties in the town hall, in which newly rich vanilla barons prove their status by paying ludicrous prices for random objects such as roast chickens.

Mananara is also the starting point for visiting Parc National de Mananara-Nord, the Nosy Atafana Marine National Park and tiny Aye-Aye Island. For a bit of snorkelling, walk along the long peninsula behind the airport, which has some white-sand beaches and coral about 100m offshore. Watch out for sea urchins here.

There is electricity in Mananara, but no telephone service.

Aye-Aye Island

This small, privately owned island in the Mananara River offers the opportunity to observe aye-ayes in their natural environment. Access to the island costs Ar10,000 per person, including car and pirogue transport. It's not an untouched wilderness, but a charming spot nonetheless, and is presided over by the friendly caretaker, Narcisse, his wife, children and dozens of chickens. You can visit the island for a couple of hours after dark, but there's also a small **gîte** (Ar8000) on the island if you want to stay overnight. Bring a torch and mosquito repellent.

You're almost guaranteed to see an aye-aye here – they have adapted to living in the palm trees, boring holes in coconuts with their sharp teeth and spooning out the flesh with their skeletal middle finger. You'll also have the chance to spot brown lemurs, tiny *Microcebus* (mouse lemurs), fat-tailed dwarf lemurs, grey bamboo lemurs and over 40 species of birds. There are no guides, but researchers are occasionally in residence and will show you around.

The best way to reach the island is by boat, arranged through Chez Roger (below) in Mananara. Alternatively, you can walk for about 4.5km along the paved road that leads west along the river from Mananara towards Sandrakatsy, then cross over to the island via pirogue.

Sleeping & Eating

Chez Roger (r Ar20,000) In the centre of town, this is the best place, especially if you want to visit Aye-Aye Island. The big and comfortable bungalows have bathrooms (bucket showers), and the restaurant does slap-up meals.

Hôtel Aye-Aye (r Ar25,000; 🗩) Near the airport, this hotel is also a good spot, with a small pool, bungalows among the palm trees, and a great selection of rums.

Entertainment

Mananara is, surprisingly, a bit of a party town. Every Friday, Saturday and Sunday night there is a disco and *bal* (party) either at the Hôtel de Ville in the middle of town or at Snack Bar restaurant, around the corner from Chez Roger.

Getting There & Around
BOAT
Cargo boats sail relatively frequently between Mananara, Île Sainte Marie, Maroantsetra and Toamasina. There are usually several departures, depending on the weather, although there are no set schedules. This journey is only really safe between September and March – at other times the sea is much too rough to make the journey.

Inquire at the small port in Mananara – boats often come in and leave again fairly quickly, so you'll have to return often on the chance of finding a ship in port. Fares between Mananara and Île Sainte Marie or Maroantsetra average about Ar50,000; the trip takes at least eight hours, often sailing through the night. Decent boats to look for include *Estilina*, *Geralda II* and *Tsiriry*. Occasional cargo boats go as far as Sambava, Antalaha or even Diego Suarez in the north. There are no facilities of any kind on the boats – bring sun protection (an umbrella is handy for shade), food and water.

Another option is to charter a speedboat from Maroantsetra.

TAXI-BROUSSE
Mananara lies 127km north of Soanierana-Ivongo. There are occasional taxis-brousses between Mananara and Toamasina in the dry season, but the road is abysmal and getting worse.

From Mananara north to Maroantsetra, the road is also in bad condition, and entails several river crossings; there are occasional taxis-brousses during the dry season. Inquire about taxi-brousse departures in the market or at Chez Roger.

MANANARA TO MAROANTSETRA
If you have the time and energy, Mananara to Maroantsetra (114km) is a beautiful walk or mountain-bike ride along the very rough coastal road, which sees almost no vehicle traffic.

Manambolosy, 20km north of Mananara, is the first major town and has a basic **hotel** (r Ar10,000). **Tanjora**, also with a **hotel** (r Ar10,000), is 15km north, followed in a further 15km by the village of **Anandrivola**, which has a sandy lagoon and bungalows at the **Jolex Hotel** (r Ar20,000); meals and motorcycle lifts can be arranged.

About 17km further on is **Rantabe**, from which you can take a pirogue trip 15km upriver through forest. South of town is a beach and some offshore coral. **Bungalows** (r Ar10,000) are available.

Just north of Rantabe you will need to cross the Rantabe River in a pirogue. Transport to Maroantsetra is sometimes waiting on the other side. If not, continue on foot for 12km to **Nandrasana**, from where there are usually at least three vehicles daily to Maroantsetra (Ar8000).

Water is sometimes available in Nandrasana, Rantabe and Manambolosy, and you can get fresh fish in all the villages, but you'll need to bring most supplies with you. If you're coming south from Maroantsetra, you can hire guides (Ar60,000) and porters (Ar45,000) for the trip – see p220 for details.

RÉSERVE DE NOSY MANGABE
The thickly forested island nature reserve of Nosy Mangabe (520 hectares) is located in Baie d'Antongil about 5km offshore from Maroantsetra. With its dark-green forested hills rising dramatically out of the surrounding sea, and a wonderful yellow sickle of beach, the island has a magical, otherworldly feel rather like a location from *Jurassic Park*. It rains a lot on Nosy Mangabe, however, so you could well end up seeing all this through a wall of water.

The main attraction of Nosy Mangabe is its flourishing population of aye-ayes, which were introduced in 1967 to protect them from extinction. Nosy Mangabe's aye-ayes are fairly elusive these days, and a sighting is by no means guaranteed. Besides the aye-ayes, the island is home to mouse lemurs, white-fronted brown lemurs and black-and-white ruffed lemurs, all of which are fairly easily spotted if you stay overnight.

Walking through the forest in the dark, your torch will pick out a host of reptiles and amphibians – Nosy Mangabe is home to the leaf-tailed gecko *(Uroplatus fimbriatus)*, one of nature's most accomplished camouflage artists; several species of chameleons; many frogs; and several snake species, including the harmless *Pseudoxyrohopus heterurus*, which is believed to be endemic to Nosy Mangabe, and the Madagascar tree boa.

There are several walking trails on the island and a small waterfall. At one end is a beach called Plage des Hollandais, with rocks bearing the scratched names of some 17th-century Dutch sailors. From July to September, you can see whales offshore.

Information
An entry permit for the Réserve de Nosy Mangabe (not included in the permit for nearby

Parc National de Masoala) costs Ar15,000 for three days. Guides (compulsory) are Ar15,000 per group per day. Night walks cost Ar12,000 for groups of up to four, plus Ar8000 for the guide's evening meal. Some guides will cook in the evenings for an extra fee.

Permits can be obtained at the Parc National de Masoala office in Maroantsetra, or on the island itself.

Sleeping & Eating

There is a very well-equipped **camping ground** (tent sites Ar5000) at the Angap station on the western edge of the island. It has picnic tables, shelters, a kitchen and toilets, and a waterfall nearby provides the showers. You'll need to bring camping and cooking equipment, food, water or purifying tablets, and cooking fuel. Camping equipment can be rented through 3M Loisirs in Maroantsetra (right), and sometimes through the guides at the reserve.

Getting There & Away

Boat transfers to Nosy Mangabe can be arranged with the guides based at the Parc National de Masoala office in Maroantsetra, or with 3M Loisirs (right). Rates for a return day trip are about Ar85,000 per boat with a minimum of three people. The trip takes 30 to 45 minutes and may occasionally be cancelled or postponed if the weather is bad, so it's best not to schedule a flight too close to your planned return from the island.

MAROANTSETRA

Maroantsetra (maro-ant-*setr*), set on Baie d'Antongil near the mouth of the Antainambalana River, is a remote and isolated place full of languid charm, surrounded by beautiful riverine scenery. It's well worth spending a day or two exploring the area on foot, quad or mountain bike. On the way you'll pass vanilla plantations, wave-pounded beaches and the occasional chameleon on the side of the road – plus, of course, dozens of waving children.

From July to September there's a good chance of seeing breeding and birthing humpback whales.

Maroantsetra's climate is one of the wettest in Madagascar, with close to 3500mm of rain annually. May to September are the wettest months, although rain can fall at any time of year. The nearest good beach to Maroantsetra is **Navana**, which has a backdrop of virgin rainforest. It's a 30-minute boat ride from town.

Information

Bank of Africa has a branch here for changing cash and travellers cheques.

Contact **Angap** (7.30am-noon & 2.30-6pm), two blocks down from the market, behind Maroantsetra's two large radio towers, to organise treks across the Masoala Peninsula, visits to Nosy Mangabe or trips to Parc National de Mananara-Nord. The Parc National de Masoala office is also located here.

Activities

KAYAKING

Sea kayaking is an excellent way to explore the shores around Maroantsetra and the Masoala Peninsula, and there are numerous excellent routes. **Kayak Masoala** (www.kayakafrica .com/madagascar.asp) has set up several kayaking camp sites on the peninsula and run trips there from Maroantsetra. Inquire at Le Coco Beach (opposite) for information.

QUAD, MOTOR OR MOUNTAIN BIKING

A great way to explore the area around Maroantsetra is by mountain bike. If that sounds too energetic, rent a quad or motorcycle, both of which are just about the only motor vehicles that can make it far along the very rough RN2. All bikes can be hired in town.

CANOEING

The tour companies listed here can organise trips by pirogue up the various rivers outside Maroantsetra. Some include a visit to a vanilla plantation and treatment plant. Maroa Tours also organises overnight camping trips by motorised pirogue to the Makira rainforest, newly added to the Parc National de Masoala. These can be a good alternative to Nosy Mangabe if the sea is too rough.

Tours

There's a lot to do in Maroantsetra, and several well-organised ways of doing it. English-speaking guides are easy to find.

Relais du Masoala, Maroantsetra's most upmarket hotel, organises overnight excursions in the surrounding area, including the Masoala Peninsula (Ar170,000 per person) and to Nosy Mangabe (Ar70,000 per person for groups of at least two).

3M Loisirs (write to Boite Postale 83, 512 Maroantsetra) Near the small bridge leading to Le Coco Beach hotel, has a selection of good-quality sporting and camping equipment for hire, including snorkelling gear, tents, quad bikes, 4WD vehicles, motorcycles and canoes. It also arranges river excursions (Ar55,000 per half day), and boat trips to Nosy Mangabe (Ar80,000 return) and the Masoala Peninsula.

Maroa Tours (☎ 57 720 06; Le Coco Beach) Rakoto, an English-speaking Angap guide and 'fixer', does excursions by pirogue to villages upriver from Maroantsetra (Ar35,000 per person for groups of two or more), along with visits to Nosy Mangabe and the Masoala Peninsula. The tours include visits to a vanilla and cinnamon farm and village weaving workshops. The best time to see vanilla is between October and June. Rakoto can also organise guided treks to Mananara.

Sleeping

Hôtel du Centre (☎ 48 via post office; r Ar3000, meals Ar4000) A basic place with rooms in wooden sheds. Meals can be arranged in the evenings.

Le Coco Beach (☎ 57 702 06; camping Ar9000, r €25) This friendly midrange hotel has comfortable, well-maintained bungalows and a good restaurant set amid coconut palms. Those of you who are arachnophobes should watch out for spiderwebs and their large occupants strung between the trees at night! Le Coco Beach is a good place to meet other travellers and get a group together for trips further afield. Cross over the small bridge and turn right, about 800m from the centre of town.

Hôtel Antongil (☎ 17 via post office; r Ar10,000, dinner Ar4500) There are big, breezy upstairs rooms with fans and mosquito nets around a wide wooden veranda at this two-storey building in the centre of town. Rooms share toilets. The small restaurant serves Malagasy meals.

Le Maroa (☎ in Toamasina 032 04 225 20; d Ar12,000, mains Ar6000) Near the Parc National de Masoala office, Le Maroa has a good restaurant (lots of varieties of *soupe chinoise*) and decent bungalows with fans and mosquito nets.

Relais du Masoala (☎ 57 721 43/42, in Antananarivo 22 219 74; relais@simicro.mg; r Ar100,000, dinner Ar10,000; **P**) This is a very tranquil and well-decorated upmarket hotel about 2.5km east of town overlooking a small canal, with the bay and the mountains in the distance. The luxurious bungalows scattered through the leafy grounds have two double beds, huge bathrooms, decks, fans and mosquito nets. A variety of excursions can be arranged from here.

Eating

Places for a good meal include Les Grillades, near Le Coco Beach, Bar Blanc Vert nearby, and the restaurant at Le Maroa.

The restaurant at Le Coco Beach is good value; try Rakoto's legendary punch coco. Meals at Relais du Masoala are more refined, and there are some delectable desserts. Rive Gauche, in a pretty spot near the harbour, is open in the early evening for ice creams and snacks.

If you're stocking up for a camping trip, Maroantsetra is good for self-caterers. It has great bread, which is available at the market, along with a modest selection of fruits and vegetables.

THE MEN WHO WOULD BE KING

The Baie d'Antongil has a peculiar history of encouraging delusions of grandeur in some of its early European visitors – at least two displayed quite staggering amounts of ambition in their plans for territorial gain and self-advancement.

The first such pretender was John Avery, a British pirate, who established himself here around 1695. One of his raids was on the ship of a Mogul maharajah on its way to Mecca; among the booty was an oriental princess, whom Avery duly married. After making treaties with neighbouring pirate leaders, he proclaimed himself governor of d'Antongil and tried to establish his own mini-state. Amazingly it isn't known what eventually became of Avery, though some historians believe he returned to England to live out his days incognito.

Almost a century later, in 1773, a Hungarian count by the name of Maurice-Auguste de Benyowski rocked up in the bay after years as a Russian prisoner of war. Having established his own town, Louisville, he proceeded to consolidate his hold in the area with a combination of diplomacy and violence, and in a stunning show of confidence subsequently declared himself emperor of Madagascar. This alone he might have got away with, but he then tried to persuade the King of France to recognise his 'empire', resulting in an instant military overthrow and exile. Sadly for Benyowski, his fate is much clearer than Avery's: when the count returned for a second attempt in 1783 his forces were defeated summarily at Foulpointe, and both he and Louisville disappeared forever.

EASTERN MADAGASCAR

NOTHING BUT MAMMALS

Every year between July and September, Baie d'Antongil, just south of Maroantsetra, is the site of the migration of hundreds of humpback whales *(Megaptera novaeangliae)*. The whales make their way from the Antarctic northward to the warmer waters around Baie d'Antongil, where they spend the winter months breeding and birthing before the long journey back to Antarctica. En route the whales swim past Fort Dauphin and Île Sainte Marie, where they are often sighted offshore.

Humpbacks can measure up to 15m in length and weigh as much as 35,000kg. Despite their size, they are exceptionally agile, and capable of acrobatic moves such as breaching (launching themselves completely out of the water with their flippers). Humpbacks are also renowned for their singing, which is presumed to be related to mating patterns. Humpback songs can last up to an hour, and are considered to be the most complex of all whale songs.

To maximise your chances of observing the whales and their acrobatics, try to go out on a day when the water is calm – although conditions on the bay vary widely, so the water may be calm in one area and rough in another.

The Wildlife Conservation Society (WCS; based in Maroantsetra) and the American Museum of Natural History (AMNH; based in New York City) have a long-term research and conservation programme for humpback whales and other marine mammals, with a field base on Nosy Mangabe. The WCS-AMNH project has drafted a set of guidelines aimed at ensuring the wellbeing and safety of both whales and whale-watchers. These have since been adopted as national law in Madagascar and local boat operators have been trained to operate within the guidelines, ensuring that disturbance to the whales by whale-watchers will be minimal.

To ensure that you go out with experienced and trained guides and boat operators, organise your trip through the office of Parc National de Masoala (p220) in Maroantsetra. Expect to pay from about Ar90,000 for a half-day trip.

For details of the whale-watching project, have a look at the website of the **American Museum of Natural History** (http://research.amnh.org/biodiversity/center/programs/whales.html).

Getting There & Away

AIR

Air Madagascar flights connect Maroantsetra a few times a week with Antananarivo (€78), Toamasina (€78), Sambava (€46) and Antalaha (€41). The Air Madagascar office (at Ramanaraibe Export) is a few kilometres from town on the road to the airport. Flights to/from Maroantsetra are often full, especially between June and November – be sure to reconfirm your ticket. Weather may affect plane schedules, particularly during the rainiest months (July to September).

BOAT

During most of the year, the only alternative to flying is to get a cargo boat to or from Maroantsetra. Boat travel is not a safe option between July and September, when the seas are rough.

There are unscheduled but regular sailings between Maroantsetra and Île Sainte Marie (10 hours), Toamasina (two days), Antalaha (12 to 15 hours) and Mananara (nine hours). Inquire at the port in Maroantsetra, and then be prepared for inevitable delays. The boats that take passengers are sometimes extremely overloaded, and some do capsize, so if the boat looks too full, don't get on. Good boats to look out for to Mananara are *Estilina*, *Geralda II* and *Tsiriry*. To Île Sainte Marie or Toamasina, look out for *Savannah, Red Rose* or *Rosita*.

Maroa Tours, 3M Loisirs and Relais du Masoala can arrange speedboat transfers to various points on the Masoala Peninsula.

TAXI-BROUSSE

Maroantsetra lies 112km north of Mananara at the end of a 'road', which is more of a rutted cart track with several river crossings en route. Occasional taxis-brousses connect the two towns during the dry season from October to December, but this is not a method of transport to be relied upon. To the north of Maroantsetra, there are no roads, and hence no taxis-brousses.

Getting Around

The airport is about 7km southwest of town. Maroantsetra has a few taxis, which all charge Ar10,000 for a trip out to the airport.

Alternatively, it's possible to get a lift in the Air Madagascar vehicle for a small fee;

ask at the Air Madagascar office when you reconfirm your ticket.

MASOALA PENINSULA & PARC NATIONAL DE MASOALA

The Masoala (mash-wala) Peninsula is the site of a 210,000-hectare national park containing one of the best rainforests in the country. It also encompasses three protected marine areas: Tampolo Marine Park on the peninsula's southwestern coast, Cap Masoala Marine Park at the tip of the peninsula and Tanjona Marine Park on the southeastern coast. Most of the park is spread across the central part of the peninsula, extending southwest to the coast by Tampolo Marine Park. There are several small discrete parcels (parcs détachés) elsewhere on the peninsula, including Andranoala, near Cap Est, Tanambao-Anjanazana, contiguous with Tanjona Marine Park, and Beankoraka, near the tip of the peninsula.

Masoala Peninsula is one of Madagascar's premier **trekking** areas. It also offers excellent opportunities for **sea kayaking**, **snorkelling** and **swimming**. At the peninsula's southernmost tip is the beautiful **Cap Masoala**, which can be reached on foot or by bicycle from Cap Est. Masoala Peninsula is exceptionally wet. The months between October and December are somewhat drier and are the best months for trekking, although you should be prepared for rain at any time of the year. June and July are the rainiest months; river levels are highest at this time.

Information

Parc National de Masoala is administered by Angap in collaboration with the Wildlife Conservation Society (WCS). Park headquarters are at the Angap office in Maroantsetra (p220). There is also a Parc National de Masoala and Angap representative based in Antalaha.

The best place to arrange permits, guides and treks across the peninsula is at the Angap office in Maroantsetra. The guides here are well organised and many speak English. Treks can also be arranged in Antalaha or in Ambodirafia, near Cap Est, although the staff and guides there don't speak English.

Permits cost Ar20,000 for three days. Guide fees start at Ar12,000/13,000 per day/night for

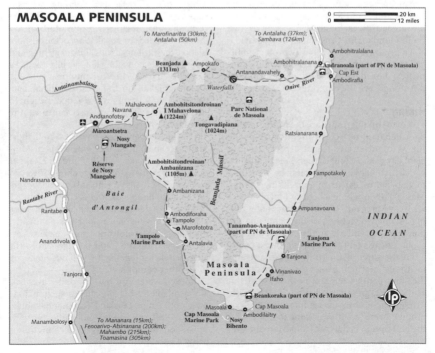

MASOALA PENINSULA

visits to the park. For trekking circuits, guide fees are Ar75,000 for the Maroantsetra to Antalaha circuit, Ar13,000 per day for a tour of the peninsula and Ar120,000 for Maroantsetra to Cap Est, plus Ar7000 to Ar 13,000 per day for a porter. Food, including for the guides and porters, is not included in these rates and is supposed to be paid by you, although there may be some room for negotiation on this. One reason for the comparatively high fees is that they include the days that the guides and porters need to walk back to Maroantsetra after depositing you in Antalaha or Cap Est (food for this return portion is the responsibility of the guides and porters themselves). Guides are also required for visiting the marine parks.

Wildlife

The Masoala Peninsula is famous for its dramatic vegetation, which includes primary forest, rainforest and coastal forest as well as a variety of palm and orchid species.

Ten lemur species are found on Masoala, including the red-ruffed and eastern fork-marked lemurs. The helmeted vanga shrike is most often seen here. There are also several tenrec and mongoose species, 14 bat species, 60 reptile species and about 85 bird species, including the rare serpent eagle and Madagascan red owl (both found on the peninsula's west coast).

The marine national parks protect mangrove ecosystems, coral reefs, dolphins and turtles. For details about whales in Baie d'Antongil, see the boxed text, p222.

Hiking

The main hiking routes are the Maroantsetra to Antalaha direct trip (three to five days); the Maroantsetra to Cap Est route (five to eight days); and a tour of the whole peninsula, which involves starting at Antalaha, travelling to Cap Est by car or bike, trekking to Cap Masoala, then taking a boat to Maroantsetra via Nosy Mangabe. Several shorter routes taking in smaller sections of the peninsula are possible, particularly if you're based at the ecobungalows on the peninsula's west coast.

Of the three main routes, Maroantsetra to Antalaha, which passes through rice paddies and gentler terrain, is the easiest but also dullest, although all the treks are fairly demanding and involve numerous slippery, muddy stretches. If you want to see forest, the best option is the trek from Maroantsetra to Cap Est.

There are river and stream crossings along both routes – primarily small, low streams on the Maroantsetra to Antalaha trek, and some deeper, faster-moving rivers between Maroantsetra and Cap Est (which means you may be wading up to waist or chest height, depending on the time of year, often over slippery rocks). Inquire at the Angap office (p220) about trail conditions when you arrive.

You need an official guide for all treks on the peninsula.

Sleeping & Eating

Ecolodge Chez Arol (http://arollodge.free.fr; Ambodiforaha; camping per person Ar3000, r Ar10,000, dinner Ar7000) Travellers rave about the good French food at Chez Arol and its wonderful position between the beach and the forest. Numerous trekking and snorkelling trips can be arranged from here. It has a booking office in Maroantsetra, 200m east of the bank.

Tampolo Lodge (d Ar16,000, dinner Ar6000) A set of bungalows on the beach near Chez Arol, at Tampolo.

Kayak Masoala (mea@dts.mg; camp sites per person Ar10,000, 9-night all-inclusive trip per person €1250) Several wilderness camp sites with bow tents and dining shelters at Cap Masoala are run by Kayak Masoala. The company organises trips here by motorboat, followed by guided sea-kayak tours of the offshore islands. Snorkelling, diving, bird-watching and fishing are also possible. For details, ask at Le Coco Beach (p221) in Maroantsetra.

Ambanizana on the west coast has **bungalows** (r Ar6000) run by Le Coco Beach in Maroantsetra. You can also camp at the Angap base here.

On the Maroantsetra to Cap Est trek, most nights are spent in villages, where it is customary to pay between Ar15000 and Ar2500 per person per night to the village chief. However, you should still carry a tent, as some villages are too small to be able to offer accommodation.

There are designated **camping grounds** (camp sites Ar3000) all the way round the peninsula, including at Marofototra, Cap Masoala, Ambodilaitry, Ifaho and Cap Est. These have wells and shelters for tents, but you'll need to bring in all other equipment.

Bottled water and basic supplies are usually available in bigger villages such as Mahavelona, Ampokafo and Antanandavahely, but you will need to be self-sufficient with most food. There are water sources en route – bring a good purifier.

CAP EST

Remote and beautiful Cap Est is Madagascar's easternmost point. Ambodirafia, southeast of Ambohitralanana on the coast, has an Angap station and is the starting point for treks down the peninsula's east coast. The walk from here to Cap Masoala takes about four days. The numerous rivers en route must be crossed by pirogue; allow at least three days for cycling one way.

Résidence du Cap (☎ 032 04 539 05; r with bathroom Ar15,000, set dinners Ar7000) is Cap Est's main hotel. It has been destroyed by cyclones and rebuilt twice in four years. Assuming it's still standing by the time you get there, it has five bungalows, electricity from a generator and a restaurant. It's located about 4km southeast of Ambohitralanana and makes a good base for trekking.

Hôtel du Voyageur (Ambodirafia; r Ar3000) has simple but picturesque bungalow accommodation with bucket showers. It also has Malagasy meals. Further towards Cap Masoala at Vinanivao is **Chez Marie** (r Ar4000), a similarly simple place.

Cap Est is linked to Antalaha by two taxis-brousses daily (Ar5000, four hours) in the dry season. You can also get there by mountain bike (four to six hours), which can be rented in Antalaha.

To travel to and from Cap Est or Cap Masoala by sea, ask in Antalaha's small harbour about cargo boats heading around the peninsula. Once in Cap Masoala it's possible to take a boat on to Maroantsetra, although this should be arranged in advance if possible or you could be in for a long wait. It's also possible, but hard walking, to continue up the western side of the peninsula by foot to Maroantsetra (four to six days).

ANTALAHA
pop 30,000

Antalaha, a prosperous coastal town, suffered significant damage during Cyclone Hudah in April 2000 and Cyclone Hiary in 2002. Numerous buildings, including the airport, were partially destroyed and vanilla production was dealt a severe blow, but little sign of the damage now remains in the town centre.

Apart from being a relaxing place to stop if you are travelling up or down the east coast, Antalaha makes a good starting point for visiting Cap Est, about 50km to the south.

Information

The Angap and Parc National de Masoala representative (for arranging permits and guides) is in town next door to the Chamber of Commerce.

Antalaha is well known in Madagascar's expat circles for its excellent dentist – inquire at the Kam-Hyo pharmacy opposite Hôtel Florida if you need his services. There are also banks in Antalaha for changing money, and a good internet café – look for the orange sign next to the Kam-Hyo pharmacy.

Tours

Hôtel Océan Momo can help organise excursions in the area, as can Le Corail restaurant and **Henri Fraise Fils Travel Service** (☎ 88 810 33; port). Le Corail also rents mountain bikes.

Sleeping & Eating

Chambres Liane (☎ 032 04 763 60; r Ar16,000) Small but well-kept rooms with mosquito nets, but no fans, and friendly staff.

Hôtel Florida (☎ 032 07 161 90; r Ar15,000, with hot water Ar35,000; ❄) On the main road opposite the white pharmacy. Some more expensive rooms with air-con are also available.

Hôtel Nany (☎ 032 40 051 89; port; r Ar24,000) Basic whitewashed rooms around a cheery courtyard full of palm trees. Cold water only in the showers.

Hôtel Océan Momo (☎ 032 02 340 69; www.ocean-momo.com in French; d Ar65,000, mains Ar10,000) This comfortable hotel about 100m south of the port is Antalaha's most luxurious option. The imposing white bungalows, in rows beside the beach, have tiled floors, dark wood furniture and four-poster beds with mosquito nets. The restaurant is equally impressive – large and tastefully decorated, with a range of seafood on offer.

Le Corail (☎ 032 04 539 05; ☽ lunch & dinner Tue-Sun) Le Corail has good French food, great desserts, and rents out mountain bikes. It's also the booking office for Résidence du Cap hotel in Cap Est, and the owner can give advice on trekking on the peninsula.

Fleur de Lotus (☽ dinner) Near Hôtel du Centre, this is one of Antalaha's better dining options; it has a good Chinese menu selection.

For inexpensive food and homemade ice cream, try Salon de Thé Joice, near the police station just south of the market.

Getting There & Around
AIR

Air Madagascar (☎ 88 813 22) has flights linking Antalaha several times weekly with Maroantsetra (€41) and Antananarivo (€99).

EASTERN MADAGASCAR

The airport is 12km north of town. Taxis between town and the airport charge a ridiculous Ar20,000 per person, so you might want to catch a taxi-brousse from the main road by the airport turn-off, which is cheaper.

BOAT

Cargo boats sail regularly between Antalaha and Maroantsetra, sometimes also stopping near Cap Est. There are no set schedules; inquire at the port about sailings. There are also cargo boats to other areas along the east coast, including Toamasina, Sambava and Iharana.

TAXI-BROUSSE

Heading north, there are usually several taxis-brousses each day between Antalaha and Sambava (Ar10,000, three hours). Departures are from the taxi-brousse stand about 2km north of town.

Heading south, two taxis-brousses daily go to Cap Est (Ar15,000, four hours) in the dry season. Taxis-brousses towards Cap Est depart from the taxi-brousse station on the way to the airport from town. If you're taking a mountain bike to Cap Est, the taxis-brousses can tie it on top.

SAMBAVA

pop 28,000

Sambava is a sprawling beach town set between the sea and the soaring Marojejy Massif on Madagascar's rugged northeastern coast about halfway between Maroantsetra and Antsiranana. The town is nothing special in itself, but makes a good base for exploring the surrounding area, which produces coffee and cloves as well as vanilla. If you want to swim off Sambava's beaches (which are long and sandy, but hot and blustery) inquire locally about sharks and currents.

All major banks have branches in Sambava and you might find yourself using them more often than expected, as everything in Sambava is fairly expensive compared with other towns in the region.

Best (☎ 88 922 48; best.sambava@wanadoo.mg; Rte Principale; per min Ar200), 100m from Hôtel Paradise, has internet access.

Tours

Sambava Voyages (☎ 88 921 10) in the centre of town can organise excursions in the surrounding area. These include visits to a vanilla factory and nearby coffee plantations,

transport to Andapa or Antalaha, and day trips along the river in a pirogue, returning on foot through the villages.

Sleeping & Eating

Sava Hôtel (☎ 88 922 92; savahotel@gasyonline.mg; Rte Principale; r with shared/private bathroom Ar30,000/34,000) A fairly uninspiring place with big, shabby rooms and a cheap restaurant.

Hôtel Orchidea Beach II (☎ 88 923 24; orchideabeach2@ wanadoo.mg; Plage des Cocotiers; r Ar46,000) A rustic, welcoming establishment that has more charm than any other in town. Just across the road from the beach, it has small but well-maintained rooms with fans but no mosquito nets. The friendly restaurant serves a good selection of seafood. Cold water only in the bathrooms.

Hôtel Paradise (☎ 88 922 97; Rte Principale; d/tr Ar52,000/64,000) This place is highly kitsch but comfortable, with a huge, flashy Chinese-run edifice, a good restaurant and obliging staff. Rooms are vast and cool, but noisy, with fans but no mosquito nets, and painted *trompe l'oeil* bedheads.

Hôtel Las Palmas (☎ 88 920 87; in Antananarivo 22 593 96; fax 88 921 73; Plage des Cocotiers; r with fan/air-con Ar60,000/72,000; ⌘) Nominally Sambava's most upmarket hotel, this place has a good position on the beach, but is decent rather than luxurious. The rather small rooms, with pink plastic bathrooms, have fans or air-con, but no nets. There's a terrace restaurant and some beach umbrellas. The hotel runs excursions to the palm and vanilla plantations outside town.

Hotel Carrefour (☎ 88 920 60; r with fan/air-con Ar64,000/100,000; ⌘) A once grand, now faded hotel, down by the beach at the north end of town. If you arrive here after 8pm you won't be able to check in.

Getting There & Around

Air Madagascar (☎ 88 920 37; Rte Principale) flies from Sambava several times weekly to Antananarivo (€99), sometimes via Maroantsetra (€177) or Toamasina. There are also several flights weekly to Diego Suarez (€62).

The airport is situated about 2km south of town. It's possible to take a taxi to the airport from town, or you could walk.

Taxis to Antalaha (Ar10,000, three hours) and Andapa (Ar10,000, 2½ hours) depart from the hectic taxi-brousse station in the market at the southern end of town. Transport to Iharana (Ar10,000, 2½ hours) and on to Diego

Suarez (Ar50,000, about 17 hours) departs from the northern taxi-brousse station.

ANDAPA

Andapa lies in an attractive agricultural valley in one of Madagascar's most important rice-growing areas. Nothing in particular happens in Andapa, but the beauty of the surrounding countryside, the cool climate and the friendly, untouristy atmosphere make it a great place to kick back and just take in a slice of Malagasy life. From town there are a couple of easy and scenic hikes, one which passes through rolling rice fields to a set of impressive rapids about 3km northeast of town. You can also walk 2km south to a waterfall, surrounded by vanilla plantations and fishponds.

There is a very helpful **WWF/Angap office** (wwfandapa@wwf.mg; BP 28, 205 Andapa) in Andapa, from which to arrange treks to the nearby Parc National de Marojejy and Réserve Spéciale d'Anjanaharibe-Sud. If you want to visit either of these areas from Andapa, you'll need at least three days.

Hôtel Vahasoa (r from Ar20,000) is a very friendly and homely hotel with a restaurant serving fantastic food. A slap-up, multicourse Chinese dinner, often including lobster, costs Ar20,000. The charming owners, Mr and Mrs Tam Hyok, can help with advice on hikes in the surrounding area or visits to the national park. Taxis-brousses will drop off or pick you up outside the door on request.

Hôtel Beanana (http://hotel-beanana.no-ip.com; r Ar25,000) is the only other place in town – it's on the way into the village. Meals are available if you order in advance (breakfast Ar6000).

There are also several *hotelys* in town serving very simple Malagasy-style meals.

Andapa lies 109km southwest of Sambava along a winding, sealed road which passes through spectacular scenery. Taxis-brousses go daily between the two towns for about Ar5000 (2½ hours). If you start early, it's quite possible to get to Andapa as a day trip from Sambava.

PARC NATIONAL DE MARO-JEJY & RÉSERVE SPÉCIALE D'ANJANAHARIBE-SUD

The rugged and precipitous Marojejy (Marojezy) Massif rises north of the road between Andapa and Sambava. It is part of a 60,050-hectare national park that protects a remote wilderness area noted for its vegetation, including over 2000 types of plants, and the spectacular views from the upper reaches of the forest. The park is also home to 11 species of lemurs, including the aye-aye, the silky sifaka *(Propitecus candidus)* and the helmeted vanga shrike, endemic to the region. There are over 100 bird species, about 70% of which are endemic to Madagascar, as well as numerous species of frog and chameleon.

The Réserve Spéciale d'Anjanaharibe-Sud (18,250 hectares), to the southwest of Parc National Marojejy, gained attention in 1997 when the Takhtajania perrieri – a small tree in the Winteraceae family, which is believed to have existed on earth about 120 million years ago – was rediscovered here.

At the park's lower elevations the landscape is dominated by thick rainforest, while above about 800m, the rainforest is replaced by highland forest. At the highest elevations, rising up to the peak of Mt Marojejy at 2133m, the primary vegetation cover consists of heath, mosses and lichens. It can get very cold at the higher altitudes. Trails in the park and up to the summit are very hard and steep, so this destination is for fit trekkers only.

Both de Marojejy and d'Anjanaharibe-Sud are administered by the World Wide Fund for Nature (WWF). Local communities on the borders of the park manage portions of the forest in partnership with WWF.

The turn-off to Marojejy is near Manantenina village, 40km from Andapa on the Sambava road (near the 66km post). Once in the park, there are three camp sites, each at different altitudes. The first two camp sites have huts with beds, but the third and highest is a camping ground only. The Réserve Spéciale d'Anjanaharibe-Sud features most of the same vegetation as the park, but walking here is easier. The best times to visit the parks are from April to May and September to December.

For information, and guides and permits, contact **WWF** (wwfandapa@wwf.mg; BP 28, 205 Andapa) in Andapa or the WWF welcome office in Manantenina. **Sambava Voyages** (☎ 88 921 10; Sambava) can also arrange visits to the park.

IHARANA (VOHÉMAR)

Iharana (commonly known as Vohémar) lies 153km north of Sambava along a mostly sealed road. It is the last stop north on the east coast before the (rough) road heads inland to Ambilobe and Diego Suarez. Like Sambava and Antalaha, Iharana is a vanilla-producing centre.

One of the main sites of interest for visitors is **Lac Andranotsara**, 7km south of Iharana. It is also known as Lac Vert (Green Lake) because of its coloration by algae. Nearby is a good beach. According to legend, there was once a village at Andranotsara, which one night sank into the earth under the weight of an irritable seven-headed monster who curled up there to sleep. This incident was followed by seven days of rain, which flooded the indentation. The crocodiles that inhabit the resulting lake are thought to be reincarnations of the villagers, and various *fady* (taboos) are in effect. It's possible to walk from Iharana to Lac Andranotsara, though you'll need to ask directions locally.

The main hotel in Iharana is the **Sol y Mar** (☎ 88 630 42; vohemarina@vohemarina.com; r Ar24,000-190,000), with decent bungalows, some more expensive rooms, and a good restaurant.

Hôtel-Restaurant La Cigogne (☎ 88 630 65) is known for its food. La Floride, not far from the Sambirano pharmacy, has good meals, although you'll need to order in advance. There are also some simple rooms here.

Another place to try is Hotely Kanto, which has good Malagasy dishes.

Taxis-brousses travel daily between Iharana and Sambava (Ar6000, four to five hours). There is usually one vehicle daily between Iharana and Daraina (four hours, 60km), northwest of Iharana en route to Ambilobe, where there's a basic *hotely*. At least several vehicles weekly continue on to Diego Suarez during the dry season, via Ambilobe. The stretch between Iharana and Ambilobe is very rough, and can take anywhere from 12 to 20 hours. The journey from Ambilobe on to Diego Suarez is only about two hours.

SOUTH OF TOAMASINA

CANAL DES PANGALANES

The Canal des Pangalanes is a collection of natural rivers and artificial lakes that stretches approximately 600km along the east coast from Toamasina to Farafangana, although it's only navigable from just north of Mananjary. More than its rather dull scenery, the canal's charm comes from the procession of boats of all shapes and sizes on its waters, and the small villages on the banks. Here you can stop to see eels drying in the sun, visit local coffee factories, or talk with fishermen mending their wooden pirogues under the trees.

The best times to tour the Canal des Pangalanes are from March to May and September to December.

TOURS

Most organised tours cruise from Toamasina to one of the nearby lakes, stay overnight at a lakeside hotel – where you may be able to do some water sports or hiking – and then return to Toamasina. Few organised tours travel along the canal for any great distance. In addition to the operators listed on pp199–200, the following companies do trips along the canal:

Boogie Pilgrim (☎ 22 530 70; www.boogiepilgrim -madagascar.com) This Antananarivo-based tour operator organises trips to and from its hotel, Bush House, on Lac Ampitabe.

Boraha-Village (☎ 57 400 71; www.boraha.com) This hotel on Île Sainte Marie organises very high-quality trips on the canal, with the emphasis on local life, agriculture and fishing. Guides speak English.

L'Aziza (☎ 032 07 008 66; l.aziza@netcourrier.com) No-frills, budget trips on flat-bottomed canal boats from any point on the Pangalanes to any other cost Ar50,000 per person per day, including lunch. It also does hotel bookings. Reduced rates for groups.

GETTING THERE & AWAY

You can travel along the canal in either direction by boat, by taxi-brousse along a parallel inland road or by cargo train. For all travel on the canal, allow plenty of time, and be prepared to spend time on boats without any amenities at all – not even seats!

To find a boat heading down the canal from Toamasina, ask around at the *gare fluviale* about 2.5km from the centre of town. There are no fixed sailing schedules, so you may have to wait a while. To continue down the canal each day, you will need to keep asking about onward public boats or pirogues, which can be chartered. Allow three to four days between Toamasina and Ambila-Lemaitso, travelling by pirogue and staying in villages en route. If you take public boats all the way, reckon on about Ar50,000 per person, not including accommodation, for the whole trip.

If you are coming from Antananarivo, the usual places to start a tour of the canal are Manombato, a tiny village on the shores of Lac Rasobe, or Ambila-Lemaitso, where there are several hotels.

Watch out for the green barge called *Imitso*, which runs between Toamasina and Vatomandry, carrying merchandise and a few pas-

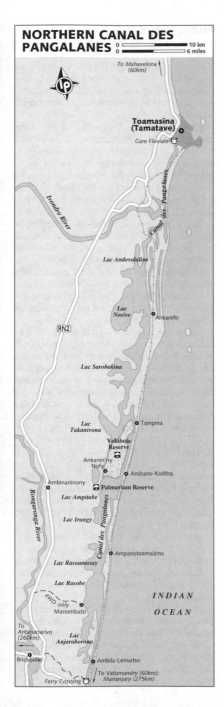

NORTHERN CANAL DES PANGALANES

0 — 10 km
0 — 6 miles

To Mahavelona (60km)

Toamasina (Tamatave)
Gare Fluviale

Ivondro River

Canal des Pangalanes

Lac Andovolaline

Lac Nosive — Ankarefo

RN2

Lac Sarobakina

Lac Takanivona — Tampina

Vohibola Reserve

Ankanin'ny Nofy

Andrano-Koditra

Ambinaninony

Palmarium Reserve

Lac Ampitabe

Lac Irangy

Canal des Pangalanes

Ampanotoamaizina

Lac Rasoamasay

Lac Rasobe

Rongaronga River

4WD only
To Manombato

INDIAN OCEAN

To Antananarivo (260km)

Lac Anjaraborona

Brickaville

Ambila-Lemaitso

Ferry Crossing

To Vatomandry (60km); Mananjary (275km)

sengers (the fare is Ar2500 from Ankanin'ny Nofy to Toamasina).

La Compagnie du Canal (☎ 53 351 48; compagnie ducanal@wanadoo.mg; Rue Maitre Nativel; ☒ 6-7am & 10am-5pm Mon-Sat, to noon Sun) runs daily boat services to Manambato (€50) via Ankanin'ny Nofy (€35); there are discounted rates for groups of five or more.

Lac Ampitabe & Vohibola

Accessible only by boat, Lac Ampitabe is a great place to go and get away after a few days on the river. It is peaceful, with white sandy beaches and a wonderful private wildlife park. The **Palmarium Reserve** (☎ 033 14 847 34; admission Ar10,000; ☒ dawn-night) recently changed ownership (it was Le Reserve d'Akanin'ny Nofy, named for the village of Akanin'ny Nofy, northeast of the lake), and protects 50 hectares of palm-tree forests. Inside you'll find wide, well-maintained trails, and several species of incredibly tame lemur, including Coquerel's sifaka and some very tame black-and-white ruffed lemurs. There's also a good selection of reptiles on another island just offshore.

The adjacent **Le Palmarium Hotel** (☎ 033 14 847 34; hotelpalmarium@yahoo.fr; bungalows from Ar70,000) is owned by the same people as the reserve. The bungalows are large with hot-water bathrooms – almost posh for the wilderness. Night-time entertainment is provided by Philibert, a tame vasa parrot, and a pair of clowning lemurs. Meals can be arranged for Ar15,000.

The German-run **Bush House** (☎ 22 258 78; www.boogiepilgram-madagascar.com; r & bungalows per person from Ar75,000), just across from the reserve, is another option. It has charming staff, a great atmosphere and simple but rustically attractive rooms. Rates include full board. Walks, boats and canoe trips can be arranged to visit local village projects supported by the hotel, as well as the lemur reserve and the sea beach on the other side of the lake. All the guests eat together in the evenings, and the food is superb. Speedboat transfers from Toamasina/Manombato cost €159/38 per boat for up to six people. Near Bush House is l'Île aux Nepenthes, an islet containing hundreds of carnivorous pitcher plants.

Don't miss a visit to **Vohibola**, the newest ecotourism initiative from **Man and the Environment** (MATE; ☎ in Antananarivo 22 674 90; www.mate .mg). A visit to this preserve is a great way to see a Madagascan-started NGO with the goal of teaching local people about conservation.

Vohibola in an interesting area between the Indian Ocean, lakes and the Canal des Pangalanes, about 45 minutes south of Ankanin'ny Nofy by boat. The project protects one of the two largest remaining pieces of littoral forest in the country, home to a number of highly endangered tree species. When MATE employees began exploring the forest they discovered a rare and extremely endangered tree, the *Humbertiodendron saboureaui*, which had not been seen in 50 years and was thought to be extinct. Visitors have the opportunity to plant an indigenous tree from the extensive nursery should they wish. You should. Placing the little tree in the ground is not only a small way to give back, it makes you feel great to boot!

For now there are just two hiking trails, the Discovery Trail and the Wetlands Trail, each with unique scenery. Other activities are planned including canoeing and mountain biking. Contact MATE for all details on access, tariffs and facilities; volunteer placements may be available.

Lac Rasoamasay
The main place to stay here is **Ony Hôtel** (☎ 030 55 850 88; http://onyhotel.free.fr; r Ar30,000), on the northern side of the lake. Camping is also possible.

Lac Rasobe & Manombato
On the southwestern edge of Lac Rasobe and about 1km south of the village of Manombato lies a beautiful white-sand beach with a number of (expensive) hotels spread along it. This is the starting point for many tours of the northern canal area. Manombato village is connected with the main road by a sandy 7km track (4WD only). The turn-off from the RN2 is about 11km north of Brickaville. There's no public transport from Brickaville, so you'll have to charter a car there or hitch or walk from the turn-off.

The best hotels are **Chez Luigi** (☎ 56 720 20; d/tr Ar40,000/50,000), which has large and luxurious bungalows and does water-skiing, transfers and canoe trips, and **Les Acacias** (☎ 56 720 35; socyin@simicro.mg; d with cold/hot water Ar30,000/40,000), which offers boat hire to Ankanin'ny Nofy for Ar150,000 per boat (up to six people). **Hotel Rasoa Beach** (☎ 56 720 18; d Ar35,000) has good-value six-person rooms, but is otherwise overpriced.

The cheapest option is the basic **Hibiscus** (r Ar15,000), which has shared bucket showers and is slightly away from the beach.

Ambila-Lemaitso
This sleepy seaside village, regularly flattened by cyclones, is a good place to start a tour of Canal des Pangalanes. There's a long, white beach, but ask about sharks and currents before swimming. Canoes (Ar10,000 per day) can be hired from **Kayak Nari** in the centre of town.

Just after the ferry crossing as you come from Brickaville is the friendly **Le Nirvana** (r Ar20,000), a very atmospheric but decaying set of bungalows on a narrow strip of land between the canal and the sea. There's a peaceful wooden jetty overlooking the canal. This is a good place to find out about transport up and down the canal.

In the village itself, **Hôtel Relais Malaky** (☎ 56 720 22; d/tr Ar18,000/25,000) has a faded, colonial air and sea views, with a decent restaurant downstairs. A bit further outside the village is **Hotel Ambila Beach** (☎ 030 23 847 85; camping Ar8000, tr Ar20,000), which has a terrace overlooking the river. **Le Tropicana** (r Ar10,000) is the cheapest option, with basic bungalows on a small beach on the river.

To get to Ambila-Lemaitso from Brickaville, you'll have to charter a private car in town to follow the sandy road from the northern edge of town east for about 18km to a small ferry crossing over the canal. From the ferry crossing, it's another 4km north along a sandy track to Ambila-Lemaitso. At Ambila-Lemaitso you can inquire about boats heading up or down the canal.

MANANJARY
pop 24,500
Mananjary (manan-dzar) is an agreeable, relaxed backwater sliced into two parts by the Canal des Pangalanes. It is also a local centre for production of vanilla, coffee and pepper.

Every seven years, the small Antambohoaka tribe holds mass circumcision ceremonies in Mananjary, known as *sambatra* (the actual operations are now performed in the hospital). Similar ceremonies are also held in surrounding villages.

North of Mananjary at Ambohitsara is the locally revered **White Elephant** sculpture. This relic is attributed to the Zeïdistes, descendants of the prophet Mohammed who first landed at Iharana on Madagascar's northeast coast and then moved south. Despite the name, it bears little resemblance to an elephant.

Sleeping & Eating

The most comfortable place in town is **Hôtel Jardin de la Mer** (☎ 72 942 24; d Ar20,000), near the water, about 1km from the centre of town with well-kept bungalows and a good restaurant. The hotel organises trips on the canal and in the surrounding area.

On the ocean side of the canal, **Hôtel Sorafa** (☎ 72 942 50; fax 72 943 23; r Ar22,000-25,000), formerly called the Solimotel, has decent rooms on the seafront and a restaurant. Mountain bikes can sometimes be hired here.

Getting There & Away

Daily taxis-brousses connect Mananjary with Fianarantsoa (Ar15,000, six hours) and Manakara (Ar12,000, four hours). For Manakara,

you may need to get off at the junction village of Irondro and wait for a connection.

There is no direct road access from Mananjary to Toamasina.

MANAKARA

pop 31,500

Manakara is a quiet Malagasy town with wide unpaved streets and an end-of-the-world feel. It is known primarily as the terminus of the train line from Fianarantsoa. Manakara has some long, pine-fringed beaches, but sharks and strong currents mean that swimming is not possible here.

Manakara is divided into two parts. In the centre, known as Tanambao, are the train and taxi-brousse stations, the market and

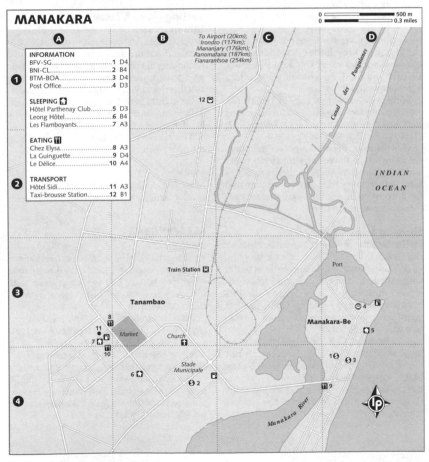

MANAKARA

```
0 ———————— 500 m
0 ———————— 0.3 miles
```

INFORMATION
BFV-SG 1 D4
BNI-CL 2 B4
BTM-BOA 3 D4
Post Office 4 D3

SLEEPING 🏠
Hôtel Parthenay Club 5 D3
Leong Hôtel 6 B4
Les Flamboyants 7 A3

EATING 🍴
Chez Elysa 8 A3
La Guinguette 9 D4
Le Délice 10 A4

TRANSPORT
Hôtel Sidi 11 A3
Taxi-brousse Station 12 B1

To Airport (20km);
Irondro (117km);
Mananjary (176km);
Ranomafana (187km);
Fianarantsoa (254km)

Canal des Pangalanes

INDIAN OCEAN

Port

Train Station

Tanambao

Market

Church

Manakara-Be

Stade Municipale

Manakara River

POUSSE OFF

The *pousse-pousse* is king in Manakara, but of all the towns in Madagascar, we never encountered as many aggressive, underhand and plain dishonest tactics as we did here. Tourists can expect to be hassled persistently, and even locals might have problems! We strongly recommend avoiding the *pousses* altogether, but if you do decide to take one, be assertive, confirm the price several times up front (it should never be more than Ar1000), and don't take any crap from anyone. Luckily it's easy enough to walk around the town, but if you do need alternative transport, ask at your hotel about hiring a bike, or look for the town's solitary charter taxi.

some hotels. Over the lagoonlike estuary of the Manakara River is the old seaside district of Manakara-Be, where you'll find BFV-SG, BNI-CL and BTM-BOA banks, a post office, a few hotels and the beach.

For bicycle, car or boat trips in Manakara's surrounding area, as well as excursions along the Canal des Pangalanes, contact **Sylvain** (☎ 72 216 68), an English-speaking guide.

One warning: the *pousse-pousse* men here are the worst in the country for cheap tricks and bullying behaviour, and they turn out in force to meet every train arrival – be prepared for the onslaught! See the boxed text (above) for advice and alternatives.

Sleeping & Eating

Les Flamboyants (☎ 72 216 77; lionelmanakara@dts.mg; r incl breakfast €6.50; 🖳) This is an exceptionally good-value guesthouse in the centre of town, with a shady 1st-floor terrace and French poetry on the bedroom walls. There's also lots of local information available. This is the first guesthouse the *pousses-pousses* from the station will take you to.

Hôtel Parthenay Club (☎ 72 216 63; Manakara-Be; bungalow Ar25,000; 🏊) A slightly decaying but still charming hotel in gardens down by the beach, with a rather forbidding-looking concrete swimming pool and a tennis court (plus racquets). The restaurant food has a good reputation.

Magneva Hôtel (☎ 72 714 73; d Ar28,000) If you don't mind being about 2km out of town, this is a very comfortable and peaceful option. The big, tiled rooms and bungalows set amid tranquil gardens have hot water, and a car is available for going in and out of town. Ring for a pickup, as it's too far to go in a *pousse-pousse*.

Hôtel Morabe and Le Délice are two good, simple local hotels near the market. The food at Le Délice is excellent.

La Guinguette (☎ 72 213 92; ⏰ lunch & dinner Wed-Mon), down by the beach in Manakara-Be, has a good selection of seafood and French dishes. Chez Elysa, diagonally opposite Les Flamboyants, serves drinks and snacks, and has a lively atmosphere. There's occasional live music.

Getting There & Away
TAXI-BROUSSE
At least one taxi-brousse daily connects Manakara and Ranomafana (Ar15,000, six hours) continuing to Fianarantsoa (nine hours). These wait until at least 4pm before setting off, so you'll arrive at your destination in the middle of the night. There is usually one direct vehicle daily to Mananjary (Ar10,000, four hours) and Farafangana (Ar8000, three hours).

The taxi-brousse station is located 2km north of town.

TRAIN
Most travellers prefer to travel at least one way by train from Fianarantsoa; see p108 for details.

FARAFANGANA
pop 22,000
Farafangana is at the southern extreme of the Canal des Pangalanes, and is 109km by road south of Manakara. It is a quiet town with nothing special to do, but it has a friendly, relaxed ambience.

Hôtel Les Cocotiers (☎ 73 911 87; ranarson@dts.mg; r Ar25,000) and its annexe **Le Coco Beach** (☎ 73 911 88) provide the best lodgings in town.

There is generally a daily taxi-brousse travelling between Farafangana and Manakara (Ar8000, three hours). There is no public transport along the 315km road to Fort Dauphin, so you'll have to fly. Air Madagascar has weekly flights for around €100.

Comoros

THOR VAZ DE LEON

234

Comoros

Haphazardly scattered across the Indian Ocean, the mysterious, outrageous and enchanting Comoros islands are the kind of place you go to just drop off the planet for a while. Far removed from the clutter that comes with conventional paradises – sprawling hotels, neon discos – the Comoros are so remote even an international fugitive could hide out here.

Rich in Swahili culture, and devoutly Muslim, the charming inhabitants come from a legendary stock of Arab traders, Persian sultans, African slaves and Portuguese pirates. The four developed islands offer everything from relaxing on white-sand beaches by turquoise seas to hiking through rainforests on the lookout for giant bats.

Nicknamed 'Cloud Coup-Coup' land because of their crazy politics, the three independent islands (the fourth, Mayotte, is still a part of France) have experienced almost 20 coups since gaining independence in 1975! In fact, a Comorian president is lucky if there's time for his official portrait to be taken before armed men are once again knocking on the door. In the last decade, however, the quarrelsome tiff-prone independent islands agreed to put their differences aside and fly under the joint banner of the Union des Comores.

Holidaying in the Comoros isn't for everyone; travel will kick your arse at times. But it teaches lessons in patience, humility and resilience. Everything moves *mora mora* (slowly slowly) and tourism facilities are far from plush. Islam, and all its traditions, is evident everywhere. Women are expected to show modesty and cover up, and alcohol is a no-no for both sexes.

But if your idea of the perfect holiday is less about drinking rum punch in a skimpy bikini at a swank resort, and more about long, lazy days sipping tea and talking politics with the locals, then a safari in the exotic Comoros will probably be the kind of unpredictable, swashbuckling adventure you've been craving.

HIGHLIGHTS

- Wandering the labyrinthine stone streets of Moroni's old **Arab quarter** (p241)
- Exploring the smallest, wildest and most interesting Comore, **Mohéli** (p245), with fabulous beaches and turquoise seas
- Hiking through the cool, misty highlands and clove and ylang-ylang scented beachside plantations of **Anjouan** (p249)
- Swimming with sea turtles off the coast of Mayotte in **Sazilé** (p261)
- Camping in the desert landscape created by the 2005 eruption of **Mt Karthala** (p237)

- HIGHEST POINT: 2360m - PRINCIPAL LANGUAGES: Arabic, French, Shimashiwa (Swahili)

GRANDE COMORE

pop 360,000

The biggest (and most politically bullying) of the three islands, Grande Comore is also dominated by the largest active volcano in the world, Mt Karthala (2360m) – over the last 200 years it has consistently erupted once every 11 years on average. The last eruption spewed lava for a full 14 days in December 2005. It flattened villages, contaminated drinking water and killed at least one child. This came on the heels of the tourism crisis of 2002, when the islands' switch to a new constitution had foreign state departments warning people to steer clear for a while. Mt Karthala's eruption only further decimated the island's already struggling tourism industry. This is a shame, because two years after the explosion Grande Comore has picked up the pieces. And the good news that has come out of the volcano's latest blast is the spectacular desert landscape it created on the mountain – the hiking is particularly fantastic, and unique, these days.

Aside from being the largest island at 60km by 20km, Grande Comore is also the most economically developed of the three independent islands that make up the Union des Comores. Grande Comore (known as Ngazidja by the Comorians) wields the most political power of the three islands from the seat of its handsome main town, Moroni. The island is fringed by solidified lava and sandy beaches of various hues, where brilliant white meets dark volcanic grey and molten black. What little agricultural land is still available is found in the south, where there are banana, breadfruit, cassava, vanilla, ylang-ylang and coconut plantations. Most of the island's population and activity is concentrated on the west coast. The sparsely populated and dramatically beautiful east coast remains quiet and traditional, with only a few tiny thatched-hut villages. Couples looking for a simple but romantic holiday away from everyone else will like it here.

History

For information on the history of the Comoros, see p29.

COMOROS

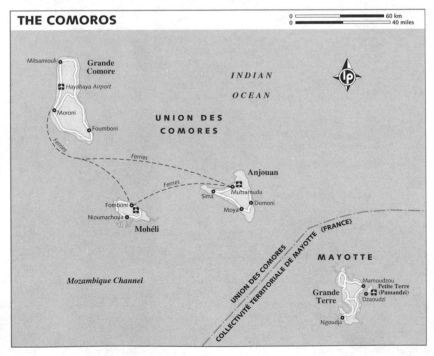

THE COMOROS

COMOROS

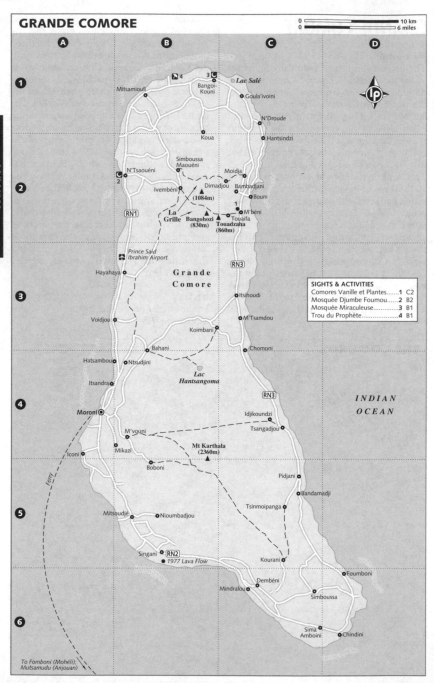

GRANDE COMORE

0 _____ 10 km
0 _____ 6 miles

A **B** **C** **D**

1

Mitsamiouli
Bangoi-Kouni
4
3
Lac Salé
Goula'ivoini

N'Droude

Koua
Hantsindzi

2

Simboussa Maouéni
N'Tsaouéni
2
Moidja
Ivembéni
Dimadjou
Bambadjani
× (1084m)
Bouni
RN1
La Grille
Bangohozi (830m)
M'béni
1
Touaifa
Touadzaha (860m)

Prince Said Ibrahim Airport

Hayahaya

3

G r a n d e
C o m o r e
Itsihoudi
RN3
Voidjou
M'Tsamdou
Koimbani
Chomoni
Bahani
Hatsambou
Ntsudjini
Itsandra
Lac Hantsangoma
RN3

INDIAN OCEAN

4

Moroni
Idjikoundzi
M'vouni
Tsangadjou
Iconi
Mikazi
Mt Karthala (2360m)
Boboni

ferry

Pidjani

5

Mitsoudjé
Nioumbadjou
Tsinmoipanga
Bandamadji

Singani
RN2
1977 Lava Flow
Kourani

6

Dembéni
Foumboni
Mindralou
Simboussa
Sima Amboini
Chindini

To Fomboni (Mohéli); Mutsamudu (Anjouan)

SIGHTS & ACTIVITIES
Comores Vanille et Plantes	1	C2
Mosquée Djumbe Foumou	2	B2
Mosquée Miraculeuse	3	B1
Trou du Prophète	4	B1

Orientation

Grande Comore's Prince Saïd Ibrahim Airport lies about 19km north of Moroni, the capital, in the village of Hayahaya. Boats arriving in Grande Comore come into the port in central Moroni. Moroni is the only place on the island with any real infrastructure, but tarmac roads in reasonably good condition run around the perimeter of the island, with those in the north being in the best condition.

After a short time travelling around Grande Comore, you will notice one annoying factor: there are no signposts anywhere. To know where you are and where you are going, you will have to guess, follow a detailed map or keep asking people.

Information

Grande Comore, like the other islands in the group, is overwhelmingly (and tolerantly) Muslim. Visitors are asked to dress modestly when away from the beach, meaning no shorts or low-cut tops for women, and no bare-chested men. Topless swimming or sunbathing are not acceptable. During the holy month of Ramadan (see p266), the population of the Comoros fasts from dawn to dusk and most restaurants are closed. Shops and other businesses open earlier and close earlier during this period as well, especially on Fridays. Travellers should respect the sensibilities of the population and refrain from eating, drinking or smoking in public during daylight hours. During the rest of the year, nearly everything in the Comoros shuts down between Friday afternoon and Monday morning – be prepared.

Grande Comore has telephone and postal services in the larger cities. The island also boasts a limited, but growing, mobile phone network. Note that even with a local SIM card calls are still very expensive. There are now internet cafés all around the island, not just in Moroni (p239), although whether they are open depends on whether Grande Comore has any power, which is never a given.

The **BIC** (☎ 73 12 04; Pl de France) in Moroni can change cash and travellers cheques and does Visa cash advances when the phone lines are working. It's best to just bring as many euros with you as you plan to spend – it saves a lot of time and they can be changed anywhere on the islands, from banks to hotels. There are no moneychanging facilities at the airport so make sure you have enough euros (or at a pinch – and be ready to get ripped off – US

dollars) to get a taxi to your hotel and to last until you get to a bank.

El Maarouf Hospital (Map p240; ☎ 73 26 04; Rte Magoudjou, Moroni) has been revamped with a large injection of overseas aid, and is now just about acceptable for minor medical problems although it still routinely runs out of plasters and medicine. If you can't get to the hospital, and you are badly hurt, you can try ringing the **police** (Map p240; ☎ 74 46 63; Ave des Ministères, Moroni) for help. They are also useful for nonmedical emergencies. You should have travel insurance, as any major medical problems will require you to be airlifted to South Africa.

Activities

Grande Comore's water activities are pretty much limited to the dive company listed here, but the island is home to some good swimming beaches and fabulous volcano hikes.

DIVING

Grande Comore is the only island of the independent Comoros that has a proper dive centre. **Itsandra Plongée** (off Map p240; ☎ 73 29 76; poumka@ifrance.com; 1 dive/5 dives CF20,000/75,300, NAUI Open Water course CF115,000), based on the beach in the village of Itsandra, is French-run and by all accounts fairly reputable. It's not always open, however, so it's best to ring or email them in advance.

HIKING

Grande Comore has some very rewarding hikes, including to Mt Karthala and La Grille.

Mt Karthala

This is one of the world's most active volcanoes and forms the base for much of the island. The volcano last erupted in 2005, which was both tragic – one child died and villages were damaged – but also beautiful, as its lava carved a stupendous desert out of the mountain landscape. It's possible to climb Mt Karthala in a very long day, but it's much more fun to carry camping equipment and spend a day or two exploring the summit. The trek should only be attempted during the dry season (between April and November). The most popular routes begin at M'vouni or further up at Boboni. However, the road between M'vouni and Boboni is almost impassable by normal vehicles, so you will have to take a 4WD or trek there. It takes at least seven hours to climb from M'vouni to the summit and about five hours from Boboni.

Although the summit and the crater are frequently clear, the slopes are normally blanketed in thick mist for much of the day. The best and most sheltered camp site is within the crater itself. Especially since the latest eruption, it's really important to take a guide along. Be sure to carry all the food and water you'll need for the trip, and don't underestimate the amount of water you'll require. Unless you are really fit, you may want to take a porter, which should cost less than half of what you end up paying for a guide.

Chauffera (☎ 73 02 16) is a Moroni guide recommended by readers who also provides sleeping bags and tents. He is very professional and friendly, and charges about CF65,000 for a two-day trip. Bartering is possible.

Comores Travel Services (☎ 77 00 55; comotour@ yahoo.fr; Mbéni; tent hire CF5000, 2-day expedition per person CF76,000) is also recommended. The company specialises in taking walkers up the volcano and hires camping equipment. When arranging a trip, be sure to sort out any particulars, such as who will provide and carry food, water and equipment, before you leave. Also make sure you find out the full price before departing, so there are no problems at the end.

Getting There & Around

Patience is the key to getting around Grande Comore particularly along the east coast. It can take hours for buses to show up, if they do, and breakdowns are frequent. Boats can be absolute death-traps, with no safety regulations enforced (if any even exist) and no life jackets. They are rickety affairs that look like their weathered wood has been patched up one too many times. Seas in the Comoros can get very rough, and boats between the three islands will not travel if the water is too rough. The independent islands don't much like French-owned Mayotte, believing it should belong to them, and boat travel between it and the other Comoros is pretty much nonexistent. Airlines, however, care more about profit than politics, so it is easy to fly.

AIR

Grande Comore is currently served by the following international airlines:

Air Austral (Map p240; ☎ 73 31 44; www.air-austral .com in French; Quartier Oasis, Moroni) Flies several times a week between Moroni, Mayotte, Mauritius and Réunion. Connections in Mayotte for flights to Madagascar.

Air Madagascar (Map p240; ☎ 73 55 40; www .airmadagascar.mg; Quartier Oasis, Moroni) Used to fly between Moroni and Mahajanga on the west coast of Madagascar, with connections to Antananarivo. At the time of research this service was suspended, but it may well be worth checking to see if it's resumed.

Air Seychelles (Map p240; ☎ 73 31 44; www.air seychelles.net; Rue Magoudjou, Quartier Oasis, Moroni) Weekly flights between Moroni and Malé and connections through Paris.

As well as the international flights listed above, Grande Comore is served by two internal airlines, Comores Aviation and Comores Air Service, which fly their small planes almost daily to the islands of Anjouan and Mohéli. Comores Aviation also provides services to Mayotte.

Comores Aviation (Map p240; ☎ 73 34 00; comores .avi@snpt.km; Blvd de la Corniche, Moroni) and **Comores Air Service** (Map p240; ☎ 73 33 66; cas@snpt.com; Blvd El Marrouf, Moroni) provide a reasonably efficient and easy way to fly between the islands. A hop from Moroni to Mohéli costs around CF20,000, and flights go three times a week. To Mayotte the fare is CF44,500 (also three flights per week). Comores Air Service does a circular ticket taking in all three islands for CF72,000. Both airlines can also fly you to Mahajanga (CF109,000) in Madagascar once a week.

BOAT

Boats regularly ply between Grande Comore and the other islands in the archipelago, although finding one to Mayotte (not in the good graces of the other three islands that claim it as their own) can be difficult. Anjouan is probably the easiest destination to get to. If you've got a bit longer to wait you could hop a boat to go further afield without too much difficulty – the usual destinations are Zanzibar, Mombasa in Kenya, or Mahajanga in Madagascar. To find a boat, head for the port in Moroni where various makeshift offices along the seafront display the latest comings and goings on blackboards outside.

Please note that the safety and quality of boats vary widely and some vessels are so shaky they are downright scary. Life jackets on any boat are a rare thing, and if the seas are too rough your driver will turn around. Try to see the vessel before you buy your ticket as some are true death-traps. One of the best ferries is *Alliance des Îles* to Anjouan (CF11,500, five hours). To Mohéli boats are smaller and less frequent, as the port is often ignored by bigger ships (CF9150, four to six hours).

CAR
Hiring a car on Grande Comore can only be arranged in Moroni. Prices are reasonably standard – €40 per day, plus petrol. Most cars come with a driver for the same price, which is a good thing since the roads are steep and winding and signposts nonexistent.

TAXI-BROUSSE
Long-distance routes are served by taxis-brousses (bush taxis), which mostly take the form of minibuses, although there are a few *bâchés* (small, converted pick-ups) too. Because the east coast is so sparsely populated, very few taxis-brousses travel between M'beni or Pidjani and Chomoni, so circling the entire island by public transport is very difficult (but not impossible). Like everything else on the island, public transport seems to slow down between 11.30am and 3pm, and after dark (or by 4pm during Ramadan) it virtually stops.

MORONI
pop 44,518

Moroni feels like another world. It is a timeless place where the air is heavy with romanticised Arabia – a great introduction to the Comoros if you've just arrived. Wandering the narrow streets of the old Arab quarter, you'll pass women in colourful wraps chatting on crumbling stone doorsteps, and grave groups of white-robed men whiling away the hours between prayers with games of dominoes played on smooth stone benches. Unfortunately, the place is quite dirty – throwing rubbish on the street is common practice, and the government has yet to figure out what to do with sewage and waste water. As a result, the odour emitting from these quaint streets can be rather disillusioning.

Moroni had its beginnings as the seat of an ancient sultanate that traded primarily with Zanzibar (in Tanzania). In Comorian, the name means 'in the heart of the fire', in reference to its proximity to Mt Karthala. At sunset Moroni harbour must be one of the most beautiful sights in the Indian Ocean. The fading orange light is reflected by the coral-walled Ancienne Mosquée du Vendredi (Old Friday Mosque, p241), the whitewashed buildings of the seafront and the dozens of wooden boats moored between volcanic rock

jetties. At dusk there are often hundreds of men and boys swimming here, with the giant silhouettes of fruit bats flapping overhead.

Orientation
From the airport at Hayahaya, the quickest and easiest way into Moroni is by hopping into a shared taxi with some other passengers, which will cost you CF1000 (about €2). If you arrive in the port, you can simply walk or hail a shared taxi to take you to your chosen hotel.

From the north a couple of main roads lead to the appropriately named Ave des Ministères, where there are some government offices, including the tourist office. The confusing *medina* (old Arab quarter), with its maze of narrow lanes, is found between the harbour and the bazaar. The Ave de Republic Populaire de China, which passes the port and stadium, is thus named because it ends at the huge, incongruous and Chinese-built Peoples' Palace, a long low building with arched windows that resembles a shopping arcade.

Information
The Comoros recently split its phone and postal services, but hasn't gone about changing names yet, and it seems to be arbitrary which post offices sell phonecards and which sell stamps. You'll probably need to try a few.

If you just need to use a card phone for a few minutes, there are always touts posted outside phone booths more than willing to let you use their phonecard – for a small commission of course. Still it works out cheaper if you're just ringing a hotel or two, as you only pay for the units (block of minutes) you use. Plus it saves you from partaking in an often frustrating search for a phonecard!

New internet cafés are opening (and closing) around town every month.

BIC (☎ 73 12 04; Pl de France; ☼ 7.15am-2pm Mon-Thu, to 11am Fri) The only place to change cash or travellers cheques. Also does advances on Visa cards for a hefty commission and has a branch of Western Union. It closes one hour earlier during Ramadan. BIC maintains two ATMs in town, but these only seem to accept local cards.

Cyber Nassib (☎ 73 25 00; per hr CF900) In the popular café of the same name; has a fast connection and headsets for internet phone calls and is popular with teenage gamers. Connections are fast and cheap for the Comoros.

Direction Generale du Tourisme (☎ 74 42 43; dg.tourisme@snpt.km; Ave des Ministères; ☼ 7.30am-2.30pm Mon-Thu, to 11.30am Fri) There's no official tourist

COMOROS

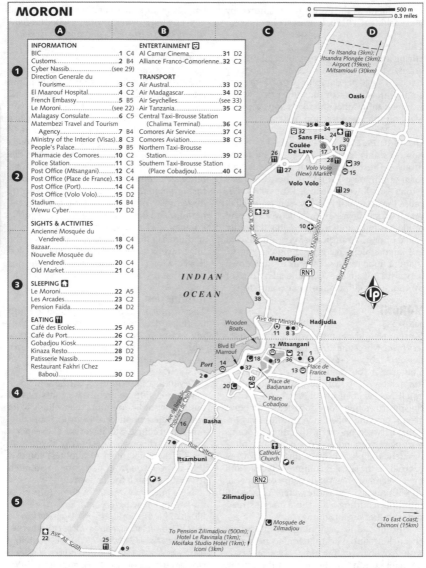

MORONI

0 _____ 500 m
0 _____ 0.3 miles

INFORMATION
BIC.................................**1** C4
Customs...........................**2** B4
Cyber Nassib...................(see 29)
Direction Generale du
  Tourisme.......................**3** C3
El Maarouf Hospital..............**4** C2
French Embassy..................**5** B5
Le Moroni........................(see 22)
Malagasy Consulate...............**6** C5
Matembezi Travel and Tourism
  Agency..........................**7** B4
Ministry of the Interior (Visas)..**8** C3
People's Palace...................**9** B5
Pharmacie des Comores..........**10** C2
Police Station...................**11** C3
Post Office (Mtsangani)..........**12** C4
Post Office (Place de France)....**13** C4
Post Office (Port)...............**14** C4
Post Office (Volo Volo)..........**15** D2
Stadium..........................**16** B4
Wewu Cyber......................**17** D2

SIGHTS & ACTIVITIES
Ancienne Mosquée du
  Vendredi.......................**18** C4
Bazaar............................**19** C4
Nouvelle Mosquée du
  Vendredi.......................**20** C4
Old Market........................**21** C4

SLEEPING
Le Moroni.........................**22** A5
Les Arcades.......................**23** C2
Pension Faida.....................**24** D2

EATING
Café des Ecoles...................**25** A5
Café du Port......................**26** C2
Gobadjou Kiosk....................**27** C2
Kinaza Resto......................**28** D2
Patisserie Nassib.................**29** D2
Restaurant Fakhri (Chez
  Babou)..........................**30** D2

ENTERTAINMENT
Al Camar Cinema..................**31** D2
Alliance Franco-Comorienne......**32** C2

TRANSPORT
Air Austral.......................**33** D2
Air Madagascar....................**34** D2
Air Seychelles...................(see 33)
Air Tanzania......................**35** C2
Central Taxi-Brousse Station
  (Chalima Terminal).............**36** C4
Comores Air Service...............**37** C4
Comores Aviation..................**38** C3
Northern Taxi-Brousse
  Station.........................**39** D2
Southern Taxi-Brousse Station
  (Place Cobadjou)...............**40** C4

INDIAN OCEAN

To Itsandra (3km);
Itsandra Plongée (3km);
Airport (19km);
Mitsamiouli (30km)

Oasis

Sans Fils
Coulée De Lave
Volo Volo (New) Market
Volo Volo

Magoudjou

Hadjudia

Wooden Boats
Mtsangani
Port
Place de France
Dashe

Place de Badjanani
Place Cobadjou

Basha

Itsambuni

Catholic Church

Zilimadjou

Mosquée de Zilimadjou

To East Coast;
Chimoni (15km)

To Pension Zilimadjou (500m);
Hotel Le Ravinala (1km);
Moifaka Studio Hotel (1km);
Iconi (3km)

---

office in Moroni, but you can get a helpful list of hotels and *pensions* from this government-run organisation.

Le Moroni (☎ 73 52 42/64/74; lemoroni@bow.snpt.km; Ave Ali Soilih) This upmarket hotel organises day trips taking in all the island's major attractions. A boat trip to the beaches in the north of the island costs €35 per person, a full-day island tour costs €45, and a two-day expedition up Mt Karthala is €200. All prices are based on a group of four.

Matembezi Travel and Tourism Agency (☎ 73 04 00; agence.matembezi@snpt.km; Rue Caltex) This very professional and friendly tour operator can organise hikes, picnics and other full- or half-day trips for around €35. It also organises hikes up Mt Karthala, and rents cars with or without a driver from €45 per day, excluding fuel.

Pharmacie des Comores (☎ 73 22 73; Rte Magoudjou; ⏰ 8am-1pm & 4-7pm Sat-Thu, 8-11.30am & 4-7pm

Fri) Try this place for minor medical problems. See p237 for details of emergency medical services in Moroni.

Post offices (☎ 7.30am-2.30pm Mon-Thu, to 11am Fri) All four post offices have phone boxes but not all sell phonecards. The post offices also offer internet access for CF500 per hour.

Sights

ARAB QUARTER (OLD TOWN)

The area around the port and the Ancienne Mosquée du Vendredi (Old Friday Mosque) is a convoluted *medina* with narrow streets lined with buildings dating back to Swahili times. It's reminiscent of a miniature version of Zanzibar's Stone Town and almost as intriguing. Here you can spend at least an hour wandering aimlessly, chatting with locals or joining in a game of dominoes or *bao* (an ancient African game played using a board carved with 32 holes). Watch for the elaborately carved Swahili doors found on many houses.

MOSQUES

The most imposing structure along the waterfront is the off-white **Ancienne Mosquée du Vendredi**, a two-storey building with elegant colonnades and a square minaret. The original structure dates back to 1427, though the minaret was added early last century.

Today Friday worship takes place at the magnificent **Nouvelle Mosquée du Vendredi** (New Friday Mosque) next to the port. In between prayers, the steps outside the mosques serve as a meeting place for the town's menfolk, many dressed in the traditional *kanzu* (long white robe) and *kofia* (skull cap). To see the interior of any of the mosques, you have to be male, appropriately dressed (in long trousers) and go through the ritual washing of the feet before entering.

BAZAAR & OLD MARKET

Moroni's bazaar and old covered market, which sprawl down the road past the BIC, are a hectic mess of noise, smell and colour. Women in gaily coloured *chiromani* (cloth wraps), their faces plastered in yellow sandalwood paste, huddle over piles of fruit, vegetables and fish, waving off clouds of flies and trying to avoid being crushed by the throngs of pedestrians and vehicles jostling through the bottleneck. In among it all are wide boys (hawkers) flogging plastic sunglasses, Muslim zealots haranguing the crowds, and toddlers playing in the dust. The men in the bazaar generally don't mind being

photographed or filmed, although it's polite to ask first. The women will either screech refusals and wave you away, or demand money for their pictures.

Sleeping

Moroni has more options than anywhere else in the independent Comoros, although all will seem way overpriced if you've just arrived from Madagascar.

Pension Faida (☎ 73 22 11; Quartier Oasis; r CF7500-15,000) The budget traveller's choice, Faida has rooms in a family home either with private bath and fan or shared facilities. It's a bit rickety (the handles fall off the doors) and lacking in polish with tatty walls, but friendly and homely. Monsieur will hire himself and his car out for excursions for CF15,000 per day, plus petrol.

Les Arcades (☎ 73 19 42; Blvd de la Corniche; r CF11,500-44,500, breakfast €4; 🗱 🛋) This big pink edifice has so many different types of rooms it's hard to get your head around them. The cheaper ones have simple décor and come with TV, mozzie nets and air-con, while deluxe rooms are super smart and huge – some even have two showers! The pool looks a bit murky, but on-site massage is offered and there are terraced gardens for strolling.

Hotel Le Ravinala (☎ 73 51 90; r CF16,000-20,000; 🗱) Although very welcoming and friendly, this *pension* is difficult to find and far out of town. Screened rooms have TV and telephones but shared bathrooms. Bigger rooms with bathroom (full-size bath) and nets are also available. There's a comfortable sitting room and a restaurant (red-bean curry CF2500) so you don't have to wander far.

Moifaka Studio Hotel (☎ 73 15 56; hmoifaka@snpt.km; s/d from CF17,000/19,000; 🗱) Moifaka is an excellent option if you can do without the extra amenities provided by Le Moroni. Rooms are modern, clean and tiled, with TV and good en suite bathrooms. The most expensive rooms have satellite TV and air-con. The only disadvantage is that it's hard to find, as it's out of town in the suburbs towards Iconi. Take a taxi.

Le Moroni (☎ 73 52 42; lemoroni@bow.snpt.km; Ave Ali Soilih; s/d from €72/102; 🗱 🖴 🛋) Moroni's only international-standard hotel is the place to stay if you're feeling homesick for Western amenities. It features a business centre, swimming pool, excursion desk, bar, restaurant and even giant chess! The new-looking rooms are comfortable, have satellite TV and come in

COMOROS

two price tags – standard and luxe. The only difference between the two is a lack of safe and minibar in the standard rooms, and neither is worth paying an extra €20 for! The terrace restaurant overlooking the sea serves recommended pizzas along with the usual steaks and seafood from CF4500. There are a couple of decent vegetarian options too. Breakfast costs CF3000.

Eating & Drinking
Eating and drinking options are limited in Moroni, especially if you're here during Ramadan. The cheapest eats in town are the little food stalls and hole-in-the-wall restaurants along Rue Caltex and Blvd de la Corniche. **Café des Écoles** (Ave Ali Soilih), on the road towards Le Moroni, is one such place. It serves delicious fresh fruit juices. Café du Port, at the roundabout, is an alternative young Comorian hang-out that serves alcohol. You'll find it packed with animated locals chatting about life and politics over beers until dawn. The best coffee, cakes and crepes come from the **Gobadjou kiosk** (street eats per item CF150), also on the roundabout. Run by a friendly old man, it has chairs under a tree, and doubles as a taxi rank.

Kinaza Resto (☎ 73 27 68; Rte Magoudjou; mains from CF500; ☺ lunch & dinner) This restaurant recommended by readers serves a wide choice of food, including samosas, Comorian rice dishes and even burgers at more than fair prices.

Patisserie Nassib (☎ 73 84 60; Rte Magoudjou; pastries from CF500, mains from CF2000; ☺ 6am-11pm; ▣) The best patisserie in town turns into a very popular little café at night, serving burgers, kebabs and rice dishes on a pleasant terrace. In the morning come for fresh fruit juice, yogurt and crispy just-baked baguettes. If it's just bread and cake you're after, there's a bustling stall selling both out front.

ourpick Restaurant Fakhri (Chez Babou; ☎ 73 21 29; Quartier Oasis; mains CF4000; ☺ lunch & dinner Tue-Sun) Run by a family of voluble Indians, this is definitely the liveliest restaurant in town, featuring a huge terrace lit up with fairy lights and an outdoor ice-cream bar. The menu includes kebabs (cooked on an open barbecue), huge curry dishes (one portion is enough for two people), samosas and sandwiches, plus lots of fresh juice. There are also vegetarian options. The ice cream is to die for, and half the town turns up to get it in the evenings.

Entertainment
Films and concerts are shown regularly at the **Alliance Franco-Comorienne** (☎ 73 10 87; afc@snpt.km; Blvd de la Corniche; ☺ 7.30am-10pm Mon-Sat). The cultural centre also offers French courses, sports classes and even cabaret and karaoke! There's a library with French books, magazines and videos, internet access (per hour CF500), regular exhibitions and a hall for concerts. Films, which are all dubbed into French, cost CF300 and are shown weekly. Some activities are only open to members. The **cafeteria** (snacks CF1200; ☺ 7.30am-10pm Mon-Sat) serves alcohol.

Getting There & Around
There are three taxi-brousse stations in Moroni. The northern taxi-brousse station, near the new market in Volo Volo, serves the north and east. Vehicles here go to Itsandra (CF300, 20 minutes), the airport at Hayahaya (CF500, 30 minutes), Mitsamiouli (CF500, one hour), and as far as M'beni on the northeast coast. For destinations in central Grande Comore, mainly Chomoni (CF500, 40 minutes), taxis-brousses leave from the Chalima terminal, which is hidden away in the labyrinthine old town – ask a local to lead the way.

To southern destinations such as Foumboni (CF700, 1½ hours), taxis-brousses leave from the southern taxi-brousse station at Place Cobadjou, near the New Friday Mosque.

Once in town, getting around is as easy as walking or flagging down one of the hundreds of shared taxis, which will pick you up and deposit you anywhere in town for CF300, or a bit more for further destinations. You can easily take a shared taxi from town to the airport (CF1000), Itsandra (CF500) or Iconi (CF500).

To hire a car, ask at one of the hotels. Many taxi drivers double as one-man rental companies and can be hired out for the day. You get the driver as well. Car hire costs around CF15,000 per day.

ITSANDRA
Much less hectic, cleaner and prettier than Moroni, yet only 4km away, the village of Itsandra is a great place to base yourself during a stay in Grande Comore. There is a startling white-sand beach with super clear water, although it is definitely not isolated – groups of locals linger here all day, but this is pretty much true for any Grande Comore beach. The village has an excellent choice of hotels.

We only had space to include a few here, so wander around (it's a very small village) and see if something else catches your eye.

Motel Vanille (☎ 73 28 08; RN1; r from CF13,000) is a very good-value place and ideal if you want to be out of Moroni. Rooms have a sitting area, satellite TV, kitchen with fridge, bedroom with fan and mosquito net, and private bathroom. There's a supermarket underneath the hotel, and the owners will arrange for a cleaner if you're staying longer than a few days. You can also order a few Comorian specialities to be cooked for you (meals from CF2000). Car hire is available for around CF15,000 per day.

Another excellent place to stay that's been recommended by readers is Pension Manguier (☎ 73 20 81; RN1; r incl breakfast CF7500). The owner, Maoulida, is very friendly and helpful, and rooms, while simple, are clean, quiet and peaceful.

Itsandra is near enough to Moroni for you to take a shared taxi (CF300) into town to eat in the evenings.

HATSAMBOU

On the coast 3km north of Itsandra is the village of Hatsambou, visible from RN1 about 20m lower than the road. The Comoros is the world's second-largest producer of vanilla (after Madagascar) and here, on the inland side of the main road, is a small shed where green vanilla is graded and sorted. The workers can explain the vanilla producing and sorting processes (in French).

The Royal Itsandra Hotel (☎ 73 35 17; itsandrahot@ snpt.km; RN1; r from €58; 🛰) is now the only up-market beach hotel in Grande Comore. It's not especially charming, but entirely acceptable and with a lovely private beach and a good restaurant (mains from CF3000) – try the fish soup. Rooms are spacious, light and have sea views as well as a telephone, TV and full-size bathtub. There's a casino and piano bar providing nightlife, and every so often the hotel does a seafood buffet outside among the palm trees. Transfers from the airport can be arranged for CF5000 per car.

N'TSAOUÉNI

The sleepy village of N'Tsaouéni is also believed to be the final resting place of Caliph Mohammed Athoumani Kouba, a cousin of the Prophet Mohammed, and one of the founders of Islam in the Comoros. The location of his tomb is the subject of some dispute, but the best case can be made for the recently renovated tomb beside the old and crumbling Friday mosque. The building housing the tomb has a magnificently carved door, and the tomb itself is inside a larger cement structure, draped in colourful cloths. To see the tomb, ask the guardian, who lives in the house opposite the door, to let you in.

MITSAMIOULI
pop 6332

With a long sandy beach that's popular with youth playing pick-up football, Mitsamiouli, on the island's northern tip, is the second-largest town on Grande Comore. However, like Itsandra, the beaches are a bit public for sunbathing or relaxing, and there isn't a lot of shade. Because Mitsamiouli was home for years to a luxury South African hotel, many of the locals here speak some English.

Le Maloudja (☎ 78 81 56; r with breakfast CF15,000; 🛰), the only place to stay in Mitsamiouli since the demise of Grande Comore's only five-star hotel, is fairly decent, with simple, no-frills rooms, although it is a bit grimy. It's in a lovely spot, however, right on a magnificent beach and next to a small pocket of forest that's good for watching birds and even lemurs.

our pick Cool Memories (Rue du Ralima; local dishes CF1200; 🕑 lunch & dinner) is an excellent place serving local food in the centre of the village. Owner Zoro organises cultural tourism excursions around town. The interior is black and white with famous quotes on the walls. The exterior has an abstract tropical paint job, and there is a great central courtyard. Look for it one block back from the sea road.

TROU DU PROPHETE

The French name of this small bay, 2km east of Le Maloudja hotel, translates rather inelegantly as 'hole of the prophet'. Its much prettier local name is Zindoni. Legend has it that the Prophet Mohammed once made landfall in the harbour, and it almost certainly once served as a haven for 17th-century pirates. It's now a popular leisure spot bordered by a few French holiday villas, including the former home of Bob Denard (p31). It's signposted off the main road, but doesn't have much of a beach.

COMOROS

THE POMPEII OF GRANDE COMORE

The village of **Singani**, on the way from Moroni to Foumboni, likes to think of itself as the Pompeii of the Indian Ocean, and with pretty good reason. During the eruption of Mt Karthala in April 1977, locals spoke of the 'sky turning red like sunset'. The lava flow swept through the village, destroying everything in its path – only the school was spared.

Two weeks before the eruption occurred, a madman had taken to running through the village streets, warning people of an impending eruption. No-one listened, but three days prior to the eruption the earth began to quake and the man's warnings were taken more seriously. After the initial eruption, the village was evacuated before the lava reached the inhabited area and no-one was threatened except the man himself, who elected to remain in the school. Strangely enough, the stream of lava parted and spared the building. There he remained for several days until rescuers managed to dig through the lava. By that time, he'd lost whatever grip he'd ever had on reality. The only people in Singani who benefited from the volcano were the local football team – the ash was levelled into a large playing field.

BANGOI-KOUNI & LAC SALÉ

No-one in the small village of Bangoi-Kouni, about 3km further on, knows the origins of the so-called **Mosquée Miraculeuse** (Miracle Mosque). According to local legend it's reputed to have constructed itself in a single night.

Another legend connected with the village is that of the nearby **Lac Salé**. A sorcerer supposedly arrived at a neighbouring village and asked for a drink of water. Refused by miserly villagers, he retaliated by sending a magic flood to drown them all, and thus created the lake. Even today villagers in Bangoi-Kouni are said to offer a coconut to thirsty travellers to prevent the same fate befalling them. The vibrant blue saltwater lake sits in a deep crater between the shore and RN3, about a kilometre or so east of Bangoi-Kouni. It's easily visible from the main road, and you can walk around the crater rim, with great views of the coast.

M'BENI

M'beni is home to Grande Comore's only official ecotourism attraction – an essential oils distillery and experimental farm known as **Comores Vanille et Plantes** (☎ 77 02 32; www.comores-online .com/cvp/ecomusee.htm in French; admission free). There's a shop selling spices, essential oils, jam, honey and local crafts; a distillery and vanilla treatment plant; an interesting collection of local plants and herbs; and even a pen full of ostriches! Most of this is designed to find new ways of improving agricultural production by breeding strains of plants and trees resistant to disease, but it's also a well-thought-out tourism project, and a green and pleasant place to visit. There's a small snack bar, too.

CHOMONI

Sheltered by a bay and with a fascinating mix of black lava and white sandy beach, Chomoni, about halfway down the east coast, is the best beach along this part of the island. You can stay at the basic **La Guinguette** (☎ 77 62 21, 33 52 40; r CF7500), which has palm-thatch bungalows with nets right on the beach, but limited toilet facilities (be prepared to squat). Excursions around the island are available and you can snorkel out front – La Guinguette has the gear. The restaurant serves curries and fish and rice dishes (mains cost from CF3000 to CF5000). Soft drinks come out icy cold.

ICONI

Arrr! Grande Comore's oldest settlement and original capital, Iconi, is rich in pirate lore. At one time the seat of the Sultan of Bambao, Iconi suffered badly at the hands of Malagasy pirates between the 16th and early 19th centuries. In 1805 a particularly determined wave of pirates sent many of the inhabitants of Iconi fleeing the town. When the invaders killed their leader, the women of Iconi threw themselves off the cliffs into the sea rather than face capture.

In March 1978, a second tragedy took place in Iconi when Ali Soilih's youth gangs massacred unarmed citizens protesting against his policies forbidding Comorian tradition and religious fervour. There's a plaque commemorating them on the wall of the sultan's palace in the centre of the village.

The most imposing buildings in Iconi are the 16th-century **Palais de Kaviridjeo** (the former home of the sultan), and the still-shiny **Nouvelle Mosquée du Vendredi** (New Friday Mosque).

MOHÉLI

pop 36,885

Mohéli is the Comoros island you go to when you want to drop off the planet for a while – the one we said even a hunted fugitive could blend into. It's wild, undeveloped and sparsely populated (except for, strangely, lots and lots of donkeys, far more in fact than on the other islands). A visit to this, the smallest and most interesting of the Comoros islands, is a highlight of any Comorian trip. There is no question about Mohéli's backwater status: this island hasn't caught up with the 20th century yet, let alone the 21st. But this is a very good thing. While the other islands offer capitals with trash-strewn streets, Mohéli is relatively clean by Comorian standards. Plus this island is home to the only national park in the Comoros, Parc Marin de Mohéli. Nature lovers looking to explore the dramatic, craggy islets off Mohéli's golden shores or snorkel amid the colourful coral reefs, splashing about in the clear aquamarine water off the southwest coast, will love it here.

Also known as Mwali or Moili, Mohéli is a favourite with fans of sea turtles and marine mammals such as dolphins and whales. All are protected in the national park. Bird-watchers will also find plenty to interest them at Lac Dziani Boundouni on the eastern edge of the island, where there's also a good chance of spotting the rare mongoose lemur in the remaining stands of rainforest.

Mohéli doesn't have many modern amenities, but it kicks too much arse in the raw-beauty department to care. For many travellers this lack of organised tourism is what makes the island so special in the first place, and many consider a visit here the most interesting and inviting in the Comoros. An excellent ecotourism project funded by the EU means that simple bungalow accommodation is easy to find in attractive spots all over the island.

History

In 1830 the Malagasy prince Ramanetaka arrived on Mohéli (up to this time the island

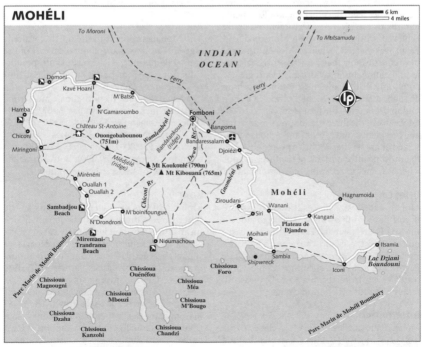

was dependent on Anjouan) and staged a coup that left him in power as sultan. He was succeeded by his young daughter, Djoumbé Saoudy, who took the name of Fatima I.

The French hoped to get a foot in Mohéli's door by sending a governess, Madame Droit, to see to the young sultaness's education, but this was to no avail. Love, however, succeeded where education failed. Fatima began an affair with the Frenchman Joseph François Lambert, a trader, adventurer and ship owner from Mauritius who had been made a duke by the queen of Madagascar. Lambert was able to gain control of great tracts of land on Mohéli and set up plantations with his British partner, William Sunley. In 1867, after the affair had begun to wane, Fatima abdicated the throne and fled the Comoros with a French gendarme, opening the way for the island to become a French protectorate.

Throughout colonialism and the independence that followed, Mohéli, by virtue of its small size and low economic value, was forced into a back-seat position in the affairs of the Comoros. In the 1990s after years of 'humiliation' by France and the independent Moroni-based government, Mohéli's leaders declared its independence from the other islands. Reconciliation with the Moroni government was only achieved in April 2000, when Mohamed Saïd Fazul was elected leader of Mohéli under a new constitution that kept the three islands as one nation, but provided each with greater autonomy. If the new constitution lasts long enough, it should be Mohéli's time to elect a Union president – the post is supposed to rotate between the three islands every four years, and presidents from Moroni and Anjouan have served or are serving. Mohéli's people also hold the most positive outlook of the three islands when it comes to retaining one nation status.

Orientation

Mohéli's small size makes it easy to explore if you have your own car, although not all the roads are tarmac. Taxis-brousses can't quite circle the island as they can't do the stretch between Mirénéni and Miringoni. The Parc Marin de Mohéli encompasses the whole south coast, from Itsamia to N'Drondroni, and the islands off Nioumachoua.

Information

Mohéli is the smallest and least developed of the Comoros. Medical facilities are severely limited

and if you develop any serious health problems, you'll need to fly to Mayotte. There are telephone, email and postal services in Fomboni, and cybercafés are slowly catching on.

Hiking

Mohéli is so small it's easy to traverse the island in one long day, or you could camp midway. A particularly fine walk begins along the Dewa River southeast of Fomboni, then climbs steeply up to the interior of the island and eventually descends to the south coast a couple of kilometres east of Nioumachoua.

Another route, across the western end of the island, begins at Miringoni, then climbs steeply through rainforest and agricultural land to the ruined mountain hut of Château St-Antoine atop the Mlédjélé ridge. From here it's about a 1½-hour walk to Kavé Hoani on the north coast. The same trek can be started at Hamba, a beach about 3km north of Miringoni.

Getting There & Around

Transport throughout the island is very, very slow and patience is mandatory – even the aeroplanes don't always fly if they're not full. Bring a good novel or four.

AIR

The Mohéli airport is in the north-coast village of Bandaressalam, about 4km east of the capital Fomboni. Taxis-brousses run sporadically along the road past it into town (CF100) or you can try to hitch.

Mohéli is served by both the Comoros' internal airlines, **Comores Aviation** (Map p248; ☎ 72 03 86) and **Comores Air Service** (Map p248; ☎ 72 01 55). Flights go at least three times a week to Mayotte (CF50,000), Anjouan (CF20,000) and Grande Comore (CF20,000). Both airline offices are in the main street of Fomboni.

BOAT

Mohéli isn't as well served by boats as the other three Comoros islands; its small size means that it is often ignored by cargo boats. Nonetheless, some boats arrive and depart reasonably regularly to and from the neighbouring islands – try *Alliance des Iles* to Grande Comore (CF9150, four to six hours).

To find out about boat movements, look for bits of paper on the **'message trees'** (Map p248) in front of the police station in Fomboni's main street. Boats usually come in to the port at Bangoma, 1.5km southeast of the town centre.

CAR & TAXI-BROUSSE

All car hires places on Mohéli cost the same – CF15,000 per day plus petrol. Most sleeping places can either hire cars themselves or find you one. Just ask at reception. Try Akmal Bungalows (right).

Taxis-brousses go from Fomboni to points across the island, including Miringoni (CF500, 1½ hours), Ouallah 1 and 2 (CF600, 2½ hours), Itsamia (CF300, one hour) and Nioumachoua (CF600, two hours). Most places only see one or two taxis-brousses per day, so it's hard to do a day trip to any of them, but there are simple bungalows in each of these villages if you need to stay the night.

FOMBONI

pop 4665

Fomboni is quiet and sleepy in the extreme. There's no old Arab town like those in Moroni and Mutsamudu, and most of the buildings are low-rise and low-tech. Once you've walked up and down the nameless main street a couple of times, cast an eye over the market and visited the jetty, you've pretty much experienced all that the town has to offer. Mohélians are a bit quieter and less outgoing than their counterparts on Grande Comore and Anjouan, but they are still unfailingly friendly and courteous. So, as long as you aren't looking for action-packed entertainment, Fomboni is a good place to just wander about, taking in everyday Comorian life.

Orientation

Fomboni has just one main street, which arrives from the airport in the southeast, meanders along past the market and the government buildings next to the shore, passes the Hotel Relais de Singani then goes west towards Domoni. Taxis-brousses can generally be found just outside the market or at the junction just past the Comores Aviation office. Standing on the appropriate side of the main street and waving at any that pass will get you where you need to go.

Information

There's no full-time bank on Mohéli, just a part-time branch of the BIC, open every second Tuesday morning, when the 'bank' arrives by plane in a canvas bag!

Centre de Ressources (☎ 72 04 60; per 10min CF450; ⏰ 8.30am-noon & 3-5.30pm) Fast and reliable internet access.

Hospital (☎ 72 80 38) Main street.
Police station (☎ 72 01 27) Main street.

Sights & Activities

There's not a lot in the way of official sights in Fomboni. You can take a look at the very overgrown gravestones of Joseph François Lambert (opposite) and his business partner, William Sunley, in the **Christian cemetery** next to the football ground; on the other side of the pitch are some even more overgrown **Shirazi (Persian) tombs**, where simple plaques are buried amid piles of waste and rubbish. Or wander around the small **market** down by the shore and marvel at the size of the fish.

Sleeping & Eating

Fomboni has a handful of places to sleep and eat. Self-catering places are very limited, however, and the market really only carries tinned sardines, cheese spread and veggies. Try the **bread shop** (⏰ 9am-noon), next door to the Comores Aviation office, for fresh loaves to make into sandwiches.

Chez Saoudata Muhadji (Pension Farsifa; ☎ 72 05 21; r from CF6000) This very friendly little B&B has nice little rooms with fans, nets and spotless vinyl floors. Grey shutters, black-and-white pillows and padded chairs add a level of thoughtful comfort. Bathrooms are shared. The building is unmarked, so you'll have to ask the way – everybody knows it. Dinner is also available (mains CF2000).

Ninga Hotel (☎ 72 08 45; Bandaressalam; r CF6500) The cheapest and most basic of Fomboni's hotels, the newly christened Ninga is right opposite the airport. It's shabby but cheerful, with a good restaurant serving main dishes from CF1500.

Hotel Relais de Singani (☎ 72 05 45; r CF11,000-17,000) This claims to be Fomboni's most upmarket hotel, and it is a bit more polished than the rest – air-con is an option in the most expensive rooms. There are also TVs, en suite bathrooms and mozzie nets. Cars can be hired here at the usual rate, and bicycles are available for CF4000 per day. Excursions to the islets are CF7500 for a day tour. A cybercafé is planned. Meals (mains from CF2500) must be ordered in advance.

Akmal Resto & Bungalows (☎ 72 00 50; akmalresto@yahoo.fr; set meals CF3000 to CF4000) Fomboni's only real restaurant serves absolutely huge meals. The dishes change nightly but usually include fish or chicken accompanied by giant salads and followed by fruit. Seafood night includes

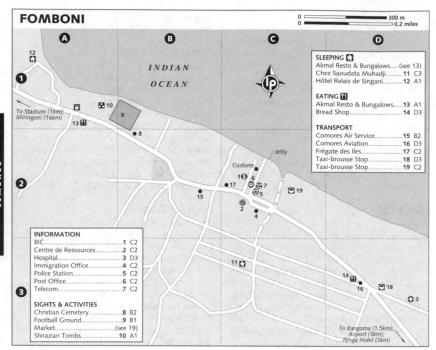

FOMBONI

0 ——————————— 300 m
0 ——————————— 0.2 miles

INDIAN
OCEAN

To Stadium (1km);
Miringoni (16km)

Jetty

Customs

SLEEPING
Akmal Resto & Bungalows.....(see 13)
Chez Saoudata Muhadji..........11 C3
Hôtel Relais de Singani..........12 A1

EATING
Akmal Resto & Bungalows.....13 A1
Bread Shop.............................14 D3

TRANSPORT
Comores Air Service...............15 B2
Comores Aviation....................16 D3
Frégate des Iles......................17 C2
Taxi-brousse Stop....................18 D3
Taxi-brousse Stop....................19 C2

INFORMATION
BIC...1 C2
Centre de Ressources..............2 C2
Hospital....................................3 D3
Immigration Office..................4 C2
Police Station...........................5 C2
Post Office...............................6 C2
Telecom....................................7 C2

SIGHTS & ACTIVITIES
Christian Cemetery..................8 B2
Football Ground.......................9 B1
Market...............................(see 19)
Shirazian Tombs.....................10 A1

To Bangoma (1.5km);
Airport (3km);
Ninga Hotel (3km)

COMOROS

massive lobster. Next to the restaurant you'll find good little straw bungalows (singles/doubles with breakfast CF10,000/16,000) with private bathrooms (cold water only), nets, fans and even TVs! The manager is very knowledgeable about the island and has cars for hire (CF15,000 per day, including driver).

Getting There & Around
For information about getting to/from Fomboni, see p246.

AROUND MOHÉLI
With sandy beaches, primary rainforests, tranquil lakes and best of all, the fascinating offshore islets of the *parc marin* (marine national park), Mohéli is a fantastic place to explore on foot or in a car. There are ecotourism projects in the villages of Itsamia, Nioumachoua, and at Ouallah 1 and 2.

Itsamia
Itsamia is a fairly substantial village with a sweep of sandy, if slightly grubby beach. **Sea turtles** visit the beach at night during high tide to lay their eggs. Visitors can observe the turtles with the

help of a local guide, and then learn more about the life of this endangered animal in the education centre, known as La Maison des Tortues (Turtle House). Guides cost CF1500 per person, and you'll need a good torch, although you mustn't shine it directly on the turtles until they have started to lay eggs (see p258).

There are simple **bungalows** (r with private bathroom CF5000) on the beach at Itsamia, and a small restaurant area. Meals can be arranged for about CF1500. You can camp here for a one-off fee of CF1000.

Nioumachoua & the Parc Marin de Mohéli
Nioumachoua is Mohéli's second-biggest community, although it's nothing more than a hot, dusty low-rise village without any proper hotels. The magnificent view compensates for the lack of human-made beauty – you can see the five islets of the *parc marin* rising steeply out of the sparkling turquoise sea just offshore. Some are ringed by tempting yellow-sand beaches. The beach in the village itself is similarly wide and golden, but fairly dirty. Instead head a little outside the villages, where

the beaches are cleaner, deserted and fronted by fantastic aqua water.

The Nioumachoua ecotourism association (known to the locals simply as L'Association) has a boat for hire that takes visitors out to the islands for snorkelling, picnics or overnight stays. The cost is a steep CF14,000 per boat, or CF17,000 if it comes back the next day to pick you up. A guide to show you the good snorkelling sites costs CF3000. There are no facilities on the islands; you will need to pack everything to take in and out.

Makwe (☎ 72 60 55) sells his handicrafts at the association and for a small fee will take you up the little hill behind the association's bungalows to check out the most massive baobab around – one reader estimated its trunk at 30m in circumference! The tree is in the middle of an old Shirazi village that's now in ruins and makes a fascinating photograph.

Speaking of bungalows, L'Association maintains a row of little **bungalows** (CF5000), which have nets, bathrooms and electricity. They're easy to find, right under the baobab trees next to L'Association headquarters. Next door is the **Restaurant Baobab** (mains CF2500), a cute-looking straw hut with local cloths on the tables. It serves fish dishes, manioc, bananas and so on. Readers have said the lobster here is the best in the Comoros.

Ouallah 2

The next village after Nioumachoua is confusingly known as Ouallah (or Wela) 2. It's a tiny little place elevated a few hundred metres above sea level, with the stunning beach of **Sambadjou** just downhill from the village. Nearby is the **Cascade de Mirémani**, a waterfall that cascades prettily on to the beach. The **bungalows** (s/d incl breakfast CF5000) are in a beautiful spot on the beach and are some of the nicest on the island – the locals who own them are making quite an effort. Facilities have been upgraded, and the bungalows have electricity and shared showers and toilets. A restaurant under the property's one tree is being constructed. For now meals can be cooked to order. There's a boat for hire.

Ouallah 1

Ouallah 1 is the last village accessible by taxi-brousse from Nioumachoua, and is home to the grandly titled Maison des Livingstones, an ecotourism centre named after the giant Livingstone's fruit bat. There is a set of well-built **bungalows** (s/d incl breakfast CF5000) with nets and a separate sanitation block. Meals can be cooked to order from about CF1500.

There's also a guide (CF3000 per person or CF5000 per couple) available to walk with visitors through the forest to the roosting place of the bats. It's a steep and slippery three-hour walk there and back, and the bats, when you reach them, are a bit far away to see clearly. But it's still worth doing for the experience of walking in the forest and the chance to learn more about the island's flora – the guide will explain the various plants used in local medicines.

Miringoni

Isolated somewhat by its lack of a decent access road from Ouallah 2, Miringoni is set among thick vegetation on the west coast of Mohéli. You can walk to town from Ouallah 2 in about three hours – ask locals for directions or hire a guide to show you the shortcuts. If you do the walk at low tide, it's possible to follow the coastline along the beach. This is a gorgeous hike that gives access to beautiful hidden coves that are hardly ever visited. You must time the walk right though, because once the water comes in it will get dangerous.

You can stay in the village's only **bungalow** (CF3000), which has lovely views of the coast. You can also find an eco-guide here to take you into the forest. Meals can be arranged. More bungalows are planned, but these are village initiatives and take money to construct. A quad-bike tour company is also in the works, and once up and running the bikes will be able to do the rough 9km dirt track leading to the Ouallah–Mirénéni highway, giving the village more tourism accessibility and possibilities.

ANJOUAN

pop 286,000

Called the 'pearl of the Comoros' by its residents, Anjouan is no doubt the most scenic of the Comoros and fulfils any lifelong fantasies of playing Robinson Crusoe on a deserted tropical island. Known by the locals as Nd-zouani or Nzwani, this is also the Comorian island that most closely resembles the image most people conjure up when daydreaming of kissing a lover in an exotic far-flung destination. The air here really is heavy with the scent of cloves and ylang-ylang, and the magic landscape includes crumbling old Arab plantations, endless rows of palms, and trees whose branches are heavy with a load of ripening yellow bananas.

Through this mosaic of green moves the rural population: the women swaying under their loads of firewood or stacks of cassava; the men, machetes in hand, setting off in the cool of the morning to cut new palm thatch for their roofs. Up in the highlands, the air is blissfully cool and mists often descend over the trees of the rainforest, dripping moisture on to the giant, swooping bats who call the trees home.

The Anjounais are fiercely proud of their identity, declaring independence from the rest of the Comoros in 1996. They have been reluctantly coaxed back into the Union – it helps when your president is the top chief in the Comoros – but relations remain uneasy with the other islands.

History

During the latter part of the 19th century, Sultan Abdallah III of Anjouan ran into problems with his long-term supporters, the British, over his continued holding of slaves. When he agreed to halt the practice, Anjouan's landowners revolted – they depended on slaves to farm their plantations. In April 1886 the ageing sultan travelled to France, which had a more relaxed approach to the issue of slavery, and signed the treaty making the island a French protectorate. In 1912 the island joined the other three Comoros in becoming a full colony of France.

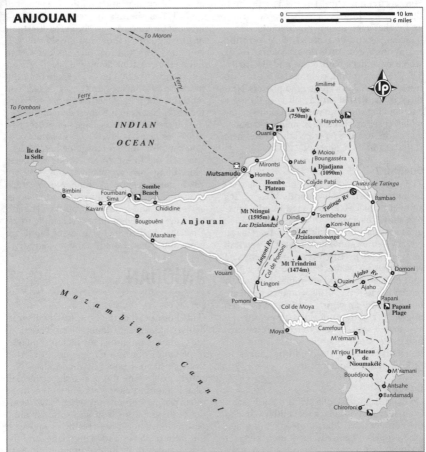

The destinies of the three islands remained on a parallel course throughout the series of coups d'état that characterised politics in the Comoros over the next 12 years. But in March 1996 the volcanic tensions created by years of federalism and centralism finally erupted.

In 1997 the Anjouan government, led by the self-elected president Ibrahim, declared full independence from the federal government in Grande Comore. Almost immediately guerrilla war broke out between the supporters of President Ibrahim and those who wanted Anjouan to remain part of the federation.

Anjouan rejected any attempt to bring the island back into the federal republic until 2001, when a new 'military committee' led by Major Mohamed Bacar seized power on Anjouan with the aim of rejoining the Comoros. Bacar survived two coup attempts in quick succession, and held on to power long enough to become president of Anjouan in the elections held in April 2002. In 2006 Ahmed Abdallah Sambi of Anjouan was elected president of the Union by a 60% majority. He has pledged to clean up Anjouan's cities.

Orientation

Anjouan's airport lies just outside the village of Ouani, about 6km north of the capital, Mutsamudu. Boats arriving in Anjouan come into the port in central Mutsamudu. Anjouan is shaped like an elongated triangle, with three main roads connecting the major towns on the island – Bambao, Domoni and Mutsamudu.

Information

The larger towns of Anjouan have telephone and postal services, but only very limited fax and email facilities are available in Mutsamudu.

The BIC (p252) in Mutsamudu can change cash and travellers cheques. There are no moneychanging facilities at the airport, so make sure you have enough euros (or US dollars) to pay for a taxi to your hotel, and to last until you get to the bank.

Medical facilities in Anjouan are extremely limited, with hardly any supplies, so you will need to fly to Mayotte should you require anything remotely serious.

Hiking

Anjouan is in many ways the best of the Comoros islands for hiking, as its wooded highlands have the coolest climate. Try to walk from the coast into the hills rather than the other way round, so that you've reached enough altitude to stay cool by the time the sun is at its height.

THE CRATER LAKES

On the slopes of Mt Ntingui are two crater lakes, Lac Dzialaoutsounga (697m) and Lac Dzialandzé (910m). Together, they make a nice day trek from the village of Bambao on the east coast or from the village of Koni-Ngani to the west. To do the walk, trek or find a taxi-brousse to Dindi, about 7km west of Bambao. From Dindi, the track climbs, passing Lac Dzialaoutsounga on the left and after 2km arrives at the Col de Pomoni. The track to the right climbs for 1km through a semi-wooded area to Lac Dzialandzé. From here you can walk around the lake, with great views of the crater and surrounding farmland, to Koni-Ngani, where you can pick up a taxi-brousse back to Bambao, and then on to Domoni or Mutsamudu.

MT NTINGUI

Normally covered by clouds, it's a hard and steep climb from Lac Dzialandzé to the 1595m summit of Mt Ntingui, the highest point on Anjouan. On a rare clear day, it affords a view over all four islands of the archipelago. At this point, you can either descend to Mutsamudu or return to the Col de Pomoni, and descend through the village of Lingoni to Pomoni on the west coast. Alternatively, you can climb up to Mt Ntingui from Mutsamudu – follow the road from Mutsamudu to the village of Hombo, then ask your way from there.

JIMILIME & THE NORTHEAST

The far northeast of Anjouan, accessible only on foot or by boat, offers another option for exploring off the beaten path. One easy day walk begins at Col de Patsi (700m), which is about 11km above Ouani. The trekking route begins by ascending 1090m-high Mt Djadjana, then following the ridge down through inhabited areas to the traditional village of Jimilime. You can also walk from Ouani directly over the ridge and down to Jimilime and Hayoho on the opposite coast.

Getting There & Around

Transport around the island is slow, just like everywhere else in the Comoros, especially along the remote east coast.

AIR

Anjouan is served by both the Comoros' domestic airlines: **Comores Aviation** (Map p253; ☎ 71 04 82; nts.mutsa@snpt.km; Mutsamudu) and **Comores Air Service** (☎ 71 12 32; Ouani). Flights go from Anjouan to Mayotte (CF50,000), Moroni (CF30,000) and Mohéli (CF20,000) almost every day, but for flights to destinations further afield, you'll have to connect in Mayotte or Moroni. There are also two flights per week to Dar es Salaam in Tanzania (CF170,000).

BOAT

The port in Mutsamudu is well served by the region's sea traffic. To find a boat to your chosen destination, check the chalked-up ship movements on the blackboards propped up at intervals along the seafront. Alternatively, just ask around in the town square or contact **Agence Tourisme Verte** (RECA Mroni; Map p253; danielmoitane@yahoo.fr; 8am-1pm & 4-9pm), also in the town square.

CAR

If you're driving around Anjouan in September, try to avoid the carpets of cloves spread out to dry on the roads! **Agence Tourisme Verte** (Map p253; danielmoitane@yahoo.fr; 8am-1pm & 4-9pm) in Mutsamudu's town square rents cars for about CF20,000 per day, including driver and fuel. If you hire a guide (some of whom speak English), it costs another CF12,000 per day.

TAXI-BROUSSE

Taxis-brousses are infrequent and slow down after 3pm. In Mutsamudu, taxis-brousses leave from the town square in front of the post office. There are regular services between Mutsamudu and Domoni (CF550), Bimbini (CF500), Ouani (CF150) and Moya (CF200) from early morning until mid-afternoon. Distances are short, but the steep and winding roads mean the journey is slow going.

MUTSAMUDU

pop 24,962

Despite a campaign to clean it up, Mutsamudu remains smelly and filthy. Shells of burnt-out cars and piles of rubbish litter the streets, choking the shoreline and the river that runs through the town square. Cattle live on the garbage, munching away on the refuse and defying veterinary science by looking surprisingly healthy.

If you can handle the stench, you might be able to enjoy Mutsamudu's attractions – plus

there are ongoing campaigns to tidy up the town. The narrow, spice-scented streets of the large and well-preserved *medina* (founded in 1492) and the views from the ruined citadel are especially wonderful. So too is the friendly, laid-back atmosphere of the seafront and the town square, where you can chat with the old men in their immaculate white robes, fingering prayer beads as they gather outside the mosques.

Orientation

Most of Mutsamudu stretches along two parallel (unnamed) main streets, from the port area to the Hôtel Al Amal about 750m away. Between the two streets is a fascinating maze of lanes and shops in the *medina* (the old Arab quarter). Next to the port is the town square, where you will find the main offices, the bank, taxis-brousses and most of the town's unemployed menfolk.

Information

Agence Tourisme Verte (RECA Mroni; danielmoitane@ yahoo.fr; 8am-1pm & 4-9pm) For car hire, excursions and information about boats; in the town square. Monsieur Daniel can also arrange homestays with local families, and provide guides for hiking (CF20,000 per day). The office is right next door to the BIC.

BIC (☎ 71 01 71; 8.30am-3.30pm Mon-Fri) The only bank on the island; in the town square.

Centre Médical Urbain de Mutsamudu (☎ 71 13 07) Medical emergencies.

Internet Shop (☎ 71 15 28; per hr CF600; 8.30am-8pm) About 70m up the road from La Paillotte, on the way to Hôtel Al Amal.

Mutsamudu police headquarters (☎ 71 02 00)

Sights

Overlooking Mutsamudu, up a steep stairway from the road above the *medina*, is the ruined, cannon-laden **citadel**, constructed with British money in 1860 to defend the town against Malagasy pirates. The citadel was damaged in a 1950 cyclone, but still affords great views across the town and the new harbour, which was financed by Arab interests.

Wandering through the narrow stone streets of the *medina* is the best form of sightseeing in Mutsamudu. You can stop to admire the **Mosquée du Vendredi** (Friday Mosque), the half-ruined **Sultan's Palace** and the occasional **covered bridges** that link one side of the street to the other. These bridges were constructed centuries ago to allow high-born Swahili women

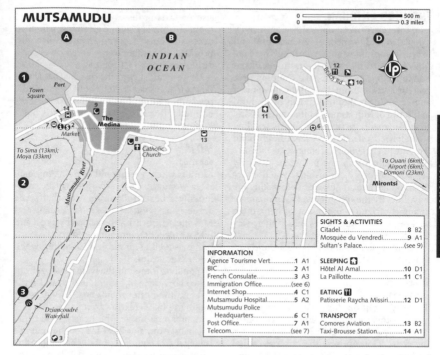

to visit friends and neighbours without having to show themselves immodestly in the streets. Likewise, the smooth **stone benches** (*barazas* in Comorian) set into the doorways of the richer houses allowed the master of the household to receive male visitors outside without compromising the propriety of his womenfolk.

There is also an easy walk from Mutsamudu up the river gorge to the pretty **Dziancoudré Waterfall**. The only decent **beach** within walking distance of town is run by the Hôtel Al Amal. Nonguests can use it for a small fee.

Sleeping & Eating

Eating and sleeping options are few and far between in Mutsamudu, and all are relatively expensive, although there are a couple of food stalls in the town square, which sell fresh bread and the occasional beef kebab most evenings. Nightlife is nonexistent.

La Paillotte (☎ 71 05 24; s/d CF12,500/17,500) The rooms behind this very good restaurant are nicely decorated, and those on the 1st floor have TVs, fans, nets and hot water. The restaurant serves a good, but limited, menu (mains CF4000 to CF6000) that includes lobster.

There are omelettes at breakfast – yummy. The owners are friendly.

Hôtel Al Amal (☎ 71 10 17; sat@snpt.km; s/d €62/82; ✖ ☐ ☎) Anjouan's only 'proper' hotel even quotes in euros! It is a rather ubiquitous western-style hotel in a huge complex just over a kilometre from the centre of town. It has a small yellow-sand beach (sometimes covered in spilled oil) and fairly modern rooms with carpet, telephones and TVs. The restaurant, with a smart bar (it even serves cocktails), has a very grand menu (mains CF4000 to CF6500) featuring dishes such as *magret de canard* (duck fillet) and tuna carpaccio, although the most exotic dishes seem perpetually unavailable. The place also has internet access, although guests have to pay to use it (CF500 per hour).

Patisserie Raycha Missiri (Beach Rd; mains from CF1500; ☽ breakfast, lunch & dinner) Readers recommend this cheap and friendly place that looks out over the water for its friendly ambience and delicious food. The restaurant has a big menu of comfort French food, including *frites* (french fries), omelettes, *brochettes* (kebabs) and skirt steaks at less than exorbitant prices.

254 ANJOUAN •• Interior Anjouan

INTERIOR ANJOUAN

The interior of Anjouan, although heavily populated and farmed, is very beautiful and excellent for hiking and exploring. There are lots of opportunities for interesting walks; if you're feeling energetic, take camping gear and turn any combination of the three main routes (west of Bambao, north of Pomoni and south of Mutsamudu) into a cross-island trek. The roads are steep and dizzily winding – you'll need a steady nerve and a heavy hand with the horn if you're driving yourself. Once off the main roads, the paths are generally seasonal and very confusing – you'll either need to take a local guide or keep asking the way. Luckily the inhabitants of Anjouan are extremely friendly and happy to help, often walking several kilometres out of their way to put strangers on the right track.

For more details about hiking around Anjouan, see p251.

DOMONI

pop 15,351

The jury is out on this seaside town – some love it, others hate it, saying the seafront is ruined by oil and rubbish. Halfway down the coast, Domoni was the original capital of Anjouan and now has the second-largest population. The embroidery found here is especially beautiful, made by very skilled craftspeople. Domoni is also the source of some of the Comoros' finest woodcarving. The town is guarded by an ancient fortified wall and a ruined tower, built to protect the town from Malagasy pirates.

The old town is even more winding and maze-like than the *medina* in Mutsamudu, with carved Swahili doors and stone relief-work lintels on the bigger houses and palaces. Look out for the women painting each other's faces with sandalwood paste on the many staircases, and the little straw rooms constructed on the roofs of the stone houses to catch the sea breeze.

A more recent addition to Domoni is the **mausoleum** to former president Ahmed Abdallah Abderemane, assassinated in 1989 by his presidential guard. With its brilliant white walls and four high minarets, it's now the most imposing structure in town, if not the entire country.

Motel Loulou (☎ 71 92 35; r CF15,000; 🔀) is a few minutes' walk up from town towards the police station and the road to Ajaho. You can

also ask taxis-brousses to drop you there. The rooms are brand new and gleaming, with tiled floors, mosquito nets and private bathrooms. Breakfast or meals can be served on order – dishes are around CF3000.

Or you can stay at the nearby **Chez Ahmed Yahaya** (r incl breakfast CF7500), about 100m up the road from Motel Loulou, close to the gendarmerie. Readers say the breakfast is huge. Rooms are simple, but fairly priced.

MOYA

pop 8100

Moya is where you should head in Anjouan. It's a wonderfully scruffy little village overlooking a beautiful white beach that some argue is as good as those on Mohéli and Mayotte. The beach is protected by a reef and offers excellent swimming and rock scrambling, as well as passable snorkelling when the seas are calm.

You'll be joined in the water by dozens of naked boys, who like to roll in the sand while wet and then offer their ghost-like faces for photographs. Be extra careful about leaving your possessions on the beach. Don't buy seashells from the local kids – the practice is illegal and environmentally harmful. Start early if you want to take a day trip on the taxi-brousse from Mutsamudu – the trip here can take up to 2½ hours. Better to stay overnight in the local hotel, enjoy a seafood feast and watch the spectacular sunset. If you're lucky you might catch a Comorian wedding – the beach is a very popular place to get married.

The only hotel is **La Sultan** (☎ 32 06 34, 71 14 33; r incl breakfast CF7500), set above the beach in a shady spot with great views. The small rooms, which have shared bathrooms (someone in the family can often boil some water for you) and mosquito nets, are hot and basic, but the management is very friendly, the drinks are cold and the food is fantastic (mains CF2000 to CF4000), even if Chef Yusaf Houmadi can be a bit too liberal with the salt for some. Enormous lobsters in vanilla and coconut sauce are the house specialities. Order your meals at least two hours in advance.

If you just want something simple, check for small local stalls selling kebabs – called *brochetties* here – along with jackfruit and cassava. If you ask around, there are usually locals willing to fry you up fresh-caught fish (around CF500 to CF1000).

SIMA & THE WEST

Twenty kilometres west of Mutsamudu, Sima is one of the oldest settlements in the Comoros and certainly the oldest on Anjouan. Its **Mosquée Ziyarani** was constructed in the 15th century over the top of a mosque built in the 11th century. From Sima, the circular island route splits; the main road heads south towards Marahare and Moya, and another continues 5km west through Kavani, with the landscape becoming wilder on the way to the sheltered fishing village of **Bimbini**.

Head north on the road from Sima past the small village of Foumbani to reach **Sombe Beach** – it's one of the best isolated beaches on the island and you'll more than likely have it to yourself. You'll find it between Foumbani and the equally small village of Chididine, which is on the road back to Mutsamudu. The water here is very calm and you can dive off black rocks, the remnants of an old lava flow, into crystal-clear and calm water – it makes a great day trip if you bring along a picnic and perhaps a bottle of local rum... To reach the beach grab a taxi in Foumbani or Chididine and get dropped off at the trail for Sombe Beach – the driver will know what you are talking about. If you don't negotiate a round-trip journey (prices vary depending on where you start) don't leave the beach too late; after 3pm, passing taxis on the main road become less frequent. To reach the beach follow the trailhead (it begins where the electricity wires cross the road) and slither down a rock and mud embankment to the strip of white sand.

MAYOTTE

pop 194,000

Yes, it has fantastic white sand, turquoise sea beaches and excellent diving, snorkelling and sailing, but otherwise Mayotte (Mahoré) is overpriced and some say over-Frenchified. A *collectivité territoriale* (overseas territory) of France, Mayotte differs from the other Comorian islands politically in that its people are French citizens governed by French law. As a result, French citizens don't need visas to holiday here, and the island is crammed with holidaymakers on packages from all over France. It also has a large expat and diplomatic community in its capital city.

Despite large infusions of money aimed at bringing the island's economy and infra-structure into parity with the Métropole (as mainland France is known), Mayotte remains economically poor, with a clear gulf between the local population and the French expatriates.

Under French administration, Mayotte has for the most part enjoyed relative peace and stability, although the other three Comorian islands feel the Mahorais (as the people of Mayotte are called) sold out, and they uncharitably refer to them as 'the spoilt children of the republic'. To the casual visitor, both the Mahorais and Mayotte's French expats seem considerably less friendly than the inhabitants of the other three islands.

Budget travellers may want to steer clear of Mayotte. Thanks to bureaucrats receiving fat government salaries in euros, and lots of upmarket resorts, prices for meals and transport are the same, if not more, than in France. Bargaining is all but impossible.

History

During the mid-19th-century 'scramble for Africa', Sultan Adriansouli, who had gained quite a few enemies during his rise to power, formed an accord ceding the island to the French in exchange for protection from his rivals. The official transfer of Mayotte took place in May 1843 and the island was transformed first from a sultanate into a haven for French planters and slaveholders, and then into a full colony of France.

A majority of Mahorais voted against independence in a 1974 referendum, and when Ahmed Abdallah Abderemane unilaterally announced the independence of all four islands, Mayotte's leaders asked France for its intervention. French Foreign Legionnaires and a couple of warships were sent to patrol the territory, and the Comoros' transition to independence went ahead without Mayotte. Another referendum was held in 1976, during the height of Ali Soilih's chaotic reign in the independent Comoros, and this time a whopping 99% of the population voted to stay with France. The UN regularly calls on France to hand Mayotte back to the Union des Comores, but faced with a population staunchly opposed to a break with France the French seem disinclined to do so.

Orientation

The 'island' of Mayotte consists of three main islands: Grande Terre (356 sq km), the central island, which contains the largest town, Mamoudzou, and the adjacent industrial zone;

COMOROS

COMOROS

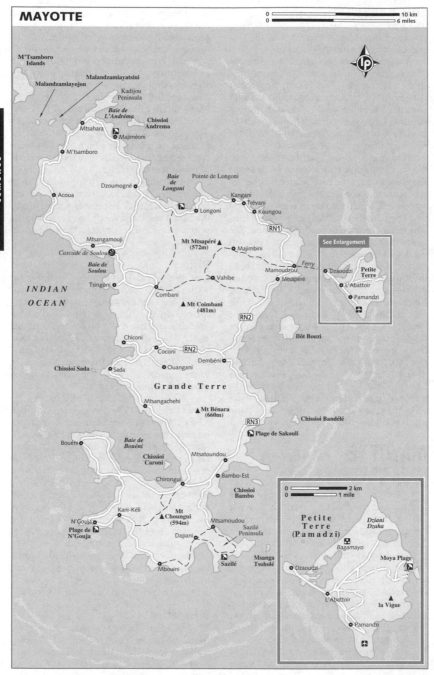

MAYOTTE

0 — 10 km
0 — 6 miles

M'Tsamboro Islands

Malandzamiayatsini

Malandzamiayojou

Kadijou Peninsula

Baie de L'Andréma

Chissioi Andrema

Mtsahara

Majiméoni

M'tsamboro

Acoua

Dzoumogné

Baie de Longoni

Pointe de Longoni

Kangani

Trévani

Longoni

Koungou

RN1

See Enlargement

Mt Mtsapéré (572m)

Majimbini

Ferry

Mamoudzou

Dzaoudzi

Petite Terre

L'Abattoir

Pamandzi

Mtsangamouji

Cascade de Soulou

Baie de Soulou

Vahibe

Mtsapéré

Tsingoni

Combani

INDIAN OCEAN

Mt Coimbani (481m)

RN2

Ilôt Bouzi

Chiconi

Coconi

RN2

Dembéni

Chissioi Sada

Sada

Ouangani

Grande Terre

Mtsangachehi

Mt Bénara (660m)

RN3

Chissioi Bandélé

Plage de Sakouli

Bouéni

Baie de Bouéni

Chissioi Caroni

Mtsatoundou

Chirongui

Bambo-Est

Chissioi Bambo

Kani-Kéli

Mt Choungui (594m)

Mtsamoudou

Sazilé Peninsula

N'Gouja

Plage de N'Gouja

Dapani

Msanga Tsoholé

Sazilé

Mbouini

0 — 2 km
0 — 1 mile

Petite Terre (Pamadzi)

Dziani Dzaha

Bagamayo

Moya Plage

Dzaoudzi

la Vigue

L'Abattoir

Pamandzi

Petite Terre (Pamandzi; 18 sq km), where the airport is located; and the rock of Dzaoudzi, linked to Petite Terre by a causeway. The latter two islands are just a short ferry ride from Mamoudzou, which has the bank and main shopping area.

Information

The various shops, offices and businesses you'll need while in Mayotte are divided between Mamoudzou, Petite Terre and various villages around Grande Terre.

In an emergency, telephone Mayotte's **police** (☎ 17), **fire service** (☎ 18) or **hospital** (☎ 61 15 15). The latter is slightly better than its counterparts on the Union des Comores.

Be aware that you *cannot* change Comorian francs or Malagasy ariary anywhere on Mayotte. There are no moneychanging facilities at the airport, so make sure you arrive with enough euros to get yourself into town.

Activities

DIVING & SNORKELLING

Dive specialists report that Mayotte is one of the most biologically diverse sites in the world, with more than 600 species of fish inhabiting the great coral reef that encircles the island. The island is also on the migration routes of various species of sailfish and marlin. Not surprisingly the island has a number of dive companies. Prices range from about €55 for one dive to €220 for five dives. The following is just a selection of the companies:

Aqua Diva (☎ 61 81 59; aquadivadive@wanadoo.fr; Kaweni)

Lagon Maoré (☎ 60 14 19; jardin.maore@wanadoo.fr; N'gouja) Attached to Le Jardin Maoré hotel on the south coast. Also does boat excursions, whale-watching and big-game fishing.

Le Lambis (☎ 60 06 31; lambis.plongee-mayotte@ wanadoo.fr; Blvd des Crabes, Dzaoudzi)

SAILING & BOAT TRIPS

With the biggest lagoon in the world, Mayotte is home to a plethora of sailing companies. Half-day excursions in the lagoon generally cost around €55; a full day on the water is €75.

Mayotte Découverte (☎ 61 19 09, 69 17 24; Mamoudzou) Does trips in an extraordinary craft called *Le Visiobul*, which has an enormous Perspex bubble underneath it!

Mayotte Voile (☎ 69 02 59; Plage de Sakouli) Based on the brown-sand beach at Sakouli, it offers sailing and windsurfing lessons, boat excursions and canoeing.

Sea Blue Safari (Map p259; ☎ 61 07 63; sea.blue .safari@caramail.com; Rue du Commerce, Mamoudzou) Specialises in dolphin- and whale-watching.

HIKING

Although not as scenic as the other islands of the Comoros, there are still a few good walks to be done in Mayotte.

Sazilé Peninsula

From the village of Mtsamoudou at the southeastern corner of the island, there's an 8km circuit track that takes in the little-visited beach of Sazilé, where you'll find sea turtles offshore and the colourful dunes of Magikavo. Just offshore is the lovely exposed sand bar known as Îlot du Sable Blanc. This is a popular destination for day trips, but be warned that the beach is very exposed, with no shade.

The route can be easily walked in a couple of hours, excluding stops, but access to Mtsamoudou can be a problem, so allow all day for the trip. To get there from Mamoudzou, look for a taxi-brousse going directly to Mtsamoudou. If you're unsuccessful, take one going to Chirongui via Mtsamoudou and get off at Bambo-Est. From there, it's a 5km walk to Mtsamoudou and the start of the circuit. The way to the beach is marked by paint on stones. Boats to the islet will be easiest to find at weekends.

Getting There & Around

AIR

Mayotte is served by the following international airlines:

Air Austral (Map p259; ☎ 60 90 90; mayotte@air-austral .com; Place du Marché, Mamoudzou) Flights to Nosy Be and Mahajanga in Madagascar, Réunion and Mauritius. Also has an office opposite the ferry terminal in Dzaoudzi.

Air France (Map p259; ☎ 61 10 52; issoufali.mayotte@ wanadoo.fr; Place du Marché, Mamoudzou) Flights to France via Réunion.

Air Madagascar (☎ 60 10 52; tsc@snpt.km; Dzaoudzi) Weekly flights to Mahajanga and sometimes Nosy Be in Madagascar.

Air Seychelles (Map p259; ☎ 62 31 00; ario-mayotte@ wanadoo.fr; Place Mariage, Mamoudzou) Flies weekly between Malé and Mayotte.

Alliance Papillon (☎ 62 54 45) Organises charter flights to Zanzibar (€390), Pemba (Mozambique, €310) and Diego Suarez (€340) in Madagascar.

Comores Aviation (Map p259; ☎ 61 62 00; comores .aviation-MAY@wanadoo.fr; Rue du Commerce, Mamoudzou) Tickets cost €100 to Moroni, €75 to Anjouan and €90 to Mohéli.

COMOROS

BOAT

Getting to/from Mayotte by boat is fairly difficult and very expensive, as the Mahorais authorities fix prices and bargaining is not possible. Boat travel in the Comoros can be dangerous. You should always inspect the vessel before boarding; most don't have any sort of life jacket on board, and some are in such dilapidated condition it doesn't seem like they'll make the trip. If the seas are too rough, boats don't run and you'll just have to wait where you are.

CAR & MOTORCYCLE

The cheapest car-hire deals are to be had at **MultiAuto** (☎ 69 22 99; location-multi-autos@wanadoo.fr; Kaweni; ✆ Mon-Sat), 1km from the town centre, which sometimes goes as low as €22 per day with unlimited kilometres. For scooters, try **Jéjé** (Map p259; ☎ 69 39 92; 27 Rue du Commerce, Mamoudzou) in Mamoudzou, which hires Vespa mopeds with helmet and lock for €20 per day. No-one on the island hires out mountain bikes.

TAXI-BROUSSE

Taxis-brousses are reasonably priced on Mayotte – the fare is €3 to points north of Mamoudzou, such as M'Tsamboro (40 minutes), or €5 if you go as far south as N'Gouja (about an hour). There are three taxi-brousse stations in Mamoudzou – the one next to the port is for vehicles south, the one on Place du Marché has departures for the centre of the island, and the one a bit further down Ave Adrian Souli is for destinations in the north.

GRANDE TERRE
Mamoudzou

Most of Mayotte's shops, restaurants and businesses are concentrated in Mamoudzou, and the neighbouring industrial zone of Kaweni. Here European-style paint warehouses and tyre emporiums sit side by side with the same rotting vegetables, open drains and piles of rubbish you'd see in any developing country's port. All in all it's a sprawl, lacking any of the charm or architectural interest of the towns of the independent Comoros.

Although it's not the prettiest city in the world, Mamoudzou is the commercial heart of Mayotte, and you will probably find yourself coming into town to grab a bite to eat or do some shopping. Plus, if you're the type of traveller to come all this way to experience the Comoros, you need to see the less attractive places as well to get the full picture. It's ironic, however, that the island controlled by one of the world's superpowers is the most neglected of all the Comoros.

INFORMATION

To make telephone calls, you'll need to buy a *télécarte* (phonecard) for one of the public telephones. Cards are on sale at most shops and kiosks or at the post office. Dial ☎ 00 before international numbers. Calls to Europe or the USA cost about €0.25 a minute.
BFC-OI (☎ 61 10 91; Rue Mariazé; ✆ 7.30am-noon & 1.30-3.30pm) The only bank that will change foreign currency or travellers cheques and do advances on Visa and

---

RESPONSIBLE TURTLE WATCHING

■ When in the water, keep your distance and avoid disturbing resting, sleeping or actively feeding turtles.

■ Approach turtles slowly and calmly, and move away if the turtle shows signs of distress.

■ Never try to feed, catch or ride turtles.

■ Don't shine torches on the female turtles on the beach until they have started laying their eggs.

■ Never shine torches or point camera flashes directly into turtles' eyes – photograph them from behind.

■ Leave turtle eggs and hatchlings (baby turtles) undisturbed.

■ Do not interfere with the hatchlings' crawl to the sea, as this could jeopardise their survival.

■ Never photograph hatchlings – they are very sensitive to light.

■ Limit your viewing to 30 minutes at a time.

■ Never buy products made from turtle shells, or foodstuffs made from turtle parts – these are illegal.

COMOROS

MAMOUDZOU

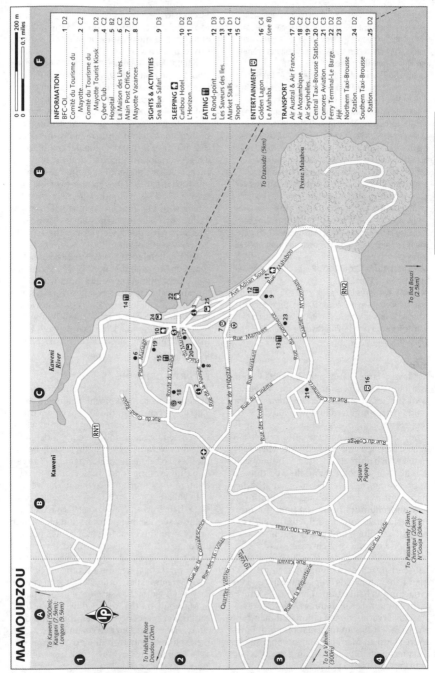

INFORMATION		
BFC-OI..1	D2
Comité du Tourisme du		
Mayotte.................................2	C2
Comité du Tourisme du		
Mayotte Tourist Kiosk............3	D2
Cyber Club............................4	C2
Hospital.................................5	B2
La Maison des Livres............6	C2
Main Post Office...................7	D2
Mayotte Vacances.................8	C2
SIGHTS & ACTIVITIES		
Sea Blue Safari.....................9	D3
SLEEPING 🛏		
Caribou Hotel.....................10	D2
L'Horizon............................11	D3
EATING 🍴		
Le Rond-point.....................12	D3
Les Saveurs des Îles............13	C3
Market Stalls.......................14	D1
Shopi..................................15	C2
ENTERTAINMENT 🎭		
Golden Lagon......................16	C4
Le Mahaba.......................(see 8)	
TRANSPORT		
Air Austral & Air France.......17	D2
Air Mozambique..................18	C2
Air Seychelles.....................19	C2
Central Taxi-Brousse Station..20	C3
Comores Aviation...............21	C3
Ferry Terminal–Le Barge.......22	D2
Jéjé....................................23	D3
Northern Taxi-Brousse		
Station.............................24	D2
Southern Taxi-Brousse		
Station.............................25	D2

MasterCard. It also has ATMs, which should theoretically give you money on a Visa card. This is the main branch and is directly opposite the ferry terminal. The bank gets horribly crowded, so get there about 30 minutes before opening to avoid the queues.

Comité du Tourisme du Mayotte (☎ 61 09 09; ctm@mayotte.tourisme.com; Rue de la Pompe; ⏰ 7.30am-4.30pm Mon-Fri) Very helpful. It also has a branch at the airport and smaller information kiosk by the ferry terminal, which is open on Saturdays. The best place to come for lists of the *chambres d'hôtes* (B&B-style accommodation) around the island, although the info isn't always up to date. Can also provide information on diving and sailing companies.

Cyber Club (☎ 62 62 1; 24 Route de Vahibé, Passamainty; per 10min €1; ⏰ 9am-10pm Mon-Sat) Internet access just outside Mamoudzou; also serves snacks.

La Maison des Livres (☎ 61 14 97; marielaure .maison.des.livres@wanadoo.fr; Place Mariage) The best bookshop in the Comoros, with maps, guides to Mayotte and the surrounding countries, novels and magazines, all in French.

Main post office (☎ 61 11 03; Rue de l'Hôpital; ⏰ 7am-5pm Mon-Fri, to 11am Sat)

Mayotte Vacances (Map p259; ☎ 61 25 50; mayotte -vacances@wanadoo.fr; Place du Marché) Organises boat trips and picnics on various islets in the lagoon, tours of Grande Terre and car hire. Prices average about €35/55 per person per half/full day.

SIGHTS

Îlot Bouzi, a large island in the Mayotte lagoon, is a fauna-conservation area for Mayotte's own species of lemur, *Lemur fulvus mayottensis*. Three hundred and fifty *makis*, as the lemurs are commonly known, roam the island, some of which are used to people and can be handled and stroked. You will be able to tell which animals are used to human contact by their lack of fear and their boldness in approaching you. Even if you are approached by a lemur, we'd advise against petting it. The more lemurs become tame, the more problems arise with the animals themselves – tourists are bitten and lemurs get hooked on junk food instead of their native nosh.

The *makis* are endangered in Mayotte because of poaching, culling by farmers (who blame them for raids on plantations) and encroaching urbanisation. The lemurs can be visited by contacting **Terre de l'Asile** (☎ 61 03 30), the conservation organisation that maintains the island. It has an information point in the tourist kiosk in Mamoudzou, just opposite the ferry terminal. A visit, including the 5km boat transfers, costs €15 per person.

SLEEPING

Most of the accommodation in Mamoudzou is aimed at visiting businesspeople and is therefore expensive.

Habitat Rose Doudou (☎ 61 04 48; rose.doudou@ wanadoo.fr; 16 Route de Majimbini; r from €35) A quiet, family-run *chambre d'hôte* with a good choice of rooms and prices, and the opportunity to self-cater – there's a well-equipped kitchen for guests to use. You can also rent studios with bathroom, kitchen and one bedroom. The disadvantage is that it's quite far out of town. To get here follow the road past the hospital, then look for the signpost at the crossroads.

L'Horizon (☎ 65 95 98; 9 Rue Mahabou; r with breakfast €55; ❄) This is another homely *chambre d'hôte* with big, modern rooms with private bathroom. It's conveniently close to town and friendly, with good views over the lagoon. Reserve, as it's often full.

Caribou Hotel (☎ 61 14 18; hotelcaribou.mayotte@ wanadoo.fr; Place du Marché; r from €85; ❄) Mamoudzou's most upmarket hotel comes with a restaurant and snack bar, business services and a slightly plasticky feel. The rooms, however, are comfortable and have satellite TV and telephones. The snack bar (sandwiches €6) is a popular meeting place for the town's French population.

EATING & DRINKING

There is a fairly good selection of restaurants in Mamoudzou, most of which double as bars. There's not much in the way of cheap eats – try the market stalls down by the port, which serve fried bananas and the occasional omelette for around €3, but get there early before the flies have done too much damage. You can also find evening food stalls around the stadium in the suburb of Cavani, to the west.

Le Vahine (☎ 61 14 49; 12 Rue du Stade; fish curries €7; ⏰ lunch & dinner Mon-Sat, dinner Sun) Excellent, friendly service, big portions and reasonable prices mean this cheerful place is often packed, although the menu is very limited. If you can't get a table, have a wander in the area, which has several cheap restaurants and cafés.

Les Saveurs des Îles (☎ 61 29 76; 10 Rue du Commerce; rice dishes €7; ⏰ lunch Mon-Sat) One of the few places in Mamoudzou that serves down-home local cooking at reasonable prices, including delicious curries, chicken and coconut rice. It's on the 1st floor, away from the exhaust fumes.

Le Rond-point (☎ 61 04 61; 2 Rue du Commerce; mains from €16; ⏰ lunch & dinner Mon-Sat) A good wine list and a cocktail menu complement the French gastronomy and lagoon view in this fairly classy establishment. It's popular with bureaucrats and expats for its authentic French cuisine.

ENTERTAINMENT

Given Mayotte is a part of France, you can drink like a sailor here. And Mamoudzou boasts two (fairly average) discos: the down-to-earth **Golden Lagon** (Rue du Commerce; admission €12) and **Le Mahaba** (Place du Marché; admission €15), next door to Mayotte Vacances, where a smart dress code is enforced.

GETTING THERE & AROUND

A regular ferry known as *le barge* takes cars, bikes, trucks and foot passengers between Mamoudzou and Dzaoudzi, with a journey time of about 10 minutes. Foot passengers cost only €1 per person, but cars are €20. You only pay on the Mamoudzou side. The ferry departs every 30 minutes between 6am and 10.30pm, then every hour until 12.30pm. There are ferries until 2.30am on Saturdays.

Within Mamoudzou, shared taxis cost a standard €1 for rides around town.

Around Grande Terre

Most of the route that encircles Mayotte is paved, but the uneven coastline, especially in the north, makes for lots of twisting and bending and is rather slow going, so don't try to cover too much ground in a day.

SIGHTS & ACTIVITIES

As you travel around Mayotte, watch out for the interesting and colourful **bangas**, small bachelor houses constructed by young men and painted with humorous sayings and philosophies such as '*la vie célibataire est la vie superbe*' (the bachelor life is a superb life). Often, several friends will share the same *banga*, each encouraging the other to complete his education before marrying and starting a family.

Off the far northwestern tip is a group of islands collectively known as **M'Tsamboro**. They are very difficult to reach by public transport, but offer superb swimming and snorkelling. Mayotte Vacances (opposite) organises day trips by boat around the islands for about €55 per person.

On the chocolate-coloured west-coast beach of Soulou is the **Cascade de Soulou**, an unusual 8m-high waterfall that plunges directly into the sea (or onto the beach at low tide). Be careful if driving down the rough track that leads to the waterfall, 2km south of Mtsangamouji – hire cars are regularly trashed on this route.

Sea turtles often come and lay their eggs on the beaches of the peninsula of **Sazilé** in the extreme southeast of Mayotte, and the sand island opposite. To get here, it's a 4km walk from the trailhead on the road between the villages of Mtsamoudou and Dapani. If you're there in the daytime, you'll need to don a snorkel and fins to see the turtles, which are fairly wild and shy.

SLEEPING & EATING

There are a few scattered B&Bs and homestays in the villages around Mayotte, but these can be very hard to find. The best thing to do is get an up-to-date list of what's available from the Comité du Tourisme in Mamoudzou (opposite) before setting out, and ring ahead to get proper directions. There are no camp sites on the island, but in some places you may be allowed to pitch a tent. Likewise there are one or two little restaurants around the island, but you're mostly confined to the hotel restaurants listed here.

Hôtel Le Sakouli (☎ 60 63 63; sakouli.hotel@wanadoo.fr; Plage de Sakouli; r from €200; 🏊 🐟) is Mayotte's most upmarket beach hotel, popular with French honeymooners. There is a fantastic horizon swimming pool, a Jacuzzi and a panoramic terrace. The rooms are big and tiled, with a TV, full-sized bathtub and balcony. If you come for lunch in the restaurant (€25) you are allowed to use the pool. Prices go up at Christmas and New Year and during school holidays.

A more rustic option is **Le Jardin Maoré** (☎ 60 14 19; jardin.maore@wanadoo.fr; Plage de N'gouja; r from €125; 🏊). Not only are the prices a bit lower, but it is also on a much better beach, with the added draw of virtually guaranteed sea-turtle viewing. During the day you can snorkel with the turtles that live just off the beach, and during the night watch them come up on to the shore to lay their eggs. The food and service in the restaurant (buffet lunch €20) are generally average, but Le Jardin's bungalows are very well decorated, with raffia walls, draped mosquito nets and platform beds. There's also a fully equipped dive and water sports centre on site. The restaurant gets very busy with French expatriates at weekends. During

COMOROS

French summer holidays and Christmas, rates increase substantially.

PETITE TERRE

The island of Petite Terre, with two villages named Pamandzi and L'Abattoir, is connected to the rock of Dzaoudzi (a sort of poor man's version of the Rock of Gibraltar) by a causeway. Until the arrival of the foreign legion in 1962, it served as the capital of Mayotte, and still functions as its military centre. Two small islands comprise Petite Terre, which, being considerably quieter and cleaner than Mamoudzou, has become the affluent high-rent district of Mayotte. It's here that most of the European community lives.

The village of Pamandzi has a pretty, tranquil beach known as **Moya Plage**, and a volcanic crater called **Dziani Dzaha**, but there's very little of interest on Dzaoudzi beyond a few handsome colonial buildings and a single hotel.

Near the coast on the western side of Pamandzi is the archaeological site of **Bagamayo**. Researchers working at the site have uncovered pottery, tombs and glass beads indicating a 10th-century Shirazi settlement.

For sleeping try Petite Terre's most upmarket option, **Le Rocher** (☎ 60 10 10; lerocher@wanadoo.fr; Blvd des Crabes, Dzaoudzi; r from €65; ☒). Expect lots of gilt, fake Grecian statues and potted palms, but the cheesy décor is actually quite fun and the prices reasonable for Mayotte. Rooms are a bit worn but still comfortable. Some have balconies and views of the lagoon, while others come with full-sized bathtubs. There's a pricey onsite restaurant and a disco called **Ningha** (☒ Mon-Sat), which charges €15 entry for men (free for women).

Villa Raha (☎ 62 03 64; 13 Rue Smiam, Pamandzi; r from €30) is the best budget option. The rooms are scruffy but acceptable overall and the location is nice and quiet. Some of the rooms share a little sitting area. Dinner (€10) can be arranged.

For typical French cuisine including frogs legs and crab specialities, try **Auberge de l'Île** (☎ 60 14 57; Rte de Moya, L'Abattoir; mains €20), which has a rotating nightly menu.

For more of a bar atmosphere on the beach, try **Le Faré** (☎ 60 13 31; Blvd des Crabes, L'Abattoir; mains from €10; ☒ dinner Tue, lunch & dinner Wed-Sun), which has a limited menu – usually a daily dish. It also has a pool table, however, and fills quickly on weekends.

Getting There & Around

The redoubtable *barge* brings passengers over to Petite Terre from Mamoudzou. Once you're there, you can whiz anywhere on the island in shared taxis, which cost between €1 and €1.50, depending on where you're going.

Directory

CONTENTS

ACCOMMODATION

In most Malagasy and Comorian towns, it's usually possible to find a decent, relatively clean room (with bathroom) starting at around Ar25,000. For more amenities – such as aircon, satellite TV and a swimming pool – in a Western-style upper midrange hotel expect to pay between Ar60,000 and Ar75,000 (unless you are staying in tourist resort areas such as Nosy Be and Île Sainte Marie, in which case prices can be double that).

In this guide, 'budget' refers to establishments charging less than Ar25,000; 'midrange' refers to places charging roughly between Ar25,000 and Ar60,000; and 'top end' usually refers to establishments that charge more than Ar60,000 per night. Some top-end places only quote in euros.

PRACTICALITIES

- In Madagascar, check out the French-language newspapers *Midi Madagasikara*, *Madagascar Tribune* and *L'Express de Madagascar*. In the Comoros, pick up the government-run *Al Watwan*, also in French.

- Madagascar TV stations include Marc Ravalomanana's MBS, as well as the semiprivate MA-TV, RTA, OTV and RTT. In the Comoros, MTV (not the American music channel!) shows local music and some films dubbed into French.

- Voltage in Madagascar and the Comoros (in those places that have electricity) is 220V. Outlets take European-style two-pin round plugs.

- Madagascar and the Comoros both use the metric system.

In tourist areas such as Nosy Be and Île Sainte Marie prices are always higher than in cities such as Fianarantsoa or Diego Suarez, but costs rise even more during the June to August high season and around Christmas, New Year and Easter. Unless otherwise noted, prices quoted in this book are high-season prices. It's better, but not essential, to make advance reservations during the high season.

Camping & Gîtes D'Étape

Camping is possible in most areas of Madagascar and the Comoros. Campsite facilities vary, from hot showers, toilets and well-equipped cooking areas, to nothing more

---

BOOK ACCOMMODATION ONLINE

For more accommodation reviews and recommendations by Lonely Planet authors, check out the online booking service at www.lonelyplanet.com. You'll find the true, insider lowdown on the best places to stay. Reviews are thorough and independent. Best of all, you can book online.

DIRECTORY

RESPONSIBLE DIVING

Please consider the following tips when diving, and help preserve the ecology and beauty of reefs.

- Never use anchors on the reef, and take care not to ground boats on coral.
- Avoid touching or standing on living marine organisms or dragging equipment across the reef. Polyps can be damaged by even the gentlest contact. If you must hold onto the reef, only touch exposed rock or dead coral.
- Be conscious of your fins. Even without contact, the surge from fin strokes near the reef can damage delicate organisms. Take care not to kick up clouds of sand, which can smother organisms.
- Practise and maintain proper buoyancy control. Major damage can be done by divers descending too fast and colliding with the reef.
- Take great care in underwater caves. Spend as little time within them as possible as your air bubbles may be caught within the roof and thereby leave organisms high and dry. Take turns to inspect the interior of a small cave.
- Resist the temptation to collect or buy corals or shells or to loot marine archaeological sites (mainly shipwrecks).
- Ensure that you take home all your rubbish and any litter you may find as well. Plastics in particular are a serious threat to marine life.
- Do not feed fish.
- Minimise your disturbance of marine animals. *Never* ride on the backs of turtles.

---

than a cleared area of bush. Some national parks also have basic hostels known as *gîtes d'étape* (also known as *gîtes*), as well as one or two tents for hire, but the tents are not always very high quality.

Homestays

In rural areas you can sometimes arrange informal homestays by politely asking around a village for a place to sleep in return for payment. Pay a fair fee (about Ar15,000 per room is appropriate) and if possible provide your own food – your hosts may barely have enough to feed themselves.

Hotels & Bungalows

Hotels in Madagascar and the Comoros are also known as *pensions, chambres d'hôte, residences* or *auberges. Pensions* and *chambres d'hôte* are the simplest. Note that the word *hotely* in Madagascar refers not to a hotel, but to a simple restaurant, although often these have basic rooms as well.

Cheaper rooms have their own shower or basin and you share a toilet (WC). Other, more expensive rooms have bathrooms including toilet. Cheapest of all are rooms with a shared toilet and bathroom, known as *salle de bain commune.*

Madagascar is just starting to tap into the luxury market – there are now a few posh 'eco-lodge' resorts scattered about, mainly on Nosy Be and the islands around it, and on Île Sainte Marie in the east. Fly-in resorts are taking off on the remote northwest coast between Nosy Be and Mahajanga.

Hot water and a decent blanket or two are luxuries worth paying for if you're staying in the *hauts plateaux* (highlands) region of central Madagascar, especially in winter, when even the posh Hilton in Antananarivo can feel freezing – hotels don't have central heating, and cheaper places are notorious for draughts. If you're travelling to Antananarivo and central Madagascar in winter, consider investing in a lightweight sleeping bag and silk liner. Also bring a hat and thermal long-johns and undershirt.

ACTIVITIES

Someone has finally lit a torch under Madagascar's untapped adventure industry, and adrenalin-pumping activities are now more readily available than ever.

Climbing

For rock climbing, head to the Diego Suarez area in northern Madagascar. There are some good technical routes up the Montagne des Français, and even a few companies offering tours and advice. Antananarivo-based adventure specialist **Les Lézards de Tana** (☎ 22 351 01; www.madamax.com), or its subsidiary **New Sea Roc** (www.newsearoc.com) in Diego Suarez, are good places to start.

If trees are more your thing than rocks, check out **Mad'arbres** (www.madarbres.com), an innovative new company with sites at Andasibe and Anjozorobe (in eastern Madagascar) that offers roped climbs and rainforest canopy tours for all levels of fitness.

Cycling

Madagascar is a good country for mountain-biking. Cheap Chinese-made bicycles can be hired in many places. For any long-distance trip you will need to bring your bike from home. For more information on cycling check the website of **Madagascar on Bike** (www.madagascar-on-bike.com).

Diving & Snorkelling

Madagascar and the Comoros are the ideal places to lower oneself over the side of a boat and into another world. Ifaty, Île Sainte Marie, Nosy Be and Mayotte are some of the best sites. There are companies in every dive spot competing to offer internationally recognised diving courses and trips for qualified divers.

Most dive operators insist on checking your general ability, health and qualifications before you can enrol in a diving course. If you are not sure if diving is for you, many places offer a *baptême*, also known as a 'try dive' or 'first dive'. Some dive instructors speak English, Italian and German as well as French. Many dive centres in Madagascar are closed between February and May, when diving conditions are least favourable.

Please note that there is no hyperbaric chamber anywhere in Madagascar, so should you have a mishap under water, you will have to go to Réunion to be depressurised.

Hiking & Trekking

Madagascar is made for trekking, and many people come for this reason alone. There are literally thousands of kilometres of virgin and varied terrain, chock full of vegetation and animals that may exist nowhere else in the world. In a single week you could easily find yourself marching in single file along a rocky, boiling ridge with acres of yellow grass on all sides, then a few days later slithering downhill through stands of giant bamboo with rainwater trickling down your neck.

The most popular hiking areas in the country include Parc National d'Andringitra, Parc National de l'Isalo, the Réserve Spéciale de l'Ankàrana and the Masoala Peninsula. Hiking highlights in the Comoros islands include the picturesque hills of Anjouan, the rainforests of Mohéli and the ascent of Grande Comore's Mt Karthala, an active volcano.

SAFETY GUIDELINES FOR DIVING

Before embarking on a scuba-diving, skin-diving or snorkelling trip, carefully consider the following points to ensure a safe and enjoyable experience.

- Possess a current diving certification card from a recognised scuba-diving instructional agency (if scuba-diving).
- Be sure you are healthy and feel comfortable diving.
- Obtain reliable information about physical and environmental conditions at the dive site (eg from a reputable local dive operation).
- Be aware of local laws, regulations and etiquette about marine life and the environment.
- Dive only at sites within your realm of experience; if available, engage the services of a competent, professionally trained dive instructor or dive master.
- Be aware that underwater conditions vary significantly from one region, or even site, to another. Seasonal changes can significantly alter any site and dive conditions. These differences influence the way divers dress for a dive and what diving techniques they use.
- Ask about the environmental characteristics that can affect your diving and how local trained divers deal with these considerations.

It's not all hard going, but a reasonable level of fitness is required for most areas. In many places, such as Parc National de Ranomafana or the Masoala Peninsula, trekking involves some mud, stream crossings, leeches and slogging through rice paddies – particularly during the rainy season. In the more dry areas of the south and west, such as Parc National de l'Isalo, the main challenge is likely to be the heat.

For most hikes you will need sturdy shoes, a water bottle, first-aid kit and waterproofs. For longer treks, you'll need to be self-sufficient with water, food and camping equipment, and in almost all cases you'll need a guide. Porters are also available in many places. For routes off the beaten track, bring along a topographical map and a compass or GPS device.

Sailing & Kayaking

Madagascar and the Comoros offer miles of coastline to explore and a variety of vessels to sail in, from tiny wooden pirogues to luxury catamarans. Nosy Be and Mayotte are the two most popular take-off points.

The water around the Masoala Peninsula in northeastern Madagascar is ideal for sea kayaking. **Kayak Masoala** (www.kayakafrica.com/madagascar .asp), a company based near Maroantsetra, runs boat-supported sea-kayak trips to beautiful Cap Masoala on the peninsula's southern edge.

Surfing & Water Sports

Surfing and windsurfing are starting to take off in Madagascar, especially around Fort Dauphin and the beaches around Toliara, which have lots of untapped potential – there are numerous rideable breaks with no one riding them. If you have your own board and gear, and know what you're doing, you'll get to surf totally virgin waves. Surfing is best from March through September and you'll need to bring all your own equipment.

Windsurfing and kitesurfing are popular in Diego Suarez' windy bays. The best windsurfing is between August and February.

Quad-Biking

Revving up the motor and hitting the trail on a quad bike (ATV) is also popular, with multiple companies in the touristy areas (especially the north and east) running guided tours.

Madaventure (☎ 032 04 782 37; www.madaventure .com) is an east coast–based adventure company specialising in quad bike and beach-

buggy tours of Île Sainte Marie and the Canal des Pangalanes; it gets good feedback.

In northern Madagascar, **MadaQuad** (Map p176; ☎ 032 40 888 14; www.madaquad.net; 9 Rue Surcouf, Diego Suarez) is one of Diego Suarez' top quad bike companies, running guided trips to an amazing red *tsingy* forest and three gorgeous bays. The overnight camping trip is unique, and includes a snorkelling stop.

BUSINESS HOURS

Offices, post offices, banks, shops and internet cafés are normally open from 8am to noon and 3pm to 6pm on weekdays. Most places are also open from 8am to noon on Saturday. In hotter areas, such as Toliara, places may stay shut even longer during daylight hours, but then remain open until about 7pm on weekday evenings.

In the Comoros, government offices and banks close around noon on Friday for prayers and don't reopen in the afternoon. During the holy month of Ramadan restaurants are closed and many businesses, shops and government offices open around 7am and close at lunchtime for the rest of the day. The dates of Ramadan change every year – to find them, check out www.holidays .net/ramadan/dates.htm.

Most restaurants are open from about 11am to 2pm for lunch, and in the evenings from about 6pm to 9.30pm.

CHILDREN

With few formal children's attractions or childcare facilities, Madagascar and the Comoros are both reasonably hard places to travel with young children, so junior travellers are a fairly rare sight. Some national parks and zoos (eg the Croq Farm in Antananarivo and the Andasibe-Mantadia, l'Isalo and Ranomafana national parks) have visitors centres with exhibitions geared towards helping children understand issues of biodiversity and conservation.

Disposable nappies are available in Antananarivo's supermarkets, but are hard to find elsewhere. Many hotels provide *chambres familiales* or double rooms with an extra single bed geared for use by parents and children. Some of the more upmarket hotels provide a *menu enfant* (children's menu) and high chairs in their restaurants.

For more information, check out Lonely Planet's *Travel with Children* by Cathy Lanigan and Maureen Wheeler.

CLIMATE CHARTS

Madagascar experiences a variety of climatic conditions. Most rainfall occurs on the east coast and in the far north, while areas southwest of the highlands remain dry for much of the year.

Average maximum temperatures vary from about 30°C in coastal areas (although the mercury has climbed as high as 44°C on occasion) to around 25°C on the *hauts plateaux*. In Antan-

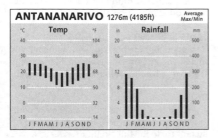

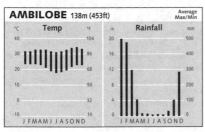

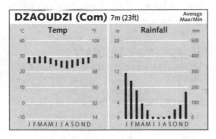

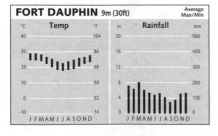

anarivo and other highland areas, temperatures during the winter months can drop to 10°C and even lower during the night. Temperatures at the country's highest elevations may be as low as -10°C during June and July – bring some warm clothing, please. Along the western coast, temperatures are high year-round.

The Comoros have a tropical climate, with a wet season from the months of October to April. The heaviest rainfall occurs between December and April and amounts can reach as high as 390mm in a month.

Temperatures are extremely hot even during the wet season, rarely dropping below 19°C at any time of year. The central, higher parts of the islands (especially Anjouan) remain significantly cooler than the coasts.

For more information on the best time to travel in Madagascar and the Comoros, see p14.

CUSTOMS

It's forbidden to take the following out of Madagascar: live plants (including vanilla), mounted insects, tortoiseshell, fragments of *Aepyornis* (elephant bird) eggshell, precious stones (in export quantities only), antique jewellery, antique coins, fossils, funerary art and antiquities. The export of coral and seashells is forbidden in the Comoros islands and Mayotte. For more detailed information, check the website of **Malagasy customs** (www .madagascar-contacts.com/douanes in French).

DANGERS & ANNOYANCES

Travelling around Madagascar and the Comoros is not inherently dangerous – there isn't a single venomous snake on any of the islands. There is no reason for you to be overly concerned about your personal safety. However, as when travelling anywhere in the world, some common-sense precautions are always warranted.

One of the most maddening annoyances here is the number of crusty old French men spied at beach resorts with their arms around beautiful Malagasy girls young enough to be their daughters. The government is attempting to fight the sex-tourism industry with signs in shop windows declaring in Malagasy, French and English that 'A child is not a toy'.

Along with underground brothels, where the youngest virgins go for the highest price, Madagascar's tourist areas – Nosy Be is particularly bad – are filled with young girls who come from the rural villages in hopes of meeting a rich European man to marry and escape with. Sadly, many men prey on this exact desperation, and seduce these girls into having sex (they usually pay for expensive meals and hotel rooms and talk about love and marriage) for a week until they return home to their lives across the planet, leaving the women brokenhearted, or, even worse, pregnant. Of course for all the tears, there are also happy endings. Genuine foreigners do come to Madagascar, fall in love with a local girl and stay forever.

Beaches & Forests
Some areas along the Malagasy and Comorian coastlines are subject to danger from sharks and strong currents. Make sure to seek local advice before heading into the water. To avoid stepping on sea urchins or nibbling crabs always wear shoes when walking on the beach or swimming in the water.

In rainforests watch for leeches in muddy areas or during the rainy season. Wear your socks over your trousers (OK, we know how freaking dorky that sounds, but it does work), apply insect repellent, and carry salt to remove any leeches that do get in. Mosquitoes are also ubiquitous – wear insect repellent, especially at dawn and dusk.

Crimes
If you've travelled in other parts of Africa you will be shocked at how safe Madagascar feels. Armed car-jacking and random violent crime aren't an issue. People are definitely poor, and you will see shack ghettos looking as raggedy as the folks huddled over the cooking fires in front of them, but on the whole the Malagasy are a reserved lot and are likely to leave you alone. Pick-pocketing and snatch-and-grab robberies are the most frequent crimes. You can usually avoid any trouble by dressing down (leave the diamonds at home), walking confidently and carrying as few valuables as possible.

Police checkpoints are random, though most usually occur on the road. We were stopped on numerous occasions but never asked to produce our passports. Supposedly it is the law to carry your passport, and you can be fined for not having it on you, so carry it to be safe.

Road Accidents
A combination of packed and unroadworthy vehicles, reckless drivers and poor-quality roads makes taxi-brousse (bush taxi) travel in Madagascar, and to a lesser extent the Comoros, fairly hazardous. To minimise the risks, try to avoid night travel if possible.

Annoyances on taxis-brousses come in the form of inadequate legroom, or any sort of personal space for that matter (rows meant to seat three never have less than five, leaving you no room to move at all), and deafening music blasting from tinny speakers. Consider an inflatable cushion and a pair of earplugs (an iPod turned high also works).

Touts & Guides
Be wary of organising trips with someone you met at the airport on arrival in Madagascar. It's always best to wait and get a recommendation from your hotel or other travellers first.

While most official guides are very competent and well trained, some guides are reluctant to do the full circuit they've been paid for, while others ask for higher fees than those set by the park. Check prices before parting with your money. If you aren't satisfied with your guide for any reason, report the matter to the **Association Nationale pour la Gestion des Aires Protégées** (Angap; National Association for the Management of Protected Areas; www.parcs-madagascar.com/angap.htm in French) or park office.

When booking an organised tour or car and driver hire, clarify at the outset (ideally in writing) what your agreement is with the tour operator. It's also a good idea to try to meet your guide in advance to gauge their language abilities.

EMBASSIES & CONSULATES
Madagascan Embassies & Consulates
Australia (☎ 02 9299 2290; tonyknox@ozemail.com.au; 6th fl, 100 Clarence St, Sydney NSW 2000)
Canada (☎ 613 744 7995; ambmgnet@inexpress.net; 649 Blair Rd, Ottawa, K1J 7M4, Ontario)
Comoros (☎ 73 18 69; consmad@snpt.km; BP 349, Moroni)
France (☎ 01 45 04 62 11; ambamadparis@tiscali.fr; 4 Ave Raphael, Paris 75016)
Germany (☎ 02 28 95 35 90; ambamad@aol.com; Rolandstrasse 53-170, Bonn-Bad Godesberg)
Italy (☎ 3 6 30 77 97; ambamad-rm@flashnet -it.netclub.mg; Viaricardo Zandonai 84, 400 194 Roma)
Japan (☎ 03 3446 72 52; 2-3-23 Moko Azabu, Minako-Ku, Tokyo)
Kenya (☎ 02 218 393; mbnbo@africaonline.co.kc; 1st fl, Hilton Hotel, BP 41723, Nairobi)

Mauritius (☎ 0686 50 15; Rue Guiot Pasceau, Floreal)
Netherlands (☎ 10 4255212; 97 Heemraadssingel, 3022 CB Rotterdam)
Seychelles (☎ 03 40 30; BP 68 Plaisance, Mahe)
South Africa (☎ 011 442 33 22; PO Box 786098, Sandton 2146)
United Kingdom (☎ 020 8746 0133; 16 Lanark Mansions, Pennard Rd, London, W12 8DT)
United States (☎ 202 265 5522; malagasy@embassy .org; 2374 Massachusetts Ave, NW, Washington, DC 20008)

Comorian Embassies & Consulates

For Mayotte, pay a visit to your nearest French embassy.
France (☎ 01 40 67 90 54; 20 Rue Marbeau, Paris)
Germany (☎ 02 2345 4444)
Kenya (☎ 02 22 29 64)
South Africa (☎ 012 343 9483)
United Kingdom (☎ 020 7460 1162; 16 Lanark Mansions, Pennard Rd, London, W12 8DT)
United States (☎ 212 223 27 11; 420 East 50 St, New York, NY 10022)

Embassies & Consulates in Madagascar

Norway, Denmark and the UK have honorary consulates near the port in Toamasina.

The following embassies and consulates are mostly in Antananarivo.
Canada (off Map pp72-3; ☎ 22 425 59; c.canada@dts .mg; Lot II, 169 Villa 3H, Ivandry)
Comoros Antananarivo (Map p76; ☎ 032 02 404 506; Rue Doktor Villette, Isoraka); Mahajanga (☼ 8am-1pm Mon-Sat) A block behind the Air Austral office in Antananarivo, this embassy can issue Comorian visas.
France (Map p76; ☎ 22 214 88; 3 Rue Jean Jaurès, Ambatomena) Near the Shanghai Hotel.
Germany (off Map pp72-3; ☎ 22 238 02; 101 Rue Pasteur Rabeony, Ambodiroatra)
Italy (Map pp72-3; ☎ 22 284 43; 22 Rue Pasteur Rabary, Ankadivato) East of the centre.
Japan (Map p76; ☎ 22 261 02; Rte Fort Duchesne Ampasanimalo)
Mauritius (off Map pp72-3; ☎ 22 321 57; Rte Circulaire Anjahana) South of the centre.
Netherlands (off Map pp72-3; ☎ 22 224 22; 88 Lotissement Bonnet, Ivandry) North of the centre.
Seychelles (Map p76; ☎ 22 632 02; 18 Rue Jean Jaurès, Ambatomena) Near the Shanghai Hotel.
South Africa (off Map pp72-3; ☎ 22 423 03; Rte d'Ambohimanga, Ambohitrarahaba)
United Kingdom (Map pp72-3; ☎ 22 273 70; Lot III, 164 Ter Alarobia Amboniloha)
United States (Map p76; ☎ 22 209 56, 22 212 57; 14 Lalana Rainitovo, Haute-Ville) East of the UCB bank.

Embassies & Consulates in the Comoros
France (☎ 73 06 15; Ave de Republic Populaire de China, Moroni, Grande Comore)
Madagascar (☎ 73 18 69; consmad@snpt.km; Moroni, Grande Comore)

FESTIVALS & EVENTS
Madagascar
Alahamady Be (March) The low-key Malagasy New Year.
Santabary (April/May) The first rice harvest.
Fisemana (June) A ritual purification ceremony of the Antakàrana people.
Famadihana (June to September) Literally the 'turning of the bones', these reburial ceremonies are held especially during August and September. See the boxed text on p37 for more information.
Sambatra (June to December) Circumcision festivals held by most tribes between June and September, and in November and December in the southwest.

The Comoros
Comorian festivals are based around the Muslim calendar, which changes from year to year. For more information on holidays, see below.

FOOD
Budget restaurants as listed in this guide are usually food stalls or small Malagasy *hotelys*; they are open only until about 8pm, and serve mainly rice dishes or snacks for under Ar6000. Midrange restaurants serve plain French food and lots of seafood, including staples such as *steack frites* (steak and chips) and calamari, shrimp and lobster dishes, costing between Ar6000 and Ar25,000 for a main course depending on whether you order calamari or lobster. French haute cuisine, which might include lobster profiteroles or goose liver pâté, usually infused with local spices, can cost as much as Ar30,000 for a main course.

For more information, see p39.

GAY & LESBIAN TRAVELLERS
Homosexual practices are illegal in Madagascar and the Comoros for persons under 21 years of age. Homosexuality is not openly practised, and there are no organisations catering to gay and lesbian travellers. Overt displays of affection – whether the couple is of the same or opposite sex – are considered culturally inappropriate.

HOLIDAYS
In the Comoros, and to a lesser extent in Madagascar, accommodation and flights are

often harder to find during French school holidays, when many expats from Mayotte and Réunion travel in the region. To find out when these holidays are, look up the website www.ac-reunion.fr/academie/calendri.htm, which is in French.

Government offices and private companies close on the following public holidays; banks are generally also closed the afternoon before a public holiday.

Madagascar
New Year's Day 1 January
Insurrection Day 29 March – celebrates the rebellion against the French in 1947.
Easter Monday March/April
Labour Day 1 May
Anniversary Day 8 May
Organisation of African Unity Day 25 May
Ascension Thursday May/June – occurs 40 days after Easter.
Pentecost Monday May/June – occurs 51 days after Easter.
National Day 26 June – Independence Day.
Assumption 15 August
All Saints' Day 1 November
Christmas Day 25 December
Republic Day 30 December

The Comoros
The main holidays for Muslim Comorians are Islamic and based on the lunar calendar, so the dates change yearly. The biggest celebration is Id-ul-Fitr, which marks the end of the Ramadan fast. The other major Islamic holiday is Id-el-Kabir, also known as Id-el-Haj, which marks the beginning of the pilgrimage to Mecca.

These four dates are designated as specific public holidays:
New Year's Day 1 January
Labour Day 1 May
Organisation of African Unity 25 May – Celebration Day.
Independence Day 5 July

In addition to those celebrated above, Mayotte also observes Bastille Day (14 July) and Christmas Day (25 December).

INSURANCE
A travel-insurance policy to cover theft, loss and medical problems is essential. Some policies specifically exclude dangerous activities, which can include scuba-diving, motorcycling or even trekking.

You may prefer a policy that pays doctors or hospitals directly rather than you having to pay on the spot and claim later.

Check that the policy covers an emergency flight home. This is an important consideration for Madagascar, given the cost of air tickets to most destinations.

For more advice about health-insurance policies, see p286.

INTERNET ACCESS
Many internet providers in Madagascar and the Comoros (including some post offices) run fast and reliable services. The cheapest services, mostly available in provincial capitals, cost about Ar50 per minute, while in more remote places the cost might be as high as Ar300 per minute; Ar100 per minute seems to be the norm.

LEGAL MATTERS
The use and possession of marijuana and other recreational drugs is illegal in Madagascar and the Comoros. If you are arrested, ask to see a representative of your country. Madagascar is strict in enforcing immigration laws, so don't overstay your visa. The legal age of consent for heterosexual sex is 15 years.

MAPS
Official maps produced by Foiben Taosarintanin'i Madagasikara (FTM) are available at bookshops in Antananarivo and major towns for about Ar20,000. The maps can be fairly dated but are generally accurate, and more than adequate for visiting the country. FTM also produces street maps of the provincial capitals, although these are increasingly hard to find.

Edicom and Carambole both publish detailed maps of Antananarivo, which are widely available at bookshops and cost about Ar15,000.

A detailed map and compass is essential when hiking without a guide. Topographical maps are hard to find in Madagascar, so buy one before you leave.

In Malagasy, *lalana* means street; *arabe* or *araben* means avenue; and *kianja* or *kianjan* means place or square. In this book, street names are given in either French or Malagasy, depending on local usage. One street often has several names depending on what map you look at, and locals basically don't use street names at all.

MONEY
Madagascar

Madagascar changed its currency from the Malagasy franc (FMG) back to the precolonial ariary (Ar) in 2004. Although the old Malagasy franc will remain exchangeable up until 2009 at banks, all the shops use and accept ariary now. One ariary is worth five FMG.

Prices are still quoted in FMGs in more remote areas. More of a problem is unscrupulous taxi drivers and tour guides who quote tourists using the old currency, but fail to tell them so, hence screwing travellers (at least those who don't ask if the high fare is in FMGs) into paying five times what the trip was worth. It's a good scam that the drivers don't even have to feel *too* guilty about – they did quote with legal tender!

Euros are also widely accepted, with the most expensive hotels quoting prices in them. Some want you to pay in euros so badly that they levy a conversion fee for using the ariary! US dollars are sometimes accepted in Antananarivo, major cities and tourist areas.

Taxi drivers and market vendors often cannot change large bills, so keep a selection of small change with you.

Madagascar is still primarily a cash economy – finding a hotel that accepts Visa, let alone one where the machine is actually working, is a real feat!

ATMS

BMOI, BNI-CL and BFV-SG all have ATMs at some branches in Antananarivo and other major towns. However, the amount you can take out is only around €150, and the machines often don't have enough cash to support multiple withdrawals. Many ATMs are only open a couple of hours later than the bank's normal opening hours.

BLACK MARKET & MONEYCHANGERS

There is no black market in Madagascar. Moneychangers may approach you on the street, but they are best avoided.

CREDIT CARDS

Credit cards are accepted at some upmarket hotels, at Air Madagascar, and at some larger travel agencies. Some places levy a commission of about 5% to 8% for credit-card payments. The most useful card is Visa, with MasterCard also accepted in a minority of places. Be aware that although a hotel may advertise that it accepts credit cards, machines are not reliable and often don't work.

Visa and MasterCard can now also be used at most banks to obtain cash advances (in ariary). Unless you are in a small city with a bad connection, authorisation is quick and easy, taking no longer than a shop transaction. Visa is more readily accepted but many banks also take MasterCard; commission rates go as high as 5%, depending on the bank.

EXCHANGE RATES

Exchange rates fluctuate daily, so it is generally best to only change what you need as you go along – as long as you are paying cash you don't pay commissions at the banks. Hotels usually change euros, and sometimes dollars, for guests free of charge. For exchange rates, see the inside front cover of this guide.

EXCHANGING MONEY

The best foreign currencies to carry are euros, followed by US dollars. Otherwise UK pounds, Swiss francs, Japanese yen and South African rand can be changed in Antananarivo, and sometimes in other major cities.

Travellers cheques are not particularly useful in Madagascar – except in Antananarivo you'll be hard pressed to find anyone who even accepts them. The banks and (few) hotels that do accept them also give a worse exchange rate than with cash, and charge a commission of up to 5% for exchanging them. At the most, take a few hundred dollars for emergencies (in case you get robbed), but otherwise euros (to change) and an ATM card are the way to go.

The major banks in Madagascar, with branches in Antananarivo and all major towns, are the Bank of Africa (BOA), Banky Fampandrosoana'ny Varotra-Société Générale (BFV-SG), Banque Malgache de l'Océan Indien (BMOI) and Bankin'ny Indostria-Crédit Lyonnais (BNI-CL).

The foreign-exchange counter at Ivato airport has exchange rates that are just as good as those at the banks, and is usually open for international flight arrivals. Madagascar's other airports do not have exchange facilities. The *bureau de change* at Ivato airport will change Malagasy currency back into euros or dollars, but requires a minimum of €50.

The Comoros

The currency of the Union des Comores (the official name of the Comoros, excluding

Mayotte) is the Comorian franc (CF), which is tied to the euro.

You can pay for major items such as accommodation, air tickets and boat fares in either Comorian francs or euros. For smaller purchases the local currency is usually preferable.

You can reconvert Comorian francs into euros at the bank if you have the original bank receipt. In Mayotte, the official currency is the euro, and Comorian or Malagasy currency is entirely useless.

For exchange rates, see the inside front cover of this guide.

CREDIT CARDS

Credit cards (Visa and MasterCard) are accepted by many hotels and restaurants in Mayotte, but in the other Comoros islands only the most upmarket establishments accept cards, and all charge high rates of commission.

EXCHANGING MONEY

The best foreign currency to carry in the Union des Comores is the euro, although you can, in theory, also change US dollars, British pounds, Swiss francs and Japanese yen at the Banque pour l'Industrie et le Commerce (BIC), which has branches on the islands of Grande Comore and Anjouan. The BIC, which is the only bank to change foreign cash or travellers cheques, can also do advances on Visa cards, although it charges a hefty commission for this.

In Mayotte, only one bank, Banque Française Commerciale Ocean Indien (BFC-OI), will change cash or travellers cheques. BFC-OI's ATMs should theoretically advance you money on a Visa card.

You cannot change Comorian or Malagasy currency anywhere on Mayotte. There are no moneychanging facilities at the airport.

POST

There are post offices in all major towns of Madagascar and the Comoros. The postal service is generally reliable, although postcards frequently go missing.

To send a letter it costs Ar1000 to Europe, Ar2500 to Australia and Ar2600 to the United States. In the Comoros, prices are CF300 to France, CF350 to Europe and CF400 to the United States and Australia. Postcards are slightly cheaper.

SHOPPING

Madagascar offers a fantastic variety of handicrafts and souvenirs, so most of the visitors queuing in the departure hall of Ivato airport in Antananarivo are laden down with newspaper-wrapped bundles and bulging carrier bags. There is something for everyone – chess and solitaire sets made from semiprecious stones; musical instruments; sandals and belts; leather bags; chic brightly coloured raffia baskets; wood carvings and wood-inlay boxes; embroidered tablecloths; handmade Antaimoro paper; and tin model Citroëns and pousses-pousses (rickshaws), perfect down to the most minute detail. You will also see a lot of intricately detailed, handcrafted wooden replicas of ships and beautifully carved wood maps of Madagascar and the world.

Most souvenirs in the Comoros are simply everyday items, and can be bought at markets on all the islands – embroidered skullcaps, carved lecterns for the Koran, brass-inlaid wooden chests, silver and gold jewellery and colourful lengths of cloth known as chiromani.

In both countries, locally grown spices – white or black peppercorns, cinnamon sticks, cloves, saffron or vanilla – are widely available, but some countries, such as Australia, may not allow you to bring them in.

If you can cope with carrying your souvenirs until you get back to the airport, Ambositra (p100) in the central highlands is the shopping capital of Madagascar, with dozens of shops selling carvings and marqueterie (objects inlaid with coloured woods).

If you want to leave your purchasing until you're a taxi ride away from the airport, the best place for shopping is the Marché Artisanale de La Digue (p87) in Antananarivo. Bargaining hard is expected – start from 50% of the price and work upwards. It makes a good stop if you have time to kill on the way out.

When shopping, bear in mind that embroidery and raffia do far less damage to the environment than wooden products, which are often carved from endangered tropical hardwoods. If you do want to buy wooden products, try to find something made of eucalyptus, which is not endangered. Don't buy anything made from tortoiseshell or seashells, which are both illegal.

SOLO TRAVELLERS

Travelling alone in Madagascar or the Comoros poses few safety problems, provided you use common sense, such as avoiding unlit streets in bigger cities after dark.

The main disadvantages of travelling solo are financial – single rooms in hotels or guesthouses are uncommon, and you will invariably end up paying for a double room. You can expect to pay very high rates for organised tours if you're on your own, so it's best to find fellow travellers to share costs.

Speaking French will make a huge difference to your travels in Madagascar or the Comoros. If you are travelling independently, a grasp of at least the basics of the French language will enable you to communicate far more effectively. If you don't speak any French, learn some.

English-speaking readers have written to tell us on more than one occasion that more English than you would expect is spoken in the Comoros, and that they got by here without French. The same cannot be said for Mayotte.

TELEPHONE & FAX
Fax
In Madagascar, the Comoros and Mayotte, faxes can be sent from telephone offices, post offices and from upmarket hotels. Some internet cafés also offer fax services.

Madagascar
The country code for Madagascar is ☎ 261, followed by 20 if you are dialling a land line, then the seven-digit number. To call out of Madagascar, dial ☎ 00 before the country code.

International telephone lines are fairly good in Madagascar, and internal telephone service across the country has improved. The best way to dial internationally is with a *telecarte* (phonecard). Cardphones are scattered around all larger towns. Cards are sold at post offices, at Agence d'Accueil Telecom (Agate) offices and at some shops and hotels. For international calls you will need at least 100 units. Calls can also be made from more upmarket hotels (although rates will be much higher). Rates for international calls are Ar2700 per minute to France and the Comoros, and about a very pricey Ar4100 per minute to the rest of Europe, the USA and Canada. Calls are 30% cheaper between 10pm and 6am, all day Sunday and on holidays. The international operator can be reached by dialling ☎ 10.

Numbers in Madagascar consist of a two-digit area prefix followed by a five-digit local number (usually given in the form of a three-digit then a two-digit number). The two-digit prefix must be dialled whether you are calling locally, from elsewhere in Madagascar or from abroad. These prefixes are listed throughout this book as part of each telephone number. If you are quoted a five-digit number, add the two-digit area prefix.

To reach remote areas that do not have direct-dialling facilities (all those telephone numbers that have only two digits), dial ☎ 15 for the local operator, then request the number.

MOBILE PHONES
Cell phone coverage is excellent across all of Madagascar – our tri-band phone got better service in Madagascar than it does in many parts of the USA.

Mobile phone prefixes are 030, 031, 032 and 033. If dialling a mobile phone number from abroad, omit the zero and the 20 prefix, but add the country code.

For calls to mobile numbers from within Madagascar, you will need to dial the zero. When calling landline numbers from a mobile phone, dial ☎ 020 before the seven-digit number.

The Comoros
The country code for the Comoros, including Mayotte, is ☎ 269, followed by the six-digit local number. To call out of the Comoros, dial 00 followed by the country code. If you need any help with international calls, dial the **operator** (☎ 10). To dial from Mayotte to the Comoros or vice versa, dial ☎ 0269 followed by the number.

Calls can be made on all the islands from phone booths and hotels. In the Union des Comores, calls can also be made from Telecom offices (known as SNPT), usually located near the post office. In both the Union des Comores and Mayotte the easiest way to make a call is to buy a phonecard and use it in a phone box. In Mayotte, phonecards are sold in kiosks, shops and supermarkets. In the other Comoros islands, you can get a card from one of the touts hanging around outside phone booths proffering cards. Simply make your call, pay for the units you've used and give the card back. International calls cost CF1325 per minute to Europe and the US, and CF1500 per minute to Australia.

TIME

Madagascar and the Comoros are three hours ahead of GMT/UTC. There is no daylight savings.

TOURIST INFORMATION

The tourist offices in Madagascar, the Union des Comores and Mayotte can all provide lists of hotels and guesthouses; see individual chapters for details. Tourist office contact details for each place:

Comité du Tourisme du Mayotte (☎ 61 09 09; ctm@mayotte.tourisme.com; Rue de la Pompe, Mamoudzou, Mayotte; ☒ 7.30am-4.30pm Mon-Fri) Also has a branch at the airport.

Direction Generale du Tourisme (☎ 74 42 43; dg.tourisme@snpt.km; Ave des Ministères, Moroni, Grande Comore, Union des Comores; ☒ 7.30am-2.30pm Mon-Thu, to 11.30am Fri, to noon Sat)

Maison de Tourisme de Madagascar (☎ 22 351 78; www.madagascar-tourisme.com in French; 3 Lalana Elysée Ravelomanantsoa, Antananarivo, Madagascar; ☒ 8.30am-noon & 2-7pm Mon-Fri)

TRAVELLERS WITH DISABILITIES

Madagascar and the Comoros have few, if any, facilities for travellers with disabilities. This, combined with a weak infrastructure in many areas, may make travel here difficult.

Public transport is very crowded and unable to accommodate a wheelchair unless it is folded up. Travelling by rental car is the best option.

The Réserve Privée de Berenty (p136), near Fort Dauphin, and Parc National de l'Isalo (p122) are the most accessible of Madagascar's nature reserves for those with a disability.

In Antananarivo and most of the provincial capitals there are hotels with either elevators or accommodation on the ground floor. While most bungalow accommodation – the most common type of lodging in Madagascar – is generally on the ground floor, there are often steps up to the entrance, and inner doorways are often too narrow for a wheelchair.

There are few bathrooms large enough to manoeuvre a wheelchair in, and almost none with any sort of handles or holds.

Organisations that provide information on world travel for the mobility impaired include the following:

Mobility International USA (☎ 541 343 1284; www.miusa.org; USA)

National Information Communication Awareness Network (Nican; ☎ 02 6285 3713; www.nican.com.au; Australia)

Royal Association for Disability & Rehabilitation (☎ 020 7250 3222; www.radar.org.uk; UK)

Society for the Advancement of Travel for the Handicapped (SATH; ☎ 212 447 7284; www.sath.org; USA)

VISAS
Madagascar

All visitors must have a visa to enter Madagascar. Thirty-day visas for citizens of most countries can easily be purchased at Ivato airport in Antananarivo upon arrival for €13. The process is very straightforward and requires no photos – but you will need proof of a return flight. Simply hop off the plane and head straight for the visa line. The most annoying bit is waiting in the very long queue. To avoid the line, you could arrange in advance at any Malagasy embassy or consulate, but it is hardly worth the extra effort.

Visas for stays of up to three months from the date of entry do need to be organised in advance through the embassy or consulate. The same is true for multiple entry visas. Both must be used within six months of the date of issue. It's best to request a three-month visa from the start if there is any chance that you may need one, as visa extensions can be time consuming and expensive.

At most Malagasy embassies and consulates, visas cost the equivalent of about €29/34 for single/multiple entry. At most places you will need to provide a copy of your ticket or an itinerary from your travel agency and two to four photos.

As long as you have not exceeded the normal three-month maximum, visas can be extended at the immigration office in Antananarivo or any provincial capital. You will need between two and four passport-size photos and a copy of your return air or boat ticket. A one-month extension costs about €13 and can take several days to process.

The Comoros

All visitors need a visa to enter the Union des Comores. If you're coming from Madagascar you can obtain a visa prior to departure from the Comorian consulate in Antananarivo or Mahajanga.

Visas are available on arrival in Grande Comore, Anjouan and Mohéli. They cost €7 for up to 45 days and €11 for 90 days. Visas must be bought at the immigration offices in Moroni, Mutsamudu or Fomboni. If you arrive after the close of business on Friday and will be leaving before the following Monday, you will be issued with a free two-day weekend visa on arrival.

Only nationals of countries that need a visa to enter France will require a visa for Mayotte. These can be obtained at your nearest French consulate before arrival.

VOLUNTEERING

More people are showing interest in paying for the opportunity to 'volunteer' for community-enhancement and scientific-research projects in Madagascar. Many travellers express a desire to give back to the places they journey to, and the working holiday allows them to do just that.

Schools, orphanages and women's shelters often take on volunteers (without charging them!), but the network is far from organised – show up in the area where you want to work and ask around.

The following organisations all offer different types of experiences; check their websites to see what fits your budget and skills.

Akany Avoko (☎ 22 441 58; www.akanyavoko.com) An Antananarivo-based children's home that cares for around 150 orphans, street kids and young teenage mums with nowhere else to turn. Akany Avoko has been around for 40 years, and is sustained entirely by charitable donations and income-generating projects devised within the centre. It welcomes volunteers with the right skills.

Blue Ventures (☎ 0208 341 9819; www.blueventures .org) Based in London, with a field site in Andavadoaka, this highly efficient and effective organisation coordinates teams of volunteers to work with local NGOs and biologists. Together they educate communities reliant on marine ecosystems for survival on how best to preserve the ecosystems.

Dodwell Trust (www.dodwell-turst.org) This British charity runs a variety of projects accepting volunteers for one- to six-month stays. Opportunities include helping out with a radio programme broadcast in rural villages that discusses family health, AIDS prevention and sustainable development issues in an engaging manner. You can also live in a small town or village and assist with teaching English, or volunteer at the zoo in Antananarivo looking after the lemurs. Inexpensive housing is arranged.

Earthwatch (☎ in England 01865 318838; www .earthwatch.org/Europe) This Oxford-based company runs upmarket scientific research trips geared at midcareer professionals that give the opportunity to work with Dr Alison Jolly on lemur research.

WOMEN TRAVELLERS

Most women do not feel threatened or insecure in any way when travelling in either Madagascar or the Comoros. Hospitality and kindness to strangers are firmly entrenched in both cultures and extend in equal measure to female travellers. The most you can expect, especially in the Muslim Comoros, is some mild curiosity about your situation, especially if you are single and/or don't have children. Meeting Malagasy or Comorian women is relatively easy – many are well educated and confident and hold responsible jobs in government-related offices, especially the offices of national parks.

That said, around holiday resorts, where most of the local girls are snapped up by male tourists, you may encounter a low level of verbal pestering from local men. Compared with similar attention in say, North Africa, it's positively lacklustre, and a polite refusal nearly always suffices. Travelling in a group, saying you are married and dressing modestly (essential anyhow in the Comoros) are all ways to minimise problems. Physical harassment and violent crime are very rare, and in fact male travellers face far more pestering from the hordes of prostitutes who frequent almost every disco.

Women shouldn't enter mosques unless specifically told they can do so.

A limited selection of tampons is available in Antananarivo and some of the larger towns, but it's best to bring your own supply, especially in the Comoros.

Transport

CONTENTS

GETTING THERE & AWAY

ENTERING THE COUNTRY

Getting to Madagascar entails nothing more complex than a bit of queuing. Immigration officials generally just check or issue your visa before letting you go on your way. Landing cards are all printed in English as well as French. If you've come from a country where yellow fever is present you may be asked for a yellow-fever certificate (see p291).

Arriving in Mayotte and the Union des Comores is also relatively hassle free. There's a simple form to fill in (printed in English and French) and you're on your way.

If you need a visa on arrival in the Union des Comores, these are not issued at the airport but at the immigration offices in each island's capital.

See p274 for more information about visa requirements.

AIR
Airports & Airlines

International and domestic flights come into Ivato airport, just north of Antananarivo. The airports in Mahajanga and Toamasina both

THINGS CHANGE...

The information in this chapter is particularly vulnerable to change. Check directly with the airline or a travel agency to make sure you understand how a fare (and ticket you may buy) works and be aware of the security requirements for international travel. The details given in this chapter should be regarded as pointers and are not a substitute for your own careful, up-to-date research.

handle flights from Réunion, Mauritius and the Comoros. International flights come into Moroni airport on Grande Comore, and Dzaoudzi on Mayotte.

Air Madagascar is the national carrier of Madagascar. While occasional upsets in airline schedules still occur, service is relatively good.

Air Madagascar, Air France and Corsair, all operating flights from France, fly directly to Madagascar. There are now a few flights per week from Milan to Nosy Be or Île Sainte Marie in addition to flights from Munich or Rome to Antananarivo. There are no direct flights from outside the East African and Indian Ocean region to the Comoros. To fly to the Comoros from anywhere else, your best bet is to fly to Réunion, Mauritius, Antananarivo, Nairobi or Dar es Salaam and get an onward flight from there.

The main regional airline linking Madagascar and the Comoros with the Indian Ocean region is Air Austral (working in partnership with Air France and Air Mauritius).

In the Comoros, two airlines are currently operating – Comores Aviation and Comores Air Service. They both fly between the three islands of the Union des Comores. Comores Aviation also flies to Mayotte, while Comores Air Service has flights to Mombasa, Dar es Salaam and Zanzibar in East Africa.

AIRLINES FLYING TO & FROM MADAGASCAR

Air Austral/Air Mauritius (ARIO; Map p76; ☎ 22 359 90; www.airaustral.com; Rue des 77 Parlementaires Français, Antananarivo)

Air France (☎ 23 230 01; www.airfrance.com; Tour Zital, Rte des Hydrocarbures, Ankorondrano)
Air Madagascar (Map p76; ☎ 22 222 22; www.air madagascar.com; 31 Ave de l'Indépendance, Antananarivo)
Corsair (Map p76; ☎ 22 633 36; www.corsair.fr; 1 Rue Rainitovo Antsahavola, Antananarivo)
Interair (Map pp72-3; ☎ 22 224 06; www.interair.co.za; Madagascar Hilton, Rue Pierre Stibbe, Anosy, Antananarivo)

AIRLINES FLYING TO & FROM THE COMOROS
Air Austral/Air Mauritius (ARIO; Map p76; ☎ 22 359 90; www.airaustral.com; Rue des 77 Parlementaires Français, Antananarivo)
Air Madagascar (Map p76; ☎ 22 222 22; www.air madagascar.com; 31 Ave de l'Indépendance, Antananarivo)
Air Seychelles (HM; ☎ 73 31 44; www.airseychelles .net) Hub: Malé, Seychelles.
Air Tanzania (TC; ☎ 73 54 26; www.airtanzania.com) Hub: Dar es Salaam.

Tickets
Since there is so little competition, there are few specials for travel to Madagascar and the Comoros. Booking online for either destination is rarely possible or cheaper – your best bet is to approach a local tour operator. Even in this case, many tour operators don't deal with either destination and you may have to

approach the airline office (if there is one) in your country directly.

Air Madagascar, Corsair and Air France occasionally offer some good deals to Madagascar, especially during the low season. The high season for air travel to Madagascar and the Comoros is June to August, December to January and around Easter.

Air Madagascar offers 50% discounts on domestic flights to anyone who has arrived in Madagascar on an Air Madagascar flight from Europe.

Air Austral offers an Indian Ocean pass, which allows passengers who have bought long-distance tickets on Air Austral, Air Mauritius and Air Seychelles to receive discounts of up to 10% on routes within the Indian Ocean region on all three airlines.

All ticket prices quoted in this book include international departure tax.

Africa & the Indian Ocean
Both Madagascar and the Comoros are well connected with the Indian Ocean islands of Mauritius and Réunion, and reasonably easy to reach from mainland Africa.

Once you're in Madagascar, **Dodo Travel & Tours** (Map p76; ☎ 22 690 36; www.dodotravel tour.com; Rue Elysée Ravelomanantsoa), in Antananarivo,

TRANSPORT

CLIMATE CHANGE & TRAVEL
Climate change is a serious threat to the ecosystems that humans rely upon, and air travel is the fastest-growing contributor to the problem. Lonely Planet regards travel, overall, as a global benefit, but believes we all have a responsibility to limit our personal impact on global warming.

Flying & Climate Change
Pretty much every form of motor travel generates CO_2 (the main cause of human-induced climate change) but planes are far and away the worst offenders, not just because of the sheer distances they allow us to travel, but because they release greenhouse gases high into the atmosphere. The statistics are frightening: two people taking a return flight between Europe and the US will contribute as much to climate change as an average household's gas and electricity consumption over a whole year.

Carbon Offset Schemes
Climatecare.org and other websites use 'carbon calculators' that allow jetsetters to offset the greenhouse gases they are responsible for with contributions to energy-saving projects and other climate-friendly initiatives in the developing world – including projects in India, Honduras, Kazakhstan and Uganda.

Lonely Planet, together with Rough Guides and other concerned partners in the travel industry, supports the carbon offset scheme run by climatecare.org. Lonely Planet offsets all of its staff and author travel.

For more information check out our website: lonelyplanet.com.

is a useful place to seek information about flights within this region.

MADAGASCAR

The main hubs for flights to Madagascar are Johannesburg in South Africa and Nairobi in Kenya. There are several weekly flights between Johannesburg and Antananarivo (about €700 return) on Interair, and twice weekly on Air Madagascar. Travel between Madagascar and Nairobi (about €640 return) generally works better if you purchase your ticket directly from Air Madagascar in Kenya or Madagascar.

Air Austral has regular flights between Réunion and Mauritius and Antananarivo (from €330).

THE COMOROS

Air Austral has regular flights from Réunion and Mauritius to Mayotte and Moroni on Grande Comore. There are also regular flights from Mahajanga in Madagascar to Mayotte (around €350).

Air Tanzania has a weekly flight from Moroni on Grande Comore to Dar es Salaam (about €500 return). Air Mozambique flies weekly between Mayotte and Pemba in northern Mozambique (about €270 return), with connections to Maputo. Comores Air Service has flights to Mombasa in Kenya (about €600 return) and Zanzibar in Tanzania (about €450 return). African Express Airlines, a branch of South African Airways, flies weekly from Mayotte to Nairobi (about €600 return).

Bear in mind that Comores Air Service flights won't show up on travel agency booking systems in the rest of the world, so if you want to use these flights, you'll have to book them yourself when you arrive in **Mombasa** (☎ 00254 41 404265) or **Zanzibar** (☎ 00255 54 2230029). It's definitely best to allow a few days' leeway if you're travelling to the Comoros via this route.

Asia

Air Madagascar flies between Singapore and Antananarivo, with connections in Singapore to other Asian countries. Otherwise the best way to reach Madagascar or the Comoros from Asia is via Mauritius or Johannesburg. Air Mauritius has flights several times a week from Singapore and Hong Kong to Mauritius, and South African Airways flies regularly to Johannesburg from both cities.

It's also easy to get flights on Kenya Airways or Air India from Bombay to Nairobi,

from where you can connect to Madagascar or Mayotte.

Australia & New Zealand

There are no direct flights from Australia to Madagascar or the Comoros. The best routes are generally via Mauritius or Johannesburg. Air Mauritius has weekly flights connecting both Melbourne and Perth with Mauritius from about A$3000. From Mauritius there are regular connections on Air Austral to Antananarivo, Mayotte and Moroni on Grande Comore.

Alternatively, Qantas and SAA both have flights connecting Sydney with Johannesburg starting from A$2200 in the low season. From Johannesburg, you can connect with an Air Madagascar or Interair flight to Antananarivo. Try these agencies:

Flight Centre Australia (☎ 133 133; www.flightcentre .com.au); New Zealand (☎ 0800 233 544; www .flightcentre.co.nz)
STA Travel Australia (☎ 1300 733 035; www.statravel .com.au); New Zealand (☎ 0508 782 872; www.statravel .co.nz)

Europe

The main European hub for flights to and from Madagascar or the Comoros is Paris. Air Madagascar and Air France fly three to four times a week between Paris and Antananarivo. Prices from Paris on both airlines usually start from about €1400. There are also some good deals available with the scheduled airline Corsair, although prices are broadly similar on all three airlines.

It's also possible to fly from many European capitals to Johannesburg, Nairobi, St-Denis (Réunion) or Port Louis (Mauritius), and from one of these cities to Antananarivo. The best connections are usually via Réunion or Mauritius, which are linked by Air Austral flights to Antananarivo (from €330), as well as by several flights weekly to other places in Madagascar and to the Comoros. To the Comoros, you can take a flight from Europe to Mombasa in Kenya or Dar es Salaam in Tanzania and connect to Moroni (Grande Comore) from there (p238). Contact one of the following agents to get you started:

Air Fare (☎ 020 620 5121; www.airfair.nl in Dutch) A well-respected Dutch travel agency.
Nouvelles Frontières (☎ 08 03 33 33 33; www .nouvelles-frontieres.fr) A good French option with group tours to Madagascar.
OTU Voyages (☎ 0825 004 027; www.otu.fr in French) Has branches across France.

STA Travel Germany (☎ 01805-456 422; www.statravel
.de in German); UK (☎ 0870 1600 599; www.statravel
.co.uk) Also has plenty of other offices across Europe.
Trailfinders (☎ 020-7938 3939; www.trailfinders
.com) Excellent, reliable UK travel agency with huge
experience.

The USA & Canada

The cheapest way to fly from North America
to Madagascar or the Comoros is generally
via Paris. It may work out cheaper to get two
separate tickets – one from North America to
Europe, and then a second ticket from Europe
to Madagascar. During the high season, however, it often ends up being the same price, and
it's much less of a hassle to book just one ticket.
Expect to pay around US$3000 return.

Another option is to fly from Atlanta or New
York to Johannesburg, with a connection to
Antananarivo – although at the time of research
this option ended up being more expensive
than flying through Europe. In the USA, the
main travel agency specialising in Madagascar
is Cortez Travel & Expeditions (see right). It
has information on good-value airfares and
can book Air Madagascar flights. The following
companies might also be able to help:
Flight Centre Canada (☎ 1 888 967 5355; www.flight
centre.ca); USA (☎ 1866 WORLD 51; www.flightcentre.us)
Contact it directly for fares.
Orbitz (www.orbitz.com) A good source of online fares.
STA Travel (☎ 800 329 9537; www.statravel.com) Good
deals to Paris.

SEA

It's possible to travel to and from Madagascar and the Comoros by boat, but for most
destinations you will need plenty of time and
determination. Travel is likely to be on cargo
ships – unless you find a ride on a yacht as a
crew member – so sleeping and eating conditions, combined with sometimes turbulent
seas, can make for a rough trip. Bring sea-
sickness tablets with you.

Mombasa (Kenya) and the island of Zanzibar (Tanzania) are the main places to look for
cargo boats to Madagascar or the Comoros.
It's also sometimes possible to find passage on
a yacht heading from South Africa, Réunion
or Mauritius – or maybe even from France to
Nosy Be or Mayotte.

TOURS

For a list of organised tour companies within
Madagascar, see p285. Following are a few

companies operating general interest tours
to, and around, Madagascar.

AUSTRALIA
Adventure Associates (☎ 02-8916 3000; www.adven
tureassociates.com) Runs tours to Madagascar, combined
with Réunion and Mauritius.

FRANCE
Comptoir de Madagascar (☎ 01 42 60 93 00; www
.comptoirdemadagascar.com in French) Tours and air
tickets to Madagascar.
Terre Malgache (☎ 01 44 32 12 87; www.terre
-malgache.com in French) A wide range of tours to Madagascar, plus one to Mayotte.

GERMANY
Madagaskar Travel (☎ 08233-75341; www.mada
gaskar-travel.de in German) General and specialist wildlife
itineraries.
Trauminsel Reisen (☎ 08152-9319-0; www.traum
inselreisen.de in German) Itineraries all over
Madagascar.

ITALY
Zig Zag Viaggi (☎ 0341 284154; www.zigzag.it in
Italian) Escorted group tours.

THE NETHERLANDS
Baobab Travel (☎ 020-6275129; www.baobab.nl in
Dutch) Longer itineraries in Madagascar. Also has a branch
in Belgium.
Summum Reisen (☎ 020-4215555; www.summum.nl
in Dutch) Group tours.

SWITZERLAND
Priori (☎ in Antananarivo 20 22 625 27; www.priori.ch)
Cultural and wildlife tours.
Zingg (☎ 41 44709 2010; www.zinggsafaris.com)
Canoe, kayak and trekking trips.

UNITED KINGDOM
Rainbow Tours (☎ 020 7226 1004; www.madagascar
-travel.net) Specialist and general-interest guided trips to
Madagascar.
Reef & Rainforest Tours (☎ 01803 866965;
www.reefandrainforest.co.uk) Focuses on wildlife
holidays.
Wildlife Worldwide (☎ 44 1962 737649; www
.wildlifeworldwide.com) Wildlife viewing tours.

UNITED STATES
Cortez Travel & Expeditions (☎ 800 854 1029, in
Antananarivo 20 22 219 74; www.air-mad.com) Well-
established operator for Air Madagascar flights and tours.

For the Comoros, the only tour possibilities are the trips to Mayotte organised by the tour operators in France listed here.

GETTING AROUND

AIR
Madagascar

Air Madagascar, Madagascar's national carrier, has an impressive network of domestic routes. While fares have leapt dramatically in recent years, tickets on 'Air Mad' flights are still relatively inexpensive, and provide a useful way of covering large distances and avoiding long road journeys. While cancellations, schedule changes and delays occur (especially during the low season, in stormy weather or on flights to more remote destinations) the airline is generally efficient.

A handy free booklet detailing timetables and routes (but not fares) is available from Air Madagascar's head office in Antananarivo and from some travel agencies.

You can pay for tickets in ariary, euros or US dollars at the head office in Antananarivo and Air Madagascar offices in larger towns, but smaller offices may only accept ariary or euros. The office in Antananarivo also accepts travellers cheques and credit cards.

The baggage allowance for most internal flights is 10kg. On Twin Otter (small plane) flights baggage is strictly limited to 5kg.

The Comoros

The Comoros is served by two reasonably efficient internal airlines, Comores Air Service and Comores Aviation. See p238 for information on routes and fares.

The Comores Aviation office in Mayotte may take credit cards (but sometimes it simply can't be bothered). The offices in the Union des Comores generally only accept Comorian francs or, at a pinch, euros, so come prepared with the right currency.

Reservations & Check-in

Air Madagascar flights are frequently full, so it's always worth booking as far in advance as possible.

While it's now officially not necessary to reconfirm your Air Madagascar tickets, it's always best to check with the airline a few days in advance and again on the day of departure, as there are frequent last-minute

schedule changes. The same goes for flights on Comores Aviation and Comores Air Service, although these flights aren't usually full. In fact, the reverse is often true, so it's best to check the day before that your flight hasn't been cancelled due to lack of passengers…

If you have checked in baggage, be sure to keep your baggage-claim ticket until you are reunited with your luggage at your destination.

BICYCLE

It may often be just as fast to travel by bicycle as by taxi-brousse (bush taxi). A mountain bike is normally essential. Carry spare parts, although inner tubes and other basic parts are sometimes available in larger towns. The terrain varies from very sandy to muddy or rough and rocky.

It's usually no problem to transport your bicycle on taxis-brousses or on the train if you want to take a break en route.

Although you are able to hire mountain bikes for around Ar3000 per day in many larger towns, including Toliara, Toamasina, Antsirabe and Ambodifotatra on Île Sainte Marie, these are not normally in good enough condition for longer journeys. The Comoros are also theoretically good for mountain biking, but mountain bikes aren't available for hire, so you will have to bring your own.

BOAT
Cargo Boat

In certain parts of Madagascar, notably the northeast coast and Canal des Pangalanes, cargo boats (sometimes called *boutres*) are the primary means of transport. There are also frequent boats between the four Comoros islands, and between the Comoros and Madagascar.

When choosing a cargo boat, keep in mind that there have been several accidents involving capsized vessels (the ferry *Samsonette*, which used to run scheduled services between Île Sainte Marie and the mainland of Madagascar, sank in 2000, killing over 20 people). Always check for lifejackets and don't get in if the seas are rough or if the boat is overcrowded.

Boat travel on the east coast is generally not safe because of cyclones, especially during the rainy season between May and September.

While some cargo boats in Madagascar and the Comoros have passenger cabins, most have deck space only. Departure delays are

MAJOR DOMESTIC AIR ROUTES

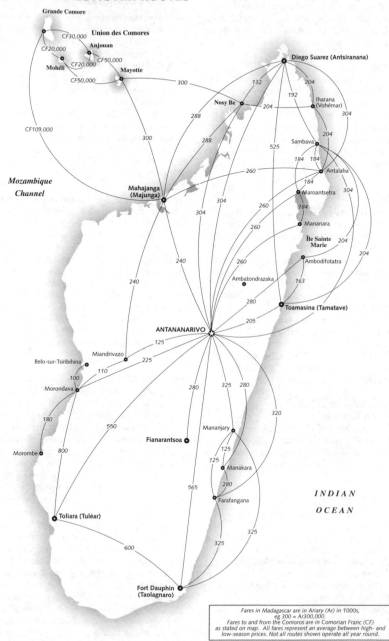

TRANSPORT

Fares in Madagascar are in Ariary (Ar) in 1000s,
eg 300 = Ar300,000.
Fares to and from the Comoros are in Comorian Franc (CF)
as stated on map. All fares represent an average between high- and
low-season prices. Not all routes shown operate all year round.

common as most boats do not have a motor and departures must correspond with the outgoing tide. Securing a space on a boat from Mahajanga to Morondava will cost around Ar65,000 per person.

Pirogue

Engineless pirogues or *lakanas* (dugout canoes), whether on rivers or the sea, are the primary means of local transport for shorter journeys in many areas of Madagascar and the Comoros (where they are known as *galawas*).

Pirogues can easily be hired, along with a boatman, but bear in mind there are no amenities on board and the ride can be quite rough.

BUS

In a few parts of Madagascar (such as the route between Antananarivo and Toamasina in the east) routes in and around major cities are served by bus. These usually use the same stations as the taxis-brousses and are generally slightly less expensive. However, taxis-brousses remain the main form of public road transport in Madagascar and the Comoros. **MadaBus** (☎ 32 42 089 69; www.madabus.com) has coach lines between the major cities, is a comfortable way to travel, and is less expensive than flying or hiring a private vehicle. Some sample fares are Antananarivo–Antsirabe (Ar25,000), Antsirabe–Fianarantsoa (Ar36,000) and Fianarantsoa–Toliara (Ar75,000).

CAR & MOTORCYCLE
Driving Licence

To drive in Madagascar or the Comoros, you will need to have an International Driving Permit. Take note that wearing a seatbelt is now mandatory for the driver of a vehicle in Madagascar.

Fuel & Spare Parts

You'll find petrol stations of some kind in all cities and in most major towns. Not all have pumps – particularly in the Comoros, petrol stations usually consist of a youth stationed at the roadside with an array of old Coke bottles full of opaque fuel. For longer trips, and for travel in remote areas, you will need to carry extra fuel with you.

Spare parts and repairs of varying quality are available in most towns. Make sure to check the spare tyre of any car you rent before setting out.

ROAD VOCABULARY

When inquiring about local road conditions in Madagascar (taxi-brousse stations are a good place to start), the following French terms might come in handy:

Nids-de-poule Potholes.
Piste (or piste de sable) Sand or earth road.
Piste amenagée Sand road with some level of surfacing.
Piste de rocaille Road or track with loose stones.
Route goudronnée Tarmac road.
Route saisonnière Seasonal road.

Hire
CAR

To rent a car in Madagascar or the Comoros, you must generally be at least 23 years old and have held a driving licence for at least one year. Rental costs include insurance.

Due to the often difficult driving conditions and road hazards most rental agencies make hiring a driver obligatory with their vehicles. For a listing of car-rental agencies in the capital see p87. See the individual destination chapters for more information. Prices average between Ar100,000 and Ar230,000 per day for a 4WD including fuel. For almost all destinations off the main routes you will need a 4WD.

CHARTER TAXI

As an alternative to high car-rental prices, it's also possible to hire a taxi on the street. Make inquiries first at the taxi-brousse stand or nearby hotels to get an idea of the going rate for your destination. Be sure to clarify such things as petrol and waiting time, and try to check that the vehicle is in decent shape before departing. Also, most taxi drivers do not relish the idea of dodging animals, potholes or drunken drivers at night, so be prepared to find accommodation when the sun sets.

For longer multiday journeys, you'll need to be more careful. In addition to the standard vehicle papers and a valid driving licence, the driver should have a special charter permit (indicated by a diagonal green stripe). It's not a bad idea to have a written contract signed by you and the driver stipulating insurance issues, the agreed-upon fee (including whether or not petrol is included) and your itinerary. An excellent choice for transport, transfers and excursions is a very knowledgeable and friendly driver named **Roger Felix** (☎ 32 0773 330, 22 328 09; Antananarivo).

MOTORCYCLE

Motorcycles can be hired by the half day or full day at various places in Madagascar, including Toliara, Nosy Be and Île Sainte Marie (for use on the islands only). At most places, they range from a Honda or Yamaha 125cc or 250cc to a tiny Peugeot *mobylette*. Some places also rent motorcycles suitable for longer, rougher journeys, and provide support vehicles as well.

Road Conditions

Of Madagascar's approximately 40,000km of roads, less than 25% are paved, and many of those that are paved are badly deteriorating. Nontarred roads are often exceptionally muddy, sandy or rocky. Roads in the far northeast from Soanierana-Ivongo to Antsiranana, and in a few other areas of the country, are prone to flooding and often have broken bridges. Routes in many areas are impassable or very difficult during the rainy season. Madagascar's government has, however, pledged to improve road conditions and already some routes have been resurfaced, with the promise of more road improvements to come.

The designation *route nationale* (RN) is sadly no guarantee of quality. Most accidents, however, are caused by human failing (especially drunkenness) rather than by dangerous vehicles and roads. Delays are more common than accidents, so always factor in a few extra hours to allow for breakdowns or military checkpoints en route.

Road conditions in the Comoros vary, but are generally good, and distances are so short that it's easy to get around on foot or by bicycle.

Road Rules

Driving in Madagascar and the Comoros is on the right-hand side. The police occasionally stop vehicles and carry out random checks, in the hope of detecting any of the 1001 possible (and probable) infractions of the vehicle code. Occasionally foreigners will be asked for their passport, but as long as your visa is in order there should be no problem.

If you aren't used to local driving conditions, watch out for pedestrians, animals, broken-down cars and slow-moving zebu carts on the road. It is particularly hazardous to drive at night, as there is no lighting, so try to avoid it.

HITCHING

Hitching is never entirely safe in any country in the world, and we don't recommend it. Travellers who do decide to hitch should understand that they are taking a small but potentially serious risk. People who do choose to hitch will be safer if they travel in pairs and let someone know where they are planning to go.

In Madagascar, traffic between towns and cities is thin, and most passing vehicles are likely to be taxis-brousses or trucks, which are often full. If you do find a ride, you will likely have to pay about the equivalent of the taxi-brousse fare. Along well-travelled routes or around popular tourist destinations, you can often find lifts with privately rented 4WDs or with hotel supply trucks. In the Comoros, hitching may be possible with tourists, but with most other vehicles you'll probably have to pay for a ride.

LOCAL TRANSPORT
Charette

In more rural parts of Madagascar and the Comoros, the *charette*, a wooden cart drawn by a pair of zebu cattle, is a common form of local transport. They're most useful for carting your luggage when you're trekking, so that you can forge ahead and leave the *charette* to bring up the rear. Fares are entirely negotiable, and breakdowns are frequent.

Pousse-Pousse

The brightly coloured *pousses-pousses* (rickshaws) seen in hordes in various Malagasy towns supposedly got their name when drivers yelled '*pousse, pousse*' (push, push) at passers-by for aid as they were going uphill.

Many travellers have scruples about using them, perceiving an association with slave labour or finding the prospect of being pulled around by another human offensive. This sympathy may wane after a few days of relentless hounding by *pousse-pousse* drivers, who seem to regard the sight of a tourist on foot as a personal slight. In any case, the *pousse-pousse* people need work, not sympathy, as they rent the rickshaws and have to pay a daily amount to the owners. If you have heavy luggage, it's polite to hire two. In

TRANSPORT

most places, locals pay between Ar500 and Ar1500 for a ride. Tourist rates are higher, and always negotiable, so agree to a fare before you climb aboard. When it's raining, the price sometimes doubles.

Taxi-brousse

Taxis-brousses are slow, uncomfortable, erratic and sometimes unsafe. But they are as much a part of daily life in Madagascar as the sight of a humped cow or a raffia hat, and you'll find it hard to travel independently around the country without wedging yourself into one at some point. Taxis-brousses are used in the Comoros, too, but distances are mercifully shorter.

COSTS

Fares for all trips are set by the government and are based on distance, duration and route conditions. Prices are the same for locals and foreigners. However, fares vary among vehicle types, with minibuses (which tend to be somewhat quicker) or *taxis-be* (which are more comfortable, and hold fewer people) being slightly more expensive than larger trucks.

If you can speak French, ask the locals boarding the bus what the fare is before paying – some opportunistic taxi-brousse drivers try to charge foreigners a much higher fare. You can also ask to see a list of official fares, sometimes posted in the ticket office. If you want to keep your backpack with you in the vehicle you'll need to pay for an extra seat.

RESERVATIONS

If you want one of the more comfortable seats on a less frequented route, it's advisable to book a seat the day before you want to travel. This can be done at the transport-company offices located at taxi-brousse stations. Prices are generally fixed and non-negotiable.

TAXI-BROUSSE STATIONS

All towns have one or more *gares routières* or *stationnements des taxis-brousse* (bus or taxi-brousse stations). Despite the general appearance of anarchy, the taxi-brousse system

TAXIS-BROUSSE GLOSSARY

The term taxi-brousse (literally 'bush taxi') is used generically in Madagascar and the Comoros to refer to any vehicle providing public transport. When you buy your taxi-brousse ticket, therefore, you could be about to climb into anything from a tiny Renault 4 packed with 10 passengers to a rumbling juggernaut with entire suites of furniture tied to its roof. Most taxis-brousses, however, are 24-seater Japanese minibuses in varying states of dilapidation. Most of the time the term taxi-brousse will suffice to describe any form of motorised public transport, but you might come across some of the following terms in the course of your road adventures. It goes without saying that all the vehicles (described below in order of size) will be carrying at least four times the number of passengers that you thought was anatomically possible, and that they will break down regularly.

The *camion-brousse* is a huge 4WD army-style truck, fitted with a bench or seats down each side, although the majority of passengers wind up sitting on the floor or each other. They are used for particularly long or rough journeys, which you may well wish you had never begun.

A *familiale* or *taxi-be* (literally, 'big taxi') – usually a Peugeot 504 or 505 – is a big jump up in comfort and generally in speed as well. In theory, *taxis-be* accommodate nine passengers – two in the front with the driver, four in the middle and three in the back – although drivers frequently manage to fit in a few more. The price for a *taxi-be* is generally about 25% higher than for the same route in a *bâché* or *camion-brousse,* and they fill up and leave much faster than minibuses.

A *bâché* is a small, converted pick-up, which usually has some sort of covering over the back and a bench down each side. *Bâché* are used on shorter, rural routes and are hideously uncomfortable.

A *taxi-ville* (town taxi) is a small car, usually an old Renault 4 or Citroën 2CV, used for transport within towns on a jump-in-and-ride basis. Fares are per person and fixed according to the distance you go, and the taxi will stop to pick up new passengers along the way. *Taxis-ville* can also be hired to take you to spots further outside the town for a negotiable fee.

A *taxi-spécial* is any kind of taxi-brousse rented by a person or group exclusively.

is a relatively well-organised one once you get the hang of it. Upon arrival in a town, you may well be besieged by pushy but harmless touts, tugging at your luggage and yelling in your ear to try and win your custom.

Vehicles display the destination in white paint on the windscreen, and fares are pinned up in the transport-company offices near the edges of the station. The choice will often come down to simply joining the next vehicle to leave, which will be packed to the roof, or holding out for a decent seat in a later taxi-brousse. If you want to speed up departure, it's sometimes effective to pay for the remaining empty seats, which will also provide more comfort for everyone (although keep in mind that other passengers are often picked up along the way regardless).

TAXI-BROUSSE TIPS

No matter what type of vehicle you are in, the two front seats beside the driver are usually the most comfortable and most sought after. To get these seats you'll need to arrive early at the station, buy a ticket the day before, or do some serious pleading, bribing, hustling or flirting.

Rear seats are designed for the more compact Malagasy physique and can be uncomfortable or simply impossible for long-legged Westerners. In desperate situations, it may be better to pay for an extra seat.

Luggage goes on the roof, so make sure your rucksack is waterproof and not liable to burst open under stress.

If at all possible, avoid travelling on a taxi-brousse after dark. Unlit roads, driver fatigue and less security for your luggage all contribute to making the journey riskier. You'll also miss the scenery en route, which is often spectacular.

TOURS

Madagascar's many tour operators and freelance guides offer mountain-bike excursions, 4WD circuits, walking tours, wildlife-viewing trips and cultural and historic tours.

An organised tour can be particularly valuable if you don't speak much French, as it can otherwise be hard to break the communication barrier with the fairly reserved Malagasy people, who rarely speak English.

The general rule of thumb for organised tours is to check as much as possible beforehand – this includes vehicles, camping equipment and even menu plans. Try to get all the

details, agreed by both parties in advance, in writing.

Following is a list of some of the reliable Antananarivo-based companies that can arrange excursions throughout Madagascar. For details about travel agencies outside Madagascar, see p279.

Boogie Pilgrim (off Map pp72-3; ☎ 22 530 70; www .boogie-pilgrim.net; Île des Oiseaux, Tsarasaotra, Alarobia) Adventurous ecotours and camps in several places in Madagascar, including the Parc National d'Andringitra and the Canal des Pangalanes. English and German speaking.

Cortez Travel & Expeditions (☎ 22 219 74; cortezmd@dts.mg; 25 Lalana Ny Zafindriandiky, Antanimena) American-based agency offering a wide range of itineraries for individuals and groups.

Espace Mada (☎ 22 262 97; www.madagascar-circuits .com; 50 Ave Ramanantsoa, Isoraka) Vehicles, guides and 4WD excursions, including Tsiribihina River and Parc National des Tsingy de Bemaraha trips.

Mad Cameleon (☎ 22 630 86; madcam@dts.mg; Lot 11-K6, Lalana Rasamoely, Ankadivato-Ambony) Tours focusing on western Madagascar, including the Tsiribihina River descent, Parc National des Tsingy de Bemaraha, and pirogue trips down the Manambolo River.

Malagasy Tours (Map pp72-3; ☎ 22 627 24; www .malagasy-tours.com; Avaradrova) Inside the Grill du Rova restaurant, this is a reliable, upmarket operator offering tours in all areas of the country, with trekking and trips along the Tsiribihina River and the Canal des Pangalanes.

Setam (☎ 22 324 31; www.setam-mg.com; 56 Ave du 26 Juin, Analakely) Bicycle expeditions, orchid tours and visits to *Famadihana* ceremonies, along with the usual circuits.

Transcontinents (Map pp76-7; ☎ 22 223 98; transco@dts.mg; 10 Ave de l'Indépendance) Tours and car hire.

Tropika Touring (☎ 22 222 30, 22 276 80; tropika@dts.mg; 41 Lalana Ratsimilaho, Ambatanakanga) Offers various tours throughout the country, including descents of the Tsiribihina River.

Za Tours (☎ 24 253 07; www.zatours-madagascar.com; Lot II J, 178 AB bis, Ambodivoanjo Ambohijatovo) Well-regarded English-speaking tour company.

TRAIN

The Malagasy rail system, known as the Réseau National des Chemins de Fer Malgaches (RNCFM), is made up of over 1000km of tracks and was built during the colonial period. The only section operating is the Fianarantsoa–Manakara line, which passes through some beautiful forest scenery. For departure and fare information for this line, see p108. There are no trains in the Comoros.

Health

CONTENTS

As long as you stay up to date with your vaccinations and take some basic preventive measures, you'd have to be pretty unlucky to succumb to most of the health hazards covered in this chapter. Madagascar and the Comoros certainly have an impressive selection of tropical diseases on offer, but you're much more likely to get a bout of diarrhoea (in fact, you should bank on it), a cold or an infected mosquito bite than an exotic disease such as sleeping sickness. When it comes to injuries (as opposed to illness), the most likely reason for needing medical help is as a result of road accidents – vehicles are rarely well maintained, some roads are potholed and poorly lit, and drink-driving is common.

BEFORE YOU GO

A little planning before departure, particularly for pre-existing illnesses, will save you a lot of trouble later on. Before a long trip, get a check-up from your dentist and your doctor if you require any regular medication or have a chronic illness, eg high blood pressure or asthma.

You should also organise spare contact lenses and glasses (and take your optical prescription with you), get a first-aid and medical kit together, and arrange necessary vaccinations.

Travellers can register online with the **International Association for Medical Assistance to Travellers** (IAMAT; www.iamat.org). Its website can help travellers to find a doctor who has recognised training in the country they are travelling to. You might like to consider doing a first-aid course (contact the Red Cross or St John's Ambulance) or attending a remote medicine first-aid course, such as that offered by the **Royal Geographical Society** (www.wildernessmedical training.co.uk).

If you are bringing medications with you, carry them in their original containers, clearly labelled. A signed and dated letter from your physician (ideally translated into French) describing all medical conditions and medications, including generic names, is also a good idea. If carrying syringes or needles, be sure to have a physician's letter documenting their medical necessity.

INSURANCE

Find out in advance whether your insurance plan will make payments directly to providers or will reimburse you later for overseas health expenditures (doctors expect payment in cash; some hospitals take credit cards, but the machines themselves often don't work, so it's best to carry an emergency supply of cash). Note that doctor's fees are going to be much less than in Western countries. It's vital to ensure that your travel insurance will cover the emergency transport required to get you to a good hospital, or all the way home, by air and with a medical attendant if necessary. Not all insurance covers this, so check the contract carefully. If you need medical help, your insurance company might be able to help locate the nearest hospital or clinic, or you can ask at your hotel. In an emergency, contact your embassy or consulate.

Membership of the **African Medical & Research Foundation** (Amref; www.amref.org) provides an air-evacuation service in medical emergencies in some African countries, sometimes including Madagascar, as well as air-ambulance transfers between medical facilities. Money paid by members for this service goes into providing grassroots medical assistance for local people.

RECOMMENDED VACCINATIONS

The **World Health Organization** (WHO; www.who .int/en/) recommends that all travellers are covered for tetanus, polio, measles, rubella, mumps and diphtheria, as well as for hepatitis B, regardless of the destination they are travelling to.

According to the **Centers for Disease Control & Prevention** (www.cdc.gov), the following vaccinations are recommended for Madagascar and the Comoros: hepatitis A, hepatitis B, rabies and typhoid, and boosters for tetanus, diphtheria and measles. Yellow fever is not a risk in the region, but the certificate of yellow-fever vaccination is an entry requirement if travelling from an infected region (see p291).

MEDICAL CHECKLIST

It is a very good idea to carry a medical and first-aid kit with you, to help yourself in the case of minor illness or injury. Following is a list of items you should consider packing.

- Acetaminophen (paracetamol) or aspirin
- Adhesive or paper tape
- Antibacterial ointment (eg Bactroban) for cuts and abrasions (prescription only)
- Antibiotics (prescription only), eg ciprofloxacin (Ciproxin) or norfloxacin (Utinor)
- Antidiarrhoeal drugs (eg loperamide)
- Antihistamines (for hayfever and allergic reactions)
- Anti-inflammatory drugs (eg ibuprofen)
- Antimalaria pills
- Bandages, gauze and gauze rolls
- DEET-containing insect repellent for the skin
- Fluids (if travelling to remote areas)
- Iodine tablets (for water purification)
- Oral rehydration salts
- Permethrin-containing insect spray for clothing, tents and bed nets
- Pocket knife
- Scissors, safety pins and tweezers
- Steroid cream or hydrocortisone cream (for allergic rashes)
- Sun block
- Syringes and sterile needles
- Thermometer

Given the prevalence of malaria, consider taking a self-diagnostic kit that can identify malaria in the blood from a finger prick.

INTERNET RESOURCES

There is a wealth of travel health advice online. **Lonely Planet** (www.lonelyplanet.com) is a good place to start. The **World Health Organization** (www.who.int/ith/) publishes a superb book called *International Travel and Health,* revised annually and available online at no cost. Other websites of interest are **MD Travel Health** (www .mdtravelhealth.com), the **Centers for Disease Control & Prevention** (www.cdc.gov) and **Fit for Travel** (www .fitfortravel.scot.nhs.uk).

You may also like to consult your government's travel health website, if one is available:

Australia (www.smartraveller.gov.au)
Canada (www.hc-sc.gc.ca/pphb-dgspsp/tmp-pmv/pub _e.html)
United Kingdom (www.doh.gov.uk/traveladvice/index .htm)
United States (www.cdc.gov/travel/)

FURTHER READING

- *A Comprehensive Guide to Wilderness and Travel Medicine* by Eric A Weiss (1998)
- *Healthy Travel* by Jane Wilson-Howarth (1999)
- *Healthy Travel Africa* by Isabelle Young (2000)
- *How to Stay Healthy Abroad* by Richard Dawood (2002)
- *Travel in Health* by Graham Fry (1994)
- *Travel with Children* by Cathy Lanigan and Maureen Wheeler (2004)

IN TRANSIT

DEEP VEIN THROMBOSIS (DVT)

Blood clots can form in the legs during flights, chiefly because of prolonged immobility. This formation of clots is known as deep vein thrombosis (DVT). Although most blood clots are reabsorbed uneventfully, some might break off and travel through the blood vessels to the lungs, where they could cause life-threatening complications.

The chief symptom of DVT is swelling or pain of the foot, ankle or calf. When a blood clot travels to the lungs, it may cause chest pain and breathing difficulty. Travellers with any of these symptoms should immediately seek medical attention.

To prevent DVT, walk about the cabin, perform isometric compressions of the leg muscles

HEALTH

(ie contract the leg muscles while sitting), drink plenty of fluids and avoid alcohol.

JET LAG & MOTION SICKNESS

If you're crossing more than five time zones you could suffer jet lag, resulting in insomnia, fatigue, malaise or nausea. To avoid jet lag, try drinking plenty of nonalcoholic fluids and eating light meals. Upon arrival, get exposure to natural sunlight and readjust your schedule (for meals, sleep etc) as soon as possible.

Antihistamines such as dimenhydrinate (Dramamine) and meclizine (Antivert, Bonine) are usually the first choice for treating motion sickness. The main side effect of these drugs is drowsiness. A herbal alternative is ginger (ginger tea, biscuits or crystallized ginger).

IN MADAGASCAR & THE COMOROS

AVAILABILITY & COST OF HEALTH CARE

Health care in the area is varied: there are excellent private hospitals in Antananarivo, but health care can be pretty patchy in both countries, although Mayotte – as part of France – has a European standard of health care. The public health system is underfunded and overcrowded. Medicine and even sterile dressings and intravenous fluids might need to be purchased from a local pharmacy by patients or their relatives. The standard of dental care is equally variable, and there is an increased risk of hepatitis B and HIV transmission via poorly sterilised equipment. By and large, public hospitals offer the cheapest service, but will have the least up-to-date equipment and medications; private hospitals and clinics are more expensive but tend to have more advanced drugs and equipment and better-trained medical staff.

Most drugs can be purchased over the counter, without a prescription. Many drugs for sale might be ineffective: they might be counterfeit or not have been stored under the right conditions. It is strongly recommended that all drugs for chronic diseases be brought from home. Also, the availability and efficacy of condoms cannot be relied upon – bring all the contraception you'll need as condoms bought in the region might not have been correctly stored.

There is a high risk of contracting HIV from infected blood if you receive a blood transfusion. The **BloodCare Foundation** (www.bloodcare.org .uk) is a useful source of safe, screened blood, which can be transported to any part of the world within 24 hours.

Unfortunately, adequate – let alone good – health care is available to very few Malagasy.

INFECTIOUS DISEASES

It's a formidable list but, as we say, a few precautions go a long way…

Cholera

Cholera is usually only a problem during natural or artificial disasters, eg cyclones, war, floods or earthquakes, although small outbreaks can also occur at other times. Travellers are rarely affected. It is caused by a bacteria and spread via contaminated drinking water. The main symptom is profuse watery diarrhoea, which causes debilitation if fluids are not replaced quickly. An oral cholera vaccine is available in some countries, but it is not particularly effective. Most cases of cholera can be avoided by seeking out good drinking water and by keeping away from potentially contaminated food. Treatment is by fluid replacement (orally or via a drip), but sometimes antibiotics are needed. Self-treatment is not advised.

Dengue Fever (Breakbone Fever)

Dengue fever is spread through mosquito bites. It causes a feverish illness with headache and muscle pains similar to those experienced with a bad, prolonged attack of influenza. There might be a rash. Mosquito bites should be avoided whenever possible. Self-treatment: paracetamol and rest.

Diphtheria

Diphtheria is spread through close respiratory contact. It usually causes a temperature and a severe sore throat. Sometimes a membrane forms across the throat, and a tracheostomy is needed to prevent suffocation. Vaccination is recommended for those likely to be in close contact with the local population in infected areas, although this is more important for long stays than for short-term trips. The vaccine is given as an injection alone or with tetanus, and lasts 10 years. Self-treatment: none.

Filariasis

Found in most parts of West, Central, East and Southern Africa, and in Sudan in North Africa. Tiny worms migrating in the lymphatic system cause filariasis. The bite from an infected mosquito spreads the infection. Symptoms include localised itching and swelling of the legs and/or genitalia. Treatment is available. Self-treatment: none.

Hepatitis A

Hepatitis A is spread through contaminated food (particularly shellfish) and water. It causes jaundice and, although it is rarely fatal, it can cause prolonged lethargy and delayed recovery. If you've had hepatitis A, you shouldn't drink alcohol for up to six months afterwards, but once you've recovered there won't be any long-term problems. The first symptoms include dark urine and a yellow colour to the whites of the eyes. Sometimes a fever and abdominal pain might be present. Hepatitis A vaccine (Avaxim, Vaqta, Havrix) is given as an injection: a single dose will give protection for up to a year, and a booster after a year gives 10-year protection. Hepatitis A and typhoid vaccines can also be given as a single dose vaccine (hepatyrix or viatim). Self-treatment: none.

Hepatitis B

Hepatitis B is spread through infected blood, contaminated needles and sexual intercourse. It can also be spread from an infected mother to the baby during childbirth. It affects the liver, causing jaundice and occasionally liver failure. Most people recover completely, but some people might be chronic carriers of the virus, which could eventually lead to cirrhosis or liver cancer. Those visiting high-risk areas for long periods or those with increased social or occupational risk should be immunised. Many countries now give hepatitis B as part of the routine childhood vaccination. It is given by itself or at the same time as hepatitis A (hepatyrix).

A course will give protection for at least five years. It can be given over four weeks or six months. Self-treatment: none.

HIV

Human immunodeficiency virus (HIV), the virus that causes acquired immune deficiency syndrome (AIDS), is an enormous problem throughout Africa. Infection rates are lower in Madagascar (in 2007 the percentage of people affected was estimated at just under 1%), but the vast majority of the estimated 39,000 people infected have no access to medication that might keep the disease under control. The virus

is spread through infected blood and blood products, by sexual intercourse with an infected partner and from an infected mother to her baby during childbirth and breastfeeding. It can be spread through 'blood-to-blood' contacts, such as with contaminated instruments during medical, dental, acupuncture and other body-piercing procedures, and through sharing used intravenous needles. At present there is no cure. If you think you might have been infected with HIV, a blood test is necessary; a three-month gap after exposure and before testing is required to allow antibodies to appear in the blood. Self-treatment: none.

Leptospirosis

This disease is spread through the excreta of infected rodents, especially rats. It can cause hepatitis and renal failure, which might be fatal. It is unusual for travellers to be affected unless living in poor sanitary conditions. It causes a fever and sometimes jaundice. Self-treatment: none.

Malaria

Malaria is present throughout Madagascar, particularly in the coastal areas; it is less common in the central highlands and Antananarivo, but outbreaks can occur. It is found throughout the Comoros. The disease is caused by a parasite in the bloodstream spread via the bite of the female *Anopheles* mosquito. There are several types of malaria, falciparum malaria being the most dangerous type. Infection rates vary with the seasons and climate, so check out the situation before departure. Several different drugs are used to prevent malaria and new ones are in the pipeline. Up-to-date advice from a travel health clinic is essential as some medication is more suitable for some travellers than others (eg people with epilepsy should avoid mefloquine, and doxycycline should not be taken by pregnant women or children younger than 12).

The early stages of malaria include headaches, fevers, generalised aches and pains, and malaise, which could be mistaken for flu. Other symptoms can include abdominal pain, diarrhoea and a cough. Anyone who develops a fever in a malarial area should assume malarial infection until a blood test proves negative, even if you have been taking antimalarial medication. If not treated, the next stage could develop within 24 hours, particularly if falciparum malaria is the parasite: jaundice, then reduced consciousness and coma (also known as cerebral malaria), followed by death. Treatment in hospital is essential, and the death rate might still be as high as 10% even in the best intensive-care facilities.

Many travellers are under the impression that malaria is a mild illness, and that taking antimalarial drugs causes more illness through side effects than actually getting malaria. This is unfortunately not true. If you decide that you really do not wish to take antimalarial drugs, you must understand the risks, and be obsessive about avoiding mosquito bites. Use nets and insect repellent, and report any fever or flu-like symptoms to a doctor as soon as possible. Some people advocate homeopathic preparations against malaria, such as Demal200, but as yet there is no conclusive evidence that this is effective, and many homeopaths do not recommend their use.

Adults who have survived childhood malaria have developed immunity and usually only develop mild cases of malaria; most Western travellers have no immunity at all. Immunity wanes after 18 months of nonexposure, so even if you have had malaria in the past and used to live in a malaria-prone area, you might no longer be immune.

Malaria in pregnancy frequently results in miscarriage or premature labour. The risks from malaria to both mother and foetus during pregnancy are considerable. Travel throughout the region when you're pregnant should be carefully considered.

Meningococcal Meningitis

Meningococcal infection is spread through close respiratory contact and is more likely in crowded situations, such as dormitories, buses and clubs. Infection is uncommon in travellers. Vaccination is recommended for long stays and is especially important towards the end of the dry season. Symptoms include a fever, severe headache, neck stiffness and a red rash. Immediate medical treatment is necessary.

The ACWY vaccine is recommended for all travellers to the region. This vaccine is different from the meningococcal meningitis C vaccine given to children and adolescents in some countries; it is safe to be given both types of vaccine. Self-treatment: none.

Poliomyelitis

Polio is generally spread through contaminated food and water. It is one of the vaccines given in childhood and should be boosted every 10 years, either orally (a drop on the tongue) or as an injection. Polio can be carried asymptomatically (ie showing no symptoms) and could cause a transient fever. In rare cases it causes weakness or paralysis of one or more muscles, which might be permanent. Self-treatment: none.

Rabies

Rabies is spread by being bitten or licked on broken skin by an infected animal. It is always fatal once the clinical symptoms start (which might be up to several months after an infected bite), so post-bite vaccination should be given as soon as possible. Post-bite vaccination (whether or not you've been vaccinated before the bite) prevents the virus from spreading to the central nervous system. Animal handlers should be vaccinated, as should those travelling to remote areas where a reliable source of post-bite vaccine is not available within 24 hours. Three preventive injections are needed over a month. If you have not been vaccinated you will need a course of five injections starting 24 hours or as soon as possible after the injury. If you have been vaccinated, you will need fewer post-bite injections, and have more time to seek medical help. Self-treatment: none.

Schistosomiasis (Bilharzia)

This disease is spread by flukes (minute worms) that are carried by a species of freshwater snail. The flukes are found inside the snail, which then sheds them into slow-moving or still water. The parasites penetrate human skin during paddling or swimming and then migrate to the bladder or bowel. They are passed out via stool or urine and could contaminate fresh water, where the cycle starts again. Paddling or swimming in suspect freshwater lakes or slow-running rivers should be avoided. There might be no symptoms. There might be a transient fever and rash, and advanced cases might have blood in the stool or in the urine. A blood test can detect antibodies if you suspect you have been exposed, and treatment is then possible in specialist travel or infectious-disease clinics. If not treated, the infection can cause kidney failure or permanent bowel damage. It is not possible for you to infect others. Self-treatment: none.

Trypanosomiasis (Sleeping Sickness)

Spread via the bite of the tsetse fly, this disease causes a headache, fever and eventually coma. There is an effective treatment. Self-treatment: none.

Tuberculosis (TB)

TB is spread via close respiratory contact and occasionally through infected milk or milk products. BCG vaccination is recommended for those mixing closely with the local population, although it gives only moderate protection against TB. It's more important for long stays than for short-term stays. Inoculation with the BCG vaccine is not available in all countries. It is given routinely to many children in developing countries. The vaccination causes a small permanent scar at the site of injection, and is usually given in a specialised chest clinic. It is a live vaccine and shouldn't be given to pregnant women or immunocompromised individuals.

TB can be asymptomatic, only being picked up on a routine chest X-ray. Alternatively, it can cause a cough, weight loss or fever, sometimes months or even years after exposure. Self-treatment: none.

Typhoid

This is spread through food or water contaminated by infected human faeces. The first symptom is usually a fever or a pink rash on the abdomen. Sometimes septicaemia (blood poisoning) can occur. A typhoid vaccine (typhim Vi, typherix) will give protection for three years. In some countries, the oral vaccine Vivotif is also available. Antibiotics are usually given as treatment, and death is rare unless septicaemia occurs. Self-treatment: none.

Yellow Fever

Yellow fever is not a problem in Madagascar or the Comoros, but travellers should still carry a certificate as evidence of vaccination if they've recently been in an infected country, to avoid any possible difficulties with immigration. For a full list of these countries visit the websites of the **World Health Organization** (www.who.int/wer/) or the **Centers for Disease Control & Prevention** (www.cdc.gov/travel/blusheet.htm). A traveller without a legally required, up-to-date certificate may be vaccinated and detained in isolation at the port of arrival for up to 10 days or possibly repatriated.

TRAVELLER'S DIARRHOEA

Although it's not inevitable that you will get diarrhoea while travelling in Madagascar and the Comoros, it's certainly very likely. Diarrhoea

is the most common travel-related illness – figures suggest that at least half of all travellers to Africa will get diarrhoea at some stage. Sometimes dietary changes, such as increased spices or oils, are the cause. To avoid diarrhoea, only eat fresh fruits or vegetables if cooked or peeled, and be wary of dairy products that might contain unpasteurised milk. Although freshly cooked food can often be a safe option, plates or serving utensils might be dirty, so you should be highly selective when eating food from street vendors (make sure that cooked food is piping hot all the way through).

If you develop diarrhoea, be sure to drink plenty of fluids, preferably an oral rehydration solution containing lots of salt and sugar. A few loose stools don't require treatment, but if you start having more than four or five loose stools a day, you should start taking an antibiotic (usually a quinolone drug, such as ciprofloxacin or norfloxacin) and an antidiarrhoeal agent (such as loperamide) if you are not within easy reach of a toilet. If diarrhoea is bloody, persists for more than 72 hours or is accompanied by fever, shaking chills or severe abdominal pain, you should seek medical attention.

Amoebic Dysentery

Contracted by eating contaminated food and water, amoebic dysentery causes blood and mucus in the faeces. It can be relatively mild and tends to come on gradually, but seek medical advice if you think you have the illness as it won't clear up without treatment (which is with specific antibiotics).

Giardiasis

This illness, like amoebic dysentery, is also caused by ingesting contaminated food or water. The illness usually appears a week or more after you have been exposed to the offending parasite. Giardiasis might cause only a short-lived bout of typical traveller's diarrhoea, but it can also cause persistent diarrhoea. Ideally, seek medical advice if you suspect you have giardiasis, but if you are in a remote area you could start a course of antibiotics.

ENVIRONMENTAL HAZARDS
Heat Exhaustion

This condition occurs following heavy sweating and excessive fluid loss with inadequate replacement of fluids and salt, and is particularly common in hot climates when taking unaccustomed exercise before full acclimatisation.

HEALTH

Symptoms include headache, dizziness and tiredness. Dehydration is already happening by the time you feel thirsty – aim to drink sufficient water to produce pale, diluted urine. Self-treatment: fluid replacement with water and/or fruit juice, and cooling by cold water and fans. The treatment of the salt-loss component consists of consuming salty fluids (as in soup) and adding a little more table salt to foods than usual.

Heatstroke

Heat exhaustion is a precursor to the much more serious condition of heatstroke. In this case there is damage to the sweating mechanism, with an excessive rise in body temperature; irrational and hyperactive behaviour; and eventually loss of consciousness and death. Rapid cooling by spraying the body with water and fanning is ideal. Emergency fluid and electrolyte replacement is usually also required by intravenous drip.

Insect Bites & Stings

Mosquitoes might not always carry malaria or dengue fever, but they (and other insects) can cause irritation and infected bites. To avoid these, take the same precautions as you would for avoiding malaria (see p289). Bee and wasp stings cause real problems only to those who have a severe allergy to the stings (anaphylaxis), in which case, carry an adrenaline (epinephrine) injection.

Scorpions are frequently found in arid or dry climates. They can cause a painful bite that is sometimes life-threatening. If bitten by a scorpion, try taking a painkiller. Medical treatment should be sought if collapse occurs.

Bed bugs are often found in hostels and cheap hotels. They lead to very itchy, lumpy bites. Spraying the mattress with crawling insect killer after changing bedding will get rid of them.

Scabies is also frequently found in cheap accommodation. These tiny mites live in the skin, particularly between the fingers. They cause an intensely itchy rash. The itch is easily treated with malathion and permethrin lotion from a pharmacy.

Water

Madagascar's water is not safe to drink from the taps anywhere in the country – including the most expensive hotels. Consequently you should avoid ice in drinks without first asking if it's been made from filtered water.

Bottled water is available throughout Madagascar, but at around €1 per bottle it's expensive. It's better to invest in a water purifier – we really liked the SteriPen (about US$130). It is small enough to fit in your pocket and uses ultraviolet light (no chlorine taste) to clean 16oz of water in less than a minute. You do need to use a wide-mouthed water bottle to get the pen in deep enough to purify. Drinking from streams also puts you at risk of waterborne diseases unless you filter or purify first.

TRADITIONAL MEDICINE

Although Western medicine is available in larger cities and towns, *fanafody* (traditional medicine or herbal healing) plays an important role in Madagascar. Many urban dwellers prefer traditional methods, visiting market kiosks to procure age-old remedies. *Ombiasy* (healers) hold considerable social status in many parts of the country, particularly in more remote areas where traditional practices are still strong. They are often consulted for a variety of ailments.

It remains unlikely in the short term that even a basic level of conventional Western-style medicine will be made available to all the people of Madagascar and the Comoros. Traditional medicine, on the other hand, will almost certainly continue to be practised widely.

Language

CONTENTS

WHO SPEAKS WHAT WHERE?
Madagascar
Madagascar has two official languages: Malagasy and French. Malagasy is the everyday spoken language while French is often used for literary, business and administrative purposes, and in many of the more upmarket sectors of the tourism industry. Unless you travel on an organised tour, stick to big hotels in major towns or speak Malagasy, it'll be essential to speak at least basic French in order to get by comfortably in cities and towns. In rural areas, where knowledge of French is less widespread, you'll almost always find someone who speaks enough French to allow communication, but you may need to learn a bit of Malagasy also.

Although more Malagasy are learning English, relatively few people speak it and you shouldn't rely on English unless you are using middle- to top-range hotels and restaurants in Antananarivo, Nosy Be and Île Sainte Marie. If your French is poor, it isn't difficult to find someone in the major towns who is willing to try out whatever English words they might have picked up at school or elsewhere.

Comoros
Arabic and French are both official languages of the Comoros, but the most commonly spoken language is Shimasiwa (also known simply as Comorian), a dialect of Swahili. There are several variations, but they are all mutually understood. The local language on Anjouan is known as Shinzuani; on Mohéli, it's Shimwali; on Grande Comore, it's known as Shingadzija; and on Mayotte, it's called Mahorais. Very little English is spoken and visitors without at least a smattering of French may find themselves at a loss in the Comoros.

FRENCH

An important distinction is made in French between *tu* and *vous*, both of which mean 'you'; *tu* is only used when addressing people you know well, children or animals. If you're addressing an adult who isn't a personal friend, *vous* should be used unless the person invites you to use *tu*. In general, younger people insist less on this distinction between polite and informal, and you will find that in many cases they use *tu* from the beginning of an acquaintance.

For a more comprehensive guide to the language, pick up a copy of Lonely Planet's *French Phrasebook*.

PRONUNCIATION
j	as the 's' in 'leisure' (**zh** in our pronunciation guides)
c	before **e** and **i**, as the 's' in 'sit'; before **a**, **o** and **u**, it's pronounced as English 'k'. When underscored with a 'cedilla' (**ç**), it's always pronounced as the 's' in 'sit'.
r	pronounced from the back of the throat while restricting the flow of air

Most other letters in French are pronounced more or less the same as they would be in

English. In any case, the pronunciation guides we've included should help make things a lot easier.

ACCOMMODATION

I'm looking for	*Je cherche ...*	zher shersh ...
a ...		
camping ground	*un camping*	un kom·peeng
guesthouse	*une pension*	ewn pon·syon
	(de famille)	(der fa·mee·ler)
hotel	*un hôtel*	un o·tel
youth hostel	*une auberge*	ewn o·berzh
	de jeunesse	der zher·nes

Do you have any rooms available?
Est-ce que vous avez des chambres libres?
e·sker voo·za·vay day shom·brer lee·brer

I'd like (a) ...	*Je voudrais ...*	zher voo·dray ...
single room	*une chambre à*	ewn shom·brer
	un lit	a un lee
double-bed	*une chambre*	ewn shom·brer
room	*avec un grand*	a·vek un gron
	lit	lee
twin room	*une chambre*	ewn shom·brer
with two beds	*avec des lits*	a·vek day lee
	jumeaux	zhew·mo
room with	*une chambre*	ewn shom·brer
a bathroom	*avec une salle*	a·vek ewn sal
	de bains	der bun

How much is it ...?	*Quel est le prix ...?*	kel e ler pree ...
per night	*par nuit*	par nwee
per person	*par personne*	par per·son

May I see the room?
Est-ce que je peux voir es·ker zher per vwa la
la chambre? shom·brer

CONVERSATION & ESSENTIALS

Hello.	*Bonjour.*	bon·zhoor
Goodbye.	*Au revoir.*	o·rer·vwa
Yes.	*Oui.*	wee
No.	*Non.*	no
Please.	*S'il vous plaît.*	seel voo play
Thank you.	*Merci.*	mair·see
You're welcome.	*Je vous en prie.*	zher voo·zon pree
	De rien. (inf)	der ree·en
Excuse me.	*Excuse-moi.*	ek·skew·zay·mwa
Sorry. (forgive me)	*Pardon.*	par·don

What's your name?
Comment vous ko·mon voo·za·pay·lay voo
appelez-vous? (pol)
Comment tu ko·mon tew ta·pel
t'appelles? (inf)

EMERGENCIES

Help!		
	Au secours!	o skoor
There's been an accident!		
	Il y a eu un accident!	eel ya ew un ak·see·don
I'm lost.		
	Je me suis égaré/e. (m/f)	zhe me swee·zay·ga·ray
Leave me alone!		
	Fichez-moi la paix!	fee·shay·mwa la pay
Call ...!	*Appelez ...!*	a·play ...
a doctor	*un médecin*	un mayd·sun
the police	*la police*	la po·lees

My name is ...	*Je m'appelle ...*	zher ma·pel ...
Where are you from?		
	De quel pays êtes-vous?	der kel pay·ee et·voo
	De quel pays es-tu? (inf)	der kel pay·ee e·tew
I'm from ...	*Je viens de ...*	zher vyen der ...
I like ...	*J'aime ...*	zhem ...
I don't like ...	*Je n'aime pas ...*	zher nem pa ...
Just a minute.	*Une minute.*	ewn mee·newt

DIRECTIONS

Where is ...?	*Où est ...?*	oo e ...
Go straight ahead.	*Continuez tout droit.*	kon·teen·way too drwa
Turn left.	*Tournez à gauche.*	toor·nay a gosh
Turn right.	*Tournez à droite.*	toor·nay a drwat
at the corner	*au coin*	o kwun

behind	*derrière*	dair·ryair
in front of	*devant*	der·von
far (from)	*loin (de)*	lwun (der)
near (to)	*près (de)*	pray (der)
opposite	*en face de*	on fas der

island	*l'île*	leel
museum	*le musée*	ler mew·zay
old city (town)	*la vieille ville*	la vyay veel
sea	*la mer*	la mair
square	*la place*	la plas
tourist office	*l'office de*	lo·fees der
	tourisme	too·rees·mer

HEALTH

I'm ill.	Je suis malade.	zher swee ma·lad
It hurts here.	J'ai une douleur ici.	zhay ewn doo·ler ee·see

I'm allergic to ...	Je suis allergique ...	zher swee za·lair·zheek ...
antibiotics	aux antibiotiques	o zon·tee·byo·teek
aspirin	à l'aspirine	a las·pee·reen
bees	aux abeilles	o za·bay·yer
nuts	aux noix	o nwa
peanuts	aux cacahuètes	o ka·ka·wet
penicillin	à la pénicilline	a la pay·nee·see·leen

antiseptic	l'antiseptique	lon·tee·sep·teek
aspirin	l'aspirine	las·pee·reen
condoms	des préservatifs	day pray·zair·va·teef
contraceptive	le contraceptif	ler kon·tra·sep·teef
diarrhoea	la diarrhée	la dya·ray
medicine	le médicament	ler may·dee·ka·mon
nausea	la nausée	la no·zay
sunblock cream	la crème solaire	la krem so·lair
tampons	des tampons hygiéniques	day tom·pon ee·zhen·eek

LANGUAGE DIFFICULTIES

Do you speak English?
Parlez-vous anglais? — par·lay·voo ong·lay

Does anyone here speak English?
Y a-t-il quelqu'un qui parle anglais? — ya·teel kel·kung kee par long·glay

How do you say ... in French?
Comment est-ce qu'on dit ... en français? — ko·mon es·kon dee ... on fron·say

What does ... mean?
Que veut dire ...? — ker ver deer ...

I understand.
Je comprends. — zher kom·pron

I don't understand.
Je ne comprends pas. — zher ner kom·pron pa

Could you write it down, please?
Est-ce que vous pouvez l'écrire? — es·ker voo poo·vay lay·kreer

Can you show me (on the map)?
Pouvez-vous m'indiquer (sur la carte)? — poo·vay·voo mun·dee·kay (sewr la kart)

NUMBERS

0	zero	zay·ro
1	un	un
2	deux	der
3	trois	trwa
4	quatre	ka·trer
5	cinq	sungk
6	six	sees
7	sept	set
8	huit	weet
9	neuf	nerf
10	dix	dees
11	onze	onz
12	douze	dooz
13	treize	trez
14	quatorze	ka·torz
15	quinze	kunz
16	seize	sez
17	dix-sept	dee·set
18	dix-huit	dee·zweet
19	dix-neuf	deez·nerf
20	vingt	vung
21	vingt et un	vung tay un
22	vingt-deux	vung·der
30	trente	tront
40	quarante	ka·ront
50	cinquante	sung·kont
60	soixante	swa·sont
70	soixante-dix	swa·son·dees
80	quatre-vingts	ka·trer·vung
90	quatre-vingt-dix	ka·trer·vung·dees
100	cent	son
1000	mille	meel

QUESTION WORDS

Who?	Qui?	kee
What?	Quoi?	kwa
What is it?	Qu'est-ce que c'est?	kes·ker say
When?	Quand?	kon
Where?	Où?	oo
Which?	Quel/Quelle?	kel
Why?	Pourquoi?	poor·kwa
How?	Comment?	ko·mon

SHOPPING & SERVICES

I'd like to buy ...
Je voudrais acheter ... — zher voo·dray ash·tay ...

How much is it?
C'est combien? — say kom·byun

I don't like it.
Cela ne me plaît pas. — ser·la ner mer play pa

May I look at it?
Est-ce que je peux le voir? — es·ker zher per ler vwar

I'm just looking.
Je regarde. — zher rer·gard

It's cheap.
Ce n'est pas cher. — ser nay pa shair

It's too expensive.
C'est trop cher. — say tro shair

I'll take it.
Je le prends. — zher ler pron

Can I pay by ...?	Est-ce que je peux payer avec ...?	es·ker zher per pay·yay a·vek ...
credit card	ma carte de crédit	ma kart der kray·dee
travellers cheques	des chèques de voyage	day shek der vwa·yazh

more	plus	plew
less	moins	mwa
smaller	plus petit	plew per·tee
bigger	plus grand	plew gron

I'm looking for ...	Je cherche ...	zhe shersh ...
a bank	une banque	ewn bonk
the hospital	l'hôpital	lo·pee·tal
the market	le marché	ler mar·shay
the police	la police	la po·lees
the post office	le bureau de poste	ler bew·ro der post
a public phone	une cabine téléphonique	ewn ka·been tay·lay·fo·neek
a public toilet	les toilettes	lay twa·let

TIME & DATES

What time is it?	Quelle heure est-il?	kel er e til
It's (8) o'clock.	Il est (huit) heures.	il e (weet) er
It's half past ...	Il est (...) heures et demie.	il e (...) er e day·mee
in the morning	du matin	dew ma·tun
in the afternoon	de l'après-midi	der la·pray·mee·dee
in the evening	du soir	dew swar
today	aujourd'hui	o·zhoor·dwee
tomorrow	demain	der·mun
yesterday	hier	yair

Monday	lundi	lun·dee
Tuesday	mardi	mar·dee
Wednesday	mercredi	mair·krer·dee
Thursday	jeudi	zher·dee
Friday	vendredi	von·drer·dee
Saturday	samedi	sam·dee
Sunday	dimanche	dee·monsh

January	janvier	zhon·vyay
February	février	fayv·ryay
March	mars	mars
April	avril	a·vreel
May	mai	may
June	juin	zhwun
July	juillet	zhwee·yay
August	août	oot
September	septembre	sep·tom·brer
October	octobre	ok·to·brer
November	novembre	no·vom·brer
December	décembre	day·som·brer

TRANSPORT
Public Transport

I want to go to ...
Je voudrais aller à ...   zher voo·dray a·lay a ...

What time does ... leave/arrive?	À quelle heure part/arrive ...?	a kel er par/a·reev ...
the boat	le bateau	ler ba·to
the bus	le bus	ler bews
the minibus taxi	le taxi-brousse	le tak·see broos
the plane	l'avion	la·vyon

I'd like a ... ticket.	Je voudrais un billet ...	zher voo·dray un bee·yay ...
one-way	simple	sum·pler
return	aller et retour	a·lay ay rer·toor

the first	le premier (m)	ler prer·myay
	la première (f)	la prer·myair
the last	le dernier (m)	ler dair·nyay
	la dernière (f)	la dair·nyair
ticket office	le guichet	ler gee·shay
timetable	l'horaire	lo·rair

Private Transport

I'd like to hire a/an...	Je voudrais louer ...	zher voo·dray loo·way ...
car	une voiture	ewn vwa·tewr
4WD	un quatre-quatre	un kat·kat
motorbike	une moto	ewn mo·to
bicycle	un vélo	un vay·lo

Is this the road to ...?
C'est la route pour ...?   say la root poor ...

Where's a service station?
Où est-ce qu'il y a une station-service?   oo es·keel ya ewn sta·syon·ser·vees

Please fill it up.
Le plein, s'il vous plaît.   ler plun seel voo play

I'd like ... litres.
Je voudrais ... litres.   zher voo·dray ... lee·trer

petrol/gas	essence	ay·sons
unleaded	sans plomb	son plom
leaded	au plomb	o plom
diesel	diesel	dyay·zel

I need a mechanic.
J'ai besoin d'un mécanicien.   zhay ber·zwun dun may·ka·nee·syun

The car/motorbike has broken down (at ...)
La voiture/moto est tombée en panne (à ...)   la vwa·tewr/mo·to ay tom·bay on pan (a ...)

The car/motorbike won't start.
La voiture/moto ne veut   la vwa·tewr/mo·to ner ver
pas démarrer.   pa day·ma·ray
I have a flat tyre.
Mon pneu est à plat.   mom pner ay ta pla
I've run out of petrol.
Je suis en panne   zher swee zon pan
d'essence.   day·sons
I had an accident.
J'ai eu un accident.   zhay ew un ak·see·don

MALAGASY

Malagasy belongs to the Austronesian family of languages; its closest linguistic relative is a language spoken in southern Borneo. Over the centuries it has incorporated numerous other influences, including Bantu (particularly in some of the west coast dialects) and Arabic. The influence of Arabic is most evident in the names of the days of the week.

Malagasy was first written using a form of Arabic script (see boxed text, right), and then only in very limited areas in southeastern coastal Madagascar. It wasn't until the early 19th century during the reign of Radama I that Malagasy developed its current written form when missionaries from the London Missionary Society began devising the modern Latin-based alphabet. This 'standard Malagasy', which is based on the Merina dialect, has since served as the national language.

If you're serious about learning Malagasy, it'll be worth investing in one of the dictionaries or instructional textbooks that are available in Antananarivo bookshops.

PRONUNCIATION

When King Radama I sent out a request for missionaries from the London Missionary Society to help with the education and development of Madagascar, two of those sent were Welshmen David Jones and David Griffiths. Together with the king himself, they set about romanising and transliterating the Malagasy language. Despite this early effort, written Malagasy bears remarkably little resemblance to today's spoken language. Syllables seem to evaporate and vowels aren't pronounced the way English (or even French) speakers might anticipate. The general advice is to 'swallow as many

---

SORABE

The Sorabe (Great Writings) are sacred manuscripts written in Malagasy using a form of Arabic script. The earliest of these were made sometime after the 8th century under the influence of stranded Arab traders who wanted to reproduce pages of the Quran. The Sorabe were later expanded to include histories and genealogies, astrologers' predictions and various works on traditional medicine. Knowledge of the script used in writing the Sorabe was primarily the preserve of specially trained scribes known as *katibo*. Most Sorabe are in the possession of the Antaimoro and Antambohoaka tribes in southeastern Madagascar.

---

syllables as you can and drop the last one'; vowels at the end of most words are dropped in pronunciation.

The Malagasy alphabet has 21 letters; the English letters 'c', 'q', 'u', 'w' and 'x' don't exist in Malagasy. In words borrowed from English, French or other languages, the 'c' is replaced by an **s** or **k**, the 'q' is replaced by **k** and the 'x' by **ks**. When **k** or **g** are preceded by an **i** or a **y** (which are pronounced more or less the same), the **i** is pronounced both before and after the **k** or **g**.

The letter **o** is usually pronounced like a double **o**; thus *veloma* (goodbye) emerges as 've-*loom*'. The letter **a** is pronounced as the 'u' in 'cut'.

You only have to glance at a map of the country and you'll notice that Malagasy place names generally contain lots of letters. Similarly, people's surnames can be a mouthful. In the interests of avoiding embarrassment or possible offence through mispronouncing family names, you may want to accept invitations to address people by their Christian names, which are often biblical.

CONVERSATION & USEFUL WORDS

Greetings/Good day.	*Salama.*
Welcome!	*Tonga soa!*
Come in.	*Midira.*
How are you?	*Manao ahoana ianao.*
I'm fine.	*Salama tsara aho.*
Very well, thank you.	*Tsara fa misaotra.*
What's new?	*Inona no vaovao?*
Nothing much.	*Tsy misy.*

LANGUAGE

DIALECTS

Despite the linguistic unity of Malagasy, regional differences do exist, and in some coastal areas, standard Malagasy is shunned. The three broad language groups are those of the highlands; the north and east; and the south and west. However, even within these areas there are local variations. The following table indicates a few of the lexical and phonetic differences between standard Malagasy and some of the regional dialects.

English	Highlands	North & East	South & West
Greetings.	*Manao ahoana.*	*Mbola tsara anarô.*	*Akore aby nareo.*
(in response)	*Tsara.*	*Mbola tsara.*	*Tsara/Soa.*
What's new?	*Inona no vaovao?*	*Ino vaovaonao?*	*Talilio?*
Nothing much.	*Tsy misy.*	*Ehe, tsisy fô manginginy.*	*Mbe soa.*
Where?	*Aiza?*	*Aia?*	*Aia?*
Who?	*Iza?*	*La?*	*La?*
spouse	*vady*	*vady*	*valy*
ancestor	*razana*	*raza*	*raza*

Goodbye.	*Veloma/Manorapihaona.*	dirty	*maloto*
See you soon.	*Vetivety.*	easy	*mora*
See you later.	*Mandram pihaona.*	good	*tsara*
Yes.	*Eny/Eka.*	interesting	*mahasondriana*
No.	*Tsia.*	little	*kely*
Please/Excuse me.	*Azafady.*	lost	*very*
Thank you (very much).	*Misaotra (indrindra).*	more	*mihoatra*
		slow	*votsa*
You're welcome.	*Tsy misy fisaorana.*		
My name is ...	*... no anarako.*	accommodation	*zavatra ilaina*
Bon apetit!	*Mazoto a homana!*	bed	*fandriana*
Bon voyage!	*Tongava soa!*	breakfast	*sakafo maraina*
Cheers!	*Ho ela velona!*	food	*hanina*
Sir/Madam	*Tompoko*	kitchen	*lakozia*
		lunch	*sakafo antoandro*
I don't understand.	*Tsy azoka.*	room	*efitra*
Alright/OK.	*Ekena.*	tariff	*tarify*
Show me.	*Atoroy ahy.*	water	*rano*
How much is it?	*Ohatrinona?*		
It's too expensive.	*Lafo loatra, lafo be.*	time	*fotoana*
It's very cheap.	*Tena mora be.*	today	*androany*
Please give me some.	*Mmba omeo aho.*	tomorrow	*rahampitso*
Where is ...?	*Aiza ...?*	yesterday	*omaly*
		beach	*morona*
chief	*lehibe*	beside	*akaiky*
driver	*mpamily*	boulevard	*arabe, araben*
father/mother	*ray/reny*	to buy	*mividy*
friend	*sakaiza*	danger	*loza*
man/woman	*lehilahy/vehivavy*	entry/exit	*fidirana/fivoahana*
name	*anarana*	forest	*ala*
traveller	*mpandeha*	guide	*mpitarika*
		help	*fanampiana*
bad	*ratsy*	island	*nosy*
beautiful	*mahafinaritra/tsara tarehy*	lake	*farihy*
big	*be*	left/right	*havia/havanana*
deep	*lalina*		

LANGUAGE

CITY & TOWN NAMES

Although most people continue to use French place names in Madagascar, since the time of independence, cities, towns and places have been officially known by their Malagasy names. The following list may help alleviate some of the confusion:

Malagasy	French
Ambohitra	**Joffreville**
Andasibe	**Périnet**
Andoany	**Hell-Ville**
Antananarivo	**Tananarive**
Antsiranana	**Diego Suarez**
Fenoarivo	**Fénérive**
Iharana	**Vohémar**
Mahajanga	**Majunga**
Mahavelona	**Foulpointe**
Nosy Boraha	**Île Sainte Marie**
Anantsogno	**St Augustin**
Taolagnaro	**Fort Dauphin**
Toamasina	**Tamatave**
Toliara	**Tuléar**

Pronunciation can be difficult; one general rule for Malagasy names is to drop word-final vowels.

map	*sarin tany*
market	*tsena*
sea	*ranomasina*
station	*gara*
street	*làlana*
to swim	*milomano*
to walk	*mandeha*
town/village	*tanana/vohitra*
waterfall	*riana*

COMORIAN

The following is a list of useful Comorian words and phrases. Unfortunately, Comorian spelling isn't standardised so you may see several different transliterations for these words.

CONVERSATION & USEFUL WORDS

Hello.	*Salama.*
Good day.	*Bariza.* (Grand Comore)
Good day. (in response)	*M'bona.*
Welcome.	*Karibu.*
How's it going?	*Njeje?* (Anjouan)
	Ndje? or *Habare sa?* (Mohéli & Mayotte)
Fine. (in response)	*Ndjema/Sijouha.*
Goodbye.	*Kwaheri.*
Good night.	*Lala ha unono.*
Please.	*Tafatvali.*
Thank you.	*Marahaba.*
Yes.	*Aiwa.*
No.	*Uh uh.*
I don't understand.	*Ntsu elewa.*
I don't speak Comorian.	*Mimi tsidji ourogowa shimasiwa.*
My name is ...	*Mi opara ...*
I'm from ...	*Mi tsila ...*
How much is this?	*Ryali nga?* or *Beyi hindri?*
That's expensive/ inexpensive.	*Ngohouzo anli/Rahisi.*
It's beautiful.	*Udjisa.*
I'd like to go to ...	*Ngamwandzo nende ...*
Where?	*Ndahu?*
shady dealings	*makarakara*
Sir	*monye*
Madam	*bueni*
mother	*mama*
father	*baba*
grandmother/ elderly woman	*koko*
grandfather/ elderly man	*bakoko*
European/foreigner	*mzungu*

road/street	*pare*
beach	*mtsangani*
to drink	*hunua*
to swim	*huyeleya*
boat	*markabu*
to fish	*mulowa*
fisherman	*mulozi*
mosque	*mukiri*
the top/peak	*liju*
town	*mjini*
post office	*poste*
paradise	*pevoni*
mosquito	*dundi*

It's hot.	*Ina moro.*
It's cold.	*Ina baridi.*
night	*uku*
day	*mtsana*
today	*leo*
tomorrow	*meso*
yesterday	*jana*

FOOD & DRINK

I'm hungry/thirsty.	*Ngamina ndzaya/nyora.*
Do you have food available?	*Kamtsina bahidrou ya houla?*

LANGUAGE

I'm looking for a place to eat/sleep.	*Tamtsaho pvahanou nililye/nilale.*
Do you have ...?	*Ngagina ...?*
It's good.	*Ya djema.*
to eat	*houla*
market	*shindoni* or *bazari*
banana	*masindza* or *ndrovi*
coconut (fresh/dried)	*idjavou/nadzi*
orange	*trundra*
sugar	*muwa*
coffee	*kafe*
milk	*dziwa*
rice	*tsohole* or *mayele*
bread	*mkatre*
meat	*nyama*
tea	*kayi*
chicken	*kuhu*
shark	*papa*
lobster	*kamba diva*
water	*madji*
fish	*fi*

NUMBERS

1	*montsi, moja*
2	*mbili*
3	*ndraru*
4	*nne*
5	*ntsanu*
6	*sita*
7	*nfukare*
8	*nane*
9	*shenda*
10	*kume*
11	*kume na mwedja*
12	*kume na mbili*
20	*shirini*
30	*mengo-mi-raru*
40	*mengo-mi-ne*
100	*djana*
200	*majana mbili*
300	*majana mi-raru*
1000	*shihwhi*

LANGUAGE

Also available from Lonely Planet:
French Phrasebook

Glossary

For a glossary of food and drink terms, see p43.

Agate – Agence d'Acceuil Télécom; telephone office
aloalo – elaborate woodcarvings used to adorn tombs
andevo – traditional underclass
andriana – noble
Angap – Association Nationale pour la Gestion des Aires Protégées (National Association for the Management of Protected Areas), the organisation that administers most of Madagascar's parks and reserves
Antaimoro – east coast tribe from the region around Manakara; also the name given to a type of handmade paper
Antakàrana – tribe from northern Madagascar
arabe/araben – avenue
ariary – Madagascar's unit of currency
aye-aye – rare nocturnal lemur

bâché – small, converted pick-up truck
baie – bay
banga – colourful temporary dwelling built by bachelors in the Comoros
bangwe – village or town square
bao – a popular game in the Comoros and elsewhere in Africa, played by dropping polished seeds into a series of holes in a wooden board
baraza – stone bench found in the Comoros
Basse-Ville – lower town
bazary – market; often designated Bazary Kely (small market) or Bazary Be (big market)
be – 'big' in Malagasy; denotes larger parts of a town
betsa-betsa – an alcoholic drink made from fermented sugarcane juice
Betsileo – Madagascar's third-largest tribe after the Merina and the Betsimisaraka
Betsimisaraka – Madagascar's second-largest tribe
Boina – Sakalava territory in the area around Mahajanga
boutre – single-masted dhow used for cargo
buxi – local term for minibus in Fianarantsoa and some other areas of Madagascar

camion-brousse – large truck used for passengers
cassava – root vegetable also known as manioc, or *mhogo* in Comorian
CFPF – Centre de Formation Professionnelle Forestière (Centre of Professional Forestry Training)
chambre d'hôtes – B&B-style accommodation, often in a family home
chiromani – cloth wrap worn by Comorian women

coelacanth – prehistoric fish, still living off the Comoros and southern Madagascar
collectivité territoriale – French overseas territory; status of Mayotte
Comorian – English term for a person from the Comoros; also spelt Comorien or Comoran
côtier – literally 'person from the coast'; the term is usually used to describe someone who is not a member of the Merina tribe
coua – bird belonging to one of nine species of coucou

fady – taboo, forbidden
Famadihana – exhumation and reburial; literally 'the turning of the bones'
familiale – a synonym for *taxi-be* (big taxi)
Fihavanana – conciliation or brotherhood
fijoroana – a ceremony invoking the ancestors
fosa – a puma-like animal and the largest of Madagascar's carnivores (not to be confused with the *fossa*)
fossa – local name for the striped civet

galawa – Comorian dugout canoe
gare routière – bus station
gargote – cheap restaurant
gasy – Malagasy (pronounced 'gash')
gîte – rustic shelter
Grands Mariages – Comorian wedding ceremonies

hajj – pilgrimage to Mecca
hasina – a force that flows from the land through the ancestors into the society of the living
Haute-Ville – upper town
hauts plateaux – highlands; the term is often used to refer to Madagascar's central plateau region
hira gasy – music, dancing and storytelling spectacles
hôtel de ville – town hall
hotely – small roadside place that serves basic meals
hova – commoners

Id-ul-Fitr – Muslim festival at the end of the fast of Ramadan; also spelt Eid-el-Fitr
Imerina – region ruled by the Merina
immeuble – building
indri – largest of Madagascar's lemur species

kabary – discourse performed by a highly skilled orator
kely – 'small' in Malagasy; often used to denote a township or satellite town
kianja – place or square; also known as *kianjan*

lac – lake
lakana – dugout canoe; synonym for *pirogue*
lalana – street
lamba – white cotton or silk scarf
lamba mena – literally 'red cloth'; used as a burial shroud, but is rarely red

Mahafaly – southern tribe
maki – Malagasy and Comorian term for a lemur
malabary – long gowns worn by dancers
masonjoany – face pack made from ground wood and water
medina – old Arab quarter of a Comorian town
Merina – Madagascar's largest tribe, centred in Antananarivo
metropole – continental France (as opposed to French overseas possessions)
mihrab – niche in a mosque indicating the direction of Mecca
minaret – tower of a mosque, from where the call to prayer is issued
mofo – bread, usually baked as baguettes
mora mora – 'slowly, slowly' or 'wait a minute'; often used to mean the Malagasy pace of life
Mosquée de Vendredi – Friday mosque
mzungu – foreigner or white person; mostly used in the Comoros

nosy – island
Nouvelle-Ville – new town

ombiasy – highly respected healers who not only prescribe herbal cures, but also carry out rituals to secure assistance from the ancestors, to balance out negative *vintana*, or to communicate with a *tromba* that has possessed a person

paositra – post office
parc marin – marine national park
parc national – national park
petit marché – small market
pic – peak
pirogue – dugout canoe
pisteur – untrained guide, often speaking Malagasy only
pousse-pousse – rickshaw

Ramadan – Muslim month of fasting from sunrise to sunset
ramba-ramba – noisy cart used for transporting produce between villages; powered only by human sweat and toil
rangani – marijuana; pronounced 'roungoun'
ranovola – drink made by adding boiling water to the residue left in pots used to cook rice; also known as *ranon'apango*
ravinala – literally 'forest leaves'; also known as travellers' palm, the most distinctive of Madagascar's palm trees
Réseau National des Chemins de Fer Malgaches (RNCFM) – Madagascar's rail system
réserve forestière – forest reserve

réserve spéciale – special reserve (often similar to a national park)
resto – commonly used abbreviation for restaurant
rhumerie – bar selling varieties of rum
RN – route nationale; national road (often still no more than a track)
rova – palace

Sakalava – western tribe
salegy – Kenyan-influenced music of the Sakalava tribe
salon de thé – tea room
sambatra – mass circumcision ceremony
sambos – samosas
Sava – region comprising Sambava, Andapa, Vohémar (Iharana) and Antalaha
sifaka – a type of lemur, known in French as a *propithèque*
sigaoma – a type of music similar to black South African popular music
stationnement de taxi-brousse – bush-taxi station

table d'hôtes – fixed menu or set meal
tapia – small red berries that taste similar to dates
tavy – Malagasy term for the slash-and-burn method of agriculture
taxi-be – literally 'big taxi'; also known as a *familiale*
taxi-brousse – bush taxi; generic term for any kind of public passenger truck, car or minibus
taxi-spécial – charter taxi
taxi-ville – literally 'town taxis'; used for shorter distances
tenrec – small mammal resembling a hedgehog or shrew
THB – Three Horses Beer, Madagascar's most popular beer
tilapia – freshwater perch (fish)
tromba – spirit
tsapika – a form of music that originated in the south
tsingy – limestone pinnacle formations; also known as karst

valiha – a stringed instrument that is played like a harp
vary – rice (Malagasy)
vazaha – foreigner or white person
Vezo – nomadic fishing subtribe of the Sakalava, found in the southwest
vintana – destiny
voay – crocodile

WWF – World Wide Fund for Nature

ylang-ylang – bush with sweet-smelling white flowers used to make perfume

Zafimaniry – a subgroup of the Betsileo people who live in the area east of Ambositra, and are renowned for their woodcarving skills
zebu – a type of domesticated ox found throughout Madagascar; it has a prominent hump on its back and loose skin under its throat

The Authors

AARON ANDERSON
Southern Madagascar, Central Madagascar, Transport

This was Aaron's second experience in Africa – his first voyage took him backpacking around South Africa researching a guidebook even before he'd actually become a Lonely Planet author (thanks, Becca). Former microbrewer, wanderer and amateur bear wrestler, Aaron originally hails from Elvis' home town of Memphis, Tennessee. He started out in the travel-writing game late in life – in his early 30s, and after a lengthy stretch of brewing beer for a living – when he realised he wanted to write, and could. *Madagascar & Comoros* is Aaron's sixth Lonely Planet title. Other projects have included *Washington DC* city guide, *Thailand* and *Western Europe*. When they're not on the road, which isn't often, Aaron and Becca live in Boulder, Colorado.

DAVID ANDREW
Destination, Getting Started, Itineraries, History, The Culture, Food & Drink, Wildlife, Environment

David took to wildlife-watching the way that some people take to religion or sport. As a biologist he has studied the Giant Panda in southwest China and seabirds in Antarctica. He has travelled extensively in Africa's wild places and was hooked on Madagascar long before he first visited *la Grand Île*. He has written about wildlife from all corners of the globe as an author of all five guides in Lonely Planet's Watching Wildlife series; as founding editor of the Whitley Award–winning *Wingspan* magazine and a former editor of *Wildlife Australia*; and as a freelance journalist in places as diverse as the Galápagos Islands, Borneo and New Guinea. His visits to Madagascar left him in no doubt that Charles Darwin was oh so right about evolution…

LONELY PLANET AUTHORS

Why is our travel information the best in the world? It's simple: our authors are independent, dedicated travellers. They don't research using just the internet or phone, and they don't take freebies in exchange for positive coverage. They travel widely, to all the popular spots and off the beaten track. They personally visit thousands of hotels, restaurants, cafés, bars, galleries, palaces, museums and more – and they take pride in getting all the details right, and telling it how it is. Think you can do it? Find out how at lonelyplanet.com.

THE AUTHORS

BECCA BLOND
Northern Madagascar, Western Madagascar, Comoros, Directory

Becca's journey through Madagascar started on the wrong foot when she tripped coming off the Air France flight, and fractured her ankle. Determined to see a lemur and do her friend Tom's work justice, she gritted her teeth and researched the title on one leg. She even enjoyed herself, although she admits this was only possible with a lot of help from co-author and fiancé Aaron Anderson. Becca's love affair with Africa began at age 20, in university, when studying in Zimbabwe. She has since visited the continent seven times – the last four trips were to research Lonely Planet's *South Africa, Lesotho & Swaziland* and *Africa on a Shoestring*. She speaks fluent French.

TOM PARKINSON
Antananarivo, Eastern Madagascar

Tom researched the whole of Madagascar for this guidebook, fuelled by his passion for African sights, sounds and particularly rhythms. Tragically, Tom passed away unexpectedly while writing up his notes in January 2007, aged 28. His loss is keenly felt by everyone who knew him and worked with him.

The Antananarivo and Eastern Madagascar chapters of this book represent just a small part of Tom's prolific body of work, which has included guides to Malaysia, Kenya, East Africa, Poland, Germany and Berlin. Tom had a long association with Africa, covering some particularly rugged corners of the continent for Lonely Planet, including Chad, Niger, Sudan and Algeria.

Madagascar was a dream destination for Tom ever since he first joined Lonely Planet in 2002. In July 2007, a tree was planted in Tom's name at the SOS Children's Village (p99) in Antsirabe, a charity supported by the Tom Parkinson Memorial Fund.

(Tom wrote the Antananarivo and Eastern Madagascar chapters, except for the chapter introductions, which were written by Becca Blond and Aaron Anderson.)

CONTRIBUTING AUTHORS

Dr Caroline Evans wrote the Health chapter. Having studied medicine at the University of London, Caroline completed general training at Cambridge. She is the medical adviser to Nomad Travel Clinic, a private travel-health clinic in London, and is also a GP specialising in travel medicine.

Patricia C Wright wrote the Environment chapter, which was updated for this edition by David Andrew. Patricia is Professor of Anthropology at the State University of New York and Director of the Institute for the Conservation of Tropical Environments. In 1986 she and her colleagues discovered a new species of lemur, the golden bamboo lemur.

Behind the Scenes

This is the 6th edition of *Madagascar & Comoros*. The 1st edition was researched and written by Richard Wilcox, the 2nd edition by Deanna Swaney, the 3rd by Paul Greenway, the 4th by Mary Fitzpatrick and the 5th by Gemma Pitcher. This edition was researched and written by Tom Parkinson, David Andrew, Aaron Anderson and Becca Blond.

THIS BOOK

This guidebook was commissioned in Lonely Planet's Melbourne office, and produced by the following:

Commissioning Editor Lucy Monie
Coordinating Editors Kate James, Michelle Bennett
Coordinating Cartographer Marion Byass
Coordinating Layout Designer Carol Jackson
Senior Editors Sasha Baskett, Helen Christinis
Managing Cartographers Shahara Ahmed, Adrian Persoglia
Managing Layout Designer Celia Wood
Assisting Editors Adrienne Costanzo, Judith Bamber
Cover Designer Carol Jackson
Project Manager Rachel Imeson
Language Content Coordinator Quentin Frayne

Thanks to Ryan Evans, Emma Gilmour, Imogen Hall, Lisa Knights, Sara LeHoullier, Adam McCrow, Naomi Parker, Raphael Richards, Marg Toohey, Gerard Walker, and our man in Antananarivo, Jackson Bloom.

Extra special thanks to Joe Bindloss for writing Tom's biography statement, and the Parkinson family for all their support in putting the pieces together.

THANKS

AARON ANDERSON & BECCA BLOND

First off we want to thank Tom. Although Aaron didn't know Tom personally, Becca did and when we were offered this project we knew we had to accept out of respect and responsibility for a friend and coworker. Second up, thanks go to Tom's parents, Dilys and Stephen Parkinson, who supported us the entire way, going as far as sending us Tom's original notes so that we could retrace his footsteps when we got to Madagascar and incorporate the places he had originally picked. Lucy Monie, who commissioned us on this title, also deserves thanks. Not only was she a patient and fabulous editor, but she also had faith that we would do Tom's last work justice. So thanks Lucy. To the rest of the editing and carto team we worked with – Kate, Shahara and Marion – thanks for all your hard work. In Madagascar we want to extend a huge thanks to the kind people at the

THE LONELY PLANET STORY

Fresh from an epic journey across Europe, Asia and Australia in 1972, Tony and Maureen Wheeler sat at their kitchen table stapling together notes. The first Lonely Planet guidebook, *Across Asia on the Cheap*, was born.

Travellers snapped up the guides. Inspired by their success, the Wheelers began publishing books to Southeast Asia, India and beyond. Demand was prodigious, and the Wheelers expanded the business rapidly to keep up. Over the years, Lonely Planet extended its coverage to every country and into the virtual world via lonelyplanet.com and the Thorn Tree message board.

As Lonely Planet became a globally loved brand, Tony and Maureen received several offers for the company. But it wasn't until 2007 that they found a partner whom they trusted to remain true to the company's principles of travelling widely, treading lightly and giving sustainably. In October of that year, BBC Worldwide acquired a 75% share in the company, pledging to uphold Lonely Planet's commitment to independent travel, trustworthy advice and editorial independence.

Today, Lonely Planet has offices in Melbourne, London and Oakland, with over 500 staff members and 300 authors. Tony and Maureen are still actively involved with Lonely Planet. They're travelling more often than ever, and they're devoting their spare time to charitable projects. And the company is still driven by the philosophy of *Across Asia on the Cheap*: 'All you've got to do is decide to go and the hardest part is over. So go!'

SOS Children's Village in Antsirabe, who took the time to show us around and let us plant a tree in Tom's honour. At home we would like to thank our family and friends for their unwavering support. We can't name you all, but Vera, Grandma Pauline, Jenny, Uncle Joe, David, Patricia, Jessica, Spanky, Brittany, and of course Duke, your faith in us is never forgotten. Aaron would also like to extend special thanks to Russell, Jon VS, Mike P, Brett, Chris, Eric Hoerske, Juan Carlos, Dr Feelgood, Captain Freedom, Mark A, the Keebler elves, Ambien and the Simpsonseads.

OUR READERS

Many thanks to the travellers who used the last edition and wrote to us with helpful hints, useful advice and interesting anecdotes:

A Carrara Achille, Brian Adair, Jane Adair, Sybrandus Adema, Kelyn Akuna, Dick Alliband, Silvia Andrea, Shabnam Anvar, Mike Asimbola, Martine & Gérard Aymonnier **B** Bierta Barfod, Inge Bartsch, Kathryn Baskerville, Patricia Bernard, Martin Bohnstedt, Catherine Brinkley, George Broché, Rebecca Brown, Andrea Brugnoli, Meti Buh, Terence Burgers, Alexis Burke, Martin J Byrne **C** Dave Carlson, Davide Castellani, Dan Cavanagh, Rita Chambers, Rory Chapple, Flavio Ciferri, Nat Ciferri, Gertie Clabbers, Lisa Cliff, Melanie Cohen, Ofir Cohen, John Connell, Richard Cooper, Ortwin Costenoble, Marie Cousens, Zsolt Cseke, Bruno Cuypers **D** Ingrid De van Ven, Frederike Diersen, Andrew Doak, Ivo Domburg, Gernot Dresch **E** Elizabeth Edwards, Na'Ama Eilat, Alink Ellen **F** Adrian Faulkner, Bianca Frei **G** Giorgio Gadola, Witek Gdowski, Marta Ghezzi, Sheena Gibson, Arend Goens, Bard & Fiona Green **H** Kevin Handreck, Graham Hardwick, Claudia Haschkovitz, Johan Hedve, Cherifa Hendriks, Jacob Hendriks, Miriam Henze, Hilmar Jobst Herzberg, Julian Hewitt, Simon Hill, Gill Hoggard, Chris Howles, Nardy Hudson, Charlie Humble, Krista Humble, Annette Hutton **I** Alison Iredale **J** Emily Jamieson, Volkmar E Janicke, Beate Jantzen, Christa Jeker **K** Fruzsina Kaiser, Alan Keeble, Michael Keller, Metka Koren, Elena Kostoglodova, Eva Królikowska, David Kromka, Ian Kutschke **L** Bruno Laforge, Benaifei Lakdawalle, Menno & Angela Lanting, Andrea de Laurentiis, Andreas Ledergerber, Yeondae Lee, Jo Leech, Laura Lefkowitz, Adam Levine, David Lewis, Margaret Lorang, Toon Luttikhuis, Hallvor Lyngstad **M** Bianka Madej, Joe Maguire, Monika & Alex Marion, Javier Marti, Brent Matsuda, James May, Beth McKernan, Silvia Merli, Francis Monck-Mason, Nick Morphet, Reinhard Mostert, Stephen Muecke, Strother Murray **N** Frick Nadja, Matthew Nelson, Fabrizio Nicoletti, Jochen Nicolini, Suzanne Nuttall **O** Sharon Orell, Gustaf Ossmer **P** Elvira Pacheco, Nicki Parnell, Jeremy Parsons, Erik Patel, Ilan Peri, Ann M Pescatello, Hans Pflug, Mark Pickens, Jean-Pierre Pignard, John Pitterle, Apurv Puri **R** Helen Randle, Susanne Rasfalk, Sarah Ravaioli, Sue Rees, Paula Jane Reid, Cindy Rimmington, John Robertson, Andrew Robson, Ayliffe Rose **S** Andrea Michele Sacripanti, Oyvind Sathre, Beth Schaeffer, Brigitte Schattner, Kyley Schmidt, Derek Schuurman, Mark Shahinian, Josef Sidler, Merli Silvia, Rieky Slenders, Elia Soutou, Georgina Starkie, A Steenstra, Vernon & Susanne Steward, Mary Sullivan, Mark Sutcliffe **T** Benita Tapster, Kim Tardy, Mara Tattarletti, Graham Taylor, Boutin Thierry, Brock Thiessen, Lesuthu Tshepo **V** Rein van Dun, Vincent van Reenen, Dominique & Anond Viki, Marinus Vissers, Harrie Vollaard **W** Iain Walker, Ken Walker, Silvia Wandl, Karin Wandschura, Michelle Warrick, Rene Wasvis, Thomas Werner, Richard H Wiersema, John Wilson, Manfred Wolfensberger, Chantal Wullimann **Y** Rodger Young **Z** Maya Zeller

ACKNOWLEDGMENTS

Many thanks to the following for the use of their content:

Globe on title page © Mountain High Maps 1993 Digital Wisdom, Inc.

Internal photographs: p4 Aaron Anderson, Becca Blond, Tom Parkinson; p52 (#5) Images of Africa; p56 (#2) DEA/C.Dani-I.Jeske/Getty Images; p58 (#4), p60 (#4) Nick Garbutt/naturepl.com; p58 (#3), p61 (#6) Pete Oxford/naturepl.com; p59 (#7), p61 (#5) Nick Garbutt/NHPA. All other photographs by Lonely Planet Images and by Anders Blomqvist p53 (#1); Olivier Cirendini p49; David Curl p50 (#1), p57 (#1), p63 (#5); Tom Cockrem p63 (#1); Karl Lehmann p 51 (#4, #6), p54 (#4, #5), p55 (#3), p57 (#4), p59 (#6), p62 (#6, #8); Andrew MacColl p53 (#4); Carol Polich p50 (#7), p64 (#1); Andy Rouse p55 (#1); Thor Vaz de Leon p52 (#2).

SEND US YOUR FEEDBACK

We love to hear from travellers – your comments keep us on our toes and help make our books better. Our well-travelled team reads every word on what you loved or loathed about this book. Although we cannot reply individually to postal submissions, we always guarantee that your feedback goes straight to the appropriate authors, in time for the next edition. Each person who sends us information is thanked in the next edition – and the most useful submissions are rewarded with a free book.

To send us your updates – and find out about Lonely Planet events, newsletters and travel news – visit our award-winning website: **www.lonelyplanet.com/contact**.

Note: we may edit, reproduce and incorporate your comments in Lonely Planet products such as guidebooks, websites and digital products, so let us know if you don't want your comments reproduced or your name acknowledged. For a copy of our privacy policy visit www.lonelyplanet.com/privacy.

Index

000 Map pages
000 Photograph pages

INDEX

INDEX

INDEX

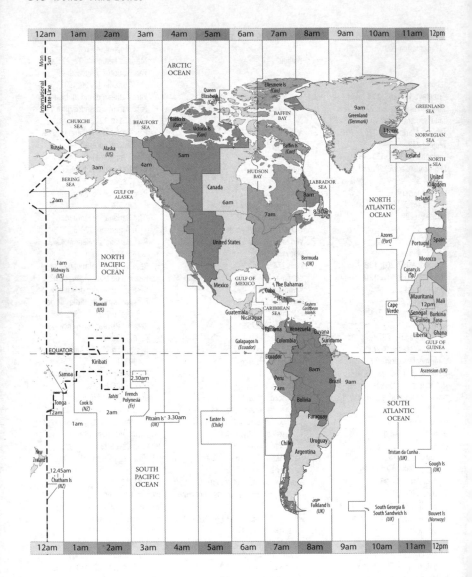

| 12am | 1am | 2am | 3am | 4am | 5am | 6am | 7am | 8am | 9am | 10am | 11am | 12pm |

Mon / Sun

International Date Line

ARCTIC OCEAN

CHUKCHI SEA

Russia

BEAUFORT SEA

Queen Elizabeth Is (Can)

Banks Is (Can)

Victoria Is (Can)

Ellesmere Is (Can)

BAFFIN BAY

9am
Greenland (Denmark)

11am

GREENLAND SEA

NORWEGIAN SEA

Iceland

NORTH SEA

United Kingdom

Ireland

Alaska (US)

3am

4am

5am

Baffin Is (Can)

HUDSON BAY

LABRADOR SEA

8am

8.30am

2am

BERING SEA

GULF OF ALASKA

Canada

6am

7am

NORTH ATLANTIC OCEAN

Azores (Port)

Portugal

Spain

Morocco

1am
Midway Is (US)

NORTH PACIFIC OCEAN

United States

Bermuda (UK)

Canary Is (Sp)

Mauritania

Mali

Hawaii (US)

Mexico

GULF OF MEXICO

The Bahamas

Cuba

Haiti

Eastern Caribbean Islands

CARIBBEAN SEA

Cape Verde

12pm

Senegal
Guinea

Burkina
Faso

Guatemala
Nicaragua

Liberia

Ghana

GULF OF GUINEA

EQUATOR

Kiribati

Panama

Galapagos Is (Ecuador)

Venezuela

Colombia

Guyana

Suriname

Samoa

2.30am

Ecuador

8am

Ascension (UK)

Tonga

12am

Cook Is (NZ)

Tahiti

French Polynesia (Fr)

2am

Peru

7am

Brazil

9am

SOUTH ATLANTIC OCEAN

1am

Pitcairn Is (UK)

3.30am

Easter Is (Chile)

Bolivia

Paraguay

New Zealand

12.45am
Chatham Is (NZ)

SOUTH PACIFIC OCEAN

Chile

Uruguay

Argentina

SOUTH ATLANTIC OCEAN

Tristan da Cunha (UK)

Gough Is (UK)

Falkland Is (UK)

South Georgia & South Sandwich Is (UK)

Bouvet Is (Norway)

| 12am | 1am | 2am | 3am | 4am | 5am | 6am | 7am | 8am | 9am | 10am | 11am | 12pm |

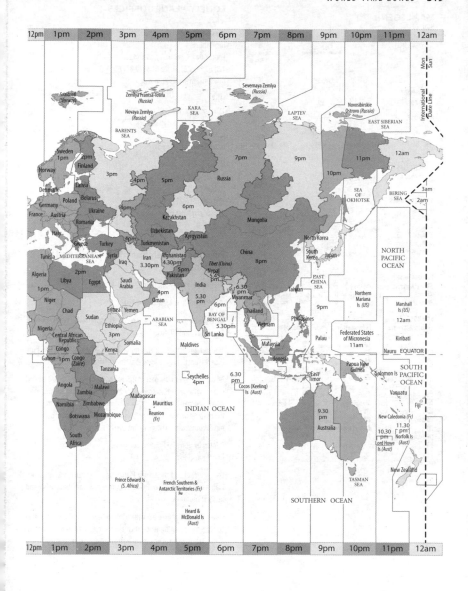

12pm 1pm 2pm 3pm 4pm 5pm 6pm 7pm 8pm 9pm 10pm 11pm 12am

Mon Sun
International Date Line

Svalbard *(Norway)*
Zemlya Frantsa-Iosifa *(Russia)*
Severnaya Zemlya *(Russia)*
Novaya Zemlya *(Russia)*
KARA SEA
LAPTEV SEA
Novosibirskie Ostrovo *(Russia)*
EAST SIBERIAN SEA
BARENTS SEA

Sweden 1pm
Norway 2pm
Finland
3pm
4pm
5pm
7pm
9pm
11pm
12am
10pm

Denmark
Latvia
Germany Poland Belarus
France Austria Ukraine
Italy Romania
6pm
Russia
SEA OF OKHOTSK
BERING SEA
3am
2am

Greece Turkey
Tunisia MEDITERRANEAN SEA Syria
Algeria 2pm Iraq Iran
Libya Egypt
Kazakhstan
Uzbekistan
Turkmenistan 4pm
Kyrgyzstan
Mongolia
North Korea
South Korea Japan
NORTH PACIFIC OCEAN

Afghanistan 4.30pm
Iran 3.30pm
Tibet (China)
China 8pm
EAST CHINA SEA

Niger 1pm
Chad Sudan
Saudi Arabia
Oman 4pm
Pakistan 5pm
Nepal 5.45 pm
India 5.30pm
Myanmar 6.30 pm
Taiwan
Northern Mariana Is *(US)*
Marshall Is *(US)*
12am

Nigeria
Central African Republic
Eritrea Yemen
Ethiopia 3pm
Somalia
ARABIAN SEA
BAY OF BENGAL
Sri Lanka 5.30pm
Thailand
Vietnam
Malaysia
Philippines
9pm
Palau
Federated States of Micronesia 11am
Kiribati
Nauru EQUATOR

Congo 1pm
Gabon Congo (Zaire)
Kenya
Tanzania
Maldives
Indonesia
East Timor
Papua New Guinea
Solomon Is
SOUTH PACIFIC OCEAN

Angola
Zambia Malawi
Namibia Zimbabwe
Botswana Mozambique
Madagascar
Mauritius
Reunion *(Fr)*
Seychelles 4pm
Cocos (Keeling) Is *(Aust)* 6.30 pm
INDIAN OCEAN
Vanuatu
Fiji
New Caledonia *(Fr)*
11.30 pm
10.30 pm Norfolk Is *(Aust)*
Lord Howe Is *(Aust)*

South Africa
Australia 9.30 pm
New Zealand

Prince Edward Is *(S. Africa)*
French Southern & Antarctic Territories *(Fr)*
TASMAN SEA
SOUTHERN OCEAN

Heard & McDonald Is *(Aust)*

12pm 1pm 2pm 3pm 4pm 5pm 6pm 7pm 8pm 9pm 10pm 11pm 12am

320

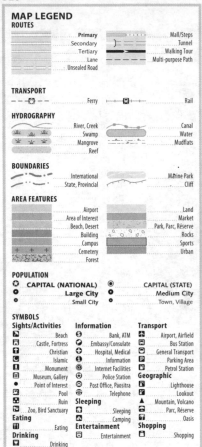

MAP LEGEND

ROUTES

Primary
Secondary
Tertiary
Lane
Unsealed Road
Mall/Steps
Tunnel
Walking Tour
Multi-purpose Path

TRANSPORT

Ferry
Rail

HYDROGRAPHY

River, Creek
Swamp
Mangrove
Reef
Canal
Water
Mudflats

BOUNDARIES

International
State, Provincial
Marine Park
Cliff

AREA FEATURES

Airport
Area of Interest
Beach, Desert
Building
Campus
Cemetery
Forest
Land
Market
Park, Parc, Réserve
Rocks
Sports
Urban

POPULATION

CAPITAL (NATIONAL)
Large City
Small City
CAPITAL (STATE)
Medium City
Town, Village

SYMBOLS

Sights/Activities	Information	Transport
Beach	Bank, ATM	Airport, Airfield
Castle, Fortress	Embassy/Consulate	Bus Station
Christian	Hospital, Medical	General Transport
Islamic	Information	Parking Area
Monument	Internet Facilities	Petrol Station
Museum, Gallery	Police Station	**Geographic**
Point of Interest	Post Office, Paositra	Lighthouse
Pool	Telephone	Lookout
Ruin	**Sleeping**	Mountain, Volcano
Zoo, Bird Sanctuary	Sleeping	Parc, Réserve
Eating	Camping	Oasis
Eating	**Entertainment**	**Shopping**
Drinking	Entertainment	Shopping
Drinking		

LONELY PLANET OFFICES

Australia
Head Office
Locked Bag 1, Footscray, Victoria 3011
☎ 03 8379 8000, fax 03 8379 8111
talk2us@lonelyplanet.com.au

USA
150 Linden St, Oakland, CA 94607
☎ 510 893 8555, toll free 800 275 8555
fax 510 893 8572
info@lonelyplanet.com

UK
2nd Fl, 186 City Rd,
London ECV1 2NT
☎ 020 7106 2100, fax 020 7106 2101
go@lonelyplanet.co.uk

Published by Lonely Planet Publications Pty Ltd
ABN 36 005 607 983

© Lonely Planet Publications Pty Ltd 2008

© photographers as indicated 2008

Cover photograph: Group of ring-tailed lemurs, Madagascar; Heather Angel / Natural Visions.

Many of the images in this guide are available for licensing from Lonely Planet Images: www.lonelyplanetimages.com.

All rights reserved. No part of this publication may be copied, stored in a retrieval system, or transmitted in any form by any means, electronic, mechanical, recording or otherwise, except brief extracts for the purpose of review, and no part of this publication may be sold or hired, without the written permission of the publisher.

Printed by Hang Tai Printing Company.
Printed in China.

Lonely Planet and the Lonely Planet logo are trademarks of Lonely Planet and are registered in the US Patent and Trademark Office and in other countries.

Lonely Planet does not allow its name or logo to be appropriated by commercial establishments, such as retailers, restaurants or hotels. Please let us know of any misuses: www.lonelyplanet.com/ip.

Although the authors and Lonely Planet have taken all reasonable care in preparing this book, we make no warranty about the accuracy or completeness of its content and, to the maximum extent permitted, disclaim all liability arising from its use.